VIATOR

Medieval and Renaissance Studies

VOLUME 8

VIATOR

MEDIEVAL AND RENAISSANCE STUDIES

Volume 8 (1977)

PUBLISHED UNDER THE AUSPICES OF
THE CENTER FOR MEDIEVAL AND RENAISSANCE STUDIES
UNIVERSITY OF CALIFORNIA, LOS ANGELES

UNIVERSITY OF CALIFORNIA PRESS
BERKELEY, LOS ANGELES, LONDON 1977

VIATOR

Medieval and Renaissance Studies

Manuscripts should be addressed to the Editors, Center for Medieval and Renaissance Studies, University of California, Los Angeles, California 90024, U.S.A. *Viator* is open to contributions from all sources. The Editors are particularly interested in considering intercultural and interdisciplinary articles. Texts, illustrations, maps, diagrams, musical examples, and the like, will be published when they are necessary to documentation. Articles that have been, or soon will be, printed elsewhere in any language in substantially the same form are not acceptable.

Inquiries concerning subscriptions and earlier volumes should be addressed to the University of California Press, 2223 Fulton Street, Berkeley, California 94720, U.S.A.

University of California Press
Berkeley and Los Angeles, California
University of California Press, Ltd.
London, England

ISBN: 0-520-03363-9

Library of Congress Catalog Card Number: 71-111417

CONTENTS

CONSTANTINE THE GREAT AND THE CULT WITHOUT IMAGES

•

by Robert Grigg

It has been widely believed that Constantine the Great introduced religious images into the churches he founded.[1] Admittedly these images have not survived.[2] Still, it is thought that the later decoration of Constantine's churches, most notably the Lateran Basilica in Rome, could hardly have been unrelated to their original decoration.[3] Moreover, a variety of later texts, often accepted at face value, purportedly

As this paper develops ideas that appeared, in germinal form, in my doctoral dissertation, I should like to use this occasion to express my gratitude to my readers at the University of Minnesota – D. Tselos, C. Sheppard, and B. Bachrach – and to the Kress Foundation whose grant made a portion of this research possible. I should like to thank the staff of the Dumbarton Oaks Center for Byzantine Studies and the Index of Christian Art in the University of California Art Library, Los Angeles, for their generosity. Thanks are due especially to M. Anastos and J. D. Breckenridge who read a draft of this paper and offered suggestions for improving it. I regret that J. D. Breckenridge's research dealing with much the same material was not yet published at the time I submitted this paper, but I should like to thank him for his willingness to provide me with a copy of his notes for his oral presentation to the College Art Association in 1975, titled "Eusebius and the Possibility of Christian Portraiture," a presentation that contained ideas that parallel some of those found in this study.

[1] J. Wilpert lent his authority to this assumption: "Konstantin widmete die Basilika dem Erlöser [the Lateran], in dessen *Zeichen* er über Maxentius den *Sieg* davongetragen. Es verstand sich daher von selbst, dass in einer solchen Votivkirche vor allem das Bild des Patrons prangen musste" – *Die römischen Mosaiken und Malereien* (Freiburg i. B. 1916) 1.189. Cf. *idem*, "La decorazione costantiniana della basilica lateranense," *Rivista di archeologia cristiana* 6 (1929) 102ff. Of the apsidal mosaic of St. Peter's in Rome, Wilpert writes, "trotz der auf den ersten Blick erkennbaren mittelalterlichen Zusätze sind alte und neue Schriftsteller einig in dem Glauben, dass die Kopie [of Innocent III, preserved in a later drawing] im wesentlichen die Symbole und Gestalten enthalte, welche schon auf dem ursprünglichen Mosaik Konstantins dargestellt waren. Müntz ["Notes sur les mosaïques chrétiennes," *Revue archéologique* 2 (1882) 143ff] lässt sogar die Möglichkeit gelten, dass einige Partien noch die des alten Originals gewesen seien" – *Mosaiken* 1.361. W. Oakeshott, *The Mosaics of Rome* (London 1967) 18, 25, and pl. III, identifies a mosaic fragment now in the Vatican Grottoes as a fragment of the original Constantinian apsidal mosaic of St. Peter's. Cf. H. Buschhausen and H. Lenzen, "Ein konstantinisches Silberreliquiar aus Jabalkovo in Bulgarien," *Jahrbuch der österreichischen byzantinischen Gesellschaft* 14 (1965) 198. For similar attributions in Constantine's churches in the Holy Land, see D. Ainalov, *The Hellenistic Origins of Byzantine Art*, ed. C. Mango, trans. E. and S. Sobolevitch (New Brunswick 1961 [1900]) 224-248, who was strongly attracted to the idea that Constantine's churches in the Holy Land were decorated with commemorative images that

describe or allude to the original decoration of Constantine's churches.[4] Probably the best known example is the biography of Pope Sylvester in the *Liber pontificalis*, which alleges that Constantine gave to the Lateran Basilica a large structure of uncertain form and function, designated a *fastidium* and described as bearing statues of Christ, the apostles, and angels.[5] Other late texts, which sometimes are given credence, simply describe the kind of Christian imagery that Constantine allegedly sponsored or was associated with.[6] Interestingly, that churchmen like Origen and

---

had a profoundly formative effect upon Christian iconography. It is clear that Ainalov 231 was tempted to attribute some of these imagined archetypal images to Constantine. His theory has been widely received. Specifically, it has been suggested that the apse of Constantine's basilica at Golgotha was decorated, perhaps in Constantine's reign, with an image combining a cross and a half-length portrait of Christ overhead – K. Schmaltz, *Mater Ecclesiarum: Die Grabeskirche in Jerusalem*, Zur Kunstgeschichte des Auslandes 120 (Strasbourg 1918) 134f., 278; C. Cecchelli, *Il trionfo della croce* (Rome 1954) 55f.; *idem* et al., *The Rabula Gospels* (Olten-Lausanne 1959) 34f.; and C. Ihm, *Die Programme der christlichen Apsismalerei*, Forschungen zur Kunstgeschichte und christlichen Archäologie 4 (1960) 85.

[2] Constantine's churches are known from contemporary descriptions and, where excavation is possible, from the remains of pavements and foundation courses of walls. With one possible exception, the archaeological evidence has nothing to say of Constantine's sponsorship of Christian imagery. This possible exception – the church of Archbishop Theodore of Aquileia – will be examined below. The pavement mosaics discovered in excavations of the Church of the Nativity in Bethlehem are today not regarded as Constantinian in date – E. Kitzinger, "The Threshold of the Holy Shrine," *Kyriakon: Festschrift Johannes Quasten*, ed. P. Granfield and J. A. Jungmann (Münster 1970) 641. For a full bibliography of Constantine's churches, see G. T. Armstrong, "Constantine's Churches," *Gesta* 6 (1967) 1-9. Important recent studies not included in his bibliography are F. W. Deichmann, "Das Oktogon von Antiocheia," *Byzantinische Zeitschrift* 65 (1972) 40-56; R. Krautheimer, "Constantine's Church Foundations," *Akten des VII. internationalen Kongresses für christliche Archäologie, Trier 1965* (Vatican 1969) 237-255; *idem*, "The Constantinian Basilica," *Dumbarton Oaks Papers* 21 (1967) 117-40.

[3] Wilpert, *Mosaiken* 1.189, 361; *idem*, "Decorazione costantiniana" 102ff. This reasoning continues to command respect – J. M. C. Toynbee and J. Ward Perkins, *The Shrine of Saint Peter's and the Vatican Excavations* (London 1956) 212; Y. Christe, "A propos du décor absidal de Saint-Jean du Latran à Rome," *Cahiers archéologiques* 20 (1970) 199-206; and J. Beckwith, *Early Christian and Byzantine Art*, The Pelican History of Art (Harmondsworth 1970) 11f.

[4] E. g., Anastasius Bibliothecarius reports that the two legates of Pope Hadrian I at the Second Council of Nicaea (A.D. 787) referred to Constantine's sponsorship of religious images: "Tale quid et divae memoriae Constantinus Magnus imperator olim fecit: aedificato enim templo Salvatoris Romae, in duobus parietibus templi historias veteres et novas designavit, hinc Adam de paradiso exeuntem, et inde latronem in paradisum intrantem figurans: et reliqua" – *Interpretatio synodi VII generalis* (PL 129.289). Wilpert, "Decorazione costantiniana" (n. 1 above) 80, accepting this report, traces the origin of picture cycles with scenes of concordance between the Old and New Testaments back to the Constantinian era.

[5] L. Duchesne, ed., *Le Liber pontificalis*, ed. 2 (Paris 1955) 1.172. The same list of donations includes references to other gifts bearing images: on the rim of the baptismal font in the Lateran Baptistery, statues of the Savior, a lamb, and John the Baptist (1.174), in St. Peter's, candelabra with images illustrating the Acts of the Apostles (1.176).

[6] Pope Hadrian I wrote a letter to the emperor Constantine V, a militant Iconoclast, alleging that Constantine the Great decorated churches with images of Christ and the saints – ed. J. Mansi, *Sacrorum conciliorum nova et amplissima collectio* (Paris 1901 [1759]) 12.1055ff. Constantine is associated with images of Sts. Peter and Paul in the story of his conversion found

Tertullian disapproved of cult images is not regarded as a serious challenge to the reliability of arguments which attribute to Constantine the introduction of Christian imagery into his churches:[7] as Norman Baynes once argued, Christian bishops were too grateful for the sudden show of imperial support to object to the introduction of images of Christ and the saints into their newly built churches.[8]

As attractive as it is to think that Constantine's support of church building overnight transformed Christian churches into large public structures, brilliantly decorated with mosaics featuring subjects drawn from the Old and New Testaments, this view has been increasingly received with skepticism.[9] Indeed, the assumptions expressed above, though held and defended in a variety of ways, do raise fundamental questions, one of which I should like to explore.[10] Is there reliable evidence that Constantine was ever associated with the kinds of images that are sometimes alleged to have constituted the original decoration of his churches? Most importantly, was he ever associated with images of Christ, like those which allegedly decorated the *fastidium* of the Lateran Basilica?

It might reasonably be expected that contemporary Christian authors would supply the answer: they certainly were not silent about Constantine's churches. On the contrary, to them his churches were of outstanding importance as visible signs of his piety and his favor for Christianity.[11] Thus it is not surprising to find in the *Vita*

---

in this letter and in the *Constitutum Constantini* 8, ed. H. Fuhrmann, MGH Fontes iuris germanici antiqui 10 (Hanover 1968) 71ff. For images of Christ that Constantine allegedly sponsored, see the *Epistola ad Theophilum imperatorem* (PG 95.348f.) quoted below and the *Patria Konstantinupoleos*, ed. T. Preger, *Scriptores originum Constantinopolitanarum* 2 (Leipzig 1906) 219f.

[7]Origen, *Contra Celsum* 4.31, 7.64; Tertullian, *De idolatria* 4. The classic studies of the hostility of the early Church towards images are C. Clerc, *Les théories relatives au culte des images chez les auteurs grecs du IIe siècle après J.-C.* (Paris 1915) 125-168; H. Koch, *Die altchristliche Bilderfrage nach den literarischen Quellen*, Forschungen zur Religion und Literature des Alten und Neuen Testaments 27 (1917); W. Elliger, *Die Stellung der alten Christen zu den Bildern in den ersten vier Jahrhunderten*, Studien über christliche Denkmäler 20 (1930); N. H. Baynes, "Idolatry and the Early Church," *Byzantine Studies and Other Essays* (London 1955) 116-143; E. Bevan, *Holy Images* (London 1940) 84-112; and T. Klauser, "Die Äusserungen der alten Kirche zur Kunst," *Atti del VI congresso internazionale di archeologia cristiana, Ravenna 23-30 settembre 1962* (Rome 1965) 223-242.

[8]Baynes 126.

[9]A. Grabar, *Christian Iconography: A Study of Its Origins*, Bollingen Series 35 (1968) 38; F. W. Deichmann, "Vom Tempel zur Kirche," *Mullus: Festschrift T. Klauser* (Münster i. W. 1964) 59 n. 27; R. Cormack, "Byzantine Cappadocia: The Archaic Group of Wall-Paintings," *Journal of the British Archaeological Association* 30 (1967) 28; and Krautheimer, "Constantinian Basilica" (n. 2 above) 120f., 130 n. 47.

[10]It might be questioned, e. g., that Constantine even made decisions regarding the details of the churches he founded. Krautheimer, "Foundations" (n. 2 above) 239-242, 251, discusses this question with particular reference to the letter written by Constantine to Bishop Makarios of Jerusalem and preserved in the *Vita Constantini* (hereafter VC) 3.31f.

[11]VC 3.25, 3.42 (for Helena's piety), 3.48, 3.50f., 4.33. Cf. W. Telfer, "Constantine's Holy Land Plan," *Texte und Untersuchungen zur Geschichte der altchristlichen Literatur* 68 (1957) 696-700, and R. Storch, "The 'Eusebian Constantine'," *Church History* 40 (1971) 145-155.

Constantini, which is today often (but not without controversy) thought to have been written shortly after Constantine's death, a lengthy description of the structures that Constantine built around the tomb of Christ in Jerusalem.[12] Strangely, though, in this description, there is not a single reference to an image. Other allusions to Constantine's churches similarly lack explicit references to images, even though they sometimes concern ornamentation.[13] One passage in the *Vita Constantini* is especially interesting, as it at first appears to indicate that images decorated the basilica which Constantine erected at Golgotha. The author describes the festivities that marked the dedication of the basilica in A.D. 335.[14] The bishops who were assembled for this occasion delivered speeches. Some praised Constantine's piety and the beauty of his church. Some spoke about religious doctrine. Then came the author's turn: "Thereupon we also honored the festival with artful public oratory, . . . aptly composing prophetic speculations with the symbols [*symbolois*] that are set forth."[15] The meaning of this passage is elusive, hinging upon the author's use of *symbolois*. Were the *symbola* to which the author refers images with anthropomorphic figures? That possibility cannot be ruled out, since he elsewhere uses the same word, *symbola*, to refer to statues of the Good Shepherd and Daniel.[16] But there are other possibilities, too, which cannot easily be dismissed. Eusebius, in his *Tricennial Oration* (*Triakontaeterikos*), writes, referring to the "sacred caves" in Palestine which Constantine commemorated with churches, "every one of these the emperor adorned, proclaiming to all the saving sign."[17] On the basis of this report, it

[12] VC 3.29-40. The authorship and authenticity of the VC, traditionally attributed to Eusebius of Caesaria, have been strongly contested. For an introduction to the history of this controversy and its enormous bibliography, the reader would do well to consult F. Winkelmann, "Zur Geschichte des Authentizitätsproblem der Vita Constantini," *Klio* 40 (1962) 187-243.

[13] VC 3.40, 3.43, 3.45, 4.47 and Eusebius's *Tricennial Oration* (*Triakontaeterikos*) 9.

[14] VC 4.45.

[15] *Ibid.*, ed. I. Heikel, *Eusebius Werke* 1, Die griechischen christlichen Schriftsteller (GCS) (1902) 136: *'ένθα δὴ καὶ ἡμεῖς τῶν ὑπὲρ ἡμᾶς ἀγαθῶν ἠξιωμένο[ι] ποικίλαις ταῖς εἰς τὸ κοινὸν διαλέξεσι τὴν ἑορτὴν ἐτιμῶμεν, τοτὲ τῶν διὰ γράμματος βασιλεῖ πεφιλοκαωημένων τὰς ἐκφράσεις ἑρμηνεύοντες, τοτὲ δὲ καιρίους καὶ τοῖς προκειμένοις συμβόλοις τὰς προφητικὰς ποιούμενοι θεωρίας.*

[16] VC 3.49. This text is quoted below in n. 25.

[17] *Triakontaeterikos* 9 (Heikel 221): *ταῦτα δὴ πάντα βασιλεὺς ἐκόσμει τὸ σωτήριον εἰς 'άπαντας ἀνακηρύττων σημεῖον.* The following passage concerning Constantine's basilica at Golgotha is also of interest, though it unfortunately is ambiguous: *νεών τε 'άγιον τῷ σωτηρίῳ σημείῳ πλουσίως καὶ δαψιλέσι κατεκόσμει φιλοτιμίαις. . . .* – *ibid*. Schmaltz (n. 1 above) 134 understands from it that the basilica was dedicated to the "saving sign." Ihm (n. 1 above) 85 evidently interprets it to mean that the basilica was decorated with this sign. The authorship of the *Triakontaeterikos* is generally uncontested. Not even Henri Grégoire challenged the traditional attribution to Eusebius; indeed, the silence of the *Triakontaeterikos* regarding Constantine's alleged vision, in Grégoire's opinion, was a reason to regard the *Vita Constantini* as a later composition – "Eusèbe n'est pas l'auteur de la 'Vita Constantini' dans sa forme actuelle et Constantin n'est pas 'converti' en 312," *Byzantion* 13 (1938) 568. For the attribution to Eusebius, also see F. Vittinghoff, "Eusebius als Verfasser der 'Vita Constantini'," *Rheinisches Museum für Philologie*, n. s. 96 (1953) 362, and W. Telfer, "The Author's Purpose in the Vita Constantini," *Texte und Untersuchungen zur Geschichte der altchristlichen Literatur* 68 (1957) 158.

is tempting to infer that Constantine's commemorative churches in the Holy Land were decorated with the Christogram (possibly, too, with the monogrammatic cross): it was referred to as the "saving sign" by the author of the *Vita Constantini*; it was interpreted as a Christian symbol by contemporaries, used sometimes on Constantine's coins, seemingly as a sign of protection, and soon thereafter widely used in church decoration, along with the monogrammatic cross.[18] This raises the interesting possibility that the author of the *Vita Constantini* was referring to instances of the Christogram or monogrammatic cross when he used the designation *symbolois*, especially since great importance was attached to Constantine's use of the "saving sign," as we shall momentarily find. It is no less possible that the author was referring to liturgical ceremonies that attended the dedication of the basilica.[19] All three of these interpretations are eligible and the difficulty of choosing decisively between them weakens the usefulness of this passage as evidence that the basilica at Golgotha was decorated with images.

The *Vita Constantini* contains references to votive offerings, made of gold, other precious metals, and jewels, that Constantine gave to the churches he founded.[20] But none of these reports supplies evidence that Constantine's churches were decorated with images. What makes this silence doubly surprising is that the author observes Constantine's public images with extraordinary attentiveness: he describes a painting that was placed over the gate of the imperial palace in Constantinople;[21] he refers to other images of Constantine that were placed in similar settings, showing him with his eyes raised to the heavens and his hands spread out in prayer;[22] he mentions paintings that were produced after Constantine's death, showing him reposing in the heavens;[23] and he even describes two of Constantine's numismatic images, one showing the emperor gazing into the heavens, the other, found on some of his consecration coins, showing him as a charioteer, ascending into the heavens and being welcomed by a divine hand which extends downward.[24]

There is only one passage in the *Vita Constantini* that is directly relevant to the question of Constantine's sponsorship of Christian imagery, if not to the question of

[18] See below for a discussion of Constantine's use of these signs. Bibliography is given in n. 91 below. For the widespread use of signs of Christ in the decoration of churches, see H. Brandenburg, "Christussymbole in frühchristlichen Bodenmosaiken," *Römische Quartalschrift für christliche Altertumskunde und für Kirchengeschichte* 64 (1969) 89ff.

[19] Eusebius's reference to the presence of "ineffable symbols [*symbola*] of the salutary Passion" – *Historia ecclesiastica* (hereafter HE) 10.3.3 – in a passage that concerns the dedication of churches, is commonly understood as a reference to liturgical ceremonies – PG 20.848 n. 94; and G. Bardy, ed. and trans., *Histoire ecclésiastique*, Sources chrétiennes (SC) 55 (Paris 1958) 80.

[20] VC (n. 10 above) 3.40, 3.43, 3.45, 4.46; cf. L. Voelkl, *Die Kirchenstiftungen des Kaisers Konstantin im Lichte des römischen Sakralrechts*, Arbeitsgemeinschaft für Forschung des Landes Nordrhein-Westfalen, Geisteswissenschaften 117 (1964) 33f., and Krautheimer, "Foundations" (n. 2 above) 241.

[21] VC 3.3.

[22] VC 4.15.

[23] VC 4.69.

[24] VC 4.15, 4.73.

the decoration of his churches. According to the author, Constantine's piety was visibly manifest in statues of the Good Shepherd and Daniel which decorated some of the public fountains of Constantinople.[25] If it can be trusted,[26] this is significant evidence. It appears to embarrass the suggestion that Constantine believed "representational images" to have no place in the Christian cult.[27] Unfortunately, though, in other important respects, its implications are not clear.

Were the statues of the Good Shepherd intended as representations of Christ or, possibly, the Lord of the Old Testament, who protects His flock, the faithful on earth?[28] The setting alone would seem to indicate that they were not conceived as figures meriting special respect; yet the author clearly implies in his report that the figures were inspired by Holy Scriptures.[29] This circumstance, plus the frequent portrayal of the Lord or Christ as a shepherd in book 10 of Eusebius's *Historia ecclesiastica,*[30] almost forces upon one the conclusion that the author did interpret the statues of the Good Shepherd as representations of Christ or the Lord. This conclusion, however, is not necessarily as strong as one might at first imagine. It is one thing to say that the Good Shepherd, like the figure of the lamb, was an image of Christ in the sense of an allegorical figure, that specifically it symbolized the solicitous guardianship which Christ manifested for the faithful.[31] It is quite another to say that the Good Shepherd was an image of Christ in the sense of a likeness. In the former case, the anthropomorphic form of the image need not have been perceived as an image of Christ in the flesh, as would be entailed in the case of a likeness. I suggest that it was just this distinction that was tacitly recognized by the author of the *Vita Constantini* and probably by other Christians, making images of the Good Shepherd less offensive than images that were unequivocally intended as likenesses of Christ, images in which one was intended to perceive Christ in the flesh. There are at least two reasons to think that the author of the *Vita Constantini* did not regard the images of the Good Shepherd as likenesses of Christ. First of all, he

[25] VC 3.49 (Heikel [n. 15 above] 98): *Εἶδες δ' ἂν ἐπὶ μέσον ἀγορῶν κειμέναις κρήναις τὰ τοῦ καλοῦ ποιμένος σύμβολα, τοῖς ἀπὸ τῶν θείων λογίων ὁρμωμένοις γνώριμα, τόν τε Δανιὴλ σὺν αὐτοῖς λέουσιν ἐν χαλκῷ πεπλασμένον χρυσοῦ τε πετάλοις ἐκλάμποντα.*

[26] Klauser (n. 7 above) 231f. questions the authenticity of the report.

[27] As Grabar (n. 9 above) 38 tentatively suggests.

[28] The New Testament passage usually cited in connection with this image is John 10.11, in which Christ identifies himself as the Good Shepherd. But the Old Testament Lord is sometimes figured as a shepherd: Psalms 23 and 78 and Ezekiel 34.11-16. For other passages from the Old Testament that express the same identification, see T. Klauser, "Studien zur Entstehungsgeschichte der christlichen Kunst IX," *Jahrbuch für Antike und Christentum* 10 (1967) 106.

[29] VC 3.49, quoted in n. 25 above.

[30] HE 10.4.4, 4.25, 4.28, 4.34, 4.46, and 4.72.

[31] For a discussion of the general nature of symbolism in art, see G. Dickie, *Aesthetics: An Introduction* (Indianapolis 1971) 122ff. I am not, by the way, suggesting that the author's use of the word *symbola* is a reason for identifying the Good Shepherd as an allegorical figure, though this would seem to be the opinion of J. Kollwitz, "Zur Frühgeschichte der Bilderverehrung," *Römische Quartalschrift für christliche Altertumskunde und für Kirchengeschichte* 48 (1953) 3f.; *idem*, "Bild III," *Reallexikon für Antike und Christentum* 2 (1954) 320.

does not designate the statues of the Good Shepherd as "likenesses," even though he easily could have done so, just as Eusebius did in his description of the statue of Christ at Paneas. According to Eusebius, "this statue was said to bear the likeness [*eikona*] of Christ."[32] It reminded him of other images, paintings, that bore "likenesses [*eikonas*]" of Paul, Peter, and even of Christ.[33] It is not unlikely that one of the reasons the author of the *Vita Constantini* failed to describe the statues of the Good Shepherd as such was his failure to regard them as intended likenesses of Christ or the Lord. Second, the sheep- or ram-bearing figure – almost certainly what our author saw – was a widely used motif in the third and fourth centuries,[34] which not infrequently appeared in pagan contexts, where it may have been intended as an allegorical figure of *philanthropia.*[35] Against this background it is hard to imagine that Christians would have interpreted it as a likeness of Christ.

Finally, were similar images found in Constantine's churches? There is hardly sufficient evidence to answer the question. What evidence there is seems contradictory. The very author who reports these statues is inexplicably silent about similar images in Constantine's churches. And, as we shall soon see, there is ample evidence of Christian hostility towards religious images in the Constantinian era. On the other hand, some churchmen were evidently willing to introduce such images into their churches. The church of Archbishop Theodore of Aquileia contains important pavement mosaics, apparently Constantinian in date,[36] which feature the story of Jonah and the whale,[37] an image of a sheep-bearer[38] (a figure which strongly tempts one to employ the designation "Good Shepherd," though Klauser believes this is a

[32] HE (n. 19 above) 7.18 (PG 20.680): *Τοῦτον δὲ τὸν ἀνδριάντα εἰκόνα τοῦ 'Ιησοῦ φέρειν 'έλεγον.*

[33] *Ibid.*: *καὶ τῶν ἀποστόλων αὐτοῦ τὰς εἰκόνας Παύλου καὶ Πέτρου, καὶ αυτοῦ δὴ τοῦ Χριστοῦ, διὰ χρωμάτων ἐν γραφαῖς σωζομέναις ἱστορήσαμεν.*

[34] Klauser, "Studien . . . I" (n. 28 above), 1 (1958) 33ff.

[35] *Ibid.* 31.

[36] Apart from considerations of style, the pavement mosaics of the south hall have been dated on the basis of the following inscription, which indicates that Archbishop Theodore of Aquileia was the builder of the church: ☧ THEODORE · FELI[X] [A]DIVVANTE · DEO OMNIPOTENTE · ET POEMNIO CAELITVS · TIBI [TRA]DITVM · OMNIA [B]AEATE · FECISTI · ET GLORIOSE · DEDICASTI – P. Zovatto, *Mosaici paleocristiani della Venezie* (Udine 1963) 64. H. Kähler, *Die Stiftermosaiken in der konstantinischen Südkirche von Aquileia*, Monumenta artis romanae 4 (1962) 8ff., 18 n. 48, provides the following argument to date the mosaics: several of the lists of Aquileian bishops record Theodore's term of office as 11 years; as his predecessor, Chrysogonus II, died in 304 or 305, this would seem to indicate, then, that Theodore's episcopacy ended in 315 or 316; it is possible, however, that the cathedra remained vacant for some time after the death of Chrysogonus; on the other hand, Theodore attended the Council of Arles in 314; therefore, the latest possible date for the termination of his episcopacy would be 325. Is it possible that parts of the pavement mosaic were added significantly later than the inscription? According to Kähler, this is unlikely since the style of the mosaics is too uniform to accommodate the possibility of a significant interruption in the laying of the mosaics. Zovatto, *Mosaici* 64, and *idem* and G. Brusin, *Monumenti paleocristiani di Aquileia e di Grado* (Udine 1957) 111f., believe that Theodore's episcopacy came to an end no later than 320.

[37] Zovatto, *Mosaici* fig. 92.

[38] *Ibid.* fig. 77.

temptation which should be resisted)[39] and what are presumably donor portraits.[40] Although there are substantial difficulties in his identification of these portraits, Heinz Kähler believes that they represent Constantine and his family.[41] This identification of course would imply that Constantine founded a church whose decoration included images that paralleled closely those reported in the *Vita Constantini* – an image of the Good Shepherd and an episode from the Old Testament, expressing God's power to deliver His faithful servants from evil. Anyone who reads book 10 of Eusebius's *Historia ecclesiastica* could easily envision Christian churches rebuilt immediately after the Great Persecution featuring such images.[42] Still, given the tenuous nature of Kähler's identification of the donor portraits, it is necessary to conclude that there is no compelling reason to think that Constantine's churches were decorated with similar images. Nor is there anything in the contemporary textual sources warranting the conclusion that Constantine's churches were

[39] Klauser (n. 28 above) 107.

[40] Kähler (n. 36 above) figs. 1-14.

[41] *Ibid.* 12ff. Some of the difficulties are pointed out by A. Grabar in his review of Kähler's study – *Cahiers archéologiques* 14 (1964) 252: it is difficult to imagine imperial portraits being placed upon the pavement, where they would be dishonored by being trodden upon; it is not clear that the entire Constantinian household was Christian, as Kähler's identifications would imply; the alleged images of Constantine and Fausta lack diadems; and the images of Fausta and Crispus, as identified by Kähler, were inexplicably untouched by their *damnatio memoriae*. Kähler 11, 13 admits that there are difficulties with his identifications: they cannot be defended on the basis of portrait resemblances and there are no identifying inscriptions. Judging from the absence of evidence of a *damnatio memoriae*, it is hard to believe that the citizens of Aquileia had Kähler's identifications in mind. Not only is it difficult to explain why the alleged portraits of Fausta and Crispus should have been left intact, it is also difficult to explain why Constans did not destroy the image of his usurping brother, Constantine II, who was defeated at Aquileia in 340 – A. H. M. Jones, *The Later Roman Empire*, 2 vols. (Norman, Okla. 1964) 1.112 – or why Magnentius did not avenge his defeat at Mursa in 351 by destroying the image of Constantius II: after that defeat, Magnentius retreated to Aquileia – Julian, *Panegyric in Honor of Constantius II*, ed. W. Wright, *The Works of the Emperor Julian*, 3 vols. Loeb Classical Library (London 1913-1924) 1.99 (Kähler 14 identified two of the portraits as Constantius II and Constantine II.). Still, it is difficult to gauge the strength of these objections. E. g., although one would not expect imperial images in a pavement mosaic, that seems to be precisely what one finds in the pavement mosaics of the villa at Piazza Armerina – see H. Kähler, *Die Villa des Maxentius bei Piazza Armerina*, Monumenta artis romanae 13 (1973) 33f., who identifies, on cogent grounds, portraits of Maxentius and his father, Maximianus Herculius. It is also of interest to note that "signs of Christ" were frequently placed upon floors – Brandenburg (n. 18 above) 74ff. This practice became so widespread by the early fifth century that it was legally banned in 427 by Theodosius II – *Codex Justinianus* 1.8. The reconstructed ceiling frescoes in Trier present a similar problem of identification: there, several striking female busts have been identified as members of the imperial family – Helena, Constantine's mother; Fausta, his wife; and the younger Helena, wife of Crispus: M. R. Alföldi, "Helena nobilissima femina: Zur Deutung der Trierer Deckengemälde," *Jahrbuch für Numismatik und Geldgeschichte* 10 (1959-1960) 79ff.; W. N. Schumacher, "Cubile Sanctae Helenae," *Römische Quartalschrift für christliche Altertumskunde und Kirchengeschichte* 58 (1963) 196ff.; I. Lavin, "The Ceiling Frescoes in Trier and Illusionism in Constantinian Painting," *Dumbarton Oaks Papers* 21 (1967) 100f.

[42] Throughout, Eusebius construes the Peace of the Church as an expression of the benevolent protection of Christ or the Lord for his flock. For passages in which either the Lord or Christ is figured as a shepherd, see n. 30 above.

decorated with likenesses of Christ, similar to those signaled by Eusebius in his *Historia ecclesiastica,* or that Constantine was ever associated with such images. This is worth noting because a radically different picture emerges if one considers later sources.

According to an anonymous report in the *Liber pontificalis* dealing with the life of Pope Sylvester, Constantine provided the Lateran Basilica with a *fastidium.*[43] The *fastidium* or *fastigium* it describes has been variously interpreted. Some regard it as an altar ciborium,[44] others as a gabled enframement facade, borrowed from imperial traditions.[45] Interestingly, the report alleges that the *fastigium* was decorated with two groups of statues: one group consisted of an enthroned Christ flanked by his apostles, the other, an enthroned Christ flanked by four angels holding spears. Though the report was composed in the first years of the sixth century,[46] it is thought to have been based upon an early list of donations from Constantine.[47] Hence, in spite of its relatively late date, it is commonly believed to provide reliable evidence of the actions of Constantine, or, at least, of actions requiring his approval.[48] Molly Teasdale Smith, for example, seems to have assumed the reliability of this report in her recent attempt to reconstruct the appearance of the *fastigium.*[49] She believes that the *fastigium* represents "an adaptation of Roman imperial forms to a new Christian use."[50] Richard Krautheimer, on the other hand, expressed doubts about the reliability of this report. "Its figural decoration . . . suggests at the present state of our knowledge a date after the middle of the century."[51] In my judgment, Krautheimer understates the evidence against the trustworthiness of the report. The

[43] Duchesne (n. 5 above) 1.172: "Basilicam Constantinianam, ubi posuit ista dona: fastidium argenteum battutilem, qui habet in fronte Salvatorem sedentem in sella, in pedibus V, pens. lib. CXX, et XII apostolos qui pens. sing. in quinos pedibus libras nonagenas, cum coronas argento purissimo; item a tergo respiciens in absida, Salvatorem sedentem in throno, in pedibus V, ex argento purissimo, pens. lib. CXL, et angelos IIII ex argento, qui pens. sing. in pedibus V lib. CV, cum gemmis alabandenis in oculos, tenentes astas; fastidium ipsum pens. lib. IIXXV, ex argento dolaticio."

[44] C. Rohault de Fleury, *La Messe* (Paris 1883) 2.2ff.; H. Leclercq, "Ciborium," *Dictionnaire d'archéologie chrétienne et de liturgie* 3.2.1589ff.; and Duchesne (n. 5 above) 1.191 n. 29.

[45] E. Dyggve, *Ravennatum palatium sacrum: La basilica ipetrale per cerimonie*, Danske videnskabernes Selskab, Copenhagen, archaeologisk-kunsthistoriske Meddelelser, 3.2 (1941) 38 n. 3; and M. T. Smith, "The Lateran *Fastigium*: A Gift of Constantine the Great," *Rivista di archeologia cristiana* 46 (1970) 151 n. 14.

[46] Duchesne (n. 5 above) 1.xxxviii-xxxix.

[47] Voelkl (n. 20 above) 22f. and Krautheimer, "Constantinian Basilica" (n. 2 above) 130 n. 47, who, however, questions the authenticity of the report of the *fastigium*.

[48] C. Davis-Weyer, *Early Medieval Art, 300-1150,* Sources and Documents in the History of Art Series (Englewood Cliffs 1971) 11 accepts it, as did A. Alföldi, "Insignien und Tracht der römischen Kaiser," *Mitteilungen des deutschen archäologischen Instituts, römische Abteilung* 50 (1935) 132 n. 4, and A. Grabar, *L'empereur dans l'art byzantin*, Publication de la Faculté des lettres de l'Université de Strasbourg 75 (1936) 196.

[49] Smith (n. 45 above) 149ff. She has recently reiterated this thesis in her "The Development of the Altar Canopy in Rome," *Rivista di archeologia cristiana* 50 (1974) 379f., again assuming the reliability of the report in the *Liber pontificalis.*

[50] Smith (n. 45 above) 151 n. 14.

[51] Krautheimer, "Constantinian Basilica" (n. 2 above) 130 n. 47.

enthroned Christ flanked by angels holding spears is a strikingly mature image that is without securely dated parallels until the late fifth or early sixth century.[52] It is exemplified in four monuments in Ravenna, all of them sixth century in date: one instance occurs in the lowest zone of the mosaics on the south wall of the nave of San Apollinare Nuovo,[53] which was erected under the patronage of Theodoric the Ostrogoth;[54] another in the apse of San Vitale;[55] another formerly in the church of Sant'Agata Maggiore;[56] and still another on the triumphal arch of the church of San Michele in Affricisco.[57] Two other examples are found in Egypt: one on the eastern wall of the sepulchral chapel of Theodosia at Antinoë, which perhaps dates to the middle of the sixth century;[58] the other in the cloister of the Monk Jeremiah, which was founded about A.D. 470.[59] This last example, according to Christa Ihm, seems to be the earliest dated instance of this image, as it could have been produced near the end of the fifth century.[60] If one were to relax the requirement that the guardian angels bear spears or staffs, then the earliest securely dated examples would appear to be those found in the mosaic on the triumphal arch of Santa Maria Maggiore in Rome (produced shortly before the middle of the fifth century).[61] In the left half of the mosaic, in the second register from the top, the Christ Child is seated upon a wide throne, behind which are four angels who flank him. Still, this is more than a century after Constantine's alleged donation to the Lateran Basilica and it is not an exact parallel. Nevertheless, it does suggest that the image described in the *Liber pontificalis* could have been produced about the time Santa Maria Maggiore was decorated.

[52] As noted by J. Croquison, "L'iconographie chrétienne à Rome d'après le 'Liber pontificalis'," *Byzantion* 34 (1964) 540.

[53] C. Nordström, *Ravennastudien*, Figura 4 (1953) pl. 20a; and G. Steigerwald, "Christus als Pantokrator in der untersten Zone der Langhausmosaiken von S. Apollinare Nuovo zu Ravenna," *Tortulae*, ed. W. N. Schumacher (Freiburg i. B. 1966) 272ff. Also see the useful study by T. Klauser, "Engel X," *Reallexikon für Antike und Christentum* 5 (1962) cat. no. 92, col. 279.

[54] Nordström 55.

[55] *Ibid.* 88, pl. 22b; Klauser, "Engel X" cat. no. 71a, col. 273; and for a justification of the approximate date of 530, a general discussion, and bibliography, see Ihm (n. 1 above) cat. no. 24, pp. 163ff.

[56] Ihm (n. 1 above) cat. no. 31, pp. 174f., pl. 7.2. As a result of an earthquake on 11 April 1668, the mosaics of this church were lost. Their iconography is known from a drawing and from Ciampini's description – Ihm 174f.

[57] In 1842 the apsidal mosaic of S. Michele (founded in 545) was purchased by King Friedrich Wilhelm IV of Prussia and is now in the Staatliche Museen of Berlin, in heavily restored condition. In the apse, 2 archangels, carrying ceremonial staffs and labeled Michael and Gabriel, flank a standing figure of Christ, who holds a gemmed cross. In the center of the triumphal arch, overhead, is an enthroned Christ, flanked by 2 guardian angels who hold long ceremonial staffs – Ihm (n. 1 above) cat. no. 23, pp. 161ff., pl. 8.2, and Klauser (n. 53 above) cat. no. 83b, col. 276.

[58] Ihm (n. 1 above) cat. no. 51, p. 198, pl. 7.3.

[59] *Ibid.* cat. no. 53n, pp. 205, 208f., and, for a general discussion of this motif, p. 28.

[60] *Ibid.* 28.

[61] Klauser (n. 53 above) col. 303 lists 19 examples of guardian angels flanking a figure of Christ or the Virgin in early Christian monuments. Of these 19 instances, 14 are dated in the sixth century. The other 5 are assigned to the fifth century. But, with the exception of the 2 examples in Sta. Maria Maggiore, these fifth-century dates are not secure. The ambo fragment,

This last observation is worth making, for the image of the enthroned Christ guarded by angels bearing spears seems to make its earliest appearance just shortly before the date of the composition of the report in the *Liber pontificalis.* This circumstance suggests that the anonymous author may have interpolated later imagery into his account of Constantine's donations to the Lateran Basilica. The interpolation conceivably could have occurred if the statuary groups came into existence later on. Is there any reason to think they may have? Another report in the *Liber pontificalis* suggests how this may have occurred. It alleges that the western emperor Valentinian III (A.D. 425-455) restored the original *fastigium* at the request of Pope Sixtus III (A.D. 432-440),[62] the pope responsible for the decoration of Santa Maria Maggiore.[63] Apparently the *fastigium* had been destroyed in the sack of Rome in A.D. 410.[64] Valentinian III is also recorded as having given Saint Peter's a golden image with twelve gates and figures of the apostles and the Savior.[65] This image is reminiscent of the other statuary group decorating the *fastigium.* Therefore, the possibility that the author was describing a later, fifth-century image, created under Valentinian III, is very real. Given the maturity of the image containing the spear-bearing guardian angels, this is a far more convincing hypothesis than one which accepts the report at face value.

It is fair to recall how unreliable the *Liber pontificalis* has proved to be in other matters dealing with Constantine. It falsely states that Constantine was baptized in

---

e. g., from Salonika, now in the Archaeological Museum of Istanbul, is dated by Klauser (cat. no. 39, col. 267f.) ca. 440. Contrast this with R. Lange, *Das Marienbild der frühen Jahrhunderte*, Iconographia ecclesiae orientalis, ed. H. Skrobucha (1968) 30f., who prefers the early sixth century. W. F. Volbach, *Early Christian Art*, trans. C. Ligota (New York n.d.) 326 prefers the second half of the fifth century. Of the other 2 examples that are tentatively dated in the fifth century, one is found upon the alabaster ciborium columns in S. Marco in Venice. But these are notoriously controversial as regards date: see, e. g., E. Weigand, "Zur Datierung der Ciboriumsäulen von S. Marco," *Atti del V congresso internazionale di studi bizantini, Roma 20-26 settembre 1936* (Rome 1940) 2.450f., who prefers to date the columns in the later Middle Ages. The last example is a relief fragment from Carthage that Klauser (n. 53 above) cat. no. 34b, col. 266, dates ca. 430. But this date rests upon comparisons with scenes of the Adoration of the Magi on other monuments and lacks precision – for this relief see *Dictionnaire d'archéologie chrétienne et de liturgie* 1.1.730, fig. 162. Only the two instances found in the mosaics of the triumphal arch of Sta. Maria Maggiore, dated ca. 435 by Klauser (cat. nos. 32b.1, 32b.3, col. 265), remain. They are apparently our earliest securely dated instances of guardian angels; I could find none that antedate them in the Princeton Index of Christian Art. But, lacking staffs or spears, they do not form a completely satisfying parallel to the iconography of the Lateran *fastigium*. For these two examples, see Oakeshott (n. 1 above) pl. 55. For bibliography concerning Sta. Maria Maggiore, see R. Krautheimer, S. Corbett, and W. Frankl, *Corpus basilicarum Romae* 3 (Vatican 1967) 1f.

62 Duchesne (n. 5 above) 1.233: "Fecit autem Valentinianus Augustus ex rogatu Xysti episcopi fastidium argenteum in basilica Constantiniana."

63 Krautheimer, *Corpus basilicarum* 3.5, 3.55.

64 Smith (n. 45 above) 156f. draws attention to this possibility.

65 Duchesne (n. 5 above) 1.233: "Ex huius supplicatione optulit Valentinianus Augustus imaginem auream cum XII portas et apostolos XII et Salvatorem gemmis pretiosissimis ornatam, quem voti gratiae suae super confessionem beati Petri apostoli posuit." Croquison (n. 52 above) 542 suggests that the image may have been an altar *antependium*. It was still in existence in the time of Pope Hadrian I (A.D. 772-795) – Toynbee and Ward Perkins (n. 3 above) 233 n. 43.

the Lateran Baptistery in Rome.[66] It states that the remains of Saint Peter were placed in a large bronze coffin, though this is now known to be false.[67] And it implies that Santa Costanza in Rome was built as a baptistery, although there is far better evidence that it was built as a mausoleum.[68]

Other, still later texts also inspire doubts. Five that reflect the influence of the Iconoclastic Controversy immediately come under suspicion: Iconodules, in their efforts to find unassailable precedents for a practice which they wanted to defend, understandably were strongly tempted to portray Constantine as a patron of religious images. Two of these reports are associated with Pope Hadrian: his letter to Constantine V, alleging that Constantine decorated his churches with images of Christ and the saints, and the testimony of his two legates at the Second Council of Nicaea (A.D. 787) that Constantine decorated the Lateran Basilica with images illustrating the Old and New Testaments.[69] A letter addressed to the Byzantine emperor Theophilus (A.D. 829-842), an Iconoclast, attempts to defend the admissibility of images by reporting that Constantine not only engraved as a token the saving and heaven-manifest cross, he also sponsored images of Christ, such as the blessed apostles handed down to the "Universal Church."[70] Another letter allegedly sent to Theophilus by a council that was held at Jerusalem in A.D. 836, attributes to Helena, Constantine's mother, a mosaic image of the Adoration of the Magi. This image allegedly adorned the exterior western wall of the Church of the Nativity in Bethlehem.[71] Finally, the *Patria Konstantinupoleos* (ca. A.D. 995) reports that

[66]Duchesne 1.174. This account is in conflict with the widely received account in the VC 4.61ff. For the literature on Constantine's baptism, see N. H. Baynes, *Constantine the Great and the Christian Church* (London 1931) 90f. (The entire monograph is reprinted from the *Proceedings of the British Academy* 15 [1929]. It has been reprinted in London in 1972.)

[67]Duchesne 1.176. After the Vatican excavations, this report is now recognized to be a "pious legend" – Toynbee and Ward Perkins (n. 3 above) 204.

[68]Duchesne 1.180f. This report is in conflict with the fourth-century historian Ammianus Marcellinus 21.1.5 who implies that the structure was used as a mausoleum. See H. Stern, "Les mosaïques de l'église de Sainte-Constance à Rome," *Dumbarton Oaks Papers* 12 (1958) 161.

[69]Mansi (n. 6 above) 12.1055ff. and Anastasius Bibliothecarius, quoted above in n. 4.

[70]*Epistola ad Theophilum Imperatorem* 3 (PG 95.348f.): γνώρισμα ἐγχαράττει τῷ βασιλικῷ τῆς πολιτείας νομίσματι, τό τε οὐρανοφανὲς σημεῖον τοῦ Σωτηρίου σταυροῦ . . . Ὡσαύτως δὲ ἐνιδρῦσθαι καὶ ἀναστηλοῦσθαι τὸν σεβάσμιον καὶ σεπτὸν χαρακτῆρα τῆς ἐνσάρκου πολιτείας αὐτοῦ, τῆς τε ἀχράντου μορφῆς αὐτοῦ τὰ χαρακτηρισικὰ ἰδιώματα . . .· ἐμφαίνοντος τὰ γνωρίσματα, καθὼς παρέδωκαν τῇ καθολικῇ Ἐκκλησίᾳ οἱ μακάριοι ἀπόστολοι· κατακοσμοῦντος αὐτὴν ζωγραφικαῖς ἱστορίαις καὶ μουσουργικοῖς ψηφίσιν . . . τὸν θεανδρικὸν χαρακτῆρα τοῦ Χριστοῦ ἐγκαθιδρύοντος. This is purportedly written by John of Damascus, but that is patently impossible, since he died long before the reign of Theophilus – J. D. Breckenridge, *Numismatic Iconography of Justinian II,* Numismatic Notes and Monographs 144 (1959) 61 n. 68.

[71]The relevant parts of the text are found in H. Vincent and F.-M. Abel, *Bethléem: Le Sanctuaire de la Nativité* (Paris 1914) 127f. The letter as a whole was edited by L. Duchesne, *Roma e l'Oriente* 5 (1912-1913) 222ff. The Persians who invaded Palestine in 614 are said to have spared the Church of the Nativity, since they recognized the Magi as their countrymen. Whatever the substance of the report, the attribution of the mosaic to Helena is questionable.

Leo III, an Iconoclast, destroyed a bronze statue of Christ, allegedly erected by Constantine the Great at the Chalke, the principal gateway to the imperial palace.[72] All of these reports are strongly suspect. Not only was there the desire to portray Constantine as a sponsor of Christian imagery, they are in conflict with the silence of contemporary sources and they are removed from the events they refer to by over four centuries.

Another text, allegedly written by Petronius, bishop and patron saint of Bologna, in the first half of the fifth century, has been used by Dmitrii Ainalov as evidence that Constantine decorated the memorial church of the Ascension on the Mount of Olives with "beautiful pictures."[73] Were this text as reliable as Ainalov thought, it would contribute important evidence, for, strangely, the late fourth-century pilgrim now identified as Aetheria was silent about images in Constantine's commemorative churches in the Holy Land.[74] Yet the text allegedly written by Petronius inspires little confidence. As its editors, Molinier and Kohler, point out, there is no corroborating evidence that Petronius ever made a pilgrimage to the Holy Land.[75] And I suspect there is reason – though not necessarily conclusive reason – to believe that the text was written later than the early fifth century. In describing the Holy Sepulcher, the author alludes to Golgotha, "where the cross on which Christ was fixed for the salvation of the world had been placed. In fact, this place is represented in different images of varied colors [*Ille vero locus variis imaginibus diversi coloris depictus est*]."[76] As the author gives no hint that these images of Golgotha were in any way unusual, it is tempting to suppose that they were Crucifixion scenes. But this inference makes it difficult to accept an early fifth-century date for the text,

---

Because Justinian extensively remodeled the church, it is generally thought that he or one of his successors was more likely responsible for the mosaic – B. Bagatti, *Gli antichi edifici sacri di Bethlemme,* Pubblicazioni dello Studium biblicum franciscanum 9 (1952) 13. For the remodeling of the church, also see J. W. Crowfoot, *Early Churches in Palestine,* The Schweich Lectures of the British Academy 1937 (London 1941) 79.

[72] Preger (n. 6 above) 2.219: Ἐν τῇ λεγομένῃ Χαλκῇ στήλη χαλκῆ ἦν τοῦ κυρίου ἡμῶν Ἰησοῦ Χριστοῦ παρὰ τοῦ μεγάλου Κωνσταντίνου κτισθεῖσα· ὁ δὲ Λέων ὁ πατὴρ τοῦ Καβαλλίνου ταύτην κατήγαγεν.

[73] "In medio autem templi atrium cum columnis pretiosorum lapidum tereti circulo mire exornavit, & vestibulum, quod erat ante atrium, vestivit variis lapidibus lactei coloris cum coelaturis suis. Parietes autem totius aedificii, atrii & vestibuli circumquaque in circuitu per girum pulchris picturis decorare studuit. A pede montis huius usque ad verticem ascensus erat per marmoreos gradus. In medio atrii est locus, ex quo, cernentibus discipulis, Christus ascendit in coelum. In eodem vero loco Spiritus Sanctus venit super eos, & dedit illis scientiam omnium linguarum . . . ." – ed. A. Molinier and C. Kohler, *Itinera Hierosolymitana et descriptiones Terrae sanctae* 2 (Geneva 1885) 146; and Ainalov (n. 1 above) 231. For Petronius see *Lexikon für Theologie und Kirche* 8.328.

[74] Aetheria, in referring to Constantine's basilica at Golgotha, simply says that Constantine honored (*honoravit*) it with a decoration of gold, mosaic (*musivo*), and marble – ed. P. Geyer, *Itinera Hierosolymitana, saeculi IIII-VIII,* Corpus scriptorum ecclesiasticorum latinorum (CSEL) 39 (1898) 76.

[75] Molinier and Kohler 147.

[76] *Ibid.* 145.

since it appears that images of the Crucifixion were not widely accepted until the sixth century.[77] It is also somewhat disconcerting to find the author believing that the descent of the Holy Spirit occurred where the disciples saw Christ ascend.[78] This is inconsistent with the testimony of other pilgrims and it increases one's doubts about the usefulness of the text.[79]

The later sources, then, present an account of Constantine's sponsorship of Christian imagery that differs strikingly from that presented by contemporary sources. Unfortunately these later sources are unreliable. As a result, there is no good evidence that Constantine either sponsored Christian images in his churches or that he was ever associated with a likeness of Christ. The contemporary sources, which speak with greater authority, are unexpectedly silent on these points, in spite of the strong desire of authors like Eusebius to portray Constantine as a devout patron of Christianity.

An unexpected silence is similarly found in the realm of public imagery. Previous emperors were eager to associate their image with that of their preferred patron deity. And they did it in many ways, one of the most striking of which on coins was to have their profile effigy overlap the profile effigy of their patron god.[80] Constantine himself used this formula on the obverses of gold medallions minted at Ticinum

[77] K. Wessel, "Frühbyzantinische Darstellung der Kreuzigung Christi," *Rivista di archeologia cristiana* 36 (1960) 45 for the retarded adoption of the Crucifixion image.

[78] See the passage quoted above in n. 73.

[79] The site of the descent of the Holy Spirit was traditionally identified with the church of Sion – H. Vincent and F.-M. Abel, *Jérusalem, recherches de topographie, d'archéologie et d'histoire* 2: *Jérusalem nouvelle* (Paris 1914-1926) fasc. 2.421, 452.

[80] For jugate profiles of the Gallic emperor Postumus (A.D. 259-268) and Hercules, see H. Mattingly and E. A. Sydenham, *Probus to Amandus*, The Roman Imperial Coinage (RIC) 5.2 (1933) 358, 360; and A. D. Nock, "The Emperor's Divine Comes," *Journal of Roman Studies* 37 (1947) 107f. Similarly for Probus (A.D. 276-282) and Sol Invictus, M. R. Alföldi, *Die constantinische Goldprägung* (Mainz 1963) pl. 22, cat. no. 274. Other examples of an emperor signaling his divine patron by means of an anthropomorphic image could be cited on coins. Examples also can be found in monumental public images. On the reliefs found near the Palazzo della Cancelleria, Rome, Domitian is found in the presence of Mars and Minerva – J. M. C. Toynbee, *The Flavian Reliefs from the Palazzo della Cancelleria in Rome*, Charlton Lectures on Art 39 (1957) 9; and E. Simon, "Zu den flavischen Reliefs von der Cancelleria," *Jahrbuch des deutschen archäologischen Instituts* 75 (1960) 136ff. The relief sculpture of the triumphal arch of Septimius Severus at Lepcis Magna is replete with similar juxtapositions – J. M. C. Toynbee, "Picture-Language in Roman Art and Coinage," *Essays in Roman Coinage Presented to Harold Mattingly* (Oxford 1956) 207ff. In the Forum Romanum, statues of the Tetrarchs stood upon columns in the company of a column-borne statue of Jupiter – H. P. L'Orange, "Ein tetrarchisches Ehrendenkmal auf dem Forum Romanum," *Mitteilungen des deutschen archäologischen Instituts, römische Abteilung* 53 (1938) 1-34; and H. Kähler, *Das Funfsäulendenkmal für die Tetrarchen auf dem Forum Romanum*, Monumenta artis romanae 3 (1964) 9. The mingling of the Tetrarchs and their divine patrons is also found on the Arch of Galerius at Salonika – K. F. Kinch, *L'arc de triomphe de Salonique* (Paris 1890) 26, pl. 6; and A. Alföldi, "Die Ausgestaltung des monarchischen Zeremoniells am römischen Kaiserhofe," *Mitteilungen des deutschen archäologischen Instituts, römische Abteilung* 49 (1934) 44.

in A.D. 313.[81] There his profile overlaps the profile of Sol Invictus, who wears a radiate crown. But, when it came to Christ, judging from contemporary Christian authors, Constantine rejected this tradition. On the one hand, even though they badly wanted to portray Constantine as a pious devotee of Christ, they make no mention of public images in which Constantine is associated with an image of Christ.[82] On the other hand, they allege that Constantine expressed his faith in the Savior's power through a sign.[83] And, if they are to be trusted, this sign was believed to possess miraculous powers of protection.[84] Constantine's position vis-à-vis the traditions of his predecessors is succinctly portrayed in the following passage, which is found virtually unchanged in both the *Vita Constantini* and the *Triakontaeterikos*:

> So those who warred against the Universal King were confident in the aid of a great many gods. As a defense they advanced idols of the spent dead in the form of lifeless statues and they attacked with a powerful military

[81] M. Alföldi, *Goldprägung* 40f., ill. 60, cat. no. 118.

[82] This is surprising since they were concerned to point to tangible evidences of Constantine's Christian sympathies. They make frequent reference to his public monuments. I cite here, without comment or (save in one instance) secondary sources, only those references to images or relevant monuments which follow Constantine's victory over Maxentius in 312: (1) Eusebius, HE (n. 19 above) 10.4 claims that Constantine and Licinius acknowledged Christ on their monuments in Rome by means of inscriptions. This reference is datable ca. 317 and thus, according to C. Ligota, "Constantiniana," *Journal of the Warburg and Courtauld Institutes* 26 (1963) 189, is our earliest reference to a Christian monument erected in Rome by Constantine. (2) Eusebius, HE 9.9 reports that, immediately after his victory over Maxentius, Constantine's statue was erected in Rome, presumably portraying him in military attire. He had it placed in the most public place in Rome and ordered the sign of the Savior's Passion to be placed in the statue's right hand. He also added an inscription which referred to the sign as the "saving sign, the true proof of courage." Eusebius, *Triakontaeterikos* 9.8, and the author of the VC (n. 10 above) 1.40 repeat this report. (3) The author of the VC 3.3 describes an encaustic panel placed over the gate to the imperial palace in Constantinople: it featured Constantine and his sons trampling underfoot a serpent, which allegedly personified the enemy of the Church. (4) The author of the VC 4.15 refers to full-length images of Constantine which were placed over palace gates in some cities, showing him in a pose of prayer, with upraised eyes and hands outspread. (5) In the same passage he refers to gold coins of Constantine that likewise showed him gazing into the heavens. (6) The author of the VC 1.8 refers to images which conquered nations dedicated to Constantine. (7) According to the same author, VC 3.49, Constantine had the "sign of the Savior's Passion" placed overhead, on a ceiling in one of the chambers of his palace in Constantinople. (8) He describes – VC 4.73 – an image on the reverses of one of Constantine's consecration issues, showing Constantine as a charioteer, ascending into the heavens with a hand stretching downward to receive him. (9) The author of the VC 4.69 also reports that, at Rome, Constantine was honored through images which showed him reposing in the heavens. (10) Finally, statues of Constantine were posthumously erected by his sons throughout the empire – VC 4.72.

[83] Lactantius, *De mortibus persecutorum* (hereafter MP) 44.5, and VC 1.31. These passages, the difficulties they involve, and the many studies devoted to them, are too well-known to bear repeating here. But the reader who is unfamiliar with these studies would do well to consult the following two discussions: A. Alföldi, "Hoc signo victor eris," *Pisciculi* (Munich 1939) 1-18; and H. I. Marrou, "Autour du monogramme constantinien," *Mélanges offerts à Etienne Gilson* (Paris 1959) 403-410.

[84] Lactantius, MP 44.5; Eusebius, HE 9.9; VC 1.29, 1.31, 2.7, 2.9, 2.55, 3.2, 4.5, 4.21.

> force. But the pious one, having armed himself with the saving and lifegiving sign, as if it were an awesome defense against evil, stood in array against the multitude of foes. Immediately he obtained the victory against enemy and demon alike.[85]

Another passage in the *Vita Constantini* is even more explicit. According to it, Constantine's armies were preceded only by the symbol of the salutary trophy, not by golden images as in the past.[86] Clearly, Constantine's Christian contemporaries contrasted the "saving sign," which was carried by Constantine's armies, with the "lifeless statues," allegedly rejected by Constantine and carried by the armies of his enemies. Evidently they saw nothing unusual in Constantine's substitution of a sign for a "lifeless statue." Indeed, as I hope to show, it may have disturbed them to see images of Christ used by the emperor. Is it not therefore possible that they deliberately misrepresented Constantine's public imagery and simply omitted to mention images of Christ which Constantine may have sponsored? Fortunately, when it comes to Constantine's public imagery, there is independent evidence against which to test the reports of contemporary Christian authors, for, even though they constitute our only source for a few of Constantine's public images,[87] they by no means control our entire sample. Abundant material is provided by coins and there the question of a biased sample does not arise. Similarly, although Christian authors provide an interpretation of the chi-rho symbol that sometimes appears in Constantine's public imagery,[88] their interpretation could be challenged by the use made of that symbol on Constantine's coins. Therefore, it is advisable to consider Constantine's public imagery in order to test the silence Christian sources maintain about images of Christ.

Not only is there no evidence of an image of Christ in Constantine's public

[85] *Triakontaeterikos* 9.5-11 (Heikel [n. 15 above] 219): ἀλλ' οἱ μὲν τῷ βασιλεῖ τῶν ὅλων πεπολεμωμένοι, πολυπληθείᾳ θεῶν θαρροῦντες σὺν πολλῇ δυνάμει χειρὸς στρατιωτικῆς ἐπῄεσαν, νεκρῶν εἴδωλα καμνόντων, ἐν ἀψύχοις ἀγάλμασι προβεβλημένοι, ὁ δ' εὐσεβείας θώρακι πεφραγμένος, τὸ σωτήριον καὶ ζωοποιὸν σημεῖον, ὥσπερ τι φόβητρον καὶ κακῶν ἀμυντήριον, τῷ πλήθει τῶν ἐναντίων ἀντιπαρατάξας, ὁμοῦ τὴν κατ' ἐχθρῶν καὶ κατὰ δαιμόνων νίκην ἀπηνέγκατο . . . . Cf. VC 2.16 (Heikel 47f.). The reference to *nekrōn eidōla kamnontōn* in this passage was probably inspired by the belief, held by Christians, that the pagan practice of worshipping images of the gods originated from honoring dead men with images. For other expressions of this belief, see J. Geffcken, "Der Bilderstreit des heidnischen Altertums," *Archiv für Religionswissenschaft* 19 (1916/1919) 293f.

[86] VC 4.21 (Heikel 125): Ἤδη δὲ καὶ ἐπ' αὐτῶν τῶν ὅπλων τὸ τοῦ σωτηρίου τροπαίου σύμβολον κατασημαίνεσθαι ἐποίει, τοῦ τε ἐνόπλου στρατοῦ προπομπεύειν χρυσῶν μὲν ἀγαλμάτων, ὁποῖα πρότερον αὐτοῖς ἔθος ἦν, τὸ μηθὲν μόνον δὲ τὸ σωτήριον τρόπαιον.

[87] E. g., Constantine's statue in Rome – Eusebius, HE 9.9.

[88] To them it was preeminently a symbol of Christ's name, but not exclusively so – see below.

images,[89] it has even been questioned that they present any Christian symbolism at all.[90] The issue is an important one for us, for, if it turns out that Christian symbolism is entirely lacking in Constantine's public imagery, then the absence of an image of Christ would be explicable in terms of a decision simply not to use Christian signs or symbols. The outcome depends largely upon the intended significance of the chi-rho symbol in Constantine's public imagery, which is best represented by his coins.[91] Scholars today disagree sharply about the intended meaning of this symbol. Some who doubt that it was adopted or used by Constantine as a Christian sign have explained its origin in his public imagery in a variety of ways that diverge from the traditional Christian interpretation.[92] It would be satisfying to have the issue decided, whatever the outcome. Unfortunately, the challenges to the identification of this sign as a Christian sign, an identification based upon the testimony of Lactantius (writing between 313 and 315 A.D.)[93] and the author of the *Vita Constantini* (writing shortly after Constantine's death in A.D. 337),[94] in my opinion,

[89] No one today maintains that images of Christ were found in Constantine's public images. As we have seen, not even contemporary Christian authors, always eager to portray Constantine as a devotee of Christ, claimed that such images existed. See n. 82 above.

[90] P. Bruun, *Constantine and Licinius, A.D. 313-337,* RIC (n. 80 above) 7 (1966) 64. Bruun would apparently be willing to extend this claim to Constantine's monumental images as well, as he doubts that the chi-rho symbol was intended as a Christian sign. This sign probably decorated the standard that Constantine's statue in Rome apparently held, judging from Eusebius's description (HE 9.9) and from later numismatic images – P. Bruun, "The Christian Signs on the Coins of Constantine," *Arctos* n. s. 3 (1962) 27f. This also is the opinion of A. Alföldi, *The Conversion of Constantine and Pagan Rome*, trans. H. Mattingly (London 1948) 42.

[91] The bibliography on this topic is too vast to cite fully. These are some of the important studies relating generally to the Christogram: M. Sulzberger, "Le symbole de la Croix et les monogrammes de Jésus chez les premiers Chrétiens," *Byzantion* 2 (1925) 393ff.; P. Bruun, "Symboles, signes et monogrammes," *Acta Instituti Romani Finlandiae* 1.2 (1963) 97f., 156-160; and Marrou (n. 83 above). Important studies of the use of this symbol on the coins of Constantine are Bruun, "Christian Signs"; W. Kellner, *Libertas und Christogramm* (Karlsruhe 1968) 81-97; K. Kraft, "Das Silbermedaillon Constantins des Grossen mit dem Christus-monogram auf dem Helm," *Jahrbuch für Numismatik und Geldgeschichte* 5/6 (1954/1955) 151-178: M. Alföldi (n. 80 above) 139ff. It has, however, also been suggested that the hand reaching down from the heavens to crown Constantine on a gold medallion struck in Constantinople during Constantine's reign possesses a Christian character – W. Seston, "La vision paienne de 310 et les origines du chrisme constantinien," *Annuaire de l'Institut de philologie et d'histoire orientales et slaves* 4 (1936) 381f., and M. Alföldi (n. 80 above) 136 n. 2. H. Stern, *Le calendrier de 354.* Bibliothèque archéologique et historique 55 (1953) 151, on the other hand, points out that the image of the divine hand was not used exclusively in Jewish or Christian contexts and therefore its alleged Christian significance is hard to demonstrate.

[92] Some of the better known alternative explanations will be outlined below.

[93] MP (n. 83 above) 44.5. The value of this important testimony is considerably enhanced by a recent, elaborate argument for dating its composition between 313 and 315, earlier than had heretofore been generally thought – T. D. Barnes, "Lactantius and Constantine," *Journal of Roman Studies* 63 (1973) 29-46.

[94] VC (n. 10 above) 1.31. The authorship and date of this source have of course been controversial. See n. 12 above.

are not very compelling.[95] Take, for example, the recent challenge offered by Patrick Bruun.[96] Bruun is impressed by the lack of convincing evidence that the chi-rho symbol was used as a Christian sign prior to its adoption by Constantine.[97] If there were a strong tradition of its use as a Christian sign previous to its adoption, then it would obviously appear reasonable to say that Constantine adopted a Christian sign for use in his public images. It now appears that there are no securely dated instances of a demonstrable Christian use of the chi-rho symbol prior to the era of Constantine.[98] Hence, Christian testimony, which conceivably could have misrepresented Constantine's intentions, remains the sole foundation of the traditional identification.

Even if Bruun is right in saying that there are no securely dated instances of the chi-rho symbol in Christian contexts before the reign of Constantine, it would be a mistake to infer from this – as I fear Bruun does – the further, more forceful conclusion that there was no tradition of Christian symbolism to which the chi-rho symbol could have been genetically related.[99]

To see why this forceful conclusion is false, it would be helpful, first, to isolate an assumption that has distracted scholars from some obvious, but important questions. The chi-rho symbol on Constantine's coins has been explained as a reinterpretation of other, similarly shaped symbols. Some have suggested that the archetypal symbol was a sign, interpreted as a promise of a thirty-year reign, which Constantine allegedly witnessed in a pagan "vision" of A.D. 310.[100] Others have suggested that it was a star symbol which Constantine allegedly used as an emblem of his patron deity, Sol-Apollo.[101] Interesting as these suggestions are, they seem to

[95] See, e. g., Kraft's criticisms of one of these challenges (n. 91 above) 157f. As we shall see below, one of the strongest reasons for rejecting these alternatives is their inability to explain the miraculous apotropaic power Constantine evidently believed this sign possessed.

[96] Bruun, "Christian Signs" (n. 90 above) 5-35, and *Constantine* (n. 90 above) 61ff. On the other hand, Bruun, "Early Christian Symbolism on Coins and Inscriptions," *Atti del VI congresso internazionale di archeologia cristiana, Ravenna 23-30 settembre 1962* (Rome 1965) 534, suggests that the chi-rho monogram may have been used in a program of imperial propaganda aimed at the Christian community and directed by Ossius of Cordova.

[97] Bruun, "Symboles" (n. 91 above) 156ff.; *Constantine* (n. 90 above) 61.

[98] E. Dinkler, "Älteste christliche Denkmäler: Bestand und Chronologie," *Signum crucis* (Tübingen 1967) 142f.

[99] Bruun, *Constantine* (n. 90 above) 64.

[100] "Vidisti enim, credo, Constantine, Apollinem tuum comitante Victoria coronas tibi laureas offerentem, quae tricenum singulae ferunt omen annorum" – *Panégyric VII*, ed. E. Galletier, *Panégyriques latins* 2 (Paris 1952) 72. Both H. Grégoire, "La Conversion de Constantin," *Revue de l'Université de Bruxelles* 36 (1930/1931) 256ff., and A. Piganiol, *L'empereur Constantin* (Paris 1932) 49ff., see the Christogram as a modification of the omen of 30 years to which the pagan panegyrist refers above.

[101] Seston (n. 91 above) 390; *idem*, "L'opinion païenne et la conversion de Constantin," *Revue d'histoire et de philosophie religieuses* 16 (1936) 252; P. Orgels, "La première Vision de Constantin (310) et la temple d'Apollon à Nimes," *Bulletin de la Classe des lettres et des sciences morales et politiques, Académie royale de Belgique*, ser. 5, 34 (1948) 179; and J. Moreau, "Sur la Vision de Constantin," *Revue des études anciennes* 55 (1953) 320.

have been advanced on the assumption that the key test of any explanation of the chi-rho symbol was the ability to point to an antecedent symbol that looked like the chi-rho and which could be plausibly connected with Constantine. This seems innocent enough, but it ignores another important consideration – the peculiar use Constantine made of the chi-rho symbol. Why did he use it on his helmet and as part of his personal standard, as his coins testify?[102] Christian testimony supplies an attractively plausible answer: Constantine believed that the sign possessed miraculous powers of protection.[103] It is difficult to imagine any other plausible reason why this sign would have been used almost exclusively in military contexts and personally connected with Constantine. Bruun himself identifies it as Constantine's personal sign of victory and believes that it was associated with his victory at the Milvian Bridge.[104] But why did Constantine adopt this particular sign? What was the source of its prophylactic power, warranting that it be placed upon a shield, a helmet, or a standard? These questions, which Bruun fails to answer, can be attractively answered by turning to Christian traditions.

It is an interesting fact that Christians traced upon their foreheads a symbol that was widely believed to possess precisely the kind of prophylactic power that was

[102] The chi-rho symbol appears upon Constantine's helmet on coins minted at Ticinum and Siscia. On the celebrated silver multiple with the reverse legend SALVS REIPVBLICAE and on a solidus with the reverse legend VICTOR OMNIVM GENTIVM, both minted at Ticinum, probably in celebration of Constantine's decennalia in 315, the obverse presents a frontal bust portrait of Constantine. His helmet appears to be decorated with a badge containing the chi-rho symbol – Bruun, "Christian Signs" (n. 90 above) 9, 32, fig. 5a; *Constantine* (n. 90 above) pl. 9, no. 36; M. Alföldi (n. 80 above) pl. 4, no. 61, pl. 5, no. 62; A. Alföldi, "The Initials of Christ on the Helmet of Constantine," *Studies in Roman Economic and Social History in Honor of Allen Chester Johnson* (Princeton 1951) 303-311; and Kraft (n. 91 above) 151-178. Some of the coins minted at Siscia, 318-319, manifest a helmeted profile bust of Constantine. The helmet, which is perhaps related to the helmet he wears on the coins minted at Ticinum, has a crossbar that, in at least 3 instances, was decorated with the chi-rho symbol – Bruun, "Christian Signs" 14ff., fig. 6a, who concludes that the rarity of this sign in the issues of Siscia "excludes the possibility that the intention of any central authority was to display the christogram on the helmet" (p. 16). Kellner (n. 91 above) 82f. provides the most satisfying explanation of these occurrences: one of the die engravers evidently was familiar with imperial images in which Constantine's helmet was decorated with the chi-rho symbol, as one sees it on the medallions minted at Ticinum; he wanted to make it visible in Constantine's profile portraits as well and therefore transposed it from the front of the helmet to the crossbar on the side. This explanation has important implications. The die engraver may have, on his own initiative, transposed the symbol from one place on Constantine's helmet to another; he did not necessarily add to the helmet an unauthorized sign, for which there was no precedent. Thus Bruun's conclusion is stated in a misleading fashion, in so far as it implies that the die engraver was acting in an unauthorized fashion. Another important occurrence of the chi-rho symbol is found on the coins minted at Constantinople shortly after 326 with the SPES PVBLIC reverse, showing the victorious standard, crowned by the chi-rho symbol, piercing a serpent; from its crosspiece hangs a banner with 3 dots, undoubtedly representing imperial effigies in roundels – Bruun (n. 96 above) 533, "Christian Signs" (n. 90 above) 22f., 31, *Constantine* (n. 90 above) 62, 64, pl. 18, no.19; Kellner 88f.

[103] Cited above, n. 84.

[104] Bruun, "Christian Signs" (n. 90 above) 17f., 23, and *Constantine* (n. 90 above) 61f.

attributed to the chi-rho symbol.[105] This symbol was nominally the sign of the cross. But it was sometimes interpreted as Christ's name, presumably because it could be inscribed in a slanted manner, suggesting the chi, the initial letter of *Christos.* [106] In fact, the letter chi was sometimes used as an abbreviation of the name of Christ.[107] Apparently, then, the simple formal identity between a cross sign inscribed in a slanted fashion and the Greek letter chi allowed the sign Christians used upon their brow to be interpreted as a sign of Christ, both in respect to his cross

[105] According to Tertullian, *De corona* 3.25-30, ed. A. Kroymann, Corpus Christianorum, series latina 2 (1954) 1043, Christians on all occasions traced the sign of the cross upon their foreheads: "Ad omnem progressum atque promotum, ad omnem aditum et exitum, ad uestitum, ad calciatum, ad lauacra, ad mensas, ad lumina, ad cubilia, ad sedilia, quacumque nos conuersatio exercet, frontem signaculo terimus." For this and related passages, see Sulzberger (n. 91 above) 361 and F. J. Dölger, "Beiträge zur Geschichte des Kreuzzeichens I," *Jahrbuch für Antike und Christentum* 1 (1958) 5-13. Origen, *Selecta in Ezechielem* 9 (PG 13.800ff.), reports the belief that the form of the Hebrew Taw resembled the cross and that it prefigured the mark which Christians traced upon their foreheads. Tertullian, *Adversus Marcionem* 3.22, like Origen, sees the ritual mark upon the forehead in Ezekiel 9.4 as a prefiguration of the sign of the cross which Christians used – J. Finegan, *The Archeology of the New Testament* (Princeton 1969) 230. The power of this sign to avert evil is made evident in the *Apostolic Constitutions* of Hippolytus, ed. B. Botte, *La tradition apostolique*, SC (n. 19 above) 11 (Paris 1968) 136: "Frontem uero et oculos per manu(m) consignantes declinemus eum qui exterminare temptat." Cyril of Jerusalem, *Catechesis IV* 14 and *Catechesis XIII* 36 provides evidence of the ubiquity of this practice among Christians; cf. Dölger, "Beiträge . . . VIII," *Jahrbuch für Antike und Christentum* 8/9 (1965/1966) 28. Since the sign of the cross was believed to be a powerful safeguard, its use was essential in times of danger. Evidently Christians signed themselves with the cross when they were near pagan rites in order to avert demons. It was this practice, alleges Lactantius, that caused pagan rites to fail, and which led pagan priests to inspire hatred in the emperors against the Christians – MP (n. 83 above) 10.1-3 and *Divinae institutiones* 4.27. Cf. Dölger, "Beiträge . . . VI," *Jahrbuch für Antike und Christentum* 6 (1963) 11f. When Julian the Apostate visited Athena's shrine at Ilium, he was greatly relieved to find that his guide did not behave as Christians normally did in such circumstances; he neither signed his forehead nor hissed at demons, the very two actions that, according to Julian, epitomized Christian theology – Julian, *Letter to a Priest*, ed. Wright (n. 41 above) 3.51. Julian, *Against the Galilaeans*, ed. Wright 3.372, accuses the Christians of engraving the cross on the fronts of their houses: *τὸ τοῦ σταυροῦ . . . ξύλον, εἰκόνας αὐτοῦ . . . πρὸ τῶν οἰκημάτων ἐγγράφοντες*. This is evidently another measure of the faith Christians had in the apotropaic power of the sign of the cross.

[106] Eusebius, *Martyrs of Palestine* 8.7 – Bardy (n. 19 above) 146 – reports that the martyr Valentina traced upon herself the name of the Savior as she was brought before the tribunal: *εἶτα σύρεται εἰς μέσον* [of the tribunal], *καὶ τὸ σεβάσμιον τοῦ σωτῆρος ἐπιγραψαμένη ὄνομα* . . . . Sulzberger (n. 91 above) 414 regarded this as an extremely important passage, as it seemed to imply the identity of the cross and the monogram of Christ. He thought that Valentina used either the chi-rho monogram or the chi to sign herself. Finegan (n. 105 above) 231 would identify this sign as a cross mark written in the form of the letter chi. Another instance of the identity of the sign of the cross and Christ's name is given in VC 3.2, discussed below.

[107] Julian, *Misopogon* – Wright (n. 41 above) 2.483 – reports that the citizens of Antioch used the letter chi to represent Christ. The sign referred to in Eusebius's account of the martyrdom of Valentina (see above) was probably understood as a chi as well as a cross and, hence, as an abbreviation of "Christos." The chi in the acrostic IXΘYC stood for "Christos" – F. J. Dölger, *IXΘYC: Das Fischsymbol in frühchristlicher Zeit* 1 (Rome 1910) 366, and E. Stommel, "Semeion ekpetaseos (Didache 16, 6)," *Römische Quartalschrift für christliche Altertumskunde und für Kirchengeschichte* 48 (1953) 38.

and his name. Here, then, is an important Christian symbol, traced by hand, with two outstanding attributes: apotropaic power and a double meaning that must have enhanced its attractiveness as a symbol. Perhaps it is more than coincidence that references in the *Vita Constantini* to the "saving sign" which Constantine used reveal a similar double meaning. The author clearly understands it as an abbreviation of the name *Christos* when he describes Constantine's personal standard and refers to the initials of Christ on Constantine's helmet.[108] Just as clearly he understands it as a cross sign when he reports that Constantine placed upon a ceiling in his palace in Constantinople "the sign of the Savior's Passion."[109] Most significantly of all, the author fails to recognize any distinction between the sign used by Constantine and the sign Christians traced upon their foreheads. He claims that Constantine did not shrink from an open profession of the "salutary name" of Christ. Instead, one of the ways in which he manifested it was by sealing his face with the "saving sign": *νῦν μὲν τὸ πρόσωπον τῷ σωτηρίῳ κατασφραγιζόμενος σημείῳ*.[110] In view of the prophylactic power this sign possessed and its ambivalent symbolism, it is not unlikely that the chi-rho symbol was adopted simply as a graphic interpretation of the symbol that Christians used to sign their foreheads in times of danger.

It has also been suggested that the chi-rho symbol was created as a modified form of the monogrammatic cross ⳨, which first appears in Christian contexts in manuscripts of the third century.[111] There it was used as a partial abbreviation of the Greek word for cross: *s⳨os = stauros*.[112] In these contexts, it does not stand alone, but later it does, possibly before the fourth century.[113] Given the identification of the cross and the letter chi, it is possible that the chi-rho symbol came into being simply as a variant of the monogrammatic cross, with no distinction between them as regards significance.

[108] VC (n. 10 above) 1.31.

[109] VC 3.49.

[110] VC 3.2. Dölger, "Beiträge . . . III" (n. 105 above) 3 (1960) 10, takes this as the second instance in which one sees the sign of the cross, which Christians traced upon their foreheads, referred to as a sign of Christ's name; as Dölger points out, this passage does not necessarily imply that Constantine was, at that time, a Christian – "Beiträge . . . VIII" (n. 105 above) 47f.

[111] K. Aland, "Neue neutestamentliche Papyri II," *New Testament Studies* 10 (1963/1964) 75-79.

[112] *Ibid.*; Dinkler (n. 98 above) 177f.; and Finegan (n. 105 above) 234, 254.

[113] This possibility rests upon one monument – the funeral inscription of Beratius Nikatoras in the Lateran Museum. It bears two isolated monogrammatic crosses, accompanied by pictorial references to Jonah, Daniel, and a shepherd: P. Testini, *Le catacombe e gli antichi cimiteri cristiani in Roma*, Roma cristiana 2 (Bologna 1966) 152, fig. 198. Since the inscription was discovered in a burial site located within the Aurelian wall, it has been thought to antedate the reign of Aurelian (270-275) – Bruun (n. 91 above) 95f., 97f., who, however, points out that at least one scholar, A. Stuiber, *Refrigerium interim*, Theophania 11 (1957) 165f., argues that the cemetery continued in use after the completion of the wall. One of the earliest securely dated instances – if not the earliest – is the monogrammatic cross on a Constantinian solidus minted at Antioch, dated 336/337 – Kellner (n. 91 above) 93; Bruun, "Christian Signs" (n. 90 above) fig. 16.

Though these remain nothing more than attractive possibilities, they are worth pointing out to forestall the conclusion that there was no tradition of Christian symbolism which might have given rise to the chi-rho symbol.

Bruun's other arguments are based upon his examination of Constantine's coins. He identifies the chi-rho symbol as Constantine's personal symbol of victory, a symbol somehow associated with the battle of the Milvian Bridge.[114] But he regards it as devoid of intended Christian significance.[115] Why? There seem to be two general circumstances upon which Bruun bases his conclusion. First, the chi-rho symbol is sometimes used as a mark of issue and, in those cases, it is hard to imagine its being used as an important religious symbol.[116] Second, its significant uses on Constantine's coins are so rare that a propaganda offensive involving the chi-rho symbol is out of the question.[117] Bruun evidently would be more inclined to accept the identification of the chi-rho symbol as a Christian sign if its significant uses on Constantine's coins were more frequent and part of an officially directed propaganda campaign. This second circumstance, however, does not amount to a strong argument against the identification of the chi-rho symbol as a Christian sign when it does appear in significant contexts, as, for example, when it appears upon Constantine's helmet. Its occurrence as a Christian symbol in these contexts need not have been motivated by a desire to proclaim a personal allegiance to Christ. Rather, its occurrence may have been incidental, merely a result of Constantine's desire to commemorate victorious struggles in which, as it happens, he used the "saving sign" as a personal apotropaic charm, both on his helmet and standard.[118] If the chi-rho symbol appeared on Constantine's coins for this reason, then one would expect its occurrence there to have been less frequent than it would have been in a campaign to announce imperial support for Christianity.

If, then, there is no compelling reason to doubt the testimony of Lactantius and the author of the *Vita Constantini,* if the chi-rho symbol on Constantine's coins was a Christian sign, then it follows that there was no decision on Constantine's part to prohibit the presence of Christian signs in his public imagery. In turn, this means that one plausible explanation for the absence of images of Christ in Constantine's public imagery is undercut. If the chi-rho symbol was the sign of Christ, then it would appear, just as the author of the *Vita Constantini* implies, that Constantine broke with the tradition of expressing an association with patron divinities by means of anthropomorphic figures, insofar as Christ was concerned. Why did Constantine do so?

[114]Bruun, "Christian Signs" 17f.

[115]Bruun, *Constantine* (n. 90 above) 61f.

[116]Bruun, "Christian Signs" 25, 31, 33; *Constantine* 62.

[117]Bruun, "Christian Signs" 23, 31.

[118]Both A. Alföldi (n. 102 above) 311 and Kellner (n. 91 above) 94f. regard the chi-rho symbol as narrowly connected with military victories that Constantine evidently attributed to Christ's aid. Kellner in fact believes that this explains why the monogram appears so seldom on Constantine's coins.

The explanation is not that images of Christ were unavailable. Eusebius saw painted portraits of the apostles and Christ.[119] And the Christian community house at Dura Europos (before A.D. 256) was decorated with images, among which were several images of Christ.[120] Nor is it altogether that Constantine feared antagonizing militant pagans, although this surely must have been a real fear: in the East some pagans were so militantly opposed to Christians that they petitioned Maximinus to continue the persecution;[121] and, when Constantine refused to sacrifice on the Capitoline Hill in A.D. 326, the pagan population is said to have greeted him with hostility.[122] Still, Constantine risked pagan antagonism by abandoning images of the traditional gods on his coins.[123] It is hard to believe that this change went unperceived by advocates of the traditional pagan deities, who could recall the conspicuous piety of the Tetrarchs and their pagan successors.[124] Constantine took other steps that alienated pagan opinion, not least of which was the founding and reconstruction of Christian churches.[125] What, then, is the explanation? It is, I

[119] HE (n. 19 above) 7.18.

[120] P. V. C. Baur, "The Paintings in the Christian Chapel," *The Excavations at Dura Europos Conducted by Yale University and the French Academy of Inscriptions and Letters: Preliminary Report of the Fifth Season of Work*, ed. M. I. Rostovtzeff (New Haven 1934) 254-283; A. Perkins, *The Art of Dura Europos* (Oxford 1973) 52ff., and Grabar (n. 9 above) 19ff.

[121] Eusebius, HE 9.2, 9.7, 9.9, 9a.4; Lactantius, MP (n. 83 above) 36.3; and Kraft (n. 91 above) 166f.

[122] Zosimus, *Historia nova* 2.29.5.

[123] The latest issue with an effigy of Sol is that published by M. Alföldi, "Die Sol Comes-Münze vom Jahre 325," *Mullus: Festschrift T. Klauser* (Münster i. W. 1964) 10-16, minted at Antioch. Other mints, however, terminated their Sol coinage much earlier – Bruun, *Constantine* (n. 90 above) 39, 48; and *idem*, "The Disappearance of Sol from the Coins of Constantine," *Arctos*, n. s. 2 (1958) 15-37. Bruun, *Constantine* 61, attributes the disappearance of the gods not to Constantine's Christian sympathies, but to a tendency towards "divine rulership." Whatever reasons Constantine may have had to abandon the gods on his coins, the point here is that he ran considerable risk of alienating pagans by doing so.

[124] Typical expressions of their piety are the five-column monument that stood in the Roman Forum and the Arch of Galerius, Salonika, both of which feature the juxtaposition of the Tetrarchs and their divine patrons; for both monuments, see n. 80 above.

[125] Constantine appears to have refused to perform the traditional sacrifices at the temple of Jupiter Optimus Maximus, not just at his vicennalia in 326, as reported by Zosimus, *Historia nova* 2.29.5, but earlier on the occasion of his triumphal entry into Rome after his victory at the Milvian Bridge – J. Straub, "Konstantins Verzicht auf den Gang zum Kapitol," *Historia* 4 (1955) 304ff.; *idem*, "Constantine as ΚΟΙΝΟΣ ΕΠΙΣΚΟΠΟΣ: Tradition and Innovation in the Representation of the First Christian Emperor's Majesty," *Dumbarton Oaks Papers* 21 (1967) 41ff. Constantine's refusal came at the price of alienating the citizens of Rome, if Zosimus is to be believed. Some of Constantine's commemorative churches entailed the disruption of traditional religious rites. St. Peter's in Rome required the desecration of a pagan cemetery – W. Seston, "Hypothèse sur la date de la basilique constantinienne de Saint-Pierre de Rome," *Cahiers archéologiques* 2 (1947) 153ff. Jerome claims that the site of the church of the Nativity in Bethlehem had been occupied by a sanctuary dedicated to Adonis – Bagatti (n. 71 above) 115. The author of the VC (n. 10 above) 3.26ff. states that Constantine ordered the destruction of the shrine of Venus that had been built over the sepulcher of Christ. The same author, VC 3.51ff., reports that Constantine ordered the site at Mambre cleared of pagan cult practices.

suggest, the attitude of Christian bishops and apologists towards images – especially the attitudes of those churchmen who were personally close to Constantine. Images of Christ not only would have antagonized supporters of the pagan gods, they also would have disturbed Christian bishops.

It is a fact that Constantine's major Christian adviser, Ossius, bishop of Cordova, took part in a church council that banned images from church – the Council of Elvira.[126] The exact date of the council is not known.[127] But most of the competing estimates differ only by a few years, placing the council roughly between about A.D. 300 and 306,[128] although Piganiol would date it A.D. 313.[129] Notwithstanding one significant issue – whether the council met before or after the Great Persecution – the question of the date of the council is simply too involved and probably too peripheral to pursue in this study.

Fortunately, the canons of the Council of Elvira have been preserved. Canon 36 states that "picturas in ecclesia esse non debere, ne quod colitur et adoratur in parietibus depingatur [there should be no pictures in church, lest what is reverenced and adored be depicted on the walls]."[130] Although the connection with Ossius and, consequently, with Constantine, has been ignored,[131] the canon itself has been much discussed and variously interpreted.[132] If there is today a generally preferred interpretation of Canon 36, it probably is that which attributes to the members of

[126] His name appears second in the list of members and his testimony in a later council seems to refer to his participation in the Council of Elvira – for this and for a general discussion of Ossius's role in the Council of Elvira, see V. C. de Clercq, *Ossius of Cordova*, Catholic University of America Studies in Christian Antiquity 13 (1954) 85-147. The canons of the Council of Elvira are available in several sources: Mansi (n. 6 above) 2.5ff. and, most recently, J. Vivés and G. M. Díez, eds., *Concilios visigóthicos e hispano-romanos*, España cristiana 1 (1963) 1ff. Comprehensive discussions of the council are found in A. W. Dale, *The Synod of Elvira* (London 1882) and G. Bareille, "Elvire," *Dictionnaire de théologie catholique* 4 (1910) 2378-2396.

[127] The question of the council's date is discussed at length by De Clercq 87-103.

[128] De Clercq 97 opts for the date ca. 300 suggested by L. Duchesne, "Le Concile d'Elvira et les flamines chrétiennes," *Mélanges Rénier* (Paris 1887) 159-174. H. Koch, "Die Zeit des Konzils von Elvira," *Zeitschrift für die neutestamentliche Wissenschaft* 17 (1916) 61-67, preferred 306. Dale 44 also preferred this year. Vivés and Díez 1 date the council ca. 300-306.

[129] Piganiol (n. 100 above) 79-83.

[130] Mansi (n. 6 above) 2.11.

[131] Only W. Lowrie, *Art in the Early Church*, ed. 2 rev. (New York 1947) 9f., and Klauser (n. 26 above) 228 connect Ossius with this evidence, but neither seems to see the connection as noteworthy. On the other hand, Deichmann (n. 9 above) 59 n. 27 raises the possibility that Ossius was in opposition to the introduction of images into the church. He does not state the grounds for this possibility, but I presume that one of them would be the fact that Ossius attended the Council of Elvira, which banned images from church. I discuss the same possibility in "The Images on the Palestinian Flasks as Possible Evidence of the Monumental Decoration of Palestinian Martyria," Ph.D. diss. (University of Minnesota 1974) 47ff.

[132] It is discussed at length by Koch (n. 7 above) 31-41, who usefully summarizes earlier opinions. Also see Elliger (n. 7 above) 34-38; S. McKenna, *Paganism and Pagan Survivals in Spain up to the Fall of the Visigothic Kingdom*, Catholic University of America Studies in Medieval History, n. s. 1 (1938) 34f.; E. Bevan, *Holy Images* (London 1940) 115f.; K. Wessel, "Bild," *Reallexikon zur byzantinischen Kunst* 1 (1963) 620f.; and Klauser (n. 26 above) 228f.

the council a fear that images might mistakenly become objects of worship.[133] But, though this interpretation may at first seem plausible, it is inadequate to explain the literal sense of the prohibition. The members of the council, as Koch and Bevan have observed, did not write that pictures were prohibited from church "lest what is painted on walls be reverenced and adored [ne quod in parietibus depingitur colatur et adoretur]."[134] Instead, they wrote that images were to be excluded from church, "lest what is reverenced and adored be depicted on the walls." This distinction, which is unmistakable in the Latin, cannot be ignored.

Why might the council members have feared the very act of painting objects of worship upon the walls as the literal sense of the canon implies? One possibility would be that the members had in mind the Old Testament ban upon images.[135] Though this is possible, nonetheless, in itself, this suggestion is also inadequate to explain the literal sense of the canon. The Old Testament prohibition is categorical: it applies to images of all things. The council, although it may have banned all images from church, did so, by its own testimony, to prevent objects of reverence and adoration from being painted or depicted on the walls. There is, however, an explanation that not only accommodates the literal sense of the final clause, but as well reflects opinions that were commonly expressed by Christian apologists in the third and early fourth centuries.

One of the traditional objections to cult images expressed by pagan philosophers was that such images possessed attributes which it would be ridiculous and ironic to ascribe to gods. Images were made of materials which either attracted temple thieves, as did statues of gold and silver,[136] or, according to Lucian, if they were made of gilded ivory over a wooden frame, attracted swarms of mice.[137] Cult images involved other ironies. They were made by men who were merely craftsmen, men of low social status. Zeno of Citium, for example, thought that nothing made by common craftsmen could be of value; therefore, in his ideal state, temples (and presumably statues) were not desired.[138] Since cult statues were inanimate, praying to them was

[133] A. von Harnack, *Die Mission und Ausbreitung des Christentums in den ersten drei Jahrhunderten*, ed. 3 (1915) 2.321, cited in Koch (n. 7 above) 33; Dale (n. 126 above) 292ff.; H. Leclercq, "Images (culte et querelle des)," *Dictionnaire d'archéologie chrétienne et de liturgie* 7.1 (1926) 215; *idem, Histoire des conciles d'après les documentes originaux* 1.1 (1907) 240 n. 4; and McKenna 35.

[134] Koch (n. 7 above) 33, who provides the alternative Latin construction, and Bevan (n. 132 above) 115. The difference in the mood of the verb forms *colitur* and *adoratur*, which are indicative, and *depingatur*, which is subjunctive, is decisive evidence of the intention of the passage.

[135] Exodus 20.4 and Deuteronomy 5.8. Koch (n. 7 above) 39, Elliger (n. 7 above) 37, and Lowrie (n. 131 above) 9f. favor this interpretation.

[136] Lucian, *Zeus elenchomenos* 8, *idem, Zeus tragoidos* 32, and *idem, Timon* 4; cf. Clerc (n. 7 above) 116.

[137] *Zeus tragoidos* 8. Cf. Geffcken (n. 85 above) 291.

[138] Geffcken 289 and Bevan (n. 132 above) 65. Sculptors were regarded with surprising disdain, considering the admiration given to some of their statues – Plutarch, *Life of Pericles* 2, and Lucian, *Somnium* 6-9.

like trying to converse with the walls of a house: those who used such images were ignorant of the true nature of the gods.[139] Not only was it futile to pray to such images, there were some, as Plutarch reports, who were of the opinion, shared by followers of Pythagoras, that it was impious even to make such images, since that was implicitly to liken exalted beings to things which were base.[140]

Christian apologists appropriated these arguments to rebut the charge that Christians were atheists.[141] They disagreed with pagans that the refusal to use cult images was evidence of atheism. Instead, they ridiculed the cult of images as an inappropriate form of worship. This, they assumed, would explain why Christians did not use cult images. Significantly, two of the most brilliant and sustained attacks upon the cult of images were delivered by Arnobius and Lactantius, both contemporaries of the Spanish fathers who met at Elvira.

Arnobius provides an elaborate rebuttal to the accusation that Christians were impious because they lacked temples and cult images.[142] How ironic it is, he begins, that the gods even need these things! Why would gods need the shelter of a temple?[143] And why do they need images? Why do not the pagans, instead, aim

[139] Heraclitus, *Fragment B5*, ed. H. Diels and W. Kranz, *Fragmente der Vorsokratiker*, ed. 7 (Berlin 1954) 1.151f. Cf. the complaints of Xenophanes and Antisthenes, as cited by Clement of Alexandria, *Stromateis* 5.14. Plutarch often referred to statues as dead – Clerc (n. 7 above) 112f.

[140] Plutarch reports that Numa Pompilius, in accordance with the beliefs of Pythagoras, forbade the Romans to use images of the gods: *Οὔτε γὰρ ἐκεῖνος αἰσθητὸν ᾽ἢ παθητόν, ᾽άορτον δὲ καὶ ᾽άκτιστον καὶ νοητὸν ὑπελάμβανεν εἶναι τὸ πρῶτον, οὗτός τε διεκώλυσεν ἀνθρωποειδῆ καὶ ζῳόμορφον εἰκόνα θεοῦ Ῥωμαίους κτίζειν* – *Life of Numa* 8.13, ed. R. Flaceliere et al., *Plutarch Vies* 1 (Paris 1957) 191f. Cf. Clement of Alexandria, *Stromateis* 5.5; Geffcken (n. 85 above) 299 n. 2; and Clerc (n. 7 above) 105.

[141] Clerc 122f. Justin Martyr, *First Apology* 9, says that Christians do not use images because their form could not possibly reveal God, whose form is ineffable. In addition, it is simply impious to call such images divine. They are made of lifeless, base materials, which not infrequently have been used for vile purposes. They are made by men who have been known to outrage even the girls who work for them (presumably as models). And men are required to guard them from theft. Clement of Alexandria, *Protreptikos pros Hellenas* 4.54, rejects the cult of images for similar reasons. In his *Stromateis* 5.5, he writes that God forbade images in the days of Moses so that men could approach the spiritual world and detach themselves from the senses, for to worship a spiritual being through matter is to dishonor it through the senses: *τὴν νοητὴν οὐσίαν δι᾽ ῾ύλης σεβάζεσθαι, ἀτιμάζειν ἐστὶν αὐτὴν δι᾽ αἰσθήσεως* (PG 9.49). Not uninterestingly, then, Clement gives a philosophical justification for the Old Testament prohibition of images. In Origen's *Contra Celsum* 1.5, Celsus accuses Christians of not regarding statues as gods, since they are made by common craftsmen, who not infrequently lapse into immorality. He also accuses them of plagiarism. They are merely repeating what Heraclitus and Zeno of Citium said before. But, to Origen, the perceptions of Heraclitus and Zeno simply show that divine law was inscribed in the hearts of men. To justify Christian refusal to use images, he also cites the authority of the Old Testament prohibition (*Contra Celsum* 7.64) and expresses the belief that God's ineffable form could not be represented by lifeless images (*Contra Celsum* 7.66). The real image of God is man's rational soul (*ibid.*).

[142] *Adversus nationes* 6.1ff., ed. A. Reiferscheid, *Arnobii Adversus nationes libri VII*, CSEL 4 (1875, repr. 1968) 214ff. Many of his arguments are anticipated by Clement of Alexandria, *Protreptikos* 4.44-47.

[143] *Adversus nationes* 6.3 (CSEL 4.216).

their prayers to heaven, where the gods are supposed to live?[144] As it is, these images have nothing to do with gods. Everybody knows that the Athenians based their images of Hermes on Alcibiades and that Praxiteles used the features of his mistress for the Cnidian Venus.[145] Everybody knows that one and the same statue can represent different gods merely with minor changes in attributes.[146] How, then, could these images possibly represent the gods? And how could pagans give them respect when they are often made from materials that are extracted from cooking pots, whores' ornaments, and other obscene objects?[147] Not even the animals show them respect: mice and cockroaches nest in them and the swallows, flitting about in the temples, spatter them with their droppings.[148] What might a pagan say to this attack? Perhaps he would say that no one really believes that these material images are the gods. Pagans, he might say, merely believe that, when a statue is properly dedicated, the god to whom it is dedicated comes to reside in it.[149] But this belief, too, involves ironies. Why would the gods want to leave heaven to be imprisoned in cult images? Are they forced to against their will?[150] And, if the gods live inside their statues, why is it necessary to guard them? Why do not the gods strike down the thieves who rob temples of their golden cult statues?[151]

Lactantius, in his *Divinae institutiones,* dedicated to Constantine, repeats some of the same arguments. It is stupid to pray to images when men could address their prayers to heaven, where the gods supposedly reside. How did this ridiculous practice originate anyway? Well, it grew out of the practice of preserving the memory of the dead. But it is foolish to worship the dead.[152] Of course, the pagans would deny this, but if their gods are gods, then there would be no need of images: the gods would be able to hear prayers wherever they were. Images would be superfluous.[153] But these really are only images of the dead and, like the dead, they are senseless.[154] Yet the pagans, in their folly, regard this senseless matter, shaped by the hands of man, as a likeness of God! It is the sentient, acting man who is the image of God.[155] And what efficacy can statues have when they are made by men who are so

[144] *Ibid.* 6.8 (CSEL 4.220).
[145] *Ibid.* 6.13 (CSEL 4.224).
[146] *Ibid.* 6.12 (CSEL 4.224).
[147] *Ibid.* 6.14 (CSEL 4.226).
[148] *Ibid.* 6.16 (CSEL 4.228f.).
[149] *Ibid.* 6.17 (CSEL 4.229).
[150] *Ibid.* 6.17 (CSEL 4.229f).
[151] *Ibid.* 6.20 (CSEL 4.232).
[152] Lactantius, *Divinae institutiones* 2.2, ed. S.Brandt, *Opera omnia*, CSEL 19.1 (1890, repr. 1965) 99.
[153] *Ibid.*: "Superuacua sunt ergo simulacra illis ubique praesentibus, cum satis sit audientium nomina precibus aduocare."
[154] *Ibid.* (CSEL 19.1.100).
[155] *Ibid.*: "Itaque simulacrum dei non illut est quod, digitis hominis ex lapide aut aere aliaque materia fabricatur, sed ipse homo, quoniam et sentit et mouetur et multas magnasque actiones habet."

undignified that one would hesitate to associate with them?[156] What benefit can they confer when they are simply earth, which can be broken, can rot away, and can be plundered by thieves?[157]

Given such strong manifestations of this apologetic tradition in the era of the Council of Elvira, given also the preoccupation it reflects with the admissibility specifically of images of the gods or the Supreme Divinity, it is not unreasonable to suggest, as Edwyn Bevan does, that it found expression in Canon 36:[158] this tradition seems to provide the only fully adequate explanation of the literal sense of the canon. Evidently, what the Spanish fathers feared was the act of depicting God. They did not simply fear that images of God might be worshipped by Christians, as if one could distinguish between a proper and improper use of such images. Rather, their fear was based upon a more fundamental consideration: the mere existence of such images was an insult to God. God has no need of lifeless images. His true image is the sentient man. It would dishonor God to have craftsmen represent Him in base, corruptible matter. Not only would this implicitly liken Him to things which are dead, these representations, like pagan idols, would be open to various kinds of natural disfigurement and, perhaps, even to deliberate desecration.

If this fairly represents what the Spanish fathers felt, then, as one who subscribed to the canons, Ossius probably shared their opinion. At the very least, he knew that this was the opinion of other bishops and that it had normative force.

This evidence assumes importance when the significance of Ossius's association with Constantine is appreciated. It was formed quite early. Ossius was associated with Constantine at least by April 313 and possibly before the end of 312.[159] For this reason, there may be a kernel of truth in the pagan tradition, which surfaces in Zosimus, that Ossius was responsible for Constantine's conversion.[160] At least it is known that Constantine entrusted Ossius with important missions to churches in the various parts of the empire. Constantine, for example, chose Ossius to act as his representative to the African church.[161] Ossius evidently acted in opposition to the

[156] *Ibid.* (CSEL 19.1.101).

[157] *Ibid.* 2.2, 2.4 (CSEL 19.1.102, 108).

[158] Bevan (n. 7 above) 115f.

[159] Evidence of this early association is found in a letter from Constantine to Caecilian, bishop of Carthage and primate of the African Church. This letter, preserved in Eusebius, HE (n. 19 above) 10.6, empowers Caecilian to distribute a donation from Constantine in accordance with a schedule drawn up by Ossius. O. Seeck, *Regesten der Kaiser und Päpst für die Jahre 311 bis 476 n. Chr.* (Stuttgart 1919) 151, 160, dated this letter in the earliest days of April 313. Baynes (n. 66 above) 66f. believes that the letter was written even earlier, in the winter of 312.

[160] *Historia nova* 2.29.5, ed. L. Mendelsohn, *Zosimi, comitis et exadvocati fisci Historia nova* (Leipzig 1887) 86: Αἰγύπτιός τις ἐξ Ἰβηρίας [clearly Ossius] εἰς τὴν Ῥώμην ἐλθὼν καὶ ταῖς εἰς τὰ βασίλεια γυναιξὶ συνήθη γενόμενος, ἐντυχὼν τῷ Κωνσταντίνῳ πάσης ἁμαρτάδος ἀναιρειτικὴν εἶναι τὴν τῶν χριστιανῶν διεβεβαιώσατο δόξαν καὶ τοῦτο ἔχειν ἐπάγγελμα τὸ τοὺς ἀσεβεῖς μεταλαμβάνοντας αὐτῆς πάσης ἁμαρτίας ἔξω παραχρῆμα καθίστασθαι· δεξαμένου δὲ ῥᾷστα τοῦ Κωνσταντίνου τὸν λόγον καὶ ἀφεμένου μὲν τῶν πατρίων, μετασχόντος δὲ ὧν ὁ Αἰγύπτιος αὐτῷ μετεδίδου τῆς ἀσεβεία τὴν ἀρχην ἐποιήσατο τὴν μαντικὴν ἔχειν ἐν ὑποψίᾳ.

[161] Evident in the letter to Caecilian, cited above in n. 159.

Donatists, since they were to hold him responsible for the repressive measures that Constantine took against them in A.D. 316 and 317.[162] When Constantine's authority was established in the eastern part of the empire, he sent Ossius to heal the divisions among the churches in the East, particularly the bitter feud between Alexander of Egypt and Arius.[163] When this mission failed, Constantine convened the Council of Nicaea, perhaps on the advice of Ossius.[164] Again, the defeated party – the Arians this time – blamed Ossius for their misfortunes. Philostorgios writes that Alexander of Egypt journeyed to Nicomedia to meet with Ossius prior to the convocation of the council. Together they allegedly made preparations, among which was the decision to proclaim the Son *homoousios* with the Father.[165] Not infrequently, modern scholars do hold Ossius responsible for the *homoousion* formula that was adopted at the Council of Nicaea.[166] It is also widely believed today that Ossius presided over this council, justifying the title Athanasius gave him – "leader of the councils."[167]

Did Ossius influence Constantine's legislation? Evidently he did. An edict of 18 April 321, addressed to "Bishop Hosius," a common variant of Ossius's name, lays down that manumission by a Christian bishop will have the same legal force as manumission by civil courts. This law was very likely granted as the result of an express request from Ossius.[168] Another law suggests the influence of Ossius. In the previous year, 320, Constantine repealed decrees issued by Augustus prohibiting celibacy.[169] This repeal would seem to have been chiefly of interest to Christian clergymen. The Council of Elvira, for example, of which Ossius was a member, prescribed celibacy for the clergy.[170] It is also interesting that one of the few things Ossius is reported to have written was an *Epistula de laude virginitatis*.[171] Thus he may have had a special interest in clerical celibacy; he may even have led the effort – unsuccessful, as it turned out – to have clerical celibacy endorsed by the Council of

[162] Augustine, *Contra epist. Parmeniani* 1.8.13 – De Clercq (n. 126 above) 175 n. 124.

[163] VC (n. 10 above) 2.63, which probably contains a reference to Ossius, though it fails to contain his name. The intent of the passage is clarified by the parallel report in Sozomen, HE (n. 19 above) 1.16, which does give Ossius's name – De Clercq 199.

[164] VC 3.5f. attributes the convocation of the Council of Nicaea to Constantine alone. Sulpicius Severus, in his *Chronica* 2.40.5, attributes the convocation of the council to the influence of Ossius – De Clercq 224.

[165] HE 1.7a, ed. J. Bidez, GCS (n. 15 above) 21 (1913) 8f: Ὁ Ἀλέξανδρος ἄρας ἀπὸ τῆς Ἀλεξανδρείας ἔπλει τὴν ταχίστην ἐπὶ τὴν . . . Νικομήδους· ἔνθα παραγενόμενος, καὶ τοῖς περὶ τὸν Ὅσιον Κουδρούβης [Ossius] εἰς λόγους καταστάς, πείθει τῆς αὐτοῦ συνεπίστασθαι γνώμης καὶ κυρῦσαι τὸ ὁμοούσιον, λόγοις δικαιοτάτοις αὐτοὺς ὑπαγόμενος.

[166] See the sample of modern opinion presented by De Clercq (n. 126 above) 258f.

[167] Athanasius, *Apologia de fuga sua* 5; De Clercq 229ff.

[168] *Codex Theodosianus* 4.7.1 – De Clercq 179f.

[169] *Codex Theodosianus* 8.16.1.

[170] Canon 33: "Placuit in totum prohibere episcopis, presbyteris et diaconibus vel omnibus clericis in ministerio positis abstinere se a conjugibus suis et non generare filios: quicumque vero fecerit, ab honore clericatus exterminetur" – De Clercq (n. 126 above) 116 n. 146.

[171] Isidore of Seville, *De viris illustribus* 5 – De Clercq 65, 75.

Nicaea.[172] Finally, it is of interest to note that Zosimus links Ossius with Constantine's disapproval of divination and, by implication, with Constantine's laws restricting it.[173]

If this picture is fundamentally accurate, then Ossius's influence upon Constantine's religious policies was substantial.[174] I find it tempting to see the influence of Ossius in another of Constantine's religious policies. When Eusebius, in his *Triakontaeterikos*, and the author of the *Vita Constantini* contrast Constantine's use of the "saving sign" with the use of "lifeless" images by his enemies,[175] they imply, rightly, I think, that Constantine was pursuing a religious policy to which Christians would have been keenly sensitive. Spokesmen for the early Church emphatically asserted that Christians neither possessed nor desired to possess counterparts to the "lifeless" images of the pagans.[176] And, when pagan critics censured Christians for lacking cult images, the Christian defense was to justify, not to disavow, the practice of aniconic worship. Whatever the nature of Constantine's interest in Christianity, he seems, from the very first, to have deferred to this desire of churchmen to represent their religion as an aniconic cult.[177] The absence of contemporary reports of images of Christ or God in the churches Constantine founded, it is true, could be discounted as pure chance – though I think not convincingly. But in the realm of public imagery, where our sample is immeasurably better, the absence of an image of Christ or God is hardly a matter of chance and is quite surprising. Not only does it represent a striking departure from the traditional practice of associating effigies of emperor and god, it also represents a repudiation of the wide-spread belief that the proper worship of divinity required cult images.[178] There is plenty of evidence to illustrate how easy it would have been for Constantine to assume that an image of Christ would be an appropriate instrument of worship. His own sister, Constantia, if the authenticity of a letter read at the Second Council of Nicaea in A.D. 787 may be trusted,[179] asked Eusebius of Caesarea for an image of Christ. He scathingly rejected

[172] Sozomen, HE (n. 19 above) 1.23, and Gelasius, HE 2.22, report such an unsuccessful effort. De Clercq 278ff. raises the possibility that Ossius was behind it.

[173] *Historia nova* 2.29.5 quoted above in n. 160.

[174] H. von Schoenebeck, *Beiträge zur Religionspolitik des Maxentius und Constantine*, Klio Beiheft 43, n. s. 30 (1939) 22, regards Ossius as having had such a decisive influence upon Constantine that one could regard Ossius "als ersten Kardinalstaatssekretär."

[175] See n. 85 above.

[176] For studies of the attitude of the Church's spokesmen towards images, see n. 7 above and J. D. Breckenridge, "Apocrypha of Early Christian Portraiture," *Byzantinische Zeitschrift* 67 (1974) 101ff.

[177] Lactantius, MP (n. 83 above) 44.5, who, according to Barnes (n. 93 above) 29-46, was writing between 313 and 315, refers only to Constantine's use of a "heavenly sign of God [*caeleste signum dei*]" and his designating Christ on shields, "Christum in scutis notat."

[178] For the ubiquity of the cult of images, see Clerc (n. 7 above) 9f.

[179] This letter, known only through excerpts preserved by the Second Council of Nicaea and by Nicephorus the Patriarch, *Antirrhetica contra Eusebium* 9, was used by the Iconoclasts in the Council of 754 – M. Anastos, "The Argument for Iconoclasm as presented by the Iconoclastic Council of 754," *Late Classical and Medieval Studies in Honor of Albert Mathias Friend, Jr.*

her request, alleging that such images were not to be found in churches. Constantia's desire for an image of Christ was not unparalleled. In the same letter Eusebius admits that he once saw images portraying Christ and Paul in the guise of philosophers.[180] This report accords well with Irenaeus's testimony that followers of the Gnostic Carpocrates set up images of Christ along with images of the philosophers Pythagoras, Plato, and Aristotle.[181] In his *Historia ecclesiastica*, Eusebius again refers to images of the apostles and Christ, presuming that they were produced by pagans, who were wont to honor their benefactors with such means.[182] Lactantius reports that the soldiers who came to destroy the Christian church at Nicomedia, at the outset of the Great Persecution, expected to find an image of God.[183] The author of the life of Severus Alexander, writing perhaps in the late fourth century,[184] apparently saw nothing inordinately implausible in his report – little trusted today, but at least indicative of the author's expectations – that the emperor had placed in his sanctuary, statues of Apollonius, Christ, Abraham, and Orpheus, along with

---

(Princeton 1955) 183f. The available excerpts were collected by Boivin and published in his edition of Nicephorus Gregoras's *History* (1702) – G. Florovsky, "Origen, Eusebius and the Iconoclastic Controversy," *Church History* 19 (1950) 84. For modern editions of the Greek text, see H. Hennephof, *Textus byzantinos ad iconomachiam pertinentes in usum academicum*, Byzantina Neerlandica, Series A, fasc. 1 (1969) 42ff., and H.-J. Geischer, *Der byzantinische Bilderstreit*, Texte zur Kirchen- und Theologiegeschichte 9 (1968) 15ff. Its authenticity was strongly asserted by K. Holl, "Die Schriften des Epiphanius gegen die Bilderverehrung," *Gesammelte Aufsätze zur Kirchengeschichte* (Tübingen 1928) 2.387 n. 1. Koch (n. 7 above) 43ff., Elliger (n. 7 above) 49ff., Baynes (n. 7 above) 121f., Florovsky 84, and Klauser (n. 7 above) 229ff. – all have regarded the letter as authentic. Still, I fear that the question of the authenticity of the letter has not been forthrightly dealt with. E.g., of all these endorsements, only Klauser (n. 7 above) 229 ventured to date the letter: according to him, it was composed shortly before 327.

[180] Hennephof 44: *Οὐκ οἶδα γὰρ ὅπως γύναιόν τι μετὰ χεῖράς ποτε δύο τινὰς φέρουσα καταγεγραμμένους, ὡς ἂν φιλοσόφους, ἀπέρριψε λόγον, ὡς ἂν εἶεν Παύλου καὶ τοῦ σωτῆρος.* I believe that this provides strong evidence of the authenticity of the letter. In early Christian art, Christ and the apostles were frequently portrayed in the guise of philosophers and poets: Grabar (n. 9 above) 12; K. Schefold, *Die Bildnisse der antiken Dichter, Redner und Denker* (Basel 1943) 186; G. Hanfmann, "Socrates and Christ," *Harvard Studies in Classical Philology* 60 (1951) 205-233; and H. P. L'Orange, "Plotinus-Paul," *Likeness and Icon* (Odense 1973) 32ff. Significantly, according to Grabar (n. 9 above) 12, this pictorial interpretation of Christ and the apostles was not long retained by artists, except for the Four Evangelists.

[181] Irenaeus, *Adversus haereses* 1.25.6. This passage, along with later paraphrases of it, is conveniently printed in E. von Dobschütz, *Christusbilder: Untersuchungen zur christlichen Legende*, Texte und Untersuchungen zur Geschichte der altchristlichen Literatur, n. s. 3 (1899) 98*.

[182] See n. 33 above.

[183] Lactantius, MP (n. 83 above) 12.

[184] The date of the composition of the *Historia Augusta* is apparently a matter of interminable controversy. For an introduction to the history of this controversy, see A. Momigliano, "An Unsolved Problem of Historical Forgery: The *Scriptores Historiae Augustae*," *Studies in Historiography* (New York 1966) 143-180. For bibliography, see R. Syme, *Ammianus and the Historia Augusta* (Oxford 1968) 220-227, and *idem*, *Emperors and Biography: Studies in the Historia Augusta* (Oxford 1971) 291-295.

images of the best of the deified emperors.[185] All of these instances give evidence of a belief that even for the worship of Christ an image was sometimes expected. It was presumably just this expectation that led the members of the Council of Elvira to forbid the introduction of images into church.

But why did Constantine respect the desire of Christian churchmen to maintain a cult without cult images? Though this question would seem to invite pure speculation, I think we may propose some answers that are more than mere possibilities. It is, first of all, not unlikely, given his participation in the Council of Elvira, that Ossius, Constantine's earliest known influential Christian adviser, acted as an advocate on behalf of the Church's aniconic worship. While advocating respect for the Church's position, he probably would have used the kinds of arguments Christian apologists used against cult images. Since some of these arguments originated with pagans and did not rest exclusively upon tenets of Christian theology, they may have seemed persuasive even to pagans, especially to those who affected an interest in Greek philosophy.[186] Perhaps, then, Constantine came genuinely to believe that an aniconic worship was more likely to gain the favor of the Supreme Divinity than a cult which attempted to circumscribe His ineffable form in base, corruptible matter. In addition, Constantine may have found, through Ossius, that the conspicuous sponsorship of images of Christ, though it might have pleased some, would have had intolerable consequences: not only would it have antagonized militant pagans, who would have resented any support given to Christians, it would have antagonized Christian bishops to an even greater degree, as they and their spokesmen, apologists like Arnobius and Lactantius, remained unalterably opposed to cult images. Although we do not know for a fact that these were the decisive considerations, they would attractively explain how Constantine was led to pursue a religious policy that reflected the desire of churchmen to preserve the traditional aniconic worship of the Christian Church.

Department of Art
University of California
Davis, California 95616, U.S.A.

[185] *Severus Alexander* 29.2, ed. D. Magie, *Historia Augusta*, Loeb Classical Library (London 1922-1923) 2.234. Among those who doubt the authenticity of this specific report are Nock (n. 80 above) 112 n. 84, and Syme, *Emperors and Biography* 26.

[186] For the favor Constantine bestowed upon Neoplatonists, see A. Alföldi (n. 90 above) 99, 105, 111. It is also interesting to note that Ossius was interested in Platonic philosophy – if he be the "Osio" to whom Calcidius dedicated his translation of Plato's *Timaeus*: De Clercq (n. 126 above) 69ff.

"THE SHEPHERD OF HERMAS" AND THE DEVELOPMENT OF MEDIEVAL VISIONARY ALLEGORY

•

by Theodore Bogdanos

Although much has been written about its doctrinal content and its apocalyptic and reformist aims,[1] *The Shepherd of Hermas* (ca. 160 A.D.) has been neglected as a significant prototype in the development of medieval visionary allegory. It is difficult to trace step by step the influence of this early Greek work on Western medieval literature. Nevertheless, its antecedent place in the history of the genre, its availability to the medieval West, and the persistent recurrence of its formal features and thematic intentions in the major Western allegorical dream visions deserve serious consideration. Furthermore, a study of these generic characteristics in *The Shepherd* would not only determine the extent of its formative influence on the allegorical tradition but also increase our understanding of the later works.

Initially regarded as Scripture and then as an apocryphal work,[2] *The Shepherd of Hermas* enjoyed greater popularity in the East than in the West, although interest in it began to decline apparently even there after the time of Origen. In the West, it soon became subject to severe attack by the Montanist Tertullian, and by the fourth century – according to Saint Jerome – the work had been practically forgotten, "paene ignotus est."[3] Other historical evidence, however, shows that *The Shepherd* continued to be available to the West from the time of its writing to the late Middle

[1] On the work's central doctrine of *metanoia* (repentance), see Martin Dibelius, *Der Hirt des Hermas* in *Die Apostolischen Väter* 4 (Tübingen 1923) 435ff.; J. Hoh, "Die Busse in Pastor Hermae," *Theologische Quartalschrift* 3 (Augsburg 1930) 253-288; F. Kattenbusch, *Das Apostolische Symbol* 2 (Leipzig 1900) 714ff.; Lage Pernveden, *The Concept of the Church in the Shepherd of Hermas* (Lund 1966) 177-277; and A. Vanbeck, "La penitence dans le Pasteur d'Hermas," *Revue d'histoire et de littérature religeuses*, n. s. 2 (Paris 1911) 389-403. On its eschatology, see Dibelius 640-644; R. Frick, *Die Geschichte des Reich-Gottes Gedankens in der alten Kirche bis zu Origenes und Augustin* (Giessen 1928) 32ff.; S. Giet, *Hermas et les pasteurs* (Paris 1963) 158; Pernveden 223-277; and R. Schnackenburg, *Gottes Herrschaft und Reich* (Freiburg 1959) 226ff.

[2] For a more detailed history of the work, see *The Ante-Nicene Fathers*, ed. A. Roberts and J. Donaldson, 2 (Buffalo 1885) 3-8; *Βιβλιοθήκη Ἑλλήνων Πατέρων καὶ Ἐκκλησιαστικῶν Συγγραφέων*, ed. *Ἀποστολικὴ Διακονία*, 3 (Athens 1955) 31-37; Dibelius 416-424; E. J. Goodspeed, *A History of Early Christian Literature*, rev. R. M. Grant (Chicago 1966) 30-34; and A. LeLong, *Le Pasteur d'Hermas* in *Les pères apostoliques* 4 (Paris 1912) xxii-lx.

[3] St. Jerome, *De viris illustribus* 10.

Ages. If we accept the prevailing opinion that its author was none other than Hermas, brother of the Roman bishop Pius (fl. 140-155 A.D.), and if we bear in mind the profuse latinisms[4] of its Greek vernacular prose, we may assume with some justification that the work was written not somewhere in the distant East, but in Rome. The survival of several manuscripts – in the original Greek and in Latin translation – in the West from the second to the sixth century, listed by Molly Whittaker,[5] indicates that the work was in circulation at least up to the time of Boethius. In addition, sixteen manuscripts of Latin translations from the ninth to the fifteenth century, listed by Oscar de Gebhardt and Adolf von Harnack,[6] can still be found in various codices in England and the Continent. As a consequence, Ernst R. Curtius came to regard *The Shepherd of Hermas* as "the most important document of early Christian literature . . . which was circulated from the second century onwards in Latin translations."[7]

The Shepherd of Hermas displays for the first time the dramatic pattern which underlies most medieval allegorical dream visions from Boethius's *Consolation of Philosophy* (ca. 524) on. This pattern might be described as follows: The dreamer-hero finds himself in a profound spiritual crisis. One or several authoritative figures appear to him in one or several visions and help the dreamer place his crisis in a new perspective of truth, thus inducing its resolution. Such truth is communicated to the visionary hero through symbolic imagery and through rational, conceptually articulate dialogue in which the authoritative figure engages the dreamer. Their encounter takes place in a visionary landscape which has an objective reality of its own (as a supernatural realm, for example), while at the same time functioning as an imagistic concretization of the dreamer's psychic reality – an objective correlative of his inner state at each stage of his spiritual development. In order to demonstrate in some specific fashion the work's contribution to medieval allegorical tradition, I shall focus on one of these elements in it, namely, the figure of the Lady Ecclesia, who appears to Hermas, the dreamer-hero of *The Shepherd*, in several visions as his spiritual guide. In studying her complexity, I hope to suggest the range of her identity and the many levels of spiritual and aesthetic experience on which she appeals to us. Furthermore, I want to define some salient characteristics which establish her as a prototype to several key visionary figures in medieval literature and, consequently, as a seminal influence on the development of medieval visionary allegory.

Hermas sees the lady Rhoda, whose slave he had been once in Rome, bathing in

[4] For example: *κερκιβέριον* (cervical) pillow; *ὁδὸς καμπανή* (via campana) country road; *στατίων* (statio) abode or watch post; *συμψέλλιον* (subsellium) an official seat or bench.

[5] M. Whittaker, ed., *Der Hirt des Hermas* in *Die Griechischen Christlichen Schriftsteller der Ersten Jahrhunderte* 1 (Berlin 1956) ix-xx.

[6] O. de Gebhardt and A. von Harnack, eds., *Hermae Pastor* in *Patrum apostolicorum opera* 3 (Leipzig 1877) xii-xxiv.

[7] E. R. Curtius, *European Literature and the Latin Middle Ages*, trans. W. R. Trask (New York 1963) 103. M. W. Bloomfield, *Piers Plowman as a Fourteenth-Century Apocalypse* (New Brunswick, N. J. 1961) 9, states that *The Shepherd of Hermas* was well known in the medieval West.

the Tiber and begins to lust after her with a consuming passion (1.3).[8] Sometime after, he journeys to the city of Cumae, wandering through the countryside and "glorifying the creatures of God" (1.3), apparently happy and at peace with himself – until sleep overtakes him. His journey continues, however, within his dream, but the landscape has been transformed into a wild, pathless place full of crags and crevices. Traversing with difficulty its final barrier, a river, Hermas comes to an open plain, whereupon the heavens open and Rhoda appears. She tells him that she has been "taken up to heaven" (possibly through her death) to become his accuser before God (1.6). Hermas protests his righteousness, but Rhoda exposes his true motives of lust toward her. Base values and moral self-deception have thoroughly corrupted and disjointed his inner life. She urges him to repent and to reform his neglected family, promising him spiritual healing by the mercy of God. Leaving him stunned with such a revelation, Rhoda disappears.

We see here certain key elements beginning to form the visionary dramatic order which I outlined earlier: Hermas, the dreamer-hero, roams about the world like Langland's carefree wanderer. He meets in his dream an authoritative figure, Rhoda, who brings to his awareness his inner crisis. Their encounter takes place in a landscape borrowed from the dreamer's waking experience but transformed to reflect his inner turbulence, functioning as a minuscule "selva oscura" in the hero's spiritual journey. By promising Hermas healing and then disappearing, Rhoda seems to prepare for the coming of a more decisive saving force. This ceaseless quest for a yet higher authority of truth within the vision becomes characteristic of several works in medieval literature, such as the *Divine Comedy* and *Piers Plowman*. It tends to reflect the complexity and magnitude of the hero's spiritual crisis.

Terrified and saddened (*πεφρικὼς καὶ λυπούμενος*) (2.1) by the discovery of his inner deformity and fragmentation, Hermas debates passionately within himself how he may be saved. Guilt and self-disgust war powerfully against his desire for redemption and inner reconciliation. It is at such a moment of intense interior dialogue that Ecclesia comes before Hermas – as if invoked by it. We recall that it is in similar instances of desperate self-confrontation in the visionary hero that the authoritative figures of the later dream visions – Boethius's Philosophia, Alan of Lille's Natura, Langland's Holy Church, and even Dante's Virgil – make their appearance. Holding a book in her hand, Ecclesia comes and sits opposite Hermas in a splendid chair (2.2), assuming immediately – like Boethius's Philosophia in a similar posture (Bk. 1, Prose 1)[9] – the role of his spiritual instructress.[10]

[8] Citations from the Greek in my text are to Whittaker's edition (n. 5 above). My translation.

[9] Citations from Boethius are to *The Consolation of Philosophy*, trans. R. Green (Indianapolis, Ind. 1962).

[10] G. B. Ladner, *Ad Imaginem Dei: The Image of Man in Medieval Art* (Latrobe, Pa. 1965) 4-5, defines this posture as a common iconographic motif in late antique and early Christian art, depicting the spiritual sage or philosopher. E. R. Curtius's discussion of the book as symbol in classical and early medieval times is highly significant here (n. 7 above) 302-315.

Ecclesia embodies certain essential characteristics of the *mater* figure which are of special interest here. From a mythological viewpoint, as E. O. James has shown, she stands at the end of a long process of synchretic metamorphosis, beginning with the figure of the Near Eastern Mother-Goddess (such as the earthbound and compassionate Ishtar), moving on to the hellenized Phrygian Magna Mater, assimilating eventually the female figures of late Jewish sapiential and apocalyptic tradition and, later, the more spiritually attenuated Hagia Sophia of the Gnostics, finally emerging as the Mater Ecclesia of the early Christian centuries.[11] Her old age and majesty invest her with venerability, wisdom, and oracular authority. In her prophesying about "the coming tribulation" and in her solicitous counseling of the dreamer, she further fuses the identity of the Old Testament prophets with that of the pagan Africanus, who comes in a dream to his grandson Scipio to warn him of the future and guide his course of action.[12] The author's intention is rather obvious: By choosing a figure of such mythic dimension and cultural breadth – an act of felicitous plundering, as Saint Augustine would see it – the author endows his visionary guide with timeless and universal validity and with a certain engaging, irresolvable complexity. By amplifying the figure's authority, he establishes his work as unimpeachable spiritual and artistic experience. His message, too, uttered by such an imposing personality – especially within the supernaturally revelatory ambience of the dream – assumes an almost divine composure against the reader's possible skepticism. The author does not risk presumption by striking an oracular stance himself. Instead, he takes on the *persona* of the dreamer, with whom we tend to identify in our common humanity and by the fact that he anticipates and voices our objections. Thus, we are gradually led to share not only his initial resistance but his eventual conversion as well. This strategy of mythic amplification and auctorial self-effacement becomes quite common to the writers of medieval visionary allegory.

To Ecclesia's archetypal characteristics of venerability, wisdom, and oracular authority is added that of maternal femininity. The complementary effect of this quality increases considerably the complexity of the figure. On the one hand, it prepares us for the cosmogonic, god-like role that she will take on presently; at the same time, it tempers the impersonality and mythic distance of her character, bringing it down to the familiar, warm level of human exchange. Upon meeting him, Ecclesia asks Hermas about his distress (2.3). Her human aspect becomes even more engaging through her wise humor. When Hermas protests his purity of intention toward Rhoda, Ecclesia regards his duplicity with some amusement: "Never such a thing [his carnal thoughts] upon the servant of God!" she exclaims with mock

[11] E. O. James, *The Cult of the Mother Goddess* (London 1959) 47-67, 78-84, 128-153, and 228-236. See also J. J. Bachofen, *Myth, Religion, and Mother Right*, trans. R. Manheim (Princeton 1967) 69-207; and Pernveden (n. 1 above) 277-281.

[12] Macrobius, *Commentary on the Dream of Scipio*, trans. W. Stahl (New York 1966) 90. Macrobius's work, as is well known, influenced considerably the development of medieval visionary literature.

indignation (2.4). She then goes on to remind him that the first step to self-expiation is unsparing self-recognition.

From the standpoint of characterization, Ecclesia seems to have served as model to several important figures in medieval visionary allegory, such as Boethius's Philosophia, Alan's Natura, and Langland's Holy Church. They combine the same mythic, archetypal, yet very human qualities as Ecclesia. They too address their dreamers with maternal intimacy, promising them spiritual guidance and healing. With the exception of the more virginal and somber Natura, the other figures brighten their doctrine with sage, often rustic humor. "Have my words inspired you at all or are you 'like the ass which cannot hear the lyre'?" Philosophia asks the lachrymose and inattentive Boethius (Bk. 1, Prose 4). When Will asks Holy Church through what faculty exactly he may perceive the truth, half-exasperated with his pedantry and dullness, she calls him without much ceremony a "doted daffe" (doting fool or idiot) (C. 2.139).[13] Through such self-deprecation, safe because exaggerated, the author wishes to display here a disarming modesty, which of course tends to enhance rather than diminish his stature.[14] At the same time, he has succeeded in humanizing his authoritative figure, saving her from unmitigated, alienating sacerdotal gravity.

Having taken on the timeless authority of the mythic archetype and yet the immediate appeal of human identity, Ecclesia begins the dreamer's spiritual education, moving from his particular existential situation to the eternal framework that surrounds it. She exhorts him to recognize his moral depravity and repent for it. Further, he must carry her message of *metanoia*, of timely repentance, to other men. The great tribulation is approaching, the end of the age is at hand, she warns with apocalyptic urgency. Thus, as typical allegorical dreamer, Hermas assumes the dual role of the naive pupil as well as the privileged transmitter of higher truth.

As if to appeal to some inexorable, age-recorded authority, Ecclesia opens her book and reads to Hermas. But the first part of her reading strikes terror in him, "*πάντα γὰρ τὰ ῥήματα ἔκφρικτα ἅ οὐ δύναται ἄνθρωπος βαστάσαι*" (for all that was spoken was terrible, that no man could ever endure) (3.3).[15] We sense immediately that Hermas has been brought here by Ecclesia *facie ad faciem* with divine reality in its awesome, apocalyptic form, baring the full voice of God's *ὀργή*, the *ira Dei.* His memory is stunned; he cannot therefore record his experience. Only the second part of her reading reaches human articulation. It is a hymn of exaltation to God's universal order, replete with images of cosmic harmony and beauty, functioning as prelude to the work's central event – the symbolic reconstruction of that order:

[13] Citations from Langland are to *The Vision of William Concerning Piers the Plowman in Three Parallel Texts together with Richard the Redeless by William Langland*, ed. W. W. Skeat, 2 vols. (London 1886; repr. 1965).

[14] See Curtius (n. 7 above) 83-85, on the topos of affected modesty and self-disparagement in late antique and medieval literature.

[15] The author recalls here with his phraseology St. Paul's encounter with ineffable divinity: "*ἄρρητα ῥήματα ἅ οὐκ ἐξὸν ἀνθρώπῳ λαλῆσαι*" (2 Corinthians 12.4).

> *Ἰδοὺ ὁ θεὸς τῶν δυνάμεων, ὁ ἀοράτῳ δυνάμει καὶ τῇ μεγάλῃ συνέσει αὐτοῦ κτίσας τὸν κόσμον καὶ τῇ ἐνδόξῳ βουλῇ περιθεὶς τὴν εὐπρέπειαν τῇ κτίσει αὐτοῦ. . . .* (3.3-4)
>
> (Behold the God of powers, who by His invisible power and great intelligence has built the world and by His glorious design has clothed His creation with splendor . . . .)

Moving from moral discourse to direct apocalyptic encounter and then to poetic utterance, Ecclesia has manifested the levels of perception on which she will communicate her saving truth to the dreamer. The utterly apocalyptic will continue to hover throughout with its powerful presence, but beyond expression, except in a rare transfixing image, as when it will peer at us again through Ecclesia's own face. Hermas must assimilate this aspect of her truth on a totally intuitive, ineffable level. In order to touch the dreamer's understanding and to allow us as readers to participate in his visionary experience, Ecclesia turns to symbol and to rational discourse as her essential means of communication. She will first create a symbolic spectacle before him and then translate its significance into conceptually articulate terms. This twofold method of presentation serves as the work's structural principle. It becomes eventually the formal scheme of early medieval allegory, as in Boethius's *Consolation* where explicit discursive *prosae* alternate with highly evocative imagistic *metra*.

In the central symbolic event of *The Shepherd* (9.7-9; 10.4-9), Ecclesia seats Hermas beside her and, pointing her shining rod to the distance, commands six young men who accompany her: "Go ye and build!" A marvelous spectacle opens before the dreamer with the cinematic sweep of Langland's "felde ful of folke." Thousands of men gather stones from the four corners of the earth and from the depths of the waters,[16] bringing them to the six young men who are building on the water a great tower. Some stones are placed on the rising structure while others are rejected for their quality of texture and shape. Although the elements in the foreground are naturalistic, there is no background, evoking a sense of timelessness and spacelessness. Location remains significantly ambiguous. The event could be taking place out in the vast cosmos and, simultaneously, in the dreamer's psyche. Spatial relationship is moral rather than realistic, as when Ecclesia commands Hermas to sit at her left rather than her right side – as he had insisted – because of his spiritual inadequacy. At the same time, spatial relationship projects imagistically the hero's intuitive sense of his relationship to the higher reality that he is encountering. Space, then, in the visionary topography of *The Shepherd* – as in *The Consolation of Philosophy*, the *Divine Comedy*, the *Pearl*, and *Piers Plowman* – functions as both metaphysical and psychological metaphor.

Like his medieval successors, Hermas as dreamer is invitingly naive but also shamelessly curious. In fact, he frequently baits Ecclesia into answering by using the

[16] They are never specified as the sea or any other body of water.

same enterprising yet often ludicrous self-effacement as the dreamer in the *Pearl*. Ecclesia, nevertheless, goes on to explain the symbolic spectacle to him by identifying the spiritual significance of each element in it. Her explanation, however, accounts only partly for the vast impression and meaning of the event. The reader is left to discover the rest on his own.

When Ecclesia lifts her rod toward the horizon and commands her companions, "Go ye and build!" she takes on the aspect of a mythic deity who, standing on her primeval hill, creates the world by sheer utterance.[17] She reenacts, in fact, the God of Genesis, identifying her companions as His six angels of creation (12.1), their number suggesting also the six days of creation. Through the symbol of the tower, she erects before Hermas God's universal order on all its levels of significance. The building stones are humanity itself.

She calls the waters, the foundation of the tower, "life-saving" (11.5), fusing in our awareness two levels of significance: They are the fertilizing waters of creation, from which natural life springs forth; at the same time, they are the purifying waters of baptism, whence life reemerges spiritually renewed. Ecclesia reinforces the latter meaning by identifying the pure white stones rising from the depths as "*οἱ παθόντες ἕνεκεν τοῦ ὀνόματος τοῦ Κυρίου*" (those who have suffered on account of the name of the Lord) (13.2-3). For these men, martyrdom became their baptism. Thus, we begin to view the tower as the symbolic reconstruction of God's universe with its cosmological and sacramental orders.

The tower as symbol, however, encompasses another order of existence, which is closer to us: the social and the moral. Ecclesia explains to Hermas that the stones that are brought for the construction of the tower are men. They are chosen for their moral excellence and their ability to live in mutual harmony, both qualities being represented by the stones' beauty of texture and fitness of shape. The construction of the tower, therefore, symbolizes also the building of an ideal society.

The symbolic significance of this construction penetrates deeper still than the larger human framework. In the stones, we view not only the various types of men but also the many facets, actual and potential, of Hermas's and each man's soul. For example, the rejected stones torn with crevices – like the torn garments of Philosophia (Bk. 1, Prosae 1 and 3) and Natura (Prosae 1 and 4, pp. 15 and 41)[18] – image not only a disjointed human society but also the dreamer's own fragmented psyche. We recall Hermas roaming through the countryside, outwardly happy but totally unaware of his inner depravity. Other stones which are rolled away from the tower into pathless places are men whose uncertain faith has taken them into endless, unknown trails. Hermas in his spiritual wanderings had become one of them. We cannot fail to notice the skill with which the author reproduces in these stones the

[17] Henri Frankfort et al., *Before Philosophy* (Harmondsworth, Middlesex 1951) 59-70.

[18] Citations from Alan of Lille are to *The Complaint of Nature*, trans. D. M. Moffat (New York 1908).

torn and pathless landscape and, hence, the hero's initial inner state at the beginning of his spiritual journey. The author's imagistic ordering is both spiritually significant and aesthetically pleasing as unifying pattern.

What has Ecclesia accomplished, then, with the building of the tower? She has reconstructed symbolically before Hermas God's universal order on its cosmological, sacramental, social and moral levels, offering it to him as a model for his inner reordering and reconciliation. As a man, Hermas must become a building block in this vast ideal structure, but, first, he must become himself that structure in a microcosmic, individual sense. He must rebuild in himself the city, the temple, an edifice of reason and order over the wild and pathless landscape of the soul, over psychic chaos. The tower emerges here as a powerful symbol of universal and personal integration.

Perhaps the most startling event in this process of symbolic integration takes place when Ecclesia announces that the tower is she herself: "Ὁ *μὲν πύργος*, *ὅν βλέπεις οἰκοδομούμενον*, *ἐγώ εἰμί*, *ἡ* Ἐκκλησία" (11.3). Through this identification, Ecclesia takes on another aspect: As spiritual guide, she has gradually built a framework of truth which the dreamer must assimilate for his inner regeneration – an ideal universal order. After accomplishing this, she steps forward and becomes herself that order, absorbing into herself the very symbol that she has created for it. She is, then, both the guide and the goal of the dreamer's spiritual quest.

The ultimate expression of Ecclesia's identity, however, does not lie only in universal expansion but also in personal internalization. As she is departing after the building of the tower, Hermas asks why her visage had altered with each appearance to him. He is told that Ecclesia appeared at first old and weak, needing the support of a chair and the arms of her companions, because Hermas's soul was withered and near moral death. She appeared progressively younger in subsequent visions as a result of his increasing inner regeneration (18.9; 19.1-4; 20.1-3; 21.1-4).

The intriguing connection that has been developing throughout between Ecclesia's outer appearance and Hermas's inner state reaches a dramatic climax in the final vision, when Hermas encounters the apocalyptic beast. The four colors of its head symbolize the whole spectrum of human history: The black color, Ecclesia explains, stands for the spiritually dark world of the present age. The red color foretells the impending destruction of the world through fire and blood. The gold color represents those men who will survive the catastrophe and, purified as gold by fire, will become fit for the rising tower. Finally, the white color symbolizes "the coming age" (*ὁ αἰὼν ὁ ἐπερχόμενος*) of God's elect, who through their endurance and purity shall gain eternal life. It is the anagoge of time (24.1-6). The beast, however, possesses another symbolic dimension besides the eschatological one. When Hermas confronts it in all its ugly ferocity, he vanquishes it not through physical, Prudentian violence, but by spiritual posture. We get a distinct sense of self encountering self, the regenerated soul finally subduing its rebellious, dark impulses. With this triumph, Ecclesia appears now to Hermas, clothed in splendid white, "as a virgin adorned, coming out of her bridal chamber" (23.1). She now images forth Hermas's almost fully regenerated soul.

The inevitability with which she reflects his inner state cannot but take Ecclesia from an external position and internalize her in the dreamer's psyche. Where does she actually reside, then? Like her descendants – Philosophia, Natura, and Holy Church – Ecclesia as allegorical personification maintains a significantly ambiguous relationship to the dreamer. On one hand, she acts as a personality external to him, descending from a supernatural realm, whose values she reflects symbolically and articulates discursively. At the same time, she functions as an innate part of the hero emerging into affirmation and identity in the form of a distinct figure in his visionary experience, seeking to become reassimilated in a more reconciled and integrated self.

The linking of the natural cosmos with moral law into one universal order and its representation through a symbolic structural center are by no means unique to *The Shepherd of Hermas*. These notions had already developed in Mesopotamian and Timaean cosmology.[19] The work's contribution lies, rather, in the fact that it is one of the earliest attempts of some magnitude to bring the Neoplatonic system of the hierarchy of being with its binding principle of restorative interaction between levels of being into the Christian scheme of man's redemption. This assimilation finds its first systematic expression later on in the writings of pseudo-Dionysius on the divine and ecclesiastical hierarchies, becoming to a considerable extent the basis of medieval cosmology.

The idea of the disordered soul finding healing in the contemplation of cosmic order also predates *The Shepherd of Hermas*; it, too, derives from Timaean cosmology.[20] The work, however, brings for the first time this process of healing not only within the Christian redemptive scheme, but also within the visionary dramatic order that I have outlined earlier. It becomes Ecclesia's unique, and at this point seminal, task to erect within a visionary context an ideal Christian universe in a symbolic form, bringing the spiritually confused hero to it for his contemplation and absorption as ordering principle, as an integrative framework of truth.

To emphasize the indestructible unity of this framework and the pervasive interdependence of all its levels of being and value – cosmological, moral, social, psychological – Ecclesia performs an act of unification which is more than a metaphoric gesture. By becoming one with the universal order, Ecclesia, as God's sacramental agent, restates here the sacramental reconciliation and, therefore, final identity of these disparate levels of reality. The world is both creation and sacrament. Since Ecclesia presents herself not only as the sum of all universal processes outside man but also as an aspect of his psychical life, we realize that this ideal order of truth is by no means external to man but an innate part of himself, often confused and corrupted but constantly seeking reaffirmation. The fully integrated psyche is pre-

[19] Paul Piehler, *The Visionary Landscape* (London 1971) 52-62.
[20] Plato, *Timaeus* 90c.

sented here, then, as an analogical reconstruction of a divinely ordered universe, and, on the sacramental level, one with it. This process of inner reconstruction in the visionary hero with its accompanying dramatic order is carried on by Ecclesia's successors in medieval allegorical literature, as a cursory glance may show.

In Boethius's *The Consolation of Philosophy* (sixth century), which is highly indebted to Timaean cosmology but closest in time to *The Shepherd of Hermas* of all the major medieval allegorical visions, Philosophia helps the hero gain the proper philosophical perspective toward his worldly misfortune and the resulting spiritual distress by placing them within the framework of universal law and order rather than the fickle oscillations of earthly Fortune. The cosmic landscape is made by the author to reflect with its turbulence the dreamer's disordered soul (Bk. 1, Poem 2), or it is offered in its harmonious beauty as model for his inner reintegration (Bk. 3, Poem 9). Philosophia identifies explicitly cosmic with moral and psychic order, cutting across the macrocosm of nature to the microcosm of man's individual spirit (Bk. 4, Prose 7). The fertile landscape and the brilliant astral vistas described in the ascent of the soul chariot image the hero's final attainment of a truer perspective and of spiritual and psychic stability.

The immense influence of *The Consolation of Philosophy* on Alan of Lille's *The Complaint of Nature* must have transmitted to Natura those characteristics which Philosophia appears to have inherited from Ecclesia – however indirectly within the allegorical tradition – as visionary guide. A more Christian and messianic figure than Boethius's mistress,[21] Natura draws closer to Ecclesia in that she becomes herself the symbolic embodiment of cosmic, social, and psychic order rather than its mere discourser. This order is upset by man alone whose spiritual perversity is depicted in sexual and therefore very elemental terms. Man's disjointed society as well as his fragmented spirit are symbolized by the violent rupture in Natura's cosmic vesture. Throughout the work, Natura persistently ties natural with moral law. Its violation by man results inevitably in the derangement of his psyche; its contemplation and reassimilation as ordering principle restores man's spiritual and mental equilibrium.

Dante's *Paradiso* is a paean to God's *ordo* on its cosmological, sacramental, social and moral levels of existence. The spiritually alienated hero is taken to its summit by a succession of authoritative figures, finally absorbing it into his own microcosm, as his "desire and will, like a wheel that spins with even motion, [are] resolved by the Love that moves the sun and the other stars" (33.143-145).[22]

In Langland's *Piers Plowman*, too, cosmic order is identified with social, moral, and individual psychic order. Anima shows the harmony of the constellations being upset by inevitable empathy with a morally depraved society, where man feels no charity toward his brother, alienating Conscience and thus fragmenting the larger

[21] See Curtius (n. 7 above) 119 and Piehler 55.

[22] *The Divine Comedy of Dante Alighieri: III Paradiso*, trans. John D. Sinclair (New York 1961) 485.

human framework as well as his inner self (B. 15.337-364). Nature (Kynde), the aggregate of all cosmic processes, gives the same answer as Holy Church, the sacramental institution, to Will's question about attaining salvation and inner reconcilation: "Loue · ys . . . most souereyne salue · for saule and for body · Loue is the plonte of pees . . . ," Holy Church tells him (C. 2.147-149). "Lerne to loue," repeats Nature at the end, echoing one common law (C. 23.208). Temperance is a virtue which must pervade the ideal universe, the ideal society, and the ideal inner self as one order of being.[23]

As we saw in *The Shepherd of Hermas*, the process of restoration of man's inner identity and of his proper relationship to God's universal order takes the symbolic form of the building of a structural center, such as the tower, by the spiritual guide. The building of the city or the temple as a structure of reason and order over threatening chaos is a motif borrowed from ancient literature too familiar to be discussed here.[24] I merely wish to point out that *The Shepherd* helps establish this structural center as a powerful symbol of universal and personal integration, appearing in various forms in the visionary literature of the Middle Ages.

Philosophia wants Boethius to rediscover the true city from which he has exiled himself. He must carry its laws within him (Bk. 1, Prose 16). Using a similar image, she instructs him elsewhere that "the strength of man is within, hidden in the remote tower of the heart" (Bk. 4, Poem 3). Alan's Natura links the great city of the universe with the human city, wherein God rules and dwells as if in His palace. Man must not live "like one foreign-born, dwelling in a suburb of the universe" but must become one with this vast city. Furthermore, man in himself is a city, where his faculties reside in harmony with one another in various "citadels" – reason in the head, feelings in the heart, pleasure in his loins, and so on (Prose 3, pp. 27-28). I shall not elaborate on the centrality of the city as symbol in the *Divine Comedy*, both in its perverse and ideal form, reflecting man's depraved soul or standing as a model for his inner reconstruction. Finally, at the most prominent place of the landscape in *Piers Plowman* stands the Tower of Truth, where Holy Church dwells, emerging from it to instruct the dreamer. At the end of the work, Piers builds the Castle of Unity – which is Holy Church, which is human society – and defends it against Antichrist's forces with the help of Conscience, "an interior abbey . . . the monastery of the heart . . . the Church within us."[25] Thus the Castle of Unity is also the inner man. When Conscience is forced into exile from it, we are left with a sense of social as well as individual fragmentation. A further study of the use of the symbolic structural center in medieval visionary allegory would show its progressive internalization in the

[23] See Bloomfield (n. 7 above) 138-142.

[24] M. Eliade, *Images and Symbols: Studies in Religious Symbolism*, trans. P. Mairet (New York 1969) 27-56, and *The Myth of the Eternal Return or, Cosmos and History*, trans. W. R. Trask (Princeton 1971) 12-21, on "the symbolism of the center."

[25] I am using here Bloomfield's description of Langland's view of conscience, according to the monastic tradition of his time (n. 7 above) 18 and 169.

human psyche and its increasing expression in terms of the integrity of the human personality.

Perhaps the most unusual contribution of *The Shepherd of Hermas* to the allegorical tradition remains to be mentioned. We may recall that, after Hermas's triumph over the apocalyptic beast, Ecclesia appears before him "as a virgin adorned, coming out of her bridal chamber" (23.1). We noted that Ecclesia's progressive rejuvenation images the gradual renewal of Hermas's soul. The virgin, however, is more than a reflection of Hermas's new spiritual state. She is also the woman he had once debased with his carnal love, missing the deeper significance she held in his life as saving force. By purifying and ordering his soul – or, to use Jacopone da Todi's words, by "ordering his loves" – Hermas has restored his beloved to her ideal place. There is no dramatic "ben son, ben son . . ." here, but the bride that steps forth now is Rhoda idealized and sanctified. This is perhaps the moment that scandalized Tertullian into concluding, with his usual acerbity, that "scripturis Pastoris . . . moechos amat."[26] Hermas was, after all, a married man. So Rhoda becomes the first historical beloved to appear in allegorical literature, acting as the incipient force of the hero's redemption. She is the first Beatrice of Western civilization.[27]

The virgin, however, is still identified as Ecclesia. By this subtle juxtaposition of two identities in the figure of the virgin, Hermas's beloved inevitably takes on the anagogical dimension of the eternal Church, the bride of Christ, while the Bride of Christ finds its most poignant incarnation in the historical beloved. As a result, Hermas too emerges as a potential Christ – which is the goal of his spiritual guide. The hero's spiritual quest, then, assumes the fervor and concrete familiarity of human passion, while his human love is redeemed and elevated to its perfect form, which is in God. Perhaps the power of the moment lies in the sense we have that somehow both loves, however different, are being simultaneously fulfilled here. It is this reconciliation and simultaneous fulfillment that Dante brings to a crowning point in his *Divine Comedy*. By placing himself in a Christ-like position – as by his descent into and ascent from the underworld – Dante, too, allows his historical beloved to stand as an analogue to Christ's *sponsa*, the Triumphant Church, investing her with the highest spiritual meaning without ever sacrificing her human identity.

Yet, Rhoda's idealization is tempered considerably by the author's eschatological mentality. The virgin never attains to Beatrice's splendor; her hair remains aged and white under the bridal veil. This is how we see her last. E. R. Curtius views this odd juxtaposition of youth and old age in several late antique and medieval personifications as symbolizing age-old wisdom mixed with perpetual vigor.[28] In the present

[26] Tertullian, *De pudicitia* 10.

[27] Rhoda's affinity to Beatrice has been noted without any elaboration by Goodspeed (n. 2 above) 32, and H. A. Musurillo, S. J., *The Fathers of the Primitive Church* (New York 1966) 89. Piehler (n. 19 above) 140-141 mistakenly sees Rhoda being abandoned by the author, after her disappearance at the beginning of the work, and replaced by a strictly allegorical figure, Ecclesia.

[28] Curtius (n. 7 above) 101-105.

context, we must consider other interpretations as well, which need not be mutually exclusive; in fact, they coexist, adding to Ecclesia's fascinating complementarity as allegorical figure. The grotesque element in Ecclesia's appearance reminds us once again of the mysterious and awesome aspect of her nature, which stuns human perception and defies articulation. We first encountered this aspect at her initial appearance to Hermas, in "the terrible and humanly unendurable words" that she uttered to him (3.3). Secondly, if we have followed closely the significance of each successive alteration in her appearance, we come to realize that neither Hermas nor his age have attained full spiritual renewal. By imagistic association – another instance of the author's literary skill – we see in Ecclesia's remaining deformity the apocalyptic beast still lurking as a potential force of cosmic and psychic chaos. This is why, at Ecclesia's disappearance, Hermas turns anxiously around, thinking that the beast has returned (24.6). He must wait now for yet another spiritual guide, the Angel of Repentance – the Shepherd himself – to come into his life and rebuild the tower, the symbol of a divinely ordered universe and, simultaneously, of a fully integrated human soul. This happens in the remaining and larger part of the book, but only as an extended repetition of what Ecclesia had effected earlier. Yet, even after that, Ecclesia never returns fully rejuvenated, the Shepherd too departs, and Hermas is left alone by the uncompleted tower as its guardian, only with the promise of the Shepherd's return someday.

The Shepherd of Hermas does not end with a blissful, naive homecoming to an ideal world. Instead, it anticipates the maturity and historical realism of a work like *Piers Plowman*, where the quest for perfection goes on as long as the work and its hero remain within historical time. Hence, Ecclesia's incomplete rejuvenation – accented by the precarious counterpoise of delicate virginal beauty and desiccating old age on her face – like the unfinished tower, and like the continuous displacement of authoritative figures, is a symbol of man's ceaseless spiritual struggle. These images of irresolution keep the work charged with an eschatological tension, which is spiritually valid and, at the same time, artistically advantageous in that it engages the reader's imagination beyond the work in search of its true ending: the emergence of the Triumphant Church at the end of time, in the world and in each man.

My presentation of *The Shepherd of Hermas* as an important prototype in the evolution of medieval visionary allegory has been obviously incomplete. I have concentrated mainly on the five Visions, omitting the Commandments and the Parables (Similitudes) – essentially a moral and Christological elaboration of what Ecclesia has shown and taught earlier in the work. More significantly for our purposes, I have not examined sufficiently two other key dramatic factors: the dreamer and the landscape. These cannot be separated from the authoritative figure as literary experience, except by the artificial dissections of critical analysis.

By focusing on the figure of Ecclesia alone, I have tried to define those elements in her character and in her spiritual and dramatic function which establish her as a model for the allegorical personifications in medieval literature and, consequently, as a formative influence on the development of medieval dream allegory. Like the major visionary personalities of the period – Philosophia, Natura, Holy Church, Beatrice – Ecclesia is more than the sum of a few crystalline theological concepts. She moves about with a metaphoric potency and multivalence of meaning that often break down the limits of conceptual stratification. The constant interplay between her mythic and human aspects endows her with a highly engaging complementarity of character. Her symbolic expansion to God's universal order on all its levels of significance – cosmological, sacramental, social and moral – with her simultaneous internalization in the hero's psyche manifests the great range of her identity. This identity must be experienced on both an articulate and an ineffable level, where symbol defies rational penetration. Part of her vitality as allegorical personification is her capacity to function simultaneously as symbol of the immutable ideal and the potential actual, that is, of both spiritual perfection outside history and the ongoing spiritual struggle within history. Finally, in her fusion with the historical beloved – emerging here as literary figure for the first time – Ecclesia serves also as a prototype to later typological practice, as in Dante, where certain historical personalities achieve an anagogical dimension without losing their human identity and, hence, meaningful proximity to us. Within this figural framework, the author of *The Shepherd* effects, though still in a germinal form, a reconciliation between human and divine love.

One cannot trace a direct connection between *The Shepherd of Hermas* and any of the authors mentioned here – a frequent handicap in comparative studies. Yet, the work's antecedent place in the Christian allegorical tradition, its availability to the medieval West, and, above all, the persistent reassertion of its thematic aims and structural features within the medieval context attest sufficiently to its seminal role.

Department of English and Comparative Literature
San Jose State University
San Jose, California 95192, U.S.A.

THE PERSISTENCE OF SCANDINAVIAN CONNECTIONS IN NORMANDY IN THE TENTH AND EARLY ELEVENTH CENTURIES

•

by Lauren Wood Breese

The emergence of Normandy as a duchy powerful in European affairs is one of the most widely studied developments of the later Middle Ages. The province had its origins in the early tenth century as a Scandinavian colony in Neustria, and by the late eleventh century it had become a formidable duchy in France whose aristocracy spilled out across Europe and the Near East from the Scottish frontier to Antioch. Some aspects of Norman emergence are well known, especially the eleventh-century evolution of political institutions. But the tenth- and early eleventh-century history, particularly that which deals with the erosion of viking relationships and cultural patterns, has received less attention.

A matter of continuing interest has been the question of the degree to which the spectacular later development of Normandy was an indirect consequence of its Scandinavian heritage. Few hold to an extreme position regarding Scandinavian immigration into and influence on the character of Normandy. On the one hand, viking numbers were clearly not so great as to displace completely their predecessors; neither, on the other hand, can it be argued that there was a mere seizure of power by a few shiploads of warriors. The proper definition of the Scandinavian impact lies somewhere between these extremes. This study is a reassessment – in terms of archaeological, linguistic, onomastic and toponymic, as well as literary, evidence – of the Scandinavian role and presence in the western Frankish realm in the tenth and early eleventh centuries. It suggests strongly that vikings were dominant militarily and politically until the middle of the century; that they exploited that dominance in joint military ventures, in commerce and by immigration in substantial numbers; that their numbers were nevertheless too small to displace the native population or seriously to modify the indigenous culture; and that the consequences by the early decades of the eleventh century were the submergence of Scandinavian language and customs in French and the emancipation of the mixed Franco-Scandinavian nobility from military and political dependence on the northern powers.

The creation of Normandy was one of the results of viking expeditions into the kingdom of the Franks in the late ninth and early tenth centuries – along the river highways of the Seine, Somme, Marne, Vire, Oise and Loire.[1] The defeat of the Norwegian viking, Rolf, by Charles III (the Simple) at Chartres in 911, and the consequent grant of land in the Seine valley by an agreement, perhaps at Saint-Clair-sur-Epte, brought to an end one phase of viking activity in France,[2] although Rolf continued his raiding expeditions eastward into the regions of Beauvais, Amiens and Noyon[3] long after he became the "first Norman count."[4] When he died (sometime between 925 and 933) the original grant had grown by conquest to include Rouen and its environs, and to extend east as far as the Bresle and west as far as the Vire.[5] By 933 and the accession of Rolf's son, William Longsword, Lower Normandy had been acquired and the western boundary of the county established at the Couesnon. *Terra nortmannorum*, as the name implies, was a Scandinavian outpost, and much of its early history developed in connection with events in the northern seas.

In view of the history of those connections and of viking activity in the English Channel, it is intriguing that so few uncontested material traces of the presence of Scandinavians in Normandy have been discovered. The argument of Bouard that there was viking reconstruction and use of the ancient Hague-Dike rampart in the Cotentin is persuasive.[6] It is unfortunate that early archaeological exploration and treasure-hunting removed or obscured the contents of what were probably viking burial sites behind the Hague-Dike and elsewhere in the peninsula,[7] since Norwegian presence not far away is verified by a burial mound and cremation grave, datable about 900, located on the Ile de Groix, off the south coast of Brittany.[8] In

[1] Viking pirates burned Rouen in 841, pillaged it in 845, 851, 876 and, between 856 and 862, occupied the valley of the lower Seine. Charles the Bald, king of the West Franks (840-77) five times convened assemblies at Pîtres between 862 and 873 in an effort to maintain security. Vikings came to Pîtres to receive tribute. See Henri Prentout, *Essai sur les origines et fondation du duché de Normandie* (Paris 1911) 105ff.; Ferdinand Lot, "Mélanges carolingiens: Le pont de Pîtres," *Le Moyen Age* 18 (1905) 2-20. A settlement in the Seine estuary can be dated as early as 896; Jean-François Lemarignier, *Recherches sur l'hommage en marche et les frontières féodales* (Lille 1945) 75.

[2] David Douglas, "Rollo of Normandy," *English Historical Review* 57 (1942) 436, pointed out that there is uncertainty concerning Saint-Clair-sur-Epte as the site of Charles's meeting with Rolf following the battle of Chartres.

[3] Michel de Bouard, "De la Neustrie carolingienne à la Normandie féodale: Continuité ou discontinuité?" *Bulletin of the Institute of Historical Research* 28 (1955) 6.

[4] Rolf was probably not given a title; tradition calls him count and duke; *ibid.* 3.

[5] Douglas (n. 2 above) 435; see also David Douglas, "The Earliest Norman Counts," *English Historical Review* 61 (1946) 129-156.

[6] Michel de Bouard, "La Hague, camp rétranché des Vikings?" *Annales de Normandie* 3 (1953) 3-14; "Le Hague-Dike," *Cahiers archéologiques* 8 (1956) 117-145; "A propos de la datation du Hague-Dike," *Annales de Normandie* 14 (1964) 270-271. There has been disagreement. See Holger Arbman, "Hague-Dike: Les fouilles de 1951 et 1952," *Meddelanden fran Lunds Universitets historiska Museum*, (1953) 191-222; *idem, The Vikings*, trans. Alan Binns (London 1961) 84-85. For further references, see François-Xavier Dillman, "Les vikings dans l'Europe franc: Bibliographie," *Revue du Nord* 56 (1974) 95.

[7] Bouard, "Le Hague-Dike" 144-145.

[8] Arbman, *Vikings*, 83-84; Johannes Brøndsted, *The Vikings*, trans. Kalle Skov (Baltimore 1965) 83; Gwyn Jones, *A History of the Vikings* (London 1968) 232 n.

Normandy itself, there are traces of the use of a new system of Scandinavian land-measurement associated with the introduction of the eight-ox plough;[9] but, on balance, the Norman soil has not been generous in the substantiating of the Scandinavian origins of Normandy or of the continuance of Norse tradition. Two bronze brooches found in a burial-site at Pîtres,[10] a boat-shaped tomb at Réville (Cotentin) of uncertain provenance[11] and some widely distributed weapons represent the physical evidence of a northern immigration.[12] The scarcity of archaeological materials may be accidental, or it may suggest that the number of colonists was so small as to be quickly absorbed into Frankish culture and society.[13] The exact number of permanent Scandinavian immigrants is, of course, unknown and is difficult to disentangle from the sizes of war-parties. There is little evidence, as will be seen, to substantiate the immigration of numbers large enough to replace the native population – either directly from Scandinavia or via the Danelaw and the Irish Sea.[14]

Toponymic evidence offers the most substantial proof of the extent of Norse settlement. Hundreds of place-names of Scandinavian origin are found or imputed in the northern portion of the province, with concentrations in the regions of Caux (centering on Fécamp) and the Cotentin (particularly the Hague).[15] The invaders who arrived with Rolf in the Seine valley were mostly Danes, although Rolf himself has been identified as Norwegian. Many of the viking invaders had arrived in Normandy via the Scandinavian settlements in eastern England.[16] The Anglo-Saxon

[9] The terminology, *bol* and *åttingar*, connected with the introduction of the new agricultural technology, however, does not appear in documents until the late eleventh century. See Lynn White, jr., *Medieval Technology and Social Change* (Oxford 1962) 52-54.

[10] Birgitta Elmqvist, "Les fibules de Pîtres," *Meddelanden fran Lunds Universitets historiska Museum* (1966-1968) 203.

[11] Michel de Bouard, "Sépultures énigmatiques à Réville," *Annales de Normandie* 14 (1964) 258ff.

[12] Lucien Musset, "Influences réciproques du monde scandinave et de l'occident dans le domain de la civilisation au moyen âge," *Cahiers d'histoire mondiale*, I (1953), 78; Jones, *op. cit.*, 232n; Holger Arbman and Nils-Ove Nilsson, "Armes scandinaves de l'époque viking en France," *Meddelanden fran Lunds Universitets historiska Museum* (1966-1968) 163-166, 171-175, 192, 197 and 200.

[13] David Douglas, *William the Conqueror: The Norman Impact upon England* (Berkeley 1964) 22 n.; P. H. Sawyer, "The Density of the Danish Settlement in England," *University of Birmingham Historical Journal* 6 (1957) 16, in reference to the ninth-century Danelaw, suggested that the numbers have been greatly exaggerated; the largest Danish army cannot have numbered more than two or three hundred men.

[14] See the discussion in P. H. Sawyer, *The Age of the Vikings*, ed. 2 (New York 1972) 120-128.

[15] See the studies of Jean Adigard des Gautries, "Les noms de lieux . . . attestés entre 911 et 1066," in *Annales de Normandie* 1-9 (1951-1959), and in *Bulletin de la Société historique et archéologique de l'Orne* 65 (1947) 95-119; F. M. Stenton, "The Scandinavian Colonies in England and Normandy," *Transactions of the Royal Historical Society* 27 (1945) 8; François de Beaurepaire, "La toponymie de la Normandie: Méthodes et applications," *Cahiers Léopold Delisle* 18 (1969) 85.

[16] Sawyer (n. 14 above) 176; Lucien Musset, *Les invasions: Le second assaut contre l'Europe chrétienne (VII-XIe siècles)* (Paris 1965) 253-256; see also Musset, "Pour l'étude des relations

Chronicler in the entry for 896, for example, stated that "those [of the Danish army] that were moneyless got themselves ships and went south across the sea to the Seine."[17] Between 924 and 933 when Lower Normandy came under the control of the Norman dukes, other Scandinavians from the Danelaw, together with some Anglo-Saxons, moved into the Bessin and into the north of the Cotentin.[18] That the Scandinavians were joined by Anglo-Saxons (or at least by anglicized dependents) is attested by the presence of some twenty-six Anglo-Saxon town-names and a few agrarian terms, such as *mansloth* (land tenure), *forlenc* (land area; furrow-length) and *delle* (parcel of land).[19] Onomastic evidence even verifies a limited immigration of Celto-Scandinavians from the Irish Sea area into the Cotentin and the Bessin (for example, *Duncan* and Doncanville; *Niall* and Néhou).[20]

The degree and nature of the earliest colonization are ambiguous. The comparative rarity of place-names combining with Old Norse *þorp* (hamlet; farmstead) and Old Norse *byr* (village) indicates that the first immigrants were not farmer-peasants to the same extent as was the case in the Danelaw.[21] That is, the number of Old Norse personal names attached to the Gallo-Roman suffix *-ville*, such as Kati (Catteville), Helgi (Heugueville), Saxi (Sasseville), Skuli (Eculleville), Toki (Tocqueville), implies that the earliest settlers were a warrior group who conquered and imposed their names on extant Frankish villages. On the other hand, the comparatively large number of place-names which apply to streams (ON *bekkr*), groves (ON *lundr*), valleys (ON *dalr*), ridges (OIcel. *haugr*), enclosures (ON *garðr*), sheds (ON *budh*), and others, does not represent the legacy merely of a handful of soldiers. In addition to the warriors many came in search of arable land and personally colonized it.[22]

entre les colonies scandinaves d'Angleterre et de Normandie," *Mélanges de linguistique et de philologie Fernand Mossé In Memoriam* (Paris 1959) 330-339; and François de Beaurepaire, "Les noms d'Anglo-Saxons contenus dans la toponymie normande," *Annales de Normandie* 10 (1960) 307-316.

[17] *Anglo-Saxon Chronicle*, ed. Dorothy Whitelock with David Douglas and Susie I. Tucker (London 1961) 57; hereafter cited as ASC. *Anglo-Saxon Chronicle: Two of the Saxon Chronicles Parallel*, ed. John Earle and Charles Plummer, 1 (Oxford 1892) 89. These editors offer the date 897 rather than 896 for this entry.

[18] Musset, "Pour l'étude" (n. 16 above) 338-339.

[19] *Ibid.* 331, 333 and 335-56; Lucien Musset, "Un type de tenure d'origine scandinave en Normandie, le mansloth," *Mémoires de l'Académie des sciences, arts et belles-lettres de Caen*, n. s. 12 (1952) 359-367; Beaurepaire (n. 16 above) 308 and 310; François de Beaurepaire, "Quelques finales anglo-saxonnes dans le toponymie normande," *Annales de Normandie* 13 (1963) 219-229.

[20] Lucien Musset, "Les deux âges des vikings: Réflexions et observations d'un historien normand," *Medieval Scandinavia* 2 (1969) 190.

[21] For discussion of *by* and *thorp* in the Danelaw, see Sawyer (n. 14 above) 154-166, and F. M. Stenton, *Anglo-Saxon England*, ed. 3 (Oxford 1971) 523-525.

[22] For the evidence of *-ville* and other connectives, see Jean Adigard des Gautries, *Les noms de personnes scandinaves en Normandie de 911 à 1066* (Lund 1954) 375-435; and Beaurepaire (n. 15 above) 83-85.

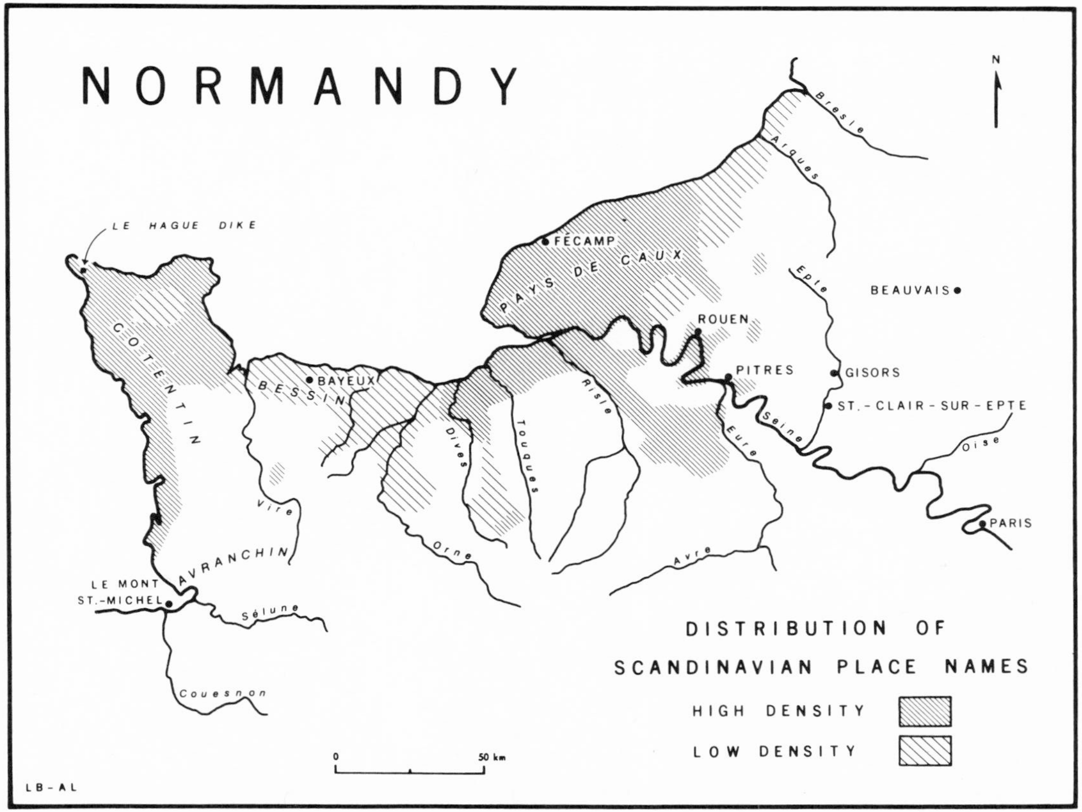

Distribution of Scandinavian place-names based on map in François de Beaurepaire, "La toponymie de la Normandie: Méthodes et applications," *Cahiers Léopold Delisle* 18 (1969) 84.

Of the approximately eighty personal names identified with the period between 911 and 1066, three were feminine – Gerloc, Gonnor and Tófa.[23] It is to be presumed that some Scandinavian women came to Normandy, as they did to the Danelaw and to Iceland. Under the circumstances it would be surprising if many Scandinavian women accompanied the early war-parties to the French coast. Even in the tenth century it is reasonable to assume that most of the settlers chose local girls, *more danico*, and that successive generations thereby increasingly lost their distinct cultural identity. The survival of Scandinavian personal names must be used with caution as historical evidence. Many Scandinavians took two names (for example, Rolf [Robert], Gerloc [Adelis], Gonnor [Albereda]) and, as Sawyer pointed out, names and ancestry are not necessarily connected.[24] Even with these qualifications, however, the frequency of Scandinavian personal names echoes the forcible substitution of an immigrant, in place of a Frankish, aristocracy during the course of the tenth century.

Information about the social arrangements of tenth-century Normandy is not much more accessible than exact population-figures. However, it is interesting to note a variation from Latin Christian marital patterns among the members of the ruling house. Although most of the counts are reputed to have contracted Christian marriages for political reasons, the succession passed uninterrruptedly through "mistresses" who were in fact wives under Danish custom (*more danico*), and who may in some cases have been Scandinavian women.[25] From the time of Rolf to that of Richard II, the children of such alliances were recognized by the ruling family and the court as legitimate heirs. It was not until 989 that the church had sufficient authority to impose its sanctification on the Norman dynasty in a Christian cere-

[23] Adigard des Gautries, *Les noms de personnes scandinaves* 71-177 and 251-253.

[24] Sawyer (n. 13 above) 13-14.

[25] The mother of William Longsword is unknown. The twelfth-century writers, Benoît and Wace, call her "Pope" (Popa), daughter of Berengar of Bayeux, count of the Bessin; Benoît, *Chronique des ducs de Normandie* 1, ed. Carin Fahlin (Uppsala 1951) 295; Wace, *Le roman de Rou et des ducs de Normandie* 1, ed. H. Andresen (Paris 1877) 59 and 85. According to Douglas (n. 2 above) 435, such a connection is unlikely. Benoît 1.351 related that Sprota, whom William Longsword took as his wife "a la danesche maniere," was the mother of the third count, Richard I. Ordericus Vitalis, *Historia ecclesiastica* 2, ed. Marjorie Chibnall (Oxford 1969) bk. 2.2 and 8, referred to the fourth ruler, Richard II, as *Gonnoridae*, son of Gonnor, Richard I's Scandinavian mistress. Judith of Brittany, the first wife of Richard II, bore him at least six children, including the heirs Richard III and Robert I; see William of Jumièges, *Gesta normannorum ducum*, ed. J. Marx (Rouen 1914) 88, bk. 5.13; Benoît 2.261; David Douglas, "Some Problems of Early Norman Chronology," *English Historical Review* 65 (1950) 303. Upon Judith's death in 1017, Richard II took a local girl, Papia, daughter of Richeldis of Envermeu, and she bore Malger (future archbishop of Rouen) and William (future count of Arques). For reference to a gift to the cathedral of Rouen by Papia and her mother, Richeldis, see *Recueil des actes des ducs de Normandie (911-1066)*, ed. Marie Fauroux, Mémoires de la Société des antiquaires de Normandie 36 (Caen 1961) 3; hereafter cited as RADN. Elizabeth Eames, "Mariage et concubinage légal en Norwège à l'époque des Vikings," *Annales de Normandie* 2 (1952) 195-208, sheds light on the legality of the Norman marriages, *more danico*.

mony. Richard I was the first Norman ruler whose successor was the issue of a Christian marriage. In 989 he married Gonnor, mother of his eight children and mistress of nineteen years.[26]

There is no evidence of extraordinary viking activity in the nine years of William Longsword's reign (933-942). The testimony of Dudo and William of Jumièges that William received Harald Bluetooth from Denmark (in approximately 940) and permitted his fleet to outfit somewhere near the Cotentin has been questioned.[27] After William Longsword's death in 942, however, there occurred a resurgence of viking movements in the Channel and in Normandy. The fact that William's son and successor, Richard I (942-996), was in his minority not only permitted rival viking factions to compete openly for supremacy in Normandy but presented a similar opportunity to the Carolingians. Louis IV d'Outremer, king of the West Franks (936-954), engaged in several military actions in Normandy in the early years of Richard's reign. In 942, Louis routed an Icelander, Sigtryg, who was cruising the Seine near Rouen with some Northumbrian vikings; Louis followed up his victory by engaging Sigtryg and an ally, Tormod, in a battle at Rouen in which both vikings were killed.[28] In 945 the king again intervened in Norman affairs ostensibly to combat "paganism," but met defeat before the combined forces of the Norman count (Richard I), the duke of Francia (Hugh the Great), and the king of Denmark (Harald II Gormsson, Blåtonn).[29] Peace was agreed upon by Louis IV and Richard I in 946.[30]

Fifteen years later in 961, a viking band camped in the Seine valley and launched raids towards the frontier of Brittany and in the region of Chartres. This situation provoked renewed hostility between Normans and Carolingians and inaugurated a four-year period of intensified warfare.[31] In 962, Richard I (referred to, interestingly enough, as *pyratarum dux* by Richer of Rheims)[32] again employed the services of the Danish king. Harald's troops assisted Richard's struggle against Louis IV's successor, Lothair, king of the West Franks (954-986), and Thibald, count of Chartres and Blois. The result was a sizable accession of territory by Richard. Finally, in 965 at

[26] Wace 2.53-54; Adigard des Gautries (n. 22 above) 306.

[27] Dudo of Saint-Quentin, *De moribus et actis primorum normanniae ducum*, ed. Jules Lair, Mémoires de la Société des antiquaires de Normandie 23 (Caen 1865) 239; William of Jumièges 3.41; Bouard, "La Hague" (n. 6 above) 5.

[28] Richer of Rheims, *Historiarum libri IV*, ed. G. Waitz (Hanover 1877) 57.

[29] Benoît (n. 25 above) 1.539; F. Clément et al., *L'art de vérifier les dates des faits historiques*. . . ed. 3, 2 (Paris 1784) 832.

[30] The precise nature of the peace treaty and of the remodeled feudal relations associated with it have been a matter of doubt and controversy. For a survey of the views of commentators, see Lemarignier (n. 1 above) 86-87, 123; and Ferdinand Lot, *Fidèles ou vassaux? Essai sur la nature juridique du lien qui unissait les grands vassaux à la royauté depuis le milieu du IXe jusqu'à la fin du XIIe siècle* (Paris 1904) 186, 187, 5 n.

[31] David Douglas, "The Rise of Normandy," *British Academy, Proceedings* 33 (1947) 107.

[32] Richer (n. 28 above) bk. 2, 54.

Gisors on the Epte, Lothair formally recognized Richard's rule over the Bessin, the Cotentin and the Avranchin and, in turn, Richard promised to rebuild and restore the monastery of Mont-Saint-Michel thus acquired.[33]

Danish intervention in the Norman-Carolingian wars of 945 and 962 contributed to Normandy's political survival by accelerating the disintegration of the Carolingian monarchy and indirectly aiding the insurgency of the house of Capet. In 968 Richard recognized the duke of Francia as his overlord.[34] One later Norman chronicler would even have Hugh Capet (son of Hugh the Great) reared in the Norman court and his sister, Emma, married to Richard I,[35] but these connections are unsubstantiated. Located in lands centering on the county of Paris, the dukes of Francia would have attached high value to closing the Seine to viking war-parties, a service most appropriate to the Norman counts. This consideration must have been a matter of frequent discussion and bargaining between the Norman and Frankish rulers.

From the death of the last French Carolingian, Louis V, and the royal coronation of Hugh Capet in 987 until at least the events at Val-ès-Dunes in 1047, Norman counts were among the chief vassals of the emergent Capetian dynasty.[36] There is no further evidence of Scandinavian penetration into the French heartland, and the pursuit by both sides of the mutual military and political advantages of the entente was the most significant cause of the gradual half-century shifting of the orientation of the Norman house away from Scandinavia and toward the Frankish area.

After the middle of the tenth century Norman economic activities, although still dependent on northern connections, also brought the county more into contact with its continental neighbors. The special location of the province, adjacent to the viking-dominated North Sea, Anglo-Saxon England, and the northwestern edge of Latin Europe, contributed to this development, as did the general European economic recovery which began in this period. In the tenth century, Normandy was the most southerly Scandinavian foothold. There Old Norse, or *dönsk tunga*, was still understood, and there viking ships and sailors could find a place of safety among those who shared a common heritage. Although there was no Norman navy before 1066,[37] numismatic finds substantiate that throughout the tenth century Norman goods were carried along the North Sea trade routes. Norman coins, datable between 960 and 1000, have been found in the Hebrides, Scotland, Denmark, Poland, Germany and Russia.[38]

[33] *Recueil des actes de Lothaire et de Louis V, rois de France*, ed. L. Halphen (Paris 1908) no. 24.

[34] RADN (n. 25 above) no. 3.

[35] Benoît (n. 25 above) 2.13-15; 1.574 and 577.

[36] Lemarignier (n. 1 above) 79-80.

[37] C. Warren Hollister, *Anglo-Saxon Military Institutions on the Eve of the Norman Conquest* (Oxford 1962) 103.

[38] Jean Lafaurie, "Le trésor monétaire du Puy (Haute-Loire): Contribution à l'étude de la monnaie de la fin du Xe siècle," *Revue numismatique* 14 (1952) 94; see also the appendix to this article, entitled "Principaux trésors enfouis de la fin du IVe siècle jusqu'au milieu du XIe siècle,

Three valuable numismatic finds of the mid-twentieth century were the coin hoard discovered in 1943 in the outskirts of Le Puy, near the Upper Loire, the monetary treasure found in 1950 near the walls of the abbey of Iona, off the western coast of Scotland, and the treasure of Fécamp, uncovered in 1963. Among the 156 pieces found at Le Puy, buried about the year 1000, were three Norman coins struck at Rouen, bearing the name *Richardus* (I); of the 350 coins in the Iona find (the burial of which dates to approximately 980) three again bore the name of *Richardus* (I) and of *Rotomagus* (Rouen), the mint.[39] In the treasure of Fécamp, hidden near the abbey between 980 and 985, 6,046 of the 8,584 coins recovered were Norman of the period 942 to 985.[40] All but two of the Norman group were unquestionably minted at Rouen and were ducal or ecclesiastical deniers. The latter two are of particular interest. They each bear the inscriptions *VGODACSC* (Hugh the Dane) and *HVALCRIV* (possibly a place-name, or the personal name, Walcherus).[41] Struck in the same period (and perhaps even engraved in the same workshop) as those of Rouen, the existence of these coins suggests that ducal concessions were granted to – or even briefly usurped by – certain individuals to mint money. Coinage in the name of "Hugh the Dane" is a provocative hint of continuing but unrecorded Scandinavian presence. The number and distribution of extant tenth-century Norman coins is impressive. The find at Le Puy is particularly interesting as possible evidence of a new era of Norman enterprise which during the eleventh century was to extend not only to the north but also to the south along the pilgrim route to Rome and, by 1016, to Apulia in southern Italy.[42]

The Norman counts enjoyed substantial revenues from trading activities. The mint at Rouen had been reopened by at least the mid-tenth century, and, as the Fécamp treasure attests, the Norman upper classes were well supplied with money – in comparison with their peers in other parts of France.[43] Rouen continued throughout the tenth century to be a commercial center and military stronghold. Rolf built the first post-Gallo-Roman fortifications on the bank of the Seine, and his grandson,

---

contenant des monnaies françaises," 109-169; for further discussion of monetary circulation in the tenth century, see A. Dieudonné, "La numismatique normande: Les monnaies féodales," *Bulletin de la Société des antiquaires de Normandie* 36 (1924-1925) 337ff.

[39] Lucien Musset, "Les relations extérieures de la Normandie du IXe au XIe siècle, d'après quelques trouvailles monétaires récentes," *Annales de Normandie* 4 (1954) 31; Dieudonné 340-341.

[40] Françoise Dumas-Dubourg, *Le trésor de Fécamp et le monnayage en Francie occidentale pendant le seconde moitié du Xe siècle* (Paris 1972) 3, 7, 14-16.

[41] *Ibid.* 101-103. The use of a Latinized name, such as "Ugo," with a Scandinavian epithet was not unusual for the tenth century; see *ibid.* 102 and n. 24.

[42] Henri Prentout, "Etudes sur quelques points d'histoire de Normandie: Le règne de Richard II, duc de Normandie (996-1027), son importance dans l'histoire," *Mémoires de l'Académie nationale des sciences, arts et belles-lettres de Caen*, n. s. 5 (1929) 86-87.

[43] Bouard (n. 3 above) 8; Lucien Musset, "A-t-il existé en Normandie au XIe siècle une aristocratie d'argent? Une enquête sommaire sur l'argent comme moyen d'ascension sociale," *Annales de Normandie* 9 (1959) 286-288; and *idem* (n. 39 above) 35, regarding the coinage of Richards I, II and III.

Richard I, constructed an additional keep and a bridge over the Seine.[44] Rouen's importance in the tenth century may be connected with the loss of Quentovic (south of Boulogne, near the mouth of the Canche), a major port for traffic from the Rhinelands and from England.[45] Quentovic was plundered initially by Danish raiders in 842.[46] This was only the beginning of the town's misfortunes. By the late ninth century, silting closed the estuary of the Canche, undermining the port's utility. The Frankish king, Louis IV, hoping to secure control of a western outlet, vainly attempted to restore it in 938.[47] The closing of Quentovic redirected some traffic southward to Rouen, and may well have influenced counts Richard I and Richard II in their choice of Fécamp, a Channel port and center of Scandinavian population north of the Seine, as the capital of Normandy.

The staple commodities of interregional trade were foodstuffs, particularly grain, plus salt, and metals, such as iron and lead.[48] Wine from hilly regions bordering the Aisne, the Oise, and the Seine, destined for England, moved through Norman ports, probably in exchange for cloth. By the late tenth century when Ethelred II fixed the tolls in London, the wine and oil[49] merchants of Rouen were so well organized and powerful that they were exempted from payment of the *tonlieu.*[50] Irish slaves and booty from Danish raids were sold in Rouen, and during the reign of Richard I, viking mercenaries in Normandy, acquainted with the Bay of Biscay and the western coast of León, provided guides for expeditions into northwestern Spain.[51] Given the scope of Norman involvements, it was important for the Norman rulers to maintain good relations on two fronts: to provide a stable market for the sale of booty and trade-goods brought to the ports by northern seamen, and, at the same time, to guard against the possibility of disruptive pirate raids on the Frankish interior by preventing viking access via Norman rivers.

Normandy also played a conspicuous and increasingly independent role in the events which culminated in the creation of the Anglo-Danish empire in the early

[44] Pierre Héliot, "Sur les residences princières bâties en France du Xe siècle," *Le Moyen Age* 61 (1955) 46-47; Jean Yver, "Les châteaux forts en Normandie jusqu'au milieu du XIIe siècle: Contribution à l'étude du pouvoir ducal," *Bulletin de la Société des antiquaires de Normandie* 53 (1955-1956) 33.

[45] Rouen and Quentovic were two principal ports for trade with England as early as the seventh century. Jan Dhondt, "Les problèmes de Quentovic," *Studi in onore di Amintore Fanfani* 1 (Milan 1962) 211.

[46] *Ibid.* 209, 215, 221-222.

[47] G. C. Dunning, "Trade Relations between England and the Continent in the Late Anglo-Saxon Period," *Dark-Age Britain: Studies Presented to E. T. Leeds* (London 1956) 221.

[48] Robert Folz, "Charlemagne and His Empire," in *Essays on the Reconstruction of Medieval History*, ed. Vaclav Mudroch and G. S. Couse (Montreal 1974) 89.

[49] *Craspicis* has several meanings: whale oil; salted or fat whale meat; and sealskin.

[50] Suzanne Deck, "Les marchands de Rouen sous les ducs," *Annales de Normandie* 6 (1956) 246.

[51] Charles Homer Haskins, *Norman Institutions* (New York 1960) 48; Archibald R. Lewis, *The Northern Seas: Shipping and Commerce in Northern Europe, A. D. 300-1100* (Princeton 1958) 259 n., 338, 386 and 447; Haakon Shetelig, *An Introduction to the Viking History of Western Europe* (Oslo 1940) 140.

eleventh century. For reasons which are unclear, viking activity in the Channel, directed against Anglo-Saxon England, intensified in the 980s.[52] Norman counts, at best indifferent to the plight of the Anglo-Saxon king, Ethelred II Unraed (978-1016), harbored viking contingents in Norman ports and, as we have seen, aided in the disposal of plunder. After the 980s, however, the gradual and halting emergence of an Anglo-Norman rapprochement may be discerned, the impetus to which seems to have come from the church. In 990, apprised of the increasing hostility between the English and Norman courts, Pope John XV sent an envoy to England to assist Ethelred's council in a treaty which provided for reparation of damages and specified that neither party harbor the other's enemies. These terms were agreed to by Richard I at Rouen on 9 March 991.[53] The extent to which the pope was concerned with the specifically religious condition of the far-away Normans is not clear, but significant ecclesiastical changes have been suggested for the same decade as his intervention in North Sea foreign relations[54] – changes which in the long run were more far-reaching than his diplomatic efforts, which broke down within nine years. In 1000, during the reign of Richard I's son, Richard II (996-1026), the treaty worked out through Pope John's intervention was violated. In the entry for that year, the Chronicler reported that in the summer the "enemy fleet had gone to Richard's kingdom."[55]

The intervention of John XV, however, is a reminder of the increasingly important role of the church in both its secular and monastic branches from the mid-tenth century onwards. Few, if any, Carolingian monastic houses survived intact into the tenth century. By the latter part of that century, however, ecclesiastical organization began to be reconstituted. Norman counts encouraged the reestablishment of monastic congregations and the filling of empty episcopal seats. Monastic reform began with a Flemish revival under the leadership of Mainard of Ghent, who spent thirty years in Normandy (ca. 961-991). In the 990s the Cluniac movement, with its centralizing tendencies, was introduced at Fécamp by William of Volpiano (Dijon).[56] It would be surprising if the Continental orientation of the church did not contribute significantly to the new independence from Scandinavian ties which is particularly to be noted during the reign of Richard II.

For example, in a reversal of a long-standing posture of mutual hostility, the

[52] ASC (n. 17 above) 80ff.; Earle and Plummer (n. 17 above) 123ff.

[53] *Memorials of Saint Dunstan,* ed. W. Stubbs, Rolls Series (London 1874) 397-398; William of Malmesbury, *De gestis regum anglorum*, ed. W. Stubbs, Rolls Series (London 1887) 1.191-193.

[54] See Jean-François Lemarignier, *Etude sur les privilèges d'exemption et de juridiction ecclésiastique des abbayes normandes depuis les origines jusqu'en 1140* (Paris 1937) 39-40; David Douglas, "The Norman Episcopate Before the Norman Conquest," *Cambridge Historical Journal* 13 (1957) 101-115.

[55] ASC (n. 17 above) 85; Earle and Plummer (n. 17 above) 133.

[56] Douglas (n. 13 above) 105-109; Donald Matthew, *The Norman Monasteries and Their English Possessions* (Oxford 1962) 5, 16; René Herval, "Un moine de l'an mille: Guillaume de Volpiano, 1er abbé de Fécamp (962-1031)," *Fécamp: Ouvrage scientifique du XIIIe centenaire, 658-1958* 1 (Fécamp 1959-1961) 27-44.

Norman and Anglo-Saxon houses were united by the marriage in the spring of 1002 of Richard II's sister, Emma, to Ethelred II. The English position in the northern seas was appreciably strengthened by this marriage.[57] In the same year, Ethelred (as it was written, "because the king had been informed that they [the Danes] would treacherously deprive him, and then all his counsellors, of life, and possess the kingdom afterwards") ordered the massacre of "all the Danish men who were in England" on Saint Brice's Day (13 November).[58] This action was probably taken to punish disloyal Scandinavian mercenaries,[59] and the securing of his southern flank by the Norman marriage would have been an important factor in Ethelred's decision to bring the sword to his opponents. After 1002, evidence of the use of Norman ports by northern warships against England is lacking, with the possible exception of a brief visit to Rouen by Svend Forkedbeard mentioned by William of Jumièges.[60]

It appears that throughout the tenth century Normans and Scandinavians often tended to cooperate on the basis of ethnic and cultural ties. The survival – or lack of it – of the Scandinavian tongue after the cessation of Scandinavian immigration (usually dated to the 980s or 990s) is important in this respect. If we are to believe Dudo, who related that William Longsword (933-942) sent his son to Bayeux to be taught the language of his forebears,[61] Scandinavian speech was nearly forgotten by the mid-tenth century. Dudo's statements, however, are to be read cautiously. Not only is the date too early, but the choice of Bayeux is surprising. Toponymic studies disclose that the Bessin was a region lightly settled by Scandinavians, making its chief center an unlikely place for young Richard I to be sent to learn the language.[62] Yet, despite Dudo's unreliability as a source, it is probable that in some areas Scandinavian speech was rapidly replaced – the differences between Frankish and Scandinavian tongues being sufficient to preclude communication between the settlers and the natives.[63] An "official" abandonment of Scandinavian speech in the Norman court was doubtless hastened by the Frankish wives and mistresses[64] and by the close relationship of the Norman counts to the kings of France.

Danish and Norwegian were spoken in the Danelaw until the late eleventh

[57] Frank Barlow, *Edward the Confessor* (Berkeley 1970) 7.

[58] ASC (n. 17 above) 86; Earle and Plummer (n. 17 above) 134-135.

[59] For example, Pallig (brother-in-law of Svend Forkedbeard) "had deserted King Ethelred in spite of all the pledges which he had given him," ASC 85; Earle and Plummer 132.

[60] William of Jumièges (n. 25 above) 80, bk. 5.7. No stipulation that Norman harbors be closed to the enemies of Richard's new brother-in-law was recorded.

[61] Dudo (n. 27 above) 221.

[62] Beaurepaire (n. 15 above) 85.

[63] Sawyer (n. 13 above) 9.

[64] Frankish wives were Gisella – if indeed she was a wife of Rolf – Leyarda, Judith; mistresses included Sprota, Gonnor and Papia.

The date when French replaced Norse as the spoken language of the Norman court is unknown. The abandonment of Norse might have occurred as early as the rule of the first count to be raised in Frankish surroundings, i. e., Richard I. This early date is questionable, and the reign of his son, Richard II, is a much stronger candidate for a "formal" change. (Although see the reference to a visiting skald in 1025, n. 70 below.) There is no evidence that Robert I or William II knew the Scandinavian tongue.

century, but it is acknowledged that immigration there was far greater than in Normandy.[65] Norman linguistic researches have disclosed that many nautical terms and names of marine life were influenced by words of Scandinavian origin.[66] The specialized vocabulary of maritime economics (ON *hvalr*; *hval* [whale]; *hvalmanni* [whaler]; *hvalseta* [whaling group or community]; *wrec; wrek* [wreck; jetsam]) can be found in Norman charters of the mid-eleventh century.[67] That documentary and other written materials in Latin fail to demonstrate the continuance of Scandinavian speech does not exclude the possible use in local areas of a *patois* rich in Scandinavian, Anglo-Saxon and even Celtic terms.[68] In an illiterate age, the absence of written testimony to this effect is inconclusive, and it would appear from the frequency of commercial and pirate traffic in Norman ports and from the connections of the family of Richard I and his Scandinavian wife, Gonnor,[69] that some familiarity with northern speech was a practical political asset. It is interesting to note here that in 1025 a visiting skald entertained the court of Richard II with verses not likely sung in Old French.[70]

By the early eleventh century, linguistic and cultural ties were clearly inadequate to prevent Norman rulers from acting in their own interests –whether such action meant cooperation with the Scandinavians or warfare against them. In 1013, after the English surrender of sizable areas (including London) to the Danish king, Svend Forkedbeard, the Norman court offered refuge to Emma and her children, then to Ethelred and finally to two Scandinavian warriors, Olaf Haraldsson and Lacman,[71]

[65]Sawyer (n. 14 above) 156; Stenton (n. 21 above) 522; H. R. Loyn, *Anglo-Saxon England and the Norman Conquest* (New York 1963) 59; see also Sawyer (n. 13 above) 1-17.

[66]Ralph P. de Gorog, "A Note on Scandinavian Influence in Normandy and in Finland," *Modern Language Notes* 76 (1961) 840-847, examines such terms as ONorm. *estiere* (rudder); *feste* (rope; cable); OF *agrier* (to rig); OF *sigle* (sail); MFr. *run* (ship's hold). Gorog and others have determined that words meaning porpoise or sea-swine (*marsvin*), lobster (ONorm. *houmar*), fish resembling the herring (ONorm. *selletan*), and whale (*hval*) are Scandinavian borrowings. See also Gorog, *The Scandinavian Element in French and Norman: A Study of the Influence on French from the Tenth Century to the Present* (New York 1958).

[67]Lucien Musset, "Aperçus sur la colonisation scandinave dans le nord du Cotentin," *Annuaire des cinq départements de la Normandie* 121e année (1954) 37; Gustave Vasse, "Le rôle du port de Fécamp dans l'avenir de l'économie nationale," *Bulletin de l'Association des amis du vieux Fécamp and du pays de Caux*, 1940-1941 (1942) 21. For the term *werec* (and varying forms: *veresc*; *verefc*; *verest*; *verses*; *veresq*; etc.) see the charters of William II in 1056-1066 and 1063-1066, in RADN (n. 25 above) nos. 214 and 224. Gorog, *Scandinavian Element*, 98, related that the term *walmannus* (*waumannus*), "whale-fisher," was used in the northern Cotentin until the twelfth century, and that the family names *Le Vauman* and *Le Gaument* (from ON *hvalmannr*) still exist in Normandy.

[68]Beaurepaire (n. 15 above) 83, refers to Celtic linguistic research.

[69]Gonnor's daughter, Emma, married the Danish king, Cnut; her sister, Aveline, married a Norman with the Scandinavian name Turulfus (of Pont-Audemer), ca. 980; another sister, Wevia, married Osbern of Bolebec; Adigard des Gautries (n. 22 above) 275 and 340.

[70]The skald, Sigvatr Thorharson, and his companion, Bergr, were from the court of Olaf Haraldsson; *ibid.* 70; Prentout (n. 42 above) 83.

[71]The identity of Lacman has not been determined. Adigard des Gautries (n. 22 above) 69 suggested that *Lacman Suavorum*, instead of being a king of the Swedes, might have been *rex Sudrorum* (king of the Hebrides). Lacman was not a personal name; rather, it was a title, meaning "man of law" – *logmadr.*

who had recently been raiding in Brittany[72] and whose forces earlier had been enlisted in Ethelred's defense.[73] Prior to leaving Normandy, incidentally, Olaf and several of his men were baptized by the duke's brother, Robert, archbishop of Rouen – an event of significance to the later history of Christianity in Scandinavia. Olaf Haraldsson became patron saint of Norway.[74]

The death of Svend Forkedbeard in 1014 was the occasion of Ethelred's return to England, but by that date the Anglo-Saxon monarchy could neither sustain the offensive nor rally in sufficient numbers to prevent the Danes under Svend's son, Cnut, from completing their conquest. The Norman count, Richard II, offered no military assistance to his brother-in-law in regaining his throne, but it is interesting that Norman troops were dispatched to Ireland in 1014 in an effort to stop the Danes at Clontarf.[75] Ethelred died in 1016; his son and successor, Edmund Ironside, died seven months later on 30 November; and in December, 1016, Cnut was able finally to gain the English throne.

* * *

Cnut's reign as king of England (1016-1035) was a more constructive interval in English development than the previous history of viking invasions seemed to promise, but it did little to smooth relations with Normandy. To buttress the new monarchy, in 1017 Cnut married his predecessor's widow, Queen Emma, sister of the Norman count. The Encomiast wrote of the occasion:

> Thanks be to God, Lady Emma, noblest of women, became the wife of the very mighty King Cnut. Gaul rejoiced, the land of the English also rejoiced, when such a great adornment was conveyed over the seas.[76]

[72] ASC (n. 17 above) 93; Earle and Plummer (n. 17 above) 144; for the raid on Brittany, see Adémar of Chabannes, *Chronicon Aquitanicum et Francicum, seu historia Francorum* 3, ed. Jules Chavanon, Collection de textes pour servir à l'étude et à l'enseignement de l'histoire (Paris 1897) iv, 136, 139-140.

[73] William of Jumièges (n. 25 above) 85-87, bk. 5.11-12. Alarmed by the reception of Scandinavian raiders at the Norman court and concerned that Richard II would employ them in his current battle against Odo, count of Chartres and Blois (datable 1013-1014), the Capetian king, Robert II (996-1031), convened an assembly at Coudres. The arbitration imposed a southern boundary between Richard and Odo at Tillières-sur-Avre, and (in view of William of Jumièges's comment that Olaf and Lacman were presented with gifts and persuaded to return to their countries) it probably required Richard to expel his northern allies. See *Encomium Emmae reginae*, ed. Alistair Campbell, Royal Historical Society, Camden Third Series 72 (London 1949) app. 3, 78, 2 n.; Prentout (n. 42 above) 79-80; Ch. Pfister, *Etudes sur le règne de Robert le Pieux (996-1031)* (Paris 1885) 214, 215. Odo II (ca. 983-1037) became count of Blois, Tours, Chartres and Meaux upon the death of his brother, Thibald, in 1005; Helgaud de Fleury, *Vie de Robert le Pieux*, ed. Robert-Henri Bautier and Gillette Labory, Sources d'histoire médiévale (Paris 1965) 65, 5 n. Helgaud, Robert's encomiast, made no mention of events at Coudres.

[74] William of Jumièges (n. 25 above) 87, bk. 5.12; Benoît (n. 25 above) 2.261; *Acta sanctorum*, July vii (Antwerp 1729) 101-113.

[75] Musset (n. 39 above) 37.

[76] *Encomium Emmae reginae* (n. 73 above) bk. 2, sect. 16, p. 33.

Emma's feelings toward her two royal spouses are not known, but after 1017, at any rate, she quickly identified herself with the new Danish dynasty. As a condition of her second marriage she renounced her children by Ethelred, and after the death of Cnut in 1035 she struggled to protect the crown for her third son, Harthacnut. Her older sons, the ethelings Alfred and Edward, were reared in the Norman court, and it is not surprising that the Norman aristocracy refused to recognize her or her championship of Harthacnut after her brother's (Richard II's) death in 1026.[77] Adam of Bremen related that sometime in the mid-1020s Cnut tried but failed to secure Danish ties in Normandy by offering his widowed sister, Estrith, in marriage to Richard II's son and later successor, Robert (1027-1035).[78] The fact of such a marriage-offer is questioned,[79] but Robert's hostility to Cnut, evidenced in the Norman championship of the ethelings and the dispossessed Saxon dynasty,[80] is understandable in view of the rapid and threatening expansion of Denmark over the North Sea world in the third decade of the eleventh century.

Emma outlived her Danish husband and son by a decade.[81] The sudden expiration of the Danish dynasty – Harald Harefoot died in 1040 and was followed by Harthacnut two years later – made possible the reintroduction of Norman influence in English affairs with the restoration of the line of Ethelred and the coronation of Emma's son, Edward (the Confessor), as king of England (1042-1066). The events which culminated in the Norman invasion of England in 1066 are well known – as are Emma's connections which supplied the ancestral legitimacy for William's claims.

As long as Scandinavian princes and Norman counts shared the same economic and political ambitions, and as long as they shared a familiar northern culture and language, Normandy remained viking in spirit and policy, even though the Normans were located on the periphery of a North Sea world. By at least the second decade of the eleventh century, Normandy had achieved a separate European identity – as independent of northern connections as of eastern (French) ones – and was no longer a satellite of Scandinavia.

Department of History
California State University
Fullerton, California 92634, U.S.A.

[77] Miles W. Campbell, "Emma, reine d'Angleterre, mère dénaturée ou femme vindicative? " *Annales de Normandie* 23 (1973) 102-103, 105.

[78] Adam of Bremen, *Gesta Hammaburgensis ecclesiae pontificum ex recensione Lappenbergii*, ed. G. Waitz (Hanover 1876) bk. 2, lii, 77.

[79] Douglas (n. 25 above) 292-295.

[80] *Encomium Emmae reginae* (n. 73 above) xlviii; Lucien Musset, "Relations et échanges d'influence dans l'Europe du Nord-Ouest (X^{e}-XIe siècles)," *Cahiers de civilisation médiévale: X^{e}-XIIe siècles* 1 (1958) 76.

[81] Emma died in her seventies on 6 March 1052. ASC (n. 17 above) 122; Earle and Plummer (n. 17 above) 176; *Encomium Emmae reginae* (n. 73 above) xlix.

MAGNATES AND "CURIALES" IN EARLY NORMAN ENGLAND

•

by C. Warren Hollister

The Norman Conquest, R. H. C. Davis recently remarked, transformed England into "the first and most perfect example of a feudal monarchy."[1] The Old English ruling class was swept away and its lands passed to William the Conqueror, to be kept or granted out much as he chose. William was thus given the opportunity, never to be repeated, of creating a new English landed aristocracy *ex nihilo.* In this sense (to misquote Burckhardt), Norman England was William the Conqueror's work of art.

The outlines of William's new design are disclosed in Domesday Book (1086): he kept about seventeen percent of the lands as *terra regis,* permitted the churches to retain about twenty-seven percent, and granted fifty percent to some 180 homage-bound lay tenants-in-chief, almost all of whom were Normans or other Frenchmen.[2] Of these lands granted to laymen, well over a third was reserved for an elite group of ten powerful magnates, all of whom held lands with annual values in excess of £750. At the top of this list of ten stood three super-magnates: the Conqueror's half-brothers Odo bishop of Bayeux (about £3000 per year) and Robert count of Mortain (about £2100), and a more distant royal kinsman, Roger of Montgomery (about £2100).

William's ten leading magnates together controlled nearly twenty percent of the land revenues of all England. These men were drawn largely from the new nobility that the Conqueror had earlier raised to positions of wealth and power in Normandy,[3] but they also included two neighboring magnates who had fought for him at Hastings: Eustace count of Boulogne and Alan of Brittany (who became lord of

I am grateful to the National Endowment for the Humanities, the American Philosophical Society, the Social Science Research Council, the American Council of Learned Societies, the Fulbright Commission, the John Simon Guggenheim Memorial Foundation, and the Warden and Fellows of Merton College, Oxford, for supporting research on this paper, to Professors Emily R. Coleman and W. Elliot Brownlee for their valuable suggestions (they do not necessarily concur in all that I say), and to my research assistants Jean Saulter, Carole Moore, Joseph Navari and Thomas Keefe.

[1] R. H. C. Davis, *The Normans and their Myth* (London 1976) 110.

[2] These percentages are derived from information gathered by W. J. Corbett, *Cambridge Medieval History* 5 (1926) 508ff., and represent land values as recorded, manor by manor, in Domesday Book. About 6% of the land was in the hands of miscellaneous smallholders.

[3] D. C. Douglas, *William the Conqueror* (Berkeley 1964) 83-104.

Richmond).[4] Although the loyalty of these ten proved to be less than total,[5] most of them remained faithful companions of the Conqueror throughout his reign.

Their activity at William's court can be measured roughly by the frequency with which they attested his charters. For obvious reasons, the correlation between charter attestations and attendance at court is imperfect: one could be at court and not attest, and it is possible that a person's name might occasionally appear on a witness list without his having been present at the time the charter was issued. Nevertheless, attestations remain our surest means of determining which people were habitually in the royal entourage. And the wealthiest of William the Conqueror's magnates were also among his most frequent attestors.

This close connection between wealth and court activity can best be shown in tabular form. Table A lists England's ten greatest lay landholders at the Conqueror's death in 1087, roughly in the order of their wealth as measured by the annual values of their Domesday manors.[6] These values are provided in column 1; column 2 lists the total number of their attestations of extant royal charters; and column 3 provides their rank-order based on the frequency of attestation among all lay witnesses of royal charters. Thus, Roger of Montgomery attested more charters of William I than any other layman; Odo of Bayeux, Geoffrey of Coutances and Robert of Mortain were second, third and fourth, and so on. In other words, William I's three supermagnates were among the four most frequent attestors of his charters. If for our purposes here we define as a *curialis* anyone among the fifteen most frequent lay witnesses of royal charters, it results that seven of William I's ten wealthiest barons in 1087 were also *curiales*. Of the remaining three, William of Warenne attested with reasonable frequency (eight known charters), Geoffrey de Mandeville served as sheriff of several counties and was the addressee of five royal charters, and Eustace count of Boulogne had responsibilities in his homeland. Table A thus presents a highly simplified profile of the model feudal monarchy to which R. H. C. Davis alludes – a polity in which

[4] Alan's presence at Hastings is not certain but is highly probable: *Complete Peerage* 10 (1945) 783.

[5] Eustace of Boulogne rebelled in 1067 but was reinstated; Odo of Bayeux was arrested by the king in 1082, for reasons that are not altogether clear, and was restored as the king lay dying in 1087: see David R. Bates, "The Character and Career of Odo Bishop of Bayeux (1049/50-1097)," *Speculum* 50 (1975) 15-18. Another very large landholder, William I's kinsman William fitz Osbern (earl of Hereford), was killed while fighting in Flanders in 1070 or 1071; his son and English heir, Roger earl of Hereford, rebelled in 1075 and was disseised and imprisoned: *Complete Peerage* 6 (1926) 447-450.

[6] Two of the ten, Odo of Bayeux and Geoffrey of Coutances, were bishops in Normandy but held their English lands as laymen. The Domesday manorial values represent the gross revenues from all lands held of the king, whether retained as demesne or granted out as fiefs; to have provided only demesne values would have been to overlook the income that a tenant-in-chief derived from his vassals. On the other hand, manors held in mesne tenancy of some other tenant-in-chief have been excluded, as have sources of income not associated with land. For these and other reasons, the figures are imprecise – yet they remain our best available indexes of English baronial wealth. For a discussion of the problems involved in using Domesday manorial values see Reginald Lennard, *Rural England, 1086-1135* (Oxford 1959) 25-29.

TABLE A
Relationship between Landed Wealth
and Frequency of Attestations among
English Magnates Alive in 1087

10 greatest Engl. lay landholders	*pounds/year*	*Wm. I attests.*	*rank/lay attestors*
Odo of Bayeux (deprived 1082)	3000	34	2
Robert of Mortain	2100	30½	4
Roger of Montgomery	2100	40	1
Wm. I of Warenne	1165	8	
Alan ld. of Richmond	1100 + waste	21	7
Hugh e. of Chester	800	15½	9
Richard of Clare	780	11	11
Geoffrey of Coutances	780	34	3
Geoffrey de Mandeville	780	0*	
Eustace II c. of Boulogne	770	0**	
Total of attestors in top 15: 7 of 10			

*Sheriff: 5 charters of Wm. I addressed to him.
**Spends much of the reign in Boulogne.

the greatest lords are joined to their king not only by homage but by companionship and royal service as well.

As in the case of many such statistical demonstrations, however, one might have guessed as much without the figures. That most of William I's wealthiest barons were also *curiales* is a predictable result of the Conqueror's having given huge English honors to his kinsmen and associates and having continued his intimacy with most of them throughout his reign. Orderic Vitalis writing some decades later, speaks with reverence of "those wise and eloquent men who for many years lived at King William's court, observed his deeds and all the great activities there, were privy to his deepest and most secret counsels, and were endowed by him with wealth that raised them above the condition to which they were born."[7]

The Conqueror's successors on the English throne, lacking his fresh start, had to deal with powerful, entrenched families not of their own choosing. The trouble began as soon as the close associations between William I and his magnates were

[7] Orderic Vitalis, *Historia ecclesiastica*, ed. Marjorie Chibnall (Oxford 1969-1975) 2.190.

severed by death. It was a classic problem of feudal regimes, bound together by personal relationships and based on the idea of governance through the cooperation of prince and magnates. Repeating the homage and fealty oaths on the succession of a new lord or vassal might restore the former moral and legal bond, but it did not guarantee the close cooperation that enabled the political order to function smoothly.

The Conqueror's successor in England, William II "Rufus," faced this problem and others as well. At William I's death in 1087, the Anglo-Norman realm was divided: England passed to William Rufus and Normandy to his older brother, Robert Curthose. Neither brother was satisfied with only half the patrimony, and to make matters worse, the great magnates – most of them with extensive lands on both sides of the Channel – now owed allegiance to two princes. From the standpoint of the princes, the undivided loyalty of their magnates could no longer be assumed. And from the magnates' standpoint, allegiance to one prince against the other involved the risk of forfeiting either their English or Norman honors. The separation of England from Normandy thus produced political instability in both lands.

Accordingly, William Rufus, in the first year of his reign (1088), faced a major rebellion involving at least six of the realm's ten wealthiest magnates (see Table A): Odo of Bayeux, his brother Robert of Mortain, Roger of Montgomery (with three of his sons), Gilbert fitz Richard of Clare, Geoffrey of Coutances (with his nephew Robert of Mowbray), and Eustace count of Boulogne (son and heir of William I's Eustace). Other wealthy landholders supporting Curthose included Roger Bigod (lands worth ca. £450 per year), William of Eu (ca. £400), Roger of Lacy (ca. £400) and Hugh of Grandmesnil (ca. £340). Only two of the magnates in Table A, William of Warenne and Hugh earl of Chester, are known to have supported Rufus.[8]

The rebels hoped to reunite the Anglo-Norman realm by putting Robert Curthose on the English throne. Their motives are suggested (in simplified form) by a speech that Orderic Vitalis puts in their collective mouths:

> What are we do? Behold that on the death of our lord two youths succeed him, and the lordship of England and Normandy is suddenly divided. How can we properly serve two lords who are so different and live so far apart? If we serve Robert duke of Normandy as we ought, we shall offend his brother William, who will then despoil us of our great incomes and mighty honors in England. Conversely, if we adhere to King William, Duke Robert will deprive us of our paternal estates in Normandy . . . . Thus let us join in a firm, inviolable agreement, and having ousted or killed King William, who is the younger and more impudent, and to whom we owe nothing, let us make Duke Robert – who is the firstborn and of pliable temper and to whom we have already sworn

[8] The rebellion is discussed in some detail in E. A. Freeman, *The Reign of William Rufus* (Oxford 1882) 1.22-89, and C. W. David, *Robert Curthose, Duke of Normandy* (Cambridge, Mass. 1920) 44-52.

> fealty in his father's lifetime – prince of England and Normandy, to the end of preserving the unity of the two realms.[9]

Although Orderic's quotation is not to be taken literally, it does represent an informed, nearly contemporary judgment of baronial motives. In 1088 the reunification of the Anglo-Norman state would clearly have been a convenience to major trans-Channel magnates, but this goal could have been achieved as well by establishing Rufus in Normandy as by enthroning Robert in England. The passage raises two points of feudal ethics in Robert's favor: that he had previously received the barons' oaths of fealty,[10] and that he deserved to inherit his father's dominions in accordance with the Norman custom of primogeniture.[11] But against these arguments there might well have been raised the *fait accompli* of Rufus's coronation and the Conqueror's deathbed designation. One gets the impression that, within the customary framework of kin-right, the magnates were apt to consult their own interests first and discover moral justifications afterwards. The leaders of the ducal party in 1088 were at once intimate advisers of the previous ruler and great territorial lords in their own right. Although they had been *curiales* of William the Conqueror, they now had the potential of exercising quasi-independent power, and one can understand how they might have preferred the pliability of Curthose to the "impudence" of Rufus. William of Malmesbury expresses this idea when he writes that the ducal faction preferred Robert, "who was of milder spirit and whose youthful follies had been melted away by many hardships," to Rufus, "fastidiously reared, ferocious in spirit, whose scornful look discloses his overbearing nature, who would risk all in defiance of faith and justice."[12] Curthose could be manipulated; Rufus could not – or not so easily. Rufus was arrogant, unpredictable, and therefore less apt to consult or defer to the wealthy, established magnates of the previous reign.

Rufus survived the 1088 rebellion as a consequence of his own skill and his brother's incompetence (Curthose, who was supposed to join his supporters in England, never quite made it across the Channel). But even though the rebellion failed, it dramatized the worrisome fact that Rufus could not trust most of his greatest magnates. Robert Curthose learned the same lesson during the next few years when Rufus campaigned with some success in Normandy, drawing a number of major Norman and Anglo-Norman barons into his camp. But despite Rufus's advances in Normandy, his hold on England remained far from secure. In 1095 there

[9] Orderic, 4.122-124. These thoughts are attributed to Odo of Bayeux, Eustace of Boulogne (who held nothing in Normandy), Robert of Bellême (who stood to inherit vast Norman lands from his father, Roger of Montgomery), *aliique plures.*

[10] Indeed he had: see David (n. 8 above) 12, 15, 18.

[11] On the 1087 inheritance see John Le Patourel, "The Norman Succession, 996-1135," *English Historical Review* 86 (1971) 225-250; cf. John S. Beckerman, "Succession in Normandy, 1087, and in England, 1066: The Role of Testamentary Custom," *Speculum* 47 (1972) 258-260.

[12] William of Malmesbury, *Gesta Regum Anglorum,* ed. William Stubbs, Rolls Series (1887-1889) 2.360.

came to light a widespread conspiracy of Rufus's magnates to depose or assassinate the king and to enthrone in his place Stephen of Aumale, a son of one of William I's sisters.

Fortunately for Rufus, the rebellion-conspiracy of 1095 misfired. The only magnate actually to rebel was Robert of Mowbray earl of Northumberland, who had inherited the huge Conquest honor of his uncle Geoffrey bishop of Coutances (d. 1093). Robert seems to have defied Rufus prematurely, and when the king moved swiftly against him, his fellow conspirators held back. They had expected a supporting invasion from Normandy, but it never materialized. And Rufus was saved from being assassinated in a well-planned ambush by the timely confession of one of the conspirators.[13] Once again Rufus survived, and once again he did so despite the wishes of his major magnates. The sources do not reveal the names of every baron involved in the conspiracy, but they do suggest that it was a large and very serious affair: "Earls and men of similar rank," writes Orderic, "had knowingly been parties to the treacherous confederacy."[14] Among the conspiring magnates whose names are disclosed were the heirs of three of William I's ten wealthiest magnate-*curiales*: Hugh of Montgomery earl of Shrewsbury, Gilbert fitz Richard of Clare and (as we have seen) Robert of Mowbray earl of Northumberland.[15] Among the other wealthy magnates known to have been involved were two more veterans of the 1088 uprising: William of Eu and Roger of Lacy. The sources fail to identify any major lay landholders who gave Rufus their unqualified support.

The magnates who conspired in 1095 were distinctly noncurial.[16] Attestations of the eight lay conspirators whose names are disclosed occur only nine times in Rufus's surviving charters. Table B provides a list of the known conspirators with their total attestations (A.D. 1087-1100) and an indication of their landed wealth. They were a rich, powerful group, and none of them was ever drawn fully into Rufus's court circle either before or after 1095.

Clearly Rufus had inherited a troublesome landholding elite. But he was by no means helpless to change the situation. Rebellious magnates might be disseised, and the king might use their forfeited lands (or his own demesne) to raise up new magnates from among his friends. Through such means a new elite group of magnate-*curiales* might in time have been created.

[13] The narrative sources on the 1095 rebellion are woven together (with abundant nineteenth-century constitutional interpretation) in Freeman (n. 8 above) 2.37-69. On the projected invasion from Normandy see *S. Anselmi Opera omnia,* ed. F. S. Schmitt (Edinburgh 1946-1961) 4.77-78, epistle 191.

[14] Orderic (n. 7 above) 4.284.

[15] Of the remaining seven magnates in Table A, Odo of Bayeux and Eustace of Boulogne had forfeited their English honors in 1088 and Robert of Mortain had died leaving a son not yet of age. The allegiances of the other four (or their heirs) are unknown.

[16] The one *curialis* who may have been involved in the conspiracy is William bishop of Durham, who attested 28 of Rufus's charters.

TABLE B
Laymen Known to have been Rebels or Conspirators, 1095

Name	*Attestations for Rufus*	*Lands worth over £750*	*Lands worth £400-750*	*Disposition of lands*	*Family rebelled in 1088*
Robert of Mowbray	2	X		to king	X
Hugh of Montgomery	2	X		retained	X
Philip of Montgomery	0			none	X
Gilbert of Clare	4	X		retained	X
William of Eu	0		X	to king	X
Roger of Lacy	0		X	to his brother Hugh	X
Odo of Champagne	1		[£200]	to Arnulf of Montgomery	
Stephen of Aumale	0			none	

There is some evidence that Rufus moved in this direction, though apparently not very far. In the aftermath of the 1088 rebellion he seized the lands of Odo of Bayeux and (probably) Eustace of Boulogne,[17] keeping their demesnes in his own hand throughout the remainder of his reign. But Rufus forgave Robert of Mortain,[18] Roger of Montgomery and his sons, Geoffrey of Coutances, Robert of Mowbray, Gilbert of Clare, William of Eu, Robert of Lacy, Roger Bigod and the rest. According to Orderic,

[17]On Eustace see the *Anglo-Saxon Chronicle,* A.D. 1101: a clause in the treaty of that year between Robert Curthose and Henry I provided that Eustace's English lands be restored to him; it seems most likely that Eustace had lost them in 1088.

[18]A. S. Ellis, "Biographical Notes on the Yorkshire Tenants Named in Domesday Book," *Yorkshire Archaeological and Topographical Journal* 4 (1875-1876) 129, states mistakenly that Robert of Mortain was disseised and banished from England in 1088, citing the *Anglo-Saxon Chronicle* (which says nothing about Robert of Mortain). William Farrer made the same point in *Victoria County History* (hereafter VCH) *Yorkshire* 2 (1912) 155 and in *Early Yorkshire Charters* 2 (1915) 236, citing Ellis and (again wrongly) the *Anglo-Saxon Chronicle.* The error was repeated by, among others, C. T. Clay (*Early Yorkshire Charters* 6 [1939] 57) and I. J. Sanders (*English Baronies* [Oxford 1960] 66), both citing Farrer, and F. J. West (*The Justiciarship in England* [Cambridge 1966] 35-36). The decisive text is Orderic (n. 7 above) 5.208, reporting that after Robert surrendered Pevensey Castle in 1088 he was restored to Rufus's friendship.

> He shrewdly spared the older barons . . . out of love of his father whom they had served long and faithfully, and out of respect for their gray hairs. In any event he knew that illness and speedy death would soon put an end to their activities.[19]

But when the Conqueror's magnates died – as most of them did during the new reign – Rufus took no steps to prevent their lands from passing to their heirs. And many of the reinstated rebels of 1088, or their heirs, were involved in the conspiracy of 1095 (see Table B).

Rufus acted with greater severity in 1095-1096, though once again he failed to break the power of the great Conquest families. His treatment of the known conspirators of 1095 is shown in Table B. Robert of Mowbray was imprisoned, and the vast honor that he had inherited from Geoffrey of Coutances remained in Rufus's possession until his death. William of Eu was blinded and castrated, and his Domesday lands likewise passed into the king's hands and remained there.[20] Roger of Lacy was banished, and his lands passed to his brother Hugh.[21] Another conspirator, Odo of Champagne (father of the 1095 pretender, Stephen of Aumale), also lost his lands; and Rufus surprisingly gave large portions of them to Arnulf of Montgomery, whose powerful family had supported Curthose in 1088 and Stephen of Aumale in 1095.[22] The other conspirators were forgiven, "out of respect," says Orderic, "for their exalted kinsmen who might have sought vengeance in Normandy." Of the very wealthiest of the conspirators, Orderic states that Rufus "spared men of this kind."[23]

Can any pattern be discerned in Rufus's policy of punishing a few rebels or conspirators and reinstating the rest? One can comprehend the harsh treatment of Bishop Odo, the leader of the 1088 rebellion,[24] and of Robert of Mowbray who alone took up arms in 1095. But beyond this, the king's motives seem to have consisted largely of vengeance (sometimes for obscure reasons) and greed. Rufus is said to have received huge fines from those whom he forgave in 1095, and we are told explicitly that he took Hugh of Montgomery back into his favor for £3000.[25]

[19] Orderic (n. 7 above) 4.134, based on Chibnall's translation.

[20] William of Eu's Domesday honor was eventually granted by Henry I to Walter fitz Richard of Clare: see Sidney Painter, *Studies in the History of the English Feudal Barony* (Baltimore 1943) 178-179; E. C. Waters, "The Counts of Eu," *Yorkshire Archaeological and Topographical Journal* 9 (1885-1886) 257-302. This honor is not to be confused with the Rape of Hastings – held in 1086 by William's father, Robert count of Eu – which remained in the hands of the counts of Eu for several generations: see Henry Ellis, *A General Introduction to Domesday Book* (London 1833) 1.463; Sanders (n. 18 above) 119-120.

[21] Orderic (n. 7 above) 4.284.

[22] J. F. A. Mason, "Roger de Montgomery and His Sons (1067-1102)," *Transactions of the Royal Historical Society*, ser. 5, 13 (1963) 16-17.

[23] Orderic (n. 7 above) 4.284.

[24] Odo's treason was compounded by his defiance of Rufus at Rochester Castle after submitting to him at Pevensey: *Anglo-Saxon Chronicle*, A.D. 1088.

[25] Orderic (n. 7 above) 4.284.

The king seems to have been interested chiefly in collecting money rather than friends from among the great families, for the sons and heirs of the wealthiest Conquest magnates are seldom found on the witness lists of Rufus's surviving charters (see Table C). William son of Robert of Mortain and Stephen son of Alan of Richmond are not known to have attested at all; William II of Warenne, adult and active throughout Rufus's reign, attested only twice; Gilbert of Clare attested only four times. The sons and heirs of Roger of Montgomery gained much land under Rufus (usually for a stiff price), yet they rarely attested.[26] In short, many magnates purchased Rufus's forgiveness, but – whether by their choice or his – they were seldom in his entourage.[27]

It is clear enough that Rufus did not make *curiales* of his magnates. But the question remains, did he give lands to his friends on such a scale as to make magnates of his *curiales*? As we have seen, the greatest honors forfeited under Rufus (by Odo of Bayeux, Eustace of Boulogne, Robert of Mowbray and William of Eu) were not granted out to royal favorites but remained in the king's hands. Nevertheless, frequent attendance and service at court doubtless brought its rewards. Indeed, Orderic goes so far as to say,

> Many of his father's nobles . . . died during his reign, and the king raised up in their place not magnates but certain underlings, whom he exalted by granting them wide honors as a reward for their flattery.[28]

In the absence of Pipe Rolls or another Domesday survey, it is difficult to tell how much Rufus gave to his *curiales*. His administrative lieutenant, the cleric Ranulf Flambard, surely grew wealthy in the king's service, and other members of Rufus's court circle prospered as well. His faithful steward Eudo is known to have received some lands,[29] and the *curialis* Robert fitz Hamon was given a substantial barony of

[26] Mason (n. 22 above) 13-20. Hugh of Montgomery, earl of Shrewsbury 1093/4-1098 (a 1095 conspirator) attested twice. His brother Robert of Bellême (a 1088 rebel) served as a military commander for Rufus in Normandy when Curthose was on Crusade and became earl of Shrewsbury in 1098, yet attested no known charter of Rufus's. Another brother, Roger the Poitevin (a 1088 rebel and major landholder under Rufus), attested only twice. Still another brother, Arnulf of Montgomery (a 1088 rebel to whom Rufus granted extensive lands seized from Odo of Champagne in 1095), attested only once.

[27] One notable exception was Roger Bigod, a 1088 rebel with Domesday lands worth about £450 per year. Roger became a royal steward under Rufus and attested twenty-six of his surviving charters.

[28] Orderic (n. 7 above) 5.202.

[29] Eudo held a considerable Domesday honor, valued at £383; Rufus granted him the manor of Dereman, Hertfordshire (worth £15 in 1086), and some minor properties in Essex; plus perhaps other lands for which the charters have not survived: *Regesta regum Anglo-Normannorum,* ed. H. W. C. Davis and others (Oxford 1913-1969) 1, nos. 399, 435, 442; William Farrer, *Honors and Knights' Fees* (Manchester 1925) 3.166; cf. Lennard (n. 6 above) 99-104. Henry I seems to have treated Eudo much more generously, granting him the city of Colchester (worth £88 in 1086), the manor of Witham, Essex (£12-9-0 in 1086) and control of three valuable manors of the Mandeville family (£163 in 1086): *Regesta* 2, nos. 519, 553, 661, 688.

TABLE C
Relationship between Landed Wealth and Frequency of Attestations among English Magnates Alive in 1100

10 greatest Engl. lay landholders	*pounds/ year*	*Wm. II attests.*	*rank/lay attestors*	*succeeds*
Robt. of Bellême	2430	0 (2)*		1098 (1093/4)*
Wm. of Mortain	2100	0		1090
Wm. II of Warenne	1165	2		1088
Stephen ld. of Richmond	1100 + waste	0**		*c.* 1093
Hugh e. of Chester	800	8½	8	*ante* 1087
Gilbert of Clare	780	4		1086/8
Geoffrey de Mandeville	780	1		*ante* 1087
Robert Malet	600	0		*ante* 1087
Henry of Ferrers	545	3		(d. 1093/1101; no attests. by heir)
Philip of Braose	455 + Wales	0		1093/6
Total of attestors in top 15: 1 of 10				

*The figure in the parentheses applies to Robert of Bellême's brother, Hugh of Montgomery, who was Robert's immediate predecessor as earl of Shrewsbury.
**Spends much of the reign in his honor in Brittany.

about £300 a year.[30] Additional acts of royal generosity have doubtless gone unrecorded, yet it does seem clear that Rufus raised nobody to the level of the greatest Conquest magnates. Occasionally he might grant earldoms to men who supported him in times of trouble: in 1088 he made William I of Warenne earl of Surrey and Henry of Beaumont earl of Warwick; and Walter Giffard was later raised to the earldom of Buckingham. But neither William of Warenne nor Walter Giffard

[30] Robert fitz Hamon, who attested 21 of Rufus's charters, had been landless in 1086; he supported Rufus in the 1088 rebellion and soon thereafter was given the estates of the late Queen Matilda (Orderic [n. 7 above] 4.220). The lands ascribed specifically to the queen in Domesday Book have a total annual value of £261, but to them should probably be added additional lands

seem to have received any additional lands in the process.[31] Henry of Warwick, landless in 1086, was enriched with the Warwickshire estates of the Englishman Thurkell of Arden (worth about £120 per year) plus the Warwickshire and Northamptonshire lands of Henry's brother, Robert of Meulan (worth about £210 per year).[32] The total value of the lands in Henry's earldom apparently came to the tidy but unspectacular figure of about £330 per year. If he received any additional lands, for which the evidence has vanished, they cannot have been worth a great deal.[33] In any event, the three new earls came from families already wealthy: the Giffard honor had a Domesday value of about £420; Henry of Warwick's Beaumont kinsmen held lands in 1086 worth about £300; and William of Warenne was, as we have seen, one of William I's ten greatest landholders (about £1165). And of the three, only Henry of Warwick can be regarded as a *curialis* of William II (eight attestations). Walter Giffard and William II of Warenne (whose father, William I, died in 1088 just after receiving his earldom) each attested only two known charters of William Rufus.

The shape of Rufus's policy toward his great men is suggested by the contrasting careers of two major magnates of his reign: the curial baron Robert count of Meulan and the eldest of the Montgomery brothers, Robert of Bellême. Robert of Meulan was one of Rufus's most active *curiales* (sixteen attestations), yet his English holdings appear from the available evidence to have actually diminished during the reign. Robert received his maternal grandfather's county of Meulan in the French Vexin and inherited the extensive Norman honor of his father Roger of Beaumont (d. ca. 1094) plus Roger's English estates in Dorset and Gloucestershire, worth about £77 per year. But Robert gave his own Domesday lands in Warwickshire and Northamptonshire (ca. £210 per year) to his brother Henry earl of Warwick.[34] It is difficult to believe that Robert of Meulan received no additional English lands under Rufus, and some acquisitions doubtless went unrecorded. But Robert became a dominating magnate only under Henry I, who gave him large chunks of the super-honor of

---

ascribed to the queen's *antecessor*, the thegn Brictric, valued at £55. Robert fitz Hamon extended his power into Wales during the reign, becoming the conqueror and lord of Glamorgan. Cf. also Urse of Abitôt, sheriff of Worcester and a *curialis* of William II (11 attestations), whose aggressions against the bishropric of Worcester during William I's reign are well recorded, and who "seems to have secured fresh lands between the survey and his death" (in 1108): VCH *Worcestershire* 1.264.

[31] *Complete Peerage* 2.386-387; 12.1.493-495; Orderic (n. 7 above) 4.180 n. 1.

[32] *Chronicon Monasterii de Abingdon*, ed. Joseph Stevenson, Rolls Series (1858) 2.20; *Complete Peerage* 12.2.358; VCH *Warwickshire* 1.277; VCH *Northamptonshire* 1.371.

[33] The Northamptonshire Survey (temp. Henry I – Henry II: *ibid.* 1.387) shows that the earl of Warwick received a crumb or two of *terra regis* in Northamptonshire from either William II or Henry I. At some point the earls of Warwick received lordship over the Domesday fee of William fitz Corbucion, worth £28 per year in 1086: VCH *Warwickshire* 1.278. Henry I made Henry of Warwick lord of Gower (South Wales): Lynn H. Nelson, *The Normans in South Wales* (Austin 1966) 122.

[34] Levi Fox, "The Honor and Earldom of Leicester: Origin and Descent," *English Historical Review* 54 (1939) 386-387; Robert's role as one of Rufus's key advisors emerges clearly in Eadmer, *Historia novorum*, ed. Martin Rule, Rolls Series (1884) 40, 62, 86.

Mortain (forfeited ca. 1104) and permitted him in 1102 to acquire extensive lands from the Grandmesnil family in and around Leicestershire.[35]

Robert of Bellême, on the other hand, had fought against Rufus in the rebellion of 1088, and two of his brothers (at least) had joined the secret confederacy of 1095 and been pardoned afterwards. Robert of Bellême himself had always tended to support Curthose against Rufus.[36] When Curthose departed for the Holy Land in 1096, pawning Normandy to Rufus, Robert of Bellême fought in the king's behalf along the Norman frontiers. In April 1098 Robert of Bellême captured Rufus's enemy (and his own), Elias count of Maine.[37] But Robert must seldom have been in the royal entourage, for he attests no known charter of William Rufus. Nor could Rufus depend on Robert's unfailing allegiance. In August 1100, when Rufus was killed in the New Forest, Curthose was known to be returning from the Holy Land, and the king was about to lead an army across the Channel to hold Normandy against its crusader-duke.[38] In the warfare that would have ensued had Rufus dodged the fatal arrow, nobody can predict what Robert of Bellême might have done. Yet Rufus had, in the meantime, raised Robert to a dominating position among the magnates of England. On the death of his brother Hugh earl of Shrewsbury in 1098, Robert of Bellême bought the earldom from Rufus for £3000 (to the disadvantage of two younger brothers).[39] This vast honor, plus the estates of Roger of Builli which he purchased "from the king for a great sum of money,"[40] made Robert of Bellême the wealthiest lord in England. He was also a tremendously powerful magnate on the continent – lord of his father's great estates in Normandy, his mother's inheritance of Bellême and his wife's county of Ponthieu. In raising him to the pinnacle of the English landholding nobility, Rufus was playing a hazardous game.

Taken altogether, the evidence from Rufus's reign suggests very strongly that the king granted lands to his *curiales* on only a relatively modest scale.[41] Most of the great Conquest families, though prone to rebellion and seldom at court, retained their honors or (*vide* Robert of Bellême) expanded them. Only a few fell, and Rufus raised up no *curiales* to take their places.

Between the Conqueror's death in 1087 and Rufus's in 1100, the royal *curia* was

[35] Fox 387-388; J. F. A. Mason, *William the First and the Sussex Rapes,* The Historical Association, Hastings and Bexhill Branch (1966) 20; VCH, *Northamptonshire* 1.371, 374, 377-378, 381-383 (Northamptonshire Survey).

[36] Mason (n. 22 above) 19-20.

[37] Orderic (n. 7 above) 5.214, 238, 242, 254.

[38] *Ibid.* 5.280.

[39] *Ibid.* 5.224.

[40] *Ibid.* 5.224-226. Robert of Bellême is said to have been Roger of Builli's kinsman, but their exact relationship is unknown.

[41] Grants of land were of course not the only means by which a king might reward his courtiers. He might also dispense such lucrative ephemera as wardships, danegeld exemptions, administrative offices, moratoriums on debts, favor in litigation before royal courts, etc. On Henry I's use of these kinds of patronage see R. W. Southern, *Medieval Humanism and Other Studies* (Oxford 1970) 206-233.

thus transformed from a court dominated by the king and his greatest magnates to a court of middling landholders and household officials in which the chief territorial magnates tended to play a minor role. The contrast is demonstrated by a comparison of Table A (1087) with Table C (1100). Whereas in 1087 seven of England's ten wealthiest landholders were also *curiales* (that is, among the fifteen most frequent lay attestors), in 1100 only one landholder among the wealthiest ten was a *curialis.* [42] Table D makes the same comparison in reverse, listing the ten most frequent lay attestors who were alive at the close of each reign, together with data on their

TABLE D
Relationship between Frequency at Court and Landed Wealth: 1087, 1101

The 10 leading lay curiales *of Wm. I alive in 1087*					
Names	*Wm. I attests.*	*Addressee*	*Office*	*Land income*	*Norman lands*
Roger of Montgomery	40	1	[earl]	2100	very large
Odo bp. of Bayeux	34	5	[earl]	3000	very large
Geoffrey bp. of Coutances	34	13		780	large
Robt. c. of Mortain	30½	7	[earl]	2100	very large
Robt. c. of Meulan	23	0		220	no (France)
Roger of Beaumont	21	0		77	large
Alan ld. of Richmond	21	1		1100 + waste	no (Britt.)
Eudo *dapifer*	16	0	steward	385	mid.
Hugh e. of Chester	15½	1	[earl]	800	large
Henry of Ferrers	12	2	Domesday commiss.	545	large
Totals:				11,107	

[42] The list of landholders in Table C concludes with three men whose families are absent from Table A. These three did not grow appreciably wealthier between 1087 and 1100; they advance into the select group only because three much wealthier landholding families of 1087 had forfeited their lands (Odo of Bayeux, Eustace of Boulogne, and Geoffrey of Coutances's heir, Robert earl of Northumberland).

TABLE D (Cont)

The 10 leading lay curiales *of Wm. II alive in 1100*					
Names	*Wm. II attests.*	*Addressee*	*Office*	*Land income*	*Norman lands*
Eudo *dapifer*	37	0	steward	415	mid.
Roger Bigod *dapifer*	28	2	steward, sheriff	450	small
Robert fitz Hamon*	21	0		300 + Wales	large
Robert c. of Meulan	16	1		?100	large
Urse of Abitôt	11	5	constable, sheriff	90	very small
Hamo II *dapifer*	9	11½	steward, sheriff	128	no
Wm. Peverel of Nottingham	9	2½	?local justiciar	250	mid.
Hugh e. of Chester	8½	0	[earl]	800	large
Henry e. of Warwick*	8	1	[earl]	325	mid.
Robert of Montfort	7	0	constable	385	large
Totals:				3,243	

*Much enriched under Wm. II

administrative activities (how many royal writs were addressed to them?), their administrative offices and their annual income from English lands. It emerges from this analysis that William I's ten chief lay *curiales* held lands of the king worth almost 3 1/2 times the lands of their counterparts under William II (£11,107 per year versus £3243 per year).[43] William II's *curiales*, on the other hand, were much more apt to be officers of the royal household (5 of 10 versus 1 of 10).

[43] These figures are subject to caution: they are based on Domesday land values in 1086, which had doubtless changed by 1100: e.g., the Beaumont manor of Sturminster (Dorset) was worth £55 in 1086; all the Beaumont lands in Dorset were worth £72 in 1086 (Domesday Book 1.80-80b); but "Sturminster" was worth £140 in ca. 1107 (*Regesta* [n. 29 above] 2, no. 843). Likewise, the values of the lands of Rufus's *curiales* make no allowances for unrecorded gifts of land. Nevertheless, the general implications of the data are clear.

For Rufus to have re-created the close personal bonds between king and magnates would have required a policy of great tact and political artistry, designed to persuade the magnates that their own best interest and advantage lay in working closely and submissively with their monarch. And Rufus lacked the capacity, or the will, to follow such a policy. His *curiales* were typically men of middling wealth, household officials and occasional royalist bishops (as the attestations show), augmented by a mixed bag of young knights of modest origin, entertainers and assorted court followers whose varied activities (on which all the chroniclers dwell) did not include the witnessing of royal charters.[44]

At Rufus's death in mid-1100 the split between magnates and *curiales* remained as pronounced as ever. And there is little to suggest that Rufus would have succeeded, had he lived longer, in drawing the young magnates into his court and administration, or that he was inclined to build a countervailing group of curial magnates through the creation of vast new honors. In the weeks just prior to his death Rufus's confidence and ambition seem to have been immense,[45] but perhaps unwisely so. The peaceful interlude of Curthose's absence on Crusade was about to end, and with Rufus's greatest magnates seldom at court, his regime was dangerously unstable. This view accords with that of Sir Richard Southern who, applying his penetrating insight to very different kinds of evidence, concluded that when Rufus died "the country was ready for a revolution, which might well have swept away much of the structure of royal government."[46]

The revolution very nearly occurred in summer 1101, a year after Rufus's death, when Robert Curthose crossed the Channel to contest Henry I's seizure of the throne and was joined by powerful magnates in England.[47] But the campaign ended with a compromise in which Henry I kept his throne while relinquishing his Norman holdings and promising Curthose a large annuity. The affair was more than simply a struggle between Curthose and Henry I; it was also the climax of the schism between Rufus's magnates and *curiales*.

Table E compares the men known to have supported Curthose in 1101 with those

[44] Walter Tirel, who allegedly fired the misaimed arrow that killed Rufus in 1100, typifies the young knights at the court, though he was better connected than most. Lord of Poix (near Amiens) and castellan of Pontoise, he had only minor holdings in England and Normandy. Having married into the Clare family (by 1086), he joined Rufus's entourage and became the king's intimate friend and constant companion: Orderic (n. 7 above) 5. 288; Eadmer, *Vita Anselmi*, ed. R. W. Southern (London 1962) 27-28. But Walter Tirel attested no known royal charters, nor did the Clare marriage bring him any appreciable lands: cf. Domesday Book 2.41, and *Pipe Roll 31 Henry I* (London 1929) 56, in which his widow, Adeliza of Clare, is recorded as holding one small manor (Langham, Essex: held by Walter in 1086 and valued at £15 per year).

[45] See, for example, William of Malmesbury (n. 12 above) 2.378-379.

[46] Southern (n. 41 above) 231.

[47] C. Warren Hollister, "The Anglo-Norman Civil War: 1101," *English Historical Review* 88 (1973) 315-334.

known to have supported Henry I.[48] Since, by happy coincidence, exactly nine names can be identified with each party, the totals in all categories in Table E are susceptible to direct comparison. There are many reasons why a baron might have opted for one faction or the other: two members of the Curthose group (Eustace of Boulogne and Ivo of Grandmesnil) had accompanied the duke to the Holy Land; several held extensive lands in Normandy; the leader of the group, Robert of

TABLE E

The Two Factions in the Succession War of 1101

Supporters of Curthose, 1101	*Family anti-Wm. II 1088*	*Family pro-Wm. II 1088*	*Family anti-Wm. II 1095*	*Approx. value Engl. lands: £/year*	*Wm. II attests.*
Robt. of Bellême e. of Shrewsbury*	X		X	2365	0
Wm. of Mortain e. of Cornwall*	X			2100	0
Roger the Poitevin c. of La Marche*	X		X	260	2
Arnulf of Montgomery e. of Pembroke*	X		X	200	1
Wm. II of Warenne e. of Surrey		X		1165	2
Walter II Giffard e. of Buckingham				425	1
Ivo of Grandmesnil	X			340	1
Robt. of Lacy ld. of Pontefract	**		**	250 + waste	0
Eustace c. of Boulogne	X			*** 770	0
Totals:	6	1	3	7875	7

*Kinsmen: Robert, Roger and Arnulf were brothers; William of Mortain was their sister's son.
**Roger of Lacy, of the Herefordshire branch of the family, opposed Rufus in 1088 and 1095.
***Not in possession of his English lands in 1100; deprived *c.* 1088, restored 1101.

[48] The names are drawn from the major English and Norman chronicles of the period. On William of Mortain's role, see also the "Chronica Monasterii de Hida juxta Wintoniam," in *Liber Monasterii de Hyda,* ed. Edward Edwards, Rolls Series (1866) 305-306; see also *Regesta* (n. 29 above) 2, nos. 530-531, 533-536, where the witnesses can almost certainly be identified as supporters of Henry I. Orderic names Robert Malet as a ducal supporter, but probably wrongly: C. Warren Hollister, "Henry I and Robert Malet," *Viator* 4 (1973) 115-122.

TABLE E (Cont)

Supporters of Henry I, 1101	*Family anti-Wm. II 1088*	*Family pro-Wm. II 1088*	*Family anti-Wm. II 1095*	*Approx. value Engl. lands: £/year*	*Wm. II attests.*
Hugh e. of Chester		X		800	8
Richard of Redvers				12	1
Robt. fitz Hamon		X		300	18
Hamo II *dapifer*				128	?9**
Eudo *dapifer*				415	31
Henry e. of Warwick		X		325	5
Robt. c. of Meulan		*		?100	16
Roger Bigod *dapifer*	X			450	26
Urse of Abitôt shf. of Worcs.				90	13
Totals:	1	3	0	2620	127

*Robert of Meulan was in Normandy during the 1088 rebellion; his brother Henry of Warwick supported Rufus.
**There is some confusion between Hamo I *dapifer* and his son, Hamo II *dapifer*. Hamo II probably succeeded in 1087/1091.

Bellême, must have resented Henry's seizure of the strategic Bellême stronghold of Domfront in the 1090s,[49] and Robert probably influenced his two brothers, Roger and Arnulf, and his young nephew William of Mortain. Whatever their reasons for backing Curthose, the nine anti-royalists had much in common. All were sons of great Conquest magnates; all had retained or expanded their lands under Rufus; yet none had entered his court circle.

Henry I's supporters, on the other hand, consisted by and large of Rufus's friends, *curiales* and administrators – men of greater age and experience and of less landed wealth than the Curthose group. Here again, other factors than wealth and service at

[49] Orderic (n. 7 above) 4.256-258, 292; *Anglo-Saxon Chronicle,* A.D. 1094.

court were doubtless involved. Robert fitz Hamon, Richard of Redvers (the only low attestor in the group), and Hugh earl of Chester (the one great magnate) held lands in western Normandy where Henry had exercised lordship prior to his accession. And Henry earl of Warwick is said to have been an old friend of Henry I's.[50]

But regardless of individual motives, the contrast between the two groups remains striking. The nine Curthose supporters held lands valued collectively at nearly £8000; the nine royalists held lands worth less than £3000. The Curthose group had attested Rufus's surviving charters only seven times altogether; the royalist group had attested more than 120 times.[51] The Curthose group included far more men whose families had plotted or rebelled against Rufus than did Henry I's group. Among the royalists were three of Rufus's stewards; the ducal supporters included no officers of the late king's household. In short, the war of 1101 pitted the *curiales* of the previous reign against the non-curial magnates.

Henry I, having survived the invasion-rebellion of 1101, seems to have undertaken a deliberate policy of closing the gulf that produced it, whether by transforming his great magnates into friends and *curiales* or by destroying them and putting others in their places. The vast Montgomery lands of Robert of Bellême and his brothers were forfeited to the king in 1102. Henry I offered his sister-in-law's hand to William of Mortain and, when William refused, gave her in marriage to Eustace of Boulogne.[52] Eustace became Henry I's friend, while William of Mortain defected in 1104 and forfeited his immense English earldom. The faithful and astute royalist Robert of Meulan was raised into the highest echelon of wealth by his acquisition of large portions of the Mortain and Grandmesnil honors. William of Warenne was disseised in 1101, reinstated in 1103, and lured into the royal *curia* (sixty-nine attestations under Henry I as against two under Rufus). And in later years Henry created new magnates and super-magnates from among his own kinsmen and closest associates – Robert earl of Gloucester, Brian fitz Count, Roger bishop of Salisbury, Stephen of Blois.

Clearly, the traditional contrast between Rufus, the "baron's king," and Henry I surrounded by faceless *curiales* whom he had "raised from the dust" requires drastic revision. The data discussed in this paper will, it is hoped, contribute to the needed reinterpretation. Attestation statistics certainly do not tell the whole story. They do not in themselves make clear, for example, the nature of the relationships between the Norman kings and the men who attested their charters. They do not tell us to what extent a king was able to impose his will on his *curiales* or they on him.[53] We

[50] Malmesbury (n. 12 above) 2.470. This friendship may well have influenced, or been shared by, Henry of Warwick's brother, Robert of Meulan.

[51] Again, these attestation statistics must be interpreted with caution: some of Curthose's supporters did not inherit or come of age until well into Rufus's reign (see Table C); others spent much time on their continental estates.

[52] "Chronica" (n. 48 above) 306; Florence of Worcester, *Chronicon ex chronicis,* ed. Benjamin Thorpe (London 1848-1849) 2.51.

[53] The chronicles suggest that William I and William II both dominated their courts but that Robert Curthose, as duke of Normandy, did not.

only know that the men most active at the Conqueror's court tended to be of a different sort than those at the court of Rufus, and that Rufus's relations with his greater magnates appear to have been far from satisfactory.

Henry I made an obvious effort to change things. In the days and months just following his accession he presented himself as a reforming king: he directed his coronation charter against Rufus's abuses, filled vacant prelacies, imprisoned the despised Ranulf Flambard and recalled Archbishop Anselm from exile. But Henry's most fundamental effort at reform has largely escaped notice, perhaps because the problem to which it was addressed has not been well understood. According to Orderic Vitalis (whose observation that Henry raised men "from the dust" is so well known),

> From the beginning of his reign he had the wisdom to conciliate all groups, drawing them to himself by his regal munificence. He honored his magnates (*optimates*) generously, bestowed on them riches and honors, and thus won their fidelity by his soothing policies.[54]

As usual, Orderic oversimplifies. Robert of Bellême and William of Mortain, for example, were by no means soothed by Henry's policies. But in time their places as super-magnates were taken by Henry's friends. To determine the degree to which Henry re-created the fusion of magnates and *curiales* that the Conqueror had achieved would require further, very extensive analyses of baronial wealth and attestations during Henry's long reign. For now, suffice it to say that the new king was aware of the problem and was coming to grips with it.[55]

Department of History
University of California
Santa Barbara, California 93106, U.S.A.

[54] Orderic (n. 7 above) 5.296.

[55] The problem is approached very tentatively in Hollister (n. 48 above) 120-122, and (n. 47 above) 331-332.

EMPEROR FREDERICK I, THE THIRD CRUSADE, AND THE JEWS

•

by Robert Chazan

On 4 July 1187, the forces of Saladin overwhelmed the army of Guy of Lusignan at the fateful battle of Hattin. In the course of this decisive engagement, the True Cross was lost and Christian knighthood in the Near East was decimated, laying all of Palestine open to Moslem reconquest. Saladin was quick to capitalize on his opportunity, sweeping across Galilee to Acre, taking a series of coastal strongholds north of Acre, then moving southwards towards Ascalon and Gaza. The greatest of his achievements – symbolically and emotionally at least – came on October 2, when the desperately undermanned defenders of Jerusalem capitulated.[1]

News of this appalling catastrophe rapidly spread westward, accompanied by strident appeals for a new Crusade to aid the beleaguered Christians still holding out and to win back some of the lost ground. This information penetrated the Jewish neighborhoods of western Europe as well, eliciting a mixed reaction of elation and trepidation. For the Jews, the Christian defeat was in one sense sweet. Having suffered grievously at the hands of exhilarated crusaders, the Jews had long despised the crusading enterprise and had prayed for a failure which would serve as retribution for its sins.[2] The reports from the East detailed just such a failure, which the Jews could well view as the longed-for retribution. On the other hand, enthusiasm over the Christian downfall had to give way to serious fears over its immediate repercussions. For the catastrophe had not broken the power of Christendom; it had in fact roused the Christian world to a new Crusade, during which the old pattern of excesses might well be reenacted.

The Jewish concern was not unwarranted. Along with the Third Crusade came a

[1] On the crusader defeats in the East, see Steven Runciman, *A History of the Crusades,* 3 vols. (Cambridge 1951-1954) 2.450-473; Kenneth Setton, ed., *A History of the Crusades*, 2 vols. (Philadelphia 1955-1962) 1.607-621; Joshua Prawer, *Toldot Mamlekhet ha-Ẓalbanim be-Erez Yisra'el*, ed. 3, 2 vols. (Jerusalem 1971) 1.526-561; Andrew Ehrenkreutz, *Saladin* (Albany 1972) 195-208.

[2] For some of these prayers for retribution, see, e.g., Adolf Neubauer and Moritz Stern, *Hebräische Berichte über die Judenverfolgungen während der Kreuzzüge* (Berlin 1892) 8, 14, 16-17, 25, 28, 30; Abraham Habermann, ed., *Sefer Gezerot Ashkenaz ve-Ẓarfat* (Jerusalem 1945) 32, 40, 42-43, 52, 56, 59.

wave of devastating attacks on the Jewish communities of England.[3] On the Continent, however, the Jews fared somewhat better. French Jewry, as was generally the case, suffered little, primarily because of strong governmental protection.[4] In Germany, where the major disasters of 1096 had taken place, the Jews were profoundly shaken. Fortunately, however, the authorities were committed to the maintenance of public peace, and serious violence was averted.

In view of the complex Jewish response to the new Crusade, the frightening dangers which threatened German Jewry, and the firm imperial protection extended, it is fortunate indeed that two most useful and revealing sources have survived. These Hebrew accounts, which have long been known but never fully analyzed, afford important information on the Jews of Germany and their fate. They also shed valuable light on some major developments in Christian society, particularly during the famed assembly of March 1188, when Frederick Barbarossa committed himself to the ill-fated expedition upon which he was ultimately to lose his life.

* * *

The first of these Hebrew records comes from the pen of one of the greatest luminaries of late twelfth- and early thirteenth-century German Jewry. Its author, R. Eleazar b. Judah, is well known both as an outstanding legalist and a key spokesman for the new German-Jewish pietism.[5] R. Eleazar left, in addition to legal and mystical writings, a brief memoir describing the tumultuous events from fall 1187, when the Christian defeat took place in the East, to late April 1188, when the Jews who had fled Mainz felt safe enough to return to their homes.[6] It is difficult to establish precisely when this narrative was composed. Most of it is written in the past tense:

> I shall write down what befell us in Mainz, in the year 4947 [=1187], during the month of Elul.
>
> In 4948 [=1188], during the month of Adar II, we fled to Munzenberg.
>
> We left Munzenberg on the twenty-seventh of Nisan [=April 26].[7]

One observation in R. Eleazar's account suggests the actual recording of events as they occurred:

[3] See Cecil Roth, *A History of the Jews in England*, ed. 3 (Oxford 1964) 18-26.

[4] See Robert Chazan, *Medieval Jewry in Northern France* (Baltimore 1973) 36-37.

[5] On R. Eleazar, see Israel Kammelhar, *Rabbenu Eleazar mi-Germaiza* (Rzeszow 1930); Ephraim Urbach, *Ba'alei ha-Tosafot*, ed. 2 (Jerusalem 1955) 321-341; *idem, Arugat ha-Bosem*, 4 vols. (Jerusalem 1939-1963) 4.100-111.

[6] The text was originally published by Neubauer and Stern (n. 2 above) 76-78; it was reprinted by Habermann (n. 2 above) 161-164. For the reader's convenience, both editions will be cited.

[7] Neubauer and Stern 76, 77, 78; Habermann 161, 162, 164.

> Today, on Friday, the second of Nisan [=April 1], Eleazar the Small reached me; he is the secretary of my brother-in-law, R. Moses b. Eleazar ha-Cohen the Cantor.[8]

Thus, while R. Eleazar may have kept some notes, his memoir was probably written after the fact. However, little time seems to have elapsed between the return from Munzenberg in late April 1188 and the composition of R. Eleazar's chronicle. Given the Jewish veneration of Emperor Frederick I and the deep appreciation for his protection, it is inconceivable that R. Eleazar's narrative could have been written after late June 1188, when news reached Germany of the sudden and tragic demise of the emperor, without some reference to this appalling loss. Our suggestion then is that R. Eleazar's brief record was composed in May or June of 1188, while memories of the incidents of late 1187 and early 1188 remained quite fresh.[9]

In R. Eleazar's account, a second – and in many ways more significant – source has been embedded. As noted, during March 1188 most of the Jews of Mainz, along with neighboring Jewish communities, fled to safety in nearby fortifications. However, important developments were taking place in Mainz, and some Jews braved the dangers involved and remained.

> The court was at Mainz. There the Christians took the Cross by the thousands and the ten thousands – an innumerable host. A small number of Jews remained in Mainz in their homes.[10]

The convocation referred to is the famed "Court of Christ," held in Mainz during the month of March 1188 and culminating in Frederick's taking the Cross, along with many of his followers. Clearly, the decision of some Jews to remain in Mainz was related to developments at the imperial court. On the first of April, R. Eleazar received a letter from his brother-in-law, one of those who had stayed in Mainz in order to carry on negotiations. This letter, which details events in Mainz from the ninth through the twenty-ninth of March – the tension-filled days of the imperial assembly – was preserved by R. Eleazar and represents a first-hand and immediate recollection of this dangerous period.[11] The epistle was composed on either Wednesday the thirtieth of March or Thursday the thirty-first of March and was sent off to the Jews in Munzenberg, where it was received on Friday the first of April. There can be no question as to the date or circumstances of the composition of this valuable source.

* * *

[8] Neubauer and Stern 77; Habermann 162.

[9] Urbach, *Arugat ha-Bosem* (n. 5 above) 101, published a series of R. Eleazar's comments on Psalms, in which the tribulations of 1188 are reflected. He suggests that these comments are more significant than R. Eleazar's chronicle, which was written somewhat later. If our suggestion is correct, there was very little time lapse between the events of 1188, the observations in R. Eleazar's commentary on Psalms, and his narrative.

[10] Neubauer and Stern (n. 2 above) 77; Habermann (n. 2 above) 162.

[11] Neubauer and Stern 77-78; Habermann 162-164.

R. Eleazar's record begins with a local incident in Mainz, in September 1187. A Christian accused a Jew of attempting to kill him. This allegation was exploited by the bishop of Mainz in order to exact from the Jews a substantial sum of money. The incident was fully resolved on the second day of Rosh ha-Shanah, when the Jews appeared at the bishop's palace, swore that there had been no attempt made on the Christian's life, and added a more general oath repudiating the common charge that Jews murdered Christians during the Easter season.[12]

At this time, Jews and Christians alike were shaken by an eclipse of the sun. It took some time before the disaster normally associated with an eclipse was revealed.

> After Sukkot and before Hanukah we heard that the Moslems had gone forth and conquered Acre, had killed all its inhabitants, and had captured all the area around Jerusalem – from Acre and Ekron to Jerusalem. We further heard that on the eve of Rosh ha-Shanah, on the day when the sun was eclipsed, the Moslems killed more than four thousand Frankish warriors. They also captured the Cross upon which Jesus – may his bones be ground up – had been crucified and brought it with them to their land. They also captured the Holy Sepulcher after Hanukah and slaughtered all the inhabitants of Jerusalem. They removed the grave of the Crucified from the Church of the Holy Sepulcher and ploughed up all the ground in the church.[13]

R. Eleazar's information, while basically accurate, is marred by vagueness and distortions. There is no knowledge of the decisive battle of Hattin; there is instead heavy emphasis on the conquest of Acre. The eclipse of the sun is correctly associated with a major Christian setback, but R. Eleazar is not aware of the specifics. He does not know that it was the important coastal fortress of Ascalon that fell on 4 September 1187, the day of the eclipse. For R. Eleazar, as for his Christian contemporaries, the two central developments of late 1187 were associated with the great religious symbols of Christendom – the loss of the True Cross and the Holy Sepulcher. In his depiction of the fall of Jerusalem, R. Eleazar introduces major distortion. His suggestion that all the inhabitants of the city were slaughtered may well have been influenced by the widely-known story of crusader behavior in 1099 or by exaggerated Christian reports filtering westward. In any case, his story is inaccurate; in fact Saladin's behavior was unusually humane. The Hebrew account of desecration of the Church of the Holy Sepulcher is likewise incorrect. While many Moslem holy places which had been Christianized were returned to Moslem control, and while some Christian churches were confiscated, the Church of the Holy Sepulcher was not affected; it was simply turned over to Eastern Christian authorities.

[12] Neubauer and Stern 76; Habermann 161. On this charge, see Robert Chazan, "The Bray Incident of 1192," *Proceedings of the American Academy for Jewish Research* (PAAJR) 37 (1969) 9-14.

[13] Neubauer and Stern 76; Habermann 161.

R. Eleazar's narrative is replete with the normal Jewish animosities of the period. Nonetheless, it is strikingly restrained. When we compare it, for example, to the chronicles of the First Crusade, where crusader defeats in Hungary are gloatingly depicted,[14] we find very little exultation over a defeat far more shattering than any other suffered by Christian forces during the entire crusading period. The reason for this restraint is not difficult to discover.

> Subsequently the news reached all of Germany. Then all the Gentiles said to the Jews: "Behold the day for which we have waited has arrived – the day for killing all the Jews." This happened during Lent. When we heard this, a very great fear fell upon us, and we took up the arts of our ancestors, decreeing fasting, weeping, and mourning.[15]

A specific incident was not long in developing. On Friday, 29 January 1188, the Jewish quarter of Mainz was invaded. Fortunately for the Jews, the authorities drove off the attackers. The Jews, however, were deeply disquieted. They redoubled their fasts, prayers, and repentance. On a more practical level, the members of the community decided to adopt time-honored techniques and to flee to fortified areas. While such flight had failed during the turbulent months of early 1096, it had proved eminently successful during the Second Crusade. Thus the Jews of Mainz, along with those of Speyer, Strasbourg, Worms, and Würzburg, left their homes and retreated to refuges which they hoped would provide the necessary safety and security.[16]

At this point, R. Eleazar's memoir comes to a close, except for a brief concluding note on the return of the Jews to Mainz in late April 1188. While he might have written of the ongoing anguish of the Jews huddled together in Munzenberg, momentous developments, from both a Christian and Jewish point of view, were taking place in Mainz. It is here that the eyewitness account of R. Moses b. Eleazar is so very useful. According to R. Moses, participants in the great assembly began to arrive as early as the ninth of March; the small Jewish group in Mainz felt itself in mortal danger down through the end of the month, particularly during the period between 25 and 29 March. At this point, the emperor announced a resolutely protective stance, and tension began to abate.

R. Moses's letter divides neatly into two segments. While his interest lies mainly in the events of March 25 through 29, he prefaces his description of these crucial days with a general portrait of mounting animosity during the previous two weeks.

> I must accord thanks and glory on every sort of stringed instrument to the Lord who has granted us life and has sustained us. This year, during the week prior to Nisan, we were suspended between life and death. For the crusaders gnashed their teeth against us, preparing to swallow us up

[14] Neubauer and Stern 29-30; Habermann 57-59.
[15] Neubauer and Stern 76; Habermann 161.
[16] Neubauer and Stern 76-77; Habermann 161-162.

> as one swallows up fish. Had it not been for the mercies of the Almighty, we would have been lost. Blessed is he who saved us from their swords. The crusaders gathered to assault us in our quarter and to attack us, but the Lord saved us, as we shall indicate. However, let us retell first all that befell us down to this point.[17]

The first section of R. Moses's report, dealing with the burgeoning animosities prior to March 25, is not clearly organized and presented. R. Moses attempts merely to convey a sense of sporadic violence, governmental protection, and deep anxiety. His recital consists of a series of disjointed incidents. The first occurred on a Friday, either the eleventh or eighteenth of March. A young boy, accompanying R. Moses to the market, was accosted by crusaders, threatened, and ordered to convert. He escaped and found asylum in a church, where the priests protected him. Fleeing a second time, he was saved by a knight.[18] This isolated incident reveals some of the deep religious fanaticism often produced by crusading fervor, as well as conflict within the Christian populace, another common development during periods of crusading exhilaration.[19] A second dangerous incident took place on a Monday, either the fourteenth or twenty-first of March, when a knight attempted to enter the synagogue. This effort, however, was foiled by the authorities.[20] The picture presented by R. Moses is one of great danger, deep trepidation, and consistent governmental protection. The question was obviously whether the authorities, particularly the emperor and his retinue, would and could maintain peace and security as the assembly approached its climax.

The climactic event was the great meeting of March 27, when Frederick Barbarossa and thousands of his followers took the Cross. R. Moses's perspective was of course a rather special one.

> More than ten thousand took the Cross – but only for self-destruction and plunder. The kings, however, continued at all times to speak well on behalf of the Jews.[21]

While much has been written concerning the gathering of March 27, the Christian chroniclers fail to note the violence that it triggered against the Jews of Mainz.[22]

> On the Sabbath prior to Nisan [=March 26], the crusaders gathered on our street to assault us and to attack us. One of them arose, sword in hand, and attempted to strike a Jew.[23]

[17] Neubauer and Stern 77; Habermann 162.

[18] Neubauer and Stern 77; Habermann 163.

[19] Note, e.g., the conflict reported in Mainz in early 1096 – Neubauer and Stern 4 and 51; Habermann 28 and 98.

[20] Neubauer and Stern 78; Habermann 163.

[21] *Ibid.*

[22] The fullest study of this assembly is that of Christian Wentzlaff-Eggebert, *Der Hoftag Jesu Christi 1188 in Mainz* (Wiesbaden 1962).

[23] Neubauer and Stern (n. 2 above) 78; Habermann (n. 2 above) 163.

This was the critical moment. Thousands were preparing to take the Cross; exultation swept through Mainz; and, as so often happened, it threatened to explode in violence against the Jews. Fortunately for these Jews, the authorities remained resolute.

> The marshall came and took the crusader by the hair, pulling it and smiting him with a staff, until his blood spilled to the ground. The others fled.[24]

While the mettle of the government had been tested, the crisis had not yet been resolved. The attackers regrouped in the marketplace, where a new threat emerged.

> They told the crusaders what had been done on account of the Jews. The crusaders then gathered by the thousands and ten thousands. They wanted to take up a standard and invade our quarter. The marshall was informed and, taking his servants with him and his staff in his hand, he smote and wounded them, until they all dispersed.[25]

The immediate danger was thus averted, although the Jews continued to feel exposed and threatened.

> We were in great distress – frightened to death – from Friday [=March 25] through Tuesday [=March 29].[26]

The Jews were of course appreciative of the government's efforts. Moreover, R. Moses was convinced that the suppression of incipient violence by the imperial marshalls made a profound impression on the assembled dignitaries.

> The barons inferred properly, saying, "Behold how dear the Jews are in the king's eyes."[27]

Nonetheless Jewish trepidation did not abate, nor did Jewish negotiations cease. Despite the *de facto* protection extended, the Jews wanted the emperor to take a formal public position on their behalf.

This stand, for which the Jews had carefully labored, was finally achieved on March 29. Unfortunately R. Moses's account is cursory. Since he obviously assumes that the details will be widely known, his report emphasizes the tribulations leading up to this significant imperial action. Despite the brevity of his account, it is clear that a number of specific steps were taken to ensure subsequent Jewish safety. These included pronouncements addressed to the crusaders, to imperial officialdom, and to the Jews.

The first warning was directed at those who had taken the Cross and who had already threatened violence. The emperor forbade attacks upon the Jews and indicated the punishments for transgression. R. Moses preserves only the heart of this declaration.

[24] *Ibid.*
[25] *Ibid.*
[26] *Ibid.*
[27] Neubauer and Stern 78; Habermann 163-164.

> Anyone who attacks a Jew and wounds him shall have his hand cut off.
> Anyone who kills a Jew will be killed.[28]

This is a striking declaration on behalf of the Jews. The penalties imposed on those assaulting Jews are clear and harsh. If the report of R. Moses is reliable, Emperor Frederick's action represents a key innovation in crusader legislation and a major achievement on the part of the Jews of Mainz.

Given the significance of this information, it is important to weigh the reliability of R. Moses's account. A number of factors lead to a positive assessment of this record. It has already been noted that R. Moses composed his narrative immediately after the imperial pronouncement of March 29. There is thus no reason to suspect the distortion often occasioned by a lengthy lapse of time. As for willful distortion, it is highly unlikely that R. Moses would have dared to fabricate such a declaration and to report it to the vitally affected Jews assembled at Munzenberg. Surely such a fabrication would have been disproved immediately. The sense is, rather, that this is a first-hand and authentic account of a most important imperial statement. It is further noteworthy that the emperor took a parallel stand against violence within crusader ranks. The major chronicle of Frederick's Crusade notes that, prior to leaving western Christendom, "some of the crusaders who have wounded their companions have had their hand severed, accorded to the accepted law; others accused of violating the law have been ordered decapitated."[29] The parallel in punishment – severing of a hand and death – is striking, strengthening further our sense of the accuracy of R. Moses's record.[30]

Execution by the emperor of the aforesaid decree would have encountered one serious obstacle, namely, the judicial privileges enjoyed by crusaders. By the Third Crusade, a substantial body of judicial rights and immunities had developed for the crusaders.[31] R. Moses indicates, again laconically, that this problem was addressed by the emperor and the assembled prelates. According to his report, "the bishops condemned anyone raising his hand against the Jews in order to harm them and indicated that his crusader status would not aid him."[32] Despite the cryptic style, R. Moses seems to be indicating ecclesiastical backing for the imperial proclamation. The church authorities gathered in Mainz seem to have announced to the crusaders

[28] Neubauer and Stern 78; Habermann 164.

[29] Ansbert's "Historia de expeditione Friderici" in *Fontes rerum Austriacarum,* MGH Scriptores 5.18.

[30] It is in fact possible that Frederick decreed decapitation as the punishment for killing a Jew. In a report on crusader violence against Jews in Austria in 1196, a Jewish chronicler depicts the strong measures taken by the duke in reprisal. "He then commanded that the two leaders be seized and be decapitated." See Neubauer and Stern (n. 2 above) 74; Habermann (n. 2 above) 131.

[31] On these rights, see James Brundage, *Medieval Canon Law and the Crusader* (Madison 1969) 170-175 and 187-189.

[32] Neubauer and Stern 78; Habermann 164.

that the imperial sanctions would encounter no opposition from them. Those guilty of attacking Jews would have normal crusader immunity removed and hence be liable to the punishments which Frederick had stipulated.[33]

Having addressed the crusaders directly, Frederick next turned his attention to the officials of his realm. As we have seen, some of these officials had already interposed themselves between the crusaders and the Jews, protecting zealously the small Jewish group in Mainz against assault. According to R. Moses, the emperor sent out communications both oral and written that the imperial officials "guard the Jews carefully, even more so than they had done heretofore."[34] This move in a sense provided real enforcement for the proclamation made to the crusaders. While the crusaders had been warned against violence and threatened with punishments, it would have to be the authorized officials of the realm who would ensure tranquillity and punish transgressors.

Finally the emperor seems to have made an effort to reassure the Jews. R. Moses reports that R. Moses ha-Cohen, the key Jewish negotiator, "rode with the king and himself wrote out a letter assuring peace to the Jews."[35] In all probability this imperial message detailed the various steps taken by Frederick. It is because of the existence of this missive that R. Moses was so cryptic in his account of the imperial actions. It is most unfortunate that the official epistle has not survived; it would obviously be a useful supplement to the unofficial letter of R. Moses, preserved by his brother-in-law, R. Eleazar b. Judah.

Having examined the various actions initiated by the emperor, we are now in a position to understand the decision by a small group of Jews to brave terrible dangers and to remain in Mainz. Clearly their main concern was eliciting precisely the governmental stance which has been depicted. After describing the imperial proclamation to the crusaders, ecclesiastical backing for the pronouncement, and the charge to imperial officialdom, R. Moses notes that "all of this was fully paid for."[36] In his subsequent portrayal of Frederick's message to the Jews, the author singles out the wealthy Jew most active in these negotiations. It was R. Moses ha-Cohen, already

[33] See Prawer (n. 1 above) 2.15 n. 19. For a series of thirteenth-century sources stripping crusaders of their jurisdictional privileges, see Brundage (n. 31 above) 189 n. 145. The aforecited account of the incident in Austria in 1196 reveals some of the pressure against prosecuting crusaders. The incident began with theft by a crusader, followed by his imprisonment. This led to a public outcry, which resulted eventually in the death of sixteen Jews. While we have noted the punishment meted out by the duke of Austria, the Jewish chronicler, after indicating the decapitation of the two ringleaders, adds: "He (the duke) did not wish to kill more of them, for they were crusaders."

[34] Neubauer and Stern (n. 2 above) 78; Habermann (n. 2 above) 164. Note the similar language used in an edict of the king of France in the wake of the Blois incident of 1171 – Neubauer and Stern 34; Habermann 145.

[35] Neubauer and Stern 78; Habermann 164. It seems highly likely that this message to the Jews was drafted in Hebrew.

[36] *Ibid.*

cited earlier in the letter as the leader among those remaining in Mainz, who rode out with Frederick and composed his epistle to the Jews. The mission with which these Jews were charged – or which they perhaps took upon themselves – was the dangerous one of staying in the eye of the storm and negotiating directly with the chief figure in this crusading army, Emperor Frederick I. The letter of R. Moses indicates that the mission almost ended disastrously, although ultimately it proved highly successful. R. Moses's missive thus reveals precious information on sensitive Jewish political negotiations during a period of tension and potential violence, an aspect of medieval Jewish existence for which we have regretably little evidence.

Finally, it seems useful to conclude with some observations on the letter of R. Moses itself. A number of epistles have survived from medieval Ashkenazic Jewry. Some of these were meant simply to pass on important political information; others lamented horrifying tragedies and memorialized the heroism of Jewish martyrs; yet others celebrated seemingly miraculous deliverance from danger.[37] The letter of R. Moses is closest to this last genre. As we have noted, R. Moses does not really attempt to inform his readers fully concerning the specific measures instituted by the emperor. This was superfluous, since R. Moses ha-Cohen, in consultation with Frederick, had composed just such a record. Rather R. Moses wished to convey a sense of the frightening dangers which beset the small band of Jews in Mainz and of the almost miraculous success of their mission. Pious phrases of praise abound. Thus R. Moses begins:

> I must accord thanks and glory on every sort of stringed instrument to the Lord who has granted us life and has sustained us.[38]

Towards the end of his missive he adds:

> May the name of the Lord be blessed from now on and for all times. May his memory be praised to all eternity. Not because of our righteousness has he done all this on our behalf, but rather for his great name which shall be blessed forever.[39]

Along with this pious desire to describe fully events in Mainz in order to sing the praises of God, there is also a wish for the rest of Mainz Jewry to appreciate the heroism of those Jews who endangered their lives in order to carry on the successful negotiations. R. Moses is particularly lavish in his commendation of the wealthy R. Moses ha-Cohen; at the same time the reader was surely supposed to emerge with the utmost respect for the entire little band that stood in the breach at a moment of impending catastrophe for all of German Jewry.

[37] For a description of such letters, see Robert Chazan, "The Blois Incident of 1171: A Study in Jewish Intercommunal Organization," PAAJR 36 (1968) 17-21 and 24-26; *idem,* "The Persecution of 992," *Revue des études juives* 129 (1970) 217-218.

[38] Neubauer and Stern 77; Habermann 162.

[39] Neubauer and Stern 78; Habermann 164.

The letter of R. Moses is then a first-hand report of events in Mainz, an example of an interesting genre of Jewish letter-writing, and, most important, the source of much valuable information on significant aspects of the Third Crusade and of the Jewish response to potential crisis.

Department of History
Ohio State University
Columbus, Ohio 43210, U.S.A.

STUDIES ON THE "ḪARǦAS": THE ARABIC AND THE ROMANCE "ḪARǦAS"

•

by James T. Monroe

INTRODUCTORY REMARKS

Whereas the discovery of the Romance *ḫarǧas* has been hailed as a significant break-through in the field of early Hispanic poetry, a sizable corpus of *ḫarǧas* in Arabic has passed almost entirely unnoticed in the West. The first to analyze some of them was Emilio García Gómez, who noted in two examples of this genre the reflection of a possible Andalusian folk poetry in colloquial Arabic.[1] He later returned to the theme in a study of the *Dār aṭ-Ṭirāz*, an anthology and poetics of the Andalusian *muwaššaḥ* compiled by the Egyptian poet and critic Ibn Sanā' al-Mulk (1155-1211).[2] More recently, Linda Fish Compton has written a stimulating analysis

This article is the second in a series exploring the relations between Romance and Arabic love poetry. See also J. T. Monroe, "Formulaic Diction and the Common Origins of Romance Lyric Traditions," *Hispanic Review* 4 (1975) 341-350, and "Estudios sobre las *jarŷas*: Las *jarŷas* y la poesía amorosa popular norafricana," *Nueva revista de filología hispánica* (in press).

For the specialist in non-Arabic fields the following definitions may be helpful:

MUWAŠŠAḤ: A strophic poem invented in Andalus in the late ninth or early tenth century. It is written in classical Arabic, but not originally in classical meters, appearing to be stress-syllabic rather than quantitative, and has from five to seven strophes with complicated rhyme schemes, all of which may, however, be reduced to the basic form ababab *mn* cdcdcd *mn* efefef *mn*, and so on. Each strophe contains a part with rhymes peculiar to that strophe (ababab), called *ġuṣn*, and another with rhymes common to the whole poem (*mn*) called *markaz, simṭ, qufl*, or *bayt* by different authors. In the final strophe the *ġuṣn* introduces the words of a speaker or singer, at times a girl, who expresses herself in colloquial language in the final *bayt*, known technically as *ḫarǧa*. If the poem begins with an odd *bayt*, the latter is called *maṭla*ᶜ ("prelude"). Otherwise the *muwaššaḥ* is called *aqra*ᶜ (lit. "bald") or "acephalous."

ḪARǦA: The final *bayt* of a *muwaššaḥ*, originally couched in colloquial diction (either Romance or Arabic) and often constituting a popular song, expressing love either from a man's or a woman's viewpoint.

ZAǦAL: A strophic form appearing in early twelfth-century Andalus, structurally related to the *muwaššaḥ*, from which it differs in being entirely in the colloquial language. In it the *ḫarǧa* tends to disappear in favor of the *maṭla*ᶜ, while the *bayts* tend to repeat only half the rhymes of the former.

[1] E. García Gómez, "Sobre un posible tercer tipo de poesía arábigoandaluza," *Estudios dedicados a Menéndez Pidal* 2 (Madrid 1951), 397-408.

[2] E. García Gómez, "Estudio del *Dār aṭ-ṭirāz*, preceptiva egipcia de la muwaššaḥa," *Andalus* (hereafter *And.*) 37 (1962) 21-104.

of the Arabic *ḫarǧas* contained in the *Dār*, accompanied by complete translations of all its Andalusian *muwaššaḥs.*[3] The main difficulty in relying upon Ibn Sanā' is that, as an Easterner who lived and died in Egypt, he never really fathomed the principles upon which the prosodic system of Andalusian strophic poetry was based. Furthermore, while aware that the *ḫarǧa* was often composed in the colloquial language, either Arabic or Romance, he included no Romance texts in his anthology, and only a few in colloquial Arabic. It would seem that his Eastern tastes, perhaps even prejudices, against the colloquial, determined a process of selection whereby he eliminated from his compilation most of the more folkish *ḫarǧas* which would have been of vital interest to the modern scholar. Any conclusions about the Arabic *ḫarǧas* based on the *Dār* collection alone, must therefore remain tentative and unrepresentative of the true picture.

In 1967 the Tunisian scholars Hilāl Nāǧī and Muḥammad Māḍūr published an edition of the *Ǧayš at-Tawšīḥ*,[4] an anthology of Andalusian *muwaššaḥs* collected by the Granadan poet and vizier Ibn al-Ḫaṭīb (1313-1374), who, being a native Andalusian as well as a composer of *zaǧals* and *muwaššaḥs* himself, seems to have been more in tune with the tastes of his countrymen, and to have compiled a more representative selection of poems than his Eastern counterpart. Furthermore, the criteria for selection in the *Ǧayš* seem to be the literary excellence of the poems, whereas in the *Dār* poems are included as samples to illustrate different prosodic combinations. In manuscript form, the *Ǧayš* has already been explored as an important source for Romance *ḫarǧas*, but its Arabic ones have so far remained unstudied.[5] Despite the possible errors and limitations of the only available edition,[6] the 165 *muwaššaḥs* from Andalus it contains, of which the majority have Arabic *ḫarǧas*, make it an important publication.

[3]L. F. Compton, "Andalusian Muwashshaḥs with Mozarabic and Arabic Kharjas," Ph.D. diss. (Princeton 1972).

[4]Hilāl Nāǧī and Muḥammad Māḍūr, *Jeich ettaouchīḥ par Ibn al-Ḫaṭīb* (Tunis 1967).

[5]See J. M. Sola-Solé, *Corpus de poesía mozárabe: Las ḫarǧa-s andalusíes* (Barcelona 1973). After this article was completed E. García Gómez published a prosodic study of *ḫarǧas* in the *Ǧayš*. See "Métrica de la moaxaja y métrica española: Aplicación de un nuevo método de medición completa al 'Ǧayš' de Ben al-Ḫaṭib," *And.* 31 (1974) 1-255.

[6]See the review of the edition by García Gómez, "Sobre una edición oriental del 'Ŷayš al-tawšīḥ' de Ibn al-Jaṭīb," *And.* 34 (1969) 205-216. The reviewer points out numerous errors in the edition, but it should be noted that many of these "errors" are the result of an underlying theoretical difference of opinion about the nature of Spanish prosody dividing the editors from the reviewer. The latter believes that medieval Spanish prosody, as well as that of *muwaššaḥs* and *zaǧals*, is based on a strictly regular syllabic count allowing for no fluctuation in the number of syllables per line, and it is his practice to emend lines in order to fit them to his preconceived notions. On this point, see the criticism of his work by T. J. Gorton, "The Metre of Ibn Quzmān: A 'Classical' Approach," *Journal of Arabic Literature* 6 (1975) 1-29. It should be added that although the nature of medieval Spanish prosody is a controversial subject, few Romanists would agree that it was strictly regular. The manuscript evidence for medieval Spanish popular poetry, as well as for that of Andalusian *muwaššaḥs* and *zaǧals*, exhibits sufficient irregularity in meter to suggest that prosodic theory should be adjusted to account for it, rather than tampering with the texts to make them fit the theory.

As a further step in the study of the *ḫarğas*, I have selected thirty-five Arabic texts from the *Ğayš*, bearing in one way or another the stamp of popular poetry, to which I have added eight from the *Dār*, and one from the *Dīwān* of al-Aᶜmā at-Tuṭīlī,[7] thereby compiling a corpus of fourty-four texts. In each instance, the author of the *muwaššaḥ* containing the *ḫarğa* is indicated, along with a brief summary of his extant biographical data, followed by the source, plus a note explaining, according to the information given in the *muwaššaḥ*, who it is that utters or sings the *ḫarğa*, and to whom, when this fact is specified. Next, I have transliterated the *ḫarğa*.

The transliteration of colloquial Arabic texts leads to certain difficulties when the dialect in question is not well known, as is to some extent the case with medieval colloquial Hispano-Arabic. In particular, the exact quality of the unmarked vowels cannot be determined. I have therefore adopted a compromise solution, and attempted to transliterate (orthographically) rather than to transcribe (phonetically), so as to allow the Arabist to reconstruct the original orthography, by marking as long those vowels so written in the Arabic script (quantity had, however, disappeared in the dialects), and attributing to the unmarked ones the quality they normally have in classical Arabic, except where firm evidence exists to the contrary. I have also supplied inflexions not usually written in Arabic when the meter requires them, or suppressed them otherwise. The original texts are followed by a literal translation, a prosodic outline of the poem indicating the rhyme scheme, number of syllables per line, stressed and unstressed syllables, a rhythmic *calque* into Spanish, and rhythmic parallels culled mostly from Spanish folk poetry, but occasionally from Galician and Latin.[8]

I have chosen to put the rhythmic *calques* into Spanish rather than English for prosodic reasons. Merely a single poem is in an Arabic meter, whereas the remainder, as will be demonstrated, exhibit stress-syllabic metrics of the Hispanic type. Hence closer prosodic parallels to these *ḫarğas* exist in Spanish than in English. The *calques* are provided to illustrate the close relationship between the Arabic *ḫarğas* and the Hispanic prosodic system.

The biographical data relating to the poets included are in most instances sketchy at best, but available evidence would indicate that the earliest author was Ibn Labbūn, who was writing around the year 1085, while one of the latest was Ibn Šaraf, who was active around the beginning of the Almohad period (1145). The poets

[7] Al-Aᶜmā at-Tuṭīlī, *Dīwān*, ed. Iḥsān ᶜAbbās (Beirut 1963).

[8] Unless otherwise stated, the Spanish rhythmic parallels are quoted from: J. M. Alín, *El cancionero español de tipo tradicional* (Madrid 1968); J. Cejador y Frauca, *La verdadera poesía castellana: Floresta de la antigua lírica popular* 1 (Madrid 1921); A. Sánchez Romeralo, *El villancico (estudios sobre la lírica popular en los siglos XV y XVI)* (Madrid 1969). I would like to acknowledge a debt of gratitude to the Romanist Dorothy C. Clarke, and to the Arabists Seeger Bonebakker and Peter D. Molan, the former for having carefully revised this article and offered many valuable suggestions having to do with Spanish prosody, and the latter two for their expert advice on problems in Arabic dialectology, and for having revised the transliterations and translations of the texts edited below.

thus range from the late eleventh century to the second half of the twelfth; in other words, the majority of them flourished under Almoravid rule (1091-1145). This, of course, is no proof that many of the *ḫarǧas* here considered may not have originated at a much earlier date.

EDITION OF TEXTS

A. COUPLETS

(1) ISOSYLLABIC

1. Abū Bakr Muḥammad ibn Aḥmad IBN RUḤAYM (born in Bocairente [Valencia], he was appointed *mušrif* of Seville by the Almoravids in 1121) (*Ǧayš* 134, p. 178). A girl addresses the poet:

kún hū ánta l-ġíllah a 6
tárā sítrī ḏúllah a 6
You be my harvest,
And you will see my veil in humiliation.
ó o ó o ó o

Spanish *calque*:

Tú se la mi guilla
que este velo humilla.

Spanish parallel:

Cuando pitos flautas;
cuando flautas, pitos. (Cejador 11, p. 81)

2. Abū Bakr Yaḥya ibn Muḥammad ibn ᶜAbd ar-Raḥmān al-Qaysī IBN BAQĪ (born in Córdoba, he died in 1145) (*Dār* 10, p. 54). The poet declares:

ḥabíbī máḍā ᶜánnī a 7
mátā naǧtámiᶜ mấᶜū b 7
My lover has left me;
When will I be reunited with him?
o ó o ó o ó o

Spanish *calque*

Mi amigo ya dejóme.
¡Ay, si nos juntaremos!

Spanish parallel:

Comamos y bebamos,
y·nunca más valgamos. (Cejador 34, p. 85)

3. Abū l-Walīd Yūnus ibn ᶜĪsā AL-ḪABBĀZ AL-MURSĪ (the dates of the "baker" from Murcia are not known, but it has been suggested that he may have lived in the Almohad period) (*Ǧayš* 104, p. 143). The poet addresses his beloved:

sídi ṣáḥbu l-banáfsaǧí a 9
ǧí li-ᶜámmik ḥabíbī ǧí a 9
Lord, endowed with violet [eyes],
Come to your uncle, love, come.
ó o ó o o ó o ó

Spanish *calque*:

Negros ojos tenéis, señor,
¡Al amigo venid, amor!

Spanish parallel:

Estos mis cabellicos, madre,
dos a dos me los lleva el aire. (Cejador 141, p. 102)

4. Abū Bakr Muḥammad ibn ᶜAbd al-Malik IBN ZUHR AL-ḤAFĪD (the grandson of the famous Avenzoar was born in Seville in 1113 and died in Marrakesh in 1198) (*Ǧayš* 155, p. 209). A friend offers the poet advice in his love affair:

man ḫấn ḥabíbuh al-lấh ḥasíb a 10
al-lấh yuᶜāqíbuh wá-yuṯíb a 10
Him who betrays his beloved will God call to account;
God will punish or reward him.
o ó o ó o o ó o ó

Spanish *calque*:

Traición de amigo castiga Dios,
castigo y premio vendrán de Dios.

Spanish parallel:

De día sol y de noche luna,
¡que solo! Dios y mi desventura. (Cejador 161, p. 105)

5. AL-ḪABBĀZ AL-MURSĪ (*Ǧayš* 106, p. 144). The poet addresses his beloved:

lays náᶜšaq ánā íllā muwấṣil a 10
bi-šárṭ an yakū́n malíḥ wa-ᶜấqil a 10
I love only those who tryst with me,
Provided they are comely and intelligent.
o ó o ó o o ó o ó o

Spanish *calque:*

Yo sólo quiero a quien, entre amigos,
es o bien quapo, o bien muy listo.

Spanish parallel:

> Lo que demanda el romero, madre,
> lo que demanda no ge lo dane. (Sánchez Romeralo 54, p. 403)

6. AL-ḪABBĀZ AL-MURSĪ (*Ǧayš* 105, p. 143). The poet addresses his lover:

ánta fī qálbī ṯámm daráyt sírrī	a	10
ā́š naqúl lak ḥabī́bī mā tádrī	a	10

You are ensconced in my heart; there you learned my secret.
How can I tell you, love, what you already know?
ó o o ó o ó o o ó o

Spanish *calque:*

> En mis entrañas, sabes secretos,
> ¿qué digo, amigo, que ya no sepas?

Spanish parallel:

> Póntela tú, la gorra del fraile,
> póntela tú, que a mí no me cabe. (Cejador 167, p. 106)

7. IBN RUḤAYM (*Ǧayš* 132, p. 176). A youth sings to the poet:

l-ay qíṣṣah tabī́t wáḥdak w-ánā wáḥdī	a	11
kámā bitt ᶜíndak ḥáttā tabī́t ᶜíndī	a	11

What happens that you spend the night alone, while I too spend it alone,
When I once spent it with you and you spent it with me?
o ó o o ó o ó o o ó o

Spanish *calque:*

> ¿Por qué duermes solo, estando yo solo?
> ¡Dormí yo contigo; duerme conmigo!

Spanish parallel:

> Venido el verano de las gavillas,
> quítanse galanes de las esquinas. (Cejador 177, p. 108)

(2) ANISOSYLLABIC

a) Lines of Increasing Length

8. Muḥammad IBN ᶜUBĀDA al-Qazzāz al-Malaqī? (The "silk merchant" of Málaga attended the court of Muᶜtaṣim of Almería, who reigned between 1051 and 1091) (*Dār* 9, p. 53). The beloved addresses the poet, denying him a kiss:

ánā qūl qū́qū	a	5
láys bi-l-lā́h taḏū́qu	a	6

I say: "The sweetmeat

You will not taste, by God! "
ó o o ó o
ó o ó o ó o

Spanish *calque:*

Digo: "¡El bocado
no será probado!

Spanish parallel:

¡Ojos, mis ojos,
tan garridos ojos! (Sánchez Romeralo 42, p. 400)

9. IBN ZUHR (*Ǧayš* 150, p. 199). The poet declares:

yā rább yā rábbī a 5
hā́ḏā l-ḥabī́b iǧmá^{c}-nī má^{c}ū b 9
O Lord, O Lord,
this lover, join me with him!
o ó o ó o
o ó o ó o ó o ó o

Spanish *calque:*

¡Ay, Dios, Dios mío,
juntadme bien con este amigo!

Spanish parallel:

Andallo, andallo:
que soy pollo y voy para gallo. (Cejador 401, p. 142)

10. Abū ^{c}Īsā IBN LABBŪN (he served as vizier to ^{c}Abd al-^{c}Azīz of Valencia [d. 1085]) (*Ǧayš* 122, p. 164). A girl sings to her lover:

samā́rak ḥúlū a 5
andáh min šā́ribán li-^{c}ádad b 9
Your dark skin is sweet;
It attracts more attention than a lip addressing a multitude!
o ó o ó o
o ó o ó o ó o ó o

Spanish *calque*:

¡Moreno dulce,
más llamativo que una boca!

Spanish parallel: Same as no. 9.

11. Abū Bakr Aḥmad IBN MĀLIK al-Anṣārī AS-SARAQUSṬĪ (this vizier lived in Valencia and Murcia, and died in Seville in 1175) (*Ǧayš* 161, p. 219). The poet sings to a youth:

usáymir ḥúlū a 5
bayā́ḍ kulli ᶜā́šiq yabī́tu máᶜū a 11
O sweet little dark-skinned lad,
The joy[9] of every lover spends the night with him.
o ó o ó o
o ó o o ó o o ó o ó o

Spanish *calque:*

¡Moreno dulce,
con cada querido su amor se acuesta!

Spanish parallel:

Miquel, Miguel,
no tienes abejas y vendes miel. (Cejador 407, p. 143)

12. Abū l-Qāsim AL-MANĪŠĪ (he was from Manīš, a village in the province of Seville, and served as a guide to the blind poet at-Tuṭīlī [d. 1126]. His dates are not known) (*Ğayš* 85, p. 118). The lover addresses the poet:

qálbī mín hadī́d a 6
fī kúlli yáwm sudū́d ğadī́d a 9
My heart is made of steel,
Every day there is a new avoidance.
ó o ó o ó
o ó o ó o ó o ó

Spanish *calque:*

¡Yo de acero soy!
¡Evítame él mañana y hoy!

Spanish parallel:

Ellos eran tres,
y las vasijas, veinte y seis. (Cejador 424, p. 146)

13. IBN BAQĪ (*Ğayš* 9, p. 15). The poet declares:

našúqq as-simā́ṭa wáḥdī a 8
wa-nárā ḥabī́ba qálbī báynī a 10
I pass through the bazaar alone,
Yet I see the beloved of my heart before me.
o ó o o ó o ó o
o ó o o ó o ó o ó o

[9]The translation of *bayāḍ* (lit. "whiteness") as "joy" is conjectural. It is based on R. Dozy: *yā bayāḍa-ka min yawmin* "what a beautiful day this is"; *Supplément aux dictionnaires arabes*, ed. 3, 1 (Leiden 1967) 135 col. A. Also, the word *sawād* "blackness" has in Andalusian Arabic the sense of "melancholy," as will be shown clearly by context in a further collection of *ḫargaš* currently being edited. Hence it is likely that *bayāḍ*, as the opposite of *sawād*, should mean "joy, happiness."

Spanish *calque:*

Yo cruzo el mercado solo:
y veo a mi amigo por delante.

Spanish parallel:

¿Qué me queréis, caballero?
Casada me soy, marido tengo. (Cejador 472, p. 153)

b) Lines of Decreasing Length

14. IBN ZUHR (*Ǧayš* 157, p. 212). The poet addresses the lover:

ᶜaláyš ḥabī́bī qaṭáᶜta z-ziyā́rah	a	11
wa-ᶜaynáyk saḥḥā́ra	a	6

Why, my love, have you suspended your visits,
When your eyes are so bewitching?
o ó o ó o o ó o o ó o
o ó o o ó o

Spanish *calque:*

¿Por qué, mi amigo, ya no me visitas?
¡Hechizan tus ojos!

Spanish parallel:

Quien nace un día/ de estrella tan dura
nunca halla ventura. (Cejador 661, p. 188)

B. TERCETS

(1) ISOSYLLABIC

15. Abū Bakr Yaḥya as-Saraqusṭī AL-ǦAZZĀR (the "butcher" of Zaragoza was writing around the time of al-Muᶜtamin of Zaragoza [r. 1081-1085], then gave up his literary pursuits to return to the butcher trade) (*Ǧayš* 30, p. 148. The same *ḫarǧa* appears in a poem by Ibn Labbūn [*Ǧayš* 124, p. 166]). A girl addresses her mother, using two Romance words:

MÁMMĀ Šṹ l-ġulā́m	a	6
lā búdd kullū lī́yā	b	6
ḥalā́l aw ḥarā́m	a	6

MOTHER, HIS slave boy
Must be all mine
By hook or crook.
ó o ó o ó
o ó o o ó o
o ó o o ó

Spanish *calque:*

Madre, su rapaz,
que sea todo mío
por bien o por mal.

Spanish parallel:

Pues mi pena veis,
miradme sin saña,
o no me miréis. (Alín 20, p. 311)

(2) ANISOSYLLABIC

16. AL-MANĪŠĪ (*Ǧayš* 84, p. 116). The poet addresses his lover:

dáynu	a	2
man ġā́ba ᶜánnū ḥabī́bū	b	8
mā sú'ila[10] *ᶜánnū*	a	6

The death
Of one whose beloved has left him,
Is not to be discussed.

ó o
o ó o   ó o o ó o
o ó o o ó o

Spanish *calque:*

Muerte
de quien perdió ya a su amigo,
no se hable de ella.

Spanish parallel:

Pues que
me sacan a desposar
quiérome peinar. (Cejador 328, p. 131)

17. IBN ZUHR? (*Dar* 4, p. 47). The poet sings:

ḥabī́bī ánta ǧā́rī	a	7
dārák bi-ǧánbi dā́rī	a	7
wá-tahǧúr-nī	b	4

Lover, you are my neighbor;
Your house is next to mine,
Yet you avoid me?
o ó o ó o ó o
o ó o ó o ó o
ó o ó o

[10] The text reads *sa'ala* which makes little sense.

Spanish *calque:*

Amigo, son vecinas
tu casa con mi casa,
¿y evitáisme?

Spanish parallel:

Ya está hecho lo medio:
porque, aunque ella no quiera,
yo ya quiero. (Cejador 616, p. 180)

18. Abū l-^{c}Abbās Aḥmad ibn ^{c}Abd Allāh ibn Hurayra al-^{c}Absī AL-A^{c}MĀ AT-TUṬĪLĪ (the "blind" poet from Tudela lived most of his live in Seville, where he died young, in 1126) (*Ğayš* 14, p. 24). The poet alludes to a girl who betrayed him:

náqaḍ ál-^{c}uhū́d wa-ḫā́na-nī́	a	10
^{c}alā́š yā qáwm,	b	5
w-ánā ^{c}álā ^{c}áhdi-hí muqī́mā	c	10

He broke our compacts and betrayed me.
Why, O people,
When I am steadfast in my pact with him?
ó o ó o ó   o ó o ó
o ó o ó
ó o ó o ó   o ó o ó o

Spanish *calque:*

Rompe pactos quien me traicionó.
Decid, ¿por qué?
gentes, siempre yo leal le he sido.

Spanish parallel:

Concertáme allá esa jerigonza,
Juan de Mendoza. (Cejador 320, p. 130)

19. IBN BAQĪ (*Dār* 27, p. 77). A girl speaks in classical diction, but the theme has a popular ring to it:

wā-ḥásratī́ wa-mā́ qad ğarā́ lī	a	10
la^{c}íbtu-hú fa-mázzaqa dā́lī	a	10
wá-dalā́lī	a	4

Woe to me; what has become of me!
I sported with him and he tore my cloak
And my curls!
o ó o ó   o ó o o ó o
o ó o ó   o ó o o ó o
ó o ó o

Spanish *calque:*

¡Ay, ay de mí; de lo que me pasa!
Con él jugué: los rizos me arranca,
y la capa.

Spanish parallel:

Pajarillo que vas a la fuente,
bebe y vente. (Cejador 319, p. 129)

20. AT-TUṬĪLĪ (*Ǧayš* 20, p. 31; *Dār* 28, p. 78). A girl sings:

lā búdda náḥḍur min ḥáyṯi yarā́-nī	a	11
laᶜálla-hú bi-s-salā́mi yabdáᶜ-nī	a	11
*ḥabī́bī yakfā́-nī**	a	6
*Var. in *Dār: mā ḥálla bī́ kafā́-nī*	a	7

I'll certainly appear where he can see me.
Perchance he will greet me.
My lover is all I need.*
*Var.: What has happened to me is all I need.
o ó o ó o   o ó o o ó o
o ó o ó o   o ó o o ó o
o ó o o ó o *
*Var.:
o ó o ó o ó o

Spanish *calque:*

Saldré sin duda por donde me vea;
deseo ver si quizá me saluda.
¡Mi amigo me basta! *
*Var.: ¡Me pasa lo que basta!

Spanish parallel:

Yo me iba, madre, / al monte una tarde. (Cejador 384, p. 139)

C. QUATRAINS

(1) ISOSYLLABIC

21. IBN BAQĪ (*Ǧayš* 8, p. 14). The poet speaks:

qád bulī́nā wá-btulī́nā	a	8
wā́š yaqū́lu n-nā́su fī́-nā	a	8
qúm bi-nā́ yā nū́ra ᶜáynī	b	8
náǧᶜal iš-šákka yaqī́nā	a	8

We have been worn out and are exhausted,
Yet what do people say about us?

Arise with me, O light of my eye,
Let us turn doubt into certainty.
ó o ó o   ó o ó o
– ˘ – –   – ˘ – –   *ramal*

Spanish *calque:*

Tristes somos y afligidos,
¿qué de nos dirán las gentes?
Vamos ya, luz de mis ojos:
dudas en verdad tornemos.

Spanish parallel:

Castigado me ha mi madre
por vos, gentil caballero:
mándame que no os hable;
no lo haré, que mucho os quiero. (Cejador 687, p. 195)

Latin parallel:

Stabat mater dolorosa
Juxta crucem lacrimosa.

(2) ANISOSYLLABIC

22. AT-TUṬĪLĪ (*Ǧayš* 11, p. 19). A girl addresses her mother, using one Romance word:

MÁMMĀ	a	2
*ya*ᶜ*šáq-nī ḏā l-fátā*	b	6
wa-lā nádrī li-mấ ḏā	c	7
wa-lā náqul la-hú lā	d	7

MOTHER,
That youth loves me,
Yet I know not why,
Nor do I say to him: "No! "

ó o
o ó o o ó o
o o ó o o ó o
o o ó o o ó o

Spanish *calque:*

Madre,
tal mozo me quiere,
¡yo no sé por qué causa,
ni le digo: " ¡Dejadme! "

Spanish parallel:

Turbias
van las aguas, madre,
ellas se aclararane. (Cejador 271, p. 122)

23. AL-ǦAZZĀR (*Ǧayš* 111, p. 151). The poet addresses the panegyrized Aḥmad in love terms:

áḥmad maḥbū́bī	a	5
bi-n-nábī táǧī	b	5
ḥabī́bī bi-l-lā́hi	c	6
ǧī́-nī ḥīn áǧī	b	5

Ahmad, my love,
By the Prophet, you come!
My loved one, by God,
Come to me when I come to you!
ó o o ó o
ó o o ó o
o ó o o ó o
ó o o ó o

Spanish *calque:*

Aḥmad, querido,
juro que vienes,
¡ay Dios, el mi amigo,
ven cuando vengo!

Spanish parallel:

Rey don Alonso,
rey mi señor,
rey de los reyes,
emperador. (Alín 283, p. 480)

24. IBN LABBŪN (*Ǧayš* 121, p. 162). A girl sings:

wáyḥī ǧafā́-nī	a	5
malī́ḥ ásmar al-aǧfā́ni	a	8
ᶜámdan barā́-nī	a	5
bi-wáṣli-hi wá-ḫallā́-nī	a	8

Woe to me, there has treated me harshly,
A handsome lad, dark of eyelids.
He has exhausted me on purpose
With his trysting; then cast me aside.
ó o o ó o
o ó o o ó o ó o

Spanish *calque:*

¡Mal que me trata,
el cejimoreno guapo!
¡Ay, que me cansa
su unión, mas ahora me evita!

Spanish parallel:

Soy lastimada,
en fuego de amor me quemo;
soy desamada
[y] triste de lo que temo. (Alín 429, p. 553)

25. Abū ^{c}Āmir Muḥammad ibn Yaḥya ibn Ḫalīfa IBN YINNIQ (1152-1186) (*Ǧayš* 139, p. 184). A girl sings to her mother, using one Romance word:

háǧar ḥabī́bī	a	5
wa-zā́da-nī hámman MÁMMĀ	b	8
ā́š kān ḏunū́bī	a	5
fa-láys lū min háǧri íṯmā	b	8

My beloved has fled,
And filled me with care, MOTHER.
What are my sins?
Isn't he to blame for avoiding me?
ó o o ó o
o ó o o ó o ó o

Spanish *calque:*

¡Fuese mi amado;
de penas llenóme, madre!
¿Dónde he pecado?
¿No es él en huïr culpable?

Spanish parallel: Same as no. 24.

26. AT-TUṬĪLĪ (*Dār* 34, p. 84). The Kingdom sings the following woman's song to celebrate a change of rulers:

wā́š kān dahā́-nī	a	5
yā qáwmu wā́š kān balā́-nī	a	8
wā́š kān da^{c}ā́-nī	a	5
nábdal ḥabī́bī bi-ṯā́nī	a	8

How he has afflicted me,
O people, and how he has tormented me!
How he has upset me!
I will exchange my lover for another!
ó o o ó o
ó o o ó o o ó o

Spanish *calque:*

¡Cuán me ha afligido,
gentes, y cuán me atormenta!
¡Cuánto he sufrido!
¡Cambio mi amigo por otro!

Spanish parallel:

Si por mi llueve
échenme en el mar y cese. (Cejador 398, p. 141)

27. AL-ĞAZZĀR (*Ğayš* 116, p. 156). A drunken youth sings:

qubbáylah fī l-ḫā́li	a	6
yā ḫā́lī	a	3
fa-qā́la fī fámmī	b	6
yā ᶜámmī	b	3

"[May I give you] a kiss on the mole of your cheek,
O maternal uncle? "*
He replied: "On my mouth,
O paternal uncle! "*
*Terms of endearment. No actual blood kinship is implied.
o ó o o ó o
o ó o

Spanish *calque:*

"¿Te beso el lunare,
materno? "
Responde: "¡En la boca,
paterno! "

Galician parallel:

Falai, miña amor,
falaime;
si no me fallais,
matayme. (Alín 267, p. 469)

28. Abū Bakr (or Abū ᶜAbd Allāh) Muḥammad ibn al-Ḥasan AL-KUMAYT AL-ĠARBĪ (he was from the Algarve, possibly from Badajoz, and panegyrized al-Mustaᶜīn of Zaragoza [r. 1085-1110]) (*Ğayš* 65, p. 93). A man addresses a youth:

mā ámlaḥ ᶜiḏā́rak	a	6
ḥabī́bī yā l-ásmar	b	6
tárā[11] *ayn dā́rak*	a	5

[11] The reading *túrī* is also possible. In this case the line would mean "Show [me] where your house is."

qul-hấ wa-lā táfkar b 6
How charming is your cheek down,
My love, O dark-skinned one.
Do you see where your house is? *
Say so without thinking!
*i.e. make yourself at home in my house.

o ó o o ó o
o ó o o ó o
ó o o ó o
o ó o o ó o

Spanish *calque:*

¡Qué bellos tus rizos,
mi amigo el moreno!
¿Ves ya tu casa?
¡Di "sí," sin pensarlo!

Spanish parallels:

Estando conmigo,
mi bien, suspiráis:
esos son avisos
de amor que me dáis. (Alín XI, p. 743)
Moza tan fermosa
non vi en la frontera
como una vaquera
de la Finojosa (Marqués de Santillana)

29. AL-MANĪŠĪ (*Ǧayš* 81, p. 114). The poet sings:

al-ᶜấšiq ál-miskī́n a 7
ṭấla hámmū b 4
láylat áš-šitấ wa-r-rī́ḥ c 8
mán yaḍúmmū b 4
The poor lover,
His cares are prolonged.
On a wintry, windy night,
Who embraces him?
o ó o ó o ó
ó o ó o
ó o ó o ó o ó
ó o ó o

Spanish *calque:*

Al pobre y amador,
largas penas:
frías noches si las ha,
¿quién lo estrecha?

Spanish parallel:

Aquel pastorcico, madre,
que no viene,
algo tiene en el campo
que le duele. (Cejador 829, p. 228)

30. Abū Bakr Muḥammad ibn ^{c}Īsā IBN AL-LABBĀNA ad-Dānī (the poet from Denia was on good terms with al-Mu^{c}tamid of Seville, and died in Majorca in 1113) (*Ǧayš* 45, p. 69). A girl speaks:

ál-lāh zắnak yā l-ásmar	a	7
zayn kúlli ^{c}áskar	a	5
qád ḫarắǧta yā šāṭir	b	7
fī l-ḥárbi ẓắfir	b	5

God adorn you, O dark-skinned one,
Ornament of every army.
You have gone forth, skillful warrior,
Victorious in battle.
ó o ó o o ó o
o ó o ó o

Spanish *calque:*

¡Dios te adorne, moreno;
la guerra adornas!
Tú, el guerrero, saliste:
victorias ganas.

Spanish parallel:

Al espejo se toca
la blanca niña,
dando luz a la luna
donde se mira. (Cejador 824, p. 227)

31. AT-TUṬĪLĪ (*Ǧayš* 10, p. 18). A girl addresses the poet:

qad ra'áytuk ^{c}ayyắn	a	7
āš ^{c}aláyk sa-tádrī	b	6
sa-yaṭū́lu z-zamắn	a	7
wa-sa-tánsā ḏíkrī	b	6

I see that you are pining.
What is your trouble? You know
That time will pass,
And you will forget me.
o o ó o o ó
o o ó o ó o

Spanish *calque:*

Ya te vi entristecer,
¿qué te pasa? sabes
que el tiempo ha de correr,
¡olvidadme, ay, antes!

Spanish parallel:

Que miraba la mar
la malcasada,
que miraba la mar
cómo es ancha y larga. (Cejador 889, p. 240)

32. Abū ᶜAbd Allāh ibn Abī l-Faḍl IBN ŠARAF (he lived at the beginning of the Almohad period) (*Ǧayš* 72, p. 103). A girl sings to her mother:

hākaḏắ yā umm nášqā	a	7
wá-l-ḥabīb sắkin ǧiwắrī	b	8
in amút yā qawm ᶜíšqā	a	7
fá-ḫuḏū úmmī bi-ṯắrī	b	8

Thus, O mother, am I made miserable,
While my lover dwells in my neighborhood.
If I die, O people, of love,
Then exact my bloodwit from my mother.
o o ó o o ó o
ó o o ó o o ó o

Spanish *calque*:

Penas tengo, mi madre,
que mi amigo es el vecino;
si de amores me muero,
¡Ay! de mi madre vengadme.

Spanish parallel:

Las mañanas de abril
¡que dulces son de dormir!
las de mayo, mejor,
si no despierta el amor. (Cejador 958, p. 255)

33. IBN YINNIQ (*Ǧayš* 138, p. 183). The poet speaks to a girl:

samrah kám ḏā s-sudúdi	a	7
bi-l-ḥúrmah yā sítti ǧúdī	a	8
samrah fí wasṭi wắdi	b	7
ṯámm salabtí-nī fu'ắdī	b	8

Dark-skinned girl, how often have you shunned me!

By the respect you owe me, lady, be generous!
Dark-skinned girl, in the middle of a valley,
There you stole my heart.
o o ó o o ó o
ó o o ó o o ó o

Spanish *calque*:

¡Morenica, evitáisme!
¡Ay, Dios, señora, queredme!
¡Morenica, en un valle,
el corazón me robaste!

Spanish parallel: Same as no. 32.

34. AL-MANĪŠĪ (*Ǧayš* 82, p. 115). The poet sings to a lady:

bí-l-lāh ^{c}*aláyki yā sámrā*	a	8
yā sítti yā záyn al-^{c}*ašī́r*	b	9
álwā bi-qálbī ^{c}*inā́quk*	c	8
fa-qúm bi-nā ílā s-sarī́r	b	9

By God, O dark-skinned girl,
O my lady, O ornament of the tribe,
Your embraces have stolen my heart,
So climb with me into bed.
ó o o ó o o ó o
o ó o o ó o o ó

Spanish *calque*:

Júrote la mi morena,
señora y adorno tribal,
¡los tus abrazos me matan!
¡Pues, vente conmigo a acostar!

Spanish parallel:

¿Qué me queréis caballero?
casada soy; marido tengo. (Sánchez Romeralo 39, p. 400)

35. AL-ǦAZZĀR (*Ǧayš* 117, p. 157). A girl calls a young boy to her:

a-mā́ táǧī yā sabī́yyu ^{c}*índī*	a	10
ḏā l-yáwma táfṭar	b	5
nūfī́k ǧamā́lī wa-náhdīk náhdī	a	10
wá-lā náqṣur	b	4

Won't you come, O child, to me?
Today you'll break your fast.
I'll grant you my beauty and give you my breasts,
And I'll not be remiss.

o ó o ó o o ó o ó o
o ó o ó o
o ó o ó o o ó o ó o
ó o ó o

Spanish *calque*:

¿No vienes pronto hijuelo mío?
Tu ayuno rompe.
Mis senos más mi belleza doyte,
sin faltarte.

Spanish parallel:

Cantan los gallos / yo no me duermo
ni tengo sueño. (Cejador 519, p. 162)

36. AT-TUṬĪLĪ (*Dīwān* 21, p. 287). A girl sings to the panegyrized Abū Bakr Aḥmad ibn Ḥayyūn:

ḫálli siwắrī wa-ḫúḏ himyắnī	a	10
ḥabī́bī áḥmad	b	5
wá-ṭlu^c má^{c}ī li-s-sarī́r ḥayyū́nī	a	10
tárqud muğárrad	b	5

Leave my bracelet and grasp my sash,
My lover Aḥmad,
And climb with me into bed, Ḥayyūnī,
You will sleep naked.
ó o o ó o o ó o ó o
o ó o ó o

Spanish *calque*:

¡Deja mi ajorca, mi faja coge,
amigo Aḥmad!
¡Monta, Ḥayyūnī, conmigo al lecho,
duerme desnudo!

Spanish parallel:

Si los delfines / mueren de amores
¡triste de mí!
¿qué harán los hombres / que tienen tiernos
los corazones? (Cejador 1060, p. 277)

37. AL-ḪABBĀZ (*Ğayš* 102, p. 141). A young man whose beloved is absent appears wearing holiday clothes and fine scents during the ^{c}Īd festival. He sings:

mā l-^{c}ī́du fī ḥúllatín wa-ṭắqi	a	10
wa-šámm wa-ṭī́b	b	5

wa-ínnamā l-^{c}ī́du fī t-talā́qī a 10
má^{c} al-ḥabī́b b 5
^{c}Īd lies not in silks and fine raiment,
Nor in scents and perfumes,
But rather, ^{c}Īd lies in meeting
With one's lover.
o ó o o ó o ó o ó o
o ó o ó

Spanish *calque*:

Vestidos de gala no es la Pascua;
perfumes no es;
más bien es la Pascua el acercarme,
amigo a tí.

Spanish parallel:

Idos acostar, marido bueno,
que yo iré luego. (Cejador 323, p. 130)

38. Anonymous (*Ǧayš* 38, p. 58). A girl speaks:

qad ġádar ḥabī́bī wá ḫallā́-nī a 10
lays náṭa^{c} ḫalī́l b 6
yā́ ḫalī́lī áyn al-īmā́n c 9
al-wáfā qalī́l b 6
My lover betrayed and abandoned me.
I'll not obey any lover.
O lover, where is your faith?
Your loyalty is scant.
o ó o o ó o ó o ó o
o ó o o ó
ó o ó o ó o o ó
o ó o o ó

Spanish *calque*:

Mi amigo traiciona y me abandona;
sumisa no soy.
¡Ay, amor! tu fe ¿dónde está?
¡Que poca lealtad!

Spanish parallel:

Ne sé qué tengo en el carcañal,
que no puedo andar. (Cejador 327, p. 131)

39. AL-ḪABBĀZ (*Ǧayš* 98, p. 136). The poet addresses his lover:

ḥáblī ḥábl [*-an*] *raqī́q kamā tádrī* a 10

wá-naḫấf man yúmlī b 6
áyš ẓahár lak yā ḥíbbī fī ámrī a 10
áyš turī́d qul-hú lī b 6
My bond is a tender bond, as you know,
And I fear one who orders me about.
What do you think, my love, of my case?
Tell me what you desire.
ó o ó o o ó o o ó o
ó o ó o ó o

Spanish *calque*:

Tú conoces mis muy tiernos lazos;
témote tirano.
¿Qué parécete, amor, el mi caso?
¡Dime lo que quieres!

Spanish parallel:

Esta novia se lleva la flor,
que las otras no. (Cejador 326, p. 131)

40. IBN ŠARAF (*Ğayš* 79, p. 111). The poet quotes a woman's song to his beloved:

ál-ḥabī́b ḥuğíb ᶜan-nī́ fī dā́r a 10
wá-nurī́du nás'al ᶜánnū ğā́r a 10
wá-naḫấf raqī́b al-ḥíbb b 8
wá-āš náᶜmalú yā rább b 8
My lover has been concealed from me in a house,
And I wish to ask a neighbor about him,
Yet I fear the spy of my love.
What shall I do, O Lord?
ó o ó o ó o ó o ó
ó o ó o ó o ó o ó
ó o ó o ó o ó
ó o ó o ó o ó

Spanish *calque*:

Una casa oculta a quien amé;
a un vecino pregunté por él.
A su espía temo yo.
¿Qué he de hacer, Dios mi señor?

Spanish parallel:

Por el río me llevad, amigo,
y llevadme por el río. (Cejador 336, p. 132)

41. AL-KUMAYT (*Ğayš* 66, p. 95). A girl sings:

ḏúbtu wá-l-lāh ásan náṭluqú ṣiyā́ḥ a 12

qad kássara náhdī	b	6
wá-ᶜamál lī fī šufáyfātī ğirāḥ	a	12
wa-náṯṯara ᶜíqdī	b	6

I melt, by God, with sorrow, emitting cries.
He has crushed my breast,
And bruised my lips,
And scattered my necklace.
ó o ó o ó o   ó o ó o ó
o ó o o ó o

Spanish *calque*:

¡Penas me disuelven; lanzo gritos yo!
¡El pecho me estrecha!
¡En mis blandos labios, llaga me dejó!
¡Collar me lo esparce!

Spanish parallel:

Troque, troque, troque / los cencerros míos
y los bueyes de otre. (Cejador 560, p. 170)

D. SEXTETS

42. AT-TUṬĪLĪ (*Dār* 30, p. 80). The poet speaks:

yā rábbī mā ṣbár-nī	a	6
nárā ḥabīb qálbī	b	6
wá-naᶜšáqū	c	4
law kān yakūn súnnah	d	6
fī mán laqā ḥíllū	e	6
yúᶜanníqū	c	4

O Lord, how patient I am!
I see the beloved of my heart
And I adore him.
If only it were customary
For one meeting his lover
To embrace him!
o ó o o ó o
o ó o o ó o
ó o ó o

Spanish *calque*:

¡Ay Dios, soy sufrido!

¡Ya veo a quien quiero!
¡Yo lo adoro!
! Si fuese costumbre,
al ver al amigo,
abrazarlo!

Spanish parallel:

Sospira Gilete
y ella duerme. (Cejador 184, p. 109)

43. Anonymous (*Dār* 16, p. 63). A girl speaks in classical diction, but the *ḫarǧa* sounds popular in theme. Kannūnī refers to a member of the Guennūn family of Berbers.

ánta l-múnā táḥlū a 6
fa-trúk kalā́ma n-nā́s b 7
wá-dḫul má^{c}ī ílfī c 6
míṯla š-šarā́b fī l-kā́s b 7
yā́ kannū́nī d 4
káymā túsallī́-nī d 6
You, my desire, are sweet;
Forget what people say,
Enter with me, my love,
Like wine in the cup,
O Kannūnī,
To divert me.
ó o ó o ó o
o ó o ó o ó
ó o ó o ó o
o ó o ó o ó
ó o ó o
ó o ó o ó o

Spanish *calque*:

Mi deseo dulce,
olvida el qué dirán;
entra, amor, conmigo,
—sed vino; copa, yo—
ay, Guennūnī,
para consolarme.

Spanish parallel:

Vi los barcos, madre,
vilos y no me vale. (Cejador 417, p. 144)

E. OCTET

44. IBN AL-LABBĀNA? (*Dār* 13, p. 58). A married lady addresses her lover in her husband's absence:

ḥúbayyíbī á^{c}*zim*	a	6
wá-qum wá-hǧum	a	4
wá-q̌abbíl fam	a	4
wá-ǧī wá-nḍam	a	4
ílā ṣádrī	b	4
wá-qum bí-ḫalḫā́lī	b	6
ílā aqrā́ṭī	b	5
qád ištáġal záwǧī	b	6

My little lover, be resolute;
Rise and embrace me,
Kiss my mouth,
Come and squeeze
My breast
And raise my anklets
Up to my earrings:
My husband is busy!

ó o ó o ó o
ó o ó o
ó o ó o
ó o ó o
ó o ó o
ó o ó o ó o
ó o o ó o
ó o ó o ó o

Spanish *calque*:

¡Amiguito, vale,
estrechadme,
dadme un beso,
abrazadme
el mi pecho,
mis ajorcas junta
con mis pendientes:
mi marido es ido!

Parallel: None found.

CONCLUSIONS

Like the Romance *ḫarǧas*, many of those in Arabic appear to be independent compositions inserted into a *muwaššaḥ*. This can easily be demonstrated by the fact that occasionally the same *ḫarǧa* is used to conclude two poems by different authors. The autonomy of the *ḫarǧa*, plus the Arabic poetic convention according to which the lover often refers to his lady in the masculine form, make it difficult to break down the poems into the masculine or the feminine type of lyric. In twenty of the *ḫarǧas* edited above, however, it is clearly a girl who is speaking, leaving twenty-four that are either masculine, homosexual, or impossible to classify.[12] In fifteen *muwaššaḥs* specific reference is made to the fact that the poem is being sung, by either a man or a woman,[13] thus providing evidence for a tradition of popular songs independent from the main body of the *muwaššaḥ*.

Linguistically, the *ḫarǧas* range from two in pure classical diction, which I have included because the sentiments expressed seem to reflect popular themes[14] (a large corpus of panegyrical *ḫarǧas* in classical diction and of a clearly artificial nature has been excluded), through thirty-nine poems in a poetic diction combining classical and colloquial Arabic in varying proportions, to three poems in colloquial Arabic containing one or two Romance words.[15] It should be noted that many of the poets in this selection also composed *muwaššaḥs* with Romance *ḫarǧas*. Indeed, a rigid distinction between Romance and Arabic *ḫarǧas* is detrimental, given the fact that many borderline examples among the so-called Romance *ḫarǧas* are almost entirely in Arabic, and can be considered Arabic poems for all practical purposes. Hence, the exclusion of the Arabic corpus from the study of the Romance *ḫarǧas* is an oversimplification that tends to obscure the very nature of the *ḫarǧa* tradition. When the corpus in either language is compared with its counterpart, it becomes apparent that we are dealing with one tradition of folk poetry that expressed itself through (1) colloquial Arabic, (2) Romance, or (3) a mixture of (1) and (2) in varying proportions. This claim can be supported both prosodically and thematically.

Prosodically, only one of the poems can be reduced to an actual Arabic meter: *Ḫarǧa 21*, containing only two colloquialisms, can be scanned as two lines of *ramal* dimeter, a meter whose rhythm and syllabic count coincide perfectly with the Romance and Latin trochaic octosyllabic line (the most common meter in Spanish). *Ḫarǧa 11* is quantitatively a perfect line in the classical meter *muḍāriᶜ* (one of the rarest in the classical Arabic repertory), although its language is almost entirely colloquial, while its rhythm is unlike that of *muḍāriᶜ*. Similarly, *Ḫarǧa 2* can be scanned quantitatively as a hemistich of *ṭawīl*, but the rhythm of the poem is clearly that of the Romance iambic heptasyllable, and not at all like the normal *ṭawīl* rhythm. Thus, apart from one clear instance where an Arabic meter is recognizable, although it has a close counterpart in Romance, and apart from two other cases where a certain hybridization may be detected, the remainder of the *ḫarǧas* repro-

[12] The *ḫarǧas* in the mouths of women are: Nos. 1, 8, 10, 15, 19f., 22, 24-26, 30-32, 35f., 38, 40f., 43f.

[13] Mention of singing is found in the *muwaššaḥs* attached to *ḫarǧas* 10f., 17, 20, 24-27, 29, 32, 34, 36f., 40f.

[14] Nos. 19, 43.

[15] Nos. 15, 22, 25.

duce many of the forms known to the Hispanic system of prosody. They have therefore been treated as stress-syllabic poems and classified accordingly. There are a total of fourteen couplets, six tercets, twenty-one quatrains, two sextets, and one octet. Of these, nine poems are isosyllabic, and thirty-five are anisosyllabic. As in Spanish poetry, the rhythms are based on the principle of stress and are often slightly irregular. For this reason, I have marked in the Arabic texts the syllables that would normally be stressed in speech (to the extent that this can be determined), [16] while below, in the prosodic outline, I have marked the stresses according to the ideal and regular pattern for each meter, from which some of the individual *ḫarǧas* occasionally deviate. By comparing the two stress patterns, the reader should be able to detect the rhythmic variations that appear in practice, insofar as they depart from theoretical regularity (rarely followed in Spanish poetry). Rhythmically, six poems are trochaic, six iambic, four dactylic, one anapaestic, and twenty-seven have a mixed rhythm in which the meter known as *verso de arte mayor* ([o] ó o o ó [o] / [o] ó o o ó [o]) often appears as either its hemistich, or its whole line. *Ḫarǧas 6* and *26* have the dactylic rhythm known as *ritmo de gaita gallega*, associated with Galician dance songs, while *Ḫarǧa 31*, with its *abab* rhyme, and its alternating lines of 7-6-7-6 syllables (by Spanish count, according to which a final stressed syllable in a line is equivalent to two syllables prosodically) reproduces the *seguidilla*, an extremely common form in Spanish popular poetry (*Ḫarǧas 30* and *38* are also close to the *seguidilla* structure). *Ḫarǧas 23* and *28* correspond to a type of popular quatrain common in Spanish, which is rhymed *abab*, and is theoretically isosyllabic in nature, but which in practice often displays an irregularity in one of the lines, particularly the first or the third. *Ḫarǧa 23* should be considered a quatrain of five-syllable lines, although line 3 is actually six syllables long (the corresponding *bayts* of the *muwaš-šaḥ* are all pentasyllabic for this segment, indicating either that the text of the *ḫarǧa* is corrupted, or that the poet chose to ignore the irregularity). *Ḫarǧa 28*, in contrast, may be scanned as a quatrain of six-syllable lines, although line 3 is actually five syllables long (because the corresponding Arabic *bayt* segments all run to five syllables we can infer that the poet retained in the classical part of the *muwaššaḥ* the original irregularity of the colloquial *ḫarǧa*). Another major feature of Hispanic poetry is the *verso de pie quebrado*, a short line alternating with a longer one (normally twice as long) that generally precedes it, and not necessarily couched in the same rhythm as the longer line. The *pie quebrado* form occurs frequently in the Arabic *ḫarǧas* (see *Ḫarǧa 29*).

In a total of 151 lines, the hexasyllable predominates (35 examples), followed by the pentasyllable (23), the decasyllable (22), the octosyllable (21), the heptasyllable (18), the tetrasyllable (12), the eneasyllable (8), the hendecasyllable (6), and the bisyllable, trisyllable, and dodecasyllable (2 examples of each). Insofar as rhyme is

[16] Largely on the basis of Arnald Steiger, *Contribución a la fonética del hispano-árabe y de los arabismos en el ibero-románico y el siciliano* (Madrid 1932).

concerned, there are eleven couplets with *aa* rhyme and three with *ab*. Among the tercets, two examples have *aba*, two *aaa*, and one *aab* and *abc* rhyme. Nine quatrains have *abab*, five *abcb*, four *aabb*, two *aaaa*, and one *abcd* rhyme. The two sextets are of the *abcdec* and *abcbdd* type, while the one octet has *aaaabbbb* rhyme.

In sum, the Spanish system of syllable count, Spanish rhythms, rhyme schemes, and strophic arrangements occur in the overwhelming majority of the Arabic *ḫarǧas* included in the present selection, whereas the classical Arabic system of scansion is notoriously inadequate to explain their prosody. We therefore conclude that the metrical system of these poems, like that of the Romance *ḫarǧas*, and that of Ibn Quzmān's *zaǧals* recently analyzed by García Gómez,[17] is predominantly of the Romance type.

In the *zaǧals*, however, the lyrical voice is essentially masculine, and it is entirely clear that their authors were learned poets who adopted a popular diction, style, and prosody for literary reasons. In other words, *zaǧal* poets were not true popular poets, but rather, literary aristocrats who affected the folk style. But if this is so, what was the popular style they adopted? The substratum out of which the *zaǧal* developed in Andalus is not well known at present, and the question arises as to whether *zaǧal* poets were imitating the Romance folk poetry of Andalus directly, or whether a folk poetry modelled upon the latter and sung in the Iberian Peninsula also existed in colloquial Arabic. In the early eleventh century, the Cordovan poet and critic Ibn Šuhayd (992-1035) speaks with disdain about certain "verses such as greengrocers and butcher chiefs are attracted by,"[18] and although he furnishes no further details, it is possible that he is alluding to some form of colloquial poetry. A study of the Arabic *ḫarǧas* leads to the suspicion that a tradition of folksongs in Arabic may have existed. The poetic diction of these poems, with its peculiar admixture of classical and colloquial elements determined by prosodic requirements, to the frequent suppression of grammatical rules (a classical inflection will be retained when an extra syllable is needed to fill out a line, or dropped colloquially otherwise), is essentially the same diction used by the *zaǧal* poets. In this respect, many of our Arabic *ḫarǧas* may be fragments borrowed from *zaǧals* now lost,[19] and could conceivably reflect a semi-learned tradition of literary pastiches rather than true folklore. But in twenty examples edited above, the *ḫarǧa* is clearly in the mouths of women who provide a lyrical voice often similar to that found in the Romance *ḫarǧas*. In these instances we can be sure that we are dealing with a special tradition of feminine poetry for which there is no documentation in either classical Arabic or colloquial Andalusian *zaǧal* poetry. Of these twenty feminine poems, *Ḫarǧas 19* and *43* are in classical diction, leaving eighteen in colloquial Arabic. This in all probability means that the classical poems are pastiches composed in imitation of an authentic folk poetry well known

[17] See E. García Gómez, *Todo Ben Quzmān*, 3 vols. (Madrid 1972).

[18] Apud Ibn Bassām, *Kitāb ad-Daḫīra* (Cairo 1939) 1.1.200.

[19] *Ḫarǧă* 37 seems to have been quoted from a *muwaššaḥ* by Ibn Mu'ahhil. See Ibn Ḫaldūn, *The Muqaddimah*, trans. Franz Rosenthal (New York 1958) 3.445.

to the Andalusians, yet which they failed to incorporate into their literary anthologies as an independent genre, because of their classicist obsession with the purity of *ᶜarabiyya*.

This assumption can be further supported from another angle. Leo Spitzer pointed out that the Romance *ḫarǧas* occasionally mention the names of cities in Andalus and seem to reflect an urban milieu, in contrast to popular Romance love songs from Christian Europe, in which the environment reflected is basically rural.[20] The same remark can be made about the Arabic *ḫarǧas* in the present selection. In fifteen instances urban life and tastes are reflected. In *Ḫarǧa 3* the poet compares his beloved's eyes to violets, a cultivated flower often used as a metaphor for eyes or glances in classical Arabic poetry of an urban type (one is reminded of the "violet-eyed Aphrodite" of the *Greek Anthology*). In *Ḫarǧa 37*, a young dandy appears elegantly dressed and wearing perfumes; in *Ḫarǧa 10*, the dark complexion of the beloved is said to be so attractive that it calls out like the lips of a preacher addressing a teeming multitude; in *Ḫarǧa 13*, the lover speaks of walking through a bazaar; finally, in *Ḫarǧas 17, 28, 32,* and *40*, houses and neighborhoods are mentioned. In these examples the girl is usually in love with her neighbor and is unable to visit him, or, as in *Ḫarǧa 28*, the lover is standing at the door of his house (again, cf. the *Greek Anthology*) and attempts to entice his beloved inside in order to seduce him.

In contrast to the higher percentage of urban poems, there are only two in which a rural setting is suggested: in *Ḫarǧa 1* the lady refers to her lover as her "harvest" (Coll. Ar. *ġillah* > Sp. *guilla*. Even here the example is ambiguous), and in *Ḫarǧa 33* the lover complains that his dark-skinned lady has stolen his heart in the middle of a valley.[21] Curiously, this *ḫarǧa* is one of the most hauntingly popular of all, with its parallelistic repetition in alternate lines of the word *samrah* ('dark-skinned girl'). Thus a predominance of the urban over the rural theme can be detected in a large number of instances. This is significant, for, assuming that Arab folk poets actually adapted the style of the Christians in Andalus to the composition of popular poetry in Arabic, the adaptation in all likelihood must have occurred in the city, where peoples of different ethnic, religious, and cultural background mingled on an everyday basis, and not in the countryside, where peasants led a far more traditional and culturally segregated life.[22]

[20] Leo Spitzer, "The Mozarabic Lyric and Theodor Frings' Theories," *Comparative Literature* 4 (1952) 1-22, esp. 10.

[21] The word *wādī*, which in classical Arabic meant "valley," came to mean "river" in colloquial Andalusian. Hence my translation of *Ḫarǧa* 33 could conceivably be modified to "Dark-skinned girl, in the middle of a river." It is also possible that the meeting of the lovers in a *wādī* is a literary allusion to the scenario of ʿUḏrite poetry, in which poets often express their nostalgia for a *wādī* where they formerly trysted with their ladies.

[22] Referring to the origin of the *muwaššaḥs* Ibn Ḫaldūn says that they spread in Andalus, and that "the common people in the cities imitated them" (n. 19 above) 3.454.

A final motif of importance is the exclusive description, in the Arabic *ḫarǧas*, of the lovers as being dark-skinned (seven instances in all).[23] This motif may be contrasted, on the one hand with classical Arabic poetry in Andalus, in which fair-haired women were preferred and blondness, associated with the Umayyads, was considered an aristocratic trait, and on the other, with Romance *Ḫarǧa LI*[24] in which the beloved is described as having blond hair.

In sum, to the prosodic features of the Arabic *ḫarǧas* may be added certain generic and thematic characteristics, such as the feminine lyrical voice, the urban milieu, and the dark-skinned, and therefore essentially lower-class, protagonists typical of popular poetry in Romance. These features make it likely that our corpus reflects to some extent a type of authentically popular poetry which was prosodically modelled upon Romance folk poetry, and which possibly incorporated some of its themes, while others, such as the veil in *Ḫarǧa 1*, are typically Arabic. Furthermore, it is likely that this poetry had its point of origin in the towns. Along with the Romance *ḫarǧas* it constitutes a single tradition, and the very fact that a poetic corpus in the same meters and couched in the same stress-syllabic system of versification could fluctuate freely between two languages must mean that the choice of words in one language or the other may often have been determined not by grammatical but rather by metrical requirements. We thus seem to be dealing with a curiously bilingual poetic diction. The reason why the Arabs adopted the Christian style may in all likelihood be determined by music; that is, if a popular poet wished to sing a poem in Arabic to the tune of a well-known native melody, his Arabic poem would, plausibly, be forced into the mold of native prosody, particularly if the poet were an oral improviser, as may often have been the case. Once this authentic folk tradition became established and took root in colloquial Arabic, it was but a natural step for learned poets to imitate it in those forms known as *muwaššaḥ* and *zaǧal*; nevertheless, these two forms are derivative, and should be viewed as semi-learned imitations of an authentic popular tradition in colloquial Arabic reflected if not recorded in the Arabic *ḫarǧas*.

Department of Near Eastern Studies
University of California
Berkeley, California 94720, U.S.A.

[23] In *Ḫarǧas* 10f., 24, 28, 30, 33f.

[24] I follow the numeration used by Sola-Solé (n. 5 above).

MUDEJAR HISTORY TODAY: NEW DIRECTIONS

•

by Robert I. Burns, S.J.

I

The past twenty years have seen a renaissance of interest in the Spanish Moors: as Muslims under Islamic rulers,[1] as Mudejars or conquered subjects of medieval Christian states, as Moriscos or nominally Christian but residually Muslim subjects of early-modern Spain,[2] and across all three chronological periods as interculturally both shaper and shaped.[3] This interest owes something to the gratifying growth of medieval studies generally (not to mention the burgeoning of Arabic studies), the

Address comprising the opening session of the annual convention of the Society for Spanish and Portuguese Historical Studies, held at the Johns Hopkins University, 9-10 April 1976. The session was chaired by Julian Bishko (University of Virginia), with John Baldwin (Johns Hopkins University) and James Boswell (Yale University) as the formal commentators. I thank the American Council of Learned Societies, and the recommending American Historical Association, for their travel grant which allowed me to accept the invitation to address the international congress discussed here and preside at its first day; also the Spanish government's Consejo Superior de Investigaciones Científicas and the Diputación Provincial de Teruel, whose grant supported my stay during the congress and my travels within Spain; and the National Endowment for the Humanities under whose past and current grants I transcribed the documentary appendix for the Teruel address.

[1] A sampling of recent works must suffice. For Granada alone, Andrew Handler has ably covered the eleventh century in his *The Zirids of Granada* (Coral Gables 1974), while the later period is extensively studied by Rachel Arié, *L'Espagne musulmane au temps des Naṣrides (1232-1492)* (Paris 1973); by Cristóbal Torres Delgado, *El antiguo reino nazarí de Granada (1232-1340)* (Granada 1975); by Aḥmad Mujtār al-ᶜAbbādī, *El reino de Granada en la época de Muḥammad V* (Madrid 1973); and more cursorily by M. A. Ladero Quesada, *Granada: Historia de un país islámico (1232-1571)* (Madrid 1969). Ambrosio Huici Miranda closed his prolific life's production with an epic *Historia musulmana de Valencia y su región*, 3 vols. (Valencia 1970), and Guillem Rosselló Bordoy gave us both *L'Islam a les illes balears* (Palma 1968) and *Mallorca musulmana* (Palma 1973). There are special topics like Pedro Chalmeta's extensive *El señor del zoco en España* (Madrid 1973) and Henri Terrasse's collection of the Leopoldo Torres Balbás articles on *Ciudades hispanomusulmanas*, 2 vols. (Madrid 1971); large text-surveys like Anwar Chejne's *Muslim Spain* (Minneapolis 1974), and Gamal ᶜAbd al-Karum's *La España musulmana* (Madrid 1974); smaller surveys like those of W. M. Watt (1965) and Juan Vernet (1961); and numerous translations and editions of sources. Relations between Christian Spain and North Africa have their own bibliography, but Charles Dufourcq's *L'Espagne catalane et le Maghrib aux XIIIe et XIVe siècles* (Paris 1966) is already a classic, and the *Actas del coloquio hispano-*

shift toward viewing the Middle Ages as Mediterranean centered,[4] and the increasing exploration of medieval "sensibility" under the rubric of Christian perceptions of and attitudes toward Muslims and Islam.[5] Medievalists also realize now that the European and Arabic worlds constantly interacted, with serious implications for today's student of European art, letters, religion, institutions, folkways, and international relations. Currently the politics of oil may be sharpening interest in this interdependent and mutually acculturative past.

Mudejar studies, having lagged behind both Spanish Islamic and Morisco research, are beginning to flower. Their wider significance for the history of the West includes the neglected story of proto-colonialism, the meshing of disparate cultures and the processes of acculturation, the evolving history of "race" prejudice and handling of minorities, and the hidden or inner chapter of the Mudejar communities, as important purely in themselves as they were in bridging East and West. Various elements involved in the Mudejar story have come into prominence again today: a revived Arab world, the spectacle of mass flight of displaced persons and conversely of immigration, the universal problem of minorities and ethnic enclaves, and a debate throughout the Third World on colonialisms and their effects. We confront analogous

---

tunecino de estudios históricos (Madrid 1973) is valuable both for itself and as a harbinger of more to come. Finally, in analytic vein we have the extensive *Al-Andalus: Estructura antropológica de una sociedad islámica en occidente* (Barcelona 1976) of Pierre Guichard, and await the imminent completion of Thomas Glick's socio-anthropological and comparative book on Christian-cum-Islamic Spain. Among several partial or continuing bibliographies, Miguel de Epalza was able to log 650 Arabist books and articles in Spanish alone for the brief period 1960-1964 as a "Bibliografía general árabe e islámica en España," *Boletín de la asociación española de orientalistas* 2 (1966) 130-175.

2 Rachel Arié surveyed the first two decades of renewed Morisco interest in "Les études sur les morisques en Espagne à la lumière de travaux récents," *Revue des études islamiques* 35 (1967) 225-229. Names like Julio Caro Baroja, Tulio Halperín Donghi, Wilhelm Hoenerbach, Henri Lapeyre, and Juan Reglá suggest something of the riches of that period; the subsequent or current decade saw solid additions to the list, including the recent *Moriscos i agermanats* (Valencia 1974) by Eduard Císcar Pallarés and Ricard Garcia Càrcel which touches too on late Mudejarism, and Miguel de Epalza and Ramon Petit, eds., *Recueil d'études sur les moriscos andalous en Tunisie* (Madrid 1973).

3 Américo Castro's *España en su historia (cristianos, moros, y judíos)* is now a little over twenty years old in the translation by Edmund King which brought the topic of interculturation front and center for many people in the English-speaking world, as *The Structure of Spanish History* (Princeton 1954). Its present reappearance, mildly revised as *The Spaniards: An Introduction to their History* (Berkeley 1971), underlines the sustained interest and debate of which it is a part, and recalls as well the counterarguments of the great Claudio Sánchez Albornoz.

4 The works of Archibald Lewis and Solomon Goitein have been particularly influential, but a wide range of authors in geographical and topical specialties are the mainstay of the movement (David Herlihy, Robert Lopez, and Lynn White, jr. immediately come to mind as examples.)

5 That widening medieval bibliography has diversified into such fields as the response of theorists and intellectuals (M. T. d'Alverny, Norman Daniel, James Kritzeck, R. W. Southern); the crusades and multi-cultural crusader states, with Islamic response (Claude Cahen, Joshua Prawer, Emmanuel Sivan, some E. K. Setton co-authors); the eschatological-conversionist reaction (A. Cortabarría, Allan Cutler, E. R. Daniel), Byzantine attitudes (Theodore Khoury, Jean Meyendorff, Speros Vryonis, Jr.), the literary reflection, the theological dialogue, and public dispute.

crises and opportunities, with which we must again come to terms in a fashion both humane and practical.

To sustain and stimulate the renascent interest in Mudejarism, the Spanish government through its Consejo Superior de Investigaciones Cientificas has now committed itself to sponsoring biennially a week-long international congress, based upon daily position-papers by invited specialists, around which multiple contributions can center.[6] When the program committee of the Society for Spanish and Portuguese Historical Studies proposed devoting "an entire session" to my own books and articles on Mudejarism and to the interculturation they imply, I suggested instead a compromise combination: a report on the recent first congress, with special attention to my position-paper there in the context of my general work. While reviewing and celebrating a landmark "happening" in Mudejar researches, this would afford a wider basis for discussion and additions. A bibliographical review can furnish background for this double enterprise.

Hardly any bibliography of materials in book form exists about Mudejars. The classic was published over a hundred years ago: *Estado social y político de los mudéjares de Castilla, considerados en sí mismos y respecto de la civilización española* by the great Francisco Fernández y González.[7] In 250 pages of text, plus some 200 of appendices and documents, he discussed most of Spanish Mudejarism from its origins to the sixteenth century, covering politics, revolts, customs, art, letters, and relations with Christians. Still useful, indeed unique, it is now little more than an erudite introductory survey. When Isidro de las Cagigas gave us his two-volume *Los mudéjares* thirty years ago, he rightly complained that Fernández y González had been his only predecessor in this difficult field.[8] (Authors like Circourt, Pedregal y Fantini, and López Martínez deserve little serious notice today.)[9] But Cagigas soon lost the thread of Mudejarism by attempting to cover the

[6] Primer Simposio Internacional de Mudejarismo (details below).

[7] F. Fernández y González, *Estado social y político de los mudéjares* (Madrid 1866).

[8] Isidro de las Cagigas, *Los mudéjares*, 2 vols. (Madrid 1948-1949) 1.11. He includes a bibliography of sources, of ancient authors, and of contemporary writings; the latter is defective, omitting even Macho y Ortega (see n. 11 below) and older documentary articles like that of Eduardo Ibarra (1904). Gual Camarena (see n. 15 below) dismisses Cagigas's contribution as "muy flojo."

[9] Anne M. J. A. comte de Circourt, *Histoire des mores, mudejares et des morisques, ou des arabes d'Espagne sous la domination des chrétiens*, 3 vols. (Paris 1845-1848); A. Delgado Hernández, *Memoria sobre el estado moral y político de los mudéjares de Castilla* (Madrid 1864); and the superficial José Pedregal y Fantini, *Estado social y cultural de los mozárabes y mudéjares españoles* (Seville 1898) 33-59. Unfortunately such authors, like Mudejarism itself, do not fall within the scope of James T. Monroe's study of scholars and trends, *Islam and the Arabs in Spanish Scholarship (Sixteenth Century to the Present)* (Leiden 1970), though Cagigas is logically included and the wider Arabic theories of Fernández y González. More useful among older authors, but light, is Celestino López Martínez, *Mudéjares y moriscos sevillanos: Páginas históricas* (Seville 1935), and the address by Narciso Estenaga Echevarría, "Condición social de los mudéjares en Toledo durante la edad media," *Real academia de bellas artes y ciencias históricas de Toledo* 6 (1924) 5-27. Florencio Janer's *Condición social de los moriscos de España* (Madrid 1857) is now of very limited use for Mudejar history.

Reconquest story, from both Arabic and Christian sides. A reading of his page-by-page chapter-outlines reveals how surprisingly little he has to say about his professed topic; valuable for Reconquest history and for nuggets of passing information on Mudejarism, he does not surpass or rival Fernández y González. As a concomitant to the current outburst of Morisco studies, at least the final generation of Mudejars who were to metamorphose into Moriscos have attracted their own authors, notably M. A. Ladero Quesada in his collection of documents, *Los mudéjares de Castilla en tiempo de Isabel I.*[10]

Most of the serious research on Mudejarism is scattered in articles or occasionally as chapters in books. Outstanding among them is the posthumously published doctoral thesis of 1917 by Francisco Macho y Ortega, "Condición social de los mudéjares aragoneses (siglo xv)," the result of intense archival searches at the Archivo de protócolos of Zaragoza and the crown archives at Barcelona, in 65 pages of text and 112 of documents.[11] Valencia has been well served by the articles of Felipe Mateu y Llopis,[12] Leopoldo Piles Ros,[13] F. A. Roca Traver,[14] and (until his untimely death last year) Miguel Gual Camarena.[15] Juan Torres Fontes has opened

[10] M. A. Ladero Quesada, *Los mudéjares de Castilla* (Valladolid 1969), with 82 pages of introductory text.

[11] F. Macho y Ortega, in *Memorias de la facultad de filosofía y letras*, University of Zaragoza, 1 (1922-1923) 137-231; his text covers historical antecedents, *aljama* organization and functionaries, relations with the crown, Christian administrators, taxes, and seignorial *aljamas*. His "Documentos relativos a la condición social y jurídica de los mudéjares aragoneses," *Revista de ciencias jurídicas y sociales* 5 (1922) 143-160, 444-464 adds over fifty more documents from this century.

[12] The *Bibliografía de Felipe Mateu y Llopis, reunida en su LXX aniversario* (Barcelona 1972) allows full recovery of his Muslim and Mudejar contributions; its thousands of items are topically organized, and indexed; the orientation is numismatic. See especially Mateu y Llopis, "Nómina de los musulmanes de las montañas de Coll de Rates, del reino de Valencia, en 1409, según el libro de la colecta del morabatí del baile de Callosa," *Al-Andalus* 5 (1942) 299-335, and his "La repoblación del reino de Valencia en el siglo xiii y las monedas de tipo almohade," *Boletín de la sociedad castellonense de cultura* 28 (1952) 29-43.

[13] From his background as the preeminent specialist on Valencia's bailiff-general, Leopoldo Piles Ros has given us "La situación social de los moros de realengo en la Valencia del siglo XV," *Estudios de historia social de España* 1 (1949) 225-274, enlightening particularly on topics such as slaves, inheritance, and travel; and a register-paraphrase of over eight hundred fifteenth-century documents from that office (some in full transcription), *Estudio documental sobre el bayle general de Valencia, su autoridad y jurisdicción* (Valencia 1970); for Mudejars see pp. 35-48 and the many documents referred to there.

[14] Roca Traver's single article is the best short overview: "Un siglo de vida mudéjar en la Valencia medieval (1238-1338)," *Estudios de edad media de la corona de Aragón* 5 (1952) 115-208, with overlay map of the *morería* and an appendix of thirty documents; the categories are standard (politics, religion, social life, law, and particularly slavery) and the chronological sweep extended, but solidly based on primary materials and with original insights, incorporating as well some of the findings of Gual Camarena.

[15] Besides his articles bearing indirectly or partially on Mudejars, two have become standard in the bibliography. Miguel Gual Camarena, "Mudéjares valencianos, aportaciones para su estudio," *Saitabi* 7 (1949) 165-199, draws almost exclusively from the capitulations and *cartas pueblas*, in which he specialized, to survey the religious privileges, freedom of movement, law, and especially

the world of Murcia's Mudejars, especially in a seminal monograph-article;[16] Elena Lourie has spoken for the Balearics,[17] Pierre Guichard for Crevillente,[18] and (in an article from his doctoral thesis based on J. M. Lacarra's documents) Jean-Guy Liauzu for the Ebro Valley.[19] Lacarra himself is a pioneer on the Mudejars of Aragon proper by the careful pages, and maps of their distribution, in his volume about that province; Enrique Bayerri and J. M. Font Rius have done a similar service in the pages they devoted to the Mudejars of Tortosa.[20]

Around these central names are a galaxy of article-writers on special topics, places, or episodes;[21] general essayists;[22] local historians with a tangential chapter on their

---

taxes or rents of the thirteenth through the fifteenth centuries, with a comparative outline of Christian and Mudejar seignorial obligations. "Los mudéjares valencianos en la época del Magnánimo," in the proceedings of the *IV Congrés d'història de la corona d'Aragó*, 2 vols. (Palma 1959-1970) 1.466-494, is really a précis of a larger work he had in hand when he died, "El asalto a la morería de Valencia en 1455," based on over a hundred new documents. He also left unfinished a major study of the Mudejar rebel al-Azraq.

[16] His stream of articles and books often touch on Mudejar themes; the central study is Juan Torres Fontes, "Los mudéjares murcianos en el siglo xiii," *Murgetana* 17 (1961) 57-90, including the effects of reconquest upon occupations, emigration, ghettoization, rents, and the diminution and decline of the Mudejar community. Restrictions are also a theme of his "Moros, judíos, y conversos en la regencia de Don Fernando de Antequera," *Cuadernos de historia de España* 31 (1960) 60-90. His "El alcalde mayor de las aljamas de moros en Castilla," *Anuario de historia del derecho español* 32 (1962) 131-182, studies the main *qāḍī*, not the frontier official of his "El alcalde entre moros y cristianos del reino de Murcia," *Hispania* 88 (1960) 255-280. For Mudejar political history in this century see his *La reconquista de Murcia en 1266 por Jaime I de Aragón* (Murcia 1967).

[17] Elena Lourie, "Free Moslems in the Balearics under Christian Rule in the Thirteenth Century," *Speculum* 45 (1970) 624-649, where she establishes their presence in great numbers, quoting liberally from manuscripts of the Archivo de la corona de Aragón and the Archivo histórico de Palma for details of their society. See too her thesis below at n. 25.

[18] Pierre Guichard, "Un seigneur musulman dans l'Espagne chrétienne: Le '*ra'īs*' de Crevillente (1243-1318)," *Mélanges de la casa de Velázquez* 9 (1973) 283-334, which discovered and from extensive documentation in the Archivo de la corona de Aragón detailed the story of this Mudejar fief, concentrating mostly on its post-Castilian period (1296-1316) under James II of Aragon, with a long concluding section on Mudejar life and an appendix of nine manuscripts transcribed.

[19] J. G. Liauzu, "La condition des musulmans dans l'Aragon chrétien au XIe et XIIe siècles," *Hespéris-Tamuda* 9 (1968) 185-200, from his doctoral thesis, marred by a misunderstanding of the *exaricus* status.

[20] J. M. Lacarra, *Aragón: Cuatro ensayos* (Zaragoza 1960). Enrique Bayerri, *Historia de Tortosa y su comarca*, 8 vols. (Tortosa 1933ff.). J. M. Font Rius, "La comarca de Tortosa a raíz de la reconquista cristiana (1148): Notas sobre su fisionomía político-social," *Cuadernos de historia de España* 19 (1953) 104-128.

[21] Rachel Arié, "Quelques remarques sur le costume des musulmans d'Espagne au temps des naṣrides," *Arabica* 12 (1965) 244-261, and "Le costume des musulmans de Castille au XIIIe siècle d'après les miniatures du *Libro de ajedrez*," *Mélanges de la casa de Velázquez* 2 (1966) 59-69; cf. her book (n. 1 above). Manuel Acién Almansa, "Dos textos mudéjares de la serranía de Roda (1491)," *Cuadernos de estudios medievales* 2 (1974-1975) 245-257, on post-conquest documents in the Granadan Arabic dialect. Manuel Ardit Lucas, "El asalto a la morería de Valencia en el año 1455," *Ligarzas* 2 (1970) 127-138, from the municipal archives. Mariano Arribas Palau, *Musulmanes de Valencia apresados cerca de Ibiza en 1413* (Tetuán 1955). Arcadio García Sanz, "Mudéjares y moriscos en Castellón," *Boletín de la sociedad castellonense de cultura*

Mudejars;[23] and panelists whose papers are moving toward publication.[24] In the English-speaking world alone, three recent doctoral theses testify to the growth of interest about Arago-Catalonia's Mudejarism: Elena Lourie's "Christian Attitudes toward the Mudejars in the Reign of Aragon (1285-1291)" (Oxford 1968), Donald Thaler's "Mudejars of Aragon during the Twelfth and Thirteenth Centuries, ca.

---

28 (1952) 94-114, which distinguishes both the geographical groupings of local Muslims and the chronological phases of their decline, with special attention to the town *morería* established in 1404 and (a second step) 1438, seen from the municipal archives. Jean Gautier-Dalché, "Des mudejars aux morisques: Deux articles, deux méthodes," *Hespéris* 45 (1958) 271-289, a review article. Fernando de la Granja, "Una polémica religiosa en Murcia en tiempos de Alfonso el Sabio," *Al-Andalus* 31 (1966) 47-72, from a fragment on Ibn Rašīq's encounter with a missionary. Manuel Grau Monserrat, "Mudéjares castellonenses," *Boletín de la real academia de buenas letras de Barcelona* 19 (1961-1962) 251-273, a disappointing summary from standard authors but with an appendix of eleven manuscripts of the fourteenth and fifteenth centuries transcribed from the Archivo histórico eclesiástico de Morella. Winfried Küchler, "Besteuerung der Juden und Mauren in den Ländern der Krone Aragons während des 15. Jahrhunderts," *Gesammelte Aufsätze zur Kulturgeschichte Spaniens* 24 (1968) 227-256, attacked by Gual Camarena as derivative in "Depiste o plagio? " *Cuadernos de estudios medievales* 1 (1973) 132-133. M. L. Ledesma Rubió, "La población mudéjar en la vega baja de Jalón," *Miscelánea ofrecida a ilmo. sr. Dr. J. M. Lacarra y de Miguel* (Zaragoza 1968) 335-351, on the economic and legal situation, from Hospitaller manuscripts. Pilar León Tello, "Carta de población a los moros de Urzante," *Congreso [primer] de estudios árabes e islámicos: Actas* (Madrid 1964) 329-343, with the Arabic text in photo, transcription, and translation. P. L. Lloréns y Raga, "Los sarracenos de la Sierra de Eslida y Vall d'Uxó a fines del siglo XV," *Boletín de la sociedad castellonense de cultura* 43 (1967) 53-67, and his "La morería de Segorbe: Rentas de su mezquita," *ibid.* 49 (1973) 303-324. Pedro López Elum, "Apresamiento y venta de moros cautivos en 1441 por 'acaptar' sin licencia," *Al-Andalus* 39 (1969) 329-380, an episode documented from the Archivo del reino de Valencia concerning the imprisonment of slaves for begging alms through the *morerías* of Valencia without a license. J. A. Mitjavila, *Mossarabs, mudèixars, moriscos* (Valencia 1963), an address. Norma Mobarec Asfura, "Condición jurídica de los moros en la alta edad media española," *Revista chilena de historia del derecho* 2 (1961) 36-52, in which the restrictions and penalties circumscribing Mudejars in the eleventh and twelfth centuries are paralleled from *fueros* (Cuenca, Sepúlveda, Soria, etc.), but seen in sum as less onerous than the thirteenth century's *despojo*. M. A. Orti Belmonte, "El fuero de Córdoba y las clases sociales en la ciudad: Mudéjares y judíos en la edad media," *Boletín de la real academia de Córdoba* 25 (1954) 5-94. Leopoldo Torres Balbás, *Algunos aspectos del mudejarismo urbano medieval* (Madrid 1954), really an extensive article or very short monograph, his *discurso* for the Real Academia de Historia, and not narrowly focused on buildings like his usual articles (see n. 1 above). Relevant to both the Arabic and Mudejar past is Juan Vernet's phone-book inquiry via modern names; see for example his "Antropónimos de etimología árabe en el levante español: Ensayo metodológico," *Revista del instituto egipcio de estudios islámicos en Madrid* 11-12 (1963-1964) 141-147.

[22] For example the thought-provoking book on Valencia by Joan Fuster, *Poetes, moriscos, y capellans* (Valencia 1963), with original reflections on themes like Mudejar-Morisco language.

[23] A handy example is Rafael Esteban Abad, *Estudio histórico-político sobre la ciudad y comunidad de Daroca* (Teruel 1959), chap. 8.

[24] M. D. Cabanes Pecourt, "Aportación al estudio de la situación social de los mudéjares valencianos," is scheduled for publication in the proceedings of the 1970 Congresso Luso-espanhol de Estudos Medievais. Two papers by Agustín Nieto Fernández, "La morería de Orihuela durante el siglo XV" (on the new *morería*, including its lawsuits against Elche), and "Hermandad entre las aljamas de moros y las villas de la gobernación de Orihuela en el siglo XV," as well as my own study of rural Mudejars, will soon appear in the central volumes of the *Primer Congreso de Historia del País Valenciano*, vols. 1 and 4 to date (Valencia 1973-1975). "Socio-

1094-1276" (Princeton 1973), and James Boswell's "The Mudejars of the Crown of Aragon in the Mid-Fourteenth Century" (Harvard 1975).[25]

The revival of Mudejar studies comprises part of a wider enthusiasm for medieval Spanish history, a movement surveyed not long ago by C. E. Dufourcq and Jean Gautier-Dalché. In the United States this has now culminated, after fifty years of having to rely on R. B. Merriman's text, in the publication of two excellent histories of medieval Spain, respectively by Joseph O'Callaghan and Jocelyn Hillgarth.[26] The Mudejar revival also has as counterpart a lively new interest in Spain's allied minorities: the Mozarabs, Jews, Marranos, and Gypsies. Only an impressionistic indication of recent activity is possible here, to add dimension to our Mudejar preoccupation. The mysterious and "undocumented" Gypsies are the least accessible medieval Spanish minority; but Amada López de Meneses is illumining their immigration and their wanderings in the guise of pilgrims under passport-safeguards.

Almost simultaneously with the first international Mudejar congress, a first international congress on Mozarabs was held at Toledo, on themes in history, art, religion, literature, and music. This Arabized remnant of Visigothic Christendom (the Visigoths were having *their* first international congress that same summer at Dublin) corresponded in Spanish Islam to the Mudejar minority of the Christian north. Mozarabic liturgical research is abundant; J. M. Pinell has recently reviewed its findings and bibliography.[27] In 1972 Rome allowed selected Spanish churches to revive the Mozarabic Mass. In art Basilio Pavón is doing exciting work on the "parallelisms" between Mozarabic and Mudejar art, and on the Mozarabic role in both Arabic and Christian art. In historical study the bizarre voluntary Martyr

---

economic Structures and Continuity: Medieval Spanish Islam in the Tax Records of Crusader Valencia," my contribution to the invitational Conference on the Economic History of the Near East, Princeton University, will appear in the published proceedings of that conference.

[25] I have not read the theses of Professor Lourie (University of the Negev) or of Professor Boswell (Yale University). In Thaler's resumé, chap. 1 supplies background; chap. 2 covers Reconquest modalities and Mudejar distribution (where the royal forces conquered, there was less guerrilla warfare and Mudejars remained in the greatest number; they probably totaled under 20% of the population by mid-thirteenth century); chap. 3 considers *aljama* officials, functions, and degree of autonomy, and factors influencing social status; chap. 4 deals with the economy, especially in agriculture, including alodial and free-*exarici* farmers; chap. 5 covers relations with Christians (legal and economic equality, but with the thirteenth century a serious decline in social status due to ecclesiastical pressures, especially in rural areas).

[26] C. E. Dufourcq and Jean Gautier-Dalché, "Histoire de l'Espagne au moyen âge: Publications des années 1948-1969," *Revue historique* 245 (1971) 127-168, 443-482, and their "Les royaumes chrétiens d'Espagne au temps de la 'reconquista,' d'après les recherches récentes (1948-1969)," *ibid.* 248 (1972) 367-402; the sections on Arabic and Mudejar studies are disappointing. See also their "Économies, sociétés et institututions de l'Espagne du Moyen âge: Essai de bilan de la recherche d'après les travaux des quelques vingt dernières années," *Moyen âge* 79 (1973) 73-122, 285-319. J. O'Callaghan, *A History of Medieval Spain* (Ithaca 1975). Jocelyn Hillgarth, *The Spanish Kingdoms, 1250-1516*, 1: *1250-1410* (Oxford 1976). On eastern Spain Jerome Lee Shneidman, *The Rise of the Aragonese-Catalan Empire*, 2 vols. (New York 1970).

[27] *Diccionario de historia eclesiástica de España* 3 vols. to date (Madrid 1972-) 2.1302-1320, a segment of the larger study on "Liturgia."

Movement, solidly reorganized as a problem by Edward Colbert in 1962, recently elicited conflicting interpretations from Allan Cutler and James Waltz. In language Manuel Sanchis Guarner has distinguished himself on Valencian Mozarabic. After a half-century of relative quiescence, fresh finds of texts as well as the leadership of Álvaro Galmés de Fuentes has revitalized the study of *aljamiado* or Romance in Arabic script. The first international congress on *aljamiado-morisca* literature met at Oviedo in 1972; in 1975 the Modern Language Association's *Corónica* was able to publish a bibliography of twenty-nine items of "Aljamiado Studies Since 1970," with a discussion of resources and problems.

Hispano-Jewish studies have experienced steady progress, much of it duly reflected in their journal *Sefarad,* but this field too has now been enlivened. The two magisterial recent surveys of the Jews under Spanish Islam and under medieval Christian Spain, respectively by Eliyahu Ashtor and Yitzhak Baer, have moved from the obscurity of the original Hebrew into English. A series of special and local studies continue to deposit historical data (the names of Haim Beinart, I. S. Révah, Pedro Riera Vidal, and David Romano Ventura come to mind). The exploration of creative and literary productions associated with the school of J. M. Millás-Vallicrosa has borne rich fruit. And a revisionist reworking of the interpretative framework (not unrelated perhaps to the larger or European revision by Blumenkranz's "history of credible explanations") has brought changes or advances. Bernard Bachrach has upset the Visigothic-persecution consensus, for example, and Cutler has completed a large volume on the Christian tendency to associate Jew with Muslim and to react in parallel according to this guilt-by-association. Broad general progress can be seen in the first international congress of Sephardic studies at Madrid, which published its proceedings in 1970, and in the second congress held at San Diego in California in 1975.

Perhaps the liveliest field of Hispano-Judaic history has been Marrano studies: the collapse and conversion around 1400, and in 1492 the expulsion of the Jews (but not of the Conversos or converts, differing in this from the Mudejar-Morisco expulsion). Luis Suárez Fernández gave impetus to this inquiry with his corpus of expulsion documents; Julio Valdeón-Baruque tied the rise of a pogrom mentality to reaction against philosemitism during the Trastamar politico-social revolution. In the United States Benzion Netanyahu proposed the revisionist thesis that most Marranos were not secret Jews but hostile to Judaism (the Inquisition being rather a cause than a consequence of such secret groups as did exist). This has led Cutler to a cross-disciplinary probing of a dozen factors involved in the mass conversion to "an attractively semiticized Christian culture" and religion. Stephen Haliczer is concurrently developing the thesis that the expulsion owed little to general religious or nationalist causes, but must be explained by the crown's policy of strength through alliance with the municipal oligarchies; the precariously powerful convert element within these conflict-ridden oligarchies helped develop a defensive antisemitic program, including expulsion. In this theory the Inquisition was in part a crown expedient to protect its convert supporters.

It is no accident that progress in studying any one group triggers further activity in the others, or that all are illumined by our expanding knowledge not only about Islamic and Christian Spain but about the medieval Mediterranean world from Turkish Anatolia to Reconquest Sicily and to Languedoc and North Africa. Multiple activity in research about all the minorities of medieval Spain suggests also that it is time for yet another "First International Congress": a joint symposium or convergence of specialties on these analogous and interrelated communities of Spain and their host-cultures.[28]

II

The first of the series of international congresses designed to foster Mudejar studies gathered in the municipal Casa de Cultura at Teruel from 14 through 19 September 1975. Clustered around its Mudejar towers in the mountains halfway between Valencia and Zaragoza, Teruel was just difficult enough of access to test the serious purpose of some two hundred symposiasts, mostly Spaniards but with representatives from a half-dozen other lands. Government patronage assured both its solid financing and the continuity of the series. Each morning saw a succession of papers from nine until noon, resuming after lunch until time for late dinner. Previous distribution of the papers in Spanish allowed each speaker to review his main points and then to enter into discussion with the many experts present. The proceedings, covered by television, radio, and press, are scheduled for eventual publication in Spanish.[29]

Subject matter divided between Mudejar history and Mudejar art, the latter often with illustrative slides. Position-papers in history covered the kingdoms of Aragon, Castile, Valencia, and Murcia, while correlative contributions focused on Mudejars of places like Calatayud, Málaga, and Seville. Two discourses were devoted to "the Mudejar legacy" in South America, and one to Mudejarism "in language and literature." In art, two authorities spoke on ceramics; several concentrated on elements of some selected church, monastery, or palace; and others delved into arcane topics such as ornamental motifs, carpentry, Almohad continuity, Mudejarism in Gothic

[28] Research on the Christian ecclesial community continues so vital and productive as to defy brief summary. Monastic studies alone, from cartularies to multi-volume histories, are formidable (represented in the United States especially by Julian Bishko). St. John's University in Minnesota has just microfilmed 3,000 monastic Spanish manuscripts, largely from eastern Spain; the University of California is conducting a similar project on canonical manuscripts. The military orders, which also had their multi-city first international congress recently in Spain, are enjoying a particular renaissance (English-language contributors include James Brodman, Derek Lomax, Anthony Luttrell, A. J. Forey, and Joseph O'Callaghan).

[29] The heads of state were listed as official presidents of the event, associated with various heads of ministries, the governor of the province, and other luminaries. Actual direction fell to the Consejo Superior and to Teruel's Diputación or provincial government; the single most important organizer was Professor Emilio Sáez of the University of Barcelona, who is also editing the *acta*.

painting, and a case history of Reconquest settlement as creating architectural forms which in turn helped shape Spanish character.

J. M. Lacarra, Zaragoza University's celebrated medievalist, opened the congress with an address on the Mudejars of the upland Kingdom of Aragon, a component of the several federated realms or Crown of Aragon. "Very little" has appeared about them, and direct studies "hardly exist," despite their "high density" from the twelfth to the sixteenth century (some 15 percent of the population at the expulsion). To correct this situation, "abundant" documentation awaits in civil and ecclesiastical archives, including parish, cathedral, military order, municipal, and family collections. These manuscripts concern farmers, though rarely of the landlord class, rather than the urban merchant or artisan Mudejars; information on royal *aljamas* is "particularly deficient."

The surrender privileges evolved early here (for example, at Naval in 1099) along the lines followed by Alfonso VI at Toledo and the Cid at Valencia; they spread widely under Alfonso the Warrior. The few unransomed captive or slave Moors tended over the twelfth and thirteenth centuries to assimilate to these privileged *mauri pacis*; Murcia's surrender closed Aragon's era of easy raid-acquisition of the *mauri capti. Fuero* codes tended to treat Christians, Muslims, and Jews roughly alike. Conversion was rarely sought, and even opposed, before the Mendicant period; distinguishing signs were not locally legislated before 1301. A Mudejar *amīn* administered each community, appointed for life by a lord or sometimes elected for a brief period (Zaragoza's *merino* system being an exception). Mudejars farmed "the richest lands," such as the riverine *vegas* of Huesca, Teruel, and Zaragoza, while Christians clustered at the strategic centers or ran stock in the uplands. Areas of mixed population seem due rather to unavailability of Muslim replacements after the damage of fourteenth-century wars. Borja's Mudejars divided the *huerta* equally with a Christian group, alternating water-distribution at week's end; they had no separate quarter in the city.

The Mudejar was as determined to keep his land as the Christian share-proprietor was anxious to retain him for his irrigation skills. We need an extended analysis of the many Muslim-Christian sharecropper contracts now in manuscript, to trace their evolution and regional varieties and to compare them with purely Christian contracts. Preconquest Islamic customs heavily influenced them. Similar study is needed on the process by which the nobles, church, and orders later absorbed Mudejar freemen into protective vassalage, involving submission to the church tithe. Taxes and rents require much clarification. An investigation of the Tarazona-Borja region concluded that Mudejars paid more than Christians and that lay lords demanded more than ecclesiastical. Royal *aljamas* there tended to pay a lump sum, sustained by bonds issued at six to eight percent interest. Throughout Aragon crown jurisdiction became increasingly more express after the *cortes* of 1300. From that period also urban Mudejars diminished; Zaragoza had 202 households in 1300, 101 in 1365, and 120 in 1495 or three percent of the city's population.

Seville University's expert, M. A. Ladero Quesada, presented to the congress the

Mudejars of Castile. Noting how Mudejar research for his regions had long since ceased and must now lurch forward from this "dead stop," he too called for wide-ranging investigation among the unstudied manuscripts in municipal, ecclesiastical, nobiliary, and military-order archives, together with a "new eye" for viewing them. As illustration he offered a demographic-geographic profile for his area and a survey of the "social situation" vis-a-vis the Christians. He found Mudejar communities flourishing from the late eleventh century to a high point at the mid-thirteenth, decaying decisively thereafter under the assimilative pressures of the crown and the lure of renascent Granada. By the sixteenth century, despite a reputation for prolific families and despite a concomitant population rise among Europeans, Mudejar numbers had become static. Analysis of 120 Mudejar places in fifteenth-century tax lists reveals 38 with fewer than twenty households each, 30 with twenty-to-fifty, 13 with fifty-to-a-hundred, and only 7 with over a hundred (2 of these with over two hundred). Breaking his figures down according to diocese-regions, Professor Ladero Quesada located 22 percent of this Mudejar population in Toledo-Cuenca, another 22 percent in Avila-Burgos-Palencia-Segovia and some military-order areas, 20 percent in Calahorra-Osma-Sigüenza, 17 percent in Cartagena, 11 percent in Cádiz-Córdoba-Seville, and 5 percent in Badajoz-Coria. The military orders had large numbers, difficult to assess exactly. Each of the six regions repays close study. Burgos for example displayed many flourishing *morerías*, probably not as holdovers from conquest but the result of relatively recent immigration north from Toledo; the artisan class and most of the important urban groups were there. Toledo's Mudejars had begun to flee from bad conditions in the twelfth century, partly to the north but much more to the south, and in the thirteenth century to both south and east.[30]

The second part of Professor Ladero Quesada's address comprised a survey of all the legislative or analogous data bearing on the social condition of the free Muslims, familiar data but industriously schematized for us. Thus we see that civil legislation began to urge or impose ghettos from 1268; from 1335 church synods reinforced the trend; by 1412 the principle was established. Practical or non-legal documentation, on the other hand, indicates that application of these laws was not only uneven but "seguramente mal." The campaign against Muslim nurses for Christian children began early, by laws of 1252, 1258, 1335, 1386, and 1465. Prohibition of Muslim surgeons, physicians, and pharmacists ran from 1322 to 1465, with the expected exceptions and defiance. Legislation curbing friendly contacts multiplied in a similar rhythm – affecting for example weddings, funerals, public baths, heirs, and executors of wills. Domestic service was increasingly restricted; intergroup prostitution or even mingling of sexes (as for a Christian woman to enter unaccompanied a Mudejar ghetto) became more stringently forbidden. From the time of Alfonso XI Muslims could not take Romance first-names. Laws progressively closed trades to them, more so than to

[30] The statistics of this part can be read with profit in conjunction with Ladero Quesada's "Datos demográficos sobre los musulmanes de Granada y Castilla en el siglo XV," *Anuario de estudios medievales* 8 (1972-1973) 480-490.

Jews; from 1412 Mudejars could not even be carpenters, merchants, butchers, or tailors. The most restrictive period for such legislation ran through the century following 1410. Yet the actual life situation did not always reflect this Platonic world of law; even the kings used Muslim carpenters for their military engineering. And there was always a measure of popular tolerance.

No advance in our knowledge of Mudejarism generally or of this debated situation of law versus life is possible, Ladero Quesada argues, until local archives are exploited for grass-roots data. In the interim he offers two general conclusions. (1) Castile's Mudejars "were a very small minority in the country," subsisting at the margin of national life and nowhere near as important as their artistic contribution or our romantic imagination might suggest. (2) "Social marginizing" of the Mudejars "was on the increase from the mid-thirteenth century, and reached its farthest point in the fifteenth century." Though law and life always diverged to some degree, the multiplication of social stigmas (in dress, housing, names, work, food, sex, and social life) in these years probably threw the balance progressively against intercultural exchange and amity.

Juan Torres Fontes, Murcia University's prolific author on the region's Reconquest era,[31] selected a more specific topic for his presentation, based on documentation in Murcia's municipal archives: "The *Hermandad* of Moors and Christians for Ransoming Captives." During the late fourteenth century the Murcia-Granada frontier had fallen into a chaos of mutual raiding. People were snatched into slavery by terrorists out for profit or for reprisal, by hooligans bent on adventure, and by indiscriminate raiding against both sides by "those sons of perdition commonly called Almugavars." No solution could be attempted on the Christian side of the border, where both Christians and Mudejars were disappearing, partly because local Mudejars conspired with Muslim raiders and targeted the wealthier victims, but mostly because the overlord nobles and cities jealously resisted any threat to their privileges which might ensue from cooperation with other elements of their faction-ridden society. King Martin I intervened; his procurator Guillem Martorell convoked Mudejar and Christian authorities in the Orihuela church of the Knights of Santiago in 1399, eventually negotiating a pact by which the region's Mudejar *aljamas* agreed to recover or ransom any Christian captives, while the Christians undertook to do the same for Muslims. Where culprits kidnapping Christians proved to be themselves Christians or mixed Christians-and-Muslims, the Christian communities would have to repay the *aljamas* the corresponding whole or partial ransom.

The pact succeeded; Granadan raids fell off sharply. In one episode, raiders bearing off a Moor of Elche were captured and hanged by Elchan Christians. When the Castilian marquis of Villena persisted in kidnapping Mudejars for exorbitant ransoms (Ahmad Arrany was recovered at the cost of 119 Aragonese florins), the agreement was extended to include Castilian frontier areas. Renegotiated every two

[31] See n. 16 above.

years under royal pressure, the terms entered into a general treaty of 1405 between Martin of Aragon, Martin of Sicily, and Muḥammad of Granada. During the growing turmoil of the fifteenth century the agreement declined into a dead letter, with partisan bands and armed Mudejars roaming the roads – a situation to which Queen Isabella addressed herself in a document of 1477 transcribed by Torres Fontes as part of his address.

Besides the *ponencias*, other history "communications" deserve passing notice. Manuel Acién Almansa and José López de Coca drew upon a half-dozen local archives to offer a paper on Mudejars of the Málaga region in the late fifteenth century, just after the general surrenders. Here the crown deliberately evacuated cities while promoting Mudejar rural presence, especially in the commercial-export farmlands; incoming Christians upset this policy by fraud and usurpation, while their greedy scramble for stock pasturage unbalanced the previous, mutually advantageous arrangements between frontier Muslims and Christians. Violations and sly reinterpretations by authorities soon killed the surrender-treaty privileges. Robbery and harrassment reflected the Europeans' freely expressed scorn for their despised ex-adversaries, so that mere coexistence became difficult. The Mudejars responded by passive resistance (moving outside the region or to the few seignorial lands inside, neglecting the obligation to mount guards or to reveal taxable goods, resisting their collaborationist colleagues and leaders) and in 1500 by revolt. Demographic and tax data help trace this story. Antonio Collantes de Terán offered a brief set of notes on Sevillian Mudejars, much of it drawn from local archives. He denied the existence, long accepted, of a separate city-quarter for Seville's Muslims before the fifteenth century, for example; and he located 65 percent of the Mudejar labor force in the construction crafts (slaves concentrated mostly at the shipyards, and free Muslims prominent in maintenance of the Alcazar).

Of the four *ponencias* precommissioned on history, my own covered the thirteenth-century Mudejars of the kingdom of Valencia – the provinces of Mediterranean Spain below Tortosa and above Murcia. Since my books and articles comprised the first extensive work on pre-Isabellan Spanish Mudejars for over a century, the first to reconstruct in detail the range of a complete Mudejar society, and the first to introduce into Mudejar study methodologies of the Bloch-Febvre school currently in vogue, my address touched those three themes: methodologies for Mudejar data, ten major general conclusions about Valencian Mudejars which emerge from two decades of archival work, and a review of illustrative narrative topics in Mudejar social history. From the first five years of King James's twenty-year run of registered documentation on this conquered kingdom, fifty unpublished documents were transcribed as appendix, each with a paraphrase-summary in Spanish. To move from the legislative and theoretical aspects of Mudejarism conceived as a univocal phenomenon, the paper insisted, a researcher must focus upon some such place and time sufficiently restricted to allow mastery of all relevant data. This involves digging relentlessly, year after year, through local archives, sifting out a kaleidoscope of

Mudejar fragments within the more unlikely documents, fitting each bit into its *Sitz im Leben*, and interrelating them to discern patterns.

III

The Valencian Mudejars under James the Conqueror and his son Peter during the second half of the thirteenth century constituted a full generation, just conquered and struggling to survive as a community against acculturative odds, evolving and coping as the rhythm of European settlement varied, and responding from diverse geographical and social backgrounds. Though King James merely followed inherited patterns of Mudejarism, common around the Mediterranean periphery in handling minorities, his project became in fact qualitatively different from other models – by reason of the sheer bulk of the Islamic majority here, the sophistication of their commercial-urban society, and the entrenched military power they retained under the deceptive overgrid of Christian administration. The Valencian situation long remained open and dynamic, unlike the progressively more static and restrictive Mudejarism of the fourteenth and fifteenth centuries. Among factors lending special fascination to this time-place sector is the carapace of Mudejar castle-fiefs, the persistence of a clerisy or educated notable-*faqīh* stratum, the circumstance that Christian settlers took land mostly by small holdings rather than by the impersonally large latifundia of the Castilian conquests, and the chiliastic temper of mid-century Europe which briefly lent the conquerors high self-confidence and conversionist hopes.

I can only indicate, not outline here, the variegated treasure recoverable from the thousands of available documents – gold not lying in traditional veins but requiring an imaginative eye to discern and novel processes to leach from its rocky matrix. Here is a task to excite the *Annales* structuralist, the "total" historian in search of a social ecology and collective psychology, ambitioning not the conquest but the re-creation of lost worlds. The 17 chapters and 225 subchapters of my *Islam under the Crusaders: Colonial Survival in the Thirteenth-Century Kingdom of Valencia* (Princeton 1974) attempted such a task. The fragments of evidence allowed reconstruction of the Mudejar administrative-physical setting (such as districts, landscapes, houses), human geography (such as population figures, ethnic strains, occupations, classes), the religious and legal "social ecology" (including the paradox of an appeals system, the working of custom, mosque education, religious personnel, and the size and number of mosques), the complex siting of Muslim lords within the Christian feudal order and their relationship to the city organisms, and even a view of the underlying establishment or political-cultural-religious-economic elite. As my previous volumes on *The Crusader Kingdom of Valencia: Reconstruction on a Thirteenth-Century Frontier* (Cambridge, Mass. 1967) had concentrated upon the Christian influx, as viewed in its use of religious institutions to transform or acculturate the environment, *Islam* in turn focused upon the Mudejar society itself, as traumatically adjusting to its subjugation.

The successor of *Islam* in my Princeton series, *Medieval Colonialism: Post-Crusade Exploitation of Islamic Valencia*, attempted something different – to penetrate more deeply the life patterns of all classes of Mudejars at specific entry points, exploiting the abundant tax documentation for thirteenth-century Valencia. Labor services, crop shares, tolls, and livestock charges help reveal the rural scene, as shop rents, fines, and commercial fees reveal the urban. Social life is reflected in baths and bakeries, prisons and prostitution, taverns, treasure-hunting, and military service. The marvelous waterworks of the Valencian kingdom appear in irrigation charges, mill rents, and land transfers. Mudejar industries appear, from cloth-dyeing and paper manufacture to ceramics and wine-making. The head tax, community levies, and general revenue lists encourage demographic investigation. As a side product, Mudejar tax documentation affords a panorama of Arago-Catalan government finance and fiscal techniques, at the moment they meshed with Almohad practice. The fourth book of this series, forthcoming from Princeton, *The Crusader-Muslim Predicament: Colonial Confrontation in the Conquered Kingdom of Valencia*, devotes itself to Mudejar-Christian interaction both antagonistic and friendly, and to the problems of intolerance and acculturation – themes which depend upon that prior reconstruction of the two conflicting local societies, if we are to transcend the easy generalizations of the past.

In my *ponencia*, instead of reviewing the narrative panorama, I stressed ten generic framing conclusions as themes for discussion. (1) King James did not break with the Mudejar pattern and inaugurate an era of harsh spoliation, as claimed by such influential authors as Fernández y González, Cagigas, and Menéndez Pidal. With rare exceptions the communities throughout the kingdom won and exercised the full range of Mudejar privileges, both after the crusade and after subsequent revolts under James or his son Peter. One must look therefore to later generations for such changes as extreme ruralization, exploitation by seignorial landlords, emigration of the intellectual and city classes, and radical redistribution of Mudejar population. (2) There was no emptying of the northern third of the kingdom, nor of cities generally, as Lapeyre, Sobrequés, and Grau Monserrat hold. Nor was there the general exiling and drifting away which characterized the neighboring Murcian conquest. On the contrary, Valencian authorities labored to retain and increase the number of Mudejar farmers and artisans, mounting a movement of Mudejar immigration which disturbed crown and church, though both eventually became willing accomplices themselves.[32]

(3) The first generation after the crusade – some forty years – differed consequently in its social psychology and institutions, or in its manner of presence, from later generations. (4) A stratum of Muslim castellans, military aristocrats, and fiefdoms flourished during the early generation in parallel to the Christian feudal and

[32] See R. I. Burns, "Immigrants from Islam: The Crusaders' Use of Muslims as Settlers in Thirteenth-Century Spain," *American Historical Review* 80 (1975) 21-42. See also *idem, Islam under the Crusaders* (Princeton 1974) chap. 7.

town structure, providing a protective backbone for this complex of attitudes or social personality.[33] Játiva and then its successor Montesa, both under the Banū ᶜĪsā dynasty, became the new center of Valencian political Mudejarism.

(5) Disintegrative acculturation of Mudejar institutions can already be discerned in these early years, altering Mudejar social forms; this is signaled for example by the rise of the *amīn* as liaison between the autonomous local *aljamas* and Christian authorities. This functionary, later to develop into effective governor of each *aljama* and the key figure in the Mudejar political system, began now as a lowly tax-collector. His evolution shows parallels with that of his counterpart in the crusaders' Holy Land, the village *ra'īs*. His assimilation to the Christian notion of bailiff, with a consequent rise in real power, can be traced during these early years. The concomitant evolution of local *aljamas* into counterfeits of the corporative Christian communes can also be seen in its beginnings at this early time; Amari noted a similar tendency in Christian-Islamic Sicily. But these extrinsic symptoms are relatively insignificant beside the essential distortions by which the conquest disoriented Valencia's Islamic self-vision and social equilibrium.[34]

(6) The conquerors did not yet exploit these Muslims economically; indeed, the Valencian Mudejar was no worse off than his Christian counterpart in the matter of taxes, and probably better off than many Muslims had been during the previous Almohad disintegration. (7) Despite or perhaps because of these circumstances, and despite an osmotic-assimilative and friendly *convivencia* of Christian with Muslim here, strong revulsion divided the two peoples. This went not only beyond the conventional attitudes or expressions of mutual contempt, but even beyond expected hostility arising from religious differences; it reflects a basic antagonism of cultures in a classic position of conflict. This antagonism eventually found violent expression in riots and pogroms against Mudejar *aljamas*, affecting every part of the Valencian kingdom around 1275. Previously dismissed as a few localized outbursts connected with the revolt of Valencia's Mudejars, the riots were a universal movement extending over several months; they wreaked widespread damage and took on overtones of revolt against the crown's Mudejar policies.[35]

(8) It is possible to map the centers of Mudejar society and assess their relative importance as well as prosperity, and to construct models at least suggesting Mudejar population totals, from tax evidence like the besant poll-tax. But this area of research is as yet troublesome and unsatisfactory. (9) By anthroponymical investigation, one

[33] Besides the chapters of part 3 in *Islam*, see R. Burns, "Le royaume chrétien de Valence et ses vassaux musulmans (1240-1280)," *Annales: Économies, sociétés, civilisations* 28 (1973) 199-225, and "The Muslim in the Christian Feudal Order: The Kingdom of Valencia," *Studies in Medieval Culture* 5 (1975) 105-126.

[34] See R. Burns, "Spanish Islam in Transition: Acculturative Survival and its Price in the Christian Kingdom of Valencia, 1240-1280," in *Islam and Cultural Change in the Middle Ages*, ed. Speros Vryonis, Jr. (Wiesbaden 1975) 87-105.

[35] The data is gathered and discussed in R. Burns, "Social Riots on the Christian-Moslem Frontier: Thirteenth-Century Valencia," *American Historical Review* 66 (1961) 378-400.

can discover many individuals from the class of city-notables, discerning in some cases the leading families of a region or town and their relative balance of representatives within the common council. (10) Far more information is available about Valencian Mudejar officials, social strata, diet, cemeteries, houses, livestock, irrigation, slaves, occupations, crops, language, money, and the mutual passage of converts between Christianity and Islam (to select topics at random) than we have hitherto imagined.[36]

Because these larger themes are fascinating and illustrate the opportunities open in Mudejar research, I have devoted more space to them here. The bulk of the *ponencia*, however, explored a range of lesser or special topics, such as the office of *mushrif* or the tax structure for the Biar *aljama*. My conclusion noted, as I note again, that the archives of Mediterranean Spain hold a great treasure of manuscripts not only for the thirteenth century but for the reigns of James II and his successors. Like the thirteenth-century crusaders and pioneer settlers, a small army of doctoral candidates might forage among these riches for many years, to their own delight and instruction and for the recovery of this fundamental chapter of our Mediterranean past.

Department of History
University of California
Los Angeles, California 90024, U.S.A.

[36] Besides *Islam* and *Colonialism*, passim, see for example R. Burns, "Baths and Caravanserais in Crusader Valencia," *Speculum* 46 (1971) 442-458. On the movement between Christianity and Islam see my articles: "Renegades, Adventurers, and Sharp Businessmen: The Thirteenth-Century Spaniard in the Cause of Islam," *Catholic Historical Review* 58 (1972) 341-366; "Journey from Islam: Incipient Cultural Transition in the Conquered Kingdom of Valencia (1240-1280)," *Speculum* 25 (1960) 337-356; and "Christian-Islamic Confrontation in the West: The Thirteenth-Century Dream of Conversion," *American Historical Review* 76 (1971) 1386-1434.

In the X Congrés d'Història de la Corona d'Aragó at Zaragoza (September 1976), Roser Argemí d'Abadal showed how the Tortosa-Ebro Valley Mudejars suffered increasing economic exploitation from their feudal lords during the thirteenth century, despite legal guarantees; and Henri Bresc traced in Sicilian "Mudejarism" the same patterns found by Burns and others in Mediterranean Spain; both papers will appear in the *acta*. The Primer Congreso Internacional Islamo-Cristiano (September 1974) offered a striking symbol of the current rapprochement in Spanish Islamic-Christian studies by opening the (mosque) cathedral of Córdoba to a solemn Islamic Friday service, for the first time since the city's conquest by King St. Ferdinand in 1236.

THE PATHWAY TO ADVENTURE

•

by D. H. Green

The polarity of the medieval romance and the resulting tension between the world of the court and the realm of adventure are well-known features and have often been commented upon. The court from which the hero sets out on his wanderings and to which he may return at intervals or at the close of the narrative may be an idealized world, its material and moral refinement may surpass contemporary reality at many turns, yet it remains recognizably the world of twelfth-century feudalism. Wolfram may show us more of this contemporary world than his colleagues (the geography of *Parzival* has room therefore for Scotland and Normandy, Aragon and Ghent, Chichester and Regensburg),[1] but he certainly does not differ from them in kind. By contrast, the realm of adventure is remote from feudal society; it is a solitary world of inhospitable woods and deserted tracts where the knight encounters giants, dwarfs and monsters and where the unexpected is the norm. These two narrative poles are familiar to us, but what is perhaps not quite so obvious is the technical problem which the author of any romance faced in constructing a bridge between them, in conducting his hero from the world of the court to a realm governed by totally different laws, since the more marvellous and exotic he made the latter the more difficult he would find it to plot a convincing route by which his hero gained his privilege of entry into such a magical realm. But to plot this route is precisely one of the functions of the knightly quest, the dominant theme of so many romances,[2] so that courtly authors could hardly shirk the question of how to establish a narrative connection between these two poles, how to describe the knight's journey from feudal reality to a world of enchantment in a manner which would invite, if not the audience's belief, at least their willing suspension of disbelief. It has been shown that Wolfram, by his employment of place-names, forged a link between his fabulous world and the world of reality.[3] The purpose of this essay is to suggest that a wider

This article develops in extended form the argument that I put forward in *Der Weg zum Abenteuer im höfischen Roman des deutschen Mittelalters*, Veröffentlichung der Joachim Jungius-Gesellschaft der Wissenschaften (Göttingen 1974).

[1] Full details are given by M. Wynn, "Geography of Fact and Fiction in Wolfram von Eschenbach's *Parzivâl,*" *Modern Language Review* 56 (1961) 29.

[2] See F. Ohly, "Die Suche in Dichtungen des Mittelalters," *Zeitschrift für deutsches Altertum* 94 (1965) 171ff.

[3] Wynn 29.

range of narrative methods was available to medieval authors and that, in different degrees, they all faced the same kind of problem: how was the crucial transition into the realm of adventure to be convincingly described? [4]

It might be objected that to picture a medieval author as worried by the narrative problem of how best to persuade his audience to put aside their doubts is to attribute to both author and audience a higher degree of critical judgment than is credible. I doubt the force of this objection, partly because of the skilled use made of rhetoric by these authors as a means of consciously controlling their listeners' reactions, and partly because Thomas of Britain, for example, expressly claims for himself a feature which is certainly present in other poets: that *raisun* is his highest criterion and that he is willing to be judged by this yardstick.[5] The poets we are concerned with were prepared to take their listeners' possible responses into account and equally anxious to control these responses in accordance with their overall intentions. Moreover, in the particular case of plotting the transition from reality to fantasy we have one piece of contemporary "autobiographical" evidence to show that one courtly author at least was perfectly aware that the realm of Celtic marvels was non-existent and that there was no means of gaining access to it from the world of humdrum reality.

I refer to the well-known passage in Wace's *Roman de Rou*[6] where the Anglo-Norman poet describes how he once set out in search of the miraculous fountain of Berenton in the forest of Brecheliant, famous in the tales of the Bretons. Wace tells us that it is usual to see fairies there[7] (if what the Bretons say is true) and his description of how a miraculous storm can be brought about by sprinkling water on a stone[8] accords not merely with a local legend attested by other authors,[9] but also with the episode of the magic well in Chrétien's *Yvain*. The poet's manner of describing what he is supposed to find at the fountain adequately reveals his own attitude to this Celtic marvel, for he stresses his distance by firmly placing it in the past (6405: "Por co soleient pluie aueir, / Issi soleit iadis ploueir"), by slyly hinting that the Bretons may not be telling the truth (6410: "Se li Breton nos dient ueir"), by referring to their accounts as mere fables (6396: "Donc Breton uont souent

[4] My approach has little in common with the short survey of O. Brückl, "Betrachtungen über das Bild des Weges in der höfischen Epik: Einführung in die Problematik," *Acta Germanica* 1 (1966) 1ff. It also differs from the approach of H. R. Patch, *The Other World According to Descriptions in Medieval Literature* (Cambridge, Mass. 1950), who is more concerned with the constituent elements of topography and their origins than with the narrative problem of plotting a credible pathway to such a realm. Nor am I concerned here with the possibility that the miraculous may impinge upon the world of the court (as in the opening of *Sir Gawain and the Green Knight*). My problem concerns essentially the knight's quest taking him into the world of the unknown.

[5] See J. Bédier, ed., *Le Roman de Tristan par Thomas* (Paris 1902-1905) v. 2151ff.

[6] Wace, *Roman de Rou,* ed. H. Andresen (Heilbronn 1877-1879) 2 v. 6395ff.

[7] *Ibid.* 6409.

[8] *Ibid.* 6399ff.

[9] Cf. the contribution by C. Foulon, "Wace," *Arthurian Literature in the Middle Ages,* ed. R. S. Loomis (Oxford 1959) 100.

fablant") and by saying outright that there is no rational explanation of the miracle which they claim (6408: "Mais io ne sai par quel raison"). These reservations prepare us for the final outburst where he accuses as foolish both the so-called miracle and himself for being credulous enough to search it out:

> La alai io merueilles querre,
> Vi la forest e ui la terre,
> Merueilles quis, mais nes trouai,
> Fol m'en reuinc, fol i alai,
> Fol i alai, fol m'en reuinc,
> Folie quis, por fol me tinc. (6415)

This evidence cannot simply be dismissed by a generalizing reference to Wace's "Norman realism," for the shrewd skepticism he reveals here is comparable with the many doubts voiced by others (clerical historians especially) about the fabulous marvels attributed to Arthur.[10] The doubts felt by Wace could be entertained by others, so that courtly authors would have to take them into account and make their narrative dispositions accordingly.

In one sense, the "geographical" difficulty facing these poets (how to plot the passage from one realm to another) may be compared with a "historical" problem with which they also had to cope. Just as the fabulous realm of adventure had to be given some kind of links with the world of geographical reality, so could their fabulous plots be given some measure of credibility by the provision of links with history. In Lamprecht's *Alexanderlied* the suggestion of historical truth is mainly conveyed by biblical references[11] (since these are generally tied to specific places it is admittedly difficult to distinguish in this case between history and geography), Thomas's *Tristan* is characterized by its frequent allusions to contemporary history under Henry II,[12] while Wolfram's *Parzival* abounds in similar allusions, some obvious, others less so (as in the case of Richard Lionheart or the crusading movement).[13] The historical references in these as in other romances act as a temporal frame in which the narrative is set and which confers a degree of historical credibility on the events which it contains.

Yet in another sense this comparison operates to the disadvantage of the "geographical" problem which we are considering, since this problem constitutes a more pressing difficulty for the author of a romance. In the case of history a few general allusions are sufficient to suggest a temporal setting for his narrative; but whereas

[10] On this see W. F. Schirmer, *Die frühen Darstellungen des Arthurstoffes* (Cologne 1958) 16ff.

[11] H. Szklenar, *Studien zum Bild des Orients in vorhöfischen deutschen Epen* (Göttingen 1966) 32ff.

[12] A. Fourrier, *Le courant réaliste dans le roman courtois en France au Moyen-Age* (Paris 1960) 1.19ff.

[13] F. Panzer, *Gahmuret: Quellenstudien zu Wolframs Parzival*, Sitzungsberichte der Heidelberger Akademie der Wissenschaften, Philosophisch-historische Klasse 1939/1940 (Heidelberg 1940); H. Kolb, *Munsalvæsche: Studien zum Kyotproblem* (Munich 1963).

there is no question of his having to describe the passage of his hero from historical time to fabulous time he certainly has to plot the transition from the world of reality to that of adventure, so that his links between the two "geographical" worlds have to be more carefully contrived if his treatment of the knightly quest in search of adventure is to be at all persuasive. Carefully contrived they have to be, both as a means of implying the general verisimilitude of his story and as a way of persuading his listeners of the detailed probability that the knight who set out on his journey found that his path imperceptibly opened out into the miraculous world of adventure. What methods are therefore available to the medieval poet? How could he register the transition imperceptibly and thereby avoid provoking the critical objections of his audience?

* * *

In the medieval romance these methods seem first to have been tried out in the case of works whose setting is the Near East, whether in classical times or in the medieval present. Such priority is hardly surprising, since for the Middle Ages, as for classical Antiquity, the unknown lands of the East were the object of fantastic speculation in which remoteness, the tall stories of travelers and such precious goods as ivory, jewels and perfume all combined to heighten the exotic wonder of these *loca fabulosa*. If the East is seen in such miraculous terms, the journey of a knight to this realm of wonder (whether he be Alexander or a contemporary taken there by the Crusades) will confront a poet treating such a theme with the task of conducting his hero from the known world of European reality to the unknown realm of oriental marvels. One method of constructing a bridge between these two worlds was suggested by the factual situation in which Western writers on an oriental setting found themselves. Although the East at large was a realm of wonder, part of this realm at least had been opened up for the West since the days of Alexander, had become reasonably well known to large numbers of Europeans, and had thereby lost some of its unknown qualities. What was true of the Hellenistic period is even more true of the twelfth century: classical geographical knowledge of the Near East survives into the Middle Ages[14] and is reinforced by acquaintance with this area provided by the Bible and by the crusading experience.

The result of this is that between the accepted reality of the West and the unquestioned marvels of the East proper there comes to be interposed a large transitional zone which shares features with both the West and the East. The Near East, as the setting of biblical events and the site of crusading occupation, endeavors and experience, could be claimed as "Western," but equally its paganism, the geographical awareness of realms still further to the East which had yet to be

[14] See J. K. Wright, *The Geographical Lore of the Time of the Crusades* (New York 1925) and G. H. T. Kimble, *Geography in the Middle Ages* (London 1938).

penetrated, as well as the military reinforcements which these realms beyond the crusaders' horizon sent to the beleaguered Moslems of the Holy Land showed that the Near East was still open to and influenced by the East itself. Because of its geographical position and history this is the area where the authors of romances are first able to set and describe a transitional zone between the everyday world of reality and the remote realm of wonder, softening the harsh contrast between the two and thereby rendering any passage from one to the other less jarringly incredible.

In doing this, medieval authors are unconsciously repeating what the Greeks had earlier done as trade or colonization came to enlarge the scope of the classical oecumene. For them, too, the area of trading posts and colonial cities became a similar transitional zone, neither wholly Greek nor completely barbarian. Herodotus knew enough of the Near East to be able to say that Asia was inhabited as far as India, but beyond that he can only confess that it is deserted and that no one can say anything about its nature.[15] His distinction between two Asian zones (one of which is inhabited and therefore closer to the oecumene) is repeated when he describes the Pontic tribes of Southern Russia, for here he distinguishes between Hellenized and non-Hellenized zones. He therefore recognizes the Callipidae, dwelling at the mouth of the Dnieper, as a Greco-Scythian tribe, while further north the land is, as far as he knows, uninhabited;[16] the Olbiopolites are known to the Greeks to extend up the river Dnieper, but beyond them lies a vast uninhabited desert and beyond that a tribe of maneaters, the Androphagi;[17] elsewhere he reports a pacific tribe of Argippaei, but the regions beyond are attributed, with some hesitation, to legendary races of goat-footed men and of men who sleep for six months in the year.[18] In other words, wherever trade brought the Greeks into permanent contact with barbarians the latter lost most of their legendary attributes (while still not being completely assimilated to the Greeks themselves), so that the dividing line between the known and the unknown, between the real and the miraculous, became blurred and gave way instead to a zone which was part barbarian and part Greek.

This creation of a neutral zone, forced upon the Greeks by the practical experience of colonization, is repeated in the Middle Ages at the time of the Crusades and is reflected in works of literature which are set in the Middle East. The Strasbourg redaction of Lamprecht's *Alexanderlied* provides a clear example of this tripartite division of the known world, since the author distinguishes between Alexander's European base (Macedonia and Greece), the Middle East as far as Persia (the scene of his combats with Darius) and India (which he penetrates only after his defeat of the Persian king).[19] The Middle East shares a number of features with Europe in this

[15] Herodotus 4.40 (ed. A. D. Godley [London 1921-1924] 2.239).

[16] *Ibid.* 4.17 (2.217f.).

[17] *Ibid.* 4.18 (2.219).

[18] *Ibid.* 4.24f. (2.225).

[19] See D. H. Green, "The *Alexanderlied* and the Emergence of the Romance," *German Life and Letters* 28 (1975) 246ff.

work, above all the fact that its place-names are frequently referred to and are understood as part of geographical reality, known to the medieval audience from classical tradition, biblical testimony and topical crusading experience.[20] Alexander's campaigns in this region are conceived as being still located in the world of reality. Yet this region is also clearly different from Europe: its paganism, the pomp of Darius's court and the immensity of the realms on which he can call for recruits are reminders that the Middle East is just as much open to the wonders of the East as it is to Alexander's West. It is in the East itself (which in this work means primarily India) that Alexander's journey first opens out into a world of marvels, however. It is in this fabulous world of fairytale that place-names become markedly less frequent, so that the Greeks now move through a world so vast as to seem almost uninhabited, and it is here for the first time that Alexander encounters the marvelous peoples of the East and undergoes adventures which, unlike his purely military exploits in the Middle East, now partake of the miraculous. To the extent that the Middle East shares some features with the East proper as well as with Europe, it is depicted in this work as the transitional zone which it was in historical fact, both for classical Antiquity and for the Middle Ages.

In Antiquity the conception of a transitional zone is reflected in uncertainty as to where the actual boundary was to be drawn between Europe and Asia, since fully six such boundaries were claimed at one time or other, of which the Hellespont and the Euphrates are the most striking.[21] For Lamprecht the Euphrates also plays a part, but in a manner which underlines the transitional nature of the Middle East for this poet. Alexander's battle by the Granicus is converted in his version into a battle by the Euphrates, both in the Vorau and in the Strasbourg redaction,[22] which leads to the confusion of Alexander, at a later stage in his journey, having to cross the same river a second time.[23] This could be simply lack of skill on the poet's part, but an alternative explanation would be to see in it a deliberate wish to obscure the actual position of any firm boundary by making the Euphrates strangely ubiquitous. This might seem too charitable towards the poet, were it not for the fact that the Euphrates recurs again in an equally unexpected way. After Alexander has reached India he comes across a wide river and inquires about its name. In the *Iter ad paradisum*, the source of the German work at this point, he is told that it is the Ganges, otherwise known as the Phison, one of the four rivers that flow out of Paradise.[24] The German text substitutes for the Ganges the Euphrates,[25] another of

[20] On these three aspects see J. Brummack, *Die Darstellung des Orients in den deutschen Alexandergeschichten des Mittelalters* (Berlin 1966) 36ff.

[21] Szklenar (n. 11 above) 62 and n. 2.

[22] Vorau text, v. 1218 (cf. v. 1165); Strasbourg text, v. 1686 (cf. v. 1603). The edition used is Lamprecht, *Alexanderlied*, ed. K. Kinzel (Halle 1884).

[23] Strasbourg text, v. 2627ff.

[24] See the Latin text given by Kinzel 357ff., esp. 361f.

[25] Strasbourg text, v. 6728ff.

the four rivers of Paradise, so that Alexander comes across this mysteriously recurrent river yet a third time, thousands of miles away from where he first discovered it. It is along this river that Alexander eventually reaches Paradise in his vain and arrogant attempt to storm its walls, but since the poet has just before described in detail the difficulties of Alexander's journey across wild terrain separating Paradise from the rest of the world,[26] the function of the Euphrates is clearly that of a boundary, guarding and concealing Paradise. But it is a miraculously fluid frontier, cropping up unexpectedly on different occasions and thereby suggesting the deliberate geographical unclarity of the zone through which Alexander passes on his way to the marvels of India. Whereas it is possible to follow his route from place to place in the geographical reality of the Middle East up to this point, the topographical ambiguity of the Euphrates (together with the growing rarity of place-names) means that we are no longer able to follow in his footsteps as he passes out of the real world in search of his fabulous adventures.

A threefold geographical division is also apparent in *Herzog Ernst.*[27] Superficially this work appears to be located in two regions, which might be said to incorporate two different aspects of the narrative: Germany (the scene of the historical conflict between the hero and the emperor) and the East (the scene of his fabulous adventures during his banishment). As with the *Alexanderlied*, however, the East really falls into two zones, one of which is closer in spirit to the Western world. This is reflected in the narrative action, since Ernst's adventures in the East are divided between his crusading exploits in Jerusalem and his more emphatically miraculous adventures in a fabulous East extending from Grippia to Arimaspi. This fabulous East, like that of Alexander, is located in or near India[28] and it is in this region alone that the hero encounters the marvelous peoples and adventures which the medieval imagination associated with the East. By contrast, the world of Ernst's crusading exploits, stretching from Constantinople to Jerusalem, is noticeably free from marvels,[29] closer to the reality of Germany which the hero has had to abandon, even though the dominant question of the pagan threat gives it an exotic flavour absent from the known world of the Empire. This neutral zone of *Môrlant* therefore shares its paganism with the East proper, while its links with the West are provided by the fact that Ernst's crusading campaigns share their political realism with the feudal dissension which drove him from Germany and also by the astonishment which the

[26] Strasbourg text, v. 6685ff.

[27] Cf. Szklenar (n. 11 above) 177: "Die Gliederung des H. E. in die Abschnitte Deutschland – Kreuzzugsorient – fabuloser Orient ist keineswegs äuβerlich."

[28] See *ibid.* 153 n. 2.

[29] *Ibid.* 179: "Dieser Kreuzzugsorient zeichnet sich vor allem dadurch aus, daβ ihm alles Fabulose abgeht. Dieser Unterschied zum märchenhaften Mittelteil der abenteuerlichen Reisen Ernsts scheint uns entscheidend, denn er zeigt, daβ 'Orient' für den Dichter des H. E. kein einheitlicher Begriff war. Er wuβte genau, wo er die Fabelwesen seiner Geschichte n i c h t ansiedeln durfte. Konstantinopel und Jerusalem stehen der Wirklichkeit näher als Grippia und Arimaspi."

retinue of strange beings accompanying Ernst on his return journey causes in *Môrlant* as well as in Europe.[30]

In this work, as in the *Alexanderlied*, it was not enough to suggest the presence of a neutral zone to soften the harsh contrast between Western reality and Eastern marvels and thus to make any passage from one to the other more credible. In addition to this, the author has depicted the hero's passage from this neutral zone to the East proper in a way calculated to allay possible objections. With the *Alexanderlied* this was accomplished by what I take to be the deliberate obscurity surrounding the actual location of the Euphrates, while the author of *Herzog Ernst* chooses a different method. Having described Ernst's land-journey from Germany to Constantinople, taking him through Hungary to Bulgaria by a route well known at the time of the Crusades, he now has him set out from Constantinople for Syria by sea and arranges for a sudden sea-storm to arise and thwart these plans, driving the would-be crusader instead to the fabulous land of Grippia.[31] That Grippia, conceived as close to India, should be reached by sea from Constantinople is not so strange as might appear, given the state of medieval geography and the belief that India, situated on the Outer Ocean, could be reached by sea.[32] By using the motif of the sudden sea-storm (well known from the Hellenistic romance) to account for this journey from Constantinople to Grippia the author has avoided the need to plot the passage from the transitional zone to the East proper and has, as it were, rendered any critical check impossible. He has, in other words, covered his tracks as effectively as did the Alexander poet in the case of a miraculously ubiquitous Euphrates. In neither case can the hero actually be followed; in neither case can his penetration into a fabulous world be discredited.

With *Graf Rudolf* the position is different. Although the hero travels to the Middle East and encounters there a society which, though pagan, is as courtly and chivalric as his own, he does not, like Alexander or Ernst, travel beyond this Middle Eastern world as far as the fabulous lands of the East. Nonetheless, the presence of these fabulous lands is hinted at, since they are represented by their exotic inhabitants who are the allies of the Moslems into whose service they have been recruited in their war against the Christians. This much is made clear in the scene where Rudolf, during the siege of Ascalon, begins to parley with the enemy leader Girabobe, a pagan whose courtly idealism rivals that of the hero himself.[33] True to his chivalry, Girabobe reveals a distaste for the crudities of warfare and expresses his wish for a truce, no matter what some of his pagan allies may think of his desire for peace. However, by depicting these allies in all their savagery Girabobe demonstrates their remoteness from the ideals which govern his life, but this cultural gulf between them is reinforced by a geographical distance, since these allies are said to live at the ends

[30] *Herzog Ernst*, ed. K. Bartsch (Vienna 1869), v. 5464ff.
[31] *Ibid.* v. 2132ff.
[32] Szklenar (n. 11 above) 154.
[33] *Graf Rudolf* Cb 34ff.; ed. P. F. Ganz (Berlin 1964) 37.

of the earth (C b 45: "dine wiezzen umme arbeite niet. / iz ist ein volch also getan, / sine achten nicht uffe man / unde ist ein rechte wilde diet / unde ne ruchen ummez leben niet / unde sizzen an des meres ende / unde heizent volc svende"). This description implicitly equates these savage pagans, so unlike the courtly pagans of Girabobe's stamp, with the subhuman, half bestial heathen of the *Rolandslied*[34] and they are looked at as much askance by Girabobe as were the fabulous pagans by the inhabitants of *Môrlant* when Ernst passed through this region on his return from the East. That such savages should be called "destroyers of peoples," living at the ends of the earth, is a partial rationalization of a tradition which we saw with Herodotus, for whom the Androphagi live at the edge of the known world, far beyond the partly Hellenized Scythians known directly to the Greeks. Rudolf may have no direct contact with these people, he may not travel to their realm, but they lurk on the perimeter of the narrative, ready to invade the scene, so that the Middle East is open to their destructive threat in a way which is not true of Europe. Their presence is enough to show that the author of *Graf Rudolf* distinguished between two types of pagan and two types of pagan region: one in the Middle East, similar to Europe in its courtliness, the other more remote, both geographically and in its savagery.

As a last example of a work with an Eastern setting I take the first book of *Parzival*, in which Wolfram describes Gahmuret's arrival in the Middle East at Pâtelamunt, where his encounter with Belakane awaits him. Wolfram does not operate here with any twofold division of the East, but he does illustrate, in another way, the problem of the hero's transition from reality to adventure.[35] Gahmuret's progress, like that of Alexander, can be followed by means of the place-names with which Wolfram pinpoints his initial journey: he sets out from Anjou (6.25ff.), enters the service of the Khalif of Baghdad (13.16), learns of a campaign at Nineveh (14.5) conducted by two princes of Babylon (14.3), fights in Morocco and in Persia (15.17), at Damascus and at Aleppo (15.19) and enjoys knightly renown in Arabia (15.21). A retrospective reference is also made to Alexandria (18.14). All these place-names designate real geographical localities, known to the twelfth century from the Crusades. Yet Gahmuret's adventures only really begin once he encounters Belakane and fights on her behalf – accordingly, it is only at this stage that Gahmuret's journey passes almost imperceptibly from the world of reality into the ideal realm of adventure, for the places which are only now mentioned (Zazamanc, 16.2; Pâtelamunt, 17.4; Azagouc, 27.29) are unreal ones, chosen for their fabulous evocativeness and not meant, like the earlier names, to be equated with any physical locality.[36] They belong to the realm of adventure and indicate that the hero has now

[34] Cf. *Rolandslied* v. 2656 or 8046, ed. F. Maurer (Leipzig 1940).

[35] I have discussed this in another context, D. H. Green, "Der Auszug Gahmurets," in *Wolfram-Studien,* ed. W. Schröder (Berlin 1970) 62ff., esp. 83f. My *Parzival* references are to the sixth edition by K. Lachmann (Berlin 1926).

[36] Cf. Wynn (n. 1 above) 30f., and also *idem*, "Scenery and Chivalrous Journeys in Wolfram's *Parzival*," *Speculum* 36 (1961) 395f.

penetrated to this new realm. In one line Wolfram implicitly describes Gahmuret's transition (16.2: "von dan fuor er gein Zazamanc"): before this he had been in the world of geographical reality, but now he has found his way into the realm of chivalric adventure.

This use of place-names to indicate a transition reminds us of the *Alexanderlied*, but Wolfram reinforces this by a method which we also saw in *Herzog Ernst*: he has his hero driven by an unexpected sea-storm to Pâtelamunt (16.19ff.), which happens to be precisely a city where a besieged lady is conveniently awaiting his assistance. It is also worthy of comment that neither Gahmuret nor any of his ship's crew should have ever heard of this mysterious city before[37] – they, like the poet's listeners, have been wafted into a novel realm, but the deceptiveness of place-names and the violence of the elements have concealed the precise place where the transition was made. Too late we realize that quite a new dimension has opened up around us: although Gahmuret may say with realistic modesty that he is only one man and that the army besieging Belakane will not be put out by his arrival (24.25ff.), the action belies this, since events now follow the typical pattern of chivalric adventure. Gahmuret is greeted as a liberator (21.2f.) sent by the pagans' gods (21.7), his mercenary aims give way to the typical compassionate wish to serve those in need (29.21ff.) and, by defeating the enemy leader, Gahmuret alone is enabled to put an end to the whole conflict (43.21ff.). These are conventional romance motifs, but by making use of them only at this stage Wolfram suggests that the sea-storm and the arrival at this mysteriously unknown city indicate a realm different in kind from the real world through which Gahmuret's travels had taken him previously.

* * *

That Wolfram should have made use of romance motifs in plotting Gahmuret's journey in the East is of interest to us in yet another respect, since it suggests that the world of the romance and that of the East, as described in works devoted to Alexander, Ernst and Rudolf, may have enough in common to make such exchanges possible. This raises the question whether the technique we have been following in the East (a knight passes from the reality of Europe to the fabulous realms of the East via the transitional zone of the Middle East) may not also be true of chivalric romances located in the fictitious landscape of the Arthurian world, whether indeed the chivalric journeys through a European landscape may not betray a similar threefold division (a knight passes from the reality of the court to the mysterious realm of adventure via a transitional zone or by means of a narrative device which serves the same function, obscuring the vital passage from one world to the other). However fictitious the landscape of these romances, it is manifestly a European

[37] *Parzival* 17.1f. The *schifman* mentioned here is meant to include the *marnære* (19.15), so that even this experienced helmsman (19.16; 55.3) knows nothing of Belakane's realm.

world in which these works are set, so that the authors' task was to show that what was commonly accepted as likely in the still largely unknown world of the East (that reality could open out into the wider dimensions of adventure) was also possible in the European setting of the chivalric romance, that chivalry could be blessed by adventure on its home ground as much as when pursued in the East.[38]

For this end the authors of romances needed above all a realm in their landscape which would correspond functionally to the *loca fabulosa* of the East, a realm where adventure was an ever present possibility. In the East this realm was similarly remote from habitation (hence the striking infrequency of place-names in the *Alexanderlied* once the journey passes beyond Persia or the wild countryside through which Alexander and his men now have to toil). The geographical symbol of such solitude and remoteness in works with an Eastern setting is the desert, not in the modern restricted sense of "desert of sand," but in the wider sense of an "uninhabited wilderness," while the European equivalent of this is the dense, uncultivated wood, remote from habitation and harboring danger in many forms (wild beasts, demons, bandits). This equation between an Eastern desert or wilderness and a European wood is nothing new in the twelfth century, since courtly authors are doing nothing other than adapt to their own literary ends a linguistic equation for which the evidence reaches back to the ninth century.[39]

Several Old High German glosses attest the common parallel between Latin *desertum* or *eremus* and the vernacular *wald;*[40] Otfrid renders the biblical phrase about John the Baptist as "stimma ruafantes in wuastinnu waldes,"[41] while the *Benediktinerregel,* in addition to translating *eremus* by *wald,* coins the word *waldlihher* as a translation of *eremita.*[42] Otfrid's phrase (in which the addition of the word *wald* is strictly superfluous) is enough to suggest that *wald* was more than merely a conventional translator's equivalent for *desertum*, but was still actively felt as the aspect of European topography that corresponded most closely to the wilderness of the East. This is confirmed by the passage in the *Heliand*[43] in which Christ's sojourn

[38] Once the Celtic West is established as a land mysterious in its own right, it can come about that a journey in search of adventure and marvels should now proceed westwards. This is demonstrated most clearly in Robert de Boron's *Joseph* (ed. W. A. Nitze [Paris 1927]) where, as the various members of Joseph's family depart for the West in search of the *vaus d'Avaron*, we leave behind us the geographical and historical reality of the Holy Land and enter a region which is by contrast exotic (v. 3263: "En estranges terres ala") and wild (v. 3219: "En la terre vers Occident / Ki est sauvage durement, / Es vaus d'Avaron m'en irai").

[39] The linguistic material has been collected and discussed by P. Ilkow, *Die Nominalkomposita der altsächsischen Bibeldichtung: Ein semantisch-kulturgeschichtliches Glossar* (Göttingen 1968) 357ff. under the heading *sin-weldi.*

[40] E. von Steinmeyer and E. Sievers, eds., *Die althochdeutschen Glossen*, 5 vols. (Berlin 1879-1922); Gl. 1.280.61, 469.26; 3.4.61, 648.11. Cf. also Gl. 1.554.15.

[41] *Otfrids Evangelienbuch*, ed. O. Erdmann (Halle 1882) 1.23.19.

[42] E. von Steinmeyer, ed., *Die kleineren althochdeutschen Sprachdenkmäler* (Berlin 1916) 196.20 and 196.13. On these translations see W. Betz, *Deutsch und Lateinisch: Die Lehnbildungen der althochdeutschen Benediktinerregel* (Bonn 1949) 39.

[43] *Heliand,* ed. O. Behaghel (Halle 1933) v. 1121ff.

in the wilderness is described: the biblical *desertum* is rendered by the compound *sinweldi* (meaning literally a dense or immense wood), but a little later the simplex *wald* is used in the same sense (1124: "Thô forlêt he waldes hlêo, / ênôdies ard endi sôhte im eft erlo gemang"). Here *wald* implies the same as *ênôdi*: a deserted, desolate place, remote from human habitation and exposed to all the dangers of wild beasts and demonic temptations (Mark 1.13), a place chosen by Christ for His first encounter with a supernatural adversary.

Described in these terms, Christ's sojourn in the wilderness (or in the wood) can be seen as the metaphysical equivalent of the knightly hero's quest for adventures in the depths of a forest which are for him, too, a form of moral testing. However important this parallel may be for the spiritual dimension of the romance or for its kinship with the saint's legend,[44] what concerns us here is the long-established belief that the forest was a place of solitude, danger and trial,[45] comparable with the oriental wilderness as a region where perils and adventures were also to be found. If this is so, our problem is to inquire into the methods employed to suggest that a knight traveling through a European landscape could imperceptibly stumble across a world of adventure in the wood, remote from the reality of the court he had left behind. How does the poet cover up his traces? How does he persuade us to suspend our disbelief, to accept his suggestion that the depths of a European forest may lead to encounters no less wondrous than those of Alexander at the ends of the world?

The simplest and least satisfactory method is for the poet to mention no more than the point of arrival of the knight errant, omitting any description of the journey itself so that we are abruptly transposed from reality to enchantment. The conventional type of phrase which this method employs is therefore "he rode until he saw . . . ," and it recurs frequently in both French and German romances. In French the usual construction is with the conjunction *tant que:*

Yvain 3485
Au matin s'an revont ansanble
Et autel vie, ce me sanble,
Come il orent la nuit menee,
Ont ansanble andui demenee
Presque trestote une quinzainne,
Tant qu'avanture a la fontainne
Dessoz le pin les amena.[46]

[44] M. Wehrli, "Roman und Legende im deutschen Hochmittelalter," in the Festschrift for B. Markwardt, *Worte und Werte*, ed. G. Erdmann and A. Eichstaedt (Berlin 1961) 428ff., esp. 435, has drawn attention to the "knightly" picture of the saint, bravely riding into the depths of the forest to engage in spiritual combat in his hermitage with the Devil, sketched by Eigil in his life of Sturmi of Fulda. Now in Wehrli, *Formen mittelalterlicher Erzählung: Aufsätze* (Zürich 1969) 165.

[45] On this traditional view of the forest see M. Stauffer, *Der Wald: Zur Darstellung und Deutung der Natur im Mittelalter* (Bern 1959).

[46] Chrétien de Troyes, *Yvain*, ed. W. Foerster and A. Hilka (Halle 1926).

Queste del Saint Graal

Si ont tant chevauchié qu'il vindrent vers le Chastel as Puceles. (52.32)

. . . il chevaucha tant par ses jornées que il vint en la Forest Gaste. (56.2)[47]

German romances use the corresponding construction, normally with *unz* (*daz*):

Erec 3106

Nû riten si beide
âne holz niuwan heide,
unz daz si der tac verlie.
. . . . .
nû wîste si der wec
in einen kreftigen walt.[48]

Iwein 274

einen stîc ich dô gevienc:
der truoc mich ûz der wilde
und kom an ein gevilde.
dem volgte ich eine wîle,
niht vol eine mîle,
unz ich eine burc ersach.[49]

Such standing phrases, although used conventionally, are unsatisfactory because, from the point of view of our problem, they provide no solution, but simply avoid the difficulty of making the transition credible. This is so even when, as in *Yvain*, the author devotes some lines to the landscape traversed:

Yvain 762

. . . Einçois erra chascun jor tant
Par montaingnes et par valees
Et par forez longues et lees,
Par leus estranges et sauvages,
Et passa mainz felons passages
Et maint peril et maint destroit,
Tant qu'il vint au santier tot droit.

The difficulty here is that the landscape which Yvain rides through is sketched in conventional terms and without any suggestion that at any stage he passes from the world of reality into the realm of adventure – without any hint of a transitional zone or any narrative device to draw our attention away from this critical point.

Yet because Wace's skepticism is representative of the kind of incredulity which courtly authors had to take into account, they were forced to devise more skilful methods than this. On rare occasions only can they turn to the motif of the sea-storm, as in *Herzog Ernst*, to help them over their obstacle, since they seldom

[47] *Queste del Saint Graal*, ed. A. Pauphilet (Paris 1949).

[48] Hartmann, *Erec*, ed. A. Leitzmann and L. Wolff (Tübingen 1963).

[49] Hartmann, *Iwein*, ed. L. Wolff (Berlin 1968).

depict their knightly hero out of his landlubber's context. Because the medieval romance is normally concerned with a hero on horseback, this otherwise welcome motif, at home in the romance since the Hellenistic age, is employed very infrequently, apart from those works in an oriental setting where geographical distances dictated the need for a sea-voyage. Just as Herzog Ernst is driven by a storm to the adventures awaiting him in Grippia or Eneas to his encounter with Dido in Carthage,[50] so is Gahmuret driven by forces beyond his control to the decisive meeting with Belakane. In each case, an apparently natural phenomenon leads the hero, in a manner which mysteriously suggests the workings of a providential guidance, to a person or place which is to have particular significance for him. In each case, the storm is much more than a factual motif, it represents a turning-point which, in a manner beyond human control and therefore inaccessible to human criticism, opens up a new realm of experience of decisive importance in the hero's career. A motif of this nature would have been obviously welcome to courtly authors if their hero had been anything other than a mounted knight rarely to be seen separated from his steed. But this is not the case, so that the sea-storm cannot be exploited so readily in romances whose action is not set in the East. We find it in Hartmann's *Gregorius* when the hero, after his departure from the monastery, sets sail, entrusts his vessel to the winds and is driven by a tempest to his mother's land where their fatal reunion takes place.[51] We find it also in Gottfried's work when the young Tristan, kidnapped by merchants who in their fear of the storm that arises [52] are forced to put him ashore, is led by such mysterious means to precisely the land of his uncle Marke, whose fate is so closely bound up with his own. These are rare examples, and they are occasioned by the particular conditions of the narrative. Gregorius, admittedly, is setting out in search of knightly adventure, but since the monastery he is forsaking is situated on an island[53] he has no choice but to begin his quest by a sea-voyage. Tristan, for his part, is rarely conceived as a knight by Gottfried, he is only a child at the time of his kidnapping and the poet has in any case gone very much his own way in granting so marked a function to the sea and to voyages over the sea[54] that his work cannot be regarded as at all typical.

If their knightly theme rendered this motif of the sea-storm unusable, despite its manifest advantages,[55] courtly authors tried to rescue something for themselves by

[50] To classify the *Eneide* as an "oriental" romance may seem perverse, but with regard to this particular detail the storm which drives Eneas off his course commences, in narrative terms, just after his departure from Troy (v. 169ff.). It still belongs therefore to the oriental background of the Trojans' origins.

[51] Hartmann, *Gregorius*, ed. H. Paul and A. Leitzmann (Halle 1948) v. 1825ff.

[52] Gottfried, *Tristan und Isold*, ed. F. Ranke (Dublin 1967) v. 2406ff.

[53] Cf. Hartmann, *Gregorius* v. 941.

[54] Cf. I. Hahn, *Raum und Landschaft in Gottfrieds Tristan* (Munich 1963) 16ff. and 86ff.

[55] How popular this motif could nevertheless be, and how automatically it could call forth the idea of reaching a fabulous realm, has been pointed out to me by F. H. Bäuml in the case of *Kudrun*, ed. B. Symons and B. Boesch (Tübingen 1954). The sea-voyage depicted in stanzas

generalizing the tempest, in which the voyager is tossed hither and thither and ultimately off his intended course by elements beyond his control, into the motif of the hero losing his way. This is a fate to which any traveler is exposed, especially one whose journey takes him through an often trackless forest rarely trodden by human foot, but it shares one decisive feature with the tempest. The rider who loses his way, like the voyager who is cast off course, loses his bearings so thoroughly that his course can no longer be plotted. In other words, the audience is as much in the dark as the traveler as to his precise whereabouts, so that if at the next station of his journey he happens now to find himself in the mysterious realm of adventure his entry into this realm will have been effected while he, and with him the audience, was temporarily lost. To cause his hero to lose his way is therefore a means for the author to deprive his audience of any chance to register where the crucial transition took place. It may also serve many other functions (to suggest the knight's loss of moral bearings or his confused estrangement from God or society), but I am only concerned here with the advantage it confers upon any author in his wary relationship with a potentially critical audience.

Two examples may illustrate the employment of this motif in the knightly romance. Wolfram depicts the complete disorientation of Parzival during his years of random wandering in pursuit of knightly exploits and the Grail in two distinct ways: he loses his bearings in time (and therefore does not know how long he has been wandering or even what day it is)[56] and also in space (he is consequently unaware of the whereabouts of Munsalvæsche and repeatedly loses his way in his attempts to approach it).[57] One early result of the knight's encounter with Trevrizent is that the hermit should be able to calculate the length of time during which Parzival has been underway,[58] but the hero's reaction to his new found reorientation in time is to experience it in spatial terms (460.28: " 'alrêrst ich innen worden bin / wie lange ich var wîselôs / unt daz freuden helfe mich verkôs' "). He now recognizes (and we with him) that his travels have been *wîselôs*, deprived of God's guidance and therefore rides at random, for all these years. We may relate this passage with a slightly earlier

1124ff. is overtaken by a tempest and exposed to the dangers of the 'Magnetberg' (1125f.), but issues in a brief description of a miraculous region (1128ff.). Echoes of *Herzog Ernst* can be detected here, but none of this is called for by the narrative plot, since what is at stake here is no more than a simple voyage to "Ormanîelant" or Normandy. The motif must therefore have been attractive enough to impose itself against the actual needs of the plot in this way.

56 The problem of time as a narrative device in Wolfram's *Parzival* has been skillfully dealt with by H. J. Weigand, "Die epischen Zeitverhältnisse in den Graldichtungen Crestiens und Wolframs," *Publications of the Modern Language Association* 53 (1938) 917ff. This valuable essay has now been reprinted in an English version in H. J. Weigand, *Wolfram's Parzival* (Ithaca 1969). See also A. Groos, "Time Reference and the Liturgical Calendar in Wolfram von Eschenbach's *Parzival*," *Deutsche Vierteljahrsschrift für Literaturwissenschaft und Geistesgeschichte* 49 (1975) 43ff.

57 The topography of Parzival's wanderings is discussed by Wynn (n. 36 above) 393ff.

58 *Parzival* 460.19ff.

remark, made by the narrator as Parzival begins to draw near to the hermit's cell (446.3: "desn prüeve ich niht der wochen zal, / über wie lanc sider Parzivâl / reit durch âventiure als ê"). Wolfram is here deliberately hoodwinking his audience by withholding information from them which Trevrizent is so soon to give, but for us the significance of this remark is that it makes clear that Parzival's quest for adventure belongs to the period of his disorientation. His quest is therefore a prolonged ride at random during which he is lost both in time and in space. His route was fortuitous and aimless in that he knew that the Grail was his goal, but not where it lay or how he might get there. A wanderer who loses his way and whose path is aimless for so many years is not likely to follow a clearly defined route, easy to retrace – which means that the audience has been deliberately led to feel lost and disorientated like Parzival, deprived therefore of any opportunity to ascertain where his path took him, where his adventures were located and where the mysterious kingdom of the Grail was to be found.

Hartmann's *Erec* provides my second example, concerning the approach of Erec, accompanied by Guivreiz, to the castle of Brandigan where his climactic adventure awaits him. They depart from the castle Penefrec with the intention of going to Arthur's court in Britain (7798: "si gedâhten rîten dâ zehant / ze Britanje in daz lant / zem künege Artûse"), but the express use of *gedâhten* provides a hint, which may not be obvious at the time, that other things are in store for them. This is reinforced immediately when the poet says that they did not know at which court, at Karidôl or at Tintajôl, Arthur was to be found at that time (7801: "ûf welhem sînem hûse / si in benamen vunden, / daz enwesten si zuo den stunden"). The result is that their journey becomes a ride at random and without certainty (7808: "sus riten si nâch wâne, / und doch der gewisheit âne"), so that when they come to a fork in their road they have no idea which path to follow (7813: ". . . an eine wegescheide: / welh ze Britanje in daz lant / gienge, daz was in unerkant"). When Guivreiz eventually sees the castle of Brandigan before them, he recognizes (as we do also) that they have taken the wrong path (7899: "ich erkenne si: wir sîn verre / geriten von unser strâze. / daz ez got verwâze! / . . . / ich hân mich übele übersehen"). We have accompanied them as the doubts grew more pronounced, but since the poet has earlier directed attention towards the path to Arthur which they meant to take we have been enticed into ignoring the wrong path which they do take until it is too late and we realize that, like Erec and Guivreiz, we have stumbled into the realm of adventure unawares.

Erec subsequently comes to see that he was led to this crowning adventure of his by the guiding hand of a providence well disposed to chivalry (just as we may now suspect that it was the author's conscious control of our responses that led us to this scene without our immediately grasping what was afoot). When he is told what awaits him at Brandigan, Erec gives thanks to God for conducting him there (8521: "ich weste wol, der Sælden wec / gienge in der werlde eteswâ, / rehte enweste ich aber wâ, / wan daz ich in suochende reit / in grôzer ungewisheit, / unz daz ich in nû vunden hân. / got hât wol ze mir getân / daz er mich hât gewîset her"). These words reveal that Erec, like Parzival in his reaction to Trevrizent, now looks back on his quest for adventure as a period in which he was lost, looking for a path which he knew must exist, but of whose whereabouts he was ignorant. Parzival travels *wîselôs*, Erec in *ungewisheit*, so that the stages of their journey are as shrouded in obscurity for us as they are for them.

Erec's words are important in another respect, however, since they are a subjective confirmation of what the narrator had objectively said at a slightly earlier stage when, after his second encounter with Guivreiz, Erec's fortunes take the upward turn which is soon to bring him to the climax of Brandigan. Guivreiz and Erec congratulate themselves on having been brought together again, but then the narrator concentrates on Erec by telling us that the period during which he was lost has now come to an end (7061: ". . . wan im vil dicke swebete / sîn lîp in solher wâge, / als ûf des meres wâge / ein schefbrüchiger man / ûf einem brete kæme dan / ûz an daz stat gerunnen. / ofte hete er gewunnen / ein leben zwîvellîchez / und disem wol gelîchez: / nû hete in an der genâden sant / ûz kumbers ünden gesant / got und sîn vrümekeit"). In this narrator's assessment of the situation Erec's past adventures are seen not simply as a period in which he was lost, but more vividly in the image of a storm at sea from which he has now been saved as if from a shipwreck. This is the same motif as in the romances with an Eastern setting (*Herzog Ernst*, Gahmuret in *Parzival*), but whereas there it was meant literally, since the knight in question had to travel overseas, here it is meant only metaphorically, as an image with which to capture something of Erec's long period of random wandering through unknown tracts in search of adventure.

* * *

The other technique which we saw utilized in oriental romances, the development of a neutral zone to act as a transition between the West and the East, between reality and marvels, is also applied to Celtic romances. In place of the desert we encounter the forest, but it is a forest in which two zones can be distinguished: a dense and dangerous woodland, the abode of adventure, and an enclosing belt of forest, less wild and more amenable to human cultivation. It is this latter zone which serves as a transition between the world of the court and the realm of adventure, so that the Western romances show a threefold pattern similar to that which characterizes those in an Eastern setting. Just as the authors of oriental romances adapt to their artistic purposes an undoubted fact of geographical experience (the Middle East was better known to Europe, and therefore less exotic, than was India), so do the authors of works with a Western setting proceed from the world as they knew it in western Europe.

It is apparent that, although the forest was regarded with awe and fear as the abode of wild beasts, of outlaws and robbers, frequented by demons, this was true only of the depths of the forest by contrast with the border zone, partly cleared for cultivation, traversed regularly in the courtly pastime of the hunt and closer in all respects to the world of the court. This division of the forest into two zones appears to go back to Germanic times, at least if we can trust the semantic evidence. We have seen that *sinweldi* in the *Heliand*, like *wald* in the same text and also in Old High German, could be used as a translation of *desertum* to denote, not a cultivated forest, but wild and uninhabited woodland, inaccessible or unamenable to human effort. By contrast, the Germanic word corresponding to Old High German *wang* appears to have denoted woodland clearings or those less dense parts of the forest which could be won for cultivation. This is suggested by the gloss rendering of *campi nemoris* by *holzuuanga,*[59] by the use of the substantive in Old High German and Old Norse as the second element in place-names,[60] but especially by its employment in Gothic, Old English and Old Saxon to render the biblical *paradisus* (in the sense of "Garden of Eden"),[61] suggesting therefore that it denoted a type of Germanic *locus amoenus*, a pleasing meadow or park landscape. This distinction between *wald*, the place of terror and awe, and *wang*, a woodland glade as a more hospitable retreat, suggests that the distinction we are concerned with is of considerable antiquity.[62]

This distinction is adapted to new literary purposes in the twelfth century. Marie de France provides the setting for the adventure in her *Guingamor*[63] by alluding to two such zones: an outer belt which is close to the city and accessible to the courtly hunt (269: "Au brueil plus pres de la cité / Sont tuit li veneor alé") and the depths of the forest which the huntsmen refrain from entering (285: "Pres de la forest l'atendront, / Mes ja dedenz nen enterront"), and where the adventure later takes place. Here it is the lexical distinction between *brueil* and *forest*, as well as the different attitude revealed by the huntsmen, which shows that, however far the court may have become reconciled or even attracted to the pleasures of the outer forest, this zone is connected, by gradations which are all the more insidious for being so subtle, with the more dangerous and miraculous zone in the depths of the forest.

Even in a romance in which knighthood plays so small a part as Gottfried's *Tristan* this distinction is still apparent. When Isolde,[64] wishing to rid herself of Brangæne as a potentially dangerous accomplice after the first deception of Marke, dispatches her in the company of two hired killers to gather herbs in the wood the episode is described in these terms:

> 12764 nu si zem walde kamen hin,
> da wurze, crut unde gras
> der volle nach ir willen was,

[59] Steinmeyer and Sievers (n. 40 above) Gl. 2.743.13.

[60] Cf. Ilkow (n. 39 above) 183, under the heading *heƀan-wang.*

[61] *Ibid.* The Gothic form *waggs* renders παράδεισος in II Cor. 12.4, and OE *neorxnawang* translates Latin *paradisus* (R. Jente, *Die mythologischen Ausdrücke im altenglischen Wortschatz* [Heidelberg 1921] 226f.). For OS see *Heliand* 3134ff., where the *grôni uuang* is said to be *paradîse gelîc.*

[62] Ilkow (n. 39 above) 183 quotes Vilmar to this effect.

[63] Marie de France, *Guingamor*, ed. G. Paris, *Romania* 8 (1879) 50ff. This lay was attributed to Marie de France by K. Warnke in the third edition of *Die Lais* (Halle 1925).

[64] Cf. Hahn (n. 54 above) 15.

Brangæne wolte erbeizet sin.
nu vuorten si si baz hin in
in die wüeste und in die wilde.

The outskirts of the forest are the region where the wood is, if not cultivated, at least amenable to human purposes, where Brangæne can hope to gather herbs, but this region is distinguished from another, further in, which is termed *wüeste* and *wilde* and where the unexpected and secret violence of the planned murder can be fittingly located. On a later occasion,[65] when Gottfried is describing the setting of what is for him the miraculous adventure of the *Minnegrotte*, he firmly places the lovers' retreat at the center of a similar double zone. It is surrounded by two different belts of landscape, on the outside by a zone traversed *über walt und über heide* (16681), clearly a transitional region between wilderness and cultivation and accessible to the hunt, but further within by a wilderness proper, rocky and completely inhospitable (17338: *über velse und über herte*).

Although the European wood lent itself to such elaboration as the Western counterpart to the two regions of the East (Middle East and India), not all the adventures of Celtic romances take place in a wood. The consequence is that, where the adventure occurs elsewhere, the poet has to contrive some transitional zone, functionally comparable to the Middle East or the outskirts of the forest, which will similarly tone down the abruptness of the knight's passage from reality to adventure. The transitional zone is now no longer provided by geographical reality; but instead the poet, imitating what nature had taught him in respect of the Middle East or European forests, now constructs his own fictitious transitional zone, suggesting its existence by the narrative techniques he employs. As an example I have chosen once again Erec's crowning adventure at the castle of Brandigan, but for the sake of variety and also because his work represents the first Arthurian romance in which this problem had to be solved I shall consider Chrétien's version rather than Hartmann's. If we ignore the other technique (the manner in which Erec lost his way and stumbled unwittingly across this adventure) we shall see that Chrétien describes Brandiganz piecemeal, revealing different aspects in succession much as they would present themselves to a newcomer who was drawing near, but in such a way that we are slowly led from realistic impressions to the final understanding that this is instead an enchanted castle. We learn the truth as belatedly as Erec, so that there is at this stage as little turning back for us as for him.

When Erec and Guivrez first catch sight of Brandiganz it is the concrete details of a feudal stronghold that are revealed to them, its towers, wall and moat (5370: "... Et vienent devant les bretesches / D'un chastel fort et riche et bel, / Clos tot antor de mur novel; / Et par dessoz a la reonde / Coroit une eve mout parfonde"). Guivrez, now realizing that they have come the wrong way, recognizes the castle and describes its strength in very real terms, claiming that France, England and the region

[65] *Ibid.* 15f.

as far as Liège could not bring it to submission (5392: "Se France et Angleterre tote, / Et tuit cil qui sont jusqu'au Liege, / Estoient anviron a siege, / Nel prandroient il an lor vies"). The reason for such inviolability is the strategic position which Brandiganz occupies, for it is situated on an island (the stream that surrounds it has already been described as deep and torrential) which is extensive enough for all the food necessary for the town to be grown there (5396: "Car plus dure de quatre liues / L'isle, ou li chastiaus est assis, / Et tot croist dedanz le porpris, / Quanqu'a riche chastel covient. / . . . / De nule part ne crient assaut, / Ne riens nel porroit afamer"). Indeed, the stream is so powerful that it alone would be protection enough (5411: "Car s'il n'i avoit mur ne tor / Fors de l'eve qui cort antor, / Tant forz et tant seürs seroit, / Que tot le mont ne doteroit").

Attracted by what be sees of the town's wealth Erec decides to seek lodging there for the night (5417f. – the words *ostel* and *chastel* here belong to the sphere of humdrum reality), but Guivrez warns him against this because of a dangerous passage in the town (5422: "El chastel a un mal trespas"). *Trespas* could have a literal meaning here, but equally it could suggest an adventure in the sense of passage of arms, a possibility which is later gradually reinforced as the key-word *avanture* comes to be used more and more (5431, 5437, 5445, 5456, 5464, 5519 = *mesavanture*). Yet even though the recurrent use of *avanture* might suggest the presence of the supernatural in this castle, this is by no means certain since the word could mean nothing more than a knightly encounter. We apparently return to this comforting level of everyday reality as we accompany Erec towards the castle, passing the listing-place and the drawbridge and proceeding along the streets of the town (5493: "Einsi vers le chastel s'an vont, / Les lices passent et le pont; / Et quant les lices ont passees, / Les janz qui furent amassees / Parmi les rues a tropiaus, / Voient Erec qui mout est biaus"). All this has the reassuring quality of feudal reality, an impression which is strengthened when King Evrains comes down the street to greet his guests (5547: "Li rois Evrains anmi la rue / Vint ancontre aus, si les salue") and courteously conducts Enide into the palace (5558: "Par la main qu'ele ot blanche et tandre, / L'an mainne anz el palés amont"). The narrative continues on the same note when Chrétien, by expressly telling us what he is *not* going to describe in the furnishings of the palace, conveys to us an impression of courtly luxury (5571: "Mes por quoi vos deviseroie / Les peintures, les dras de soie, / Don la chanbre estoit anbelie? / Le tans gasteroie an folie"). However, whether we realize it or not this remark is ambiguous and contains a hint of the future, for the narrator takes up the point about not wanting to waste time and varies it repeatedly over the next few lines (5576: "Einçois me vuel un po haster"; 5579: "Por ce ne m'i vuel arester"; 5582: "Por ce ne vuel feire demore"). Such insistence introduces a note of urgency which the apparent realism of the description so far seems not to justify, but this is dismissed immediately when the narrator falls back on his everyday level in mentioning the food they were served (5585: "Orent plenieremant la nuit, / Oisiaus et veneison et fruit / Et vin de diverse meniere").

This continuous reversion to reality may have allowed us up to this point to dismiss the slight hints to the contrary, but we are now reminded that Erec, at any rate, was still turning them over in his mind and guided the conversation with his host in this direction (5594: "Si comança a remantoivre / Ce qui au cuer plus li tenoit; / De la Joie li sovenoit, / S'an a la parole esmeüe"). Again, however, we fall back on a level remote from enchantment when his host tells Erec that he is quite free to withdraw from the adventure (5636: "C'est une chose que vos loist / A repantir et a retreire, / Se vos volez vostre preu feire"), but no sooner is this said than we are again given a hint of the marvelous, for the word *avanture* is now mentioned for the seventh time in this episode, but this time in conjunction with *mervoille* (5644: "Mes con plus granz est la mervoille / Et l'avanture plus grevainne, / Plus la covoite et plus se painne"). Erec's reply to the host's remark about his liberty to draw back from this adventure is also informative: he says that his mind is made up and that he will carry on (5652: "Ci an est la broche tranchiee; / Car ja de rien que j'aie anprise, / Ne ferai tel recreantise"). The die is indeed cast, but whereas we may take this *subjectively* as an expression of the knight's persistence (he therefore replies directly to Evrain's remark about the free choice he may still exercise), it later emerges that *objectively* it is already too late (for a knight of Erec's quality in such a situation there can be no possibility of turning back).

On the following morning things seem for a brief while to have returned to everyday normality, even though we know that an encounter awaits Erec: he dons his armour in the hall (5691: "Si s'an fet armer an la sale"), descends the steps to find his horse saddled (5692: "Quant armez fu, si s'an avale / Trestoz les degrez contre val / Et trueve anselé son cheval") and rides through the crowded, noisy streets (5702: "A l'esmovoir a mout grant noise / Et grant bruit par totes les rues"). After they have left the town Evrains leads the knight to a nearby garden (5731: "An un vergier qui estoit pres"), but it is only at this point, after numerous partial hints and apparent denials of what these hints suggest, that the narrator finally drops his mask and tells us, as he says, the truth about the matter (5735: "Mes ne fet pas a trespasser / Por langue debatre et lasser. / Que del vergier ne vos retraie / Lonc l'estoire chose veraie"). This remark harks back to a similar one by the host in answer to Erec's inquiry, for he says that it would be wrong for him not to tell his guest the whole truth (5639: "Por ce vos di que traïson / Vers vos feroie et mesprison, / Se tot le voir ne vos disoie"). Chrétien's words do not mean that what he has told his audience is not the truth, but rather that it is not the whole truth, that there is still something to be made unambiguously clear. He now tells them about the garden to which Erec has been conducted: it had no wall or fence, but was enclosed by magic so that no one could enter it;[66] it is in fact an enchanted garden, a site for a

[66] Chrétien, *Erec* v. 5739ff. The magical protection which this garden enjoys reminds us of Guivrez's earlier remark (v. 5411ff.) that the tactical position of the castle, situated on an island, rendered it so inviolable that further defenses were hardly necessary. These two passages between them plot the whole way along which Chrétien has been conducting us: an initial realistic description in terms of feudal tactics ultimately gives way to the admission that a magic spell lay over this place. Likewise, the natural wealth of the castle (v. 5396ff.), seen at first as a military advantage, points forward to what we later grasp is the miraculous wealth and beauty of the enchanted garden (v. 5746ff.).

miraculous adventure. With that we have been told the full truth and we now realize that, like Erec, we have gained entry into the world of adventure, but in such a way that, since the moment when Brandiganz was first mentioned, the balance between reality and marvel has been slowly, but imperceptibly shifting towards the latter. Chrétien has in fact provided us with enough clues to alert us to the possibility of what eventually comes to pass, but nowhere are we given enough clearcut certainty to be able to pin him down.

So far, with the exception of what I called the primitive technique of constructions with *tant que* in French and *unz* in German, the methods we have been considering in Western romances have been derived from those employed in works with an Eastern setting. The motif of the sea-storm has little application to a knight riding through a European landscape; it therefore occurs infrequently or only metaphorically, but is made relevant to the new context by being generalized to the motif of a knight losing his way on his wanderings. Similarly, the suggestion of a transitional zone between West and East is transferred to a fully Western setting in the form of a transitional zone in the Celtic forest or the creation by the poet of a neutral zone of descriptions where we are deliberately left in doubt whether we are still in the world of reality or may not have already strayed unwittingly into the realm of adventure. The application of these two methods to the different conditions of a European landscape clearly made demands on the aesthetic skills of these authors – they have to suggest that their knight errant has lost his way over far longer narrative intervals than was the case with a tempest which arose suddenly, but which could die out equally quickly; they have to insure that their audience is as spatially disoriented as their hero if the transition to a new realm is to be acceptable; and, as Chrétien's description of Erec's approach to Brandiganz makes clear, they occasionally have to call upon all their rhetorical skills in order, when describing an adventure outside the forest, to manufacture a fictitious transitional zone by purely aesthetic means, without any model in geographical reality. In short, even though these two methods have been derived from elsewhere and have been simply applied to a different setting, the authors who do this show some skill and awareness of the demands made by this new setting. In view of this it is hardly surprising that they should exercise their skill in other ways and devise other means of persuading their listeners to suspend their disbelief, to accept the presence of a realm of adventure even in a Western landscape. These new techniques have, as far as I know, no precedent in oriental romances and were evolved by the authors of romances set in the West as a means of coping with their particular problem. It is these I now wish to consider.

* * *

The first of these new techniques concerns the narrative problems which confront an author who, not content with the simple challenge of following one narrative strand through from beginning to end, operates with two or more strands and must therefore decide how to make the transition from one to another and what to do about the action of the strand which he is temporarily abandoning. Is it to stand still while it is not being narrated? If not, at what point in the subsequent action of this strand are we to rejoin it and how much of the action we have missed is to be recapitulated? These are problems which have been discussed recently in connection with the medieval poet's attitude to narrative time,[67] but they also have a bearing on our question, since an author can solve his problem of making the knight's entry into the realm of adventure convincing by having this take place while the knight is lost to view and we are preoccupied with another strand of the complex action. We therefore rejoin the knight too late to witness the decisive moment and since in most cases he is already engaged, or soon about to be engaged, in a new exploit we come to him with an eager concern for his future, not a critical interest in his immediate past. *Parzival* and *Iwein* will provide us with examples of this method.

Two narrative strands are present in *Parzival* because of the important part played by Gawan alongside Parzival; but this is not their only explanation, since Wolfram often betrays a tendency to follow a secondary episode briefly to its subsequent conclusion before reverting to the main line of the narrative. However small-scale this may be, it confronts the author with the same kind of technical problem, but also gives him the opportunity to solve other problems at the same time. A first example is provided by an episode whose multiplicity of strands had already caused Chrétien some trouble in organizing it,[68] namely the single combats by which Parzival assists the besieged inhabitants of Pelrapeire. Parzival first defeats the seneschal Kingrun, spares his life on the condition that he go immediately to Arthur's court and place himself at the disposal of the lady Cunneware, and then the two knights separate (199.14: "die helde man sich scheiden sach"). Instead of following Kingrun on his way to Arthur, we remain with Parzival at Pelrapeire for his marriage and then take up the new strand of Clamide's preparations for the final assault on the city. Only after these two distinct actions at Pelrapeire have been set in motion do we eventually return to the strand dealing with Kingrun, who by now, however, has already arrived at Arthur's court (206.5: "Kingrûn scheneschlant / was komen ze Bertâne in daz lant / und vant den künec Artûs"). The use of the pluperfect indicates that Kingrun had already reached Arthur by the time we rejoin him, so that we come too late to learn anything of his way there and how he managed to discover the king while he was out hunting (206.8).

A similar technique is employed when Wolfram describes how Parzival himself later came to rejoin the Round Table temporarily in Book 6. On this occasion its effect is increased by the addition of the further motif of Parzival having lost his way. An apparently natural explanation for this is given (an unexpected snowfall),

[67] H.-H. Steinhoff, *Die Darstellung gleichzeitiger Geschehnisse im mittelhochdeutschen Epos* (Munich 1964).

[68] This has been shown in detail by Weigand (n. 56 above).

but even this is later revealed by Trevrizent as having metaphysical and temporal implications far beyond the appearances of this episode when we, with Parzival, first experience it.[69] Because of the snow Parzival has lost his way in the wild forest (282.1: "Die naht bî Parzivâle er stuont, / dâ in bêden was der walt unkuont / und dâ se bêde sêre vrôs. / dô Parzivâl den tac erkôs, / im was versnît sîns pfades pan: / vil ungevertes reit er dan / über ronen und über manegen stein"). We are, however, not even allowed to witness Parzival's journey up to the point where he is seen to be lost, so that he is not merely lost himself, he is also lost to us in the further sense that we have no precise idea whereabouts he was[70] when he recognized he had gone astray. The poet achieves this effect by concluding the previous book with Parzival's defeat of Orilus in single combat, as a result of which the defeated knight is sent to Arthur's court, just as Kingrun (and later, Clamide) had been. All this, and the reception of Orilus at Arthur's court, is described at the end of Book 5, while Book 6 opens by continuing the strand dealing with Arthur, showing us his departure in search of Parzival whom he knows to be nearby. It is only at this stage that we return to Parzival, for Wolfram now asks his audience (281.10: "Welt ir nu hœren war sî komn / Parzivâl der Wâleis? / von snêwe was ein niwe leis / des nahtes vast ûf in gesnît"). With this question the author is in fact teasing us, since the snowfall, the wild depths of the forest and the fact that we have lost Parzival to view since he dispatched Orilus to Arthur's court all mean that we can never learn where exactly Parzival was when he stumbled upon Arthur's court again. This example is instructive since it shows us the author combining two conventional motifs (the knight loses his way; the inner depths of the forest) with the rhetorical technique of deliberately withholding certain information from the audience by switching to another narrative strand at a well chosen point.

Yet it is primarily in the interplay between Parzival and Gawan in their separate quests for adventure that Wolfram can most effectively employ this technique.[71] When both set out on their travels after the double disgrace at Arthur's court Parzival's departure is mentioned first in quite vague terms (333.15: "hin reit Gahmuretes kint"), but with the promise of countless adventures to come (333.16: "swaz âventiure gesprochen sint, / diene darf hie niemen mezzen zuo"), although we are warned that we are not to learn of these immediately (333.18: "irn hœrt alrêrst waz er nuo tuo, / war er kêre und war er var"). Accordingly, the start of the next book makes it clear that the narrative strand we are now to follow is Gawan's (338.1: "Der nie gewarp nâch schanden, / ein wîl zuo sînen handen / sol nu dise âventiure

[69] See W. Deinert, *Ritter und Kosmos im Parzival: Eine Untersuchung der Sternkunde Wolframs von Eschenbach* (Munich 1960) 12ff. and 21ff.

[70] We know admittedly (from 281.23f.) that he was near the Plimizœl, but no more than this. Even this cannot help us since the Plimizœl has only been mentioned twice before (273.10 and 277.3), and quite recently, in connection with the dispatch of Orilus to Arthur.

[71] The chronological interplay between these two strands has been particularly well analyzed by Steinhoff (n. 67 above) 44ff.

hân / der werde erkande Gâwân"). With that we are told no more about Parzival; he now travels in search of adventure for what is at the moment an indefinite period of time and along a path whose stations are equally withheld from us for the time being. When he next emerges briefly from the obscurity of time and place which now envelops him it is during Gawan's exploits at Bearosche. We catch sight of Parzival therefore from the vantage-point of Gawan's adventure (since it is Gawan whom we have been following in the meanwhile), but significantly we see him not *as* he emerges from obscurity, but only some days afterwards (383.28: "er was zuo Meljanze komn / dâ vor ame dritten tage"). Parzival's elusiveness (Wolfram does not allow us to see where he comes from) has a counterpart in the way in which he also eludes Gawan when he departs from Bearosche. This time we are allowed to witness Parzival setting out again (390.7: "dô kêrte der gehiure / dâ grôz gemach was tiure: / ern suochte niht wan strîten"), but as with his departure from the Round Table we are given no idea where he intended to go. Gawan learns only later (392.24ff.) that Parzival had been present on the other side in the combat at Bearosche, but that he has now passed beyond his ken. Since we still remain with Gawan he has also passed beyond ours.

Parzival's adventures, unlike those of Gawan, are hinted at without being directly described;[72] they take place behind the scenes dominated by Gawan's exploits, so that the hero's adventures retain an element of mystery which is denied to a knight such as Gawan whom we keep much more constantly before us. The topographical obscurity of Parzival's adventures is an obvious advantage for an author whose central symbol, the Grail, is kept in deliberate obscurity as befits its mystery; but it also has the technical gain that, unable to follow Parzival, we are not allowed to desecrate the mystery of the Grail and his quest for it by asking awkward questions as to where all this may be said to have taken place. Wolfram makes use of the personified figure of *Frou Âventiure* at the beginning of Book 9 for this purpose: as a projection of the poet's imagination she provides an acceptable reason for his own ignorance of Parzival's travels and adventures since he was last seen (434.4: "wie hât Gahmuretes sun gevarn, / sît er von Artûse reit? "). This is of course fictitious ignorance on Wolfram's part, but this personification allows him to get away with it more effectively, so that behind the narrator's ignorance we may detect a poet consciously manipulating his audience, keeping them from prying too closely into the hero's exploits and from asking any embarrassing questions as to where such adventures were to be encountered. One of the many purposes of the narrative strand dealing with Gawan is therefore to give Wolfram an excuse for maintaining his ignorance about Parzival's adventures at such critical moments.

My other example of this same technique comes from Hartmann's *Iwein*, where it is elaborated in nothing like the detail which we find in *Parzival*, but still allows the

[72] This has been discussed by H. Zutt "Parzivals Kämpfe," in *Festgabe für F. Maurer*, ed. Werner Besch et al. (Düsseldorf 1968) 178ff.

author to sidestep any awkward question. The passage I have in mind concerns the search for Iwein undertaken first by the younger daughter of the Graf vom Schwarzen Dorn, and then by a relative who acts on her behalf, because only Iwein will be able and willing to fight on behalf of the daughter in her legal conflict with her elder sister. Before this episode had started we last caught sight of Iwein, the victorious champion of Lunete, departing from Laudine's court where his earlier judicial combat had taken place and accompanied for only part of his way by the grateful Lunete (5548: "nû heter rîtennes zît: / im envolgete von dan / weder wîp noch man, / niuwan vrou Lûnete, / diu im geselleschaft tete / einen guoten wec hin"). Exhaustion and the wounds of his lion soon compel him to seek refuge in a castle for fourteen days, but after that we see him under way again (5621: "hie twelter vierzehen naht, / unz daz er sînes lîbes maht / wol widere gewan, / ê daz er schiede von dan"). It is at this point that the episode of the two sisters begins so that while this episode is being narrated we are given the clear impression that Iwein was traveling in search of further adventures.

When the younger sister recognizes that she can only win her case if she can gain Iwein's assistance in judicial combat, she sets out in an attempt to find him, riding through many lands (5761: "Sus reit sî verre durch diu lant") and at random (5765: "und muote sî ir irrevart") in her attempt to come across his path. Indirectly, by learning of the difficulties and extent of her travel we learn something of Iwein's own journey. Exhaustion soon compels the younger sister to ask a relative to take over the task for her, so that the sufferings of this messenger are then described in their turn. After a time, however, the messenger stumbles across Iwein's track – first she comes to the castle (5803) where the knight, in his adventure immediately before championing Lunete, had defended the lord of the castle against the giant Harpin. The lord is able to put her on the path which Iwein took when he had earlier ridden away, and this path now takes her, as it had taken him, to the magic well and to Lunete, who is able to guide her to the spot to which she had earlier accompanied Iwein before taking leave of him. From this spot the messenger next finds her way to the castle where the knight and the lion had stayed for two weeks to recover from their wounds, and at this stage we realize that the two journeys, that of the messenger and that of Iwein, are beginning to draw closer in time, too, since we learn that Iwein has only recently left this castle (5952: "er sprach: der hât an dirre vrist / von uns hie urloup genomen"). Since she is now so hot on his trail she is advised to follow the hoofmarks (5961: "setzet iuch rehte ûf sîne slâ: / und gerâtet ir im rehte nâ, / so habt ir in vil schier erriten").

With this comforting advice she gallops after him until she catches sight of him (5967: "unz daz sî in ane sach") and can tell him of her request (5997ff.). The two converse for some time while she tells Iwein of the plight of the younger daughter and he expresses his willingness to act on her behalf. At this point Iwein tells the messenger to show him the way (6071: "nû rîtet vür und wîset mich: / swar ir mich wîset, dar var ich"), but as they ride they spend their time in conversation, thus distracting their attention from the journey at this particular point as effectively as

Hartmann intended his listeners' mind to be distracted (6076: "vil manec wehselmære / sagetens ûf ter heide: / sus vertriben sî beide / mit niuwen mæren den tac"). This distraction is vital, for it is at this point that they catch sight of the castle (6080: "nû sâhen sî wâ vor in lac / ein burc ûf ter strâze") where, we soon learn, Iwein is to undergo the decisive *Pesme Avanture.*

We should realize how skilfully Hartmann has gone to work in all this. If he had straightforwardly described Iwein's journey from Laudine's court to this castle he would have faced the difficult task of suggesting how a miraculous castle, housing such an adventure, was to be expected not in the mysterious depths of a forest (where it might have been credible), but on the main highway (*ûf ter strâze*). By describing the messenger's journey at such length Hartmann switches our attention from Iwein to her: when we leave Iwein, he has just recently left Lunete and when we rejoin him, he is on the brink of discovering this castle. Furthermore, the messenger's journey is described with its own tension, which increases when it is hinted that she is beginning to catch up with him (will she discover his path? will she be able to ride fast enough? will she be able to persuade him?), so that the reader's tension is finally resolved by the narrator when he describes Iwein's acceptance of the request (6073: "Sus wart der bote enpfangen, / und was vil gar zergangen / ir zwîvellîchiu swære").

With the tension resolved and with the messenger's search at an end the audience is invited to relax, an invitation which is made even more insinuating by the sociable conversation which now ensues between messenger and knight. Our defences are down and it is just at this point, when we have been lulled into sitting back and no longer paying close attention, that the poet strikes by introducing his enchanted castle when all seemed plain riding. We have been cajoled into relaxing at the crucial moment and have thereby lost the chance of observing critically how and where Iwein's path took the turn towards adventure, into a world where marvels happen. In this episode Hartmann's technique is quite different from Chrétien's in describing the approach to Brandiganz, but with both the result is the same: each creates an artificial transitional zone which obscures the boundary between reality and marvels. With Chrétien the castle and town are described ambiguously in terms which slowly shift the balance towards the marvelous, while Hartmann creates his smokescreen by deliberately drawing our attention in the wrong direction.

* * *

Another method employed equally involves a change in the point of view from which the action is narrated. In the case of Iwein, as we have just seen, Hartmann achieved his effect by drawing our attention away from the hero and focussing it on someone else at the precise moment when Iwein was making his decisive approach to a new realm of adventure. Yet the same effect can be achieved by the opposite method, by focussing so closely on the hero alone that we miss the wider implications and are made aware of them only when it is too late.

We saw something of this in Hartmann's description of the ride to Brandigan, instead of Arthur's court, by Erec and Guivreiz. He takes care to show us how, despite their intentions, they take the wrong path and how Guivreiz, once he recognizes Brandigan, sees that they have gone disastrously astray. Yet this is only a subjective assessment and Hartmann intends us to recognize it as only partial. The full truth is revealed to Erec, and thereby to us, only later when he learns of the adventure that awaits him in the castle, for he thanks God for the privilege granted to him and acknowledges that God has in fact guided him to this climactic adventure. What at first appeared to be a simple case of taking the wrong path and losing one's way is later revealed as an example of providential guidance. When the listener is led to believe that the hero has taken the wrong path by accident he will assume (wrongly, as it later turns out) that nothing vital or central to the narrative will occur on this sidepath and will relax his attention, as Hartmann also intended him to in the episode of Iwein's approach to the *Pesme Avanture*. He is not meant to realize, until it is too late to subject the scene to a critical scrutiny, that supernatural forces were at work behind the appearance of a mere mistake.

This argument can be taken further in the case of *Erec*, for Hartmann has so carefully articulated the cases where God intervenes and offers His guidance that the listener is unlikely, at least on a first hearing, to realize when it is that a decisive change comes about and Erec begins to enjoy the privileges that are conferred on the knight who has gained admittance to the realm of adventure. Throughout this work there are numerous references to God's guidance or assistance, but up to a certain point in the narrative these references all share the feature that they are subjective expressions of a wish or a hope (by Erec for himself or by someone else who wishes him well).[73] They are not objective statements by the narrator to the effect that God actually did assist or guide Erec in this way.

The nature of these references changes, however, in the scene where Erec rescues the knight Cadoc from the giants. Only now are we told explicitly and as an objective fact by the narrator, rather than by a character within his narrative, that God actually assisted Erec (5561: ". . . wan daz der mit im was / der Dâvîde gap die kraft / daz er wart sigehaft / an dem risen Gôlîâ: / der half ouch im des siges dâ"). This is

[73] Examples of such references are Hartmann, *Erec*, vv. 657, 750ff., 973f., 1141, 2498f., 2531, 2837f., 3188 (this wish needs to be contrasted with v. 3235f.), 4232ff., 4341, 4399ff. (what is important here is the impersonal construction with *gewern*: there is no explicit suggestion that it is God who grants them what they had asked Him for), 4885f. (said of Gawein, but in connection with Erec), 5309ff., 5372ff.

Such examples also occur after the turning point of the Cadoc episode: vv. 6698ff. (said by the narrator, but as a wish, not as a statement of fact), 6845, 6851, 6901 (narrator's wish), 7059f., 7077 (narrator's wish), 8044, 8147ff., 8350ff., 8527ff., 8534ff., 8560ff., 8636ff., 8812ff., 8859, 8891f. (narrator's wish), 9047, 9129f. (narrator's wish). But *after* the turning point they have a different effect, since now we know from the narrator's objective statements that God does in fact answer such prayers. Furthermore, the frequency of these examples in the climactic adventure with Mabonagrin is meant to underline Erec's trust in God.

only the first of such objective allusions,[74] for they recur also in the episode where God sends Erec his horse to make good his escape from Limors, and in his second encounter with Guivreiz.[75] Although wishes for divine protection are still expressed on Erec's behalf after his rescue of Cadoc,[76] this exploit clearly marks a critical turning-point in that only now does God begin to intervene as a fact of the narrative.

Since the Cadoc episode is also the first encounter in which Erec actively intervenes out of compassion with those in need rather than passively suffer the assaults of others, this turning point indicates that God's guidance and assistance are given to those whose virtue merits it. Significantly, Erec no longer has to be warned by Enite of the dangers that await him ahead;[77] it is he who notices the next adventure and is given unfailing guidance.[78] The hints that suggest this new state of affairs are subtly made, so that the audience runs the risk of being temporarily as blind to the overall truth of the situation as Erec was himself until, after his encounter with Guivreiz, he recognizes that God has in fact been guiding him along the right path. This retrospective revelation can only be said to open up a new dimension to those who have failed to take the earlier hints, but its force is to show us that the conditions of Erec's journey changed in mid-career, that a ride at random gave way to preternatural guidance in a way so subtle that we may not have noticed

[74] In fact, the first objective reference to God's assistance comes earlier than this, in connection with the horses for which Erec forces his wife to accept responsibility: Hartmann's God is so courteous that He cannot refrain from helping a lady in such distress (v. 3460ff.). However, since we are concerned with the knight on his travels and since Erec is the hero of Hartmann's work we can justifiably ignore this reference as irrelevant to the providential control of Erec's journey.

[75] We are now told by the narrator at the start of the Oringles episode that God is intervening to exercise control over events (vv. 6069ff., 6115ff.). At the close of the episode, when Erec and Enite make good their escape, the narrator expresses his wish for God's help (v. 6698ff.), but this wish is immediately answered by Erec's providential discovery of his horse (6709ff.), which is at first put down to Erec's *sælekeit* (6713), but then explicitly to God's will (v. 6726). Hartmann is similarly explicit in the second Guivreiz episode. Erec's success may be wished for by an actor within the story or by the narrator himself, but this does not stop the narrator from describing events as under the control of *diu geschiht* (v. 6868) and from attributing Erec's good fortune both to his own valor and to God's will (v. 7070ff.). This cooperation between God and knightly *vrümekeit*, at a stage when the knight has merited divine protection, forms an effective contrast with Erec's first adventure with the robbers where, as we saw (n. 73 above), there is an antithesis between the wish for God's help (v. 3188) and the statement that his success was due to his own valor alone (v. 3235f.).

Although there are no similar objective statements in the Mabonagrin episode, there are numerous tacit allusions to the David and Goliath theme (vv. 9059f., 9157f., 9190ff., 9237, 9303, 9318) which refer back to the narrator's own explicit comments on this theme when describing Erec's fight with the giants in the Cadoc scene (v. 5561ff.). We can be sure therefore that when Mabonagrin finally comes to realize that Erec has been sent by God to release him from his slavery (v. 9585ff.; cf. also 9454f., 9582, 9671f. and 9740ff.), he is voicing an opinion which is shared by the narrator.

[76] See n. 73 above.

[77] Hartmann, *Erec*, vv. 5295ff. and 6587ff.

[78] *Ibid.* vv. 5378ff., 5570ff., 8754ff., 8881ff., 10054f., 10085ff.

it at the time. If so, we shall have deprived ourselves, as the author intended us to, of the chance of observing Erec's actual transition to a new realm governed by novel conditions.

We see the same method employed in *Parzival*, but here the presuppositions are reversed. Whereas Erec first rode at random and only later came to merit God's guidance, Parzival sets out as the beneficiary of providential assistance, but then forfeits this by his failure at Munsalvæsche. We retrospectively learn with Erec that he has come to merit guidance, whereas our belated recognition in the case of Parzival is that he has now lost such assistance. The fact that, on both occasions, the truth is revealed to us only subsequently means that, as listeners, we no longer have the means of testing earlier episodes in the light of knowledge acquired only later. In *Parzival* our initial uncertainty about the scenes in question means that we fail to grasp that they illustrate the hero's providential guidance, so that our subsequent enlightenment parallels that of Parzival as he learns the truth from Trevrizent. Wolfram's technique amounts therefore to giving us the requisite information about the knight's travels, but in such a way that we can be expected not to grasp its significance at the time; by rhetorical means he is therefore putting us in the same position as his hero, who witnesses and experiences events without seeing their meaning.

The poet's methods in implying, without explicitly stating, that Parzival was preternaturally guided at the start of his journey, have been analyzed in detail elsewhere.[79] They comprise suggestions that Parzival's single-minded effort, the haste and speed of his travel, constantly take him along the correct path,[80] as well as the use of gradation to strengthen the impression that he heads unwittingly, but without the slightest deviation, for the next event that awaits his coming.[81]

The significance of these passages is that they are deliberately ambiguous and that on a first hearing an audience is likely to take them only in their innocuous sense. The haste with which Parzival travels from point to point could be simply a sign of the eagerness with which a young boy sets out in search of Arthur and chivalry; it need point to nothing more than this. The same is true of the gradations with which his actual speed is suggested, for even when Wolfram implies extraordinary feats in covering such immense distances there is still no reason for us to see in this the miraculous intervention of providence. Parzival may cover a great distance on leaving Graharz (161.17: "gewâpent reitz der tumbe man / den tac sô verre, ez hete lân / ein blôz wîser, solt erz hân geriten / zwêne tage, ez wære vermiten"), but this may be just the inexperienced enthusiasm of one just introduced to knighthood, riding his horse to death, where another would have spared it more prudently. Condwiramurs

[79] The details of Wolfram's technique have been well established by Wynn (n. 36 above) 393ff. My approach differs slightly from hers, however, in that I am more concerned to show that Wolfram first suggests Parzival's preternatural guidance by remarks which are deliberately ambiguous and only later allows us to grasp their full implications.

[80] *Ibid.* 399f.

[81] *Ibid.* 400f.

may wonder at the speed with which he covered the distance between Graharz and Brobarz (189.22: "Hetz anders iemen mir gesagt, / der volge wurde im niht verjehn, / deiz eines tages wære geschehn") and his speed may be even more remarkable on his way to Munsalvæsche (224.22: "uns tuot diu âventiure bekant / daz er bî dem tage reit, / ein vogel hetes arbeit, / solt erz allez hân erflogen"), but with an author so given to hyperbole[82] we have no grounds for not believing that here too Wolfram has his tongue in his cheek, especially if we realize that his reference to his source conceals the fact that Chrétien makes no mention of the speed or distance of Perceval's journey on this occasion.[83]

Even when the narrator refers to these journeys with apparent explicitness he still remains fundamentally ambiguous. Parzival, we are told, does not lose his way in the wild country between Graharz and Brobarz (180.15: "Doch reit er wênec irre") or even on his ride from Lake Brumbane to the Grail-castle (226.10: "Parzivâl der huop sich dan, / er begunde wackerlîchen draben / den rehten pfat unz an den graben") even though the risk is great enough here for Anfortas to feel it necessary to warn him (226.6ff.). But there is still no reason to assume anything but a happy chance here, the good fortune that accompanies the chosen hero of a fairy-tale and no one else.[84] Finally, conscious ambiguity seems to lurk behind Wolfram's phrasing in describing Parzival's journey to Munsalvæsche (224.19: "mit gewalt den zoum daz ros / truog über ronen und durchez mos: / wandez wîste niemens hant"). If the knight's horse is directed by no one's hand, this could quite well imply that Parzival allowed the horse to take its own path (precisely because he is riding at random and does not know the way) or that there was nobody to show Parzival the way[85] (so wild and deserted was the region). But behind these two obvious readings there stands another which we are not meant to perceive quite so readily – and here for the first time we touch upon the other possibilities, ambiguously present in all these references but clarified only later.

If no one's hand (or better in this context: no man's hand) guides Parzival's horse and if nonetheless the horse takes Parzival through wild country straight to the kingdom of the Grail, then it is possible to see in this phrasing a suggestion that it was the hand of God that guided Parzival on this last critical stage of his journey,[86] the God for whom one of Wolfram's circumlocutions is *diu hœhste hant*[87] and who

[82] E.g. Wolfram, *Willehalm* 62.11ff.

[83] Chrétien, *Li contes del Graal*, ed. A. Hilka (Halle 1932) v. 2976ff.

[84] In other words, Parzival's good fortune in finding the way on these two occasions could be a sign of the *sælekeit* or *geschiht* which Hartmann was ready to invoke in Erec's case (vv. 6713, 6868). But just as Hartmann in each case has to go further and mention God explicitly for his point to be made (vv. 6726, 7070ff.), so is it impossible to be sure with Parzival whether he has actually received divine guidance. Wolfram may hint at this possibility, but he refuses to pin himself down.

[85] See M. O'C. Walshe, "Notes on *Parzival*, Book V," *London Mediaeval Studies* 1 (1939) 343.

[86] Wynn (n. 36 above) 401.

[87] Cf. H. Adolf, "Die Wolframsche Wendung *diu hœhst hant*," *Neophilologus* 19 (1934) 260ff.

later answers Parzival's plea by guiding his horse to Trevrizent's cell (452.9: " 'nu genc nâch der gotes kür.' / den zügel gein den ôren für / er dem orse legte, / mit den sporn erz vaste regte. / gein Fontân la salvâtsche ez gienc"). Such explicitness is lacking in the earlier passage, because the poet wishes to reveal the fact of Parzival's guidance only retrospectively, after it is already forfeit. At the point when the knight approaches the Grail-castle we cannot know that God's hand is at work. Even though no one's hand may guide his horse, we know nothing of the significance of Lake Brumbane or of the castle to which he finds his way[88] and therefore cannot see miraculous guidance in his arrival there, by contrast with his being led to Trevrizent's cell. Equally, we know nothing at this stage of God's readiness to guide a knight who places his trust in Him to the extent of abandoning his reins. Both these points are made clear in the scene when Parzival comes to Trevrizent, but in the earlier scene they are only implicit and become apparent only retrospectively.

But how does Wolfram make this subsequently clear, how does he show us that Parzival was not, as we thought at the time, riding through a world of reality which was governed by chance or by human explanations, but was instead being miraculously guided through the realm of adventure? The turning-point, we are made to realize, is Parzival's failure at the Grail-castle, for when he departs on the following morning, thinking that he might catch up with the Grail-knights and offer them his military assistance, he loses track of them and for the first time in his travels fails to keep to the right path (249.5: "do begunde krenken sich ir spor: / sich schieden die dâ riten vor. / ir slâ wart smal, diu ê was breit: / er verlôs si gar: daz was im leit").[89] If this remark simply stood alone, it could be seen as purely fortuitous (like the earlier passage showing that Parzival had found his way, apparently by chance), but Wolfram shows that this is not the case by prefacing it with his first explicit statement about the hero's journeying (249.1: "Der valscheite widersaz / kêrt' ûf der huofslege kraz. / sîn scheiden dan daz riuwet mich. / alrêst nu âventiurt ez sich"). The auspices for Parzival finding the right way seem to be good, in fact they are better than before, for now he has horsetracks to follow, whereas earlier he had struggled through wild, trackless terrain (180.6: "vil ungevertes er dô reit, / dâ wênic wegerîches stuont") and followed unknown paths (226.6: "dâ gênt unkunde wege"). Nonetheless, it is only now that Parzival loses his way, a fact which is explicitly

[88] Our ignorance is heightened by the manner in which Wolfram withholds topographical names from us at this stage. We know that Parzival comes to a lake in the vicinity of the Grail-castle, but this is simply termed a *sê* (225.2) and its name *Brumbâne* occurs for the first time only very much later (261.27) when Parzival encounters Jeschute and Orilus. Similarly, although Parzival has now penetrated into Grail territory and soon comes to the Grail-castle itself, the names *Terre de Salvæsche* (251.4) and *Munsalvæsche* (251.2) are first mentioned to him, and to us, by Sigune, once he has left the Grail behind him. Initially, therefore, we realize as little of the meaning of this realm as does Parzival himself.

[89] Wynn (n. 36) 402.

stressed by the author's unmistakable use of *alrêst* to make the novel comment about this knight: now for the first time he rides at random, subject to the vagaries of chance[90] and therefore liable, like any other knight, to lose his way. This is borne out by what we are told of the hero's travels from this point on: he has so far forfeited the miraculous guidance which he unconsciously enjoyed earlier that he spends years trying to find Munsalvæsche again, now unwittingly riding further and further away from it, now stumbling into Grail territory, but failing to reach the goal of his quest. The journey to Munsalvæsche which Parzival had earlier accomplished with miraculous speed and directness now becomes a blind groping, extended over years and apparently leading nowhere.

In the scene of Parzival's departure from the Grail-castle Wolfram brings it home to us that his hero had previously benefited from miraculous guidance. By letting us learn of this only now, at the moment of his actually forfeiting it, Wolfram lets us feel the full magnitude of Parzival's loss, but at the same time he allows us to realize belatedly that his earlier remarks had been ambiguous and that, like Parzival, we had failed to realize the true facts of his situation. We can now appreciate that Parzival's haste and speed were not just the hallmark of an eager, youthful knight (although they may have been that as well) or simply examples of poetic hyperbole (although this is also an undeniable feature of Wolfram's style), but primarily indications of the miraculous guidance which takes him unerringly through the realm of adventure, avoiding every sidetrack and conquering every obstacle. Even the remark that no man's hand guided Parzival's horse to Munsalvæsche now begins to reveal the possibility that it was a concealed allusion to divine guidance.

At the point when Parzival leaves the Grail-castle, when we realize that he has now lost the guidance which was his before, we know for certain only that his guidance must have been miraculous, but not necessarily divine. For this further certainty we have to wait several years, during the period of Parzival's rides at random, until his approach to Trevrizent's hermitage. The pilgrim-knight has just recommended Parzival to seek out the hermit's cell nearby, pointing out that he has only to follow his track (448.21: "rîtet fürbaz ûf unser spor! "). But for Parzival, whose thoughts have been turned towards God again by this encounter with the pilgrims and by learning from them that it is Good Friday, this offer of a track to follow is not

[90] I take the verb *sich âventiurn* to imply the element of chance, a meaning which is also present in other cases where Wolfram employs the noun *âventiure*, for example with regard to Feirefiz's random journey to Europe in search of his father (748.24: ". . . dar inne diu reise mîn / nâch âventiure wart getân"). In this pagan's view of things, however, his journey has not been ultimately fortuitous, since it is crowned with the unexpected success of meeting, not his father, but his half-brother, a success for which he thanks the pagan divinities that guided him (748.14ff.). But Feirefiz is not the hero of this work and Wolfram can therefore allow us in his case to catch sight of the providential framework immediately, whereas with Parzival we have to struggle, like him, to recognize the fact of guidance at all.

enough, since it is as ambiguous as Wolfram's initial remarks about his journeying [91] and need not imply that God is intervening in his life again. He therefore rides away (451.3: "Hin rîtet Herzeloyden fruht") considering once again the possibility that God might help him and it is in this mood that he deliberately turns back from the track which the pilgrim had pointed out to him (451.23: "er kêrt sich wider, dannen er dâ reit"). By doing this he is deliberately issuing a challenge to God (452.5: "mac gotes kunst die helfe hân, / diu wîse mir diz kastelân / dez wægest umb die reise mîn! ")– he loosens his reins, abandons the horse to God, and it is in this light that we have to understand the fact that the horse now takes him, with a simplicity and directness that rival Parzival's initial journey under guidance to Munsalvæsche, to nowhere else but the hermit's cell (452.13: "gein Fontâne la salvâtsche ez gienc"). Whereas Parzival's departure from the Grail-castle had made it clear that his former guidance had been miraculous, the scene where it is restored to him as he approaches the hermit's cell shows the divine nature of such guidance. We learn the facts about this guidance retrospectively and in consciously controlled instalments, so that we partly share our ignorance with Parzival[92] and are consequently in no position to ask critical questions of an author who is manipulating our reactions as remotely, but as surely as God is guiding Parzival.[93]

* * *

But Wolfram's artistry is even more subtle than this. He is not content with arranging for us to learn the nature of Parzival's initial divine guidance retrospectively, during

[91] One might even argue that Parzival, like Hartmann in his description of Erec's good fortune (see n. 84 above), is not content with an ambiguity and can only be satisfied by an unmistakable indication. Just as Hartmann has to add the word *got* explicitly, so must Parzival be convinced by an obviously miraculous intervention. If this is so, it suggests that Wolfram's references to Parzival's initial journeying (see above between nn. 78 and 89, and especially the argument of Wynn [n. 36 above] 393ff.) are left deliberately obscure and are not in themselves enough to imply that his travels at this stage were providentially controlled. Final certainty is only provided retrospectively – we are in as much need of proof as Parzival himself.

[92] Although our growth to certainty largely parallels Parzival's, Wolfram has not failed to exploit the ironic possibilities of a discrepancy between our knowledge of the situation and his. We therefore learn, as he does not at that stage, that miraculous guidance was withdrawn after he left Munsalvæsche (249.4: "alrêst nu âventiurt ez sich"), as we are also informed that God was in control as Parzival began to approach the hermit's cell (435.12: "sîn wolte got dô ruochen").

[93] Parzival's reorientation (illustrated in his restoration to divine guidance) is expressed not merely in spatial, but also in temporal terms; for it is only after he has been guided to Trevrizent that he learns from the hermit how long he has been wandering and what day it is, and is thus given his bearings in the liturgical year. It is not by chance that Wolfram should depict Parzival's reorientation in time and place (as two aspects of the same thing) in this one episode. This can be confirmed if we recall that the episode where Parzival first began to go astray and lose his way (his departure from Munsalvæsche in pursuit of the Grail-knights) is also the first occasion (as is clear from Weigand's discussion) when Parzival "falls out of the time-pattern" of the work, since Wolfram now suddenly ceases to give us the time-references which he had so carefully provided in his earlier adventures. In other words, the ignorance which is now forced upon us is meant to reflect the beginning of the hero's temporal disorientation.

the period when it is withdrawn from him, for he suggests that even during this period of estrangement and rides at random God was still in control of events, however indirectly and however much behind the scenes. On this different level of God's intervention in the course of events Wolfram illustrates how the wrong path taken by his hero (and it is during this period that we come to expect him to take the wrong path) should ultimately turn out to be the correct path for him, however circuitously it may lead him to his goal.[94] On such occasions Wolfram takes care to alert us to the fact that the path taken was the wrong one– here his explicitness, given in the episode itself and not retrospectively, differs radically from his technique when describing Parzival's preternatural guidance. The reason for this difference is clear, for by telling his listeners early the poet may hope to disarm and lull them into a sense of false security, into the belief that, since this is the wrong path, no predetermined adventure can await the knight at the end of it; since the mistake is presented as a human error or incapacity, we cannot yet be in the miraculous realm where the hero is guided unerringly to the adventure meant for him alone. This is a method which we saw Hartmann exploit when describing Erec's approach to Brandigan, but Wolfram skilfully compounds its effectiveness by using it, not in the period when Parzival rides successfully from adventure to adventure, but in the period when he is deprived of guidance and prone to go astray anyhow, in the period when the listener's defenses are already down. Since we have been concerned with the crucial scenes when Parzival departs from Munsalvæsche and when he comes to the hermit's cell, I shall take my examples from the same episodes.

When he leaves Munsalvæsche on the morning after his failure Parzival is under the impression that Anfortas is in need of his knightly assistance.[95] On noticing the hoofmarks outside the castle he readily assumes that the Grail-knights have ridden out in the military service of their lord and, unhesitatingly, he sets out in pursuit of them, meaning to join them and render his host and benefactor the same service. However, the tracks he follows soon fade away, Parzival loses them and thereby loses his own way (249.5ff.)– for the first time in the whole work, as we have already seen. However important this point is (for it shows that guidance has been withdrawn from the hero as a result of his behaviour at the Grail-castle, even though the listener may still have no idea why this should have merited such a punishment), it conceals another detail of Wolfram's artistry. Parzival may have set out hoping to assist Anfortas and may have lost his way in the attempt, but, on quite another level, he does find his way.

At the moment when we learn that he has lost the tracks of the Grail-knights we are also told that, guided by the voice of a woman lamenting, he comes across Sigune for the second time (249.11: "dô erhôrte der degen ellens rîch / einer frouwen

[94] This problem, both in connection with the period of Parzival's rides at random and elsewhere in the work, has been briefly discussed by M. E. Gibbs, "Wrong Paths in *Parzival*," *Modern Language Review* 63 (1968) 872ff.

[95] Cf. Wolfram, *Parzival* 246.1ff. and 248.19ff.

stimme jæmerlîch"). This meeting is a disastrous one for Parzival, since Sigune curses him roundly to his face when she learns of his omission at Munsalvæsche and it is from her that he learns something of what was at stake at the Grail-castle, something of the enormity of his error. But in learning of the opportunity which he has so irresponsibly squandered Parzival is also learning something positive about the mysteries of the Grail for the first time, something about his own kinship with the world of the Grail. It is not by chance that in his first meeting with Sigune, in the worldly Arthurian setting of Bertane, Parzival should learn from her details which are connected with his pursuit of chivalry (his noble birth and his feudal obligations), whereas the second encounter, in Terre de Salvæsche, should be concerned with the mysteries of the Grail-castle.[96] In other words, although he may be cursed in this second meeting, Parzival is now being judged (and found wanting) on a higher level than on any earlier occasion and the accusation which Sigune launches against him has a vital part to play in the long journey that lies ahead of him before he finally comes to Munsalvæsche again. It is in fact the first station on his way to realizing that the help he is to bring Anfortas is not the military assistance which he naïvely imagines to be required, but the simple question of compassion which he eventually asks.[97]

In short, Parzival may have lost track of the Grail-knights, but this is because he himself is not yet ready to give Anfortas the only kind of help that can miraculously serve him. In losing their track, however, he finds the way to Sigune who, by her very accusation, teaches him vital truths about himself and the Grail. In losing the track which he intended to follow (but which was the wrong one for him, for it could have led him nowhere in his wish to serve his host) he finds a path which, however irrelevant it may seem to his wishes at the time, eventually leads him, by a roundabout way necessitated by his own folly, to the goal of his wishes. We may not realize this at the time, since we cannot yet grasp the paradox that the path *away* from the Grail-castle is the only path which will lead him back to it. Equally we are meant by Wolfram to miss the vital point that, although his hero seems to have lost his path at this stage, his way is still through the realm of adventure in which preternatural guidance, even if more indirectly than before, is granted him.

A similar impression (the faint outlines of guidance behind the appearance of losing his way) is conveyed by Parzival's next meeting with Sigune, placed in the narrative just before the knight's sojourn with Trevrizent in his hermitage.[98] The anger which Sigune had displayed towards him at their last encounter has now evaporated and she is genuinely touched by the constancy of his endeavor to find his way back to Munsalvæsche. In an attempt to help him she tells him that, since her

[96] This point has been well made by Wynn (n. 1 above) 41f.

[97] See W. Mohr's valuable demonstration of this, "Hilfe und Rat in Wolframs *Parzival*," in *Festschrift für J. Trier*, ed. B. von Wiese and K. H. Borck (Meisenheim 1954) 173ff., esp. 187 and 190.

[98] *Parzival*, 435.15ff.

food is brought to her in her retreat by Cundrie from the Grail-castle (438.29ff.) and since this messenger has only recently left her, there is every hope that Parzival might be able to follow her track and thereby reach Munsalvæsche again (442.9: "si sprach: nu helfe dir des hant, / dem aller kumber ist bekant; / ob dir sô wol gelinge, / daz dich ein slâ bringe, / aldâ du Munsalvæsche sihst, / dâ du mir dîner freuden gihst. / Cundrîe la surziere reit / vil niulîch hinnen").

This is a repetition of the earlier situation when Parzival departed from Munsalvæsche, for there too he had set out by following clear, fresh tracks (248.17: "Parzival der huop sich nâch / vast ûf die slâ dier dâ sach"). There too he had hoped to catch up with the Grail-knights ahead of him, just as Sigune now tells him that he has every chance of overtaking Cundrie (442.21: "ich rât daz du ir rîtes nâch: / ir ist lîhte vor dir niht sô gâch, / dune mügest si schiere hân erriten"). But, as on the earlier occasion, Parzival soon loses these tracks, however hopeful things had seemed when he set out (442.24: "dane wart niht langer dô gebiten, / urloup nam der helt aldâ: / dô kêrter ûf die niwen slâ. / Cundrîen mûl die reise gienc, / daz ungeverte im undervienc / eine slâ dier hat erkorn. / sus wart aber der grâl verlorn"). In contrast to the knight's journeys through wild country before he came to the Grail-castle, the desolate, trackless landscape now really does represent an obstacle and it is seen as the cause of his losing his way, a fact which the narrator sums up resignedly (443.5: "nu lât in rîten: war sol er? ").

But if this scene, in which Parzival leaves Sigune hoping to catch up with Cundrie, resembles the earlier scene when, hoping to catch up with the Grail-knights, he came to Sigune, we may press the parallel further. Is it not possible that, although he lost track of Cundrie, he found another path which, however indirect, was the only path for him – just as his earlier path to Sigune was the necessary one for him at this stage? Just after Wolfram has stated that Parzival has lost track of Cundrie he describes his encounter with a Grail-knight (443.6: "dort gein im kom geriten her / ein man . . .") and their combat. This brings it home to us that Parzival was actually in Grail territory at this time and that he can only narrowly have missed being led by Cundrie to Munsalvæsche, but after this joust Parzival rides on at random (445.27: "do reit er, ern wiste war"). Even though an unspecified lapse of time comes between this encounter and the next (446.3ff.) it is in fact only a few lines later (seconds later in narrative time, rather than narrated time) that Parzival meets the pilgrim-knight who, as we have seen, is the means whereby he comes to Trevrizent's cell in the vicinity. In terms of Wolfram's narrative there is an unbroken continuity in these encounters with Sigune, the Grail-knight, the pilgrim-knight and Trevrizent. We are led to the conclusion that if Parzival had not lost his way after leaving Sigune he may never have come across Trevrizent, but since it is Trevrizent who absolves him from sin (502.25: "er sprach: gip mir dîn sünde her: / vor gote ich bin dîn wandels wer") and reconciles him with God (741.26: "der getoufte wol getrûwet gote / sît er von Trevrizende schiet"), the ironic truth is that only by losing the way which Sigune had pointed out to him does Parzival find his way back to God.

This again provides a parallel with the scene in which Parzival came across Sigune after leaving the Grail-castle. In this earlier scene the reason behind his losing track of the Grail-knights and consequent inability to give Anfortas the military assistance he thought was required was that assistance of this kind was out of place, that Parzival had to learn, at great cost to himself and to the suffering Grail-king, precisely what manner of assistance was called for in the context of the Grail. Similarly, although Sigune reveals her new-found sympathy for the hero by putting him on Cundrie's tracks she does not realize the extent of his estrangement from God. Only when this has been healed by Trevrizent can there be any possibility of Parzival being worthy of the Grail, so that his path to Munsalvæsche leads not in Cundrie's tracks, as Sigune thought, but indirectly via Trevrizent's cell. In both cases he appears to lose his way because he is not yet ready for any direct approach to his goal. The path along which he wanders when we (and he) think that he has hopelessly lost his way is in fact the only path which will bring him in his present condition to the destination he seeks.

* * *

This last method, which I have illustrated from Hartmann's *Erec* and Wolfram's *Parzival*, reveals a narrator who in each case deliberately leads his audience astray (just as God appears to do the same with Parzival), allowing them to think that the hero was lost, had unwittingly strayed so far from the realm of adventure that their critical attention was no longer demanded for the time being. In reality, of course, the episodes in which these misleading suggestions are made are scenes which illustrate the knight's providential guidance, even if this now takes place on a level which we had not expected. Hartmann and Wolfram are therefore both exploiting the ambiguity of these situations to put us off our guard precisely when our critical faculties should be exercised most carefully. Yet the same effect can be achieved when an author exploits the ambiguity of language, as we saw in the case of *Parzival* 224.21 (*wandez wîste niemens hant*), where we learn only retrospectively that, if the hero's steed was guided by no human hand, this must be because of divine control of Parzival's travels. These wider dimensions of the action, lurking behind the apparent simplicity of the pronoun *niemen*, are revealed too late for the listeners to be able to scrutinize the scene critically and by the time they realize what is afoot the knight has long been at large within the realm of adventure. I shall discuss two examples of such verbal ambiguity to illustrate this further method of deliberately obscuring the knight's entry into this miraculous realm.

For the sake of continuity I choose one of these examples from *Parzival* again, indeed from the same crucial scene where Parzival loses his way (or so we are allowed to think) after leaving Sigune in pursuit of Cundrie. Sigune points out the way which the Grail-messenger has just gone (442.12: ". . . daz dich ein slâ dar bringe, / aldâ du Munsalvæsche sihst / . . . / Cundrîe la surziere reit / vil niulîch hinnen"), her tracks are fresh so that the knight may hope to follow them without difficulty (442.25: "urloup nam der helt aldâ / dô kêrter ûf die niwen slâ"). So far this seems quite simple and above board and this no doubt is how we are meant to take these lines at this point. But doubts begin to stir when, after the meeting with the pilgrim-knight and the telling scene in which Parzival challenges God when he slackens his reins and God accepts this challenge by guiding his horse to the hermit's cell, the path which takes the hero to Trevrizent is also called a *slâ*, in fact three times (455.23: "der rît nu ûf die niwen slâ, / die gein im kom der rîter grâ"; 456.1: "Diu slâ in dâ niht halden liez"; 457.10: "ich reit sîn slâ, unz ich iuch vant"). Again the reference to *die niwen slâ* has a straightforward explanation on which we are meant to seize, because the pilgrim-knight, like Cundrie along her path, has only recently ridden this way, so that his tracks are still fresh. But we know enough about Wolfram's use of thematic repetitions to suspect that there is more here than meets the eye.[99]

Although the realism of Cundrie's and Kahenis's fresh tracks may be quite convincing in the context of each separate scene, the recurrence of this motif, together with the use of the key-word *slâ* five times in all, in so small a space is meant as a signal to us. As G. Weber has suggested,[100] the phrase *diu niuwe slâ* highlights a turning point in Parzival's journeys, since now God's guidance extended to him is made clear both to us and to the knight who finds that God has indeed accepted his challenge and conducted his horse to Trevrizent. We in the audience are given a hint in advance, so that we come closer to the poet's omniscience and move away from Parzival's ignorance, when Wolfram tells us of his journey at the start of Book 9 (435.10: "der junge degen unervorht / reit durch âventiur suochen: / sîn wolte got dô ruochen"), but this is then illustrated in narrative terms when the horse is led to the hermit. But, as we have just seen, Parzival would not have been guided on to this *niuwen slâ*, left by Kahenis and leading to Trevrizent, if he had not earlier lost another *niuwen slâ*, left by Cundrie and leading, so he hoped, to Munsalvæsche. The loss of one *slâ* results in his finding the other, in being guided to an encounter which issues in a reconciliation with God without which he could never gain access to the Grail. In that God's guidance is shown to be operative here again for the first time after Parzival's omission at the Grail-castle this guidance really does lead the knight on to a *niuwen slâ*, but this is a new path in a spiritual or symbolic sense and no longer in the physical sense of "a freshly made track," which was all that seemed to be involved when we first came across this phrase as Parzival set out in the hope of catching up with Cundrie.

For my second example of linguistic ambiguity exploited deliberately by an author I turn once again to the first Arthurian romance, *Erec*. We have seen something of the crucial importance of the Brandigan adventure from the point of

[99] Mohr, in particular, has taught us to pay close attention to such thematic repetitions (n. 97 above) 173ff., and also "Parzival und Gawan," *Euphorion* 52 (1958) 1ff.

[100] G. Weber, *Parzival: Ringen und Vollendung* (Oberursel 1948) 58. Weber refers to four examples of *slâ* in this passage, but has obviously missed 456.1. On this same phrase and its symbolism see also W. Harms, *Homo viator in bivio: Studien zur Bildlichkeit des Weges* (Munich 1970) 235ff.

view of our problem and have analyzed Hartmann's version with regard to Erec losing his way and Chrétien's with regard to the actual approach to the castle. I now wish to consider Chrétien's depiction of the manner in which Erec loses his way. The French poet is markedly more pithy than the German, for he describes the journey from the castle of Guivrez to Brandiganz in no more than four lines (5367: "Chevauchié ont des le matin / Jusqu'au vespre le droit chemin / Plus de trante liues galesches, / Et vienent devant les bretesches . . ."). Hartmann cannot avoid a lengthier treatment, because he makes no use of the ambiguity of Chrétien's phrase *le droit chemin*. In place of this the German text says simply (7816: "die rehten strâze si vermiten: / die baz gebûwen si riten"), so that Hartmann, if he wishes to make the transition gradual, has no choice but to introduce a fork in the road (a detail missing in Chrétien) and to motivate his transition to this adventure by having Erec and Guivreiz take the wrong road and lose their way. This is in fact the outcome in Chrétien's version, too, but here the element of doubt concerns not the actors (which road are they to take?), but the listeners (which meaning are they to attribute to *le droit chemin*?).

The phrase could mean either "the path to the right" or "the correct path, because it is the path that leads directly to one's goal." We know that Chrétien's Erec, like Hartmann's, sets out with the intention of going to Arthur (5280: ". . . Tant qu'a la cort serai venuz / Le roi Artu, que veoir vuel / Ou a Robais ou a Carduel"), but we soon learn that, on taking this path, he arrives somewhere else, namely at Brandiganz (5387: "Sire! fet il, mout bien le sai, / La verité vos an dirai. / Brandiganz a non li chastiaus"). From this remark of Guivrez we are allowed to draw the conclusion that, since Erec has come to a place quite other than his intended destination, the words *le droit chemin* can only have the physical meaning of "path to the right," they cannot possibly imply "the correct path," since that would have taken the knight to Arthur's court. But if so, the phrase is used in a strangely absolute sense whereas, as E. Auerbach has pointed out in a similar context,[101] the physical sense demands a relative usage, at least a choice between a path to the left and one to the right (it is probably this consideration which led Hartmann to introduce the detail of the *wegescheide*).[102]

This doubt about the stylistic adequacy of the phrase in the physical sense is reinforced much later, however, when we come to the outcome of Erec's combat with Mabonagrain and his victorious return to Arthur's court. From this it emerges that only this final adventure really qualifies him to return with honor to Arthur, that this path to Brandiganz, which at first seemed to be the wrong one since it led him away from his goal, did in fact lead him to the Round Table, indirectly but on a higher level of accomplishment.

The position of Chrétien's Erec, following his *droit chemin*, closely resembles that

[101] E. Auerbach, *Mimesis* (Bern 1946) 126.

[102] This is not meant to exclude other possibilities as well, such as the traditional image of the *bivium*, discussed by H. Siefken, "*Der sælden strâze*: Zum Motiv der zwei Wege bei Hartmann von Aue," *Euphorion* 61 (1967) 1ff. On this image at large see Harms (n. 100 above).

of Wolfram's Parzival on his *niuwen slâ*: both start out on what we are persuaded into thinking is the right path, both lose their way and both are taken on what seems the wrong path to their ultimate goal. Both are led on the wrong path so that they may prove themselves worthy of their goal, a possibility of self-fulfilment which would not have been their lot if they had remained on what they took to be the right path. The technique, as regards the author's manipulation of his listeners, is in both cases the same: a phrase which at first we imagine to be a pointer in the world of physical topography is later seen to possess symbolic implications, but by the time this is clear to us we have long since left the crucial episode of the transition into the realm of adventure behind us.

* * *

The methods we have been considering (the creation of a deliberately blurred transition, the belated widening of the narrative dimensions or the exploitation of verbal ambiguity) all have one thing in common: they all represent different ways, open to the author, of distracting the audience's attention at the critical moment. The same is true of the last possibility I wish to look at, namely the motif of the courtly hunt after the stag or hind.[103] How relevant this motif is to our problem may be shown by a modern parallel. Imagine that you have an appointment at an office in a large building unknown to you and that you have to make inquiries as to your way there at the reception desk. Armed with these instructions you set off and because you are determined to find your way and are not distracted you will probably pay such close attention to the details of the meandering corridors that you would be able to find your way there again. But if the reception desk had sent someone with you to conduct you to your appointment you would probably have been so engaged in polite conversation that the details of your way would almost certainly have escaped you. The presence of a guide is therefore sufficient to distract attention from the route followed and the same applies to the motif of the hunt: the knight follows the animal, but the presence of the animal is enough to draw our attention temporarily away from the hero. Instead of asking a question concerning the knight (where is he heading for? where precisely does he cross into the magic realm of adventure?), we begin to wonder about his quarry (where did it spring from? will it manage to escape from the hunter?), and it is precisely at this stage, when our attention is diverted, that the author situates his crucial transition. This motif obviously combines well with the elaboration of two zones in the forest, an outer belt where the courtly hunt takes place and the mysterious and forbidding depths, for the sudden appearance of a stag in the hunting zone can easily be used to

[103] For a wide-ranging treatment of this motif see A. T. Hatto, "Poetry and the Hunt in Medieval Germany," *Journal of the Australasian Universities Modern Languages Association* 25 (1966) 33ff. and also C. Pschmadt, "Die Sage von der verfolgten Hinde," Ph.D. diss. (Greifswald 1911).

lure the eager huntsmen (and the audience) by stages of which he may not be aware into the inner zone where he is exposed to the workings of adventure.

However, this aspect is only part of the problem, for the observed fact that a huntsman may easily get lost and taken far from his path in the heat of the chase is crossed with another detail of quite a different order. By this I mean that there is a long tradition in myth and folklore about the deer leading the hunter into a miraculous new world, even into the Other World, where he engages in adventures of a novel kind.[104] The path to this esoteric world is bound to be a secret one, for otherwise the realm of adventure would no longer be esoteric or at all mysterious, and the function of the deer is to serve as a miraculous guide to this mysterious realm, moving at such speed that in the excitement of hunting him down neither the huntsman nor the listener has time to spare for the mundane question of the actual route taken.

The myth of a miraculous deer leading to a new realm is particularly ancient and widespread. In Greek tradition it is the Hind of Ceryneia which lures Heracles into the miraculous Garden of the Hesperides;[105] by the Huns it was believed that their hunters were led by a hind through the Sea of Azov and thus to the new Scythian lands beyond;[106] in the *þiðrikssaga* þiðrek and Hildibrandr are out hunting when þiðrek, in pursuit of a deer, comes across the dwarf Alfrigg.[107] That the myth was widely known in Germania is attested by its occurrence in several of the histories of the age of migrations, it survives in popular folklore in Europe at large[108] and its miraculous function in medieval literature has been summed up in these terms: "Es wird aus dem gejagten, ein (von Gott gesandtes) weisendes Tier."[109] In other words, the deer has a double function, for it appears to be an animal hunted down, but is in reality a guide to the supernatural realm. Like the path so often followed by the literary knight, the new dimension is revealed only subsequently – it is only now that the huntsman is led to giants, magicians, witches, to an enchanted land.

The motif is frequent in Arthurian literature, in such lais as *Guigemar* and *Guingamor* and in the romance as well (Chrétien introduces his *Erec* with Arthur's hunt for the white stag). In *Guigemar*[110] the miraculous origins of the theme are still clear: the huntsman shoots a white hind, but is wounded on the rebound, is told by the miraculously speaking animal of the supernatural terms of his cure and is carried by a mysterious boat to the scene of his love adventure. In courtly dressing, this is

[104] In addition to Pschmadt's dissertation, see also Baechtold-Stäubli, *Handwörterbuch des deutschen Aberglaubens* 4 (Berlin 1931) 86ff.

[105] Hatto (n. 103 above) 41.

[106] *Ibid.*

[107] *þiðriks saga of Bern,* ed. H. Bertelsen (Copenhagen 1905-1911) 1.34ff.

[108] Baechtold-Stäubli (n. 104 above) 4.90ff.

[109] Pschmadt (n. 103 above) 31.

[110] J. Rychner, ed., *Les lais de Marie de France* (Paris 1966) 5ff.

the traditional story of the fairy who has attracted a mortal into her realm to which he has been conducted by the hind as a miraculous guide.[111]

Chrétien's first romance has undergone the further process of rationalization: the fairy has become Enide, the fairest of them all, and Erec is conducted towards his encounter with her not by pursuing a miraculous deer, but precisely by *not* doing this, by leaving this courtly pastime to Arthur and the rest of his court. It has been remarked that in this episode the hunt which had earlier led to an adventure in the realm of wonder has become no more than a courtly pastime, that Chrétien, by simply announcing the theme of the hunt without a word of explanation, is following a well-known convention which would certainly have been familiar to his audience.[112] This may be true, but the French poet is also using this time-worn motif very consciously and in a novel way. The hunt may well be termed a *costume* of Arthur's court, the pursuit of the deer may well be the traditional bridge to the Other World, but the surprising innovation is that Arthur's hunt should lead to no such expected conclusion.

As the episode is set under way the audience observes the Round Table depart for the hunt, while the narrator forces them to remain behind with Erec in the company of Queen Guinevere. The listeners impatiently strain after Arthur's companions, for it is one of them, so they are led to assume, who will pursue the deer and penetrate into the realm of adventure. But this is just what does *not* come about, for while our gaze still follows the departing knights the decisive event has taken place elsewhere and the adventure has befallen Erec, even though all the traditional appearances were against this.[113] It may be that the motif of the hunt was too conventional by this time for Chrétien to be able to employ it in depicting the unobserved entry into another realm, but if so his compounding of its ambiguity by switching the emphasis to a non-participant achieves the same effect of surprise.

* * *

If I were asked for an aesthetic feature common to the various methods we have been considering I should see this in the function of irony as a rhetorical strategy whereby the courtly poet controls the reactions of his still unwitting listeners. By showing them part of the truth, while allowing them to imagine that it is the whole truth of the situation, by inveigling them into concentrating their attention on one detail while the decisive change takes place elsewhere and by revealing all the facts only

[111] J. Frappier, *Chrétien de Troyes* (Paris 1957) 93; E. Hoepffner, *Les lais de Marie de France* (Paris 1959) 84f.

[112] Frappier 93.

[113] This point, in connection with Hartmann's version, has been made by K. Ruh, *Höfische Epik des deutschen Mittelalters* (Berlin 1967) 1.114.

belatedly at his chosen moment he is ensuring that their uncertainty as to what is really happening shall parallel the knightly hero's rides at random and temporary loss of way. Only by undergoing the experience of such loss of bearings, by coming to realize that events are not what they seem to be can the audience, like the knightly hero, be persuaded to accept the suggestion that the European world of twelfth-century reality can at all turns unexpectedly open out into the ideal world of chivalric adventure.

Trinity College
Cambridge CB2 1TQ, England

THE PREFACE TO THE "SPECULUM ECCLESIAE" OF GIRALDUS CAMBRENSIS

•

by R. W. Hunt

I. The Manuscript

The *Speculum ecclesiae* was edited from the only known manuscript, British Library, MS Cotton Tiberius B.XIII, by J. S. Brewer for the Rolls Series in 1873 in volume 4 of the works of Giraldus Cambrensis. The manuscript had suffered serious damage in the fire of 1731. As Brewer says,[1] "The top and bottom, and in many instances the side margins, have been so much destroyed that column after column of the manuscript is mutilated or defaced. . . . The worst injury of all is the almost total destruction of the introductory epistle." A further misfortune, which Brewer did not know, is that the first three surviving fragments of leaves were bound up in the wrong order when the leaves were mounted in 1884. In order to make up for the lost passages, Brewer printed the extracts quoted by Anthony Wood in his *History and Antiquities of the University of Oxford.* Brewer naturally assumed that Wood had consulted the manuscript;[2] but the researches of Andrew Clark into Wood's methods have shown that Wood habitually in his printed works took over materials collected by others.[3] Clark's catalog of the materials used by Wood not only guides us to his source, but enables us to find others which have hitherto remained unknown.

The source of Wood's information about Giraldus's works is revealed in his catalog of manuscript authorities used in the *History and Antiquities*:[4]

> Sylvester Gyraldus Cambrensis
>
> Distinctiones lib. 4. Initium [copied from Pits]: Nunc ad ea quae contra naturam etc.[5]

[1] *Giraldi Cambrensis Opera* (hereafter Opp.), ed. J. S. Brewer et al., 8 vols., Rolls Series (London 1861-1891) 4.xi-xii.

[2] *Ibid.* xiii.

[3] A. Clark, ed., *The Life and Times of A. Wood* 4, Addenda, Oxford Historical Society 30 (1885).

[4] Oxford, Bodleian Library, MS Wood E.4 (S.C. 8561), p. 95; see Clark 273. I have only included what is relevant for the present purpose.

[5] This is in fact the beginning of *Top. hib.* 2 (Opp. 5.74).

> Quondam in manibus M. Hen. Parry CCC. Est nunc in Bib. Cotton. Tyberius B.13 in quibus distinctionibus mirifice insectatur vitam et mores monachorum.

In the margin are the references "γ 164.163e. Collect. inde 229. Qu. Bib. Cott. pro initio Dist." These references are to a volume of Brian Twyne's collections designated by this symbol, which is now MS Twyne XXII in the Bodleian Library. It is a collection of materials for the history of Oxford, mainly arranged according to the sources from which the extracts were taken. For pages 162-167 the general heading is:

> Excerpta ex quibusdam Manuscriptis Lantoniensis cenobii prope Glocestr. quae vidi apud Magistrum Henry Parry 1617.

There follow excerpts from five manuscripts, of which the third is that of the *Speculum ecclesiae.* The extracts from it begin on page 164 with the heading

> In altero MS^{o} qui continet opera quaedam Sylvestri Giraldi, viz eius Distinctiones libris 4.[6] Ubi in praefatione ad librum primum Distinctionum suarum sic loquitur Gyraldus. "Proinde etiam . . . nec faciam."

There follows the story about Martinus, which was printed by Rashdall from this source,[7] though he did not realize that it came from the *Speculum ecclesiae.* Then come excerpts from the *Vita Gyraldi,* that is, the *De rebus a se gestis,* which is also contained in Cotton Tib. B.XIII. That this is the manuscript used by Twyne is not in doubt, since the running title "Sylvestris (Syl., Sylv.) Giraldi (Gyral:, Gyrald.) Distinct. 2 (3)" now seen in the manuscript from fol. 32 was written by him. He also numbered the chapters, and added occasional notes, for example on fols. 37, 38, 39 and so on. This was not the only manuscript seen by Twyne in Parry's collection that found its way into the library of Sir Robert Cotton.

The greater part of Twyne's extracts were copied by Gerard Langbaine in the collections relating to the study of civil law at Oxford, which he made for Arthur Duck.[8] From them Duck derived his knowledge of the story of Martinus, which he summarized in his *De usu et authoritate iuris civilis Romanorum in dominiis principum Christianorum* (London 1653) 141. Langbaine did not consult the Cotton manuscript, and his extracts therefore have no independent authority, but he made one happy correction to the text. He had access to Twyne's notebooks as Keeper of the University Archives, where the notebooks were kept until they were placed on deposit in the Bodleian Library in the present century.

[6] This was the title by which the *Speculum ecclesiae* was then known. There was probably no title in the manuscript which is not completely rubricated.

[7] H. Rashdall, *Universities of Europe in the Middle Ages* (Oxford 1895) 2.2.753; in the edition by F. M. Powicke and A. B. Emden (Oxford 1936), 3.476-477.

[8] Bodleian Library, MS Tanner 211, fols. 222-225. There is a note in MS Twyne XXII, fol. 164, in Langbaine's hand, which is repeated in MS Tanner 211, fol. 222.

Other excerpts from the preface are contained in one of the notebooks of Richard James in the Bodleian Library (MS James 2, pp. 11-45). Richard James was librarian to Sir Robert Cotton from about the year 1628 till his death in 1638. His excerpts are headed "Giraldus Cottoni," and they certainly came from Cotton Tib. B.XIII. The page references which he gives to the manuscript he was copying correspond to the early seventeenth-century pagination (not foliation) of the Cotton manuscript, which is now first visible at page 255.[9]

This was not the only manuscript of the *Speculum ecclesiae,* as has sometimes been supposed. Bale had seen a copy at Norwich and owned one himself,[10] perhaps the Norwich manuscript. He quotes from it in his *Catalogus*[11] and *Index,*[12] and more extensively, though mostly in translation, in his *Actes of the Englysh Votaries.*[13] It was one of the manuscripts he was compelled to leave behind in Ireland.[14] Leland also refers to the work, but he may have owed his knowledge of it to Bale.[15] Further, Sir John Prise quotes from the work in his *Historiae brittannicae defensio* (London 1573);[16] and he appears to quote from a manuscript other than Cotton Tiberius B.XIII.

Cotton Tiberius B.XIII is written in a hand of the early thirteenth century, in two columns of 36-38 lines. A line contains on the average 19 letters. The common abbreviations found in literary texts are used, but not very systematically. Chapter headings are in red, but none of the initial letters have been filled in. The *Speculum ecclesiae* occupies fols. 1-153v, the *De rebus a se gestis* fols. 154-185v, and another *Speculum ecclesiae,* by Roger abbot of Glastonbury (1256-1261), according to the catalog, fols. 186-237v. This last item is most probably part of a different manuscript, first bound up with the rest by Sir Robert Cotton, according to his

[9] The present foliation, which is used in this paper, was added after the manuscript was restored.

[10] John Bale, *Index Britanniae scriptorum*, ed. R. L. Poole and M. Bateson (Oxford 1902) 420, 422.

[11] John Bale, *Catalogus* (Basel 1559) 1.524 (where the passage is in its original form, though in the *Index*, p. 97, it is altered in a Protestant sense), and 2.54 (which shows that this MS contained the chapters in Dist. 2 which are missing from the Cotton MS).

[12] Bale, *Index* 4, 37 (= 33, p. 106 + 2.25, p. 80f.), 56, 97, 108, 157, 286, 407, 412, 421, 425, 467, 511.

[13] J. Bale, *The Second Part of Contynuacion of the Englysh Votaries* (London 1551) fols. lxxii^{b}, lxxix^{b}, ci,* cii,* cv,* cv^{b},* cxii^{b}. (The pages marked with an asterisk contain extracts from the burnt parts of the Cotton manuscript.) Twyne (MS XXII, p. 229) quotes the verses from 4.19 (p. 304) from this source. Bale also listed it among the authorities used in the first part, but I have not noticed any direct references to it.

[14] Bale, *Catal.* 2.160. The books were unfortunately dispersed, and all but a few have disappeared; see Honor McCusker, "Books and Manuscripts formerly in the Possession of John Bale," *The Library*, ser. 4, 16 (1935-1936) 147.

[15] John Leland, *Commentarii de script. Britann.* (Oxford 1709) 225, De Simone Fraxinio. He does not mention it in his list of the writings of Giraldus.

[16] Prise, *Historiae britann. defensio* (London 1573) 130-133, from 2.8.9 (Opp. 4.47-50), cf. 109f. I owe this reference to Mr. N. R. Ker.

well-known custom. Brewer declared that the manuscript "was that very original and came from the hands of Giraldus himself." He assumed, wrongly as we have seen, that there never was another manuscript, and thought that the fact that the *notulae,* which are referred to in the preface, were in the manuscript put the matter beyond doubt; but these marks are not all of the same form, and some are in ink and others in "pencil," and do not appear to be all from the same hand. The manuscript has now lost all traces of former owners; but, as we have already seen, it can be identified with the copy that belonged to Henry Parry in 1617. He was the eldest son of Henry Parry, bishop of Gloucester and Worcester. He came up to Corpus Christi College, Oxford, matriculated in 1607, and became a fellow in 1614.[17] His father died 12 December 1616 and bequeathed him his manuscripts.[18] They were therefore a recent acquisition, when Twyne, who was also at this time a fellow of Corpus, made his extracts. Parry gave manuscripts to the college at different dates between 1619 and 1623;[19] thirty are still there, of which ten can be assigned to Lanthony;[20] one came from Malvern (MS 157), one from Lapworth Church (MS 394), and fourteen have no trace of provenance. The five manuscripts of the group excerpted by Twyne can be identified as MSS C.C.C. 32, 55, 116, Cotton Tib. B.XIII and Domit. A.XI, fols. 107-179.[21] None of these manuscripts has any trace of origin. What then was Twyne's reason for saying that they came from Lanthony? It is possible that they then had marks which have since been lost. For most of them were bound soon after they came into the possession of the college. But this is unlikely, since many of them must have been in very bad repair before their rebinding. For example, MS C.C.C. 32 has lost leaves at the beginning and the end, and parts of the leaves have been eaten away. Others, such as MS C.C.C. 55, do not appear to have lost any flyleaves. Twyne therefore presumably had other and more general grounds for his statement, and it may be suggested that he was told by Parry that the manuscripts came from Lanthony. This is not inconsistent with what is known or conjectured about the other books that came from there.[22] They were less widely dispersed among a multitude of owners than the books of many monastic houses. One large group of nearly a hundred is in Lambeth Palace Library. It is not known how they came there.

[17] I am much indebted to Mr. J. R. Liddell for help in elucidating the story of Parry's MSS, and to the late Dr. J. G. Milne, librarian of C.C.C. for making the study of these MSS, which were then still in the library of C.C.C., so easy. They have since been deposited in the Bodleian Library.

[18] London, Somerset House, P.C.C., 36 Weldon.

[19] The list in M. R. James, *Manuscripts in the Library at Lambeth Palace*, Cambr. Antiqu. Soc. 8º Publ. 33 (1900) 58f. is incomplete.

[20] N. R. Ker, *Medieval Libraries of Great Britain*, ed. 2 (London 1964) 112.

[21] I owe this last identification to Mr. W. A. Pantin. The inscription of gift to C.C.C. can still be made out, despite erasure. Extracts were made by R. James while the MS was still at C.C.C.; see V. H. Galbraith in *Snappe's Formulary*, Oxford Hist. Soc. 80 (1924) 355 n. 3. A third MS which is now in the Cotton collection, but which was given to C.C.C. by Parry, is Cotton App. 20; see the extracts in MS Twyne XXII, p. 419f., and MS James 36, p. 147.

[22] See James (n. 19 above).

A group of four is in the library of Trinity College, Oxford. They were the gift of Fr. Baber, chancellor of Gloucester, in 1633. Parry's father was bishop of the same diocese.

Whatever may be the origin of Cotton Tib. B.XIII, we know that there was a copy of the *Speculum* at Lanthony, for a chapter of it is incorporated in the brief chronicle of the house, which was compiled in the thirteenth century.[23]

II. Analysis of the Text

The general subject of the preface is described by Henry Wharton[24] as faults in education (*de defectu literaturae*). The two main faults are said to be wrong pronunciation of words and the excessive attention paid to dialectic. The first is leveled especially against monks, the second is more general, and is connected with the lack of patronage by princes. How Giraldus connected the two remains obscure. All his arguments tend to go off at a tangent, and the incompleteness of the text of the preface makes him appear to wander more than usual. It may therefore be useful to attempt an analysis.

The first leaf has perished, and we have only meager excerpts. Wharton states that it was addressed to Stephen Langton. In the opening words Christ Church Canterbury is mentioned, and it appears that the charge against the monks was their faults in the pronunciation and accentuation of Latin. Whether the archbishop was urged to take a hand in the reform we do not know. When the text becomes legible, Giraldus is dealing with the faults, which must be corrected, lest they spread to all the clergy of England, who have always hitherto excelled in learning. By an abrupt transition we are told that if the chorus of wrong pronunciations ceased, so also would logic cease to deprave. As will be seen from the sequel, the probable connection is that both defects arose from insufficient grounding in literature.

Giraldus then turns to another reason for the decay of the study of letters. Civil Law has stifled the Arts. The prophecy of the Sybil which Giraldus heard from the pupil of Peter Abelard, Master Mainerius, has come true. The study of law is more lucrative. But in olden times honors and rewards given by princes were generally bestowed on philosophers and poets. The liberal arts were held in high esteem. Even

[23] The greater part is printed in William Dugdale, *Monasticon* (London 1846) 6.128-134 from Cotton Julius D.X fols. 31-53. In this edition the arrangement of the work is obscured. The preface is omitted, and the list of chapters (for which, however, compare Wharton [n. 24 below] 2.321f.). The chapter divisions are ignored. Two irrelevant chapters, "De prelatis" and "De subditis" with another passage are omitted, as shown by an "etc." Finally the last chapter on the sixth prior, Roger of Norwich, is not given. It is mainly a reproduction of the story about him in *Spec. eccl.* 2.26. There are some differences of reading from the text as we have it in Cotton Tib. B.XIII, but these may be due to the compiler of the Chronicle.

[24] H. Wharton, *Anglia Sacra* (London 1691) 2.xxiii: "Initium illi facit Epistola prolixa ad Stephanum Cant. Archiepiscopum de literaturae defectu."

in times nearer to our own the appointment of prelates versed in letters encouraged such studies. But nowadays princes are unlettered men and do not care for such things. Prelates are promoted by favor and intruded instead of being canonically elected – [and so the counterbalancing influence has gone and students go on to the study of law without a proper foundation.][25] It will not be irrelevant to put in here the remarks of Master Martin to the Pauperiste, who abounded at Oxford when Vacarius's *Liber pauperum* stood in high honor. At a large gathering of students, at which cases and disputes were discussed in the presence of judges, when all the other advocates who were present objected to a certain law which seemed to be expressly directed against him (for they all used to take sides against him and he against them), they all cried out and mocked him: "You will jump through this law, Martin, (as is said of a jumping monkey), and through this law you will make a jump, whether you like it or not." He replied wittily and caustically and elegantly enough: "If I must jump, I will, but the jump you have all made from the Distichs of Cato to the Institutes, even if you have to . . .(?),[26] I never have made and never will." In these days students before they have even learned their rudiments properly go straight on to the Digest, Code and Institutes; and as they have laid no proper foundations, the whole structure of their education totters at the first puff of wind. . . . Master Ralph of Beauvais, the eminent grammarian, used to divide clerks into three classes. The first are the *superseminati* who without the necessary grounding in the arts proceed to study different sciences and so turn out to be superficial in their knowledge. The second are the *pannosi* who gather together odds and ends of knowledge and do not attain the comprehension of any one subject. The third are the *massati* (and they are few in number today) who gain a thorough grounding in the arts, theology, law and other sciences and have a firm foundation.

A further reason for the decay is that students in the trivium nowadays neglect grammar and rhetoric almost entirely and hurry on to dialectic. They become masters in three or four years, with the result that they teach badly what they have themselves imperfectly mastered, so that they may go on to teach the lucrative sciences of law and medicine. We and our contemporaries never attempted this until we were thoroughly grounded, not only in the trivium, but also in the classical authors and philosophers, in versification and dictamen by twenty years study or more. . . . They make matters worse by turning out pupils like themselves . . . and become too deeply involved in dialectic. To avoid this the wise man will not have more than a nodding acquaintance with it.

To return to the faults in pronunciation of the Canterbury monks. . . . They have no reverence for the precepts of Antiquity. Thus they pronounce words such as "dederitis" with the penultimate long . . . [they defend this by reference to isolated authorities.] . . . But it is clearly arrogant to try to revive obsolete words and reject

[25] I have enclosed in square brackets phrases not in the original, but which seem to be required by the sense.

[26] I cannot make anything of "et corpore medii."

those that are current. . . . It is to be noted that the Cistercians, who are supposed to be reformed and to avoid the errors of the Black Monks (*Cluniacenses*),[27] follow them in these false pronunciations. So do the Carthusians and Grandimontanes and Regular Canons. . . .

It is also to be noted that almost all monks in reading the Gospels say "Dominus Jesus" instead of "Jesus," whenever the name occurs, though the combination is only found twice in the Gospels, and then is used for special reasons of emphasis. [The same is true] of its occurrence in the Acts and the Epistles. We should not make additions to or alterations in the Gospels. The phrase should be kept for the special occasions on which it occurs. For rarity increases the value of all things.

So the rarity of men versed in letters may bring literature into favor again, and teachers rush to it, especially if it is supported by princes. . . . Would that these false pronunciations might cease in England, and would that letters might return to their former place of honor! There is some hope of this since Pope Honorius recently issued a decree regulating the enjoyment of benefices by those engaged in study, and forbidding all priests and beneficed clergy to study law and medicine. In consequence students will not be able to make that jump from the rudiments to law; and it is to be hoped that they will turn to letters and will proceed further to the study of canon law and theology on a sound foundation.

There is something else that may partly help the revival of sounder studies. There have been found at Toledo recently and translated certain books said to be by Aristotle. Ostensibly and at first sight they are concerned with logic, but really they discuss intricate questions concerning the nature of things. To these the students of our times, rejoicing in novelty, have eagerly rushed, deserting the books of Aristotle they had before. They have taken to them too fondly and have been led into heresy, and recently in France they were forbidden to be read in the schools. There is therefore a hope that they will leave them and return to saner studies.

Although it is not fitting that a letter should rival a book in length, I must add something here from a commentary on a certain book of Aristotle, called *De anima,* which was written to attract students to these subtle questions: "It is indeed unworthy that a man should not know that by which he is a knower, and should not understand by reason that in virtue of which he is rational. For how will he be able to love God or himself, who is seen to be ignorant of that which is best in him?" Solomon warned men against indulging in such subtleties, which lead to error; and many authors have spoken to the same effect. Mortal minds were not made to comprehend such things. Therefore do not indulge in them.

As I have made mention of my own labors at the end of this treatise, the reader should recognize the two main reasons for my almost continuous application to study. . . . Do not hide your light, for many may be able to profit from your labors.

[27] Professor D. Knowles demonstrated that in the writings of Giraldus the term "Cluniacenses," denotes the Black Monks; see his *Monastic Order in England* (Cambridge 1940) 719, app. 22.

It is to be noted that as there are two things necessary to a philosopher, wisdom and a competence, so there are two others required by a writer, knowledge and unceasing diligence. And this last must be accompanied by genius. . . . As I said in the preface to my *Topographia hibernica,* by applying ourselves to classical authors, and, so to speak, sitting on their shoulders, we may become great. Nothing hinders a man so much as diffidence, and many men grow old without knowing their powers. Such scruples have not held me back, and if I cannot do what I want, I want to do what I can. To urge us to write and make some great endeavor there is the saying that we should turn from what is transitory to lasting goods. . . . Moreover everlasting life is won by good works rather than by laborious writings. But the latter are not by any means to be despised. For that which is written down is much more durable than that which is spoken. . . . One should not write for praise alone. Those who do have their reward. However for all good endeavors praise can hardly be avoided, and often praise that is sought is not won, and that which is avoided is gained. May God grant that all who are engaged in study may do so for the advancement and glory of the church and not like proud men and fools . . . .

III. Commentary

The *Speculum ecclesiae,* in the form in which we have it, is one of the works of the old age of Giraldus. He calls it "the fruit of three years' continuous study,"[28] but like the *De principis instructione* it was planned long before it was executed. In the *Itinerarium Kambriae*, written about 1191, after reviewing the merits of various orders, he says that the Augustinian Canons are the best "sicut in libro quem de ecclesiasticis ordinibus, deo annuente, scripturi sumus, plenius explicabitur." [29] There is nothing in the text to show how early it was begun, but it cannot have been finished before 1215, since there is a reference to the Fourth Lateran Council which was held in that year.[30] This fits in with the statement of Giraldus in the *De iure et statu Menevensis ecclesiae* that he was about seventy when it was published.[31] But in one of the newly recovered passages in the preface there is mention of a later document. Giraldus refers to the Bull of Honorius III "Super speculam" of 22 November 1219 as having been issued "[die]bus his nostris ultimis." The preface cannot therefore be earlier than 1220. It is not certain whether we should date the whole work later, or whether we should suppose that the preface belongs to a revised edition. That there was more than one edition of this, as of so many of the works of Giraldus, we know from the letter to the chapter at Hereford, in which he asks for

[28] Opp. 1.415.
[29] 1.3 (Opp. 6.47).
[30] Opp. 4.94.
[31] Opp. 3.373.

the return of a copy which he had given them almost a year ago, so that he might revise it.[32]

Since the *Speculum ecclesiae* is a work of the old age of Giraldus, it is important to try to distinguish between the repetition of facts and opinions found in his earlier works and new material. To begin with the repetitions: in a long chapter in the *Gemma ecclesiastica* which was written while he was studying at Lincoln between 1196 and 1199,[33] he criticizes at length the shortcomings of education in the schools. He gives two of the illustrations which are repeated in the preface to the *Speculum*; the threefold division of clerks made by Ralph of Beauvais, and the prophecy of Mainerius. The latter is repeated verbally, with the additional detail, not known from other sources, that Mainerius was the chief pupil of Peter Abelard. The former is given in a less logical order than in the *Gemma*, and with considerable verbal changes. The *superseminati* in the *Gemma* are said to be those who skip over the poets, the *auctores* and the philosophers, and generally lack a grounding in the *artes*. They pass straight from Donatus and Cato, that is elementary grammar, to civil and canon law. In the *Speculum* this jump has already been described in the story of Martinus, and the description of the *superseminati* is generalized. They are said to bypass a grounding in letters, and to oversow or build on "scientias varias et facultates," words that seem to have no clear meaning in this context.

In the *Gemma* the burden of the criticisms of Giraldus is the abuse of logic. The pull of law away from letters under the stimulus of greed and ambition is there mentioned in a single sentence.[34] In the *Speculum* the jump from the rudiments of grammar to the study of civil law is placed first, and is illustrated by the story of Master Martinus who taught law at Oxford when the *Liber pauperum* of Vacarius was in vogue. Rashdall[35] dismissed this story as a confused recollection of the stories told about the disputes between the greater Martinus and the other Bolognese jurists at the court of the emperor Frederick I. The phrase "imperatoriam maiestátem," (p. 205 line 28), he said betrayed its origin. Now that we have a fuller text it is obvious that this interpretation will not stand. Master Martin who taught law at Oxford and who had studied at Bologna cannot be dismissed as a figment, and Professor Kuttner and Miss Rathbone have suggested that he may be the Master Martin who witnessed with Master Honorius, another English lawyer, an award of John of Cornwall at Oxford in 1192.[36]

[32] Opp. 1.415. He asks for its return "ad corrigendum adhuc plenius, et utilia quaedam locis competentibus adjiciendum." Dimock pointed out that this letter was written not earlier than 1219 (Opp. 5.lv).

[33] See Dimock's note in Opp. 5.liii.

[34] Opp. 2.349: "Episcopus autem ille . . . inter superficiales numerari potuit, cuiusmodi hodie multos novimus propter leges Justinianas, quae literaturam, urgente cupiditatis et ambitionis incommodo, adeo in multis iam suffocarunt."

[35] See n. 7 above.

[36] S. Kuttner and E. Rathbone, "Anglo-Norman Canonists of the Twelfth Century," *Traditio* 7 (1949-1950) 323.

These stories of Giraldus can be dated approximately. Not only Mainerius,[37] but also Ralph of Beauvais[38] was a pupil of Peter Abelard who ceased to teach after the condemnation at the Council of Sens in 1140. Their teaching activity cannot therefore be later than the third quarter of the twelfth century, and the stories which Giraldus tells were presumably gathered by him while he was studying in Paris, probably during his first stay from 1165 to 1172, since he was then studying the *artes* and law. The story about Master Martin may be a little later. We do not know precisely when the *Liber pauperum* flourished at Oxford, but it seems that it did not survive beyond the early years of the thirteenth century.[39]

In the *Gemma* the criticisms are all negative. There are no suggestions for remedying the deplorable state of affairs which is described. In the preface to the *Speculum* Giraldus is more optimistic: "[Forsan a]utem in brevi litteratura resurget" (p. 209 line 15). He gives two reasons: the first is the recent constitution of Pope Honorius III "Super speculam"[40] which was addressed to the masters of the University of Paris and was concerned with means for furthering the study of theology. Unfortunately the text is broken at the point where Giraldus characterized the terms of the constitution. The pope had begun by deploring the increasing popularity of the *scientiae lucrativae*, that is, law and medicine. To counteract it he decreed that masters and students of theology should be allowed licenses to receive the revenues from their benefices while they were studying at the University, and that the school of civil law at Paris should be closed. Giraldus had referred to "leges aut phisicam, lucrosas scilicet pro tempore scientias" in an earlier passage (p. 206 line 23). At the present point he probably mentioned the provision relating to the enjoyment of revenues from benefices, since the incomplete word "bene-" has survived. It is certain from the comments which follow that he mentioned the provision relating to the closing of the school of civil law at Paris,[41] but he used it to support his argument without much regard to the terms of the constitution. He hoped that the prohibition of the study of civil law at Paris would lead students back

[37] The fullest collection of references is given by N. Häring, "Chartres and Paris Revisited," in *Essays in Honor of A. C. Pegis*, ed. J. R. O'Donnell (Toronto 1974) 325-326. Dated references run from 1154 to 1174. He was one of the "greater luminaries" whose lectures and disputations William of Tyre heard at Paris in the middle of the century. Fr. Häring did not note that C. R. Cheney, *From Becket to Langton* (Manchester 1956) 16 n. 3 suggests that he was the *iurisperitus* who acted as a judge in the court of Louis VII.

[38] See R. W. Hunt, "Studies on Priscian in the Twelfth Century," *Mediaeval and Renaissance Studies* 2 (1950) 11-16.

[39] *The Liber pauperum of Vacarius*, ed. F. de Zulueta, Selden Society 44 (1927) xix, cxlviii; cf. S. Kuttner, "Dat Galienus opes et sanctio Justiniana," in *Linguistic and Literary Studies in Honor of Helmut A. Hatzfeld* (Washington, D.C. 1964) 241; E. Rathbone, "Roman Law in the Anglo-Norman Realm," *Studia Gratiana* 2 (1967) 257f.

[40] For the text see H. Denifle and E. Chatelain, *Cartularium Universitatis Parisiensis* (Paris 1889) 1.90-93. For the literature on it see Kuttner 238 n. 6.

[41] There can hardly have been more comment, since only eight lines of approximately nineteen letters each are missing.

to letters and to the liberal arts, and that on this sound foundation they would build up their studies of canon law and theology. The constitution was not concerned with questions of curriculum, and does not contain any mention of the liberal arts.

The second reason for hope of improvement (p. 209 line 24) was that lectures on certain works ascribed to Aristotle ("libri quidam tamquam Aristotelis intitulati"), which were discovered at Toledo and translated into Latin, had been forbidden in the schools in France. This refers either to the condemnation at the synod held in Paris in 1210 or to the statutes drawn up by the papal legate, Robert de Courçon, in 1215. The description of them is not very clear, and we might be inclined to suppose that he was talking of books which he only knew by hearsay, but in the next paragraph there is a quotation from a work which he calls "Super librum Aristotelis quendam de Anima" (p. 210, line 55). In fact it is a quotation from the translator's preface to the *De anima* of Avicenna.[42] Giraldus can hardly have obtained this at second hand, even though his quotation is not quite accurate. He must have had in his hands, perhaps not for very long, a manuscript containing some part of the Avicennian corpus. It is one of the earliest testimonies to the reception of the work in England.

We may not think that the hopes of Giraldus were well founded. He was taking an old fashioned view of the state of studies, even though he has found supporters among modern historians of the period. But it is surely very remarkable that at the age of seventy or thereabouts, and after a life of disappointments, he should be following so closely the most recent enactments affecting the University of Paris, and that he should be looking at a book which can have only just reached England. It is tantalizing that we know almost nothing of the movements of Giraldus in his later years. Did he know John Blund, who was teaching at Oxford in the opening years of the thirteenth century, and who had written a *Tractatus de anima* in which extensive use was made of Avicenna and Aristotle? Did he know Alexander Nequam, abbot of Cirencester, who in his *Speculum speculationum*, written about 1213, had made a "timid" use of the *De anima* of Avicenna? How deeply was Hugh de Mapenore, dean of Hereford from about 1201 and bishop from 1215 to 1219, interested in the new scientific learning?[43] At present we can only ask questions. We have already seen that Giraldus was in touch with the cathedral chapter at Hereford at the time he was

[42] This mode of referring to Avicenna, *De anima* is closely paralleled in the *Tractatus de anima* of John Blund, ed. Callus and Hunt (n. 43 below) nos. 64, 193.

[43] For John Blund and Alexander Nequam see D. A. Callus, "The Introduction of Aristotelian Learning to Oxford," *Proc. British Academy* 29 (1943) 229-281, and "The Treatise of John Blund 'On the Soul,' " in *Recueil d'études . . . offert à Monseigneur A. Mansion* (Louvain 1955) 471-495. In the edition of the *Tractatus* by Fr. Callus and myself, Auctores Britannici medii aevi 2 (London 1970), I have confirmed the view of Fr. Callus that Alexander Nequam derived his knowledge of Avicenna, *De anima* from John Blund; but this will not hold for Giraldus, since John only takes a short phrase from the translator's preface; see the edition, no. 1. For Hugh de Mapenore see B. Lawn, *The Salernitan Questions* (Oxford 1963) 35; in the Italian translation, *I quesiti Salernitani* (1969) which is revised and enlarged, p. 54.

writing the preface, and if we knew more about the interests of the chapter and of the cathedral school, we might be in a position to give a more definite answer.

* * *

The fragmentary state of the text makes it more difficult to comment on the strictures of Giraldus on the vices in pronunciation of the monks of Christ Church, Canterbury. Two whole pages are missing from the beginning of the preface. When the text begins, it appears that their fault was the wrong accentuation of words, and when the subject is resumed (p. 207), the text is again broken; but it appears that here too the chief complaint is about accentuation. This was a subject to which much attention was paid by medieval grammarians, but it is a part of grammar which has scarcely been explored by modern scholars.[44] It was a matter of practical importance in the proper rendering of the liturgy and in the reading of books in the refectory, and it is not uncommon to find that accents are carefully marked in manuscripts of the twelfth century.

The one surviving example in the preface of Giraldus is the lengthening of the "i" in the penultimate of "dederitis" (p. 207 line 19). His discussion is lost, but we may compare a passage in the *Corrogationes Promethei* of his contemporary, Alexander Nequam,[45] a work which contains a substantial section "De dictionibus dubiis in accentu":

> Queritur a multis de accentu huiusmodi dictionum "dederitis," "transieritis." Ovidius enim aliter utitur his verbis quam usus modernorum teneat. Dicit enim:
>
> [Met. 6.357] Vitam dederitis in undis,
>
> et rursum alibi:
>
> [Ex Ponto 4.5.6] Et maris Ionii transieritis aquas,
>
> et rursum:
>
> [Ars Am. 1.447] Si dederis aliquid poteris ratione relinqui.
>
> Dicunt quidam has dictiones "dederitis," "transieritis" non posse subire legem metricam, et ideo non esse mirum si causa metri Ovidius in his auctoritate, immo licentia, usus sit poetica. Possumus et nos dicere, ut in scolis dicere consuevimus, quod "do," "das" componitur "indo," "indis," "indidi." Mutatur enim coniugatio in compositione. Adam indidit nomina rebus. "Do" etiam componitur "dedo -dis," "dedidi."

[44] There is some material in C. Thurot, *Notices et extraits . . . pour servir à l'histoire des doctrines grammaticales au moyen âge, Notices et extraits* 22.2 (Paris 1868) 392-407.

[45] Extracts were printed by P. Meyer, *Notices et extraits* 35.2 (1897) 665-668. I quote from Oxford, Bodleian Library, MS Bodley 550 (S.C. 2300), fols. 17vb-18ra.

> Constat autem primam esse productam. Sic igitur Ovidius in libro Herodum ait:
>
> [7.118] Quodque tibi dedi perfide litus emi,
>
> ponens "dedi" pro hoc verbo "dedidi" per sincopam. Ita ait per sincopam:
>
> Vitam dederitis in undis.
>
> Est enim integrum verbum "dedideritis." Est ergo spondeus "-tam de-." Proceleumaticus autem est "-deritis in," scilicet pes constans ex quattuor brevibus, et equipollet dactilo. Una enim longa ex equo respondet duabus brevibus, et ita de hoc nulla est obiectio quin dicendum sit "dederitis."

It will be seen that the example which Giraldus quotes from Ovid's *Metamorphoses* (p. 207 line 19) is also dealt with by Alexander Nequam. The pronunciation of the word "videritis" was also giving trouble in monastic circles in England later in the thirteenth century. It is included in a short list of words wrongly pronounced in the liturgical section of the statutes drawn up by the General Chapter of the English Benedictines in 1277.[46]

Giraldus was less than fair to the Cistercians in his strictures. They had very early turned their attention to the securing of uniformity and correctness of accentuation.[47] Alberic, the second abbot of Cîteaux (d. 1109) had consulted Lambert, abbot of the Benedictine abbey of Pothières in the diocese of Langres. Lambert replied by sending a Psalter in which he had marked the accents together with a letter in which he set out some of the problems of accentuation. Later in the century an unknown Cistercian wrote a fuller treatise on the subject. In his preface he expresses very well the spirit in which the attempt at uniformity was made:

> Utinam nos qui sub regula vivimus et regulariter cantamus, etiam regulariter legeremus. Si enim lectio nostra nusquam a regula discreparet, nihil apud nos extra regulam fieret.[48]

Part of this treatise had a fairly wide circulation.[49] The Cistercians were followed by the Carthusians, and by the Victorines among the Regular Canons.[50] Giraldus seems to have been wholly unaware of all these attempts to ensure regularity.

* * *

[46] *Documents Illustrating the Activities of the General and Provincial Chapters of the English Black Monks*, ed. W. A. Pantin, Camden Ser. 3, 45 (1931) 70.

[47] J. Leclercq, *Analecta sacri ordinis Cisterciensis* 7 (1951) 64-70.

[48] *Ibid.* 67.

[49] In addition to the manuscripts mentioned by Leclercq, Thurot (n. 44 above) 25 mentions Paris B.N. MS lat. 5102. I have noted Leiden, B.P.L. 120, fol. 143, saec. xiii.

[50] Erlangen, Univ. Bibl. MS 186, fol. 221: "Incipit prologus in opusculum fratrum cenobii S. Victoris Parisiensis de dictionibus . . . Quoniam in eisdem dictionibus diversi diversos accentus pronunciant . . . ego Gilduinus cenobii S. Victoris Parisiensis dictus abbas . . . electis de ipsorum fratrum numero . . . iniunxi ut ipsam varietatem . . . sub unitatis leges et iura redigerent." See the catalog by H. Fischer (Erlangen 1928) 1.208.

One final comment. Every reader of the works of Giraldus soon becomes conscious that not only single quotations but whole clusters recur in many of his works. The preface to the *Speculum ecclesiae* is no exception. One long passage with a string of quotations is repeated from the *introitus* to the *Topographia hibernica*, as Giraldus probably indicated (p. 211 line 27). One of these quotations, attributed to the Philosopher, comes from a source uncommon at this time, namely from Seneca, ep. 104.26. The letters of Seneca have come down to us in two halves, one containing letters 1-88, the other letters 89-104. Letters 1-88 were generally available in the twelfth century, letters 89-104 were uncommon. A copy however did reach England. A free quotation from ep. 123 is found in the *Liber confortatorius*[51] which Goscelin wrote in 1082-1083 for Eve, the nun of Wilton, who became a recluse at Angers. A twelfth-century manuscript from Gloucester, in which both parts are put together, is extant (British Library, MS Harley 2659); and two English writers from the same part of the country, William of Malmesbury and Robert of Cricklade, knew them.[52] It is therefore not surprising to find a quotation in Giraldus. The problem is whether he knew them at first hand. Giraldus can be shown to have drawn on *florilegia*. Warner showed long ago that he "makes free use" of the *Moralium dogma philosophorum*·[53] and Richard and Mary Rouse have proved up to the hilt that he used the *Florilegium Angelicum*;[54] they have also made it probable that he used the *Florilegium Gallicum.*[55] The compilers of these three *florilegia* did not draw on letters 89-124. There is, however, an English *florilegium*, the so-called *Florilegium morale Oxoniense*,[56] extant in one late twelfth-century manuscript, in which there are a dozen or more extracts from letters 89-124. Our quotation is among them (p. 114, 12-13). It is followed by "Optimum est sine murmure pati quod emendare non possis." This is found in another work of Giraldus, the *De principis instructione.*[57] It is from Seneca ep. 107.9 with a difference. Seneca wrote: "Optimum est pati quod emendare non possis, et deum, quo auctore cuncta proveniunt, sine murmuratione comitari." It would be premature to conclude, on the strength of this one instance, that Giraldus drew on the *Florilegium morale Oxoniense*, but the coincidence

[51] Edited by C. H. Talbot, *Studia Anselmiana* 37 (1955) 79. The quotation was already noted by A. Wilmart, "Eve et Goscelin," *Revue Bénédictine* 50 (1938) 69.

[52] L. D. Reynolds, *The Medieval Traditions of Seneca's Letters* (Oxford 1955) 111, 120, 123.

[53] Opp. 8.xiii.

[54] R. H. and M. A. Rouse, "The *Florilegium Angelicum*" in *Medieval Learning and Literature: Essays Presented to R. W. Hunt*, ed. J. J. G. Alexander and M. T. Gibson (Oxford 1976) 89-90; and with full detail, A. Goddu and R. Rouse, "Gerald of Wales and the *Florilegium Angelicum*," *Speculum* (forthcoming).

[55] Rouse and Rouse 91 n. 1.

[56] Edited by C. H. Talbot, *Analecta mediaevalia Namurcensia* 6 (Louvain 1956).

[57] Opp. 8.17. Identified by Edward E. Best, Jr., "Classical Latin Prose Writers Quoted by Giraldus Cambrensis," Ph.D. diss. (University of North Carolina 1957) 117.

between the form found in the *florilegium* and in Giraldus makes it probable that Giraldus was not drawing directly on a text of Seneca's letters.

IV. TEXT

The leaves of MS Cotton Tib. B.XIII were mounted when the volume was repaired. Before the work was undertaken the leaves were numbered between the columns. This numeration begins at the present fol. 4. The present fols. 1, 2, 3 were not numbered. It is clear therefore that the order of these leaves was then uncertain. The page references given by Twyne and Richard James enable us to reconstruct the original order, and so to correct that in which they are now bound, as follows:

original order	James's pagination	present foliation
1r	1	burnt
1v	2	burnt
2r	3	3r
2v	4	3v
3r	5[58]	1v
3v	6	1r
4r	7	2v
4v	8	2r
5r	9	4r
5v	10	4v

In the following transcript the spelling of the manuscript has been kept, but the punctuation is modernized. Where the text depends on Twyne or James, I have restored the medieval spelling, which Twyne usually follows. Dots represent the approximate number of spaces for letters, but it should be remembered that the scribe is not very regular. Dashes (- - -) represent gaps in the text of more than two lines. Supplements derived from Twyne and James, and from other works of Giraldus or my own conjectures, are enclosed in square brackets. The omitted letters of the beginnings of paragraphs, which the rubricator should have filled in, are enclosed in pointed brackets.

[58] Twyne by a slip writes f. 5 for p. 5.

[De planctu lacrimabili.]

[Quoniam ad Cantuariensem sancte trinitatis ecclesiam] – – – [In dicto namque tam celebri celebique loco sanctorumque in terris habitaculo, in conventu monachorum ex litteraturae defectu usus inolescit, immo revera radices firmas fixit abusus.] – – – (3 ra) .ba . . . . tri .ta . . . . res sunt . . . . ill'. est . . . . .melicas . . . . st' et prosai. . . . . .atque fit . . . . .tantus et . . . . quod. . .ca .in versu . . . . orum. . . .litione [p]unctoque fit in prosa, ut .st fieri in legendo et sur . . . . . aliquid pronuntiando . . hac autem sola pronuntiatio[ne] observantur proprii accent[us] dictionum. In primis . . . . duabus nequaquam . . . . . iuntur dictiones ad . . . .as, melicas scilicet vel me. . . .s modulaciones. <P>ro[inde] ne peccatum unius loci [i]ncuria proveniens solum [mag]is quam impericia in uni[vers]itatem forte redundent, [et] ne clerus Anglie totus ex culpa quorundam contami[n]atus, tanta litterature singularis prerogativa ceteris [c]unctis semper hactenus lon[ge] precellens, lapsus in defectu[m] de novo videatur. Cessen[t in] sede regni suprema barbarismorum vicia et delatorum protinus ac maledicorum cessabunt convitia. (3rb) C[e]sset, inquam, in loco [tam ce]lebri chorus male pron[untiantium], et cessabit incontin[enter lo-]gica depravans. [Nec mirum] tamen si in mona. . . . . nis obsequiis et des. . . . . . . .in. . . . .ex toto. . . . . . . .tus interdum hui. . . . . reperiatur, cum etiam i. . . . . . . .lastico litteraliumque d[octri]narum tam magistris qu[am] discipulis similis hodie d[efectus] passim proh dolor et dam[pnum] inveniatur. Causam [vero] tanti defectus huius [et tam] generalis hanc esse no[veritis] quod litterature radicem [et fun]damentum [eatenus inconcus]sum leges imperiale[s] in regnis occiduis iam prope modum, immo preter modum, hodie suffocarunt. Tempus enim de quo Sibille vaticinium olim mentionem fecit quod magistrum Meinerium, principalem Petri Abailardi discipulum et rethorem incomparabiliter exim[i]um in auditorio suo Par[i]sius coram multitudine scolarium recitantem audivimus et plangentem, dampnisque futuris [val]de conpatie[ntem iam ad]venit. Erat autem vati[cinium ta]le: "Venient dies, [et] vhe illis, quibus leges obliterabunt scientiam litterarum." <Pro>inde enim (3va) . . . . pre ceteris hod[ie] . . . . magis est lucros. et . . . . commodiores . . [univ]ersorum sententiam . . . . . .s precipuis fructuo- .ant . . . . agere gratia . . . . nicolai . . . . .catervatim . . . . ur. <A>ntiquitus

1-2 De planctu . . . ecclesiam. Bale, *Index* 420, 422. 2-4 In dicto . . . abusus. J, p. 11. James adds: "Vid. et p. 3, 7." These pages are now fols. 3r, 2v, where the reference is to mistakes in pronunciation and accentuation. 13-17 et ne . . . convitia T, p. 192. 13-16 et ne . . . videatur J, 2-30 Causam . . . litterarum T, p. 191. 24-30 leges . . . literarum. J, p. 11.

13-16 cf. De libris (Opp. 1.414); "clerici litteratiores et laudabiliores totius Anglie ubi tot sunt boni." 22 cf. De invest., p. 197 Davies. 22-30 cf. Gemma eccl. 2.37 (Opp. 2.349).

enim . . . . imperatorum et principum . . . . qui per honores quos [philos] ophis atque poetis lin [gue L] atine moderatoribus lar [ge ref] erebant et artes nu [triebant], studiososque labores . . . .[re] munerabantur, litterature decus summopere tunc floruit, et liberalium artium [in] arduo celsitudinis vertice [sci] entia stetic. Item et propio [r] ibus nostro tempori diebus dum et ecclesiastice dignitates dignis et iuxta merita bona viris [v] idelicet eruditis et liberali [t] er instructis conferebantur, [lit] terarum studiis plurimum [i] ndulgebatur. Verum modernis [h] iis tempestatibus quibus [pri] ncipes r [ud] es et illiterati . . . . .que nec largi . . . . ignorant, [s] ic et . . . . quoque viros iure debito non honorant, si per eorum . . .a opera et seculares curias, per tirannicam scilicet intrusionem et non per ca(3vb)n [onicam electionem] . . . . . . tric. . . . . .no. . . . . .pro. lego . . . . t.s . . . . [Unde Y] sai [as] defectu [m temporis huius] longe pro [spiciens, ait: Ubi est] litteratu [s?] Ubi [verba legis prepon] derans? Ubi [doctor parvulo] rum? <P>roinde [etiam ver] bum illud quod apud Ox [on] iam nostri [s] die [bus a] quodam clerico [cui] nomen [Mar] tinus qui et [Bo] nonie in [l] egibus aliu [andiu] studuerat et litteris tamen [antea] provectus fuerat, P [auperistis], quorum ibi tunc copia f [uit], dum Pauperum scilicet li [ber il] le sic dictus in precio stetit, [res] ponsum erat, hic re [citare] preter rem non puta [vimus.] In quodam enim scolariu [m] conventu non modico, ubi et cause coram iu [dici] bus ventilabantur et c [on] troversie, cum ab aliis cu [nc] tis qui aderant advoca [tis] qui contra ipsum om [ne] s [esse] consueverant, et ipse quoque contrarius univ [ersis], lex una que contra ipsum expressa videbatur, obiecta fuisset; et conclamantibus cunctis et insultantibus (1va) ["Per hanc legem, Martine, salies, sicut et symie saltanti dici solet, perque legem istam velis nolis saltum facies," curialiter ab ipso, mordaciter tamen et lepide, satis responsum est in hunc modum: "Si saliendum est mihi, saliam quidem, sed saltum quem vos fecistis omnes a *Cum animadverterem* scilicet usque ad *Imperatoriam maiestatem,* si nempe debeatis et corpore medii, nec feci revera nec faciam." Solent enim miseri moderno tempore litteris addicti, terreni nimirum lucri cupidine ducti, protinus a primis litterarum rudimentis priusquam aut syllabicare recte noverint aut accentuare seu barbarismi quoque [sive solecis] mi [vi] tia [vi] ta [re, s] tatim ad libros imperi [ales], tam ad Digesta scilicet quam [ad] Codices necnon et Elemen [tor] um librum Institutiones [sa] ltu prepropero trans-

1va top 20 lines gone. 15-33 Proinde . . . transvolare T, p. 164. 25 saltanti: saltandi T *corr.* Langbaine 30 priusquam: postquam T

13-15 cf. Is. 33.18; cf. *Itin. Kambr., praef.* (Opp. 7.4 n. 2), where the passage is only found in a sixteenth century manuscript. 18 for the *Liber pauperum* of Vacarius see above, p. 198. 27-28 *Cum animadverterem* are the opening words of the Disticha Catonis, and *Imperatoriam maiestatem* the opening words of the Institutes. 33 for *Elementorum liber* as the title cf. *De princ. instr.* 1.10 (Opp. 8.32).

volare. [P] ropter quod edificio abs[que] fundamento constructo . . . . .no venti impulsu . . . . . . .nte statim et titu. . . . . quociens a verbis legalibus studio firma. . . . [a] d propria fortě trans[ib] un [t] . . . .minus la. . . . . .am. . . . . .risus at. . . . .(1vb) - - - [Magister Radulfus Belvacensis qui in artis litteratorie peritia grammaticaque doctrina singulari perogativa nostris diebus ceteris cunctis longe preminebat, trimembrem facere consuevit distinctionem talem: Clericorum nostri temporis alii superseminati sunt qui pretermisso scilicet litterature fundamento pernecessario superedificant et quasi superseminant scientias varias et facultates tantum in apparentia quadam et superficiales exi] stentes. A[lii vero pannosi] nomin [e] qui particula[tim et qua] si per panniculos comparant sibi scientias, in singulis solum apparentes, et absolutam in nullis omnino perfectionem habentes, et iuxta versus huius sententiam non incedentes:

Artes per partes, non partes disce per artes.

Alii vero massati quorum ho[die perpauci q] ui super litteratu[re fundamentum solidum tam divine legis quam humane ceterarumque facultatum stabile edificium construunt et inconcussum] . (1ra) [Alia litterature defectus causa est quod scholares diebus istis in trivio studentes, pretermissis omnino fere duabus facultatibus pernecessariis, quarum prima recte, secunda vero lepide loqui docet et ornate, ad studium logices et garrule loquacitatis apparentiam, quatinus acuti videantur et diserti, se cursu veloci transferre deproperant; cathedramque magistralem solum triennii spatio seu quadriennii, quatinus quod male didicerunt et imperfecte doctrina prorsus inutili ceteris insinuent, et ut magisterii nomine tumescant et ad leges aut physicam, lucrosas scilicet pro tempore scientias, illico transean] t, scandere [non erub] escunt. Quod nos quidem et coetanei nostri tempore sereniori et feliciori, donec non solum in trivio verum etiam in auctoribus et philosophis necnon et metricis ac dictaminum studiis massati plenius essemus consummati viginti annorum [au] t [plurium] labore continuo non attemptavimus. - - - (1rb) - - - . . . . .in artibus scilicet et maturi quod didicerunt et inutilit [er] alios docentes similesq [ue] magistris discipulos effic [ien] tes, tantum et tam e[nor] mem hodie defectum in li [t] teratura facere presumpserin [t] . Nec mirum quia iuxta illud Plauti elogium:

[Ex in] sensibili ne creda[s sensile] nasci.

<V>erumtamen qu. . s[co] lasticos non circa mo. . . . . . set. . .rcitie etatis . . . .

1vb top 20 and bottom 5 lines gone. 4-17 magister . . . inconcussum T. p. 191. 1ra top 20 and bottom 5 lines gone. 17-28 Alia . . . attemptavimus. T, pp. 191-192. 1rb top 20 lines gone.

4-17 cf. *Gemma eccl.* 2.37 (Opp. 2.348-349). 14 Walther, *Sprichwörter,* no. 1488. The verse was current in England in Gerald's time. It is found in the *Distinctiones monasticae* (Pitra, *Spicil. Solesmense* 2.482), and in Bodleian Libr. MS Digby 53, fol. 43v. 32 Cited anonymously in *Gemma eccl.* 2.34 (Opp. 2.336f.), and as Plautus in *De invect.* 4.3, p. 171 Davies. It is a slightly altered version of Lucretius 2.888: "Ex insensibilibus ne credas sensile nasci," which is quoted by

ca prima viros .d . . . . tam admiratio. . . . . .que eximiis. Quis (2va) - - - [Unde Agellius: Dialetice discipline cognitio in principiis quidem insuavis, aspernabilis et inutilis videri solet. Sed ubi aliquantum processeris, tunc eius emolumentum animo tuo dilucebit, sequeturque discendi quedam voluptas insatiabilis, ac nisi modum feceris periculum eri] t non m[edi] o[c] re, [ne vel] ud alii [p] lerique tu qu[oque in ill] is dialetice giris atque [m] eandris tamquam apud [Si] reneos scopulos consenes[c] as. Ideoque propter incommodum tale vitandum dialecticam a limine salutandam sapiens n. .ciet.

<P>orro quatinus ad prescripta monacorum [Cantua] riensium in pronunci[ando v] icia denique reverta[mur, di] fficile est a consu[etudine] . . . . . . usus omnis . . . . . .at et ab. . .iscitur .gre serm. . . . . .m quod . .molita di. . . . . .uus Thomas pronun. . . . . .quamvis valde v. . . . .(2vb) - - - Nulla m. . . . . .tem hab. . . . . .quitatis . . . . g. stantes . . . . poeta nullius addictus] in verba magistri [iurare, at] que nullorum addicti iurare in] verba priorum sive maiorum deberent. <H>aut aliter etiam hoc verbum auc. . . . . . et similia penultima sillaba quasi producta pronuntiare consueverunt. Poeta v[ero dicit:

V] itam dederitis [in undis].

. .status u. . . - - - (2ra) - - - . . . . .at. . . . . .ro. Similiter et ["alio" pro "alii" in dativ] o, sicut [illud in Ewangelio:] Dico hu[ic, Vade, et vad] it, et alio, Ve[ni, et venit.] <N>onne igitur . . . . [c] uiusdam signum . . . . et p[resu] mptuose species videtur arrogantie antiquata vocabula et tamquam [vetu] state sepulta contra usum puplicum resuscitare conari, et ea que stantia sunt et communi favore pollentia . . . . cere prorsus eniti . . . . .n. . . . . .e- - - - (2rb) - - - representare . . . . . .

[Verb] a minus memor[es vete] rum, magis exprime m[ores],

Quorum si memor es, diligi[s et] memores.

2va top 19 lines gone. 2vb top 16 and bottom 6 lines gone. 2ra top 16 and bottom 5 lines gone. 20-22 Similiter . . . venit, J, p. 11 21 J adds antiquitus after dativo, but the word was not in the MS at this point. Perhaps it occurred in the preceding sentence which is lost. 2rb top 19 lines gone.

Priscian, *Inst. gramm.* 4.27, whence it no doubt came into circulation. It is quoted often by William of Conches; see the edition of his *Glosae super Platonem* by E. Jeauneau (Paris 1965) 120. It is also found in Daniel of Morley, *Liber de naturis inf. et sup.*, ed. Sudhoff, *Archiv für Gesch. d. Naturwissenschaften* 8 (1917) 10, and in Alexander Nequam, *Speculum speculationum* 3.9 (London, British Library, MS Royal 7 F.I, fol. 52vb). 2-7 *Noctes Atticae* 16.8.16-17, quoted in *Gemma eccl.* 2.37 (Opp. 2.351), and in Ep. 24 (Opp. 1.286), and in a condensed form in *Itin. Kambr., praef.* (Opp. 6.4). 15-19 Hor. *Ep.* 1.1.14.6 Ovid, *Met.* 6.357. 21-22 Matt.8-9; Lk. 7.8. 27-28 By Giraldus, Symb. electorum 2.18 (Opp 1.364). In one manuscript the title is: "Cuidam verbis veterum utenti, mores eorum non preferenti."

<N>otandum autem quod monachi Cistercienses qui iuxta primevam ordinis institutionem et intencionem superflua Clu[n]iacensium et abusiva vit[an]da dixerunt, in dictis pronunciationum viciis ipsos imitantur, sicut Grandimontani . . . . Cartusienses, Canonici . . . . . . que regulares . . . . singula vis. . . . . regulares in. . . . . regula . . . . .cesserit antiquata (4ra) – – – [Notandum hoc etiam quod monachi fer]e [cuncti abusivis pro]nuntia[tionibus pre ceteris viris] ecclesi[asticis plus uten]tes quo[tiens evangelia] legunt, [huic dictioni] "Iesus" hanc dic[tionem "Dominus" iu]xta casuum [inflexiones] adicere solent, [in hunc] modum: "Dixit dominus [Iesus disc]ipulis suis," cum tamen [in e]wangelicis scripturis to[tis], quattuor scilicet ewangeliis, talis iunctura preterquam duobus in locis minime reperiatur. In Luca scilicet iuxta finem ewangelii sui, ubi loquitur de sanctis mulieribus illis ad monumentum venientibus, dicens: "Et ingresse non invenerunt corpus domini Iesu." Item et in Marco similiter, in fine scilicet ewangelii, ubi ait: "Et dominus quidem Iesus postquam locutus est eis assumptus est in celum, [et se]det a dextris dei." Ubi . . . . . . [q]uoque notandum quod . . . . . . [re]surrectionem tant. . . . . . . [e]w[an]geliis in . . . . .a dictionum . . . . quia ex tunc primo evidenter apparuit Iesum et dominum et deum esse. Sicut Moy[ses] . . . .(4rb) – – – . .1. . .p. . . . . ullam verb. . . . . in ewangelica . . . . tiando faciunt . . . . ewangeliis in. . . . . Non enim sic . . . . .do sacras scripturas, [preser]tim ewangelicas, quibus aut verba Christi recitantur aut opera, cuius nimirum cuncta operatio nostra quidem est instructio, nulla fieri ad[dit]io debeat, sic nec substractio seu varietatis illius alteratio. <Pre>cisum est itaque superfluumque penitus et supervacuum tali substantivo cui non opus est adiectivo vel exteriori quolibet adminiculo quicquam adicere, cuius quippe significati gratia substant omnia et subsistunt universa. Novit hoc Paulus, et maiestatem nominis huius non ignorans, ait, eidemque nomini nichil addendo sic proposuit: "Ut in nomine Iesu omne genu flectatur etc." Iesus enim salvator sonat aut salutaris. Unde cum nemo in Christi fide fundatus atque nutritus Iesum rerum omn[ium et] creaturarum dominum [et d]ominatorem existere, cuius . . . in- (4va) – – – . . . . .domine Iesu . . . . .dum asseve-. . . . . .aliter Lucas . . . . in Actibus Gau[dentes] . . . . scripsit, "quoniam dig[ni habiti] sunt pro nomine Iesu contumeliam pati." Ecce qualiter non pro nomine domini Iesu, [set Ies]u simpliciter, dignos pati contumeliam dixit.

Sane quoniam ex ipsa raritate plerumque preciositatis augmentum rebus accrescat, iuxta illud Ieronimi elogium: Pulegium apud Indos pipere preciosius est, litteraturam

4ra top 2 and last lines gone. 5-11 Notandum . . . reperiatur J, p. 11. 4rb top 3 lines gone. 4va, 4vb top lines gone.

12-13 Lk. 24.3. 13-15 Mk. 16.19. 27 Phil. 2.10. 30 There may have been here a quotation of Acts 7.59: "Domine Iesu suscipe spiritum meum." 31-32 Acts 5.41. 35 Ep. 146.2 (C.S.E.L. 56.311); also cited in *Speculum duorum,* ed. J. Lefèvre and R. B. C. Huygens (Cardiff 1974) 230.

de qua loquimur, cuius etiam quasi carmen querulum et planctum quoque tamquam epithalamicum hic emisimus, litteratorum raritas ipsa virorum futuris forte diebus coniectura probabili denuo preciosam efficiet et gloriosam, quatinus ad ipsam iterum, tamquam ad lingue Latine matrem atque magistrum, viri scolastici irreparabilium plangentes dampna dierum caterva[tim] accurrant. Presertim [au]tem si principes litterati [et la]rgi regna et inperia (4vb) – – – re. . . . . .regn. . . . . prescript. . . . . .si tamen . . . . suspiriosis . . . . quam a long. . . . . .studiosos labor. . . . . .mam litterarum so. . . . . .quarum radix quid[em est ama]ra fructus autem dul]cis for]san ex parte redolentes sa[l]tem apud posteros, quoniam et livore vacuos et litteris forte reversis ac resuscitatis affatim erudiendos dignis efferri laudibus affectamus. <U>tinam igitur in regni Anglicani sede supprema et ecclesiarum eiusdem omnium digne debiteque tamquam superlativa de cetero cesset in choro viciosa dictionum prolatio cuncta, litterarumque decus et gloria saltem in fine temporum ad pristini status hon[ore]m sit reversura. [Forsan au]tem in brevi litter[atura resu]rget, illud quidem . . . . . tandem dar. . . . . [die]bus hiis nostris ultimis a summo pontifice Honorio [qu]i mandatum nuper [ema]navit, ut clerici red[ditus] . . .stitis bene- (5ra) – – – . . . . .te. . . . . .ntendere le. . . . . .sint consequens . . . . . .detur, ut cum saltum predi[ct]um a litteris scilicet et sillabis stat[i]m ad leges more solito face[re] nequeant, pretermissis laicorum legibus et verbosis atque clamosis absque medulla constitutionibus, ad litterales scientias artesque liberales, canonicas demum theologicasque superedificando disciplinas humane saluti pernecessarias felici mutacione convertantur.

<A>d litterature quoque reparationem et tempestativam sanioris doctrine reversionem illud etiam ex parte facere posse videtur quod libri quidam tamquam Aristotilis intitulati Toletanis Hispanie finibus nuper inventi et translati, logices quodammodo doctrinam profitentes et tamquam prima fronte preferentes, set philosophicas longe magis de rerum scilicet naturis inquisitiones et subtiles quoque discussiones, quam (5rb) [locales et complexionales argumentorum habitudines studiosis mentibus et valde laboriosis experimentis, ad quos scolares nostri temporis novitate gaudentes cursim protinus et certatim accurrerunt, relic]tisque libr[is eius]dem prioribus et [antiquioribus] doctrine sanio[ris et solidioris] novitatibus ill[is in errores etiam] et hereses in[ducentibus, ni]miis affectibus adher[en]tes indulserunt, nuper in Fran[cia], ne legerentur amplius in scolis, sunt prohibiti. Quapropter relictis vanis disciplinis illis et erroneis ad saniores doctrinas, solidiores et salubriores, deo inspirante, convertentur.

5ra top 6 lines gone. 24-p.210.2 Ad litterature . . . convertentur, J. p. 12. 5rb, 5va top 6 lines gone.

10 Cited as Jerome in *Top. hib.* 3.48 (Opp. 5.191) and *Itin. Kambr.* 1.8 (Opp. 6.75); cf. Ep. 107.2 (C.S.E.L. 55.290) and Ep. 125.12 (C.S.E.L. 56.131). 15 cf. *Spec. eccl.* 4, *proem.* (Opp. 4.263). 16-17 The bull of Honorius III "Super speculam"; see above, p. 198. 17 emanavit cf. Opp. 3.373. 34 See above, p. 199.

<Q>uamquam autem indecens sit plurimum ut epistola libellum prolixitate redoleat, adiciendum hic tamen quod ad provocandum et a[ll]iciendum sco[la]rium mentes ad studia pres[c]ripta, subtilia quidem longe magis quam utilia, super librum Aristotilis quendam de Anima intitulatum, hoc scriptum quidem est inventum: "Indignum revera est valde ut id quo est sciens homo nesciat et quo rationalis est nulla ratione comprehendat. Quomodo enim deum vel se poterit diligere q[ui] quod in se melius est convincitur ignorare?" <A>d det[err]en [(5va) dum autem a studiis huiusmodi subtilibus magis quam utilibus, in errorem quippe manifeste ducentibus, Salomon ad filium ait: Fili, altiora te ne scruteris et fortiora te ne exquisieris, set] q[ue precepit tibi deus illa c]ogita semper, [et in pluribus operi]bus eius ne fuer[is curiosus.] Item Ieronimus ad quen[dam . . . . s] uper pennas ven[torum] . . . . . .ibus inquisitionibus ambulare volentem, quinimmo tanquam pernicibus alis presumptuosis pariter et perniciosis longe trans nubes et astra volare nitentem. Quid te torques, inquit, et maceras in illa questione quam subtilius est et utilius contempnere quidem quam vel solvere vel ratione discutere? Item ad Timotheum: Stultas autem et sine disciplina questiones devita, sciens quia generan[t lites. Servu]m autem domini non oportet litigare, sed mansuetum esse ad omnes. Item ad Titum: Stulta[s autem questiones et genealogi]as et contentiones et pugnas legis devita. Sunt enim inutiles et v[ane. Item ad Timotheum: Noli ver]bis contendere, ad nichil enim utile nisi ad subversionem audientium. Item <ad> Ti[motheum: Erit enim tempus cum sanam d]octrinam non sustinebunt, set ad sua desideria coacervabunt sibi m[agistros prurientes auri]bus. Et a veritate quidem auditum avertent; ad fabulas autem conv[ertentur]. Item et Augustinus ad monachum quendam querentem quit faceret deus antequam mundus fieret, sic respondens, Gehennam, inquit, stulte querentibus preparavit. Circa inicialia namque mundi tempora vel ante, sicut et finalia vel post, humana deficiunt prorsus ingenia, que se tamen exercent utrumque circa media. Quod per angelos signatur qui sicut Ysaias [t]estatur duabus quidem [alis f]aciem velabant seden- (5vb) – – – d. . . . . .qu. . . . . .eleg. . .ns et Esau repre. . . . . . et similia, nec sensibus h[uma]nis pervia nec compreh. . . . ullatenus mortalib. . . . .te permissa. O altit[udo diviti]arum sapientie et [s]cientie dei! Quam

7-9 Ad deterrandum . . . exquisieris J. p. 12. 15-23 Item ad . . . convertentur. These lines were written by the scribe in the bottom margin, and connected with the text by a *signe de renvoi.* 5 vb top 7 lines gone.

5-7 From the translator's preface to Avicenna, *De anima,* which was not included in the edition of Avicenna's works (Venice, 1508), but was first printed by A. Jourdain, *Recherches critiques* (Paris 1819); see M. T. d'Alverny. "Avendauth," in *Homenaje a Millas-Vallicrosa* (Barcelona 1954) 1.20, 33. The quotation is not exact. The original reads: "Indignum siquidem ut illam partem sui qua est sciens homo nesciat, et id per quod rationalis est ratione ipse non comprehendat. Quomodo enim iam se vel deum poterit diligere, cum id quod in se melius est convincitur ignorare?" 9-11 Eccli.3.22. exquisieris: scrutatus fueris Vulg. 13-15 Seneca, Ep. 49.6, also cited in *Gemma eccl.* 2.37 (Opp. 2.356). 16-17 II Tim. 2.23-24. 18-19 Tit. 3.9. 19-20 II Tim. 2.14. 20-23 II Tim. 4.3-4. 23-25 Augustine, *Confessions* 11.12.14. 27-28 Is. 6.2 30-p. 211.2 Rom. 11.33-34.

incomprehsibilia sunt iudicia eius et investigabiles vie eius! Quis cognoscit sensum domini, aut quis consiliarius eius fuit? etc. Noli ergo circiter hec et huiusmodi nimis subtiliter investigare, neque proterve disputare, si non volueris errare et plectibiliter exorbitare, teque scienter in penale periculum precipitare.

<V>erum quia de studiosis laboribus nostris tamquam in talo et calce tractatus huius mentionem inter cetera fecimus, duas tam vehementis tamque continui fere studii nostri causas lector agnoscat, posterorum scilicet futuris diebus si litterature laus et honor livore sopito sive sepulto quandoque resurgat, ex nostro for- (6ra) - - - . . . . est nos . . . . non inv-. . . . . quandoque vixisse testemur. Quoniam, ut ait Cassiodorus, noli celare speculum mentis tue ubi te possit omnis etas futura perspicere, multique valeant ex tue diligentie labore proficere. <N>otandum hoc autem quod sicut philosophanti cuilibet duo sunt necessaria, sapientia scilicet et sufficientia, iuxta illud poete:

> Quis locus ingenio est nisi cum se carmine solo
> vexant et dominis Cirre Niseque feruntur
> pectora nostra duas non admittentia curas?

Item et illud:

> Nam si Virgilio puer et tollerabile desit
> hospicium caderent omnes a crinibus ydre,

sic et alia quoque duo scribere volenti sunt pernecessaria, litteralis scientie scilicet habundans copia et infatigabilis studiosi laboris diligentia. Necesse est etiam ut mentis studiose conatum licet arte suffultum comitetur ingenium, iuxta illud. In- (6rb) - - -

> [ego nec studium sine divite vena
> nec rude quid prosit video ing]enium; [alterius sic
> altera] poscit op[em res et coniu]rat amice.

. . . . [in Hiber]nice Topogra[phie pro]emio quedam . . . . noverit et l. . . . . tantis auctori[bus] et [tot] antiquis scilicet et autenti[cis stu]diosis mentibus inn[iten]tes eorumque tamquam humeris insidentes, multiplicate maiestatis beneficio magni fieri possumus, si magnanimi. Nobiles nimirum ausus nichil eque impedit ut diffidentia. Omnis appetendi conatus perit ex desperatione consequendi.

6ra top 4 lines gone. 6rb top 4 lines gone.

6-7 cf. *De princ. instr.* 1 *praef.* (Opp. 8.6). 7-8 cf. *Spec. eccl.* 4, *proem,* (Opp. 4.263). 9-10 vixisse testemur: cf. the end of the original preface to *De princ. instr.* (Opp. 8.1xvii). 10-11 Cassiodorus, *Variae, praef.* (MGH Auct. Ant. 12.4.24). 14-16 Juv. 6.63-65. 18-19 The two quotations are found together in *Top. hib. introitus* (Opp. 5.4). 24-26 Hor. *Ars. poet.* 409-411. 27-p. 212.15 Taken from *Top. hib. introitus* (Opp. 5.5), with additions. 29 This is an allusion to the saying of Bernard of Chartres that we are giants standing on the shoulders of dwarfs, on which see E. Jeauneau, *Vivarium* 5 (1967), 79-99. 30-31 Jerome, according to *De princ. instr.* 1.9 (Opp. 8.32).

Multa nempe, ut ait philosophus, non quia difficilia sunt non audemus, set quia non audemus difficilia sunt.

Latet ob hoc sub ocio laudabilis plerumque virtus et eruditio, et dum se probandi formidat exercitium occulta manet lux [to] ta meritorum. Hinc accid[it u] t scientissimi plerique [se n] esciendo senescant, [et dum] vires ingen[ii] non experiu[n] tur igne [ani] mi vacui (6va) [veluti pecora pereunt, et nomen eorum non memorabitur ultra. Unde et quoniam

Paulum sepulte distat inertie
celata virtus,
Degeneres an] imos [timor arguit,
Dimidium] facti qui [cepit habet,
Audace] s fortuna iu[vat,

scribere pro] posui et livido[rum malitia r] idiculosus cen[seri potius qu] am bonorum [arbitrio me] ticulosus elegi. [Illo quo] que Ciceronis exemplo retardari non potui. Ea, inquit, re poemata non scribo, quia qualia volo non possum, qualia possum nolo. Michi enimvero ea mens est , et in hanc partem tam vehemens, cum

neque corda sonum reddat quem vult manus et mens,
nec semper feriat quodcumque minabitur arcus.

Si qualia volo non possum, qualia possum volo. <I>nvitare nos etiam ad scribendum arduumque conatum aliquem aggrediendum illud sapientis cuiusdam elogium plurimum potuit: Provide mentis est et a natura bene institute, quoniam pretereuntia sunt cuncta q[ue ce] rnimus et pereuntia, ad [sta] bilia ac permanenita bona [tot] is nisibus anelare et . . . . . . ac transitoriis ad . . . . . conv[erte] re, contraque (6vb) - - - gare. . . . . .nione de su. . . . .po. . . . . .tum primo stabiliore . . . . veriore vivere vita vid. .

<H>anc autem vitam vere vitalem plus per opera bona et bene meritoria quam per opuscula laboriosa sibi mens provida comparare nitatur. Nec tamen opuscula studiosaque conamina sunt aspernanda. Non enim contempnenda sunt omnia quibus aliqua reperiri poterunt prestantiora. Multo plures etenim agiographi nostri tam posteros quam presentes libris et litteris quam labiis et linguis seu lectionibus erudierunt, multoque pluribus Origenes et Ieronimus studendo scribendoque quam loquendo sive legendo profuerunt. Scripta nimirum literarumque vinculis alligata

6va, 6vb top 5 lines gone.

1-2 Seneca, Ep. 104.27. The two quotations are found together in *De princ. instr. loc. cit.* 3-4 cf. Cassiodorus, *Variae* 1.24 (ed. cit. 27.4). 6-7 cf. Zach. 13.2.8-9 Horat. *Od.* 4.9.29. This quotation and that of Cassiodorus are also found together in *De princ. instr.* 1.15 (Opp. 8.52). 10 Verg. *Aen.* 4.13. 11 Horat. *Ep.* 1.2.40. 12 Verg. *Aen.* 10.284. 14-15 not identified. 17-18 Horat. *Ars poet.* 348, 350. 21-23 not identified. 29-31 *Gemma eccl. proem.* (Opp. 2.4), *De libris* (Opp. 1.418).

puplicataque semel et approbata tenaciter herent, et tanquam successione quadam et reparacione continua posteritati totum profutura per evum perseverant. Non igitur inutilis, non infructuosus studiose mentis videri debet (7ra) - - - . . . . .laudis appetitum scribendo laborant. Qui enim hoc faciunt, mercedem utique suam iam receperunt, premioque prorsus fraudantur eterno. <V>erumtamen vix evenire solet ut quamvis non appetatur, in bonis actibus arduisque conatibus suis laus evitetur. Mirum enim in modum laus cum appetitur, amittitur, cumque vitatur, adquiritur. Gloria namque virtutes, ut ait Ieronimus, ac virtuosos tamquam umbra sequitur, et appetitores sui deserens, diligit et dirigit contemptores. <D>ictam autem laudis et umbre naturam hii duo versiculi satis expresse declarant:

Laus umbre similis quam non fugiendo fugabis,
si fugis, en sequitur, fugit aspernata sequentem.

<D>et igitur omnipotens et misericors deus quatinus illi qui doctrinalibus in studiis ad sponse Christi decorem et decus mente manuque laboriose desudant, fructum laboris qui non more superborum et insensatorum (7rb) - - - gentium . . . . eterne glorie no. . . . . . . transitorie, vi. . . . . .tia pura felic. . . . . constituant . . . .

Well Close
Blackbridge Road
Freshwater Bay
Isle of Wight

7ra top 6 lines gone. 7rb top 6 lines gone.

4-5 cf. Matt. 6.2 7-12 cf. *Vita Remigii et Hugonis proem. ed. secunda* (Opp. 7.5); 7-9 *Expugn. Hib.* 1.4 (Opp. 5.235). 7-8 cf. Jerome, Ep. 22.27 (C.S.E.L. 54.183.9). 8-9 Jerome, Ep. 108.3 (C.S.E.L. 55.309). The two quotations are found together also in *De princ. instr.* 1.15 (Opp. 8.53). 11-12 not identified.

LORD NOVGOROD THE GREAT: ITS PLACE IN MEDIEVAL CULTURE

•

by Henrik Birnbaum

1

Much has been said and written about the numerous manifestations of the largely homogeneous civilization that evolved among the Eastern Slavs during the period which in European history is sometimes referred to as the High and Late Middle Ages. In Russia, the Middle Ages were not followed by an epoch qualitatively distinct from the preceding times and unequivocally identifiable as that of the Renaissance, some traces of a "Pre-Renaissance" spirit in ideological content and aesthetic form – briefly discussed below – notwithstanding.[1] In this context it should be noted, then, that medieval Russian culture (or, more accurately, the culture of ancient Rus, *drevniaia Rus'*) did not emerge, for all intents and purposes, prior to the late tenth century. It was ushered in by the official conversion of the Kievan state in 988 under the ruler who, because of this political decision and not in recognition of any particular Christian piety or charity (of which, to judge by the historical record, he seems to have had very little), was to be canonized by the Orthodox Church and thus has entered Russian history as Vladimir the Saint (or simply Saint Vladimir, ca. 980-1015). If, therefore, medieval Russia did attain a level of intellectual and artistic accomplishment deserving of the label "culture" only by the turn of the first millennium A.D., it is by the same token a fair assessment to claim that, except for certain Southwest Russian or, rather, "Ruthenian" (that is, subsequently Ukrainian and Belorussian) territories then held by Lithuania, the "medieval" period of Russian history lasted until the end not of the fifteenth but of the seventeenth century. It came to a definitive close only in 1682 with the ascendancy to power of Peter the Great. It was this czar of the Romanov dynasty who, by founding the modern city

This is the revised and expanded version of a paper read on 24 February 1976 at the Center for Slavic and East European Studies, University of California, Berkeley.

[1] See further H. Birnbaum, *On Medieval and Renaissance Slavic Writing* (The Hague 1974) 48-55 (in the essay: "Some Aspects of the Slavic Renaissance"); cf. also the pertinent remarks in my paper "On the Significance of the Second South Slavic Influence for the Evolution of the Russian Literary Language," *International Journal of Slavic Linguistics and Poetics* 21.4 (1975) 23-50, esp. 26-28, 39-42.

on the Neva that for two centuries bore his name, figuratively speaking pushed open a permanent "window to Europe" and who introduced a number of sociopolitical and cultural reforms which once and for all spelled an end to the previous life style of Old Russian society.

Moreover, it is not an exaggeration or even a gross oversimplification to propose that Russian medieval culture was primarily indebted to, if not almost entirely patterned on, the rich and refined though increasingly stereotyped and petrified civilization of Byzantium. It was from here that Russia had received its particular brand of Christianity and, along with it, the gift of literacy as well as, consequently, the chief thematics and genres of its literature and the leitmotifs of its art. Thus it can be said that Old Russian icon painting and chanting in the only superficially Russian-tinged archaic Church Slavic language used in the Mass were but echoes and extensions of artistic forms of expression first developed and cultivated in Byzantium. The ecclesiastic architecture of Kievan, Appanage, and Muscovite Russia emulated the forms of construction and ornamentation of Byzantine churches and monasteries, with the magnificent Saint Sophia cathedrals of Kiev and, on a somewhat smaller scale, Novgorod reminiscent of the Hagia Sophia providing the most obvious and striking examples. In addition, the inexhaustible flow of theological and historiographic writing of ancient Rus, its abundant hagiographic, homiletic, and patristic literature as well as its many chronicles couched in a more or less unadulterated form of Russian Church Slavic, can be traced, for the most part, to readily ascertainable Byzantine sources or models. As is well known, by the fourteenth and fifteenth centuries, Byzantium itself crumbled and its immediate Slavic neighbor states in the Balkans, Bulgaria and Serbia, too, were unable to withstand the onslaught of the Osmanli conquerors. It was then that Russia and its new central political force which at that time was about to emerge from under the cracking "Tatar yoke," the young principality of Muscovy, laid claim to the spiritual, but not really the secular (contrary to occasional contentions) heritage of Byzantium; see the essentially theological doctrine of Moscow as the Third Rome, first propounded in 1510 in a letter to Vasilii (Basil) III by the Pskovian abbot Filofei (Philotheus). As concerns the purely political tradition of the state, the rulers of late medieval Muscovy rather conceived of themselves as being the successors to the grand princes of Kiev of an earlier – glorious – epoch in Russian history.[2]

It can be said, therefore, that the essence of Russian medieval culture is, in broad outline, fairly clear and its heavy dependence on Byzantine sources and prototypes generally well established. It goes without saying, that very many details of this rather monolithic culture have been filled in and elaborated while, as must be expected, numerous other problems of Old Russian intellectual and artistic life still remain obscure, controversial, or even unresolved altogether. By contrast, relatively little has as yet been accomplished by way of serious research to differentiate, within

[2] Cf., e. g., N. V. Riasanovsky, *A History of Russia*, ed. 2 (New York 1969) 137-138.

this culture sphere and evolution spanning seven centuries, among specific geographic, and usually at the same time politically definable, larger sub-areas. Such regions were as a rule characterized by their particular traits and can therefore be identified and singled out as more closely knit, internally dependent and cohesive "cultural landscapes" (to resort to the equivalent of the German notion of *Kulturlandschaft*). Thus, while general descriptions and interpretations of the cultural profiles of earlier Kievan Russia as a whole and of later, rapidly growing Muscovite Russia abound, emphasizing shifting theoretical approaches and reflecting diverse scholarly aims and interests, much less has been done in this vein for other portions of ancient Rus. Removed from the capital city or flourishing at a time when Russia had no central capital, these areas frequently show a remarkable degree of inner cohesion in their cultural microstructure, usually matching a particular political constellation. This applies, for example, to the southwestern region of Galicia-Volhynia where the principality – briefly the kingdom – of Galich or Halych, bordering on Poland and Hungary, developed a hectic if short-lived political activity matched by an intense cultural flowering after the capture and sacking of Kiev by the Mongols in 1240; to the principality of Vladimir-Suzdal, the immediate predecessor of Muscovy, maintaining some literary and intellectual ties with Galich as well as firm political and cultural links with Novgorod; and, above all, to Novgorod itself and to the territories it controlled.

In particular when it comes to Novgorod, the "father of Russian towns" (in contradistinction to Kiev, their folkloric "mother"), the relative paucity of coherent approaches to, and holistic analyses of, its cultural achievements in a wide range of fields is acutely felt.[3] For the commercial center on the Volkhov River has undoubtedly played a major, partly independent role in the intellectual and religious life of ancient Rus. In the earlier period of Russian medieval history, its contribution was second only to that of Kiev, the exceedingly Byzantinized capital in the south. After the Mongol invasion and the subsequent occupation of most of Russia and up to Novgorod's formal annexation by Muscovy in 1478, it assumed the leading part in Russian cultural evolution eventually to be outshone only by the rising star of Moscow itself which had begun to "gather" the Russian lands around its own territory and ultimately unified them within the confines of a new, politically ever more potent state.

Prior to its incorporation by Muscovy, Novgorod could play this important role in

[3] Among the rather few attempts at a comprehensive analysis of the particular contribution made by Novgorod to Old Russian culture, the following monographic treatments deserve mention: N. G. Porfiridov, *Drevnii Novgorod: Ocherki iz istorii russkoi kul'tury XI-XV vv.*, ed. 2 (Moscow 1947); V. L. Ianin, "Velikii Novgorod," in *Po sledam drevnikh kul'tur. Drevniaia Rus'* (Moscow 1953) 217-252 (emphasizing archaeological finds); D. S. Likhachev, *Novgorod Velikii: Ocherk istorii kul'tury Novgoroda XI-XVII vv.*, ed. 2 rev. (Moscow 1959); K. Onasch, *Gross-Nowgorod: Aufstieg und Niedergang einer russischen Stadtrepublik* (Vienna 1969) esp. 131-190 ("Kulturgeschichte Nowgorods").

Old Russian culture, to a large extent at least, as a result of the north Russian merchant republic's ability to keep the Tatar occupant out of its own territory at the high but prudently paid price of recognizing the suzerainty of the khan of the Golden Horde, residing most of the time in his capital of Sarai (also, New Sarai) near the Lower Volga. This formal recognition entailed, among other things, the annual payment of a tribute to the Mongol ruler; see the similar arrangement reached by the merchant patricians of Dubrovnik with the Turkish sultan a century and a half later. In addition, and no less an achievement, Novgorod, prior to the time of Peter the Great, constituted Russia's major link with the West. At first, these contacts were mainly with the Scandinavian Varangians, later with the German and Swedish merchant guilds of Visby on the Baltic island of Gotland and, shortly thereafter and growing out of this latter connection, with the many cities of the Hanseatic League, headed by Lübeck, and through them with northern and western Europe in general.[4] Thus, besides making its own significant impact on various facets of Old Russian culture proper, Novgorod, situated at the crossroads of some of Eastern Europe's most important trade routes, became instrumental in transmitting, along with material goods, cultural values of various kinds, that is, ideas, motifs, and aesthetic concepts in oral, written, and artistically fashioned form. It therefore does not appear as an inappropriate overstatement to speak of "Lord Novgorod the Great" (*Gospodin Velikii Novgorod*, as the proud merchant boyars referred to their city at the height of its political and commercial success) as the fountainhead and disseminator of medieval culture: Byzantine, Balkan and West Slavic, German and Scandinavian, in part even that of the Near East.

The following brief account is aimed, primarily, at outlining the set of relevant phenomena and the specific attendant problems and at tentatively grouping and classifying them as forming, in one sense or another, a self-contained coherent whole. The purpose of this essay is therefore programmatic in nature rather than purporting to summarize, except in a few instances, any particular, in-depth research carried out by the present writer. Essentially it is conceived as a preview of sorts of a book-length treatment of the specifically Novgorodian variety of medieval Russian culture and its further interrelations with civilizations of other areas, currently in preparation.[5]

[4] Most recently, Novgorod's connections with the Hanseatic League were surveyed and, in part, reinterpreted in my contribution "Die Hanse in Novgorod (Neuumriss einer Problematik)," to appear in the testimonial volume for D. Gerhardt (Hamburg). For a more detailed account particularly of the material side of Novgorod's trade with the Baltic provinces (Curonia, Livonia, Estonia) and western Europe at the height of its flourishing, see A. L. Khoroshkevich, *Torgovlia Velikogo Novgoroda s Pribaltikoi i Zapadnoi Evropoi v XIV-XV vekakh* (Moscow 1963), and lately further N. Kazakova, *Russko-livonskie i russko-ganzejskie otnosheniia: Konets XIV-nachalo XVI v.* (Leningrad 1975).

[5] H. Birnbaum, *Medieval Novgorod: A Cultural History* (to be published by the University of California Press, Berkeley).

2

Before going into a discussion of the primarily cultural aspects of life in Novgorod during the Middle Ages, a brief recapitulation of the political developments pertinent to the Volkhov city and the area under its control may prove useful by way of background information. The history of the more or less free city of Novgorod with its dependent territories, that is, from the dawn of Russian history until Novgorod's complete and final surrender to and annexation by Muscovy in 1478, can conveniently be divided into four periods:

(1) From the prehistoric and legendary beginnings of the city up to the year 1136. Possibly, Novgorod was founded in the eighth century A.D. (see below). The Varangian ruler Riurik's arrival is dated, according to the Primary or Nestor Chronicle – *Povest' vremennykh let* – to 862, that is to say, the same year that Prince Rastislav of Moravia turned in a letter to the Byzantine emperor Michael III asking for the dispatch of Slavic teachers, a request triggering the so-called Moravian mission of Constantine-Cyril and Methodius, undoubtedly the single most important event in Slavic cultural history of the early Middle Ages. An uprising of the boyars of Novgorod in 1136 put an end to the effective rule of the prince. Henceforth he had to reside outside the city limits, usually at *Riurikovo Gorodishche* or simply *Gorodishche*, roughly "(Riurik's) hill-fort," south of the city at the point where the Volkhov River emerges from Lake Ilmen. From that time on, the prince held only nominal power (at least in regard to matters of immediate consequence to the citizenry of Novgorod) as a sort of viceroy for the grand prince of Kiev, acting, in most instances, as an elected and paid official of the city with narrowly circumscribed authority and rights. Only exceptionally in the course of Novgorodian history after 1136 do we meet with politically charismatic, militarily skilled princes who rule, to be sure, with the consent of the people of Novgorod. Alexander Nevskii (1239-1263), who became prince of Novgorod at the age of twenty and at a time of extreme and imminent danger from the Mongols, was such an exceptional true ruler. In the early fourteenth century Novgorod abolished the office of prince altogether and, without a prince of its own, merely recognized the sovereignty of an outside grand prince, for example, that of Tver (Mikhail Iaroslavich Tver'skoi) who, however, never wielded any power in Novgorod. It was only Novgorod's conqueror, Grand Prince Ivan III of Moscow, who formally reintroduced the title of prince of Novgorod. The legislative power was in 1136 transferred or returned to the *veche*, the general assembly, meeting at Iaroslav's Yard (see below), and its delegated body, the Council of Notables with, as the term suggests, an aristocratic, wealthy membership. The executive power resided from this time on in essentially two public offices. One was the office of *posadnik*, the approximate equivalent of mayor, who in name only functioned as the chief adviser to the prince. In turn, the *posadnik* was aided by the *tysiatskii* (literally, "chiliarch," that is, the military commander of a unit originally consisting of one thousand men) who was also entrusted with settling

certain, especially commercial, disputes and who by some specialists is considered to have acted as the spokesman of the lower social strata as well. The other powerful office was that of the bishop, by 1156 virtually independent of the metropolitan see of Kiev and in 1165 elevated to archbishop, who, in addition to being the spiritual leader of his (arch)diocese, wielded considerable secular power. For example, he presided over the Council of Notables and officially represented the Republic of Saint Sophia in its external dealings; compare also his Russian title, *vladyka*, literally "ruler," an official designation, incidentally, identical with that used centuries later by the spiritual leader and, at the same time, secular ruler of a Balkan Slavic principality, the lord-bishop of Montenegro (Crna Gora).

(2) From 1136 to 1238/1240. During this time Novgorod, for all practical purposes was an autonomous merchant republic within the loosely organized federation of Russian principalities constituting the Kievan state, only formally acknowledging the suzerainty of the grand prince of Kiev.

(3) From 1238/1240 to 1386/1387. The earlier date (1238) marks the fall of the town of Torzhok, halfway between Moscow and Novgorod, to the Mongols followed by the miraculous halt – caused by poor weather and difficult ground conditions – of their march on Novgorod; the later date (1240) is that of the fall of Kiev. This period lasted until 1386/1387 when Dmitrii Donskoi, the Muscovite prince and victor over the Mongols in the battle of Kulikovo (1380), turned against Novgorod, defeating and humiliating the Republic of Saint Sophia to the degree of imposing on it a fine of 8,000 rubles and installing in the city of Novgorod a Muscovite governor or lieutenant (*namestnik*).

(4) From 1387 to 1478. During this period Novgorod and the territories forming part of the republic (which, in the north, extended all the way to the shores of the White Sea but in the southwest no longer included Pskov with the adjacent area, acknowledged as Novgorod's independent "younger brother" since 1348) could no longer steer a successful middle course between, on the one hand, the ever more menacing political formation of fellow countrymen in the east, Muscovy, and, on the other, the wide-spreading Grand Duchy of Lithuania, the merchant republic's southwestern neighbor, reaching from the shores of the Baltic to those of the Black Sea and holding vast territories of Russian land while increasingly closely linked with the kingdom of Poland (the "Crown"). Consequently, Novgorod was formally annexed and incorporated into the Muscovite state after having surrendered in effect to its ruler, Grand Prince Ivan III, in 1471.

As was mentioned above, the very beginnings of Novgorod, its foundation and earliest existence, are shrouded in a cloud of prehistoric legend and lore. Thus, for example, even the implication of its name, Novgorod, meaning "New Town," is not readily clear and has been the cause of some controversy. Was there ever a place called "Old Town" or simply "Town" that was the predecessor of historical Novgorod? We cannot tell for sure. Archaeological finds and the testimony of non-Russian, primarily Old Scandinavian, sources do not permit more than a few educated guesses. For some time, it was believed that Novgorod was perhaps a relatively recent settlement, a relocation, as it were, of some old commercial and, in part, political center such as Ladoga (today, Staraia Ladoga, 120 miles to the north, near the estuary of the Volkhov River into Lake Ladoga), the *Aldeigia* or *Aldeigjuborg* of several of the sagas of Norwegian kings in Snorri Sturluson's monumental *Heimskringla;*[6] or Staraia Russa on a smaller river a few miles south of Lake Ilmen; or possibly even Kholm on the upper Lovat River, approximately fifty miles south of Lake Ilmen (compare the name *Hólmgarðr* for Novgorod in the Old Norse historical sources). It is also quite conceivable, however, that the fortified town (Russian *gorod*) originally was located on the Merchant Side (compare the remnants of Iaroslav's Yard; see below) and only subsequently was transferred to the hill of the citadel or kremlin on the Sophia Side; compare similar relocations in other medieval Slavic cities, for example, in Prague from the original site at Vyšehrad to Hradčany on the other side ("Small Side") of the Vltava River (late tenth century).[7] The earliest systematic account of local origin, the so-called Synodal copy of the older redaction of the First Novgorod Chronicle, does not give us any information in these matters as it only begins abruptly – with the initial portion obviously missing – by reporting on some events of 1016, that is to say, when Iaroslav (later called the Wise), one year after the death of his father, Grand Prince Vladimir (the Saint), was still prince of Novgorod and only about to ascend to the grand-princely throne of Kiev, briefly occupied by his half-brother Sviatopolk, the villain of early Russian history and folklore.[8] But in the younger redaction of the same First Novgorod Chronicle, some reference is indeed made to the earliest developments in the area, including the founding of its first towns. Thus, we read under the entry for the year 6362, that is, 854, bearing the heading "The Beginning of the Land of Rus":

> In the times of Kyev [error for Kyi, H. B.] and Shchek and Khoriv [there were] the Novgorodian people, called Sloveni [more correctly: Slovene] and the Krivic[h]i and Meria: The Slovene had their territory, and the Krivic[h]i theirs, and the Mere theirs; each ruled over their tribe; and Chud [ruled] over their own tribe; and they paid tribute to the

[6] Cf. Snorri Sturluson, *Heimskringla*, ed. B. Aðalbjarnarson, 3 vols., Islenzk fornrit XXVI-XXVIII (Reykjavik 1941-1951) 1.338-339 (in the Saga of Óláf Tryggvason); 2.147-148 and 415 (in Saint Óláf's Saga); 3.3 (in the Saga of Magnús the Good), 91 (in the Saga of Harald Sigurtharson [Hardruler]). For an English translation, see Snorri Sturluson, *Heimskringla: History of the Kings of Norway*, trans. L. M. Hollander (Austin 1964) 223, 342-343, 537-538, 590. On early medieval contacts between (Staraia) Ladoga and Scandinavia (as well as other parts of northern Europe, esp. Friesland and the Frisian islands), see also *Varangian Problems: Scando-Slavica*, suppl. 1 (Copenhagen 1970) 79-94 (O. I. Davidan, "Contacts between Staraja Ladoga and Scandinavia," with discussion).

[7] Cf., e. g., *Novgorod the Great*, ed. M. W. Thompson (New York 1967), x (in Thompson's preface) and 12 (in the chapter "The Archaeological Study of Novgorod," by A. V. Artsikhovsky).

[8] Cf. *Novgorodakaia Pervaia Letopis' starshego i mladshego izvodov* (Moscow 1950) 15; English version, *The Chronicle of Novgorod, 1016–1471*, trans. R. Michell and N. Forbes, with an introduction by C. R. Beazley and an account . . . by A. A. Shakhmatov (London 1914) 1-2.

> Varangians, a squirrel [skin] per man. And those [Varangians] that were among them exerted force upon the Slovene, the Krivichi, and the Meri and Chud. And the Slovene and the Krivic[h]i and Meria and Chud rose against the Varangians and drove them out beyond the sea. And they began to rule themselves and to set up towns. And they rose to fight against each other and there was a great war and feud among them, and town rose against town, and there was no justice among them. And they said to themselves: "Let us look for a prince who would rule over us and govern us according to the law." And they went beyond the sea to the Varangians and said: "Our land is vast and abundant, but there is no order among us; come to us to rule over us and to govern us." They [that is, the Varangians] chose three brothers with their kinsmen, and they took with them a large and marvelous retinue, and they came to Novgorod. And the oldest settled in Novgorod; his name was Riurik . . . . And from these Varangians, these arrivals, Rus got its name, and it is from them that it is called the land of Rus; and the Novgorodian people are of Varangian stock to this very day.[9]

Nothing, except the last remark, is contradicted by any archaeological or historical evidence. Yet it has not been established with any degree of certainty where Riurik's Novgorod was situated. The name Novgorod itself suggests, as was already indicated, the possibility of an earlier different location. There is some indication to support the assumption that Gorodishche, south of present-day Novgorod, rather than any more distant place (Ladoga, and so on; see above), is the original site of Novgorod or, to be exact, its immediate predecessor unless, of course, this was the fortified settlement of the local East Slavic tribe of the Slovene. It was therefore in the course of moving the town a few miles down the river, perhaps precisely at the time of and in connection with the arrival from across the Baltic and the more permanent settling of the Norsemen, that the "New Town" – at first on the Merchant Side (see above) – was founded, the designation "Riurik's hillfort" notwithstanding. Note in this connection also the Old Norse name for Russia, *Garðar* or *Garðaríki*, literally "yards, enclosures, courts" or "realm of ditto." (Russian *gorod* "town, city" either is directly derived from the Old Scandinavian common noun *garðr* or, at any rate, reflects a semantic evolution suggesting the original notion of "enclosure, fortified yard.") Finds of Byzantine enamel work of the tenth or early eleventh century and remnants of ceramics dating from the ninth and tenth centuries, unearthed at Gorodishche, unequivocally point to a relatively sophisticated level of material culture and artistic taste at this place in pre-Varangian or early Varangian times.

As for the ethnic composition of the city population of Novgorod, we can assume that the Nordic element in the ninth through eleventh centuries must indeed have been significant and politically influential, not the least in view of the prince's and

[9] See *Novgorodskaia Pervaia Letopis'* 106; the literal English rendition is mine.

his kinsmen's Scandinavian ancestry and relations. Thus it is known, for example, that Prince Iaroslav of Novgorod, prior to ascending the Kievan throne, on at least two occasions went to Sweden to recruit additional, auxiliary Varangian troops for his struggle with his half-brother Sviatopolk. Such an assumption is further supported by records noting the presence of a permanent Varangian garrison stationed in Novgorod and of Varangian merchants ("guests," as they were usually referred to) who, during the earlier period, enjoyed special privileges. Some of these rights and exceptions applicable only to Varangian merchants were laid down and in some detail specified in the core portion of the earliest Russian legal code, the *Russkaia Pravda*, "Russian Law" (though more correctly, perhaps, rendered by "Justice of Rus" or "Law of the Rus," *Lex Rusorum*), also known as *Iaroslav's Pravda.*[10] Although soon binding for all of Kievan Russia, the *Russkaia Pravda*, or actually its central section, may originally have been designed specifically for the city of Novgorod and the Novgorodian lands (see below). In this context, it should be mentioned, incidentally, that the best etymology available for "Varangian" (Russian *varjag*, Sweedish *väring*, German *Waräger*, and so on) derives from the Old Scandinavian word *vár* "vow, oath," here probably referring to a particular formula that had to be solemnly pronounced by new members when being admitted to one of the Old Swedish (or generally Old Scandinavian) fellowships or trade guilds operating in Russia.[11] But it is highly unlikely that the Varangians should have ever outnumbered the Slavic townspeople of Novgorod. Likewise, it cannot be assumed that

[10] Cf. *Medieval Russian Laws,* ed. and trans. G. Vernadsky (New York 1969, paperback; ed. 1, 1947) 14. See further, H. G. Lunt in *Russian Linguistics* 2 (1975) 279 n. 23, who (271) accepts O. Pritsak's assumption that "the term *Rus* was not at first an ethnonym, but the designation of a social group," originally referring "to an international merchant organization" (cf. the etymology of *Hansa*). I do not know whether Lunt (following Pritsak) bases this new etymology on any linguistic evidence or merely on historical considerations. As is well known, the until now most widely accepted etymology of *Rus* derives this name from OSwed. *Rōþs* (gen. sg.); cf. Swed. *Roslagen* "area in eastern Sweden," *Rospiggar* < *Roþs-byggjar* "inhabitants of that area." For a fairly recent discussion of the traditional etymology of *Rus*, and some of the attendant linguistic difficulties, see *Varangian Problems* (n. 6 above) 138-139, 141-142.

[11] Cf. A. Stender-Petersen, *Varangica* (Aarhus 1953) 89-99; see further s. v. *varjag* in M. Vasmer, *Russisches etymologisches Wörterbuch* (Heidelberg 1953) 1.171; *idem* [M. Fasmer], *Etimologicheskii slovar' russkogo iazyka*, ed. O. N. Trubachev and B. A. Larin (Moscow 1964) 276 (with additional references). On a possible Old Nordic form **varangr* (rather than *varingr*) as underlying both Russian *varjag* and Byzantine (Middle Greek) *βάραγγος*, cf. G. Jacobsson, "La forme originelle du nom des varègues," *Scando-Slavica* 1 (1954) 36-43. Lunt (n. 10 above) 277 n. 8, again referring to O. Pritsak's unpublished work *The Origins of Rus*, suggests that *viking* and **varing* ("Varangian") were merely regional variants of the same notion, one of Germanic, the other of Finnic origin. Thus, it is proposed that *viking* can be derived from Indo-European **wīk-* "village, settlement, encampment" (cf. Latin *vicus*, Slavic vьsъ – the correct form of the underlying Indo-European root must thus be **wīk'–*, with palatal *–k'–* which underwent the so-called *satem* palatalization, rather than **wīk–*, with pure velar *–k–*) while **varing* would be derivable from Finno-Ugric **var* with roughly the same meaning (cf. Hungarian *város* 'town'). Both on linguistic and historical grounds the suggested etymological parallel is rather doubtful, however.

the Middle Low German speaking ethnic component that in the late twelfth century and increasingly during the late Middle Ages (thirteenth-fifteenth centuries) replaced the Scandinavian and mixed Scandinavian-German element (first the largely undifferentiated Varangians, subsequently the Swedish and German merchants of Gotland, notably Visby) ever reached any major proportions. Yet Middle Low German must undoubtedly have been spoken and heard, along with Russian, in and around the quarters of the Court of Saint Peter (*Petershof*), near Market Square and right across the street from Iaroslav's Court (see below), the Hansa's branch office in Novgorod, closed down by Ivan III in 1494.[12]

3

At this point, then, we can turn to culture proper and to the contribution that Novgorod made to medieval civilization both in terms of generating its own cultural values and forms and in transmitting foreign *Kulturgut* and traditions from one major geographic area engaged in intellectual and artistic activities to another. The north Russian city-state could do so by dint of being located at the crossroads of two important trade routes. On the one hand, these routes connected the European North with southeastern Europe and the Near East; and, on the other hand, they linked central and western Europe with the interior of Russia and – along the Volga waterway and across the Caspian Sea – the countries of central and southern Asia. In this commerce, Novgorod played the role of an active partner, sharing in the exchange of merchandise as well as in that of ideas, motifs, and artistic forms of expression, verbal as well as visual. It seems appropriate in this context to attempt to group and classify this cultural contribution according to several broader and, to be sure, occasionally overlapping categories. Here we may adopt a concept formulated over a hundred years ago by Jacob Burckhardt and applied by him to a cultural region which displayed some similarities to the north Russian merchant republic, namely, to the city-states of the Italian Renaissance. (This parallel will be pursued a bit further, below.) Following Burckhardt, we will therefore include in culture the notion of "the state as a work of art," to cite the heading of part one of his classic essay. In these terms, a sensible division of Novgorod's cultural achievements might be as follows: (1) political ideology and institutions; (2) language, literacy, literature, including some "sub-literary" folkloric genres of oral tradition; (3) visual arts, including architecture; (4) religion. In briefly discussing these categories in the present preliminary study, we cannot endeavor even to sketch, at least in any systematic fashion, all the manifold relevant phenomena but will merely attempt to illustrate them with a few select examples and to point to some particularly intriguing, if in

[12] Cf. also the relevant remarks in my forthcoming essay "Die Hanse in Novgorod," referred to in n. 4 above.

part controversial, problems falling into these various domains of Old Russian culture.

When it comes to the prevailing state ideology and the political practices of medieval Novgorod, it has in some quarters become something of a commonplace to assume that it had, by and large, a democratic form of government and to suggest broad participation of its citizenry in the conduct of the public affairs of the Volkhov city. Nothing, however, could be farther from the truth. At least some of the people of Novgorod did indeed enjoy a certain measure of political self-determination, but only when compared to other areas of Kievan Russia and its successor states (during the Tatar rule and after its gradual abolition in the "appanage" period of feudal division), that is, by comparison with the purely autocratic petty principalities ultimately absorbed by equally autocratic Muscovy. This almost proverbial freedom of Novgorod was in actual fact limited to a small elite, to the uppermost stratum of society, which set the tone and made the crucial decisions in this republic dominated by boyars and wealthy merchants. For, as I have earlier had occasion to quote from a recent critical assessment of the traditionalist view of Novgorodian history in another context, the center of the city republic was not "a town inhabited primarily by merchants and artisans but . . . a town of wealthy boyars upon whose estates the urban craftsmen lived, usually behind closed walls. – The craftsmen were economically dependent on the boyars for their homes and shops. They lacked – as did the merchants . . . – protective guilds and were effectively barred from government. – Not only was Novgorod a boyar republic which lacked a guild structure, but its population . . . contained slaves and cannot be described as an island of freedom in a sea of serfdom, a characterization which is often made of the western medieval town."[13] Too bright a picture of the internal freedom of Novgorod would therefore be quite distortive. Yet the passage just quoted also calls for some qualification. True, medieval Novgorod sometimes evokes the image of the wealthy, far-traveled merchant symbolized, as it were, by the legendary, adventurous Sadko of the Novgorodian cycle of *byliny* or *stariny*, the epic songs of ancient Russia recorded primarily in the last two centuries. (The figure of the rich Novgorodian merchant-traveler Sadko has subsequently been immortalized in Rimsky-Korsakov's famous opera by the same name.) And no doubt, many a rich and powerful lord of Novgorod was engaged in large-scale, long-distance, often international trade dealings. It was not this relatively small number of wealthy merchant boyars, however, that the above-quoted reviewer primarily referred to when speaking of that other group of petty merchants who were not organized in any professional guilds and who, to a large extent, were barred from participating in the city-state's government, as were the economically still worse-off, dependent

[13] See Birnbaum, "On the Significance" (n. 1 above) 46; the quotation is from the review article by L. N. Langer, "V. L. Ianin and the History of Novgorod," *Slavic Review* 33 (1974) 117-118.

craftsmen whose immediate needs the shopkeepers and peddlers served. Clearly, the most suitable designation for the form of government practiced in the medieval republic of Novgorod would be oligarchy, not too unlike the various forms of "self-government" known to other city-states, from ancient Greece to the Italy of the Renaissance.

In a way, the very topography of Old Novgorod can be said to reflect the division of political power and influence on the affairs of the republic. As was mentioned above, the prince of Novgorod had to reside outside the city limits once he was deprived of his earlier, indigenous political influence. In part, this loss of princely power was undoubtedly the result of the withdrawal from Novgorod of the special Varangian guard which previously had served as the prince's personal power base. Prior to 1136, the residence of the prince was in the *Detinets* (citadel or kremlin) which after this political changeover became the home of the new holders of power: the *posadnik* (approximately, mayor, but better, perhaps, compared to the *podestà* of medieval and early-Renaissance Italy) and the *vladyka* (bishop, after 1165 archbishop). Characteristically, Saint Sophia cathedral was located within the confines of the citadel. A study of the *posadniks* of Novgorod reveals a series of at first appointed, subsequently elected city officials many of whom turn out to have been politically imaginative and culturally concerned and committed civic leaders;[14] on the role of the *vladyka* as the chief patron of the religiously inspired arts and, in the person of Archbishop Gennadii, a driving force in theological learning, see below.

The city itself consisted of five boroughs or "ends" (*kontsy*), three of them on the left bank of the Volkhov River, surrounding the citadel, the so-called Sophia Side of town, and two on the opposite bank, the so-called Merchant (or Commercial) Side. South and southwest of the *Detinets* was *Liudin* or *Goncharskii konets* (People's or Potters' End) which on the north was bounded by *Zagorodskii konets* (Suburban End), west of the citadel, and, north thereof, *Nerevskii konets* (Nerev End), the place of some remarkable archaeological excavations (see below). On the other side of the river, the Merchant Side, grouped around Market Square with, at its southern end, the architectural complex known as Iaroslav's Yard (or Court; formerly, Prince's Yard – *Iaroslavov* or *Kniazhii Dvor*, the meeting place of the *veche*), once connected with the citadel area by the Great Bridge; the northern portion was taken up by *Plotnitskii konets* (Carpenters' End) while the southern borough of that side was known as *Slavenskii konets* (Slavno End). It was here, at Slavno, that the Varangians

[14] Cf. V. L. Ianin, *Novgorodskie posadniki* (Moscow 1962). In this context it bears mentioning that the name of one of the earlier *posadniks* of Novgorod, Ostromir, is linked to the first dated text known to have been written in Russia, the famed so-called Ostromir Gospel-Book (*Ostromirovo Evengelie*) of 1056/1057, an illuminated Russian Church Slavic manuscript copied by one deacon Gregorii for Ostromir from an Old Church Slavic (Early East Bulgarian) evangelistary (or *aprakos*-gospel text, i. e., a selection of gospel readings for Sundays and holidays). Regarding the renewal of an old hypothesis (first advanced by A. A. Shakhmatov) that the Slavic population of Novgorod originally may have had some West Slavic linguistic or even ethnic component, see below, with n. 30.

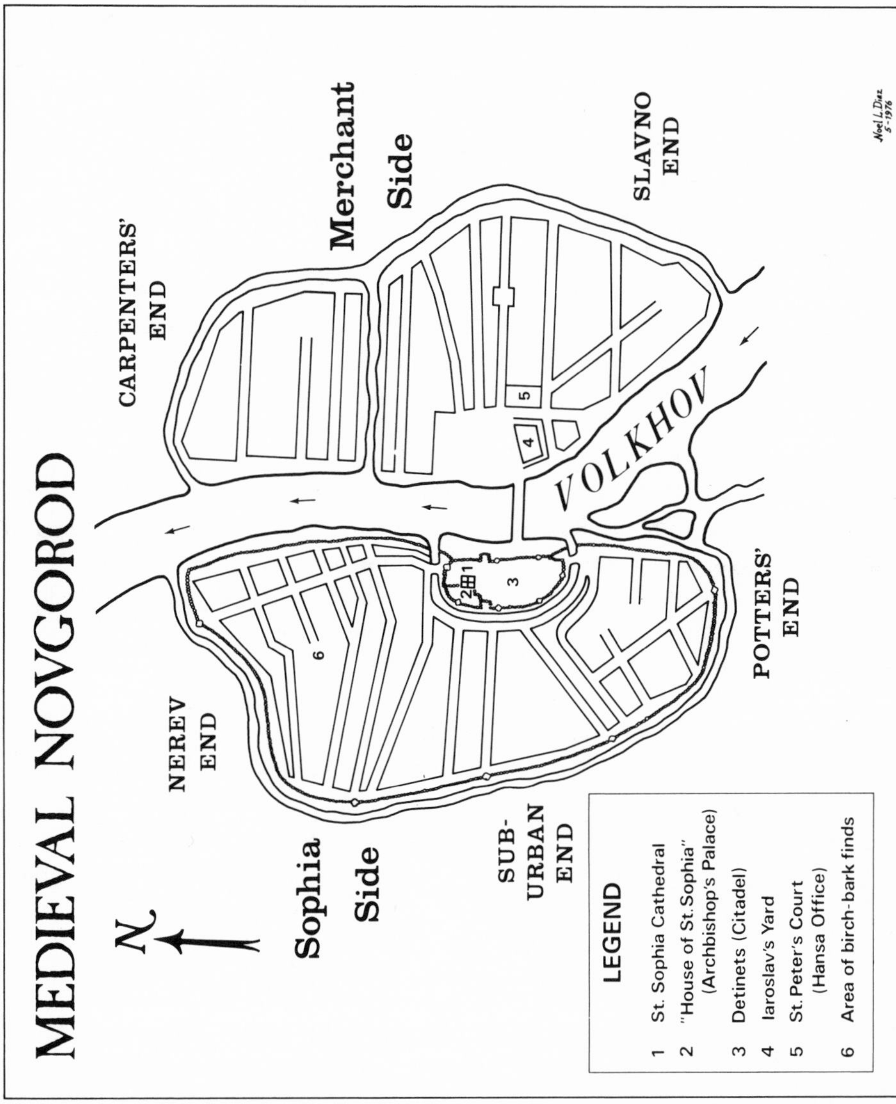
MEDIEVAL NOVGOROD
N
Sophia Side
Merchant Side
CARPENTERS' END
NEREV END
SUB-URBAN END
POTTERS' END
SLAVNO END
VOLKHOV
1
2
3
4
5
6
LEGEND
1 St. Sophia Cathedral
2 "House of St. Sophia" (Archbishop's Palace)
3 Detinets (Citadel)
4 Iaroslav's Yard
5 St. Peter's Court (Hansa Office)
6 Area of birch-bark finds
Noel L. Diaz 5-1976

first settled. It has been suggested that Novgorod's three original boroughs reflected the city's earliest ethnic makeup. According to this view, Novgorod, located at an accessible and convenient point on the Volkhov River, was the original meeting and trading place of several local tribes, Slavic as well as non-Slavic. Thus, V. L. Ianin has advanced the theory that members of the tribe of the Slovene were the first to comprise the *Slavenskii konets*, those of the Finnic tribe of Meria (the ancestors of today's Mari or Cheremis, now an East or Volga Finnic people but in ancient times perhaps reaching farther west) and possibly also people from Chud (that is, the forebears of the present-day Estonians) originally formed the *Nerevskii konets* while the *Liudin (Goncharskii) konets* in the beginning could have been populated by elements of the Krivichi tribe.[15] Be this as it may, each borough originally formed a larger unit with the immediately adjoining district outside the city proper. Together, these administrative entities made up so-called "fifths" (*piatiny*, after the five "ends" of Novgorod), each situated on both sides of some major thoroughfares leading out of Novgorod and administered by its own "end board" (*konchanskoe upravlenie*) headed by an elderman of the "end" (*konchanskii starosta*). Only the more distant territories controlled by the Volkhov city were centrally supervised.[16]

It has already been mentioned that Novgorod in all likelihood was the first Russian town whose everyday life was regulated by its own, specially designed law, the original core portion of the *Russkaia Pravda* usually referred to as *Iaroslav's Pravda* after the prince under whose rule it was instituted. (In the same vein, the next-oldest portion of the *Russkaia Pravda* is commonly known as the *Pravda of Iaroslav's Sons*.) Though influenced, it seems, in some of its legal terminology as well as in the overall conception underlying its injunctions and rulings by medieval Swedish law, a linguistic and stylistic analysis undertaken some years ago yielded little that would suggest in the specific formulations found in this earliest codification of Old Russian (and Varangian) customary law, previously handed down orally from generation to generation, the presence of any direct echoing of or outright dependence on any of the particular law collections designed for the various provinces (each originally with its own jurisdiction) of medieval Sweden. (These laws, the so-called *fornsvenska landskapslagar,* were superseded only by the *allmän landslag*, "common country law," introduced by King Magnus I, called Ladulås, literally "Barnlock," but possibly a folk-etymological distortion of the Slavic name Vladyslav or its latinized form Ladislas, in the last quarter of the thirteenth century.[17])

[15] See V. L. Ianin and M. Kh. Aleshovskii, "Proiskhozhdenie Novgoroda (k postanovke problemy)," *Istoria SSSR* 2 (1971) 32-61, esp. 42-55.

[16] Cf. Onasch (n. 3 above) 63-80. For details regarding the acquisition and extent of the Novgorodian territories (*Novgorodskaia zemlia*), see now A. V. Kuza, "Novgorodskaia zemlia," in *Drevnerusskie kniazhestva X-XIII vv.* (Moscow 1975) 144-201, with ample further references.

[17] Cf. Birnbaum, *Slavic Writing* (n. 1 above) 234-259 ("On Old Russian and Old Scandinavian Legal Language: The *Russkaja Pravda* and Medieval Swedish Laws," first published in 1962; see *ibid.* 368), with further references. For details on the various versions and chronological layers of the *Russkaia Pravda*, see, e. g., *Pamiatniki russkogo prava*, ed. S. V. Iushkov, 1: *Pamiatniki prava*

Whereas there can be at least some legitimate doubt as to whether the oldest section of the *Russkaia Pravda* was indeed at first exclusively designed for the needs of the city (and area) of Novgorod and not from the very outset applicable – once it was codified in written form – to the Kievan state as a whole, we know of a number of city ordinances, penal codes, treaties couched in legal terms, and other legal instruments which were explicitly written for Novgorod and its territories. Even a cursory perusal of the representative texts contained in the second volume of the historical survey of Russian laws under the general editorship of S. V. Iushkov, covering the period of the "feudal division of Rus," that is, the twelfth through fifteenth centuries, shows that the bulk of the law texts and legally ratified treaties reproduced, including commentaries and bibliographic notes, originated in Novgorod or were applicable to the Volkhov city. Legal documents from Novgorod's formerly dependent "suburb" (*prigorod*) and subsequently independent "younger brother" Pskov come second (for the thirteenth-fifteenth centuries), in addition to some less extensive but no less important pertinent texts from the principalities of Smolensk and Galicia-Volhynia (both twelfth-thirteenth centuries).[18]

It is often not easy to draw a sharp line between the documents that were officially drafted for and legally ratified by the appropriate bodies of the Republic of Saint Sophia and some other semi-official or even largely private documents couched in a legal language, such as officially entered deeds, donations, or agreements between two legal parties. Again, while documents of this kind – in Russian referred to as *gramoty* – are known from many parts of medieval Russia, those from Novgorod are largest in quantity and of particular prominence and interest as to their contents. When it comes to the trade treaties with one or several of the Hanseatic towns, many of the legal instruments exchanged are preserved in both their Old Russian and Middle Low German version, thus providing additional insights into questions of terminology and practice as understood and implemented by the partners involved. The best published collection of Novgorod *gramoty* contains a total of 330 such official and semi-official texts (from the twelfth through fifteenth centuries), subdivided into various categories, namely, documents relevant to (a) Novgorod's relations with Russian princes or principalities (27 *gramoty*); (b) Novgorod's relations with the West (the Hansa, Livonia, Gotland, Lithuania, Sweden, and so on; 50 documents); (c) Novgorod's internal administration (24 texts); and (d) private dealings (229 items, further subcategorized by areas of

---

Kievskogo gosudarstva X-XII vv., ed. A. A. Zimin (Moscow 1952) 71-232. Cf. also the introduction by Vernadsky (n. 10 above) 3-25, esp. 9-19 (on the *Russkaia Pravda* and on the political organization and administration of medieval Novgorod). On the possible identification of some medieval Swedish surnames with Slavic counterparts, see the important though controversial study by K. Axnäs, *Slavisch-Baltisches in altnordischen Beinamen* (Uppsala 1937) 83-88 on *Ladulås* = **Ladislās.*

[18] Cf. *Pamiatniki russkogo prava* 2: *Pamiatniki prava feodal'norazdroblennoi Rusi, XII-XV v. v.*, ed. A. A. Zimin (Moscow 1953) esp. 99-273 (Novgorod); 275-383 (Pskov); 35-98 (Smolensk); 23-33 (Galicia-Volhynia).

application: Novgorod proper with outskirts, *gramoty* nos. 102-122; Dvina land, nos. 123-278; Vaga land, nos. 279-282; Obonezh'e, nos. 283-330).[19] All these *gramoty*, written on parchment or, rarely, paper, testify not only to a well developed administrative and legal system prevailing and smoothly functioning in medieval Novgorod but also to a certain level of literacy which, it would seem, in Novgorod embraced a somewhat larger segment of the population than elsewhere in the feudal Russian society of the Middle Ages, relatively small as it no doubt must have been even in this commercially active, contact-prone, and in many ways open-minded city.

This impression of a, relatively speaking, widespread literacy (or, at any rate, semi-literacy) is further both corroborated and somewhat qualified by the discovery, in the early 1950s, of another sort of written record in Cyrillic, limited primarily to Novgorod. Within the city, the finds are almost all located in the so-called Nerev End. I am referring, of course, to the numerous (currently over 500) incised birch-bark letters or messages (Russian *berestianye gramoty* or simply *beresty*) unearthed in the course of archaeological excavations which began in Novgorod as far back as the 1930s (and in Gorodishche as early as 1929) but yielded substantial relevant results only after World War II. This, however, brings us to a largely different facet of Old Novgorodian culture than the city-republic's state ideology, institutions, and administration, namely, to its language, its level of literacy, and in particular, its specific literature, including its recorded oral tradition.

4

The archaeological digs, started in the 1930s under the directorship of A. V. Artsikhovskii, at first were intended to shed some much-needed light on the controversial origins of Novgorod. As for Novgorod's recorded history, it was thought that the generally sober local annalistic writings (First to Fifth Novgorod Chronicles as well as the two so-called Sophia Chronicles, not counting later, secondary chronicle compilations, in Russian *svody*) provided all the largely accurate, if occasionally politically or ideologically tinged, information necessary about the day-to-day or year-to-year events of the Volkhov city. All this changed drastically when, in 1951, archaeological cuttings at present-day Dmitriev Street brought to light the first birch-bark document. Since then major excavations have been conducted primarily in the block bounded by Dmitriev, Garden, Tikhvin, and Decembrists' Streets where the remnants of the Old Novgorodian settlement along what was once High, Serf, and Saints-Cosmas-and-Damian Streets (*Ulica Velikaia, Kholop'ia Ulica, Kuz'modem'ianskaia Ulica*) was unearthed and partially reconstructed. It is in these quarters that the vast bulk of the birch-bark documents was discovered. It could be established that

[19] See *Gramoty Velikogo Novgoroda i Pskova*, ed. S. N. Valk [podgotovili k pechati V. G. Gejman, N. A. Kazakova, A. I. Kopanev, G. E. Kochin, R. B. Miuller i E. A. Rydzevskaia] (Moscow 1949) esp. 7-313.

there were twenty-eight street levels throughout the excavation site, and that each street had been laid and relaid at approximately the same time along its whole length. It also became evident that these levels or strata (*iarusy*, in Russian technical language) were to serve as the basis for all further dating. While at first the chronological correlation between these stratigraphic findings (each street level yielding its own set of archaeological objects) and other data, including events recorded under specific dates in the chronicles, seemed to match perfectly, subsequently some voices have been raised which cast considerable doubt on the reliability of these absolute datings as they had been proposed, in particular, by the chief local investigator, B. A. Kolchin. Dendrochronology, or tree-ring-dating, provided the answer, corroborative and in some instances corrective. The half-logs forming the street deckings (a method known from as early as the Bronze Age and used in provincial towns and villages of Russia until quite recently) were about 150 years old at the time of felling, and they were well arranged in chronological order to within a decade or so. Outside California, this is perhaps the instance where the dendrochronological method of dating has produced the most satisfactory results, with the difference, to be sure, that while in California the sequence is tied to the present situation and the most recent past, in the archeological site of Old Novgorod it can be correlated, for its absolute dating, to five churches whose construction dates are reliably recorded in the local chronicles. It is further a fortunate accident of nature that thousands of birch-bark scraps, hundreds of them bearing carvings made with a pointed implement of metal or bone, mostly on the inner, softer side of the birch-bark piece, have been preserved virtually intact in most of the twenty-eight archeological layers due to the appropriate level of moisture in the soil. Only in the uppermost and the lowest strata no birch-bark letters have been found. The earliest are believed to date back to the late eleventh-early twelfth centuries, some belong to layers of the fifteenth century while the bulk is thought to date from the mid-to-late twelfth-fourteenth centuries.

It should be noted in this context that the medieval birch-bark letters from Novgorod have not been preserved in any orderly fashion. No archive or particularly arranged collection of these materials ever existed prior to their discovery and classification. The pieces of carved bark were found in the ground at random, just as by chance they had been thrown away or lost. Whereas in some cases these birch-bark letters were addressed, though not explicitly so, to public officials, feudal landlords, or church dignitaries, most of them are private messages which presuppose some degree of more widespread literacy in Novgorod, especially if one takes into account the fact that many of the objects unearthed during the excavations have the names or initials of their owners marked on them. Thus, for example, twenty-eight birch-bark letters were found that had been sent to Posadnik Ontsifor Lukich, his son, and grandsons, all of the wealthy Mishinich family who in the fourteenth-fifteenth centuries had its residence at the corner of High and Saints-Cosmas-and-Damian Streets. The writers and, in particular, the recipients of the birch-bark letters must in most cases have been members of the laity even though it cannot be ruled out, of course, that in some instances such messages may have been the work of a commissioned professional scribe, usually a low-ranking clergyman, a deacon or monk. In fact, the rather impersonal wording of some of these letters suggests strongly that the message may have been dictated at one end to a literate or (as the spelling often reveals) only semi-literate messenger who could read it out at the other end, both sender and receiver being illiterate themselves; or the message could have been read by some other literate person to the illiterate addressee.

Was the nonetheless relatively widespread literacy peculiar to medieval Novgorod due, perhaps, to its position as a major trading center? It is hard to tell. How did the degree of literacy among the townspeople of ancient Novgorod compare to that of their contemporaries in the towns of central and western Europe? Again, we can only guess, at best. Perhaps, reading and writing were somewhat more advanced and known in the Romance and Byzantine world where Latin (and its adapted, "vulgarized" medieval form) and Greek (classical, koinē, and Byzantine) were the written languages. But can we assume that the broad, uneducated masses – not the intellectual elite – of the Germanic peoples or the Western and Southwestern Slavs, expecially the Poles and the Czechs, the Croats and the Slovenes, were more knowledgeable than their counterparts in a city such as Novgorod? There is little to support such a conjecture.

Tree bark was widely used for writing since ancient times. Latin *liber* means both "book" and "bark." It is known that at least two emperors, Domitian and Commodus, wrote booklets on bark; and Pliny the Elder and Ulpian inform us that tree bark was the material used for writing by other ancient authors as well. Birch bark, not known in the Mediterranean region, must have been a particularly suitable substitute for the costly parchment or vellum. In Russia, the land of the birch, birch bark was used instead of paper for regular writing, not carved lettering, up to the nineteenth century if not longer, mostly in Siberia. Outside Novgorod, incised birch-bark documents in small numbers have been found at Smolensk, Pskov, Vitebsk, and Staraia Russa. It is conceivable that in the future some such medieval scripts may turn up elsewhere, for example, in Poland, Germany, or Sweden. (In Sweden, in particular, the earliest capital and trading center of Birka, on the island of Björkö in Lake Mälar, until now archaeologically insufficiently examined, may offer a good ground to search. The first Swedish birch-bark text was recently discovered in the Uppsala University Library. It contains some Latin poetry by a fifteenth-century monk from Vadstena Monastery. However, this particular text was written with ink, not carved into the bark as others may have been, to judge by a statement made by Olaus Magnus.)

It would lead too far to attempt here to give a more detailed description of the physical shape, size, state of preservation, paleography, linguistic peculiarities, and contents of the birch-bark documents from Novgorod. It needs no stressing that these texts are of utmost value as a source of information about everyday life in and around Novgorod and that, as they often refer to legal matters, they at the same time provide a telling illustration of the application of the regulations and injunctions of the *Russkaia Pravda* and other legal rulings relevant to Novgorod and the *Novgorodskaia zemlia*. A few general remarks characterizing this "subliterary" genre of Old Russian writing will therefore have to suffice here. Attempts to read an "epistolary style" into the linguistically and stylistically least awkward of these specimens, or even to posit, on the basis of them, something like an "epistolary genre" of its own for Old Russian literature, once proposed by N. A. Meshcherskii, have been rightly refuted by V. V. Vinogradov and other historians of Russian language and literature. In addition, the text of one *beresta* – no. 9, generally held to be among the oldest – will be adduced here in English translation.[20]

The great majority of these documents are evidently brief messages sent by someone outside or at the outskirts of the city, read by the recipient, and subsequently discarded. In a few instances they are memoranda (for example, lists of debts or payments owed by serfs) or even the scribblings of an almost illiterate schoolboy. Being written, for the most part, outside the city limits, they tell us more about life in the surrounding countryside than about the situation in Novgorod itself, the usual place of the addressee. The letters are never signed, nor is there any explicit indication of any address on the outside or in the opening phrase of the message. Most probably, they were handcarried by a servant or paid messenger, very possibly the scribe, from the sender to the recipient. Usually, they open with a set formula of the type "From X to Y," "Petition to Lord A from B," "Order from Y to Z," and so on. As a rule only first (Christian) names were used, at any rate before the fifteenth century, so that in most cases these are messages exchanged between people otherwise unknown to the historian except in a few instances where a particular person was prominent enough to have his name recorded in one of the Novgorod chronicles.[21]

[20] There exists already an extensive secondary literature on the Novgorod birch-bark letters. For an excellent general survey in English, including relevant information concerning the archaeological excavations which have revealed these documents, see *Novgorod* (n. 7 above), esp. xi-xii (Thompson), 6 (Artsikhovsky), and 55-63 ("Birch Bark Documents from Novgorod," written by Thompson but based entirely on an account by Artsikhovsky). For the historian, of further importance are V. L. Ianin, *Ia poslal tebe berestu* . . ., ed. 2 (Moscow 1975), and L. V. Cherepnin, *Novgorodskie berestianye gramoty kak istoricheskii istochnik* (Moscow 1969). Here, the reader will find additional references, among them also to the definitive editions of the birch-bark letters by A. V. Artsikhovskii and M. N. Tikhomirov (*gramoty* nos. 1-10, 1953); Artsikhovskii (nos. 11-83, 1954); Artsikhovskii and V. I. Borkovskii (nos. 84-136, 137-194, 1958; 195-318, 1963); and Artsikhovskii (nos. 319-405, 1963; 406-424, 1964). Since then, additional birch-bark letters were found, partly also outside Nerev End, and published bringing the total, as of this writing, to over 520 items. On the most recent finds, cf. especially Ianin 211-235. For some discussion of the relevance of the birch-bark letters for the level of literacy in Novgorod, see also *Varangian Problems* (n. 6 above) 101-102 (D. A. Avdusin, "Material Culture in the Towns of Ancient Rus' ") and 209-210 (discussion).

[21] The nomenclature of medieval Novgorod, especially the system of personal (Christian) names in use and recorded in the Volkhov city, is revealing, among other things, as to the general cultural level of its citizenry. For a thorough study of these names (other than those found in the birch-bark documents), see A. Baecklund, *Personal Names in Medieval Velikij Novgorod* 1:

The style – if style is indeed the appropriate term in this context – of these messages is usually exceedingly laconic. The laborious method of producing the birch-bark letters was certainly not conducive to verbosity. Usually, they were written with a view to a specific action required or requested, not simply for the purpose of conveying some news or expressing a sentiment or mood. The very brevity of their style and contents makes the reading of the birch-bark documents both rewarding and difficult. The tone is direct and, often, intimate. By the same token, however, their very succinctness sometimes renders it difficult to understand or interpret unambiguously a given message, particularly if fragmentary, as is often the case, and with spelling and grammar frequently haphazard and far from approximating a general norm (such as, for example, the written language of the chronicles would usually strive for). Being unique documents, the birch-bark *gramoty* do not allow for any comparison with parallel texts as is possible with many other literary pieces of Old Rus. Thus, many of these highly personal documents remain to some extent obscure or enigmatic, still awaiting a fully satisfactory and persuasive interpretation.

What follows is the tentative English rendition (provided by this writer) of what is generally considered one of the oldest extant specimens of these birch-bark texts – *gramota* no. 9 – about which a whole body of secondary writing has evolved as its wording and contents are highly controversial and full of legal and other implications, lending themselves to various interpretations. Among these is the very question of the sex of the sender, Gostiata, who seems to be either an abandoned and wronged wife or a deprived, potentially disinherited son from a previous marriage of the accused.

> From Gostiata to Vasilii. What my father has given me and [my] relatives left me, that is with him. And now, taking a new wife, he gave [or: gives] me nothing; having broken the [marriage] contract [or: having gotten rid of me], he has abandoned me and taken another one [another woman]. Come, to put [literally: putting] [things] right [literally: well].[22]

The Novgorod birch-bark letters are frequently quoted as a sort of textbook example of the fact that the local vernacular of medieval Novgorod was supposedly

---

Common Names, Acta Universitatis Stockholmiensis 9 (1959); a few of the names attested in the birch-bark documents are briefly listed in an Addendum (191-192); see further relevant portions of T. Skulina, *Staroruskie imiennictwo osobowe*, 2 vols, Komitet Językoznawstwa PAN, Prace Onomastyczne 20-21 (Wrocław 1973/1974). Generally on Russian names, especially surnames, their history and formation, see now B. O. Unbegaun, *Russian Surnames* (Oxford 1972).

[22] For some possible interpretations and discussion of the obscure wording and phraseology of this *gramota*, see e. g., W. Kuraszkiewicz, *Gramoty nowogrodzkie na brzozowej korze*, Zeszyt A: *Opracowanie językowe* (Warsaw 1957) 51-54; Cherepnin (n. 20 above) 103-106 (both with further references). For additional examples of some of these birch-bark letters with English translations, cf. *Novgorod* (n. 7 above) 57-63.

virtually free of Slavonisms, that is, of elements ultimately originating from closely related – but not genuinely East Slavic – Old Church Slavic. The latter, as is well known, was a literary language of South Slavic or more precisely Macedo-Bulgarian provenience, even though it was never really used in everyday life. Other relevant examples adduced to prove the purely East Slavic character of the language of Old Novgorod are the local annals (especially the First Novgorod Chronicle of both the earlier and the later versions), the official and semi-official documents (*gramoty*, in this instance, those not incised on birch bark), and the *Russkaia Pravda*. In other words, it is usually assumed that the written language of the northern and northwestern provinces of ancient Rus was by and large more purely East Slavic, less affected by foreign influences, notably less permeated by (Old) Church Slavic. To some extent, this is undoubtedly a correct assessment. Yet, the actual linguistic situation seems to have been far more complex; it cannot simply be postulated that the farther to the north and northwest one goes, the more purely Old Russian, that is, unadulterated East Slavic, the language of medieval Russia becomes. Particularly when it comes to the written language of ancient Novgorod, a more subtle analysis and interpretation is certainly called for.

There is in fact substantial evidence to suggest that (Old) Church Slavic was well known and, in its Russian adaptation, also widely used in Novgorod, as early as the eleventh and twelfth centuries. To begin with, it is safe to assume that Glagolitic writing was, to some extent, at least, known in Novgorod during the eleventh century, presupposing the presence of Old Church Slavic texts there. The very fragmentary Glagolitic graffiti, along with some other, more numerous ones carved out in Cyrillic on the walls of Saint Sophia Cathedral in Novgorod, attest to the familiarity of people in Novgorod with the oldest Slavic script probably as early as within years or decades of the cathedral's consecration in 1052. (The stone construction replacing an earlier wooden cathedral church was erected in 1045-1050.) It should be noted, though, that only one Glagolitic inscription bears an incompletely legible date: ". . 61" which may imply either 6561 (= 1053) or, somewhat less likely, 6661 (= 1153).[23] Another, related instance is the Russian Church Slavic translation or adaptation from an earlier Old Church Slavic version of the twelve so-called Minor Prophets made by an otherwise unknown Novgorodian priest Upyr Likhoi in 1047. His work, preserved only in manuscripts of the fifteenth-sixteenth centuries, contains a revealing note to the effect that Upyr copied his text "from the Cyrillic" (*is kurilovicě*), suggesting that he attributed the oldest Slavic script (that is, Glagolitic) to Saint Cyril (Constantine) – and rightly so, of course.[24] Moreover, some of the not too numerous palimpsests known from medieval Russia where the erased original text can be identified as having been written with Glagolitic characters seem to originate from Novgorod.

[23] Cf. V. Kiparsky, *Russische historische Grammatik* 1: *Die Entwicklung des Lautsystems* (Heidelberg 1963) 26; W. K. Matthews, *Russian Historical Grammar* (London 1960) 74.

[24] See Kiparsky 87; Matthews 73-74.

Of the earliest more or less complete dated Russian Church Slavic texts, the Ostromir Gospel-Book (see note 14 above) was most probably written in Novgorod, commissioned as it was by the Novgorod *posadnik* to whose name it has ever since been linked. However, the only very slightly Russianized Church Slavic language form of this evangelistary is so free of any significant dialectal features that, theoretically at least, the scribe, Deacon Grigorii, might also have been active elsewhere in ancient Rus, for example, in Kiev.[25] More than that, even a cursory glance at Kiparsky's broadly selective listing of early (eleventh-fourteenth centuries) texts written in Old Rus reveals very many of them to be composed in Russian(ized) Church Slavic or in a mixed, hybrid Church Slavic–East Slavic ("Old Russian") language. This presupposes that the two can be distinguished qualitatively and not only quantitatively, that is to say, by measuring the relative share of more or less unequivocally identifiable Slavonisms or, conversely, genuinely East Slavic features. At the same time, quite a few of these texts are either clearly localizable to Novgorod and to monasteries in its immediate environs or, in some less obvious instances, they are more vaguely traceable to the Novgorod region on linguistic, that is, dialectological, grounds. Above all, this applies to the many biblical and liturgical texts. Thus, not even counting the *Ostromirovo Evangelie* (for reasons indicated above), Kiparsky lists over twenty Russian Church Slavic literary pieces from the eleventh through fourteenth centuries and belonging to the purely ecclesiastic genres that definitely originated in or near Novgorod. They include several gospel texts (of both kinds, the select, *aprakos*, and the complete, *tetra* type), *menaea, sticheraria* and *hirmologies* (that is, hymnaries, plain or with musical notation), *triodia, tropologia, synaxaria* (also known as *prologs*, containing brief lives of saints), missals, lectionaries (with excerpts from the Old and New Testaments), *euchologia* (prayer-books), and epigraphic material on church walls and ecclesiastic objects.[26]

All this of course suggests a veritable flourishing of Church Slavic writing in Novgorod. Possibly – and the residual traces of Glagolitic script here are particularly telling – Novgorod may have had some early direct contacts with Bohemia where literature in Church Slavic of the Czech recension was produced until the end of the eleventh century. Here, therefore, continued an unbroken tradition from the Moravian beginnings of Old Church Slavic until 1096/1097 when the abbey of Sázava was closed down and the Slavonic liturgy came to an end, only to be revived by Emperor Charles IV in the fourteenth century. But the main influx of Church Slavic texts to Novgorod during the earlier period undoubtedly came from Bulgaria and later also from Serbia, partly by way of Kiev. It is thus quite conceivable that certain elements of the Church Slavic language in its only superficially Russianized form had penetrated into the local vernacular of Old Rus, and this may have been the case particularly in Novgorod where the pace of linguistic integration and assimilation

[25] Cf. Kiparsky 26-27.

[26] For details, see Kiparsky 32-64.

seems to have been faster than elsewhere in medieval Russia. It is along these lines, apparently, that we have to interpret the not so few Slavonisms encountered in otherwise more or less secular or at most semi-ecclesiastic documents and works, with Novgorod figuring prominently in this context.[27] In other words, there appears to have been a certain amount of Slavonisms, easily identifiable as such by phonological, grammatical, or lexico-phraseological criteria, that may have "sunk in," as it were, to the spoken language of Old Novgorod. Recently, H. G. Lunt has gone even a step further and advanced the plausible hypothesis that there existed in ancient Rus not only a written form of Church Slavic (Slavonic, in his terminology) but also a spoken variant of this standard language, limited as its use may have been.[28]

Church Slavic literature reached new heights of stylistic sophistication bordering on the abstract and the artificial during the so-called Second South Slavic Influence whose assessment both in terms of its overall cultural impact and its significance for the evolution of the literary language in Russia remains controversial.[29] There can be little doubt that in its later phase this new heavily ornate style developed into full-blown artificiality and petrification in the Muscovite state of Ivan IV. One of its chief representatives of a somewhat earlier period was Pakhomii Logofet (Pachomius Logothetes), an immigrant from Serbia and the first known professional writer of Russia, living by his pen alone and occupied mostly with rewriting and editing the body of accumulated hagiographic literature, including the writings of Russia's foremost late-medieval hagiographer, Epifanii Premudryi (Epiphanius the Wise), to conform with the linguistic and stylistic standards of his times which amounted to a far-reaching re-Slavonization or partly re-Bulgarization. While not much is known about Pakhomii's background other than that he was a native of Serbia who had escaped, along with others, from the Turkish occupation of his country, it has been established that he was active in Moscow and, characteristically, Novgorod in the years between 1440 and 1480. Other Church Slavic writers working in Novgorod had either cultivated a much simpler, straight-forward style, such as the early sermon-

[27] Cf., e. g., L. P. Iakubinskii, *Istoria drevnerusskogo iazyka* (Moscow 1953) 273-284 ("O tserkovnoslavianizmakh v drevnerusskom iazyke").

[28] Cf. H. G. Lunt, "On the Language of Old Rus: Some Questions and Suggestions," *Russian Linguistics* 2 (1975) 269-281, esp. 274-275 and 276 n. 1 (for a discussion of the merits of the term *standard language* over *literary language* as applicable to the situation in ancient Russia).

[29] Cf. Birnbaum, "On the Significance" (n. 1 above). While in my article I have tried to strike a balance in assessing the positive (enriching) and negative (retarding) effects of the Second South Slavic Influence in Russia, more extreme appraisals are represented in recent writings by the Soviet medievalist D. S. Likhachev (positive) and the Austrian Slavist A. V. Issatschenko (negative). Cf. further A. V. Isačenko [Issatschenko], "Esli by v konce XV veka Novgorod oderzhal pobedu nad Moskvoi (Ob odnom ne sostoiavshemsia variante istorii russkogo iazyka)," *Wiener Slavistisches Jahrbuch* 18 (1973) 48-55, hypothesizing – persuasively in linguistic terms, but unrealistically as regards the actual historical situation – about the conceivable positive repercussions for the evolution of literary Russian had Novgorod and not Muscovy come out winning in the struggle for the domination of the Russian lands at the close of the fifteenth century.

writer, bishop Luka Zhidiata (d. 1059), or they frequently made use of the treasures of the popular lore, whether indigenous or imported. This would apply to the anonymous fifteenth-century author of the bizarre life-story of a historically attested archbishop of Novgorod, Ioann (said to have traveled to Jerusalem in one night riding on a devil), reminiscent in more than one way of motifs otherwise found in the cycles of folk epics and tales from Novgorod, marked by a particularly rich imagination and a keen sense for entertainment. This striking fantastic and adventurous element in Novgorodian literature and oral tradition is explicable, one should think, by the Volkhov city's far-reaching international connections. See, among many other examples, the songs about Sadko "the rich guest" (that is, merchant) and about the giant Vasilii Buslaevich; the tales about the Novgorod *posadnik* Shchil; those about the end of Novgorod, a premonition of events to come, put in final literary form only after Novgorod's annexation by Muscovy; and that of the white hood from Novgorod. While some of the motifs of these genres of Novgorodian literature had undoubtedly deep roots in local tradition, much of this literary and subliterary stuff moved (as *Wandergut*) along the main trade routes at the crossroads of which Novgorod was located, borrowing, perhaps, only some particular feature or a general tinge from the atmosphere of the city of Saint Sophia.

The predominant component in the vernacular language of Old Novgorod was without any doubt East Slavic. There is no linguistic evidence to controvert this fact even if in recent times earlier claims, made by Shakhmatov and others, have been modified and, to be sure, buttressed with new arguments suggesting that the first Slavic settlers of Novgorod may not have been Eastern Slavs but rather Western Slavs – Wends – coming from the southern littoral of the Baltic.[30] Thus, H. G. Lunt writes in his recent contribution "On the Language of Old Rus," with appropriate caution subtitled "Some Questions and Suggestions":

> The Slavic settlers in the territories of Ladoga, Novgorod, and Izborsk-Pskov in Igor's time, *c.* 900, were very likely relative newcomers from the southern coast of the Baltic – West Slavs rather than East Slavs. These are the unsophisticated *Slověne* whose silken sails, booty from the Greeks, rip – to the apparent amusement of the presumably aristocratic narrator of the episode [viz., one of the authors of the Nestor Chronicle, H. B.].

[30] By contrast, according to Shakhmatov's now dated theory, based on the account of the Nestor-Chronicle, the tribes of the Radimichi and Viatichi, usually considered East Slavic, were actually of West Slavic (Lekhitic) origin. The northern East Slavic ("North Russian") tribes, while of East Slavic stock, are said to have been influenced in their speech by these "displaced" West Slavic tribes whose territory they had to cross in their northward migration and with whom they partly remained in touch after having reached their place of permanent settlement. These Eastern Slavs of the northern branch were, in the northwest, the Krivichi of Smolensk, Polotsk, Vitebsk, and Pskov and, in the northeast, the Slověne of Novgorod, Beloozero, and the upper Volga region (where they supposedly were in continued contact with the "displaced" Western Slavs); cf. A. A. Shakhmatov, *Ocherk drevněishago perioda istorii russkago iazyka*, Entsiklopediia slavianskoi filologii 11 = Russian Reprint Series 61 (The Hague 1967), (Petrograd 1915) xviii-xix, xxi-xxii.

But in the accompanying note, Lunt himself qualifies his somewhat bold, though not new, assumption by stating:

> I know of no purely linguistic evidence of importance, apart from personal names and toponyms, but historical accounts, including the repeated association of the terms *Wend/Venedes* and *Slověne* (e.g. in Livonian chronicles . . .), and archeological data (. . .), are more convincing. My acceptance of this hypothesis rests largely on the discussions given by Omeljan Pritsak in a comprehensive work, *The Origins of Rus*, now being prepared for publication.[31]

While archaeological data may indeed point to – but only point to – the consecutive presence or possibly coexistence of various Slavic ethnic groups in the north Russian area (between Lake Ladoga and Lake Peipus or Chud), it is hard to guess what evidence Lunt is referring to as regards personal names and toponyms. Certainly none of the Christian and pre-Christian names examined in A. Baecklund's previously cited monograph (see note 21 above) would suggest West Slavic rather than East Slavic (and, in part, ultimately Greek) origin. But perhaps the Harvard Slavist had some other onomastic data in mind. As for place names, again I would not know precisely what Lunt was thinking of when pointing to toponymic material as supporting evidence. There are, as far as I can see, only two names of towns, one real, the other wrapped in legends but probably once also real and subsequently presumably submerged, that come to mind in this context. One is the old town of *Ventspils* (German *Windau*) in northwestern Latvia (Curonia) on the Baltic, just across from the island of Gotland. Though located in the heartland of the ancient as well as present Baltic settlement, the name of that town – most probably an old commercial port – displays its Slavic origin or connection: *Ventspils* literally means "the town of the Wends" (compare also the similar meaning of its German name form; Latvian *pils* is a cognate of Greek *polis* "town"). The other toponym is the semi-legendary rich merchant town of *Vineta* (this being the latinized name form), believed to have been situated somewhere on the southern shores of the Baltic, along with other Baltic-Slavic coastal settlements, in all likelihood on the island of Wolin in the estuary of the Oder River, opposite the present-day city of Szczecin, also of ancient date. Founded, probably, in the ninth century, the West Slavic town of Vineta flourished particularly in the tenth and eleventh centuries, extending its trade to the Baltic provinces (perhaps present-day Ventspils was its "colony"), to Novgorod, to the merchant towns of Lake Mälar in eastern Sweden, especially Birka and Sigtuna, to Haithabu (Hedeby), Norway, and the lower Rhine valley.[32] It is therefore highly

[31] Cf. Lunt (n. 28 above) 270 and 277 n. 7; similarly though more briefly in a review in the *Slavic and East European Journal* 19 (1975) 262.

[32] Cf. J. Herrmann, *Zwischen Hradschin und Vineta: Frühe Kulturen der Westslawen* (Munich 1971) 158-159. Possibly this was also the site of the Jómsborg of the Old Icelandic *Jómsvíkinga Saga*; see *The Saga of the Jomsvikings*, ed. and transl. N. F. Blake (London 1962) vii-xv; but cf. also *Słownik starożytności słowiańskich* 2 (Wrocław 1964) 339, s. vv. *Jóm* and *Jómswikingowie*.

conceivable that West Slavic merchants from Vineta, and possibly also from other Wendish towns as well as from the predecessor of Ventspils, visited Novgorod regularly and perhaps even temporarily settled there. Adam of Bremen after all refers to Vineta-Wolin as "the greatest of all the cities that Europe harbors." But this does not necessarily mean that the first Slavic settlers of Novgorod must have come exclusively from that area. The close association of the ethnonyms *Wends* (Latin *Veneti/Venethi, Venedi,* Greek *Uenédai*, and so on, transferred to the Slavs from another, by then extinct Indo-European people) and *Slověne*, meaning generally "Slavs," in addition to being the designation of the particular Slavic tribe inhabiting the region around Lake Ilmen, proves very little indeed. *Wends* (with variants) had become just another term for Slavs, with the two ethnic names used in some areas concurrently. Compare, for example, German *Lausitzwenden*, along with *Sorben*, for the Slavs of Lusatia in present-day East Germany; and, in particular, the frequent parallel, if much criticized, usage of *Wenden* and *Slovenen* for the Slovenes of Carinthia in southern Austria.

Returning now to the problem of the co-occurrence and combination of Church Slavic and East Slavic elements in many texts from medieval Novgorod, it should be noted, above all, that in addition to the purely religious – biblical, liturgical, patristic, homiletic, and hagiographic – texts briefly referred to above for which the use of an only slightly Russianized Church Slavic was both natural and appropriate, there existed other genres which, though usually considered secular, show a mixture of vernacular Old Russian and Church Slavic. Here belong the annalistic writings of Novgorod: the five Novgorod Chronicles, some of them in more than one version, and the two Sophia Chronicles. They employed, to be sure, a rather dry, straightforward style and their narrative lacked much of the imaginative, often truly artistic component, at times amounting to whole inserted stories and tales, that can be found in their equivalents of the south, in Kiev (Nestor-Chronicle and Kiev Chronicle) and the principalities of Galich and Volhynia (Galician-Volhynian Chronicles), as well as the northeast, in the territory of Vladimir-Suzdal (Suzdal Chronicle). It can be surmised that the Novgorod Chronicles, too, were written by members of the clergy. Yet their Church Slavic is, generally speaking, not as pure and unadulterated as that of their counterparts elsewhere in Russia. This may in part be explicable as due to the greater demands for a down-to-earth, realistic presentation, rather than for a fanciful and entertaining one, that the reading public of Novgorod may have had on

---

See further, e. g., *Enzyklopädisches Handbuch zur Ur- und Frühgeschichte Europas* 2 (L-Z), ed. J. Filip (Prague 1969) 1591, s. v. *Vineta.* Generally on the problems connected with the semi-legendary town of Vineta, see further in particular R. Kiersnowski, *Legenda Winety: Studium historyczne*, Biblioteka Studium Slowiańskiego Uniwersytetu Jagiellońskiego, Ser. A no. 6 (Cracow 1950). In fact, there is some direct indiction of trade contacts between early medieval Novgorod and Vineta. Thus, in the Chronicle of Adam of Bremen, chap. 22, K14, we read: 'Ab ipsa urbe vela tendens XIIII-cimo die ascendes ad Ostrogard Ruzziae," indicating that fourteen days of sea travel separated Vineta from Novgorod.

the recording of the events pertinent to their city's past. Another contributing factor can of course have been the lesser sustained mastery of the norms of Church Slavic, particularly where these norms had not been fully integrated into the spoken "standard" language (see Lunt's reasoning referred to above), at least among the lower clergy who probably were primarily entrusted with the task of keeping a record of the happenings that took place in and around Novgorod. To give just one telling example: A. V. Issatschenko, in his forthcoming, insightful and unorthodox treatment of the history of Russian (shortly to be published in German under the title *Geschichte des Russischen*, by Carl Winter Universitätsverlag, Heidelberg) has shown that the frequently odd, if not incorrect, use of the simple past tense forms, imperfect and aorist, in the First Novgorod Chronicle can be best accounted for if one accepts the view that these inherited tense forms (now extinct in Russian) had largely dropped out of use at the time the earliest extant copies of that chronicle were written so that, here, they can be considered essentially artificial and archaic Slavonisms. Another text to which similar considerations apply is the so-called *kormchaia* or *kormchaia kniga*, literally "steering book" (in the sense of navigating guide), which contained both the Russian Church Slavic version of the Canon Law of the Eastern Orthodox Church (Nomocanon) and various civil law codes in a predominantly, though not exclusively, vernacular language. The oldest known Russian *kormchaia* dates from 1282 and seems to have been written in Novgorod; among other pieces, it contains the earliest extant text of the previously mentioned *Russkaia Pravda* in its so-called expanded version.[33]

But the basically alien, though to a certain extent comprehensible, Slavonisms had penetrated even deeper into the written language of Old Novgorod. We can find many of them, as well as the Grecisms which they often reflect, also in such by and large worldly texts as some of the legally entered documents (*gramoty*) previously referred to. Thus, it is again Issatschenko who has shown that the *gramota* that is usually considered the earliest attested specimen of this kind of writing, the so-called *Mstislav* (or *Iur'evskaia*) *gramota* of 1130 or thereabout, a donation instrument drafted by Prince Mstislav Vladimirovich and his son Vsevolod, or on his behalf as well, naming Saint George Monastery near Novgorod the beneficiary, contains a considerable amount of Slavonisms and, in the last analysis, Hellenisms.[34] Similarly, Church Slavic elements, along with purely East Slavic features, can be found in the so-called *Khutyn gramota*, a deed for the monastery of that name outside Novgorod, written in 1192 or shortly thereafter. And a close scrutiny of the language of the birch-bark letters,* usually considered the texts most closely reflecting the spoken language of medieval Novgorod, reveals that even these documents, serving purely

[33] Cf. Kiparsky (n. 23 above) 46; for a detailed study of the whole genre and related legal texts, see P. I. Žužek, S. J., *Kormčaja Kniga: Studies on the Chief Code of Russian Canon Law*, Orientalia christiana analecta 168 (Rome 1964) esp. 38-41.

[34] See A. V. Isačenko [Issatschenko], "Die Gräzismen des Grossfürsten," *Zeitschrift für slavische Philologie* 35 (1970) 97-103; cf. also Kiparsky 34.

practical purposes, are not always entirely free of Church Slavic linguistic usage; this applies, for example, to birch-bark text no. 9, cited above.

Summing up what has been said here on the language, the level of literacy, and the literature of Novgorod the Great, it can be stated that the extent of literacy seems to have been at least somewhat greater than had been previously assumed. Still, this does not suggest that the ability to read and write was truly widespread; various degrees of semi-literacy were the norm, in all likelihood. Moreover, the language of Old Novgorod was most probably not uniformly East Slavic. Though it has so far not been possible to demonstrate the existence of any West Slavic linguistic elements in Novgorod, the East Slavic vernacular had, here as elsewhere in Old Rus (granted slightly different proportions), a good deal of Church Slavic, that is, South Slavic, admixture. As for the popular literary genres, including certain "subliterary" kinds of oral tradition recorded only long after the "waning of the Middle Ages," Novgorod had its share – and, in fact, more than its share – of the traditional religious literature. Novgorod's secular and semi-secular writing, on the one hand, displays a more dry-realistic tone than much of the rest of comparable Old Russian literature but was, on the other hand, not altogether alien to a particularly fantastic streak. The latter is represented, in addition to the folk songs (*byliny*) featuring Novgorodian heroes, by some of the hagiographic or hagiographically styled writings of Novgorod with a marked penchant for story-telling and exotic adventure. This latter feature may have its explanation, to some extent at least, in Novgorod's character as an international trading center, with traveling merchants from many countries passing through the Volkhov city and meeting here with their Russian partners and exchanging with them more than merely their merchandise and their money.

5

Some of this dichotomy in form and perception, the contrast between realism and imagination, noticeable in the literature of medieval Novgorod is also characteristic of Novgorodian art and architecture.[35] It is fair to say that religious themes dominated the literature of medieval Novgorod, particularly if we include here the Novgorod chronicles for which, after all, the Church was primarily responsible and which, therefore, reflect the official ecclesiastic point of view. But some topics, such as those of the Life of Prince Alexander Nevskii[36] or the still more supernatural adventures of Archbishop Ioann of Novgorod, were only superficially disguised in the ornate style and paraphernalia of hagiographic pieces while others, such as the folksongs about Sadko and Vasilii Buslaevich, did not even pretend to carry any particular religious message (not to speak of the vast body of writing which does not

[35] The best general introduction to the art of Novgorod is still the monograph by V. N. Lazarev, *Iskusstvo Novgoroda* (Moscow 1947).

[36] On the semi-secular character of the literary biography of Alexander Nevskii and some related works, see Birnbaum, *Slavic Writing* (n. 1 above) 330-332, with further references.

qualify as literature proper). By contrast, art in Old Novgorod, as almost everywhere in medieval Europe, was entirely and exclusively in the service of the Christian Church.

Second only to the capital city of Kiev, Novgorod was a major center of the arts already in pre-Mongol, Kievan Russia. In fact, it soon outshone even the capital in the south in that it could boast a larger number of churches per square mile within its city limits and a greater concentration of monasteries in the city and its immediate vicinity than any other medieval Russian town and, for that matter, probably any particular area east of the Vistula and north of the Danube. The wooden structures of ordinary medieval dwellings have long since disappeared together with the log-decked streets which they lined. Later, a vastly different network of modern streets, dating back, in their oldest parts, to the time of Catherine the Great, were superimposed over the layout of the original city plan; and only many of the medieval stone structures, especially the stone churches of Old Novgorod, have either remained more or less intact to this day or were destroyed or severely damaged (and in part since reconstructed) during World War II when the front line for some time coincided with the Volkhov River.

The stone cathedral of Saint Sophia was built between 1045 and 1050 and consecrated in 1052 during the reign of Prince Vladimir, the son of Iaroslav the Wise, with the latter at that time residing and ruling as great prince of Kiev. Whereas Iaroslav's earlier refusal in 1014 to pay any tribute to Kiev as demanded by his father, Vladimir the Saint, was tantamount to a first declaration of independence on the part of Novgorod vis-à-vis Kiev, Iaroslav the Wise, formerly prince of Novgorod and since 1019 grand prince of Kiev, remained in control of, and in friendly relations with, Novgorod after his move to Kiev and the appointment of his son Vladimir as prince of Novgorod. Thus, it was Iaroslav, rather than Vladimir, who in 1044, one year before work began on the new cathedral in the Novgorod citadel (*Detinets*), ordered the construction of protective stone walls to surround the kremlin of Novgorod. The cathedral of Saint Sophia, which replaced an earlier wooden church, is the second largest major church building of medieval Russia and a somewhat simplified and modified version of its immediate model, Saint Sophia Cathedral in Kiev, the latter, in turn, patterned on the prototype of Hagia Sophia in Constantinople. Combining Byzantine architectural concepts with some Romanesque elements, imported, obviously, from central and western Europe, the Novgorod cathedral is particularly remarkable for its helmet-shaped (rather than fully onion-like) cupolas, typical of medieval Russia's architectural landscape. In all, there were six cupolas of which in particular the largest, gold-plated one, represents the transitional stage between the more flat Byzantine domes known from Saint Sophia Cathedral of Kiev, and the more markedly onion-shaped cupolas of northern Russia of a later date.[37] (The

[37] Generally, on the historical architecture of Novgorod, see M. Karger, *Novgorod the Great: Architectural Guidebook* (Moscow 1973); Russian edition: *Novgorod Velikii: Arkhitekturnye pamiatniki*, ed. 2 enl. (Leningrad 1966). See now further *Novgorod*, edited and photographed by

original shape of the domes of the Kiev Sophia can actually only be reconstructed, since the cathedral was radically modified in the style of the Ukrainian Baroque and subsequently almost completely destroyed during World War II.) Throughout the Middle Ages, Saint Sophia Cathedral was the symbol of the city's or, rather, the city-state's sovereignty and liberties. This is borne out by the frequent reference to the Republic of Saint Sophia as a synonym for Novgorod and its territories, the function of the archbishop of Novgorod as the chief dignitary to represent the republic in its external dealings, and the symptomatic fact that the administrative-ecclesiastic center on the left bank of the Volkhov in Novgorod was referred to as the Sophia Side (*Sofiiskaia storona*; see above).

A particularly interesting and, in fact, unique instance of the impact of Central European art and craftsmanship on Novgorod in the earlier part of the Middle Ages is provided by the famed cast bronze doors known as the Korsun (or Sigtuna, occasionally also Swedish, but more appropriately Magdeburg) Gates on the western side of the Novgorod Saint Sophia Cathedral. The origin of those doors has been a matter of much controversy. However, it now seems fairly certain that they were executed at Magdeburg in the German duchy of Saxony (also the see of an important archbishopric) in the middle of the twelfth century. Originally, apparently, commissioned by the Polish bishop of Płock on the lower Vistula, the center of the diocese of Masovia, the doors were subsequently purchased by merchants from Novgorod to adorn their cathedral. Scenes from the Old and New Testament fill most of the square plaques except at the top. The plaques are separated by garlands of stylized foliage. The door handles are held in the mouths of lions, as known from comparable bronze doors in Italy. The sculptor, undoubtedly an artist of considerable skill and originality, has left us with a self-portrait at the bottom of the left leaf of the doors, immediately adjacent to the scene depicting the Fall of Man. Standing next to Eve, the relief shows him dressed in the fashion of his time, holding the tools of his craft. Several other figures in the various reliefs are portrayed in a similar vein. In particular, the lower scenes display a naive, almost primitive style, full of spontaneity and picturesque fantasy. Some of the episodes represented are said to be rare in Romanesque iconography. Latin as well as later Cyrillic (Russian) inscriptions – the latter in part translating the former – were added after the reliefs were cast, presumably at different times. The misnomer Korsun Gates seems at first to have referred to another set of doors of the same cathedral worked in Byzantine style with motifs reminiscent of such from Salerno, Amalfi, and Venice and wrongly also labeled Swedish Gates on occasion. The incorrect reference to Sweden and particu-

B. S. Skobel'cyn, intro. M. K. Karger (Leningrad 1975). On the art of medieval Novgorod viewed as the northernmost component of an essentially Byzantine artistic style (with local and western admixtures), cf. also D. Obolensky, *The Byzantine Commonwealth: Eastern Europe, 500-1453* (New York 1971) 354-335 and 357-360. Western influences on Old Russian, notably Novgorodian, art were treated in an illuminating essay by M. V. Alpatov, "K voprosu o zapadnom vliianii v drevnerusskom iskusstve," *Slavia* 3 (1924/1925) 94-113.

larly, as regards the cast bronze doors from Magdeburg, the town of Sigtuna, briefly the capital of Sweden, is due to a mistaken mention of some magnificent city gates of Sigtuna, supposedly carried away to Russia as a result of a Russian raid on Sigtuna in 1187; the mention is found in an early-seventeenth-century Swedish history of that town, written in the period when the Swedes (under King Gustavus Adolphus, his brother, Prince Philip, and his military commander, Governor Jacob De la Gardie) had temporarily occupied Novgorod in 1611-1617, that is, toward the end of the so-called Time of Troubles (*Smuta*) and the first years of the reign of Czar Michael Romanov. Moreover, at the place where the Korsun (Magdeburg) Gates are now located, another set of doors seems to have been found earlier which were subsequently brought to the monastery of the Holy Trinity at Alexandrov (near Vladimir) at the orders of Grand Prince Ivan III. While displaying certain Byzantinesque features and resembling the doors of the church of San Paolo in Rome, these doors also share some characteristics with the cast bronze doors brought to Novgorod from Magdeburg, perhaps by way of Płock, and were, by contrast, probably manufactured in Novgorod.[38]

Generally, the twelfth-century churches of Novgorod and its region were decorated with highly accomplished frescoes mostly, it would seem, executed by native artists who combined the style and standards of Byzantine iconography with Romanesque (central and west European) as well as locally developed art forms. The imposing frescoes of the church of Saint George at Staraia Ladoga or, in medieval times, simply Ladoga, represent the farthest point in northern Europe ever to be reached by practitioners of wall painting of the Byzantine school; they date from about 1167.[39] The marvelous frescoes of 1199 in the church of Our Savior (Sv. Spas) on the Nereditsa, near Gorodishche, tragically and irreparably destroyed in World War II, constituted a uniquely complete sequence of wall paintings covering all available surfaces. To judge from preserved reproductions, their style was austere, solemn, and monumental, again blending Byzantine traditions with elements of Romanesque and local Russian artistic conceptions. It should be pointed out in this context that it is the admixture of local traits in the architecture and fresco painting of Novgorod and its surrounding area that, while retaining a generally Byzantine style, make these northwestern specimens of Old Russian art noticeably different from the more purely Byzantine type of art of early (pre-1240) Kiev or that of the

[38] For further details, see the excellent description and analysis by A. Goldschmidt, *Die Bronzetüren von Nowgorod und Gnesen*, Die frühmittelalterlichen Bronzetüren 2 (Marburg 1932) 7-26 and 39-41, with ample illustrations. Cf. further also F. Souchal, *Art of the Early Middle Ages*, intro. H. H. Hofstätter (New York 1968) 194-197; and Alpatov, 98-99. On the episode of the Swedish occupation of Novgorod, see, e. g., H. Birnbaum, "Novgorodiana Stockholmiensia," *Scando-Slavica* 10 (1964) 154-173, esp. 157-159.

[39] For details concerning the frescoes of Staraia Ladoga, see V. N. Lazarev, *Freski Staroi Ladogi* (Moscow 1960), with a French résumé and numerous illustrations. Additional information is contained in V. N. Lazarev, "Novye fragmenty rospisi iz Staroi Ladogi," *Kul'tura i iskusstvo drevnei Rusi. Sbornik v chest' . . . M. K. Kargera* (Leningrad 1967) 77-81.

Russian northeast (Vladimir-Suzdal). The fact that Novgorod was particularly saturated with ecclesiastic art by comparison with other parts of medieval Russia and, indeed, eastern Europe, was already mentioned.

It has been said that the century between about 1250 and about 1350 represents an almost complete blank in Russian art history. These were the times of the most severe Tatar rule in Russia, and although Novgorod and its territories escaped actual occupation by Mongol military units and posts, the Republic of Saint Sophia, too, felt its share of the hard and troubled times. In this connection it should be noted, though, that it was not so much because of any particular religious intolerance and fanaticism on the part of the Tatar occupant (or, in the case of Novgorod, overlord) that religous art came to a virtual standstill at that time. It has been argued and in recent years increasingly corroborated by substantial evidence that the "infidels" who had invaded and taken over military and/or political control of most of Russia during the latter part of the European Middle Ages (for chronology, see above) were in fact anything but particularly militant and demanding when it came to the Church and its local institutions. Once having recognized the strength and efficacy of the administrative infrastructure built in preceding centuries by the then still young and vigorous Eastern Church of the Kievan state, the Tatar administrators now showed considerable leniency and granted far-reaching economic exemptions and other privileges to monasteries and local church dignitaries without showing much interest for or zeal in attempting to supress the Christian faith in the areas they controlled. Obviously, the exceedingly negative image of the Tatar rule projected by the Russian Orthodox Church must be viewed to a large extent as a notion about the infidel intruders designed by the Church who associated herself with the national cause of liberation (particularly after the first decisive victories over the Tatars beginning with the battle of Kulikovo in 1380). At any rate, the actual practices of the Tatars, particularly as regards their relationship to the, by and large, very cooperative ecclesiastic establishment of ancient Russia would hardly have warranted such an image. If the production of art nonetheless came to a temporary halt, this is primarily explicable in terms of the general material hardships inflicted upon Russia by the Mongols more than as a result of any fundamental ideological clash. Also it should be noted that a major portion of southwestern Russia, the Ruthenian lands (including Kiev), were soon incorporated into the Roman Catholic Grand Duchy of Lithuania, shortly thereafter closely associated and ultimately united with the kingdom or "Crown" of Poland.

Not unexpectedly, it was Novgorod that was the first Russian town to recover from this decline in the arts. Several factors contributed here. Above all, its political and geographical position was more advantageous and relatively safer than that of other Russian areas, especially vis-à-vis the distant Mongol rulers. Leaning heavily on the powerful neighboring state of Lithuania and keeping up and continuously developing its traditional trade connections with the West, now especially with the cities of the Hanseatic League, Novgorod could afford to call in, as early as in 1338, and to commission a Byzantine master to paint the interior walls of one of its many churches. Soon, in the second half of the fourteenth century, fresco painting was to reach a new peak in Novgorod, and other art forms followed suit. It was again, and this time perhaps in a more unadulterated form, the Byzantine style of fresco painting that came to prevail in the Volkhov city. To be sure, this was no longer the largely schematic and stilted, typifying style of earlier Byzantine painters that was imported now to the Russian northwest and soon also to Vladimir-Suzdal and Moscow. The new stylistic vein in Byzantium was that occasionally referred to as the Palaeologan or Last Byzantine Renaissance. The style of painting and mosaic design had become more mellow and emotional, influenced, it would seem, both by the prevailing ill-boding atmosphere in Byzantium itself, now threatened by the advancing Ottoman Turks, and by the renewed, partly politically motivated contacts with the West, especially Italy. Outside Byzantium, this new, more unsettling style can be found especially in the Russian north (Novgorod, Pskov, Vladimir-Suzdal, Moscow) and, in the Balkans, in Romania, or what were then rather the principalities of Wallachia and Moldavia, and in Serbia.[40] In Novgorod, the art of the monastery church of the Nativity at Kovalevo near Novgorod (1380) still retained its classic harmony whereas the deliberately archaizing frescoes of the church of the Dormition at Volotovo outside Novgorod, painted in the 1380s, already display the characteristic features of "expressive ugliness" and "psychological emotionalism" which sometimes have been labeled late Gothic and which are also associated with the so-called Second South Slavic Influence if this term is used in its broader cultural, not merely narrowly linguistic, sense.[41] Unfortunately, both churches were destroyed during World War II.

There can be shown to exist an unmistakable affinity between the now lost murals of Volotovo and the art of the greatest fresco painter of Novgorod, Theophanes the Greek or, in Russian, Feofan Grek. Not much is known about his life, but he has left behind at least two major lasting monuments of his artistic mastery: the frescoes of the Novgorod church of the Transfiguration, painted in 1378 (so the chronicle tells us), and the iconostasis of the cathedral of the Annunciation in the Moscow Kremlin. Theophanes seems to have left Constantinople in the early 1370s at the latest and to have come to Russia, like many Byzantines, by way of the Crimea. Prior to coming to Novgorod, he had painted the inside of approximately forty churches, as we learn from his friend Epiphanius the Wise. He is believed to have died sometime between 1405 and 1415.[42] In a sense, Theophanes can be considered the immediate predecessor and artistic mentor of the greatest Old Russian painter, Andrei Rublev, although

[40] Generally on the Palaeologan Renaissance in Byzantium and the sphere of Byzantine cultural influence, see, for art and aesthetics, e. g., G. Mathew, *Byzantine Aesthetics* (New York 1971) 135-161, esp. 142-161 ("The Harmony of Colours"); further, K. Papaioannou, *Byzantine and Russian Painting* (London 1965) 76-82 ("The Palaeologue Style").

[41] Cf. Birnbaum, "On the Significance" (n. 1 above) 27-28 and 39.

[42] The definitive work on Theophanes is the fundamental monograph by V. N. Lazarev, *Theophanes der Grieche und seine Schule* (Vienna 1968); Russian original: *Feofan Grek i ego shkola* (Moscow).

their teacher-disciple relationship remains controversial (see note 44 below). In Theophanes's paintings the pure Byzantine art of the early Palaeologan period has been adapted to and fused with locally inspired experiments in artistic expressionism and emotionalism. Theophanes's elongated, ascetic saints bring to mind the art of another, later Greek expatriate, from the island of Crete where Byzantine-style art continued to be produced long after the fall of Constantinople, who, after having studied in Italy, ultimately wound up in Spain – El Greco. Clearly, Theophanes's portraits of saints and church leaders have been influenced by the spirit of Hesychasm, the mystical movement in Eastern Christianity that emphasized ecstasy, to be achieved by rigorous rules (including holding one's breath and contemplating one's navel), as a means of direct communication with God. Possibly, Theophanes could have been present at the Synods of 1341 and 1351 when the teachings of Gregory Palamas, the chief advocate of the Hesychasts, were officially vindicated. As is well known, Hesychasm, or rather its Russian variety, has had a major impact on Russian religious life, especially the north Russian hermit movement whose adherents used the virtually impenetrable forest belt on and beyond the upper Volga as their refuge. Theophanes's Hesychast topic of the Transfiguration, showing Christ on Mount Tabor being transfigured by the Uncreated Light, gained in popularity: an increasing number of churches all over Russia were consecrated to that theme.

In Novgorod, Theophanes did not make an impact of any consequence. The paintings of the church of Volotovo and those of the church of Saint Theodore Stratelites were ascribed to him on doubtful grounds.[43] Once in Moscow, where he went from Novgorod, he did have a following and several other Muscovite art works are known to have been accomplished by him.[44] Only indirectly from a letter written by Epiphanius do we know that in addition to painting frescoes and icons, Theophanes was also considered an "important book painter," that is, a miniature painter of illuminated manuscripts.[45]

In the late fourteenth-fifteenth centuries, Novgorodian art returned more and more to an art form earlier cultivated especially in the twelfth-thirteenth centuries: the panel-painting of icons. The Novgorod school of the fifteenth-early sixteenth centuries marks one of the absolute peaks in Old Russian icon painting. Its style remained essentially Byzantine, that is, that of the classic iconography of the Eastern Church. Only in the choice of themes and motifs did local preferences and influences prove decisive. Thus, for example, the selection of saints painted by masters of the Novgorod school reveals a clearly local bias: Saint George; Elijah; Saint Blasius (also the patron saint of Dubrovnik); Florus and Laurus; Paraskeve, the guardian saint of merchants; Anastasia, the saint of childbirth; and so on. Here, however, we are

[43] Cf. Lazarev, *Theophanes* 46-68.

[44] *Ibid.* 10-12. On Theophanes's influence on Muscovite painting, notably on the art of Anrei Rublev, see 103-111, esp. 105-108.

[45] *Ibid.* 12.

reaching a period partly after 1478, that is, beyond the end of the free Republic of Saint Sophia.[46]

In closing this section, it should be mentioned that the art of miniature painting and manuscript illumination was indeed well developed in Novgorod. The earliest dated Russian Church Slavic text, the Ostromir Gospel-Book, testifies to the elaborate accomplishments in this highly demanding minute art form, and numerous are the handsomely illuminated and richly decorated manuscripts that can be traced to the scriptoria of medieval Novgorod. Generally, though, it should be noted that it is not so much the miniature proper that is particularly innovative or artistically refined in the illuminated manuscripts from Novgorod. Rather, it is the decorative ornamentation that was imaginatively developed in the medieval Novgorodian codices. Here, it was the rich tradition of Eastern Christianity, as cultivated in Asia Minor, especially Cappadocia, in Palestine, and in Egypt, that reached Novgorod by way of Bulgaria while the direct influences from Byzantium played but a secondary role. Compared to this influence of the Christian art of the Near East, traces of European Romanesque and, later, Gothic miniature painting in the manuscripts of medieval Novgorod are almost negligible. The human face was introduced in Novgorodian book illumination as part of teratological decorative art only in the early thirteenth century.[47]

6

Art and architecture in medieval Novgorod were, as we have seen, almost exclusively in the service of the Church; in fact, they were but the visual expression of the various facets of religious life in the Volkhov metropolis and the territories over which it ruled. Yet, only the dignitaries of official Orthodoxy could – and would – act as patrons of the arts. If there was an art of religious dissidents in Novgorod, we know virtually nothing about it. But what we do know is that such dissidents or "heretics" did in fact exist in late medieval Russia. Toward the end of its history as an independent merchant republic and shortly thereafter, Novgorod was the scene of two heretic movements of which the second, in particular, shook the very foundations of spiritual and, to some extent, political and social life in fourteenth-fifteenth century Russia. These movements were the group known as *strigol'niki* who first seem to have developed in Pskov before spreading on to Novgorod (although it may only have been in the latter place that they acquired their particular name) and the so-called Judaizers or "Judaizing heresy" (*zhidovstvuiushchie* or *zhidovstvuiushchaia*

[46] For further details on Novgorodian easel painting, especially in the twelfth-thirteenth and late fourteenth-fifteenth centuries, see V. N. Lazarev, *Novgorodskaia ikonopis' – Novgorodian Icon-Painting* (Moscow 1969), with numerous color plates.

[47] Cf. Lazarev (n. 35 above) 47-50. On applied arts and crafts in medieval Novgorod, see N. G. Porfiridov, "O nekotorykh voprosakh istorii prikladnogo iskusstva drevnego Novgoroda," *Kul'tura* (n. 39 above) 96-101.

eres') which possibly was brought to Novgorod from "Lithuanian Russia" (that is, Ruthenia, notably Kiev), though it is very doubtful that it can ultimately be traced to the then Genoese-administered town of Kaffa in the Crimea, and to a not otherwise identifiable Jew Skharia or Zacharia, as claimed by the biased Joseph Volotskii; see below. Only subsequently, after having been introduced in Novgorod, the Judaizing heresy appears to have flared up in Moscow, affecting some very highly placed people such as Ivan III's chief adviser on foreign policy, Fedor Kuricyn, who had visited Hungary and Moldavia and probably is the author or at least the translator from the Hebrew of one of the few remaining pieces of genuinely "Judaizing" literature, the "Laodician Epistle" (*Laodikiiskoe poslanie*). The heresy also seems to have attracted Princess Helen, a member of Ivan's ruling family by marriage, in 1483, and daughter of the successful prince of Moldavia (and lord of some fiefs in Transylvania), Stephen the Great (Ştefan cel Mare, d. 1504). Possibly, though less likely perhaps, the "Judaizing" ideas and practices may have entered Russia by way of Muscovy, the Judaizers having strong links, one can surmise, with the Hussite refugees of the Taborite wing in Moldavia, given some of the connections just indicated. However, it is also known that Hussite refugees appeared in Pskov and Vitebsk, that is, in areas not far from Novgorod, as well as elsewhere in Russia.[48]

The terms *strigol'niki* and *zhidovstvuiushchie* need some comment. The former is usually believed to be derived from the Old Russian verb *strichi* "to shear, to cut," the Russian designation thus presumably meaning "shearers" or "cutters," but possibly also "the shorn ones" (compare *strishka*, "tonsure"). No definite agreement has yet been reached among specialists as to whether this term actually makes reference to the, at least originally, major profession of the adherents of this late-fourteenth century movement, namely to the trade of the cloth-cutters, a profession also widespread among earlier heretic groups of southern and western Europe, particularly the Bogomils of the Slavic Balkans, primarily Bulgaria and Bosnia,[49] and the Cathars or Albigensians of northern Italy and southern France. Ideologically and socially, though, the *strigol'niki* seem to have been closer to the Waldensians, known also as the Poor Men of Lyons, and to the Hussites of Bohemia, Moravia, and, subsequently, Hungary with Transylvania, and Moldavia. Another

[48] Generally on religion in medieval Novgorod, official Orthodoxy as well as the heretic movements (and their reflexes in art), see Onasch (n. 3 above) 150-185 ("Ketzergeschichte Gross-Nowgorods," "Bügerfrömmigkeit im Spiegel der Malerei," "Die kirchliche Kultur im Schatten der Katastrophe," "Bildungsrenaissance und neue Ketzerei"). On the Judaizers in particular, cf. also H. Birnbaum, "On Some Evidence of Jewish Life and Anti-Jewish Sentiments in Medieval Russia," *Viator* 4 (1973) 225-255, esp. 246-253 and 255, with further references.

[49] For some new revealing findings and intriguing conjectures on the Bogomils, also with respect to their legal ecclesiastic status and intellectual and social background, see now D. Dragojlović, *Bogomilstvo na Balkanu i u Maloj Aziji* 1: *Bogomilski rodonačalnici*, SANU, Balkanološki institut, Posebna izdanja 2 (Belgrade 1974); J. Sidak, *Studije o "Crkvi bosanskoj" i bogumilstvu*, with German résumés (Zagreb 1975); and F. Snajek, O. P., *Bosanskohumski krstjani i katarsko-dualistički pokret u srednjem vjeku*, with a French résumé, Analecta croatica christiana 6 (Zagreb 1975).

explanation for the name *strigol'niki* is that the term originally referred to the procedure of tonsuring a certain class of low-ranking Novgorodian clergy, the deacons and subdeacons. As for the term *zhidovstvuiushchie*, corresponding precisely to the common derogatory *Judaizantes* of the late Middle Ages and the following period, there can be no doubt as to its origin. It was the label used to brand this intellectually more challenging movement of the decades preceding Novgorod's definite loss of independence and of the last years of the fifteenth century not – as far as we know – by their contemporaneous condemners and adversaries, Archbishop Gennadii (Gennadius) of Novgorod and Abbot Joseph Volotskii foremost among them, but by some later critics of indeterminable date.[50] What remains largely controversial is the extent to which the Judaizers may indeed have adhered to some of the beliefs and rituals of the Mosaic faith favoring them over traditional Christian practices and dogmas such as the divine nature of Christ whom the Judaizers rather likened to one of the prophets or to Moses. However, having studied this matter in some detail, I, for one, cannot see that the Judaizers thought of themselves as not remaining within the fold of the true Christian Church, granted that they rejected much of what the official Russian Orthodox Church stood for at that time. Sharing to some extent the social concerns of their predecessors, the *strigol'niki*, who had assailed the institutionalized wealth and power position of the Church, the leading figures of the Judaizers were by and large to be found less among the lower strata of society as was the case with the *strigol'niki* but rather in the more well-to-do circles of the upper classes, the merchants of Novgorod as well as the boyars and, in part, even the officials of Muscovy. Clearly, there is a humanist and rational tenet discernible in much of the Judaizers' undertakings and activities. Their interest for the books of the Old Testament and its Jewish commentaries in their Hebrew original, as well as for some other Jewish writings, and for learning in general was, it would seem, as much motivated by purely religious conviction as it was dictated by a genuine search and craving for knowledge as such. Unfortunately, due to its ultimate total suppression and our distorted pertinent information, the true teachings and practices of the Judaizers can only be fragmentarily reconstructed and the full extent of their adherence hardly ever accurately assessed. Our own information about the Judaizers is derived primarily from the presentation of the "enemy camp," most eloquently represented by Joseph Volotskii's collection of polemic treatises (*slova*) which has come to be known under the title *Prosvětitel'* ("The Enlightener"), written, as we now have reason to believe, only in 1502-1504, that is, after the heresy's final defeat not only in Novgorod but also in Moscow.[51] This is not the place to

[50] Cf. Birnbaum (n. 48 above) 248 n. 81. Archbishop Gennadii had characterized the members of this new sect merely as people "pondering over things Jewish" (*zhidovskaa mudrъstvuiushchi*).

[51] Cf., in addition to Joseph's *slova*, his *poslaniia* ("epistles"). See *Poslaniia Iosifa Volotskogo*, ed. A. A. Zimin and Ia. S. Lur'e (Moscow 1959), with two most informative introductory essays by I. P. Eremin and Ia. S. Lur'e.

elaborate on the subject, especially as I have dealt with it previously on the pages of this journal (see note 48 above), and scholarship has since made further significant advances in this particular field.[52]

Early humanist trends were not characteristic of the Novgorodian and Muscovite Judaizers alone. The group most strongly opposing them, that of Archbishop Gennadii and the learned men with whom he had surrounded himself, the "Gennadius circle," exhibits interests and a degree of learning that can only be labeled humanist and bear comparison with similar trends evolving at about the same time in western and central Europe, in particular in the Italy of the quattrocento. The group of humanists that visited and worked for the richly endowed and politically powerful "house of Saint Sophia" in Novgorod has, in fact, occasionally and not inappropriately been likened to the "republics of scholars" such as we know them especially from Renaissance Florence.[53] The tangible result of the scholarly endeavors of Gennadii and his group was the so-called Gennadius Bible, the first complete translation of the Latin text of the Vulgate into Russian Church Slavic. The manuscript of this translation was completed in 1499, more than twenty years after Novgorod's loss of independence, and is now housed in the State Historical Museum in Moscow (sign. Sin. 915).[54]

It was certainly not by accident that the Russian Church Slavic Bible translation of Archbishop Gennadius and his associates was made primarily from Latin and that it was based on the received text of the authorized Roman Catholic version of the Bible. The instrumental mind behind the Bible translation, if not the sole translator, was a Croatian Dominican monk by the name of Benjamin (Veniamin) who had come to Novgorod in 1491 fleeing to Russia from his native Croatia, threatened and in large part occupied by the Turks. In addition to the text of the Vulgate, there is reason to believe that earlier, Old Church Slavic renditions of parts of the Bible were consulted as were some of the Greek originals and the writings of Nicholas of Lyra (fourteenth century) who in turn was familiar with the Hebrew sources of the Old Testament and the relevant commentaries made by Jewish exegetes.[55] Benjamin may also have been Gennadius's chief source of information about the Inquisition, an institution for which Gennadius showed great admiration and sympathy and whose practices he subsequently adopted in his persecution of the Judaizers. It can be assumed that Joseph Volotskii's enthusiasm for the Spanish Inquisition dates from his contacts with the Gennadius circle. Another member of this learned group was a

[52] Cf., in particular, the new important monograph by E. Hösch, *Orthodoxie und Häresie im alten Russland* (Wiesbaden 1975).

[53] Cf. esp. Onasch (n. 3 above) 177-179.

[54] On the Gennadius Bible, see most recently G. Freidhof, *Vergleichende sprachliche Studien zur Gennadius-Bibel (1499) und Ostroger Bibel (1580-81)*, Frankfurter Abhandlungen zur Slavistik 21 (Frankfurt a. M. 1972) esp. 11-18; see further *idem, Auszüge aus der Gennadius-Bibel (1499)*, Specimina philologiae slavicae 5 (Frankfurt a. M. 1974).

[55] Cf. Onasch (n. 3 above) 183.

Greek, Demetrius Trachaniotes, brother of George (Iurii) who was instrumental in negotiating and arranging the marriage of Ivan III to the Byzantine princess Sophia (Zoe). Demetrius is probably identical with Dmitrii Gerasimov, called the Interpreter (*tolmach*), who composed the first version of the "Tale of the White Hood" referred to earlier.[56] In addition to *literati* from the south, Gennadii also cultivated his contacts with the Baltic provinces, with Lithuania, and with the cities of the Hanseatic League. Thus we know of at least a few of his associates and co-workers from Lübeck. Among them were Nicholas Buelow, physician, Catholic theologian, and astrologer, and Bartholomew Gothan, a printer who, in addition, seems to have been active as an interpreter mediating between the Novgorod officials and the local representatives of the Hansa at Saint Peter's Court. These men, too, may have played some role in the work on the Bible translation, and they certainly influenced the archbishop's position in religious and other intellectual matters as well as his political orientation, leaving some traces of their north German freethinking spirit in his mind. In general, the *vladyka* of Novgorod was watched with jealous suspicion by his superiors, the grand prince and the metropolitan of Moscow, both for his barely disguised Catholic leanings and his general xenophile attitude, neither of which fit particularly well into the concept of the new state and church ideology now being shaped in Moscow. In fact, Gennadii had to make a great effort to convince the Muscovite potentates that his somewhat independent maneuvering did not actually jeopardize the interests of the state and the Church which he, too, was supposed to serve.[57]

7

We have already gone slightly beyond the point in time which, at the beginning of this essay, we had set as the limit for the period to be discussed here, the year 1478 when Novgorod lost its last semblance of independence and was formally incorporated into the Muscovite state. What remains is to add a few words about Novgorod's cultural legacy, its continued effect on Russia's cultural evolution. Who, if any, were the Volkhov city's spiritual heirs?

The immediate beneficiary of Novgorod's decline and ultimate collapse was, of course, Moscow. In literature and art this transition and transfer of the cultural center of gravity is symbolized by the fact that both Pachomius Logothetes and Theophanes the Greek, two leading figures of late medieval Russian culture, had already shifted their activities from Novgorod to Moscow. And in art, Theophanes was followed by Andrei Rublev who was active exclusively in the Moscow-Vladimir-Suzdal area. As for political ideology and theological doctrine, Moscow, the victor,

[56] Cf. *ibid.* 178; see further N. K. Gudzii, *Istoriia drevnei russkoi literatury* ed. 7 (Moscow 1966) 302.

[57] Onasch (n. 3 above) 178-179.

set the tone. In this context it may perhaps be considered symptomatic, though, that two of the most significant advocates for the new autocratic political and religious outlook were men coming from what once had been part of the *Novgorodskaia zemlia*, Iosif Volotskii and another abbot, this one from Pskov, Philotheus (Filofei) who in the same year as his city lost its independence to Moscow – 1510 – first formulated the doctrine of Moscow as the Third Rome (see above). Yet even in its most advanced form the new autocratic state ideology was determined not only by the model of Byzantium but by that of its conqueror, the well-organized Osmanli state, and by Western thinking: Ivan Peresvetov, the political guide of Ivan IV, was strongly influenced by Machiavelli and more than merely impressed by the achievements of Sultan Mehmet II. But of course, the kind of political and cultural development most typically represented by the ancient free republic of Novgorod, with its sensitivity to impulses from the West and its perceptive open-mindedness, was stifled as a result of the end of Novgorod's independence.

The "window to the West," which the Volkhov city had in fact been, was permanently pushed open, but only after more than two hundred years, when Peter the Great founded his new capital, Saint Petersburg. At the practical, commercial and technological level, Peter was the first to resume – with his contacts to the West, especially Holland but also Germany and England – Novgorod's old tradition of foreign trade as it had flourished, above all, in the period of the Hansa. But what was only begun by Peter came to fruition with his successors, Elisabeth and, even more so, Catherine the Great who are to be credited with Russia's "catching up" with the rest of Europe. This might never have become as urgently necessary had the cultural tradition of Novgorod been allowed to continue. In the final analysis, therefore, Saint Petersburg, the new capital of Russia and the scene of its greatest intellectual achievements throughout the eighteenth and early nineteenth centuries, can be considered the true heir of Novgorod.

Center for Russian and East European Studies
University of California
Los Angeles, California 90024, U.S.A.

THE QUEEN IN CHARLES V'S "CORONATION BOOK": JEANNE DE BOURBON AND THE "ORDO AD REGINAM BENEDICENDAM"

•

by Claire Richter Sherman

I. Introduction

Both the text and illustrations of the remarkable manuscript now in the British Library (London, Cotton Tiberius B. VIII) called the *Coronation Book of Charles V of France* have long been familiar to liturgical scholars and to historians concerned with the development of the French monarchy. Commissioned by Charles V himself and completed in 1365 according to the unusual and significant colophon, the manuscript remained in the royal library after his death in 1380, when it passed to his son Charles VI, who reigned until 1422. In 1424 the manuscript passed into English hands as part of the collection of John, duke of Bedford upon the sale and dispersion of the royal library. On the basis of paleography in the oath of allegiance to the king of England on fol. 80, the evidence is that the manuscript was in England about 1450. It next appeared in the seventeenth century in the collection of Sir

The impetus for this study grew out of a talk given in the fall of 1972 at the Folger Shakespeare Library on the miniatures of the *Coronation Book of Charles V* (London, British Library, MS Cotton Tiberius B. VIII). The occasion was a meeting of the seminar, sponsored by the Folger Institute of Renaissance and Eighteenth-Century Studies, on "Royal Ceremonial in Renaissance France." The leader of the seminar was Prof. Ralph E. Giesey of the University of Iowa, with whom I made the presentation on the political and constitutional significance of the program of illustrations in the manuscript.

For their help with problems relating to the text of the *Coronation Book of Charles V,* I am grateful to Victor Thuronyi of Trinity College, Cambridge and to the Rev. Dom Hilary Hayden, O. S. B., and the Rev. Dom Anselm Strittmatter, O. S. B., of St. Anselm's Abbey, Washington. I wish to thank also Prof. Ellen Ginsberg, Mrs. Ruth Spiegel, and Dr. Mical Schneider for their assistance with linguistic, critical, and historical matters. Mr. Peter Petcoff of the Reference Division of the Library of Congress was extremely helpful in solving bibliographical problems. I am particularly obliged to Prof. Richard A. Jackson of the University of Houston for sharing with me many of his discoveries regarding the sources, dates, and significance of the texts of medieval French coronation *ordines.* I have referred in nn. 7, 20, and 22 below to several of his forthcoming publications on the manuscript sources of the *ordines* and their relationships to one another.

I should like to thank the British Library Board, the Archives photographiques, and the Bibliothèque Nationale for allowing me to publish the photographs of works in their collections.

Robert Cotton, and large parts of the text were printed by Robert Selden in the second edition of *Titles of Honor* published in London in 1631.[1] In turn, Selden's publication was used by the Godefroys for their collection of French coronation *ordines* gathered in the first volume of *Le cérémonial françois.*[2] It was not until the very last year of the nineteenth century that the complete text and a facsimile of all the miniatures were published by E. S. Dewick in the series of liturgical texts sponsored by the Henry Bradshaw Society.

The text of the *Coronation Book of Charles V of France* has been studied extensively as far as it relates to the king, particularly by P. E. Schramm, the foremost modern scholar of coronation *ordines*. Schramm recognized the great importance of the changing aspects of the coronation ceremony in the development of medieval political thought and institutions. Beginning in the Carolingian period in forms blending secular protocol, liturgical formulas, and mystical symbols, the coronation ceremony enunciated the spiritual and constitutional obligations and prerogatives of the ruler vis-à-vis the church and the people. In a series of valuable publications Schramm studied the *ordines* of various European countries stressing both their similarities and their national differences. Especially in his article "Ordines-Studien 2: Die Krönung bei den Westfranken und den Franzosen" Schramm discussed in detail the significance of the *ordo* comprising the main body of the text of the *Coronation Book.*[3] He recognized very clearly and indeed emphasized an important and prominent feature of the manuscript: an extensive cycle of thirty-eight miniatures which accompanies the text.[4] The presence of these illustrations is helpful to the historian in several ways. First, the miniatures furnish important information on the particular details of an actual ceremony. And in conjunction with the date of 1365 on the colophon, the illustrations confirm that the particular coronation ceremonies represented are based upon those of Charles V and his queen Jeanne de Bourbon, which took place in Rheims on Trinity Sunday,

[1] For the history of the manuscript, which was formerly bound with an English Pontifical of the early thirteenth century, see *The Coronation Book of Charles V of France* (Cottonian MS Tiberius B. VIII), Henry Bradshaw Society 16, ed. E. S. Dewick (London 1899) ix-xi. This publication will henceforth be cited as Dewick CB, and the manuscript itself will be referred to as either the *Coronation Book of Charles V of France,* or simply as the *Coronation Book.* For other nineteenth-century discussions of the manuscript, see L. Delisle, "Notes sur quelques manuscrits du Musée brittanique," *Mémoires de la Société de l'histoire de Paris et de l'Ile-de-France* 4 (1877) 226-229, and G. Leroy, "Le livre du sacre des rois, ayant fait partie de la librairie de Charles V, au Louvre, actuellement conservé au British Museum à Londres," *Bulletin historique et philologique du Comité des travaux historiques et scientifiques* (1896) 613-625.

[2] Théodore and Denis Godefroy, *Le cérémonial françois,* 2 vols. (Paris 1649) 1.31-51.

[3] P. E. Schramm, "Ordines-Studien 2: Die Krönung bei den Westfranken und den Franzosen," *Archiv für Urkundenforschung* 15 (1938) 42-47. See also *idem, Der König von Frankreich: Das Wesen der Monarchie vom 9. zum 16. Jahrhundert, ein Kapitel aus der Geschichte des abendländischen Staates,* ed. 2, 2 vols. (Weimar 1960) 1.237-241.

[4] Schramm, "Ordines-Studien" 47.

19 May 1364.[5] It is true that nowhere are these particular rulers identified verbally in the *Coronation Book.* Yet, on the basis of the consistent portrait type of the king, which can be verified by comparison to well-documented images of Charles V in various media, it is clearly the portraits of this particular king which illustrate the text of the *Coronation Book* (fig. 1).[6] And therefore it almost goes without saying that the *ordo ad reginam benedicendam* refers to the specific consecration and coronation of Charles V's consort Jeanne de Bourbon (fig. 2).

Yet, although there are nine miniatures representing the ceremony of the queen – almost twenty-five percent of the total program – this part of the *Coronation Book* has received almost no attention from the point of view of either text or images. Indeed, when one considers that the Jeanne de Bourbon cycle is the first extant historically documented and illustrated account of the coronation of a French queen, this neglect seems even more surprising. Furthermore, the cycle of the queen's ceremony on folios 66 to 72 of the manuscript shows a density of illustration comparable to the twenty-seven images of the Charles V program spread over folios 33 to 65. And while Schramm and others have recognized that the text of the *ordo* devoted to the king's coronation has increased in length in comparison with previous coronation *ordines,* little notice has been taken that this is also the case for the Jeanne de Bourbon portion of the text. A comparison with *ordines* of the queen's ceremony going back to 980 shows that the text for Jeanne de Bourbon's consecration and coronation includes thirteen prayers, almost twice the number included in previous examples.[7]

[5] It was traditional, although not absolutely necessary, that the coronation ceremony take place on a Sunday or on a great feast day of the church. See R. Holtzmann, *Französische Verfassungsgeschichte* (Munich 1910) 120 and 180. According to Prof. R. A. Jackson (letter of 16 August 1974), François II, whose coronation took place on Monday, 18 September 1559, was the only exception to this practice. Charles V's choice of Trinity Sunday as the date of his coronation may have been influenced by at least two considerations. The first is that Philippe VI, the first king of the Valois dynasty, had also been crowned on Trinity Sunday. Charles V may have thus wanted to emphasize the continuity of dynastic tradition. Secondly, Charles V is known to have had a special devotion to the Trinity. See "The *Traité du sacre* of Jean Golein," ed. R. A. Jackson, *Proceedings of the American Philosophical Society* 113.4 (1969) 309. Prof. Jackson's edition of this work will hereafter be cited as Golein, *Traité.* The folio number mentioned in forthcoming citations will be understood as referring to Bibl. Nat., MS fr. 437, the manuscript on which the edition was based. The page number included in brackets in these citations will refer to the specific issue of the periodical named above in which Prof. Jackson's edition appeared. For further information on the history and significance of the *Traité,* see in the text below, passages between nn. 36 and 43.

[6] For other images of Charles V with a close resemblance to the portrait type in the *Coronation Book,* see C. R. Sherman, *The Portraits of Charles V of France (1338-1380),* Monographs on Archaeology and the Fine Arts Sponsored by the Archaeological Institute of America and the College Art Association of America 20 (New York 1969) pls. 1, 2, and 45.

[7] Prior to a new critical edition of the texts of French coronation *ordines,* which Prof. R. A. Jackson intends to undertake, it is necessary to continue to refer to the often inaccurate early printed versions. The citation of manuscript sources and their dates are based on Prof. Jackson's

This lack of interest in both the text and images of the Jeanne de Bourbon *ordo* probably has an obvious explanation. Although evidence exists that queens had exercised considerable political power in the late Carolingian and early Capetian periods, their influence diminished almost totally in this sphere beginning in the middle of the twelfth century.[8] Furthermore, in the crises of the succession to the French throne which occurred from 1316 to 1328 when the last Capetian kings failed to provide direct male heirs to succeed themselves, it was decreed first that no woman could sit on the French throne and then that the succession to the throne could not be transmitted through the female line. Historians are divided in their assessment of the real justification for the exclusion of women from the French throne, which fifteenth-century theorists rationalized by their ex post facto application of the Salic Law.[9]

Nevertheless, the myth of the Salic Law, coupled with the lack of direct political power of French queens in the later medieval and modern periods, has had an extremely unfortunate effect in leading to an underestimation of the considerable roles which French queens continued to play in political and cultural life. For

---

recent research summarized in his paper, "A Reappraisal of the French Coronation *Ordines* of the Middle Ages," read at the Colloque international d'histoire sur les sacres et couronnements royaux, held at Rheims, 9-12 October 1975. The texts of coronation *ordines* which include the ceremony for the French queen begin with that contained in the Fulrad *ordo* dating from about 980 (Paris, Bibl. Nat., MS lat. 12052). See E. Martène, *De antiquis ecclesiae ritibus,* ed. 2, 3 vols. (Antwerp 1736-1737; repr. 1967) 2.609-610. The next text with an *ordo* for the queen to which I shall refer is a French translation of the *ordo* of Rheims (Rheims, Bibl. Municipale, MSS 328, 329, and 330, ca. 1230), probably dating from ca. 1320; Godefroy (n. 2 above) 1.29. A third text containing the ceremony for the queen is found in the *ordo* called by Schramm, "Ordines-Studien" (n. 3 above) 30-33, the Compilation of 1300, now dated ca. 1240 to 1250 (Paris, Bibl. Nat., MS lat. 1246). For the text of this *ordo,* see Godefroy 1.23-25. Another text describing the queen's ceremony is part of the last Capetian *ordo*, dating from about 1250 to 1270 (Paris, Bibl. Nat., MS nouv. acq. lat. 1202), which is also identified as the *ordo* of Sens. For the text, see Martène 2.636. Furthermore, according to Schramm, *Der König* (n. 3 above) 2.4, there is also a French translation of the last Capetian *ordo* with the *ordo* of the queen. For this text, see Godefroy 1.11-12. All the page references to printed sources apply only to the portions of the *ordines* containing the texts of the coronation ceremonies of the queens.

[8] For an informative study of the institutional and social positions of French queens, see M. F. Facinger, "A Study of Medieval Queenship: Capetian France, 987-1237," *Studies in Medieval and Renaissance History* 5 (1968) 3-48.

[9] The Salic Law was "the earliest legal monument of the Frankish people," and the passage in it relating to royal succession pertains to the prohibition against women inheriting land. The law, however, "does not specify that it applies in respect to succession to the throne." See R. E. Giesey, "The Juristic Basis of Dynastic Right to the French Throne," *Transactions of the American Philosophical Society* (TAPhS) n. s. 51.5 (1961) 17-18. This study offers a useful summary of the history of the invocation of the Salic Law with references to the older literature. For the view that the exclusion of women from inheriting the French throne was based on purely political considerations, see P. Viollet, "Comment les femmes ont été exclues, en France, de la succession à la couronne," *Mémoires de l'Institut national de France, Académie des inscriptions et belles-lettres* 34.2 (1895) 125-178. For an opposite argument that the sacerdotal character of French kingship would by definition exclude women from the office, see F. Lot and R. Fawtier, *Histoire des institutions françaises au moyen âge,* 3 vols. (Paris 1957-1962) 2.19.

example, French queens did have direct influence in the political sphere when they acted as regents in the event of the king's absence or death when the heir to the throne was a minor.[10] Moreover, queens frequently exercised political power indirectly because of their close relationship with the king, and in this way had considerable influence.[11] In his pioneer compilation the *Recueil des roys de France* written in the sixteenth century, Jean du Tillet outlined the special legal rights and standing of French queens.[12]

In addition the very significant roles of French queens as patrons and promoters of the arts in the medieval and later periods demand further identification and study. Certainly considerable visual evidence exists of their important part in the social and cultural life of their time. French queens were often honored in monumental sculpture as donors or benefactors of religious institutions, while their images also appear in Books of Hours or other volumes destined for their own use. Their *gisants* lay next to those of their husbands and relatives not only in the royal necropolis of Saint-Denis but in other religious foundations to which the royal family had strong ties. In his section on the authority and prerogatives of French queens, Du Tillet emphasized their high moral and spiritual status.[13] Not only are their likenesses in works of art concrete proof of their high status, but another indication of it occurs when, along with the kings of France, queens were honored on the portals of Saint-Denis and of Chartres in the guise of Old Testament rulers and heroines.[14] In the ceremonies of their consecration and coronation, connected in the earlier medieval period with marriage vows and blessings, the wives of French kings became royal persons endowed with high social prestige and with spiritual and moral authority as well.[15]

Thus, a general purpose of this study is to suggest that the visual and verbal evidence concerning the historical roles of medieval French queens must be assembled and considered together in a fresh spirit of inquiry. I have focussed here on one such example. The text and images describing the consecration and coronation of Jeanne de Bourbon in 1364 constitute one section in the *Coronation Book of Charles V of France.* Yet in order to solve the central problem of the unusual prominence of both the verbal and visual elements of the *ordo ad reginam benedicendam,* I had first to address in Parts II and III of this study a series of both narrow and wider considerations. My purpose in these two sections is to place the

[10] For a discussion of queens of France as regents, see P. Viollet, *Histoire des institutions politiques et administratives de la France,* 4 vols. (Paris 1890-1912; repr. 1966) 2.86-96.

[11] Facinger (n. 8 above) 47.

[12] J. du Tillet, *Recueil des roys de France, leurs couronne et maison* (Paris 1607) 255-259. (The book was published posthumously.) See also A. Luchaire, *Manuel des institutions françaises* (Paris 1892) 478.

[13] Du Tillet 255.

[14] A. Katzenellenbogen, *The Sculptural Programs of Chartres Cathedral* (Baltimore 1959) 28-32.

[15] Luchaire (n. 12 above) 477; Facinger (n. 8 above) 17-18.

subsequent interpretation of both the text and the images of the queen's cycle within a meaningful critical and historical framework.

An obvious priority was the need to examine certain key relationships pertaining to the manuscript as a whole. For this reason, Part II of the study centers chiefly on the *Coronation Book of Charles V.* Among the topics discussed are the history of the manuscript, the motives of the patron and his role in its production, as well as the underlying relationships between text and miniatures. In addition, another primary source, essential also to our understanding of the *ordo ad reginam benedicendam* in the *Coronation Book,* required an introduction. Commissioned directly by Charles V himself, this commentary interprets the symbolic and political meaning of the coronation rites of French rulers. A short work, it is inserted in Jean Golein's translation from Latin into French of Durandus's *Rationale divinorum officiorum* (Paris, Bibliothèque Nationale, MS fr. 437). Golein's commentary, known as the *Traité du sacre*, has a close, if somewhat complex, relationship to the *Coronation Book.*[16]

The relatively narrow focus of Part II contrasts with Part III of the study, which is concerned with a general examination of the character and symbolism of practices and texts regarding the coronation of medieval French queens. Then, with the perspective gained from both the specific study of the manuscript itself and from the outline of the historical traditional underlying it, Part IV offers in an integrated manner an analysis of the text and images of the Jeanne de Bourbon cycle. Where relevant, comparisons to analogous sections of the king's portion of the manuscript are also included. In Part V the outstanding characteristics of the *ordo ad reginam benedicendam* are related to the historical situation of the monarchy in 1364. The concluding remarks of Part VI summarize the methods followed and the results obtained in the study as a whole.

II. The Coronation Book of Charles V as a Whole: History, Patron, Program, and Text-Image Relationships

The *Coronation Book* begins with a translation into French dating from about 1320 of the Rheims *ordo* of a century earlier, the texts of the coronation oaths, and a list of the peers of France on folios 35v to 42v. But the main part of the manuscript in Latin from folios 43 to 74 is devoted to the coronation ceremonies of the king and queen of France concluding with the blessing of the oriflamme and the litanies. From folio 75 to the end of the manuscript on folio 80, there follow the oaths of the peers of France and of high officers of the crown. The manuscript has intact forty-six of its forty-eight folios, which were written in six quires of eight folios each. The seventh folio of the second quire (between folios 48 and 49) and the fifth folio of

[16] For further discussion of the *Traité*, see n. 5 above and n. 37 below.

the third quire (between folios 53 and 54) are missing. In addition, the lower margins of folios 45 and 71 have been cut off, probably for the sake of the miniatures. The size of the folios is 11 by 7 1/2 inches, with twenty lines of text per page.[17]

Despite these minor losses, the *Coronation Book* is largely intact and generally in very good condition. Nevertheless, certain problems remain primarily in relation to the text. For example, there is no external proof one way or another that the *ordo* in the *Coronation Book* was actually used during the coronation of Charles V and Jeanne de Bourbon in 1364. Schramm believed it unlikely in the less than two months between the death of Charles V's father Jean le Bon on 8 April 1364 – the news of which did not reach Paris until the sixteenth of that month – and the date of the coronation on 19 May that there was enough time to compile such a complex body of material.[18] Schramm recognized the dependence of the Charles V *ordo* on the text of the last Capetian *ordo*, the so-called *ordo of Sens*, now dated from between about 1250 to 1270.[19] The extent of the derivation of the Charles V *ordo* from the last Capetian *ordo* has been reinforced both by the recent discovery of a manuscript of this text with possible royal connections as well as by the current research of Professor R. A. Jackson in official archival sources.[20] Although the Charles V *ordo* shows significant departures from the last Capetian *ordo*, as Schramm pointed out, they are substantially limited to a few key areas.

Furthermore, the colophon may yield some insight into the question. Charles V wrote in his own hand the following words found on folio 74v of the manuscript:

> Ce liure. du. sacre. dez Rois. de france/ est a nous Charles. le ve. de. Notre nom. Roy. de france. et le. fimes. Coriger. ordener. Escrire. et. istorier. lan. m.ccc.lx.v.
>
> Charles[21]

[17] Dewick CB (n. 1 above) xi.

[18] Schramm, "Ordines-Studien" (n. 3 above) 43-44.

[19] *Ibid.* 45.

[20] For an incomplete manuscript containing the last Capetian *ordo*, see H. Bober, "The Coronation Book of Charles IV and Jeanne d'Évreux," in *Rare Books: Notes on the History of Old Books and Manuscripts Published for the Friends and Clients of H. P. Kraus* 8.3 (1958) 1-12. For further discussion of the association of this manuscript with these two rulers, see n. 28 below. For the close relationship of the various portions of MS Cotton Tiberius B. VIII to the now destroyed register of the Chambre des comptes in Paris called *Croix*, see R. A. Jackson, "The Manuscript Coronation *Ordines* in the Library of Charles V of France," *Le moyen âge* (forthcoming). For an older evaluation of the dependence of the Charles V *ordo* on the last Capetian *ordo*, see R. Delachenal, *Histoire de Charles V*, 5 vols. (Paris 1909-1931) 3.66-67 n. 3. In this note, Delachenal mentioned that the Charles V *ordo* may have been derived from a specific manuscript containing this text, a pontifical identified as belonging to Guillaume II de Melun. archbishop of Sens (British Library, MS Egerton 931). See G. Leroy, "Note sur *le pontifical de Guillaume II de Melun*, archevêque de Sens (1346-1378)," *Bulletin historique et philologique du Comité des travaux historiques et scientifiques* (1896) 557-62. Prof. Jackson does not agree with Delachenal's thesis.

[21] The translations of cited passages have been provided by me. "This book of the consecration of the kings of France belongs to us, Charles the fifth of our name, king of France, and we

As Schramm stressed, no other extant *ordo* shows such direct evidence of the ruler's participation in its composition. In addition, the colophon states that Charles V's first step in overseeing the execution of the manuscript was to have the book corrected before arranging for its organization, its copying, and its illustration. This phrasing suggests that Charles V may have had a pre-existing text – probably based on a manuscript of the last Capetian *ordo* – corrected to conform to the ritual which took place at his coronation. Indeed, Jackson's latest work on the liturgical additions to the last Capetian *ordo* in the king's portion of the *Coronation Book of Charles V* tends to confirm the hypothesis that the *ordo* in the *Coronation Book* (but not MS Cotton Tiberius B. VIII itself) was actually used for the ceremony of 1364.[22] As is the case with the text of the queen's *ordo* in the *Coronation Book,* the political and symbolic significance of these liturgical additions can be directly related to the historical situation of the monarchy in 1364.

Furthermore, throughout his reign Charles V was to excel in using royal ceremonial as a means of restoring the prestige of the monarchy following the disastrous first phase of the Hundred Years' War. What could have marked a more suitable beginning for this effort than the coronation ceremony, and a means of commemorating it in the *Coronation Book,* a kind of perpetual memory of its grandeur? The pomp and splendor attached not only to the ritual itself but to the king's *entrée* into Rheims and to the events following the coronation were clear indications that a new and splendid phase of the French monarchy, and of the Valois dynasty in particular, had begun. Secondly, the text of the coronation ceremony offered opportunities by way of the symbolism of protocol and of certain regalia to emphasize the special status of the monarchy. One example is the section in the *Coronation Book* in which the king dons gloves like those of a bishop, thus bolstering the claim that the king has a quasi-clerical status.[23] Two miniatures illustrating this procedure emphasize its meaning in a direct and specific manner.[24] In short, Charles V's active role in composing and arranging the *ordo* and its illustration are consistent with his use of all types of royal ceremonial and with his patronage of art to raise the prestige of the monarchy. The ceremony of 19 May 1364 and its commemoration in the *Coronation Book* marked the initial stage of such efforts at the beginning of his reign. During this same period, Charles V set in motion two commissions of monumental sculpture honoring the Valois dynasty.[25]

---

had it corrected, arranged, written, and illustrated in the year 1365." See Dewick CB (n. 1 above) fol. 74v, col. 54, and pl. 39.

[22] For Schramm's view on the colophon of the *Coronation Book,* see "Ordines-Studien" (n. 3 above) 43. The changes in the liturgy of the king's portion of the Charles V *ordo* from that of the last Capetian *ordo* will be discussed in chap. 3 of Prof. Jackson's forthcoming book tentatively entitled *Vivat Rex: The French Coronation Ceremony from Charles V to Charles X.*

[23] Schramm, *Der König* (n. 3 above) 1.238.

[24] For the miniatures on folios 56-57 showing first the anointing of the king's hands, followed by the archbishop's blessing, and the king's donning of the gloves, see Dewick CB (n. 1 above) pls. 18-20.

[25] See P. Pradel, "Art et politique sous Charles V," *Revue des arts* 1 (1951) 89-93, and Sherman (n. 6 above) 58-60 and 66-68.

It is perhaps appropriate at this point to define more concretely the place and functions of the illustrations within the *Coronation Book*. As we recall, the colophon informs us that Charles V had an active role in arranging for the illustration of the manuscript. The king's fondness for illuminated manuscripts in his magnificent library of about a thousand volumes is well known.[26] His appreciation extended from the lavishly decorated volumes inherited from his Capetian and Valois ancestors to new works especially commissioned by him. These included texts previously without any, or with only sparse, programs of illustrations. I do not mean, however, that French coronation texts were not previously illustrated. In a pontifical manuscript in Paris (Bibliothèque Nationale, MS lat. 1246) dating from before 1250, fifteen miniatures divided into thirty separate scenes represent the various steps in the coronation ceremony in a detailed but general fashion without specific references to individuals or to a particular historical event.[27] Furthermore, in a manuscript dated by Professor H. Bober to the year 1326 by virtue of his association of the text and heraldic emblems with the coronation of Charles IV and Jeanne d'Évreux on the occasion of their marriage, a series of twenty-two historiated initials also represent in a general manner the various stages of the coronation ceremonies of a king and queen.[28]

If miniatures on the missing folios of the *Coronation Book* are included, there were well over forty representations of the narrative sequence of the parts of the ceremony. In conjunction with the rubrics of the text, the miniatures of the *Coronation Book* offer a step-by-step guide on how the ceremony proceeded. Indeed, the illuminations act as visual equivalents of the instructions in the rubrics, which are the specific sources for almost all the illustrations in the manuscript. The miniatures are placed in close proximity to the rubrics, on the same or on the next folio. Although occasionally two acts listed successively in the rubrics are combined in one miniature, the individual illustrations usually permit the reader to follow the exact sequence of actions indicated in the rubrics. In contrast, the various liturgical segments of the text are not illustrated at all. The miniatures also serve to supplement the information given in the rubrics as to important details of costume, of attendants, and of the physical positions of the principal actors in relation to one

[26] The standard work on Charles V's library is L. Delisle, *Recherches sur la librairie de Charles V*, 2 vols. (Paris 1907). For an excellent recent study, see the exhibition catalog, Bibliothèque Nationale, *La librairie de Charles V*, ed. F. Avril (Paris 1968).

[27] V. Leroquais, *Les pontificaux manuscrits des bibliothèques publiques de France*, 3 vols. (Paris 1937) 2.145-146, pls. 30-36, cited by Bober (n. 20 above) 7.

[28] Bober (n. 20 above) 7. See also Jackson (n. 7 above) at nn. 41-42. Prof. Bober's identification of this manuscript with the actual *ordo* used on the occasion of the marriage and coronation of Charles IV and his third wife, Jeanne d'Évreux, on 11 May 1326 at the Sainte-Chapelle in Paris is not convincing. Charles IV had already been consecrated and crowned at Rheims in 1321. It was not the practice for the entire ceremony to be repeated in the case of the king's subsequent marriage, when the queen would be crowned separately. On such an occasion, the king would simply don his crown; Du Tillet (n. 12 above) 264. See also H. Pinoteau, "La tenue de sacre de saint Louis IX, roi de France," *Itinéraires* 162 (1972) 128-129 n. 20.

another. Sometimes essential details of protocol not specifically mentioned in the text are furnished in the miniatures. In short, the illustrations function as supplements to the narrative information supplied in the text by giving specific details of how the complex ceremony was enacted in a dignified and majestic manner. The illustrations, then, serve as *exempla* in particular of the general instructions found in the rubrics, and generally appear to be founded on the procedures followed in the coronation ceremonies of Charles V and of Jeanne de Bourbon.

The elaborate program of miniatures accompanying the text may not have been intended when the book was first designed. Only six of the more than forty illustrations which ultimately were executed occur in the body of the text. The rest are located in the space originally left for the lower margin of the page. Evidence that the miniatures in the lower margin may not have been part of the original design of the book occurs in the several instances where the top of an illustration's frame extends into the penscroll of an initial in the line of the text directly above it (fig. 8). Furthermore, the crooked lines of the bottom of the frames and the uneven placement of several illustrations in the king's cycle – two examples are found in the lower margins of folios 56v and 57 – indicate that these miniatures may not have been included in the first design of the book. Possibly it was Charles V himself who was dissatisfied with the limited number of miniatures and then called for the present greatly augmented program of illustration. These remarks do not imply that the additional miniatures were executed at any great interval after the first illustrations were inserted in the text. The prevalence of the same types of background patterns, consistency in costume, and execution of miniatures both in the text and in the lower margins by the same members of the workshop would argue for an intervention by the king at an early stage in the preparation of the book.

Another question is the identity of the person who may have furnished a set of detailed instructions to the chief illuminator of the workshop. These instructions, founded on the rubrics, were probably provided by the same man who compiled the text under Charles V's supervision and who must have been an eyewitness at the coronation in Rheims cathedral on 19 May 1364. Although extant evidence is all too rare, enough remains to suggest that the master of the text would be the likely candidate to provide a written set of instructions for the illuminator to follow.[29] In the case of the *Coronation Book,* where accuracy was essential in details such as the peers' identifying heraldic mantles or the king's regalia, one would assume the need for a very specific set of verbal instructions probably accompanied by visual models. Unfortunately, I am unable to identify conclusively the individual responsible both

[29] For an excellent example, dated ca. 1417, of a verbal set of instructions provided by the master of the text for the benefit of the illuminator, see J. Lebègue, *Les histoires que l'on peut raisonnablement faire sur les livres de Salluste,* introd. J. Porcher (Paris 1962). For the possible role of a translator employed by Charles V acting in this capacity, see C. R. Sherman, "The Programs of the Miniatures in the Oldest Illustrated Copies of Aristotle's *Nicomachean Ethics* in the French Translation by Nicole Oresme," *Codicologica* 7 (forthcoming).

for the compilation of the *Coronation Book* text and the program of illustrations. Likely candidates might come from the group of clerics who operated a kind of "public relations" bureau for Charles V. These men translated existing texts or wrote new ones favorable to the theoretical or institutional bases of monarchical power.[30] Prominent in this circle were Raoul de Presles, who translated Augustine's *City of God* in the early 1370s, and Nicole Oresme, translator in the same decade of various Aristotelian texts, and whose relationship with the royal family was of long standing. Another obvious candidate is the Carmelite monk Jean Golein whose *Traitê du sacre* forms an important part of this study. Golein was a Norman, established in Paris first as a student and then as a professor of theology at the university beginning in 1349. Golein wrote a now-lost life of the natal patron saint of Charles V, Saint Agnes, before he began to translate at the king's command several surviving texts of historical works. These translations apparently date from the late 1360s.[31] And Charles V's later request that Golein write a commentary on his coronation might possibly indicate a prior personal familiarity with the events of 19 May 1364.[32]

The veristic treatment of the individual miniatures in terms of an accurate narrative description of specific historical events and personalities nevertheless owed a great deal to the Master of the *Coronation Book of Charles V,* as he has been called by F. Avril.[33] Although to modern eyes the rendering of space or the movement of figures in the *Coronation Book* miniatures looks quite primitive, it would be a mistake to underestimate the degree of artistic innovation present in the cycles depicting the coronations of Charles V and of Jeanne de Bourbon. One of these outstanding characteristics is the portrait likeness of the king, which extends also to other leading personalities such as the archbishop of Rheims (fig. 15). A naturalistic approach includes attempts to render such complex settings as those of Rheims cathedral (fig. 4), the archiepiscopal palace, and the platform which the king ascended for his enthronement (fig. 17). Particular attention is devoted to the representation of the high altar, decorated in various fashions with altarpieces of clearly identifiable subjects (figs. 6 and 8). A carefully controlling hand must have been responsible for the consistency of the portrait types of Charles V and of Jeanne de Bourbon, the groupings of the main actors, and the carefully delineated costumes. This achievement is all the more impressive in view of the varying quality of the different hands involved in the execution of the thirty-eight surviving miniatures. The dry, incisive style of the Master of the *Coronation Book of Charles V,* so appropriate in view of the almost diagrammatic nature of the illustrations, was much appreciated both by Charles V and his father. According to Avril, this master worked for the

[30] See Schramm, *Der König* (n. 3 above) 1.242-43.

[31] For Golein's early career and the beginning of his literary commissions for Charles V, see J. P. Williman, "*Le racional des divins offices:* An Introduction and Partial Edition," Ph. D. diss. (University of North Carolina 1967) 43-47 and 49-59.

[32] See below in the text at nn. 41-42.

[33] Avril (n. 26 above) 89.

royal family from the 1350s until the end of Charles V's reign, on texts ranging from a *Bible historiale* to Aristotle's *Politics* and the *Grandes chroniques de France.*[34] As G. Schmidt has observed, the Master of the *Coronation Book of Charles V* does not seem to come from the contemporary Paris tradition of manuscript illumination.[35] Nor does his harsh, linear style have any of the painterly qualities associated with Netherlandish artists such as Jean Bondol of Bruges. Furthermore, the Master's interest in details of setting and costume does not necessarily suggest a specific national or regional origin.

One more topic related to the *Coronation Book* as a whole needs further discussion: Jean Golein's commentary on the coronation. As we may recall, Golein inserted it in the first book of his translation of Durandus's liturgical encyclopedia of about 1291, the *Rationale divinorum officiorum.* The title, *Traitê du sacre,* is a modern one given to it by Marc Bloch when he published for the first time large portions of Golein's commentary as an appendix to *Les rois thaumaturges.*[36] The complete text of the *Traitê* was made available only in the late 1960s by two scholars working independently of one another.[37] Golein's *Traitê* follows the section in the *Rationale* on anointments and sacraments; and in its use of diverse kinds of symbolism to explain the meaning and significance of the coronation ceremony of French rulers, it is very much in the spirit of the original work.

The *Traitê du sacre* occupies folios 43v to 54v in Charles V's own copy of the *Rational des divins offices* (Paris, Bibliothèque Nationale, MS fr. 437). The colophon in the king's own hand carrying the date 1374 again bears witness to Charles V's active role in the commissioning and writing of manuscripts:

> Cest livre nomme Rasional des divins ofises est à nous Charles le Ve de notre nom, et le fimes tranlater, escrire, et tout parfere, etc., l'an mil CCCLXXIIII.[38]

Furthermore, in the *Traitê* Golein himself tells us that the king wanted Golein's commentary to be included in the translation of the *Rationale*:

> Et say bien que le grant prudence du souverain seigneur qui me fait translater ceste consecracion. cest assavoir le sage piteux Roy charles le quint . . . .[39]

[34] *Ibid.* nos. 167, 170, 195, 196, and 203.

[35] G. Schmidt, review of C. R. Sherman, *The Portraits of Charles V of France (1338-1380), Zeitschrift für Kunstgeschichte* 34 (1971) 76.

[36] M. Bloch, *Les rois thaumaturges: Étude sur le caractère surnaturel attribué à la puissance royale particulièrement en France et en Angleterre* (Paris 1961) 479-489.

[37] See n. 5 above for the edition of the *Traité* by R. A. Jackson, which is used in this study. The second complete version of the *Traité* is found in the yet unpublished dissertation of J. P. Williman (n. 31 above) as part of his edition of Golein's translation of the *Rationale divinorum officiorum* of Durandus.

[38] "This book called *Rational of Divine Offices* belongs to us, Charles, the fifth of our name, and we had it translated, written, and brought to completion in the year 1374." Paris, Bibl. Nat., MS fr. 437, fol. 402v.

[39] "And I acknowledge the great prudence of the sovereign lord who had me translate this consecration, that is, the wise and merciful king Charles V." Golein, *Traité* fol. 53v [323].

In this connection, the word *tranlater* probably connotes a paraphrase or commentary rather than an exact translation of a work from a foreign language. Although in general the *Traitê* follows the liturgical sequence of the ceremonies of Charles V and Jeanne de Bourbon in the *Coronation Book,* there are enough divergencies in Golein's commentary to support his statement that the specific source for his treatise was a pontifical which belonged to the archbishop of Rheims:

> La quele fu faite en ordenance si comme il est mis ou pontifical de larcevesque de Reins. de la quele ci ensuyvant sera declare la signifiance.[40]

In addition to the still unidentified pontifical, Jackson believes that Golein also consulted the *ordo* of Rheims, as well as a copy of the last Capetian *ordo.*[41] Of course, it is also possible that Golein may have consulted the *Coronation Book,* as well as other *ordines* in Charles V's library without mentioning them. Indeed, as we shall see, in several instances Golein's commentary suggests his familiarity with the miniatures of the Jeanne de Bourbon cycle, or with the actual events of the coronation ceremony.

Golein's account of the queen's coronation occupied folios 50 and 51 of the *Traitê.* At the beginning of this section, he mentioned specifically Jeanne de Bourbon's consecration, confirming evidence that his point of reference was the particular ceremony of 1364.[42] In the concluding section of the *Traitê* devoted to a discussion of the symbolism of the fleur-de-lis and the oriflamme, Golein returned to the subject of the queen's coronation in connection with the important contemporary issue of the exclusion of women from the French throne.[43] Golein's commentary offers an official contemporary reading of the political and theoretical implications of the queen's coronation emanating directly from the king's own circle. The value of the *Traitê* for our analysis of the Jeanne de Bourbon cycle in the *Coronation Book* accounts for our inclusion of the relevant sections in our discussion of these miniatures.

As a necessary introduction to the Jeanne de Bourbon cycle, the history and significance of the *Coronation Book* as a whole have been reviewed. The circumstances of its commission, the role of the patron, and the relationship of the manuscript's text to the actual ceremony held in 1364 were points important to our

[40] "Which was done according to the arrangement as it is found in the pontifical of the archbishop of Rheims, the significance of which will be explained below." *Ibid.* fol. 44 [310].

[41] Letter of 16 August 1974. Prof. Jackson does not think, however, that Golein was acquainted directly with the Charles V *ordo*.

[42] "Et pource est aussi la Royne sacree. et le fu avec mon dit souverain seigneur Madame Jehanne de bourbon fille de noble prince le duc de bourbon qui estoit descendu dycelle sainte lignie et estoit sa cousine. mais par la dispensacion de leglise il lot a espouse." ("And for this reason the queen is also consecrated, and so [along] with the afore-mentioned sovereign lord, was consecrated Madame Jeanne de Bourbon, daughter of the noble prince, the duke of Bourbon, who was descended from this noble line and was his cousin; but by the dispensation of the church he had married her.") Golein, *Traité* (n. 5 above) fol. 43v [309].

[43] See text passages below at n. 54, between nn. 76-77, and preceding n. 140.

understanding of the *ordo ad reginam benedicendam*. Other topics touching on the production and character of the manuscript involved a discussion of the general relationships between the text and the images in the *Coronation Book*, as well as the problem of identifying the person responsible for furnishing the program of verbal instructions to the illuminator. The latter was a personality very much in favor with Charles V throughout the reign. Finally, the significance of Jean Golein's *Traitê du sacre* for this study was proposed and defined.

III. The Character and Symbolism of Practices and Texts Regarding the Coronation of Medieval French Queens and Their Relationship to the Jeanne de Bourbon Cycle of Miniatures in the Coronation Book

Beginning in the Carolingian period with the marriage in 856 of Judith, daughter of Charles the Bald, to Aethelwulf, king of East Anglia, it became the practice to crown queens in the context of marriage vows and nuptial blessings.[44] Later, under the Capetian dynasty, the coronation of French queens continued, first in connection with the marriage ceremony. After the end of the twelfth century, however, the two ceremonies were separated.[45] Although the political authority of the queen almost disappeared after 1200, she nevertheless continued to play an important role in the official and ceremonial life of the reign and "to function both as an agent and as a symbol of royalty."[46] The importance of the queen's coronation did not diminish, since emphasis on more elaborate forms of royal ceremonial continued to develop. When circumstances permitted the queen to be crowned together with the king, the joint ceremony took place at Rheims cathedral, with the archbishop of Rheims as the chief officiant, more or less regularly from about 1223 to 1364.[47] If the queen was crowned separately from the king, her coronation would not take place at Rheims. During the thirteenth and fourteenth centuries, the separate coronation of the queen

[44] Schramm, *Der König* (n. 3 above) 1.21.

[45] Facinger (n. 8 above) 17-20.

[46] *Ibid*. 46 and 47.

[47] Although the right of the archbishop of Rheims to be the chief executant of the coronation ceremony was recognized earlier, it was only at the beginning of the twelfth century that the privilege of Rheims cathedral to be the established place for the king's coronation was definitely acknowledged. Beginning in 1129 with the consecration of Philippe, eldest son of Louis VI, all the kings of France except Henri IV were crowned there. See G. Péré, *Le sacre et le couronnement des rois de France dans leurs rapports avec les lois fondamentales* (Bagnères-de-Bigorre 1921) 24. In the period 1223-1350, the following queens were crowned together with their husbands at Rheims: Blanche de Castille and Louis VIII in 1223, Jeanne de Navarre and Philippe IV in 1286, Clémence de Hongrie and Louis X in 1315, Jeanne de Bourgogne (also known as Jeanne I d'Artois) and Philippe V in 1317, Jeanne de Bourgogne and Philippe VI in 1328, and Jeanne de Boulogne and Jean le Bon in 1350. See Du Tillet (n. 12 above) 264, and G. Marlot, *Le théâtre d'honneur et de magnificence préparé au sacre des roys* (Rheims 1643) 429-432.

took place several times at Saint-Denis and also at the Sainte Chapelle in Paris. But beginning in the fifteenth century, Saint-Denis was almost exclusively the coronation church of French queens.[48] Indeed, Jeanne de Bourbon was the last French queen to be crowned at Rheims with her husband.[49]

Aside from its purpose in serving to give the queen the status of a royal person, the coronation ceremony had some practical aspects as well. Among them were the consequent affirmation of the dynastic rights of existing or future offspring, or the ability of the queen to act as regent if need should arise. As in certain prayers in the coronation ceremony of her husband, the liturgy emphasized the queen's obligations vis-à-vis the people, mainly of a moral nature. For instance, her acceptance of a ring, symbol of the Holy Trinity, obliged her to combat heresy, and she also undertook to look out for the interests of the poor.[50] On the other hand, spiritual help in carrying out her responsibilities came to the queen through the liturgy. The paradigmatic prayers in the coronation *ordines* in which the hope was voiced that the virtues of the kings of the Old Testament would be bestowed on their descendants, the rulers of France, had their counterpart in the analogous prayers for French queens.[51] Among their models were Sarah, Rebecca, Leah, Rachel, Judith, and Esther. The first three particularly had specific relevance to an essential function of a queen: her ability to bear children. It was appropriate in the context of marriage followed by consecration and coronation that the unction particularly was supposed to assure the fertility of the queen in a supernatural, almost magical fashion.[52]

Actual texts of *ordines* for French queens from the thirteenth and fourteenth centuries followed temporally those of the kings and generally adopted the same sequence in receiving the unction and then the regalia. But because of the limitations on her temporal sovereignty, certain essential parts of the king's ceremony, such as his oaths to the church and the people, were not included in the queen's *ordo*. Thus

[48] Among the queens crowned separately from the king in the thirteenth and fourteenth centuries in the Sainte Chapelle, Paris, were Marie de Brabant, second wife of Philippe III, in 1275, and the second and third wives of Charles IV, Marie de Bohème in 1323 and Jeanne d'Évreux in 1326; Godefroy (n. 2 above) 1.468-469. On such occasions the archbishop of Rheims or of Sens would officiate. See Holtzmann (n. 5 above) 181. Although consecration was usually part of the coronation ceremony for the queen, it was not always included. On this last point, see also Schramm, *Der König* (n. 3 above) 1.203, n. 1. For a recent summary of the dates and places of the coronations of French queens, see F. Barry, *La reine de France* (Paris 1965) 79-84. In 1610 Marie de' Medici became the last French queen to be crowned (*ibid.* 81 and 84).

[49] See Jackson (n. 5 above) 318 n. 102.

[50] Dewick CB (n. 1 above) fol. 68v, col. 47.

[51] Katzenellenbogen (n. 14 above) 31.

[52] For an important discussion of the relationship between the anointing of the queen and fertility, see E. H. Kantorowicz, "The Carolingian King in the *Bible of San Paolo fuori le mura*," in *Selected Studies*, ed. R. E. Giesey and M. Cherniavsky (Locust Valley, N. Y. 1965) 87-88. For an interesting discussion of the treatment of Old Testament women in medieval thought and literature, see E. Brown, Jr., "Biblical Women in the *Merchant's Tale*: Feminism, Antifeminism, and Beyond," *Viator* 5 (1974) 387-412.

the coronation ceremony for the queen was much shorter than her husband's. Moreover, the *ordines* traditionally specified that several of the symbols of the queen's rank and office should be different from and inferior to those of the king.[53] To begin with, the queen's throne was traditionally smaller than the king's, and it was placed on the less honorable, or left side of the choir, rather than on the right. The most important differences between the ceremonies of the king and the queen lay in the procedure regarding the unction. Unlike the king, the queen was not anointed with balm contained in the Sainte Ampoule, miraculously sent from heaven on the occasion of the baptism of Clovis and carefully preserved in Rheims at the abbey of Saint-Remi.[54] This heavenly balm was the source of the superiority of French kings over those of other nations, as well as of their thaumaturgic powers to cure scrofula, and of their quasi-sacerdotal status. The queen, however, did not share in these powers, as she was entitled only to be anointed with ordinary consecrated oil. Moreover, the queen was anointed just on her head and chest, in contrast to the far more extensive anointings of the king on other parts of his body.[55]

Although the text of the *ordines* seem to make no distinction regarding the form of the ring the king and queen received, her scepter – symbol of royal temporal authority – was traditionally smaller than and different from that of the king.[56] While the *ordines* state that the queen's rod could be like the king's, he was usually depicted with the *main de justice,* symbolizing his essential responsibility for carrying out justice.[57] Evidence is lacking that the queen was entitled to don the blue mantle of state emblazoned with the fleur-de-lis, at least in the Charles V period.[58] The final royal symbol was the crown, which the archbishop of Rheims only placed on the queen's head. In the king's ceremony, the peers of France were required to support his crown and to escort him to his throne. In contrast, the rubrics for the queen's *ordo* stipulate that only barons supported her crown, and together with her "more noble women" they led the queen to her throne. The queen was accompanied by these attendants during the closing part of the ceremony during which the Mass was celebrated. Unlike the king, she received no kiss of homage or acclamation when she was enthroned. But the queen took part in making the traditional gifts during the

[53] For an example of the rubrics which specify inferior regalia symbolic of the queen's lesser rank, see the French translation of the Rheims *ordo* in Dewick CB (n. 1 above) fol. 40, col. 10.

[54] For the legend of Clovis and the Sainte Ampoule, see Bloch (n. 36 above) 224-229.

[55] See Dewick CB fol. 68, col. 46. Although the number of and places for the king's anointing varied in different periods, Charles V received a seven-fold anointing. The Charles V *ordo* specifies anointing on the top of the king's head, on his chest, between his shoulders, on his elbows, and on his hands. See *ibid.* fol. 53v, col. 28.

[56] For this specification, see *ibid.* fol. 40, col. 10.

[57] Lot and Fawtier (n. 9 above) 2.289.

[58] H. Pinoteau, "Quelques réflexions sur l'oeuvre de Jean du Tillet et la symbolique royale française," *Archives héraldiques suisses* 70 (1956) 19. For Golein's statement that the queen is not entitled to the king's fleur-de-lis banner, symbol of sovereignty, see *Traité* (n. 5 above) fol. 54 [323], and below at n. 141.

offertory procession, and she was entitled along with the king to receive communion in both kinds, a particular privilege of French rulers.[59]

These traditional distinctions between the consecration and coronation of the French king and queen continued in the text of the *Coronation Book of Charles V.* Though the ceremony for Jeanne de Bourbon occupies seven folios (fols. 66 through 72) compared to twenty-three for Charles V's portion (fols. 43 through 65), the text for the queen's rite has been greatly expanded. It contains almost twice the number of liturgical elements as do other *ordines* for the queen dating from the thirteenth and fourteenth centuries.[60] Although Schramm and others have strongly emphasized the greatly increased length of the Charles V *ordo,* it did not necessarily follow that the Jeanne de Bourbon section also show such a dramatic increase. Moreover, the queen's cycle is slightly more densely illustrated than the king's, if one compares the nine miniatures in the seven folios of the queen's *ordo* to twenty-seven miniatures in twenty-three folios of the king's portion. It is worth noting that only one of the Jeanne de Bourbon miniatures in the queen's *ordo* occurs in the text. The rest, added very possibly because of the king's intervention, are found on the bottom margins.

The ten or eleven original miniatures of the Jeanne de Bourbon cycle – one or two have been lost – were not, however, the first illustrations of an *ordo* for a French queen. One recent precedent was the fragment of the coronation book now in the University of Illinois at Urbana. As we may recall, Bober has associated the book with the occasion of the marriage and coronation of Jeanne d'Évreux in 1326.[61] Eight small historiated initials, including seven connected with the narrative sequence, decorate the text for the queen's rite. But these representations of a queen are extremely generalized in character, with no apparent individualized portraits or specific setting.[62] In contrast, as in the preceding Charles V cycle in the *Coronation Book,* the Jeanne de Bourbon miniatures are distinguished by narrative clarity and an attempt to create consistent portrait-types of the leading actors and of specific costumes and settings.

In order to avoid unnecessary repetition in the discussion of the individual scenes of the Jeanne de Bourbon cycle, I should like now to review certain constant elements in these representations. Perhaps the most striking feature of the queen's appearance is her long hair, which falls freely around her face (fig. 3). In contrast, her female attendants, with the exception of the women with a widow's coif, have the fashion-

[59] Dewick CB fol. 40 rv, cols. 10-11. For the significance of the communion as a royal privilege, see Schramm, *Der König* (n. 3 above) 1.239, and Bloch (n. 36 above) 205-208.

[60] For identification of these *ordines*, see n. 7 above.

[61] For my reservations about this association, see n. 28 above.

[62] For a reproduction of one of the narrative historiated initials in the University of Illinois manuscript showing the queen receiving the scepter and the rod, see Bober (n. 20 above) pl. 7. Other initials in the manuscript depicting stages of a queen's coronation show her being anointed on the head, receiving the ring, being crowned, and being supported on the throne. The head of a queen on fol. 23, reproduced in pl. 9 of the Bober article, is too conventional to be identified with a specific person.

able side-plaits which Jeanne de Bourbon wears in her well-known portraits (fig. 2). The requirement of unbound tresses is not found in the rubrics of the *Coronation Book* itself, but *crine soluto* is specified in another *ordo.*[63] The need to anoint the queen on her head is probably the practical reason for loose hair. Yet, in a symbolic sense a woman's long hair has often been associated with her reproductive functions. Although the significance of both masculine and feminine hairstyles varies in different societies and historical periods, the relationship between free-flowing locks and a woman's fertility would seem consistent within the context of the queen's consecration.[64]

Jeanne de Bourbon's costume also needs some description. According to Jean Golein, she wore three separate garments: a robe, a tunic, and a shirt. The *Coronation Book* also mentions the two latter items, the *tunica* and the *camisia.*[65] The robe probably corresponds to the uppermost garment, a kind of sleeveless mantle held together across the chest by two segments of red cord (figs. 3, 14, and 18). The tunic seems to correspond to the long-sleeved garment which is being removed in figure 7. The shirt, seen in figures 7 and 8, was also a floor-length, long-sleeved garment. But it had distinctive openings or rings held together by a red thong or cord which extended to just below the waist. The rubrics state that these openings were intended to facilitate the anointing of the queen's breast. The king's shirt was not only open in the front but also in the back, as he was also anointed between the shoulders. At the

[63] Martène (n. 7 above) 2.636, identified as a pontifical manuscript from Arles written before 1400. For the correspondence of this *ordo* to Paris, Bibl. Nat., MS lat. 1220, see Leroquais (n. 27 above) 2.116-122. The ceremonies on fols. 154v to 161 of this manuscript, which were printed in Martène, refer to the coronations of kings and queens of Burgundy and are now considered to be texts from a much earlier period. C. A. Bouman, *Sacring and Crowning: The Development of the Latin Ritual for the Anointing of Kings and the Coronation of an Emperor before the Eleventh Century,* Bijdragen van het Instituut voor middeleeuwse Geschiedenis der Rijks-Universiteit te Utrecht 30 (Groningen 1957) 158, favored a date in the tenth century for this Burgundian *ordo*, while R. A. Jackson thinks either the late eleventh or the early twelfth century to be more likely. A later precedent for flowing tresses is afforded by the representations of the queen in the University of Illinois *Coronation Book.* On the occasion of her first coronation at Saint-Denis in 1492, Anne, duchess of Brittany, was described as having long, free-flowing tresses. See Godefroy (n. 2 above) 1.469, and J. Nicolai, "Sensieult le couronnement et entrée de la royne de France en la ville de Paris . . .," ed. J. de Gaulle, *Bulletin de la Société de l'histoire de France* (1845-1846) 112. It should be noted that Anne de Bretagne was married successively to two kings of France, Charles VIII, and his successor, Louis XII. After her second marriage, Anne de Bretagne had a second coronation at Saint-Denis in 1504. See Godefroy (n. 2 above) 1.692, and H. Stein, "Le sacre d'Anne de Bretagne et son entrée à Paris en 1504," *Mémoires de la Société de l'histoire de Paris et de l'Ile-de-France* 29 (1902) 268-304.

[64] For a popular but informative and entertaining treatment of the historical and cultural implications of hairstyles, see W. Cooper, *Hair: Sex, Society, Symbolism* (London 1971) esp. 66-67.

[65] For the relevant passages from the *Coronation Book* and the *Traité*, see below in the text at nn. 73-74. For further information on the three items of costume, see E. Viollet-le-Duc, *Dictionnaire raisonné du mobilier français*, 6 vols. (Paris 1914) s.v. "Chemise," 3.173-176, and V. Gay, *Glossaire archéologique du moyen âge et de la Renaissance,* 2 vols. (Paris 1887-1928) s.v. "Côte," 1.449-450, and s.v. "Robe," 2.301-304.

end of the red cord, the shirts had a white or silver metal aiguillete or tag to aid in the opening and closing of the garment. The *Coronation Book* rubrics specify that the rings on the king's shirt be made of silver, and the queen's seem also to be of a similar design.[66] The French translation of the Rheims *ordo* at the beginning of the *Coronation Book* states that the queen should be clad in silk garments.[67] Nothing in the appearance of Jeanne de Bourbon's apparel contradicts what may well be a traditional requirement. The red color of the queen's garments was similar to the hue of the king's tunic and shirt. Of course, the queen did not don such symbolic items of costume as the buskins or the gloves, related respectively to the king's knightly or sacerdotal character.

The spectators and attendants of Jeanne de Bourbon's ceremony are also distinguished from those surrounding Charles V in the minatures illustrating his coronation. The great officers of state did not preside over the various phases of the queen's rite. Instead the "more noble ladies" who surrounded her at the enthronement played an important role in many of the miniatures of the queen's cycle. Two in particular stand out as Jeanne de Bourbon's constant companions in the nine surviving miniatures. The first is a woman in brown widow's garb who in six scenes occupies a place next to the queen (figs. 5, 7, 10, 11, 14, and 18). On the basis of her active participation in the coronation ceremony, one can accept Delachenal's identification of this personage as the countess of Artois, peeress of France in her own right, and by marriage and the subsequent death of her husband, dowager countess of Flanders.[68] The other constant attendant of Jeanne de Bourbon is a young woman in contemporary dress, first glimpsed through a portal of Rheims cathedral in the opening miniature (fig. 3). The *Grandes chroniques* mentioned Jeanne de Bourbon's attendants for her *entrée* into Paris following the coronation ceremonies. Among the great ladies who escorted her on that occasion were the duchess of Orléans, the duchess of Anjou, and Marie de France, the king's sister.[69] One of these three women may have been the young person shown in the Jeanne de Bourbon cycle as a favored attendant.

Not only the attendants but their specific position vis-à-vis the queen vary according to the demands of the separate stages of the ceremony. But several constant features, also characteristics of the king's cycle, merit some attention.

[66] Dewick CB fol. 47v, col. 20. For a description of the red thong or cord ending in a pointed metal tag, see Gay (n. 65 above) s.v. "Aiguillette," 1.16-17.

[67] Dewick CB (n. 1 above) fol. 40, col. 10. For descriptions of later changes in the coronation garments of French queens from those represented in the *Coronation Book*, see Pinoteau (n. 58 above) 19; Stein (n. 63 above) 272; and Barry (n. 48 above) 87-88. See also H. Pinoteau, "Une représentation du sacre de Claude de France (1517) et quelques considérations préliminaires sur les 'insignes de Charlemagne'," *Hidalguia* 18 (1970) 320-321.

[68] Delachenal (n. 20 above) 3.93. Dewick CB, notice for pl. 30 had identified this personage incorrectly as the queen's mother, the dowager duchess of Bourbon.

[69] R. Delachenal, ed., *Les grandes chroniques de France: Chronique des règnes de Jean II et de Charles V*, 4 vols. (Paris 1910-1920) 2.3.

Jeanne de Bourbon usually occupies the near center of the rectangular picture field, whatever her actual physical position (figs. 5, 7, 8, 10, 11, 13, 14, and 18). Not only is she the focal point of the composition, but her central placement also symbolizes the roles of the king and the queen as intermediaries between the secular sphere of the nobility on the left and of the clerical sector on the right. With the exception of the architectural setting of the first miniature in the queen's cycle, the clerical sphere is elsewhere denoted by the high altar placed at the extreme right of the miniature and by the chief executants of the liturgy, most notably the archbishop of Rheims and his assistants.

Finally, we should note the predominant color harmony of the queen's cycle, based on red, blue, and gold. Indeed, as in the Charles V section, the lavish use of gold for accessories and regalia is another indication of the great care and expense lavished upon the manuscript. Apart from the less distinguished portraits of the queen, what is different from the miniatures of the Charles V cycle is the constant red of the queen's costume throughout the nine scenes in which she figures. Charles V's blue state mantle emblazoned with the fleur-de-lis, which he wore in the later stages of the ceremony, gives a more somber tone to these scenes. In contrast, the vivid crimson garments of Jeanne de Bourbon lend an intensity and resonance to the scenes of her cycle which often compensate for her lack of decisive physical movement or facial expression.

IV. THE MINIATURES OF THE JEANNE DE BOURBON CYCLE IN THE CORONATION BOOK

The opening miniature of the queen's cycle on folio 66 is placed within the text, immediately below the closing lines describing Charles V's ceremony (fig. 3). The other eight surviving illustrations of the consecration and coronation of Jeanne de Bourbon are found on the bottom margins of the separate folios, often opposite one another in a double sequence. As I have already noted, originally only the text miniature may have been planned for the queen's cycle, and the far more complete existing program of illustration may be due to the early intervention of Charles V himself in extending its scope in the entire manuscript.

The rubrics which appear below the miniature and which furnish the verbal sources of the opening illuminations follow closely those of earlier texts, including the translation into French of the Rheims *ordo* with which the *Coronation Book* begins.[70] Among the important points is the statement that the ceremony for blessing the queen begins immediately after the conclusion of the king's coronation.

[70] For the rubrics beginning the *ordo* for the blessing of the queen, see Dewick CB (n. 1 above) fols. 66rv, col. 44. For the comparable instructions at the beginning of the French translation of the Rheims *ordo*, see *ibid.* fol. 40, col. 10.

The rubrics in the Jeanne de Bourbon cycle do not specify the location of the queen's throne but only that it should be smaller than the king's. Furthermore, these instructions state that king, bearing his regalia, should remain seated on this throne during the ceremony. It is from the last part of the rubrics that there come the directions which supply the texts for both the first and second miniatures:

> Regina autem adducta in ecclesiam debet prosterni ante altare. et prostrata debet orare. qua eleuata ab oratione ab episcopis debet iterum caput inclinare et archiepiscopus hanc orationem dicere.[71]

Within the only architectural setting in the queen's cycle, Jeanne de Bourbon approaches the altar, escorted by a bishop on her left and one on her right. Although the representations of Rheims cathedral in the manuscript are very simplified, one can distinguish between the rendering of the main portal on the west at which Charles V is greeted in the first miniature of the 1365 *ordo* and the much simpler structure suggesting a side door through which Jeanne de Bourbon has entered before making her way toward the high altar (figs. 3 and 4). Stationed next to the altar, the archbishop of Rheims, Jean de Craon, extends his hand in blessing toward the queen. The tonsured head of an assisting cleric is visible, while on Jeanne de Bourbon's side we catch our first glimpse of her two constant attendants. The younger woman is seen through the door, while the head of the countess of Artois is directly behind that of the queen. The usual division of groups in the cycle does not apply in this introductory miniature; two members of the clergy appear in the left sector usually reserved for lay figures. In fact, the center of the composition is unoccupied. The void thus created is no index of the physical distance between the main actors. Yet, it does enhance a certain air of tension visible in the group on the left. Jeanne de Bourbon represented in a three-quarter pose, has a rather apprehensive expression on her face, an impression reinforced by the timid, contained gestures of her hands. Furthermore, she seems almost reluctant to move forward. Only the urging of the two attending bishops, conveyed by the position of their gloved hands, seems to encourage her to advance. By way of contrast, Charles V, in the corresponding miniature of his cycle, steps forward confidently to greet the welcoming procession of clerics (fig. 4).

Jean Golein's commentary in the *Traitê* on the opening phase of the queen's ceremony adds to the information in the *Coronation Book* rubrics the location of the

[71] "But after the queen has been conducted into the church, she must prostrate herself before the altar, and in this position she must pray. After having been raised from prayer by the bishops, she must again bow her head, and the archbishop must say this prayer." Dewick CB fol. 66v, col. 44. According to an observation of Golein, it was the bishops of Laon and Beauvais who escorted the queen to the altar (Paris, Bibl. Nat., MS fr. 437, fol. 3v of the *table des matières*). But in fig. 3, the two bishops do not wear identifying heraldic copes, as they do in the comparable miniature of the king's cycle on fol. 44v. See Dewick CB p1.3.

queen's throne on the left side of the choir. His injunction that the two bishops should fetch her with the solemnity due the king emphasizes her high social status.[72]

In the next illustration on folio 66v, the queen kneels against the faldstool placed next to the high altar (fig. 5). The archbishop is reading the prayer mentioned in the last sentence of the opening rubrics cited above, while the queen is again bowing her head in prayer. At this point, Golein interpolates several private prayers appropriate for the queen to address to the Virgin and to Christ. This second miniature is more typical of the cycle as a whole than the introductory one. For one thing, there is no architectural setting. Secondly, the queen now occupies the center of the composition. She is the foil between the secular personages on the left and the clerical group on the right, composed of the archbishop of Rheims, one of the escorting bishops, and a tonsured cross-bearer. The former group is formed by five masculine attendants in fashionable contemporary dress and the queen's two faithful female companions. The countess of Artois, by virtue of the direction of her glance and the gesture of her hands, seems closely involved in the proceedings. The younger attendant, the second figure on the right, seems more detached. At the right, the queen's crown and a covered chalice precariously rest on the altar's sloping surface. Jeanne de Bourbon is again depicted in three-quarter view, but the features of her face and the contours of her head lack the sharp definition of the first representation of the queen (fig. 3). The queen's kneeling pose enhances our impression of her modesty. Even the gesture of her folded hands appears retiring in comparison to the more forward, aggressive motion of Charles V's hand in a similar miniature from his cycle (figs. 5 and 6).

The most interesting and unusual miniature of the Jeanne de Bourbon cycle follows on folio 67v. The scene represents the preparations for the anointing of the queen (fig. 7). The rubrics on the top of folio 68 supply only general instructions which do not strictly account for the specific actions occurring in this third miniature:

> Notandum quod tunica regine. et camisia debent esse aperte usque ad corrigiam. et dominus archiepiscopus debet inungere eam oleo sancto in capite et in pectore.[73]

They merely specify that the queen's tunic and shirt should be opened as far as the waist in order to permit her to receive the anointing on her breast. Jean Golein's commentary in the *Traitê* provides a more adequate guide to the meaning of the scene:

[72] Golein specified that the queen's throne was placed on the same platform which supported the king's throne: "On li doit appareillier une chaere sur l'eschaufaut du Roy a la senestre partie devers le cuer senestre." ("A throne must be prepared for her on the king's platform to the left side toward the left choir.") Golein, *Traité* (n. 5 above) fol. 50 [318].

[73] "It should be noted that the tunic and shirt of the queen must be open to the bodice, and the lord archbishop must anoint her with holy oil on the head and the chest." Dewick CB fol. 68, col. 46.

> Et quant vient a linonction la robe de la Royne doit estre noulee par devant. et pour la vergoingne femenine elle ne doit mie estre despoillee comme le Roy. mais en grant honestete la plus prochaine et familiere de elle li doit deslacier sa robe sa cote et sa chemise.[74]

In other words, the queen in the miniature is preparing to "unlace" her garments before the anointing can take place. She is shielded by her female attendants who form a protective circle around her both to preserve her modesty and to help her unfasten her garments. Jeanne de Bourbon's crouching posture is designed to achieve some degree of privacy; the distress on her face is not due to resistance to the attentions of her attendants, as Dewick claimed.[75] Rather, the queen's expression stems from her difficulties in preserving her dignity during this awkward activity.

The queen and her group of six attendants in the center dominate the composition. The empty space on either side of them further emphasizes the necessity for privacy from the curious eyes of the masculine bystanders, both lay and secular. The two female attendants on the outside of the central group function as vertical accents contrasting with the queen's stooping form. Lending additional excitement to the scene is the large, wavy gold-scroll pattern of the blue background. The sharp outlines of the queen's features, like those in the first miniature of the cycle, heighten the general tension of the scene.

The pendant illustration on folio 68 represents one of the anointings mentioned in the rubrics last cited (fig. 8). The archbishop of Rheims is anointing the queen on the breast with a golden style, as she again kneels before the faldstool. In order to preserve her modesty, two of her attendants hold a veil stretched in front of her.[76] The four male bystanders on the left of the miniature are separated from the women by some undefined distance. The countess of Artois is entrusted with guarding this flank. Yet, the clerical group on the right forms part of the main action, because of the importance of the archbishop of Rheims's role in this scene.

We should note that the anointing of the queen's head is not depicted. Perhaps the choice of subject was influenced by the more problematic unction of the queen's breast and ways of demonstrating how her privacy could be respected. As we recall, the anointing of the queen was restricted to two parts of her body. Her unction was

[74] "And when it comes to the anointing, the queen's dress should be tied in the front, and for the sake of feminine modesty, she should not be undressed like the king, but with great decency her most intimate attendant should unlace her robe, her tunic, and her shirt." Golein, *Traité,* fol. 50v [319].

[75] Dewick CB (n. 1 above) notice for pl. 31.

[76] It is interesting that the miniature representing the anointing of the queen's breast in Charles V's copy of the *Traité*, inserted in Golein's translation of the *Rationale divinorum officiorum* (Paris, Bibl. Nat., MS fr. 437, fol. 50), shows a lack of concern about the queen's privacy (fig. 9). Furthermore, here the queen is anachronistically crowned, and she wears an inappropriate fleur-de-lis mantle. One can conclude, therefore, that the analogous miniature from the *Coronation Book* did not serve as a model for the illustration of the anointing of the queen in the *Traité.*

accomplished only with sanctified oil, instead of with the balm preserved in the Sainte Ampoule. These limitations had the effect of depriving the queen of the quasi-sacerdotal character bestowed on the king by the mode and number of his anointings. Nevertheless the queen's anointing had considerable importance in two different ways. According to Golein, the unction – like baptism – had a cleansing effect of wiping away past sins and of bringing spiritual renewal. Furthermore, in regard to the queen, the unction was supposed to have the extra-sacramental effect of assuring her fertility.[77]

Following her anointing, the queen received the regalia. Although the rubrics remain silent on this point, we must assume that the queen's garments were immediately refastened upon the completion of the anointing ritual. Indeed, the miniature on folio 68v which represents Jeanne de Bourbon receiving the ring does indeed depict the costume in its original state (fig. 10).[78] The rubric which is the source of the illustration specifies only: "Tunc debet ab archiepiscopo anulus immitti digito."[79] The ring, traditional symbol of Christian faith, stands for the queen's duty to the church, her belief in the Holy Trinity, and her obligation to fight heresy. In the king's *ordo,* the ring was presented to Charles V in the same context. In his case, however, the archbishop blessed the ring in connection with the king's donning of the gloves, in a manner analogous to the consecration of a bishop. Thus, the ring in Charles V's ceremony was also related to the king's quasi-sacerdotal character.[80]

In the *Coronation Book* miniature, Jeanne de Bourbon extends her right hand to the archbishop, while she again kneels against the faldstool. He is ready to place the ring either on her first or second finger. To judge from the miniature, the ring seems to be a simple band. The separate male and female groups on the left of the two previous scenes have now merged. In this illumination the countess of Artois stands directly behind Jeanne de Bourbon, while another woman in blue widow's garb is interposed between the countess and the queen's other constant companion. Jeanne

[77] Golein, *Traité* (n. 5 above) fol. 50v [319]. For previous and forthcoming discussions of the relationship between fertility and the queen's anointing, see text passages between nn. 51-52 and preceding n. 140.

[78] Golein (*Traité*, fol. 51 [319]) mentioned the refastening of the queen's garments, but only at the point in the ceremony when she had already been crowned and was about to be led to her throne. After the king's anointing in the Charles V *ordo*, however, the rubrics specifically instructed the archbishop (or priests or deacons) to refasten the king's tunic. See Dewick CB fol. 55, col. 30, and pl. 16.

[79] "Now the ring must be placed on her finger by the archbishop." Dewick CB fol. 68v, col. 47. The queen had received the ring as part of her regalia in the Fulrad *ordo* dated ca. 980. The custom was revived in *ordines* of the fourteenth century. See H. Schreuer, *Die rechtlichen Grundgedanken der französischen Königskrönung* (Weimar 1911) 125.

[80] Dewick CB fols. 56v-57, cols. 32-33, pl. 21. For the significance of the glove ceremonial, see above in the text at nn. 23-24. From the miniature, it appears that the king's ring was intended for the fourth finger of his right hand and that a stone was set on top of the band. See also Dewick CB col. 83. In the opinion of Baron Hervé Pinoteau (conversation of 8 October 1974), there were no specific rings traditionally set aside for use in the coronations of the king or queen.

de Bourbon's likeness is of the soft, undefined type noted in the previous miniature (fig. 8). Here, however, the queen's head is more upright and her posture more confident.

The next miniature of the Jeanne de Bourbon cycle shows the queen receiving the scepter and the rod, two symbols of royal temporal authority (fig. 11). As in the comparable scene from the king's cycle, the two separate acts of receiving these regalia have been combined into one (fig. 12). The rubrics in the queen's ceremony state:

> Post istam orationem datur ab archiepiscopo sceptrum modicum alterius modi quam sceptrum regium et uirga consimilis uirge regie.[81]

Following the tradition of older French *ordines,* Golein specified in the *Traitê* that the queen's scepter should be smaller than the king's, signifying her secondary temporal authority.[82] Indeed, a comparison of her scepter with the king's in the *Coronation Book* miniatures makes the size differences very clear (figs. 11 and 12). Although silent on the precise symbolism of the queen's scepter, the liturgy relates the rod to the queen's spiritual and charitable responsibilities. Indeed, the relevant prayer in the text associates the rod with virtue and justice, bidding the queen to be "merciful and generous to the poor and to widows and orphans."[83] Although the rubrics say that the queen's rod can be like the king's, in the *Coronation Book* miniature Jeanne de Bourbon does not carry the *main de justice* held by Charles V as a symbol of his essential function to dispense justice.

The distinctive form of Jeanne de Bourbon's scepter in the *Coronation Book* has been identified as a specific object formerly in the collection of coronation regalia kept at Saint-Denis and which disappeared during the French Revolution.[84] The so-called "scepter of Dagobert" held by Jeanne de Bourbon is reproduced in Montfaucon's *Monumens de la monarchie françoise* published in 1733.[85] It is very distinctive in shape and overall form. Above the stem, a man is seated on an eagle

[81] "After this prayer the archbishop gives her a smaller scepter of a different kind than the king's and a rod similar to the king's." Dewick CB fol. 69, col. 47.

[82] Golein, *Traité*, fol. 50v [319]. See also the French translation of the Rheims *ordo*, in Dewick CB fol. 40, col. 10. For indications that in later periods the queen's scepter and rod may have changed from those represented in the Jeanne de Bourbon cycle, see Stein (n. 63 above) 278; Pinoteau (n. 67 above) 321-322; Godefroy (n. 2 above) 1.474; and Barry (n. 48 above) 87.

[83] Dewick CB fol. 69, col. 47.

[84] Pinoteau (n. 58 above) 15, and *idem* (n. 28 above) 155 n. 78. For Charles V's scepter, the so-called scepter of Charlemagne, see Pinoteau (n. 58 above) 13-14; Viollet-le-Duc (n. 65 above) s.v. "Sceptre," 4.320-327; and Schramm, *Der König* (n. 3 above) 1.213.

[85] B. de Montfaucon, *Les monumens de la monarchie françoise*, 5 vols. (Paris 1729-1733) 1.pl.3. See also, M. Félibien, *Histoire de l'abbaye royale de Saint-Denys en France* (Paris 1706) pl. 2Q 538, and 539. The scepter of Dagobert was stolen in 1794. See B. de Montesquieu-Fezensac and D. Gaborit-Chopin, *Le trésor de Saint-Denis, inventaire de 1634* (Paris 1973) 46 n. 4 and no. 87, 168-169. I am grateful to Prof. R. A. Jackson for calling this valuable publication to my attention.

with wings ending in eight-pointed stars. The eagle in turn rests on a globe held by a hand issuing from the scepter's stem. Pinoteau has persuasively explained the structure of the scepter in terms of an ascension and apotheosis of a ruler, a traditional symbolic intermediary between heaven and man.[86] The rod in the queen's left hand is shorter than the scepter and is composed of a heraldic gold rose resting on three knobs. Jeanne de Bourbon is shown with the same scepter and rod in two miniatures illustrating a copy of the *Grandes chroniques de France* executed for Charles V.[87] In this manuscript, the scène of her enthronement – copied from that of the *Coronation Book* – shows her carrying them in the same way as in the model. But in the miniature of the queen's funeral procession in the *Grandes chroniques,* the scepter is shifted to the left hand and the rod to the right.

In the *Coronation Book* miniature, the queen holds the rod and scepter in a strict vertical fashion next to her body. But because these insignia are so short, their forms emerge less strongly than the king's much longer scepter and *main de justice* (fig. 12). As far as the bystanders go in figure 11, men now predominate in the single group standing on the left of the miniature. Yet, the gesture of the countess of Artois shows her active pleasure in the proceedings. The queen's face and hair are more strongly delineated than in the previous scene, and her expression is somewhat grimmer.

The climactic scenes of the Jeanne de Bourbon cycle are the next two pendant miniatures on folios 69v and 70 (figs. 13 and 14). The first shows the archbishop placing the crown on the queen's head with the assistance of the barons, and the second represents her formal coronation. The rubrics furnish the program for both these miniatures:

> Tunc debet ei imponi a solo archiepiscopo corona in capite ipsius quam impositam sustentare debent undique barones. archiepiscopus autem debet dicere in impositione orationem.[88]

As Dewick pointed out, the instruction in the rubrics that the archbishop of Rheims alone should place the crown on the queen's head does not seem to be followed in the miniature (fig. 13).[89] Perhaps the gestures of the right hands of the count of Toulouse and of the bishop of Beauvais were intended to convey their attempt to steady the crown after it was placed on the queen's head.

The queen's attendants have now changed from largely unidentified bystanders to the barons mentioned in the rubrics. They are required as witnesses and supporters of the queen's coronation and enthronement. Except for the countess of Artois, the

[86] Pinoteau (n. 58 above) 15.

[87] Paris, Bibl. Nat., MS fr. 2813, dated 1375-1379. For the enthronement scene on fol. 439 and the funeral procession on fol. 480v, see Sherman (n. 6 above) pls. 21 and 36.

[88] "Then must the crown be placed on her head by the archbishop alone. Then when this has been placed on her head, the barons must support it on all sides. The archbishop, moreover, must say this prayer while placing it [on her head]." Dewick CB (n. 1 above) fol. 69, col. 47.

[89] *Ibid.* notice for pl. 35.

female attendants have been banished to the rear of the group on the left of the miniature. As we recall, it is symbolic of the queen's traditionally less honorific status that the rubrics call for barons as the queen's witnesses and escort, rather than the peers of France who surround the king (fig. 15).[90]

Jeanne de Bourbon, as in the previous three scenes, is kneeling before the faldstool in a three-quarter pose (fig. 13). The angle at which she holds the scepter and rod now make them stand out clearly against her body. Indeed, her posture is far more upright than in the previous three scenes. Her features are not clearly defined by contour lines, although more of her head is visible here. For the second time in the cycle, the gold and blue spiral pattern of the background lends a note of excitement to the scene, heightened by the scarlet curtains of the altar.

The actual coronation of the queen on the next folio shows further changes in the posture and placement of Jeanne de Bourbon and her attendants (fig. 14). For the first and only time in the cycle, the queen is seated in a frontal position, the traditional format in which rulers, both earthly and heavenly, exhibit their full majesty. The frozen formality of the queen's posture stands out all the more because her attendants are involved in active movement. In order to stress its throne-like character, the faldstool has been covered with a gold fabric. The countess of Artois stands on the queen's right and is actively supporting Jeanne de Bourbon's crown. The bishop of Beauvais, who extends both his hands toward the crown, is active in the sector reserved for the clergy. The presence of a young woman on that side of the miniature is, however, difficult to explain. All in all, this scene is somewhat lacking in animation, particularly in comparison to the analogous miniature from the Charles V cycle (fig. 15).[91]

At this point, it is worthwhile discussing the crowns used for the coronations of the kings and queens of France in the period under consideration. Although the three medieval French coronation crowns preserved in the treasury of Saint-Denis until 1794 no longer exist, written descriptions and engravings provide considerable information about them.[92] Perhaps I should explain that there were really two sets

[90] Prof. R. A. Jackson has explained (letter of 16 August 1974) that although several peers of France are present in the miniature on fol. 69v, they are assisting in this phase of the queen's ceremony as barons. The peers have been identified by Dewick CB, notice for pl. 35, as the duke of Bourbon, the duke of Burgundy, and the count of Toulouse.

[91] One reason for the greater liveliness in the scene of the peers supporting Charles V's crown is that the king is not seated in a completely frontal position, as is the queen. For a recent discussion of the symbolic and expressive connotations of frontality as a "theme of state," see M. Schapiro, *Words and Pictures: On the Literal and the Symbolic in the Illustration of a Text* (The Hague 1973) esp. 41.

[92] For a basic work on the crowns of various European nations, see P. E. Schramm, *Herrschaftszeichen und Staatssymbolik: Beiträge zu ihrer Geschichte vom dritten bis zum sechzehnten Jahrh.*, MGH Schriften 1-3 (Stuttgart 1954-1956) 2. For short studies of the medieval French crown, see *idem, Der König* (n. 3 above) 1.205-210, and Pinoteau (n. 58 above) 11-12. For illustrations of two of the medieval crowns in the treasury of Saint-Denis, see Félibien (n. 85 above) pl. 3P 540 for the crown of Saint Louis, and pl. 4T 543 for the crown of Jeanne d'Évreux.

of crowns used in the course of the coronation ceremony. The first set, donned for the coronation proper, was much heavier than the second pair, which the king and queen put on at the end of the ceremony and which they continued to wear during the subsequent festivities. For the coronation of the king, the so-called *couronne de Charlemagne* was used. In a recent important study, Pinoteau dated this crown to the year 1180 and identified its donor as Philippe II. With three exceptions, this crown was used for all the coronations of French kings including that of Louis XVI.[93] For the coronation of the queen, the "sister" crown to the *couronne de Charlemagne* was the *couronne de la reine*. Pinoteau believes that the *couronne de la reine* was also created in 1180 for the same occasion: the anointing and coronation at Saint-Denis of Philippe II's first wife, Isabelle de Hainaut. This crown remained in the treasury of Saint-Denis until 1590, when it was removed and later melted down by the Catholic League. For the one remaining coronation of a French queen after that date, that of Marie de'Medici in 1610, the crown left to Saint-Denis by Jeanne d'Évreux at her death in 1370 was substituted.[94]

Both the *couronne de Charlemagne* and the *couronne de la reine* were exhaustively described in an inventory of the treasury of Saint-Denis dating from 1634, which in turn relied on a previous one drawn up in 1534. Both official coronation crowns were open gold circles of four separate elements surmounted by four fleur-de-lis. Each one was encrusted with rubies, sapphires, and emeralds distributed in an identical pattern. The stones in the king's crown were, however, more valuable. Both official coronation crowns had separate interior caps. The queen's was a flat skullcap, designed to keep the crown on her head. Until the seventeenth century, the king's cap, or bonnet, was of a distinctive conical shape and was also decorated with pearls and precious stones. Other features of the official coronation crowns were rings for silver chains from which they were suspended over the altar of the treasury of Saint-Denis.[95]

As far as the crowns in the *Coronation Book* go, there is not too much consistency in their representation. If we compare the crowns worn by Jeanne de Bourbon in the miniatures on folios 69v and 70 (figs. 13 and 14), we note that the former has *fleurons* of the same size, while the crown in figure 14 has alternating large and small

[93] H. Pinoteau, "L'ancienne couronne française dite 'de Charlemagne' (1180? -1794)," *Bulletin de la Société archéologique, historique, et artistique: "Le vieux papier"* fasc. 243-245 (1972) 305-312, 351-362, and 381-399. For the specific references to the history, use, and dating of the *couronne de Charlemagne*, see *ibid.* 305, 306 n. 4, and 359.

[94] For the identity of the *couronne de la reine*, see *ibid.* 306 n. 2, and 355-357.

[95] For the description of the two official crowns in the documents, see Montesquiou-Fezensac and Gaborit-Chopin (n. 85 above) 76-84. For a modern account of the *couronne de Charlemagne*, see Pinoteau (n. 93 above) 308-310, and for illustrations of it, *ibid.* 307 (figs. 2 and 3) and 311 (figs. 6 and 7). There are apparently no known illustrations of the *couronne de la reine*. For the cap or bonnet of the king's crown, see *ibid.* 351-354 and 383-393; for the queen's cap, *ibid.* 355-357 nn. 31-32.

forms.[96] Discrepancies also occur in the forms of the crown worn by Charles V in the miniatures of his cycle.[97]

The royal family had, according to the inventory of Charles V's possessions, a treasure of great value in their collection of about fifty-five crowns, because of their precious metals and stones. One of the most famous was the new crown Charles V had made to serve as the second and lighter one to be worn at the end of the coronation ceremony. Some of the varying designs of these crowns are shown in the portraits of Charles V and Jeanne de Bourbon. One type, made of four alternating large and small *fleurons* elaborately decorated with jewels, as was the band below, is seen in the images of the king and queen in the *Parement de Narbonne* (figs. 1 and 2). Another kind of crown design favored by Charles V was one composed of eight slender *fleurons* of equal length.[98]

The liturgy of the *Coronation Book* emphasizes the responsibilities which "the crown of glory and regal excellence" placed upon its wearers. Its splendid external form called for equally outstanding spiritual qualities on the part of the queen: "Unde sicut exterius auro et gemmis redimita enites. ita et interius auro sapientie uirtutumque gemmis decorari contendas."[99] Furthermore, the queen should be aware that she is "the consort of the kingdom" and that she must "always take favorable counsel for the people."[100] Another prayer asks that God send a wide range of virtues to aid the queen in discharging her obligations: "auctoritatem regiminis consilij magnitudinem. sapientie. prudencie et intellectus habundantiam. religionis ac pietatis custodiam."[101] This section of the liturgy, then, affirms the

[96] A third type of crown worn by Jeanne de Bourbon in the *Coronation Book* occurs on fol. 72 (fig. 18). Here, above a narrow band, the two central *fleurons* are much higher than those surrounding them on either side.

[97] For example, in three miniatures in which the king wears a crown, the one on fol. 59 shows the type with five slender fleur-de-lis of the same size and jewels on the band below (Dewick CB pl. 23). On fol. 59v (fig. 15), the crown has one small *fleuron* on the left and three large ones above a band studded with jewels. The crown on fol. 64 (fig. 17) has two large *fleurons* alternating with two small ones in a single, undecorated band.

[98] For the collection of crowns belonging to Charles V and the royal family, see Schramm, *Der König* (n. 3 above) 1.206, and J. Labarte, *Inventaire du mobilier de Charles V, roi de France*, Documents inédits sur l'histoire de France, ser. 3 (Paris 1879) 12-29, nos. 1-55. The famous and precious crown ordered by Charles V for the end of the coronation ceremony and the subsequent festivities is no. 1, 12-14 in the *Inventaire*, while the *grant couronne* of Jeanne de Bourbon is no. 9, 16-17. (Whether the latter was the second crown used in her coronation is not clear.) For an illustration of the crown with slender *fleurons* of equal length, see Sherman (n. 6 above) pl. 5. For valuable information on the different types of crowns worn by Charles V, see Viollet-le-Duc (n. 65 above) s.v. "Couronne," 3.312 and 316-319.

[99] "Thus just as you shine forth crowned with gold and gems, thus also may you strive to be decorated internally with the gold of wisdom and the gems of virtue." Dewick CB (n. 1 above) fol. 69v, col. 48.

[100] *Ibid.* fol. 69v, col. 48.

[101] "Authority of command, greatness of judgment, an abundance of wisdom, prudence, and understanding, a guardianship of religion and piety." *Ibid.* fol. 70, col. 48.

high moral character of the queen's responsibilities associated with her status as a royal person.

Certainly one, and possibly two, miniatures illustrating the next phase of the queen's ceremony are missing from the *Coronation Book,* since as Dewick pointed out, the lower margin of folio 71 has been cut off.[102] The relevant rubrics from the queen's *ordo,* as well as the analogous miniatures from Charles V's cycle, can supply the possible subjects of the lost miniature or miniatures. One miniature, based on the first half of the rubrics, could have appeared on the recto of folio 71, and a second illustration conforming to the second part could have been placed on the verso of the same folio:

> Post istam orationem barones qui coronam eius sustentant deducunt eam ad solium ubi in sede parata collocatur circumstantibus eam baronibus et matronis nobilioribus.[103]

Thus, the first scene may have represented the barons leading Jeanne de Bourbon to her throne. The equivalent scene in Charles V's cycle on folio 63 shows him, escorted by the peers, climbing the steps of the platform to his prepared throne (fig. 16). In the second scene of the sequence on folio 64, he is formally enthroned. Surrounded by the peers, he receives the kiss of homage from the archbishop of Rheims (fig. 17). In the same way, a miniature on folio 71v could have represented the enthronement of Jeanne de Bourbon, surrounded by the barons and the "more noble" ladies. But there would have been no kiss of homage or acclamation for the queen. Of course, verification of this hypothesis would depend on the reappearance of these miniatures, or alternatively, on a cycle of miniatures depending on the *Coronation Book* as its model.

Golein's commentary on this stage of the ceremony generally repeated the information in the rubric but added some information on protocol:

> Les queles oroisons finees les barons doivent prendre la Royne ainsi coronnee et sa poitrine reclose et refermee avec la compaignie des nobles seigneurs et dames en soustenant la coronne la doivent mener en sa chaere devant dicte a la senestre du Roy appareilliee. et avant quelle sassiee elle se doit encliner vers le Roy a .i. genoul. et envers dieu a .ii.[104]

Aside from his comment that the queen's garments have been refastened, Golein

[102] *Ibid.*, notice for pl. 36.

[103] "After this prayer, the barons who support her crown lead her to the throne where she is placed in the seat prepared for her and is surrounded by the barons and more noble dames." *Ibid.* fols. 70v-71, col. 49.

[104] "These prayers completed, the barons must take the queen thus crowned and her breast covered up and [her garments] refastened, accompanied by the company of the lords and dames. While supporting the crown, they must lead her to the prepared seat mentioned above to the left of the king. And before being seated, she must bow with one knee to the king and towards God with two." Golein, *Traité* (n. 5 above) fol. 51 [319].

mentioned that before she was seated on her throne she bowed to the king with one knee and to God with both. This remark could be interpreted as an eyewitness observation by Golein of this practice during the coronation ceremony of 1364. A less likely hypothesis is that the information may have been a marginal note in a text which he consulted, such as the pontifical of the archbishop of Rheims mentioned by Golein as the source of his commentary.

The last miniature of the Jeanne de Bourbon cycle shows the queen receiving communion from the archbishop of Rheims (fig. 18). The taking of communion is a joint temporal experience of both the king and queen, unlike the previous parts of the ceremony, which were carried out separately. Indeed, the communion rite was one of a series of events following the enthronement of the queen which focussed on the celebration of the Mass. After the opening prayers of the Mass were sung, the king and queen removed their crowns while the Gospel was being read. Then, first the king, followed by the queen, kissed the Gospel book, which was brought to their thrones. After the offertory antiphon, the peers led the king to the altar, with the queen following them. Both then made the traditional offerings of bread, wine, and thirteen gold coins, called besants.[105] The king and queen returned to their thrones for the final part of the celebration of the Mass. After the blessing of the king, queen, and people and the *pax domini*, the king and queen received communion in both kinds.[106] Then the archbishop of Rheims removed the large crowns from the heads of the king and queen and replaced them with smaller ones. The royal pair, preceded by an official carrying the king's sword, then returned to the archiepiscopal palace.

Jean Golein offered an explanation in the *Traité* as to why the communion rite was the only part of the coronation Mass chosen for depiction both in the Charles V and the Jeanne de Bourbon cycles:

> Le Roy et la Royne doivent descendre de leur eschaufaut et venir humblement a lautel et prendre de la main de larcevesque le corps et le sanc de nostre seigneur. Et en ce est demonstree la dignite Royal et prestral. car on ne baille a nul autre sil nest prestre le sanc separeement.[107]

[105] For the offering of the thirteen gold besants, which Prof. Jackson has traced to the reign of Saint Louis, see Dewick CB col. 87. As Prof. Jackson pointed out, Golein (*Traité*, fol. 51 [319] and n. 107) seems to have erred in making the number of the besants eleven, instead of the thirteen specified in the Charles V *ordo*.

[106] The archbishop of Rheims, the celebrant of the Mass, passed the *Pax domini* (a liturgical object to be kissed) to the prelate of next highest rank, who kissed the king directly. The queen, however, received the kiss of peace from this second prelate via a Gospel-book. The *ordo* then called for all the archbishops and the bishops to give the kiss of peace one-by-one only to the king who was seated on his throne (Dewick CB fol. 65v, col. 43, and col. 70, note on col. 11, line 18). I am grateful to the Rev. Dom Hilary Hayden, O. S. B., and to the Rev. Dom Anselm Strittmatter, O. S. B., for explaining this procedure to me.

[107] "The king and queen must descend from their platform and come humbly to the altar and take from the hand of the archbishop the body and the blood of our Lord; and in this is shown the royal and priestly dignity. For to no other, unless he be a priest, is the blood given separately." Golein, *Traité* fol. 51 [320].

In other words, receiving communion in both kinds signified the quasi-sacerdotal character of French kings, as well as their special "dignity" and status as rulers. [108]

Jeanne de Bourbon is shown receiving communion as she kneels to the left of the altar (fig. 18). The archbishop of Rheims, standing alone, holds the chalice and proffers a large wafer stamped with an image of the Crucifixion with Saints Mary and John. [109] The queen's two attendants stand next to her. As usual, the countess of Artois, whose hands are raised in prayer, is more involved in the action. The queen's crown is held by the duke of Bourbon and the count of Toulouse on the left and by the count of Étampes on the right. Jeanne de Bourbon's features are somewhat more clearly defined and her head of a rounder shape than in the preceding miniatures.

A fuller account of my conclusion as to the place of the queen's cycle in the manuscript as a whole will appear in a later part of this study. But it is appropriate to indicate here several salient features emerging from our discussion of the miniatures in the Jeanne de Bourbon cycle. First, the program of miniatures extends our understanding of the ceremony because of the clear narrative sequence, the well-organized composition, and the consistently repeated details of costume and accessories. It is also evident that the illustrations function as *exempla* in particular of the general instructions furnished by the rubrics. In addition, Jean Golein's commentary contributed information both on details of protocol and on the symbolic significance of various parts of the ceremony which further enhanced our knowledge of the contemporary interpretation of the ritual for the queen.

In comparison with representations of the coronations of French queens in pontifical manuscripts, or the fragment of the University of Illinois *Coronation Book,* the Jeanne de Bourbon cycle stands out because it so obviously embodies an attempt to give a historical and individualized version of the ceremony. Furthermore, the greatly increased length of the text of the queen's *ordo* in the *Coronation Book* in relation to earlier French *ordines* of the thirteenth and fourteenth centuries is also highly significant. Of course, the Charles V portion of the *Coronation Book* is also distinguished by the same characteristics of lengthier text and an expanded program of images treated in a historical sense. But it was not inevitable that the Jeanne de Bourbon part of the *Coronation Book* should also be so extensive in both respects. We must now consider whether any specific historical circumstances which prevailed in 1364 regarding the relationship between Charles V and Jeanne de Bourbon and the state of the monarchy at this time can account for the degree of attention paid to the queen in the king's *Coronation Book.*

[108] See n. 59 above.

[109] The rubric for the queen's communion reads as follows: "In oblatione. in pace ferenda. in communione. penitus est ordo regis superius annotatus obseruandus." ("The king's *ordo* above should be followed accurately as to the offertory, the conferring of the *Pax,* and Holy Communion.") Dewick CB (n. 1 above) fol. 71, col. 49.

V. The Prominence of the Jeanne de Bourbon Cycle and Its Relation to the Situation of the Monarchy in 1364

Evidence of a very close and happy relationship between Charles V and Jeanne de Bourbon comes from many different contemporary sources. First, they were almost exactly the same age, as they were both born at the beginning of 1338, and at the same place, the castle of Vincennes.[110] Jeanne de Bourbon was the oldest daughter of Pierre I, second duke of Bourbon, and of Isabeau de Valois, sister of Philippe VI, the first Valois king, who was Charles V's grandfather. So on the Valois side, Jeanne de Bourbon was the first cousin of Charles V's father, Jean le Bon. On the Bourbon side the relationship was somewhat less close. Jeanne de Bourbon's great-grandfather, Robert de Clermont, was a son of Saint Louis, as was Charles V's great-great-grandfather, Philippe III.[111] Furthermore, the future king and queen knew one another from a very early age. Indeed, Charles's parents, who at that time bore the title of duke and duchess of Normandy, served as godparents for Jeanne at her baptism, which, like Charles's, took place at the church of Saint Pierre de Montrueil, near Vincennes. Thus, before their marriage could take place it was necessary to receive a papal dispensation both on the grounds of their close blood relationships

[110] For the account of the personal and genealogical relationship between the future king and Jeanne de Bourbon, see Delachenal (n. 20 above) 1.25-26.

[111] The following diagram summarizing the relationships between the families of the future king and queen comes from *ibid.* 1.26 n. 1.

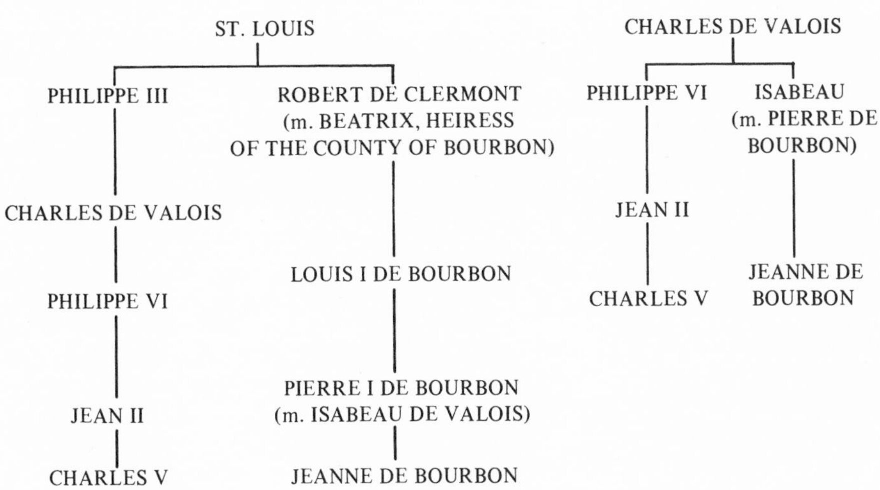

and because of the "spiritual affinity" between them due to the fact that his parents served as her godparents.[112]

The marriage was celebrated at Tain near Lyons on 8 April 1350 when they were twelve years old. But the couple had not always been "destined for one another." Indeed, before her engagement to Charles, Jeanne de Bourbon had been twice betrothed – at the age of six to Amadeus, known as the Green Count of Savoy, and then when she was eleven to Humbert, the *dauphin* of Viennois. When for financial reasons the Dauphiné was ceded to the French crown in 1349, the title of *dauphin* was given to Charles as the eldest son of the heir to the French throne. As a result of these developments, Jeanne de Bourbon was then betrothed to Charles.[113] The dynastic and political causes of the marriage did not detract from an unusually happy relationship for the twenty-eight years during which they were wed.

Charles V's high regard for Jeanne de Bourbon is revealed by her very prominent role in the official social and ceremonial life of the reign. Not only her coronation but her separate *entrée* into Paris and the brilliant social events following them are described in detailed fashion in the *Grandes chroniques.*[114] On 9 and 11 May 1369 at the extraordinary assembly of the *parlement* of Paris convened by Charles V in connection with deliberations to break the treaty of Brétigny and to declare war against the king of England, Jeanne de Bourbon sat at the king's right hand. Her presence at this very distinguished gathering was another sign of the high esteem in which Charles V held his spouse.[115] In the ordinances of 1374 in which Charles V provided for the governance of the kingdom if he died before the royal heirs reached their majority at the age of fourteen, Jeanne de Bourbon was singled out for an important role. The queen was appointed chief guardian and keeper of the royal children, assisted by two co-guardians and a council whose members were designated in advance.[116] Jeanne de Bourbon was also the focal point of a prominent incident during the climactic event of Charles V's reign: the visit of his uncle, the Holy Roman emperor Charles IV, which occurred at the end of 1377 and the beginning of

[112] *Ibid.* 1.9 n. 3. The dispensation was given by the archbishop of Lyons, Henri de Villars, by virtue of a special commission of Pope Clement VI (Archives nationales, P. 1367[1], no. 1549 – Romans, 2 August 1349). For the relevant part of the papal bull, see *ibid.* 1.43 n. 3.

[113] *Ibid.* 1.26-27.

[114] Delachenal (n. 69 above) 2.3-4.

[115] For a contemporary account of the assembly of May 1369, see *ibid.* 2.72-76. Sarah Hanley Madden, in her recent doctoral dissertation, "The *Lit de justice* of the Kings of France: Historical Myth and Constitutional Event in Medieval and Early Modern Times" (University of Iowa 1975), has concluded that the term *lit de justice* was incorrectly applied to the extraordinary assembly of May 1369 by scholars such as F. Aubert, *Le Parlement de Paris de Philippe-le-Bel à Charles VII (1314-1422): Son organisation* (Paris 1887) 196. Dr. Madden believes that the *lit de justice* was a revival in the sixteenth century of the Renaissance antiquarians, who with their seventeenth-century counterparts, created a mythical medieval *lit de justice* having pristine origins in the French historical past.

[116] D. F. Secousse, *Ordonnances des roys de France de la troisième race recueillies par ordre chronologique*, 21 vols. (Paris 1746-1829) 6.49-54, cited in Delachenal (n. 20 above) 4.538-540.

1378. The section in the king's copy of the *Grandes chroniques* describing the state visit appears to have been written under Charles V's supervision in order to emphasize the splendor of the French court. And the account of Charles IV's call on Jeanne de Bourbon at the *hôtel* Saint-Pol is one of the fullest and most intimate sections of this part of the manuscript. The *Grandes chroniques* provided many details of Jeanne de Bourbon's crown, dress, and attendants. Also described is the long conversation she enjoyed with the emperor on the occasion of a second meeting during which she bestowed her own personal gift on him.[117]

Moreover, contemporary sources went beyond the citation of official marks of esteem which Charles V showed Jeanne de Bourbon to include various manifestations of their profound spiritual relationship. The *Chronique des quatre premiers Valois* noted that in 1373 Jeanne de Bourbon had suffered a severe illness which affected her mentally. To aid her recovery, the *Chronique* reports that "le roy de France qui moult l'amoit en fit maint pelerinage; et la mercy de Nostre Seigneur revint en sa bonne santé et en son bon sens."[118] When shortly after the emperor Charles IV's visit on 6 February 1378 the queen died after childbirth, the *Grandes chroniques* devoted four chapters to the description of the elaborate funeral rites held for her. This lengthy account was accompanied by a very prominent miniature depicting the funeral procession.[119] Of course, one can interpret this emphasis on Jeanne de Bourbon's funeral in the *Grandes chroniques* as a continuation of Charles V's use of every ceremonial occasion to express the dignity and power of the monarchy. But this source also specifically mentioned the deep emotional loss which the king felt at his wife's death:

> La dicte Royne trespassa de ce siecle, ou dit hostel de Saint-Pol, dont le Roy fu moult troublez et longuement, et si furent moult d'autres bonnes personnes, car ilz s'entreamoient tant comme loiaux mariez pevent amer l'un l'autre.[120]

Christine de Pisan, who grew up at Charles V's court, gave an eyewitness description of Jeanne de Bourbon's household in her biography of the king, which she wrote in 1403. Stressing the elegance of the court, Christine spoke glowingly about the dignity and splendor of the queen and her attendants. Christine marveled at the

[117] Delachenal (n. 69 above) 2.258-263. For a miniature illustrating the meeting of the emperor Charles IV and Jeanne de Bourbon in Charles V's copy of this manuscript (Bibl. Nat., MS fr. 2813, fol. 477), see *ibid.* 4, pl. 44.

[118] "The king of France who loved her very much made many a pilgrimage because of it [her illness], and thanks to the favor of our Lord, she regained her health and reason." S. Luce, ed., *Chronique des quatre premiers Valois (1327-1393)* (Paris 1862) 244.

[119] Delachenal (n. 69 above) 2.278-282. For the miniature of the queen's funeral procession in the king's copy of the manuscript (Paris, Bibl. Nat., MS fr. 2813, fol. 480v), see Sherman (n. 6 above) pl. 36.

[120] "The said queen departed this world at the afore-mentioned hôtel de Saint-Pol, whose death greatly disturbed the king for a long time, as well as many other good people, for they loved one another as much as loyal spouses can." Delachenal (n. 69 above) 2.278.

many changes of Jeanne de Bourbon's costume and accessories according to the time of day.[121] The inventories of the queen's possessions, including her own library of some twenty-three manuscripts, indeed confirm that Jeanne de Bourbon lived in a truly regal style.[122] Charles V's generosity in maintaining the queen and her household in proper splendor is shown in his many payments to merchants and artisans for clothes, jewels, and other valuable objects.[123]

Christine did not, however, neglect to describe the pleasant social atmosphere at court. She mentioned specifically Charles V's frequent visits and his enjoyment of Jeanne de Bourbon's company, as well as his many presents to her. Indeed, Christine's verbal account of the relationship between Charles V and Jeanne de Bourbon stressed both their compatibility and their respect for one another founded on their mutual love and friendship:

> En sa compagnie souvent estoit et tousjours à joyeux visage et moz gracieux, plaisans et esbatans, et elle, de sa partie, en lui portant l'onneur et reverence, qui à son excellence apertenoit, semblablement faisoit; et ainsi cellui en tous cas la tenoit en souffisance, amour, unité, et paix.[124]

There remains one additional source of information about the prominent role of Jeanne de Bourbon in the public events of Charles V's reign: the large number of portraits of the queen.[125] The iconography of Jeanne de Bourbon includes works in all media, from small-scale manuscript illuminations and drawings in charters to tapestry and monumental sculpture. At this time, my research indicates that there were well over thirty images of Jeanne de Bourbon, including a number which have disappeared.[126] Although quantitative comparisons with the portraits of earlier or

[121] Christine de Pisan, *Le livre des fais et bonnes meurs du sage roy Charles V*, ed. S. Solente, 2 vols. (Paris 1936-1940) 1.53-57.

[122] Among the items belonging to the queen mentioned in the inventory of the king's possessions (see Labarte [n. 98 above]) were jewelled belts and brooches (nos. 57, 71, 72, and 73), rings and other jewelry (nos. 505 and 532), altar furnishings (nos. 978, 984, 999, 1012, and 1072), table and household furnishings (nos. 1418, 1525, and 1527), and the queen's fur capes (nos. 3896-3906). For the books in Jeanne de Bourbon's own library, which came into Charles V's hands, see Delisle (n. 26 above) vol. 2 nos. 103, 112, 121, 122, 149, 163, 184, 186, 187, 248, 249, 271, 282, 331, 373, 459, 526, 930, 1106, 1119, 1131, and 1147.

[123] For the king's payments to meet the expenses of Jeanne de Bourbon and her household, see the entry "Jehanne de Bourbon, reine de France," in the index of L. Delisle, *Mandements et actes divers de Charles V (1364-1380) recueillis dans les collections de la Bibliothèque Nationale* (Paris 1874) 1000.

[124] "He was often in her company, always with a happy face and gracious words, pleasant and diverting; and she for her part, awarding him the honor and reverence which were due his rank, did the same; and thus in every way he maintained her in ample style, and in love, unity, and peace." Christine de Pisan (n. 121 above) 1.57.

[125] For a convenient collection of images of Jeanne de Bourbon, see Sherman (n. 6 above) pls. 3, 11, 21, 23, 24, 29, 36, 42, 44, 46, 47, 63, 66, 67, and 68.

[126] I am reluctant to assign a definitive number to the portraits of Jeanne de Bourbon, particularly in view of the necessity for further research in respect to the many images of the queen which have been lost.

contemporary French queens are difficult to make because of the lack of previous research, still the number of Jeanne de Bourbon's portraits appears quite considerable. To be sure, Charles V's active patronage of the arts would in many cases account for Jeanne de Bourbon's prominent iconography. Indeed, it is interesting that the most distinguished portraits of this queen are pendants of the most outstanding images of Charles V – those of the *Parement de Narbonne* (figs. 1 and 2) and the donor statues in the Louvre. The homely and distinctive features of the royal couple may lack something of the majesty we might expect from Christine's description of their appearance, but their good-humored and pleasant mien are generally in agreement with her evaluation of their personalities.[127] It is worth noting, however, that about half of the extant images of Jeanne de Bourbon show the queen engaged in official events of the reign. Several images dated between 1372 and 1374 can be related to the important role which Charles V assigned Jeanne de Bourbon as chief guardian of the royal children.[128] Of this type of "official" image, the largest group is concentrated in the cycle representing the coronation of Jeanne de Bourbon in the *Coronation Book of Charles V.*

It is fair to conclude from this array of contemporary verbal and visual evidence that Jeanne de Bourbon enjoyed a strong and enduring relationship with Charles V. Moreover, official records indicate that from the king's accession to the throne in 1364 to the queen's death in 1378, Jeanne de Bourbon played an important role in the public events of the reign consistent with both the limitations and the prerogatives of contemporary queenship. Undoubtedly the high esteem in which the king held Jeanne de Bourbon, as well as the dignity with which he wished to invest every aspect of royal ceremonial, can account in large measure for the emphasis on the queen's cycle in the *Coronation Book.* Yet, there remains one other crucial element in Jeanne de Bourbon's position at the time of the coronation which particularly relates to the question of the prominence of the cycle of miniatures representing her consecration and coronation in this manuscript. At the time of the king's accession to the throne, and indeed in 1365 when the *Coronation Book* was finished, the queen had no living offspring, although she had borne since her marriage in 1350 two girls and a boy who had subsequently died.[129] It was not until December of 1368 that the heir to the French throne, the future Charles VI was born. Under these

[127] For the donor statues in the Louvre, see Sherman (n. 6 above) pls. 45-46.

[128] For images of Jeanne de Bourbon and the royal children, see the upper right miniature of the Brussels *Ethics* dated after 1372 (Bibl. Royale, MS 9505-06, fol. 2v), the frontispiece of the *Rational des divins offices* dated 1374 (Paris, Bibl. Nat., MS fr. 437, fol. 1), and a drawing in a charter of the same year, probably by the *Rational* master (Paris, Arch. nat. J. 465 no. 48). See Sherman (n. 6 above) pls. 3, 11, and 24. The breakdown of other "official" representations of Jeanne de Bourbon is as follows: one in the *Rational des divins offices* (Paris, Bibl. Nat., MS fr. 437, fol. 50), nine in the *Coronation Book,* three in one of Charles V's copies of the *Grandes chroniques de France* (Bibl. Nat., MS fr. 2813), and another drawing in a charter (Archives de Tournai, document of 6 February 1371).

[129] These children were Jean (dates of birth and death not given), Jeanne (b. September 1357 and d. 21 October 1360), and Bonne (d. 7 November 1360). After the coronation, another girl –

circumstances would not the coronation rites for Jeanne de Bourbon have had special significance – particularly in view of the traditional function of the consecration of the queen as a kind of fertility charm?

The emphasis on fertility in the paradigmatic prayers included in the text of the queen's *ordo* lends validity to this idea.[130] Indeed, three of the thirteen prayers which make up the liturgy for the consecration and coronation of the queen in the *Coronation Book* contain references to women of the Old Testament. As we may remember, most earlier *ordines* which included the ritual for the queen's ceremony did not emphasize these paradigmatic prayers as strongly.[131] The first of this series in the *Coronation Book ordo* comes at the beginning of the ceremony when the archbishop of Rheims prays:

> Et una cum sarra. atque rebecca. lya. et rachel. beatis reuerendisque feminabus fructu uteri sui fecundari seu gratulari mereatur. ad totius decorem regni. statumque sancte dei ecclesie regendum. necnon protegendum.[132]

Although the second paradigmatic prayer in the *Coronation Book* focuses on Esther and Ahasuerus and does not specifically mention fertility, hope is voiced that this particular queen too will join in a worthy union with the king which will assure the safety of their people.[133] But the third paradigmatic prayer, which comes after the queen has been crowned, again mentions fruitfulness among the many other virtues and blessings which will accrue to her:

> Et augmentari in nomine ut sara. uisitari et fecundari ut rebecca. contra omnium muniri monstra uiciorum ut iudich. [sic] In regni regimine eligi ut hester. Ut quam humana nititur fragilitas benedicere celestis potius intimi roris et sacri olei repleat infusio.[134]

Moreover, the continued connection of fertility with the anointing of the queen is apparent from the nature of the devotions suggested by Jean Golein in the *Traité* as appropriate for the queen to address privately to the Virgin and to Christ. The text

---

also called Jeanne – was born on 7 June 1366 but died on 21 December of that year. See Père Anselme de Sainte-Marie, *Histoire généalogiqúe et chronologique de la maison royale de France*, ed. 3, 9 vols. (Paris 1726; repr. 1967) 1.110.

[130] For the tradition of paradigmatic prayers in coronation *ordines* see Katzenellenbogen (n. 14 above) 31.

[131] For the identification of these *ordines*, see n. 7 above.

[132] "And together with Sarah and Rebecca and Leah and Rachel, all blessed and revered women, may she be worthy of being made fruitful and rejoice in the fruit of her womb in order to rule and protect the glory of the whole kingdom and the state of the Holy Church." Dewick CB (n. 1 above) fol. 67, col. 45.

[133] See *ibid.* fol. 67v, col. 45.

[134] "To be increased in name as Sarah was; to be visited and made fruitful as Rebecca was; to be defended against the prodigies of all vices as Judith was; to be chosen for the command of the kingdom as Esther was; so that the pouring out of sacred oil and the inner dew of heaven may all the more fill her whom human frailty endeavors to bless." *Ibid.* fol. 70, col. 48.

which Golein supplied for this occasion made an analogy between the queen and the Virgin who was anointed "souveraine royne par le mistere du saint esperit."[135] In this prayer, the queen then asked for the blessings of motherhood as a means of securing the well-being of the nation:

> Je vous requier humblement de cuer et supplie quil vous plaise a moy empetrer grace par devers lui que je puisse au jour duy recevoir tele beneicon et onction par quoy mon cuer soit de vertuz aourne. et que je puisse faire son plaisir. et de mon seigneur aussi. et que nous puissions telement le Royaume gouverner. et telz enfans ensemble engendrer norrir et eslever que son nom en soit honnore et le pueple en paix garde.[136]

Golein had the queen mention in the prayer to Christ, which immediately followed, the several desired effects of the anointing, of which the ability to have children was the concluding benefit:

> Et au jour duy ceste beneicon de sainte inonction telement recevoir que ce soit en augmentacion de vertuz et destruction de pechiez. et que je puisse de mon seigneur tele lignie avoir qui soit ordenee a vous servir et sainte eglise.[137]

In short, both the paradigmatic prayers in the text of the queen's *ordo* in the *Coronation Book* and Golein's commentary in the *Traité* emphasized the continued meaning of the anointing as a kind of fertility charm. Its significance in view of Jeanne de Bourbon's childless state in 1364 would therefore have had particular relevance. Moreover, the cycle of images accompanying the lengthened text of the queen's *ordo* in the *Coronation Book* would also have enhanced the importance attached to this part of the ceremonial in the particular historical circumstances of 19 May 1364.

VI. Conclusion

Although the *Coronation Book of Charles V* has been widely studied since the seventeenth century, most of the research devoted to it has centered on the king's

[135] The queen refers to Mary as one who was "anointed sovereign queen by the mystery of the Holy Spirit." Golein, *Traité* (n. 5 above) fol. 50v [318]. Golein made another connection between the Virgin and the queen in regard to the offertory ceremony. See *ibid*. fol. 51 [320].

[136] "I ask you humbly from my heart and beg that it pleases you to grant me grace before Him so that I may today receive such blessing and unction by which my heart will be adorned with virtues, and that I may do His pleasure, and also that of my lord, and that we may govern the kingdom in such a way and together bring into the world, raise, and educate such children that His name will be honored and the people kept in peace." *Ibid*. fol. 50v [318-319].

[137] "And today may I receive in such a way the blessing of the holy unction as to increase my virtues and destroy my sins, and so that I may by my lord have a line of descendants who will be ordained to serve you and the Holy Church." *Ibid*. fol. 50v [319].

ordo. The central purpose of this study was to direct attention to the almost totally neglected *ordo ad benedicendam reginam* and its rich cycle of illustrations. Indeed, the prominence of the queen's *ordo* appeared all the more puzzling in view of the persistent lack of interest in its verbal and visual contents. Yet, in order to understand the relationship of the queen to the king's *Coronation Book,* it was necessary first to study the manuscript as a whole. MS Cotton Tiberius B. VIII of the British Library was revealed to have been produced under the close supervision of its royal patron and noted bibliophile, Charles V of France. At the very beginning of his reign, Charles V had commissioned both the text and the extensive cycle of miniatures in the *Coronation Book* as part of a conscious campaign to use every aspect of royal ceremonial to reassert the power and prestige of the monarchy. Moreover, the colophon of the manuscript gave strong evidence of Charles V's active role in supervising the correction, writing, arrangement, and illustration of the *Coronation Book.* The forthcoming publication of Professor Jackson on the French coronation ceremony, in which he discusses the changes in the liturgy of the king's portion of the Charles V *ordo* – in conjunction with my own discussion of the liturgy for the queen – seem strongly to suggest that the text (but not the manuscript itself) of the *Coronation Book* was actually used during the ceremony of 19 May 1364.

There also seems to be convincing internal evidence that Charles V may have intervened at an early stage in the production of the book to assure the *Coronation Book* of one of its most distinctive features: an extensive series of individualized and historically-treated illustrations. These illustrations were closely related to the text, specifically to the rubrics, which furnished the verbal sources for the individual miniatures. In turn, the illuminations served as *exempla* in particular of the generalized instructions of the rubrics. By providing essential details of costume and protocol, the illustrations could aid in fulfilling the essential purpose of the manuscript to serve as a model for the procedures of future coronations. In an appropriately dry and concise style, a favored royal atelier headed by an artist called the Master of the *Coronation Book of Charles V* provided consistent portrait types of the king, queen, and other principal actors, as well as accuracy in important details of costume and accessories.

In view of the complexity of the illustrations, it also seemed reasonable to postulate an intermediary who furnished a verbal set of instructions to the illuminator for the sake of achieving the kind of accuracy and consistency essential to the larger commemorative purpose of the manuscript. Such a person probably would have compiled the text of the *ordo* under the king's supervision and would have probably been an eyewitness at the actual coronation ceremony. Among the clerics working in Charles V's "public relations" office, Jean Golein seemed a possible choice. For, as Golein himself told us, early in the next decade, the king himself commissioned as part of Golein's translation of Durandus's *Rationale divinorum officiorum* a commentary on the coronation of French rulers based on the actual rites held for Charles V and Jeanne de Bourbon. Indeed, the *Traité du sacre,* as Golein's commentary is now called, contains several passages which suggest – although not conclusively – that Golein was present at the coronation. Finally,

Golein's ties with the royal family go back to the 1360s, and there is also some evidence that at one time he had been the queen's confessor.[138] While no sure proof exists that Golein was involved in the production of the *Coronation Book,* we do know that at least later in his career he was active in the Paris book trade.[139]

Whether Golein was the person who provided verbal instructions to the illuminator or not, the *Traité du sacre* was extremely valuable in expanding our understanding of the Jeanne de Bourbon miniatures in the *Coronation Book.* Moreover, the direct connection of the *Traité* with the views of the official royal circle, and indeed with Charles V himself, makes Golein's interpretation of the queen's ceremony in political and propaganda terms all the more significant. This is especially true of Golein's views on one of the most crucial dynastic questions of the fourteenth century, the exclusion of women from inheriting the French crown. Thus, to demonstrate conclusively that the claim of the English kings to the French crown through the female line was entirely without foundation, Golein interpreted the symbolism associated with the consecration and coronation of French queens to show that they lacked the attributes essential to the basic character of French kings. The central difference was embodied in the distinction in the anointing of the king and queen. Because she was not entitled to be anointed with the heavenly balm preserved in the Sainte Ampoule, the queen lacked the sacral qualities of the king, including his ability to cure scrofula. Golein claimed that both historical tradition and divine will lay behind this crucial difference in the anointing, as well as in the consequence that the succession to the crown could be transmitted only through the closest male heir.[140] Golein further maintained that the queen's exclusion from the crown was based on other limitations in the symbolism of the coronation rite. Because the queen was blessed neither with the fleur-de-lis banner nor the oriflamme at the conclusion of the ceremony, this shows that the office was traditionally associated with a man rather than with a woman.[141] Thus, Golein's arguments seem to confirm the views of those scholars who have maintained that women were excluded from the French throne in the fourteenth century because they lacked the necessary sacerdotal – hence male – character essential to contemporary concepts of French kingship.[142] At the same time, Golein's interpretation shows that differences between the ceremonial of the king and queen were emphasized and employed for the distinct propaganda purpose of disallowing the English claim to the French throne in favor of the reigning Valois dynasty.[143]

[138] For a legal document dated 1386 stating that Golein had been the queen's confessor, see Williman (n. 31 above) 73. Although another man is known to have occupied the post in 1375, Golein may have been confessor to Jeanne de Bourbon before or after this date.

[139] See *ibid.* 77, and Delisle (n. 26 above) 1.69 and 103.

[140] Golein, *Traité* (n. 5 above) fol. 54 [323].

[141] *Ibid.* fol. 54rv [323-324].

[142] See n. 9 above.

[143] Nicole Oresme, one of the most distinguished thinkers in the entourage of Charles V, included his arguments for the exclusion of women from the French throne in a lengthy gloss on the respective merits of elective and hereditary kingship in his translation from Latin into French

In one sense, the analysis of the Jeanne de Bourbon cycle confirmed the inability of the queen to exercise sovereignty in her own right. Such elements as the queen's place of entrance, the location and smaller size of her throne, and the restrictions on her costume and regalia showed that her symbolic status was inferior to that of the king. Yet at the same time, both the text and images of the *ordo ad reginam benedicendam* in the *Coronation Book* indicated both the high social and moral status of the queen. With all due recognition of Charles V's conscious exploitation of all phases of royal ceremonial to enhance the prestige of the monarchy, one must also acknowledge that the length and character of the queen's *ordo* – to say nothing of the prominence of the densely-illustrated cycle of accompanying miniatures – had additional motivations. A considerable range of contemporary sources revealed the long-standing attachment between the king and queen, as well as the official manifestations of the great esteem which Charles V had for Jeanne de Bourbon. Furthermore, the traditional association of the anointing of the queen with her fertility had particular relevance to the situation of the royal couple at the time of the coronation. For, after fourteen years of marriage, they still had not produced an heir to the throne. The shaky situation of the new Valois dynasty, whose first two rulers Philippe VI and Jean le Bon had led France in the disastrous first phase of the Hundred Years' War, was thus increased. Therefore, the changes in the liturgy of the queen's *ordo* in the *Coronation Book,* particularly the emphasis on the paradigmatic prayers, can be traced to the traditional connection between anointing and fertility in its application to the historical situation in 1364. The prominence of the cycle of the miniatures depicting the consecration and coronation of Jeanne de Bourbon is surely due to the singular importance of the ritual for the queen in the particular historical context just described.

Although this study does not pretend to provide definitive answers to all the questions which it may have raised, I would hope that several points regarding methodology have been persuasive. The first one concerns the necessity of examining the relationship of the images to the text of a manuscript and their function, particularly when new or greatly expanded cycles of illustrations are involved. In this case, the role of the patron, documented by the colophon, was particularly important both in regard to the writing and arrangement of the text and most probably also in terms of an expanded program of illustration. The second area involved in this study led me into various problems concerning the nature of medieval French queenship. Aside from several pioneer efforts, the lack of research on the institutional and cultural influence of French queens shows the need of a

---

of Aristotle's *Politics*. See *Maistre Nicole Oresme: Le livre de politiques d'Aristote*, ed. A. D. Menut, TAPhS n.s. 60.6 (1970) 155-156. Since Charles V himself had commissioned the translation of this text, one can conclude that Oresme's views on the exclusion of women from inheriting or transmitting the succession to the French crown expressed an official royal "propaganda" position.

great deal more effort in this field on the part of historians.[144] The same lack of focus on the contributions of medieval French queens as patrons of the arts, or to the development of portraiture and to certain types of illuminated books was also obvious. As an art historian, I am particularly concerned that the roles of French medieval queens become the subject of renewed research within a broadly-based multi-disciplinary framework. It is in this spirit that I offer the example of my study of "The Queen in Charles V's *Coronation Book*" as a possible guide to a reexamination of a rich body of verbal and visual material which can substantially add to our understanding of the cultural history of the Middle Ages.

4516 Que Lane, N.W.
Washington, D.C. 20007, U.S.A.

[144] Among recent studies by historians are those by Facinger (n. 8 above) and Barry (n. 48 above).

ILLUSTRATIONS

All the illustrations, except where noted to the contrary, are from British Library, MS Cotton Tiberius B. VIII, the *Coronation Book of Charles V of France,* and are reproduced by permission of the British Library Board.

Figure 1. Charles V. Lower left compartment of central section, *Parement de Narbonne.* Paris, Musée du Louvre. Courtesy of Archives photographiques.

Figure 2. Jeanne de Bourbon. Lower right compartment of central section, *Parement de Narbonne.* Paris, Musée du Louvre. Courtesy of Archives photographiques.

Figure 3. The Entrance of Jeanne de Bourbon, fol. 66.

Figure 4. The Reception of Charles V at the West Portal of Rheims Cathedral, fol. 43.

Figure 5. Jeanne de Bourbon in Prayer, fol. 66v.

Figure 6. The Archbishop Prepares for the Unction of Charles V, fol. 50v.

Figure 7. The Preparation for the Unction of Jeanne de Bourbon, fol. 67v.

Figure 8. The Unction of Jeanne de Bourbon, fol. 68.

Figure 9. The Unction of a Queen (Jeanne de Bourbon?), *Rational des divins offices,* Bibliothèque Nationale MS fr. 437 fol. 50. Courtesy of Bibliothèque Nationale.

Figure 10. Jeanne de Bourbon Receives the Ring, fol. 68v.

Figure 11. Jeanne de Bourbon Receives the Scepter and the Rod, fol. 69.

Figure 12. Charles V Receives the Scepter and the Hand of Justice, fol. 58.

Figure 13. The Crowning of Jeanne de Bourbon, fol. 69v.

Figure 14. The Barons and Other Nobles Support the Crown, fol. 70.

Figure 15. The Spiritual and Temporal Peers Support the Crown, fol. 59v.

Figure 16. Charles V Conducted to the Throne, fol. 63.

Figure 17. Charles V Enthroned, fol. 64.

Figure 18. Jeanne de Bourbon Receives Communion, fol. 72.

FIG. 1

FIG. 2

FIG. 3

FIG. 4

FIG. 5

FIG. 6

FIG. 7

FIG. 8

FIG. 9

FIG. 10

FIG. 11

FIG. 12

FIG. 13

FIG. 14

FIG. 15

FIG. 16

FIG. 17

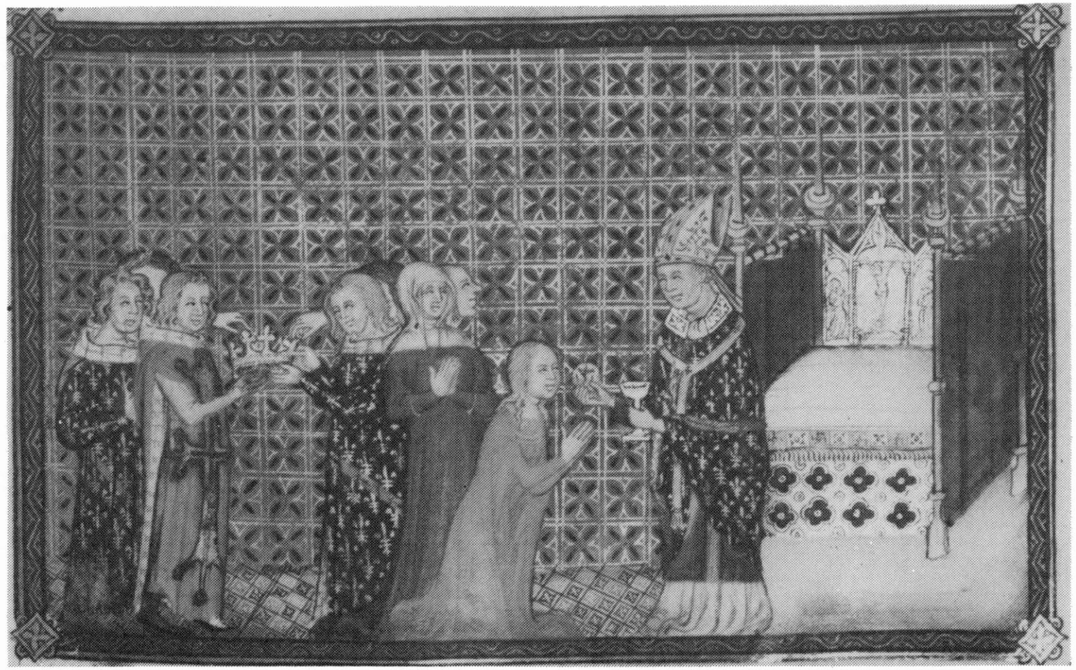

FIG. 18

A LETTER OF GIOVANNI DONDI DALL' OROLOGIO TO FRA' GUGLIELMO CENTUERI: A FOURTEENTH-CENTURY EPISODE IN THE QUARREL OF THE ANCIENTS AND THE MODERNS

•

by Neal W. Gilbert

The Quarrel of the Ancients and Moderns had its beginnings, for modern Europe at least, in the rich soil of fourteenth-century Italy: it did not wait for the achievements of seventeenth-century science to break out. This fact, which has been suggested by several scholars, emerges very clearly from the consideration of a letter written by Giovanni Dondi dall' Orologio (d. 1389) – a gifted and versatile friend of Petrarch – who taught medicine at Padua and Pavia.[1] Dondi exchanged letters and even sonnets

It is a pleasure to acknowledge the help of scholars and librarians who assisted in this research, beginning with Prof. Paul O. Kristeller, who reviewed my transcription of Dondi's letter while in Venice and supplied many readings that would have been far beyond my meager abilities as a paleographer. Any errors that remain in the text are mine. I am grateful to Signora Tullia Gasparina Leporace, then *direttrice* of the Biblioteca Marciana, for permission to reproduce the letter, as well as to the Stiftsbibliothek in Schlaegl, Austria, and to Prof. Julian G. Plante, curator of the Monastic Manuscript Microfilm Library in St. John's University, Collegeville, Minnesota, for allowing me to consult another manuscript of the letter. Prof. H. A. Kelly of the University of California, Los Angeles, and my colleague Prof. David Traill of the Department of Classics, University of California, Davis, as well as Prof. Kristeller, made many improvements in the English rendering of Dondi's letter. My thanks also go to the Centro Studi of the University of California located in Padua and to the University of Padua, its generous host; the center provided me with study facilities. While there I was assisted a great deal by Prof. Paul Castelfranco and Signorina Bianca Tonini. Prof. Lynn White, jr., another admirer of Dondi's clock, has encouraged me in this research.

The following libraries generously facilitated the consultation of rare works: Biblioteca Marciana, Biblioteca universitaria di Padova, Museo civico di Padova, Seminario di Padova, Biblioteca capitolare di Padova, Biblioteca Ambrosiana, Biblioteca apostolica Vaticana, Archivio di Stato, Mantua, University of Aix, British Library, Bodleian Library, Oxford, University of California (Davis, Berkeley, Los Angeles), Huntington Library, Newberry Library, University of Michigan, University of Minnesota, University of Rochester, Yale University, Columbia University, Library of Congress.

Finally, my thanks go to that marvelous institution, the John Simon Guggenheim Memorial Foundation, for the fellowship that enabled me to pursue this research.

Since I prepared this edition of Dondi's letter, I have been told by Professor Giuseppe Billanovich that an edition of all the letters of Dondi is being prepared in Italy by S. Albricci and E. L. Figini. This edition will fill an obvious gap in fourteenth-century scholarship.

[1] *Name.* The form of our author's name that has come to be accepted in Italian scholarship is "Giovanni Dondi dall' Orologio"; one also sees "Giovanni de' Dondi." Valuable testimony as to

with Petrarch, and this exchange has brought him to the attention of literary historians. But he was also a scientist of considerable attainments who developed an instrument, called by him a *planetarium*, which showed the positions of the sun, the moon, and the five planets. By this achievement Giovanni earned the right to the sobriquet "Of the Clock" (dall' Orologio), which had first been applied to his father Jacopo, also a teacher of medicine and inventor of an earlier *astrarium*, which did not, however, show the position of the five planets as did Giovanni's. Giovanni Dondi was an admirer of the ruins of ancient Rome; his notes on Roman buildings and inscriptions have been of interest to archaeologists and historians. As a teacher of medicine at the University of Padua, Giovanni was an influential figure, chosen by his

---

the way in which he was called in his lifetime is given by his friend, Philippe de Mézières, who knew him in the 1380's when Giovanni was in the service of Giangaleazzo Visconti: "Lequel est appelle Maistre Jehans de Dons, de la cite de Pade. Et pour sa profunde science d'astronomie son seurnom est perdu et est appelle Maistre Jehan des Orologes"; Philippe de Mézières, *Le songe du vieil pelerin*, ed. G. W. Coopland, 2 vols. (Cambridge 1969) 1.605. Philippe's observation is borne out (except for the plural "clocks") by the records of the University of Pavia: when Giovanni's name occurs among the presenting or examining masters, it usually appears in its common form, as "Iohannes de Orologio." Only in the formal wording of degrees does the full form appear: "Iohannes de Dondis dictus de Orologio de Padua" (this from a degree awarded on 9 Aug. 1383); Rodolfo Maiocchi, *Codice diplomatica dell' Università di Pavia,* 2 vols. (Pavia 1905) 1.93. The formal version of his name also appears in a letter of recommendation written by Dondi that I believe to be autograph (see below at n. 60). It is not clear to me whether the addition of the word *dictus* was intended to suggest, as De Mézières implies, that Giovanni was called "Of the clock" in place of his family name, or that he was called "Of the clock" by ordinary people who did not know the difference between Giovanni's elaborate instrument and a common clock. We know from Petrarch's testament that the designation "Of the clock" was felt to be somewhat demeaning to a man like Giovanni Dondi who was able to design a planetarium that showed much more than the mere time of day: see Theodor Mommsen, *Petrarch's Testament* (Ithaca, N. Y. 1957) 84; also Theodor Mommsen, "The Last Will: A Personal Document of Petrarch's Old Age," *Medieval and Renaissance Studies*, ed. Eugene Rice (Ithaca, N. Y. 1959) 223. Giovanni's father was also called simply "magister Jacobus ab Orlogio" as well as "magister Jacobus de Dondis nominatus ab Orlogio." See Andrea Gloria, "I due orologi meravigliosi inventati da Jacopo e Giovanni Dondi," *Atti del R. Istituto Veneto di scienze, lettere, ed arti* 7 (1896) 710-713.

Birthdate. It is disconcerting to learn that two birthdates are reported for Giovanni Dondi in the secondary literature – and even more disconcerting to find that this awkward situation is seldom recognized. One tradition, that Giovanni was born in 1318, apparently derives from family archives, as reported by a descendant: "Nato Giovanni del 1318 da Jacopo Dondi . . . in Chioggia," Francesco Scipione Dondi dall' Orologio, "Notizie sopra Jacopo e Giovanni Dondi dall' Orologio," *Saggi scientifici e letterari dell' Accademia Patavina di scienze, lettere, ed arti* 2 (1789) 469-494 at 476. He gives no precise evidence for this statement, but we are led to believe that he was relying on family papers (which may still exist in the Museo civico of Padua). Without laboring the facts, suffice it to say that this account was accepted by Colle, Vedova, Thorndike, and Bedini and Maddison. Another view, strongly represented in the secondary literature, has it that Giovanni was born in 1330. This tradition seems to derive mainly from Bellemo: "Giovanni Dondi naque in Chioggia intorno all' anno 1330," *Jacopo e Giovanni de Dondi dall' Orologio* 109 (see complete ref. later in this note). We find this date repeated, with some hesitation, by a local historian of Chioggia, the coastal village south of Venice that is presumed to be Dondi's birthplace: "Giovanni [Dondi] nacque a Chioggia nel 1328 o circa il 1330," Domenico Razza, *Storia popolare di Chioggia* (Chioggia 1898) 1.155. This date, 1330, is

peers to represent the faculty of arts in a dispute with the law faculty. His literary remains include a treatise on the *astrarium*, extant in several manuscripts and recently published from one of them; a short work on avoiding the plague, published by a medical historian; some *sermones* or academic speeches, now lost and known only by their titles; a few stray letters on routine subjects, scattered and unpublished, as well as a set of letters, some of which have been published from a manuscript in Venice; some disputed questions on the *Tegni* of Galen, unpublished; and a group of sonnets and ballads which have been published, some of them many times.

The letter that we publish here was first noticed in print by Giacomo Morelli, the

---

accepted by Antonio Barzon in the Vatican ed. of Dondi's *Tractatus astrarii* (Vatican City 1960) 6, who cites Andrea Gloria's *Monumenti della Università di Padova* 1 (Padua 1888) entry 728. In the passage cited, however, Gloria does not give a birthdate for Giovanni. In another work Gloria does mention the date, but with reservations: "Giovanni sarebbe nato in Chioggia nel 1330 circa, giusta i computi fatti dallo stesso Bellemo"; Andrea Gloria, "I due orologi meravigliosi" 718. In the *Monumenti* (1.386), Gloria acknowledges that Colle had suggested the date 1318, but seems to have misgivings about endorsing it himself: "E il Colle . . . che fa nato Giovanni nel 1318 . . . ." In short, Gloria was probably aware that neither of the two dates advanced for Giovanni's birth rests on solid evidence – and that is exactly where we stand today. Scholars seem to believe that by discrediting one of two suggested dates they have established the other. But both dates could be wrong. This situation is annoying: it would be useful to know how much junior to Petrarch Dondi was, and where he stood in relation to other contemporaries such as Fra' Guglielmo Centueri (whose birthdate, incidentally, is also not known).

Bibliography. Information on Giovanni Dondi is extensive but scattered. Until the *Dizionario biografico degli Italiani* reaches him, it would be best to begin with the exellent bibliography appended to Silvio Bedini and Francis Maddison, "Mechanical Universe: The Astrarium of Giovanni de' Dondi," *Transactions of the American Philosophical Society* 56 (1966) 63-66, which focuses chiefly upon the *astrarium* and discusses Jacopo as well as Giovanni Dondi. The basic biography is still the obsolete work of Vincenzo Bellemo, *Jacopo e Giovanni de Dondi dall' Orologio: Note critiche con le rime edite e inediti di Giovanni Dondi* (Chioggia 1894). Bellemo gives the text of Giovanni Dondi's letter of 24 Oct. 1370, to Petrarch ("Debui nec ignoro. . .") 295-310, which answers *Seniles* 12.1 ("Obtulist michi"). Other letters of Dondi had been published previously by Antonio Zardo, *Il Petrarca e i Carraresi* (Milan 1887): one to Petrarch ("Zilius noster. . .") which answers *Sen.* 13.15 ("Ex mea sospitate") and the famous letter of 19 July 1374 on the death of Petrarch ("Heu mestam ac lugubrem epistolam. . .") 282-285. All of these were published from the Venetian miscellany to be discussed subsequently. To complete the picture, three other letters of Petrarch to Dondi must be consulted in sixteenth-century eds.: *Sen.* 12.2 ("Video amice"), *Sen.* 13.15 ("Ex mea sospitate"), and *Sen.* 13.16 ("Incolumitas tua"), which answers Dondi's "Zilius noster."

The letter to Fra' Guglielmo Centueri that we publish here was mentioned briefly by Giacomo Morelli, *Epistolae septem variae eruditionis* (Padua 1819) 84-85; again in *Operette,* 3 vols. (Venice 1820) 2.289 and 2.302-304; and again in *Di Giovanni Dondi dall' Orologio, medico di Padova, e dei monumenti antichi da lui esaminati a Roma, e di alcuni scritti inediti del medesimo* (Padua 1850) 12. After Morelli, and usually echoing him, the letter was mentioned by the following: Eugène Müntz, *Les précurseurs de la Renaissance* (Paris 1882) 39, who remarks, after quoting a passage given by Morelli: "Il est facheux que Morelli . . . n'ait pas reproduit intégralement ce document si curieux"; Victor M. Massena, Prince d'Essling, and Eugène Müntz, *Pétrarque, ses études d'arts, son influence sur les artistes, ses portraits et ceux de Laure* (Paris 1902) 44-45; Pierre de Nolhac, *Pétrarque et l'humanisme*, ed. 2, 2 vols. (Paris 1907) 1.139-140 (ed. 1, 1892); Erwin Panofsky, *Renaissance and Renascences in Western Art* (Stockholm 1960) 208-210; and Richard Krautheimer, *Lorenzo Ghiberti* (Princeton 1970) 295-297.

prefect of the imperial and royal library of Saint Mark, now the Biblioteca Marciana, in the early nineteenth century. It has never been printed in its entirety, even though Morelli's account was interesting enough to whet the appetites of historians of literature and art, beginning with Eugène Müntz in 1882 and continuing with Pierre de Nolhac, Erwin Panofsky, and Richard Krautheimer. While complaining occasionally about the meagerness of Morelli's report, later scholars have so far contented themselves with citing excerpts from this letter. The reason for this will soon become clear to anyone who examines the manuscript in Venice: it is written in a hand that is not at all pleasant to read ("a monstruous apograph," one discouraged student called it), and it is quite lengthy. Yet it is extremely significant for the light that it throws upon the attitude of the circle around Petrarch in his later years toward their hero and toward Antiquity. Giovanni Dondi felt the deficiencies of his Age very keenly, and deplored its shortcomings. This mood he shared with Petrarch – indeed, as we shall see, he probably inherited it from his distinguished friend. The juxtaposition of the failings and shortcomings of the present Age with the achievements of the ancient Romans helps to set the stage, of course, for the *Querelle des ançiens et des modernes* three centuries later. What is surprising about this preliminary phase of the Quarrel is that the defender of the Ancients is Dondi, the man of science, while the defender of the Moderns, his correspondent, is a theologian! For the intended recipient of Dondi's letter was Fra' Guglielmo Centueri of Cremona (d. 1402), a Franciscan divine and administrator, who, at the time when Dondi wrote his letter, was teaching at Pavia.[2] This "William of Cremona" has only recently begun to be distinguished from another William of the same city, Guglielmo degli Amidani, an Augustinian who lived somewhat earlier. Dondi's correspondent, the Franciscan, was clearly a busy administrator, as we learn from the letter itself. Equipped with a

[2] Possibly not in the university but in the *studium generale* of the Franciscan convent in Pavia, according to A. Corbellini, "Appunti sull' umanesimo in Lombardia," *Bolletino della Società Pavese di storia patria* 15 (1915) 362. There was only one chair of theology in the University of Pavia for many years, and it was occupied by Fra' Bonifacio Bottigella, an Augustinian. However, Fra' Guglielmo Centueri was clearly active in university affairs in some collegiate capacity. Corbellini (356-357) finds an analogous situation with respect to Petrus de Candia, who had affiliations with the University of Pavia, but left no sign of having ever officially taught theology in the university. Fra' Guglielmo began his association with the University of Pavia at least as early as 9 June 1381, when he awarded a medical degree acting in place of the bishop (of Pavia, presumably): Maiocchi (n. 1 above) 1.69. It would seem that the bishop was already ailing and unable to preside, for we find other masters substituting for him as well, including, on 18 April 1382, Giovanni Dondi (Maiocchi 1.77). After Fra' Guglielmo became bishop of Pavia, he awarded degrees by his own authority. When Fra' Guglielemo died, Giangaleazzo Visconti appointed the bishop of Piacenza to serve as his successor as chancellor of the university (Maiocchi 2.16), so presumably Guglielmo had also served in the university at the pleasure of the *Conte di Virtù*.

Giovanni Dondi's association with the University of Pavia had already begun at least as early as 3 November 1379, when he was an examiner for a candidate in medicine (Maiocchi 1.60). It continued with entries for the early months of 1380 and then again those of 1382. Meanwhile Dondi was still active in examinations at the University of Padua, e.g., in April of 1380 and again in April of 1381 (Gloria [n. 1 above] *Monumenti* 1.382).

theological degree from Paris, Guglielmo eventually rose to the office of bishop in Pavia and became chancellor of the University of Pavia as well. We may briefly recapitulate his life.[3] He was the son of a doctor, a fact that may help to explain his friendship with Dondi, a medical man and himself the son of a doctor. Cenci conjectures that he must have been born about 1340, since he was a bachelor of theology by 1365, when he took part in a general chapter of the Franciscan order at Florence, a fact mentioned by Saint Bernardino of Siena.[4] We owe to Saint Bernardino, who mentions Fra' Guglielmo's views in a sermon, the preservation of fragments of Guglielmo's commentary on the *Sentences* of Peter Lombard. Bernardino owned Guglielmo's own copy of this commentary, from which he transcribed sections.[5] Other writings of Guglielmo exist in Fribourg; they are fragments of a *solemnissima quaestio* held by Guglielmo when he was a bachelor of theology at Bologna in 1368.[6] In them Guglielmo discusses the views of Brinkel, an English Franciscan who was cited also by another Franciscan with whom Fra' Guglielmo seems to have been closely associated, namely, Petrus de Candia, who later became Pope Alexander V. Guglielmo also mentions the presence of his own brother at the chapter meeting in Florence in 1365, when the brother argued with an English Franciscan, Master John Mardeslay.[7] These references are interesting for the light they throw upon the intellectual milieu of Dondi's correspondent. Clearly there must have been close intellectual and personal ties between Franciscan study houses in Italy and their counterparts in England. For example, Petrus de Candia studied in England: at Oxford, in the Franciscan *studium* there, and probably also at Norwich. Peter returned to the Continent as a champion of Oxford thought. Other non-English Franciscans who were exposed to British subtlety did not, as we know, find it so much to their liking. To judge from the admittedly scanty evidence available in print, Guglielmo Centueri may have been one of those not so favorably disposed toward contemporaries of an Ockhamist persuasion, although he does seem to have been

[3] Fra' Guglielmo's biography has been presented by Cesare Cenci, *Fr. Guglielmo Centueri da Cremona: Trattato "De Iure Monarchiae"* (Verona 1967) 12-38, from which most of the following details have been drawn.

[4] Discussing the issue of usury as it applied to the Florentine *monte*, Bernardino remarked: "Spectabiliores viri saepe de materia ista dubitant et inquirunt, sicut manifeste apparuit Florentiae in nostro Capitulo generali inibi celebrato anno Domini 1354 [actually 1365] ad quod utique convenerunt multi valentes viri, inter quos fuit magister Guillelmus de Cremona, qui postea fuit episcopus Papiensis, vir utique ingentis scientiae et magnae famae." Bernardinus Senensis, *Opera omnia* (Quaracchi 1956) 4.326.

[5] Extant in MS 102 of the University Library of Budapest: see Cesare Cenci, "Un manoscritto autografo di San Bernardino a Budapest," *Studi francescani* 61 (1964) 334. Fra' Guglielmo's commentary on the *Sentences* survived until at least the end of the seventeenth century, for it was seen in the Franciscan convent of Cremona by Franciscus Arisius, *Cremona literata* (Parma 1702) 1.184.

[6] Damasus Trapp, " 'Moderns' and 'Modernists' in MS Fribourg Cordeliers 26," *Augustinianum* 5 (1965) 241-270 at 259.

[7] Active 1355-1380, according to Andrew Little, *The Grey Friars in Oxford* (Oxford 1892) 242.

intrigued by them. The Bologna *quaestio*, for example, makes reference to William of Ockham and also to some "contemporaries" (*moderni*) "who have one great man in arts at Oxford who says that the opinions of Aristotle on the eternity of the world do not conflict with the dicta of the Catholic faith."[8] It is not clear from this brief reference whether these *moderni* are simply contemporaries or duly-acknowledged followers of Ockham. It is just possible that by this late date in the fourteenth century (1368) the rivalry between Wyclifites and contemporary logicians had reached the stage at which labels had begun to crystallize.[9] The general chapter of the Franciscans held at Naples in 1370 sent Fra' Guglielmo to Paris to read the *Sentences*.[10] He was in Paris at least for the scholastic year 1372-1373, although he was unable to complete the year because he was sent to the general chapter at Toulouse in 1373. Nevertheless Pope Gregory XI requested the university on 7 March 1373 to declare Fra' Guglielmo a master of theology.[11] In 1374 Guglielmo assisted in the conferring of a doctorate at the University of Bologna. We are not certain where Fra' Guglielmo spent the years between 1378 and 1381; Cenci suggests that he may have been in Piacenza. He was at any rate then invited to Pavia by Pasquino Capelli, his fellow Cremonese, who was secretary and chancellor of Giangaleazzo Visconti[12] (and also, incidentally, a correspondent of Giovanni Dondi, as we shall see). In Pavia, Guglielmo became one of the circle of advisers of Giangaleazzo, and was described by a chronicler of Piacenza as "a man most acute in logic, philosophy, and the liberal arts" and hence as very congenial to Giangaleazzo because of his similarity to him "in form and stature."[13] Guglielmo is referred to by Dondi in the

[8] Trapp 258.

[9] See Neal W. Gilbert, "Ockham, Wyclif, and the 'Via Moderna'," *Miscellanea mediaevalia* 9 (1974) 85-125.

[10] Cenci (n. 3 above) 16.

[11] H. Denifle and E. Chatelain, eds., *Chartularium Universitatis Parisiensis*, 4 vols. (Paris 1889-1897) 3.211.

[12] Cenci 19.

[13] *Ibid.* Although we are aware of personal relationships among Pasquino de' Cappelli, Guglielmo Centueri, Giovanni Dondi, and Petrus de Candia, I am not certain which of these men had the most influence with the Visconti: one would naturally assume it to be Pasquino, since he was Giangaleazzo's chancellor and secretary. It is worth noting that several of these men, including our two correspondents, Giovanni and Guglielmo, had connections with Cremona, the native city of Pasquino de' Cappelli. Fra' Guglielmo was the last of a Cremonese family, while the Dondis, according to family tradition (which, however, has been disputed), originally stemmed from Cremona. The records of the University of Pavia show that one of the most influential lecturers in grammar and rhetoric there in the fourteenth century was Giovanni Travesio, also from Cremona (Corbellini [n. 2 above] 331). One of the letters of Giovanni Dondi in the Venetian miscellany is addressed "Ioanni de Cremona artium liberalium magistro."

We tend to follow the lead of fourteenth-century court flattery in thinking that princes like Giangaleazzo appreciated talent and went to great lengths to attract it to their service. Thus Dondi's biographers assume that the ruler of Milan learned of his ability and summoned him personally. But perhaps we should exercise caution in accepting statements about the motivation behind Giovanni Dondi's move to Pavia. Lazzarini has suggested that Giovanni may have fallen into disfavor with Francesco II, of the ruling Carrara family in Padua, for having shown the Venetians a map of the territory involved in a border dispute between Venice and Padua. The

address of his letter as "magister sacrae paginae": as we have seen, he probably taught in the *studium* of the Franciscan order rather than in the university, although this may have changed after 1386 when our theologian obtained from Pope Urban VI permission to establish a faculty of theology at the University of Pavia.[14]

When the bishop of Piacenza died in 1381, Giangaleazzo Visconti immediately suggested to the canons of the cathedral that they elect Fra' Guglielmo as his successor, making the same "suggestion" to Pope Urban VI. The rival pope, Clement VII, had meanwhile notified the canons of his own choice, Andrea Serazoni of Milan. Giangaleazzo settled the issue by informing the canons that any of them who persisted in obeying the wrong bishop would be burnt. Fra' Guglielmo remained in Pavia despite being named bishop of Piacenza officially in 1383; finally he was translated to the see of Pavia in 1386.[15] From a reference in Dondi's letter to heavy duties recently assumed (lines 7-8), it could be assumed that the letter, which is undated in the manuscript, was written after Guglielmo became bishop of Piacenza. On the other hand, Fra' Guglielmo was previously a provincial minister of his order, and Dondi may have been referring to his duties in that post. In any event we know that Dondi's letter was written after the death of Petrarch in 1374, since he speaks of their mutual friend in tones applicable only to one who has not been on the scene for some time.

Various documents attest to the confidence placed in Fra' Guglielmo by Giangaleazzo Visconti, and it is possible that it was through his good offices that Giovanni Dondi, apparently a close friend, was lured to Milan. As bishop of Pavia, Centueri was the chancellor of the University of Pavia, where his name appears often in the official acts, as does that of Giovanni Dondi after the latter moved to Pavia.[16] Centueri apparently took an active role in recruiting faculty for the university: of

---

map had been drawn by Jacopo Dondi, and somehow favored the Venetian side in the dispute, of which Giovanni Dondi was one of ten arbitrators in 1372 (Vittorio Lazzarini, "Di una carta di Jacopo Dondi e di altre carte del Padovano nel Quattrocento," *Scritti di paleografia e diplomatica* (Padua 1969) 120. A bit of light is thrown on Dondi's attitude about leaving his native city for the court of the Visconti by a remark quoted by Uberto Decembrio (who may at the time have been secretary to the archbishop of Milan, Petrus de Candia): "The tendency to stay in one's native birthplace, even when it is lowly and obscure," Dondi is reported as saying, "must be attributed to the ignorance and inexperience of men." (Corbellini 36). Was Giovanni thinking of himself and Chioggia or Padua? The tone is slightly defensive.

[14] Cenci (n. 3 above) 23.

[15] Cenci 21-22, 24.

[16] See the many entries given for both men in the index of Maiocchi (n. 1 above). Of special interest is the degree in medicine awarded to Tommaso Parati of Crema on 15 June 1383, with Fra' Guglielmo presiding as bishop of Piacenza. Giovanni Dondi was one of the masters who presented Tommaso for the degree. MS 1065 of the Biblioteca Palatina of Parma contains medical notes taken on lectures by Albertino da Salso maggiore and also questions on Hippocrates by Giovanni Dondi: Piero Giacosa, *Magistri Salernitani nondum editi* (Turin 1901) 414-416. Another degree of interest is that awarded on 22 Feb. 1387 to Fra' Facino Bazzani of Casale. It spells out the requirements satisfied by the candidate (who was in theology) in great detail. He had spent at least eight years in philosophy in study houses of the Franciscan order, and had spent three years in England studying theology (Maiocchi 1.121-122). This further

particular interest to us is his calling of the youthful Ugo Benzi in 1396 to teach logic.[17] Ugo Benzi had studied logic at Bologna under Peter of Mantua with great eagerness, but soon, so his son tells us, exhausted the master's arguments and annoyed him by inventing new arguments of his own.[18] From shreds of evidence such as this, it might be tempting to assume that Fra' Guglielmo was an advocate of the "spidery logic of the British moderns" and for that reason tended to look more favorably on things "modern". Such an assumption would, in my judgment, be premature, for we know far too little about the whole ambience of intellectual currents at Pavia and Milan during this period. Still it would seem that Fra' Guglielmo was at least intrigued by British logic and science and it is possible that, in inviting Ugo Benzi to Pavia, he hoped to promote that logic and science.[19] If this was the case, Guglielmo de' Centueri may not have been too removed in outlook from his successor as bishop of Piacenza, the so-called "Nominalist" Petrus de Candia, with whom he was closely associated in the service of Giangaleazzo Visconti.[20] Petrus seems to have been Fra' Guglielmo's direct student in theology.[21] In the Fribourg questions, Guglielmo mentions the British theologians Duns Scotus, William of Ockham, and Thomas Bradwardine, as well as an "Anglican doctor of our order," whom a marginal note identifies as "Brinkil Folvil," a conflation of two

---

confirms the exposure to British philosophy and theology among Italian Franciscans of this period.

[17] "For he [Ugo Benzi] was immediately invited to Pavia [in 1396] to teach logic in the University. His invitation to that . . . city . . . came from the bishop . . ., famous for the sanctity of his morals as well as for the profundity of his learning." Dean Lockwood, *Ugo Benzi, Medieval Philosopher and Physician (1376-1439)* (Chicago 1951) 24. The Latin text, which comes from a life of Ugo by his son, actually reads "a Bernardo Centuero," correctly identified by Lockwood (151) as a mistaken reference to Guglielmo de' Centueri.

[18] Lockwood 23-24 (Latin text 151).

[19] On Peter of Mantua, see Cesare Vasoli, "Pietro degli Alboini da Mantova, 'Scolastico' della fine del Trecento e un' Epistola di Coluccio Salutati," *Studi sulla cultura del Rinascimento* (Manduria 1968) 11-34.

[20] Cenci (n. 3 above) 28-29.

[21] In his commentary on the *Sentences* of Peter Lombard delivered in Paris in 1380, Petrus de Candia remarks that he had heard a certain opinion (against John of Ripa) expressed by "William of Cremona" when he was lecturing "here" on the *Sentences*: Franz Ehrle, *Der Sentenzenkommentar Peters von Candia, des Pisaner Papstes Alexanders V, Franziskanische Studien,* Beiheft 9 (1925) 71-72. In the body of the text, Cardinal Ehrle assumes (279) that this "William of Cremona" was the Augustinian Guglielmo Amidani of Cremona, but later (344) realizes that his identification could not be correct, since the Augustinian William died about 1355. Ehrle then suggests, without pursuing the suggestion, that the "William" referred to was the man mentioned by John of Basel as "frater Wilhelmus de Cremona, baccalaureus Minorum." Ehrle's suggestion was, of course, correct: This Franciscan William was indeed Gullielmus de Centueris de Cremona, the recipient of Dondi's letter. Some difficulties remain, however. According to Ehrle (8-9), Petrus de Candia studied at Padua, Oxford, and Norwich, and possibly in central Europe, before being sent to teach at Paris in the years 1378 to 1380. But Fra' Guglielmo Centueri had already lectured at Paris on the *Sentences* sometime before 1373, when the pope ordered the chancellor of the University of Paris to grant him his degree (cf. n. 11 above). Either Petrus had been at Paris before his stay of 1378-1380, or he must have heard Fra' Guglielmo lecture elsewhere. Or possibly the mention of Paris in the manuscript may be an interpolation.

little-known British writers.[22] It was while Fra' Guglielmo was bishop of Pavia that he asked Giovanni Dondi to write a treatise, which still exists, on avoiding the plague.[23] Fra' Guglielmo died on 26 June 1402.[24]

The letter of Giovanni Dondi that we present here is part of a continuing correspondence between the two men, who had exchanged vernacular rhymes on various subjects. Most recently, Giovanni had been deploring the "defect and misery of our present age," and comparing it with the more fortunate times under Caesar Augustus (lines 34-40). Undoubtedly Giovanni is referring to a sonnet that begins "Oh wretched stench of manners, Oh miserable days of our age!" and ends "How much happier were natures in the Augustan empire, when the whole world possessed minds, virtues, and peace!"[25] It has been said by an editor of Dondi's poetry that his verse reflects themes that were current among poets of his day.[26] For example, Francesco Vannozzi (d. 1389), with whom Dondi also exchanged sonnets, was

[22] Trapp (n. 6 above) 28-29.

[23] In MS 1219 of the Riccardiana in Florence. It has been published by Karl Sudhoff, "Lebensregeln für Pestzeiten von Giovanni dei Dondi," *Archiv für Geschichte der Medizin* 5 (1911) 351-354. Since the treatise says specifically that it was "composed at the request and demand of the bishop of Pavia," we may date it after 1386 and before 1389 when Dondi died – assuming, of course, that the bishop mentioned is Guglielmo Centueri.

[24] Maiocchi (n. 1 above) 2.17. Lazzarini (*Scritti* [n. 13 above] 258) says that this treatise on the plague was accompanied by the letter to Fra' Guglielmo as bishop of Pavia also contained in the Venetian miscellany, fols. 66v-67r. In the Venetian MS the letter is headed, "Reverendo patri domino frat. Gulielmo dei gratia praesuli Papiensi."

[25] The sonnet is addressed "Religioso viro M^{O} G^{O} de ordine minorum sacre pagine magistro." There can be no doubt that this is Magister Gullielmus de Centueris.

O puzza abominabel de costumi
o maleditti di de nostra etade
o gente uman senza humanitade
piu che senza splendor li obscuri fumi!
Chonvien ch'el mondo in brive se consumi
poi che Justicia et innocencia cade,
et sol quel arte et studio par che agrade,
per qual l'un l'altro ofenda, ingani, et spiumi.

Qual cieli infortunati, qual figure
qual inimiche stelle o gravi segni
an ogni nostro ben or si disperso?
Quanto beate for piu le nature
ne l'imperio d'Augusto, quando ingegni
vertute et pace hebbe l'universo!

Poems of Giovanni Dondi, MS Marc. lat. Cl. XIV, 223 (4340), fol. 29. It has been published by Morelli, *Operette* (n. 1 above) 2.308, and by Antonio Medin, *Le rime di Giovanni Dondi dall' Orologio* (Padua 1895) 11.

[26] "Il Dondi tratta gli stessi argomenti communi a tutti i poeti di questa scuola [the Venetian or Paduan school of poets]; morali, filosofici, gnomici, amorosi, politici e altri d'indole affatto confidenziale e privata, che sono il soggetto di molte corrispondenze in sonetti"; Medin, preface.

A Florentine *ballata* written (or perhaps reported) by Giovanni Dondi was set to music by Fra' Bartolino of Padua: it appears in a famous musical manuscript in the Laurentian library in Florence. The *ballata* begins "La sacrosancta carità d'amore . . ." and is presented in modern musical notation by Johannes Wolf, *Der Squarcialupi-Codex Pal. 87 der Biblioteca Medicea Laurenziana zu Florenz* (Lippstadt 1955) 162-163 (I owe this reference to my colleague Prof. Sydney Charles of the Department of Music, University of California, Davis). It is of interest to note that the same codex contains settings by Francesco Landino, the blind organist and

capable of praising a prince whose favor he sought (for example, Giangaleazzo Visconti), but also of disparaging the "tyrants or *signor moderni*," who stay shut up with their books day and night, reckoning their accounts, with effeminate blood and with hands of *pasta.*[27] The fact that Dondi first presented his praise of the Ancients and disparagement of the Moderns in poetic form suggests that this theme may have been a familiar one among contemporary poets. The tone of the *canzone* of Vannozzi just quoted bears comparison with Giovanni's sonnet to Fra' Guglielmo. The opening remarks of Dondi's letter, in which he says that Fra' Guglielmo had urged him to defend his position in serious prose, suggests that vernacular poets in the fourteenth century did not necessarily expect their every utterance to be taken with deadly seriousness. At any rate Dondi finds it necessary to defend at some length his decision to expand on the theme of the poem he had sent to the Franciscan friar. Obviously Fra' Guglielmo also wrote poems, possibly on the same subject, although we cannot be sure of this. We know that he wrote sacred poetry,[28] but no vernacular or secular poetry has as yet been attributed to him. Among the commonplace themes of poetry, surely the inevitable decline of the human individual must be a standard one, especially with middle-aged or elderly poets. An example of this genre is the sonnet of Dondi that has been given the title *Deploratio declinationis nostre vite* in one manuscript.[29] Since every mortal thing (*ogni cosa mortal*) fails, the only hope of man for escape from decline is the love of God, which alone confers peace.

Giovanni's defense of the Ancients begins with a disclaimer: he admits that people of the time of Augustus wandered in a "dense and black cloud of errors" concerning religion. On this point the physician and the theologian agree, and Giovanni does not need to argue, since all loyal Christians would accept this qualification. It is when the comparison turns to the "cultivation of virtues, the reward of duties, the robustness and efficiency of souls, and finally the excellence of minds" that Dondi parts company with his friend. With respect to moral traits, Dondi is scathing in his denunciation of the underhanded devices by which his contemporaries strive to earn the favor of princes and to cheat one another. The worst of it is that those who succeed at this miserable competition seem to earn the respect of other men as well. Sound moral judgment, in other words, is entirely lacking in the fourteenth century,

---

champion of Ockham (see Vasoli [n. 19 above] *Studi* 16). Both Fra' Bartolino and Francesco Landino appear, along with Marsiglio da Santa Sofia of Padua, in the *Paradiso degli Alberti,* a work that cries out desperately for reexamination in the light of what we now know of the participants.

27
La quarta setta ch'oggi el mondo guasta
son i tiranpni, over signor moderni,
che stan con suo' quaterni
en camera di e notte a far ragioni
con sangue feminil, con man di pasta."

Le rime di Francesco di Vannozzo, ed. Antonio Medin (Bologna 1928) 23.

28 Latin hymns, to St. Siro and to the bishops of Pavia (Cenci [n. 3 above] 43).

29 Medin (n. 25 above) 19.

in Dondi's view: tangible rewards and esteem are showered upon the morally unfit and undeserving. By contrast, one need only consult the historical writings of the Ancients in order to find what sorts of actions were admired and rewarded in those days. Dondi suggests that his correspondent has also read Roman history (a fact which is borne out by the historical references in Fra' Guglielmo's work *De iure monarchiae*) and has admired the deeds of the Ancients. As for the reward of duties, one need only glance at the statues, triumphal arches, and sculptured columns of Rome to see how deeds of valor were regarded by the Ancients. Though these monuments have now been ruined by time and lie for the most part in fragments, one can gather from them even in their present condition what honor and respect must have been accorded to those "who had established peace . . . or liberated the fatherland from imminent peril or had extended empire over subject peoples." Dondi's interest in Roman inscriptions, which he took the trouble to transcribe, must have derived from his admiration for the moral fiber of the men honored by those inscriptions. In this respect Dondi carried his admiration for the Ancients one practical step further than did Petrarch, who never bothered to transcribe inscriptions from monuments or buildings but limited himself to reading, emending, or emulating historians such as Livy or moralists such as Valerius Maximus. Dondi also shared with Petrarch an admiration for military prowess: he compares the exploits of Scipio, Cato, Alexander the Great, and Hannibal with the fearfulness of his contemporaries, who are unwilling to storm a fortification or attack an enemy line. It is interesting to note that Fra' Guglielmo apparently also was interested in inscriptions, and indeed for the same reason as Dondi ("You also, I suspect, have noticed these inscriptions in passing, and have stopped a while with some amazement, and have perhaps said to yourself, 'Surely these are proof of great men' "). If any fortifications are captured today, laments Dondi, they are taken by fraud (obviously the legend of the Fall of Troy, with its record of Ancient fraud, had not impressed him).

The fact that the relative merit of the Ancients and the Moderns was not a new topic is clear from Dondi's reference to views held by others (lines 141-143): "I realize *what many people are accustomed to say* on this topic"; namely, that the Ancients were driven to perform impressive deeds by anger or ambition rather than by a commitment to virtue. Notice that Dondi does not attribute this conviction to Fra' Guglielmo but rather to "many people."

As for the caliber of minds, this is to be judged by the high level of Ancient sciences and arts and by the books and other monuments which they have produced. Here we come to the sector that occupied the center of the stage in the later phases of the *Querelle*. The merits of Ancient medical science had already been touched upon by Dondi in his correspondence with Petrarch, in an exchange which has been frequently edited and is well known.[30] It has not so often been noticed that Dondi is

[30]Petrarch's letter of 13 July 1370 to Giovanni Dondi ("Obtulisti michi materiam iocandi in malis . . .") is now available in facsimile and careful transcription by Armando Petrucci in *Francesco Petrarca, Epistole autografe* (Padua 1968) 40-51. This letter (Seniles 12.1) represents

quite correct in insisting that Petrarch should recognize that a respect for the Ancients ought, in all consistency, to be extended to their scientific as well as to their literary works. In this sense the authority of physicians, to the extent that it rested on Hippocrates and Galen, should have been acknowledged by Petrarch – who, however, had no use at all for medical men, dead or alive. Although Dondi was, as has been observed, not only a competent but even an outstanding scientist for his day, he was by no means an admirer of contemporary scientific achievement. All the scientific work of his day derived, so Dondi felt, from the work of the Ancients: "It is quite enough for moderns if they can just scratch the surface of the subjects that the Ancients treated in depth" (lines 166-167).

Of particular interest in this context is Dondi's recognition of the claim that some of his contemporaries were making for innovations in logic. He refers to "some dialecticians in our days" who have tried to find out something new or have presumed to change what has been handed down from the past (lines 167-170). Their much-vaunted innovations hardly survive their creators. This is a precious if oblique reference to the attitude of medieval logicians toward their subject, on which they are usually extremely reticent (or perhaps "complacent" would be a better term, since like most academicians they took for granted the need for their subject and did not feel any compulsion to argue its merits). Dondi again indicates that Fra' Guglielmo was familiar with these claims ("*As you know*, some dialecticians claim . . ."). This suggests, what we know from other evidence to be the case, that the so-called Terminist logic, to be found in Peter of Spain and other thirteenth-century writers, had penetrated northern Italy by the middle of the fourteenth century. Fra' Guglielmo need not have met this logic in Italy: he would certainly have encountered it at the University of Paris, where he had studied theology. However, he might very well have become familiar with Terminist logic at the University of Bologna or in a *studium* of the Franciscan order. The logic of the properties of terms was, in fact, inescapable in the fourteenth century. Most medieval observations about logic (as opposed to statements within logic) come from hostile witnesses – proponents of the literary culture of Orleans or other proto-humanists. It is instructive to learn from Dondi's reference that at least some medieval logicians thought of themselves quite explicitly as adding to an Ancient science, or modifying it. The modifications which they introduced into Aristotle's logic derived in fact from an equally Ancient source,

one of the unquestionable autographs of Petrarch: on it, see Ernest H. Wilkins, *Petrarch's Later Years* (Cambridge, Mass. 1959) 194-195. Dondi's reply ("Debui nec ignoro ingeniosissime hominum . . .") of 24 Oct. 1370 was published by Bellemo (n. 1 above) 295-310 from the Venetian miscellany. Part of the same letter was published by P.O. Kristeller, collated with Vat. lat. 5223, as Appendix II of his article, "Il Petrarca, l'umanesimo, e la scolastica a Venezia" (cited in n. 51 below) 173-178. It will be noticed that Kristeller (178), when comparing the Venetian version with that in the Vatican, considers the latter to be closer to the letter as originally sent, and suggests that the Venetian miscellany may therefore not be autograph as some scholars believe. Both manuscripts should, however, be compared with MS 358 of the Seminary in Padua, believed by Lazzarini (*Scritti* [n. 13 above] 257) to be autograph. On Dondi's letter, see Wilkins, 194-195; and for Petrarch's rejoinder, 195-196.

namely, the Stoics. It is barely possible that some medieval logicians may have been perceptive enough to have noticed that this was the case, but evidence for such a degree of historical sophistication has not yet been found. In any event, it is curious that Dondi makes no claim whatever for his own technological contributions to the science of time-keeping. This is in keeping with the spirit of his *Treatise on the Astrarium*, which he modestly presents as simply a graphic way of illustrating the achievements of Ancient astronomers. Dondi's admirers were by no means so modest, as we shall see. Nor does Giovanni mention the contributions of Arab medicine, although like every other medical man of his time he was conversant with Arab works in medicine and in fact relied upon them heavily. In his letter to Petrarch defending the authority of medical men, Dondi did not put forward the claims of Avicenna or other Arab writers, perhaps out of deference to Petrarch's notorious dislike of Arab science, as voiced in his invective *On his own ignorance and that of many others*. On 13 July 1370, Petrarch had playfully refused to comply with three of Dondi's six recommendations for his health. Dondi, while acknowledging that appeals to one's own "authorities" might be out of place in a dispute between faulties such as law and medicine, nevertheless defended the propriety of an appeal to the basic experts in each field: in grammar, Priscian; in eloquence, Cicero; in poetry, Homer or Virgil; in Roman history, Livy; in natural philosophy and dialectic, Aristotle; in geometry, Archimedes or Euclid; in astronomy, Ptolemy. "I see no reason why the most outstanding and generally approved men of a given discipline should not be given preference and consulted primarily before others – which does not mean that they should never be repudiated nor held suspect," remarked Dondi. He offers the following version of the stand Petrarch might take: "But I (you might say) hold an opinion opposed to that of these experts, an opinion which reason, or experiment, or both has confirmed for me, so that I am not prepared to credit to the same extent the authority or mere assertion of any man, no matter how skilled, whether this man be an ancient, a contemporary, or even someone yet to come (*seu prisci seu moderni, imo forsitan et futuri*) – in fact, not even if he is one of those famous medical men whom I might previously have been inclined to trust, since they supported in part the opinion about which I was wavering before, at a time when the balance was not yet tipped in either direction by any cogent reasoning, and I might have yielded on account of the respect and authority of men. But now, since an adverse opinion has been concluded with weighty reasoning, I feel myself under no moral obligation whatever to receive them or to accept their dicta and authority, but am allowed to argue against them, and to support and bolster the opinion I favor. Let them bring forward valid reasons, if they have any – or you for them." Dondi, by way of contrast, urges a stance of initial deference to authorities such as Hippocrates, the most Ancient and most skilled of all medical writers, who laid down the basic principles of medical knowledge.[31]

[31] Dondi, letter to Petrarch of 24 Oct. 1370, ed. Kristeller 174-175; my translation, reading "eximiorum" for "eximios" in the Latin text.

After this digression, we may now return to Dondi's letter to Fra' Guglielmo. Dondi disposes of the literary claims of the fourteenth century by adducing the example of Petrarch. He admits that Petrarch is the leading writer of the day, and concedes that he would have been outstanding even if he had lived in Antiquity. But if anyone were seriously to compare Petrarch's poetry with that of Virgil, he would be displaying an utter lack of sensitivity. At this point Dondi introduces an anecdote that has strongly impressed literary scholars. Petrarch himself, on being asked about a volume in his library which contained Virgil's poetry and some of his own verse, had replied, "Here you have some rags bound in with velvet" – thus indicating, says Dondi, that his work was considerably surpassed by the Ancients. There is no modern writer to compare in history with Livy or Sallust, in oratory with Cicero, in poetry with Virgil, Horace, or Ovid, in philosophy with Varro and Seneca, Dondi adds. The list is exclusively Roman, which accounts for the absence of Plato and Aristotle and the presence of those two philosophical lightweights, Varro and Seneca. Even with respect to the next category, that of "interpreters of Scripture," the fourteenth century has no one to compare with Augustine and Jerome, whom Dondi, a stickler for chronological accuracy, includes among the Ancients.

The next category begins to anticipate the Renaissance. Dondi has already mentioned the statues, columns, and arches of Rome from the point of view of their value as testimony to the regard in which noble deeds were held by the Ancients. Now he considers them as works of art and as indicative of superb technical craftsmanship. Again we have an anecdote, this time one that has intrigued historians of art. It concerns a "well-known worker in marble famous for his ability in that art among all those whom Italy then had, especially in the creation of figures." This artist used to wax eloquent on the merits of Ancient sculpture: he once lagged behind his companions while walking past some Ancient statues and remarked, "If only the breath of life were not lacking in them, these statues would be better than life! " (lines 208-219), thus indicating, Dondi observes, that "nature had been not only imitated but even surpassed by the genius of such artists." Ancient statues and buildings demand our utmost respect.

This concludes Giovanni Dondi's survey of the relative merits of the age of Augustus and the fourteenth century. When confronted with such an array of evidence from various fields, Fra' Guglielmo will be helpless, Dondi thinks, to defend his position that the Modern age is to be preferred. Dondi concedes that Augustine and Orosius, with their accounts of barbarian invasions, might seem to lend support to Fra' Guglielmo's cause, in the sense that they demonstrate that Antiquity had its own share of troubles and misfortune. But Dondi thinks that this claim can be written off, since no age is ever free from the misery brought on by war and pestilence. Dondi concedes that these two afflictions may not be worse now than they have ever been at any other time. As a physician in the century of the Black Death, Dondi must have seen his share of illness and misery, and the same goes for Fra' Guglielmo, at whose instance, we recall, Dondi wrote a little treatise on how to avoid the plague. Dondi argues that the drastic reduction of the population can be dramatized by comparing the census figures for Rome under Augustus or Claudius with the population of the whole of Italy in the fourteenth century. He ends on a note of religious concern: "We Christians prevail only by a certain sluggishness or inertia"; in most respects we act like sheep rather than men. Here Dondi rests his case, and apologizes to Fra' Guglielmo for over-extending his diatribe.

With so many of Dondi's letters still unpublished and unstudied, it would perhaps be premature to analyze this letter in very great detail. But with the reader's indulgence I would like to speculate a bit concerning the intellectual currents represented in it, if only for the purpose of stimulating further inquiry.

We are in the fortunate position of having a list of the books that Giovanni Dondi left at his death.[32] The list is fairly extensive, although not as detailed as we might like, so that some items cannot be conclusively identified. But the general outlines are clear. Scientific works – medical and astronomical – predominate, as we would expect from their owner's professional status. Hippocrates, Aristotle, and Galen are present in force, but the Arabs are even more strongly in evidence. Contemporary or near-contemporary colleagues in medicine (for example, Pietro d'Abano and Gentile da Foligno) are included; we know from one of Dondi's letters that he worked over some of these treatises with great care. The Greek scientific works are not exclusively medical: included are many works on natural philosophy, some on ethics and politics, and certain "books of Porphyry," not further characterized but most likely the *Isagoge*. There are a few Scholastic theologians (Albertus Magnus, Thomas Aquinas, and Egidius Romanus), but the works selected seem to be mainly those having some medical bearing; they are not strictly theological in character. It should be noted that *sophismata*, the "properties of terms," and the "intension and remission of forms" are conspicuously absent; Dondi seems to have had no interest whatever in Peter of Spain, William of Ockham, Walter Burley, Jean Buridan, or other writers of this type. That the absence of such works is not accidental is suggested by the vague but deprecatory remarks about "innovations in dialectic" in Dondi's letter to Fra' Guglielmo. Dondi's non-professional interests obviously lay in a more literary, humanistic direction: Pliny, Vitruvius, Terence, Livy, Cicero, Suetonius, Statius, Ovid, a book *de ystoriis Romanorum*, are here to supply the foundation for the extraordinary tribute to the literary remains of the Ancients in Dondi's letter to the Franciscan theologian. He also enjoyed, apparently, some "songs in the French language" and, of course, the writings of his great friend, Petrarch. On the whole, however, the general impression that remains from a perusal of this list is that Dondi's library was mainly a professional one,[33] with an over-

[32] Vittorio Lazzarini, "I libri, gli argenti, le vesti di Giovanni Dondi dall' Orologio," *Scritti* (n. 13 above) 265-270.

[33] Dondi's library may be compared with that of another medical man, Guido da Bagnolo, one of Petrarch's four notorious Venetian friends, who died in 1370: Ridolfo Livi, "Guido da

whelming preponderance of technical works translated from the Arabic sources. There is an unusually wide range of Arab authors, but of course Avicenna and Averroes are conspicuous.

Now let us ask ourselves where Dondi might have derived his respect for the Ancients and his unusually severe disparagement of the Moderns – if in fact he derived them from any literary source. The most obvious source by far would be Petrarch, whose dissatisfaction with his own age is a recurring theme throughout his later writings. The passage most often cited on this subject is in the *Letter to Posterity:*[34] "I applied myself especially to the knowledge of olden times (*vetustatis*), since this age was always displeasing to me; so that had not the love of those dear to me directed me otherwise, I would rather have been born in any other age and have forgotten this, driven by my mind always to put myself in other ages." But this black mood is spelled out more fully by Petrarch in a letter to Guido Sette in 1367, just seven years before his death, at about the time when Giovanni Dondi was acquainted with him. Written from Venice, where he had gone to seek "peace

---

Bagnolo, medico del re di Cipro," *Atti e memorie della R. Deputazione di storia patria per le provincie Modenesi* 11 (1918) 83-91. By contrast with Giovanni's library, literary or historical works are absent from Guido's collection – as we might have expected from Petrarch's hostile sketch in *On his own ignorance and that of many others.* Considerably more "enlightened" is the library of Giacomo Zanetini, another medical contemporary, who taught at Padua and died in 1402: M. C. Ganguzza-Billanovich, "Giacomo Zanetini († 1402), professore di medicina: Il patrimonio, la biblioteca," *Quaderni per la storia dell' Università di Padova* 5 (1972) 29-44. Among Giacomo's books are quite a few moral treatises, by Aristotle, Cicero, and Seneca, as well as works by Cassiodorus, Apuleius, Sallust, and Petrarch, indicating the wider cultural horizons of the Paduan physician (whose father, Giovanni, was a *professor grammaticae*). On the other hand, Giacomo's library was more "up-to-date" than Giovanni Dondi's, in the sense that it included works of British and French logic and physics: Oresme, Buridan, and Dumbleton, together with the older works of Grosseteste, Albertus Magnus, and others. Of particular interest is the presence in his collection of a commentary on the physics by Facino d'Asti. Some works of this little-known author were among the manuscripts of Frederick Amberg (d. 1432) in Fribourg, who also had, be it noted, Paris lectures from 1380 by Petrus de Candia as well as a commentary on the *Sentences* by our friend Fra' Guglielmo Centueri: Bernard Fleury, "Le couvent des Cordeliers de Fribourg au moyen âge," *Zeitschrift für schweizerische Kirchengeschichte* 15 (1921) 96-97; more detail in Trapp (n. 6 above). It would be hazardous to characterize this group of writers before they have been thoroughly examined in detail, but I suspect that we have here what might be called the "foreign fringe" of Oxford and Parisian nominalism. Giovanni Dondi may well be referring to this movement and Fra' Guglielmo's acquaintance with it in lines 167-170.

[34] Petrarch, Letter to Posterity: the most accessible edition is now that of G. Martellotti et al., Francesco Petrarca, *Prose* (Milan 1955) 2-18. Petrarch's mood is captured even more vividly and succinctly in his metrical letter to Francesco Nelli, *Rime, trionfi e poesie* . . . (Milan 1951) 802:

> Vivo, sed indignans quod nos in tristia fatum
> secula dilatos peioribus intulit annis.
> Aut prius aut multo decuit post tempore nasci;
> nam fuit et fortassis erit felicius evum;
> in medium sordes. . . .

On Petrarch's sense of himself vis-à-vis the Ancients and his contemporaries, see Arnaud Tripet, *Pétrarque ou La connaissance de soi* (Geneva 1967) 117-125.

and quiet," this letter, which bears the subtitle, *De mutatione temporum*, is a veritable harangue on the deterioration of the times, or the "changing of the age for the worse and into ruins" ("de etatis mutatione in peius ac ruina"). Petrarch agrees with Horace that old men such as he (aet. 63) are inclined to be "difficult, querulous, and praisers of the times of their boyhood," but believes that he can convince Guido, his correspondent, that things really are worse in the 1360s than they were when he and Guido were young.

He then leads Guido on a dismal travelogue featuring various formerly-pleasant or at least tolerable cities, including Carpentras, Montpellier, Bologna (where Petrarch had a good time, even if he did not learn much law), and other places where he had visited or studied. He contrasts the present condition of these cities with their former glory – Paris no longer studious, Bologna no longer "fat," and so on – and adds Milan and Pavia to the list. Deterioration is not just an Italian phenomenon, Petrarch is careful to add. It is the same story everywhere: things are not what they used to be ("una omnia conditio est; non sunt hodie quod heri"). He could continue the lugubrious listing for all of Europe; indeed, all countries in the world are deteriorating. Everywhere one finds the same recent and obvious *mutatio* or "decline," to use Gibbon's word. If he were asked to consider the condition of countries remote in place and time, says Petrarch, he would have to admit that he knows nothing about the Indies, for example, but certainly Egypt, Syria, and Armenia have suffered the same decline as we. "For the calamity of Greece is an old story, but that of the Scythians is recent." Petrarch recognizes that this state of affairs might be considered justified by the wretched moral condition of mankind, and he has no inclination to challenge the righteousness of a God who could visit such afflictions upon them: presumably they deserve whatever they get. "I do know that this is the universal condition. I am not asking for the causes why things used to be so much better in former times. This indeed would be a foolish question, as Solomon has already pointed out [Ecclesiastes 7.10]: 'Say not thou, what is the cause that the former days were better than these, for thou dost not enquire wisely concerning this.' " Petrarch admits that there can be many causes, known to God and a few perhaps even to man, for this decline. "I do not complain about the fallen times (*mutata tempora*), nor do I seek causes, but I assert the decline against the opinion of those among us who, born in evil times, contend that times have never been otherwise; since they, being incredulous and not themselves learned, unhesitatingly impute the manifest and deplorable decline of the times to changes in our studies and moods (*mutatis studiis nostris atque animis imputant*)." "I admit that I have changed," remarks Petrarch, alluding to his own spiritual experience, "and I rejoice in the fact, but this change has nothing to do with the other." He compares the situation to a huge wheel revolving; on the wheel there is a tiny ant, moving counter-clockwise while the wheel turns the other way. Petrarch, making minuscule moral progress, is getting better, although he suffers like everyone else from the general worsening of the times. He admits that the decline may not be of "the times" or "the world" but of men, and that the whole root of evil may be in men ("in hominibus radicem mali totam esse"). He then gives a catalogue of woes: bands of armed marauders, the Black Death, the earthquake of 1348 that brought him out of his library at Verona into the streets where people were panic-stricken, the earthquake at Rome in 1369, and so on. This series of natural disasters (if we may include the marauders in that category) have their roots in men, presumably, because they represent visitations of God's wrath upon the iniquitous.

Such was the mood of Petrarch toward the end of his life. To quote his own words, "piety, truth, faith, and peace have been exiled" and their places taken by impiety, falsehood, perfidy, discord, and war. In the face of such an indictment, it would be of little use for anyone to object to Petrarch that he has overlooked significant developments in painting, music, architecture, or even logic or natural philosophy (it would have taken a brave man indeed to advance the claims of the latter subjects to Petrarch!). Petrarch's reference to "those among us" who attribute the gloomy assessment to subjective factors is very interesting, for it suggests that there existed in the latter part of the fourteenth century a faction (of younger men?) who held that "Things Have Always Been Just as Bad," possibly because their earliest memories were of pestilence, war, and famine. These "incredulous" men cannot be convinced by the testimony of their elders, living or dead, that things had ever been better. Such skeptics are incorrigible. True scholars, however, know Things Have Been Better – Much Better, in fact, in Antiquity. This is the distinctively "Renaissance" version of this hackneyed theme. The ordinary, nonscholarly approach would be to reiterate the superiority of the Immediate Past, recoverable in memory if not in fact by older citizens. Only scholars could have achieved the leap into the distant past that constitutes the recovery of Antiquity, or, as Erwin Panofsky so convincingly put it, the "distancing" of Europe's classical antecedents that called forth a nostalgia for Antiquity. We are all capable of nostalgia for our own past, but it takes scholarship to be nostalgic for the Ancient Past. And this, by and large, is what the humanists contributed to the Italian Renaissance. Certainly Giovanni Dondi had absorbed this mood utterly. He had even taken over, perhaps unwittingly, the disparagement of personal accomplishment that marked Patrarch's mature attitude toward his own literary productions. For Dondi need not have been so modest about his own scientific achievements – had anyone ever found a *planetarium* among the ruins of Rome?

After Petrarch died, he would find supporters who were not as willing as he to write off his literary achievement: the "battle of the Three Crowns" and Coluccio Salutati's long letter of 1405 to Poggio Bracciolini survive as testimony to this fact. Modesty and self-deprecation are all very well for a poet (or at least a reformed Christian poet), but the poet's friends need not subscribe to his modest self-appraisal. Giovanni Dondi, however, had absorbed too faithfully the mood of his friend: even after Petrarch's death, he was not able to bring himself to set his friend on the same level as Virgil and Cicero, not even by dint of splitting him up into Petrarch the prose-writer (better than Virgil *qua* prose-writer) and Petrarch the poet (far better than Cicero *qua* poet), as Petrarch's later admirers did. Dondi accepted Petrarch's verdict and refused to overrule it by elevating his friend above the Ancients, or even to their level.

Thus the influence of Petrarch was basic in promoting Dondi's mood of rejection of the present – although of course we need not deny that Dondi was capable of his own observations and reflections. The anecdotes about Petrarch's book and about the sculptor admiring ancient statues show a certain empirical bent, almost in a sociologist's sense, to Dondi's approach, for in each case we find him soliciting or reporting the opinion of a contemporary expert in the field under consideration. In the field of medicine, Dondi could offer himself as an expert witness acceptable to anyone – except, that is, for Petrarch, who regarded all medical men as untrustworthy. Dondi, unlike Petrarch, accepts the basic principles of Greek medicine (for example, the doctrine of the four humors), and seems to be an admirer of the most Ancient of all medical writers, Hippocrates. Nor would Dondi think of challenging the credentials of Euclid or Archimedes in mathematics. In his attitude toward the Authorities in all fields, Dondi was not in agreement with his distinguished friend, whom, as we have seen, he tried unsuccessfully to convert to his point of view. In this issue, Dondi surely has some show of justice on his side. For in parading his sequence of unbeatable Ancients in every possible field, Dondi was being more consistent than Petrarch, who refused to acknowledge Hippocrates or Galen in medicine but bowed in humble awe before Virgil. Hence we cannot attribute Dondi's total commitment to the Ancients entirely to Petrarch's influence. Could there be another source?

One possible clue has already been offered, in the form of the book list previously mentioned. We have noted how heavily stocked Dondi's library was with Arab medical and astronomical treatises. Now, everyone acknowledges that the Arabs were the main channel for the transmission of Greek science to the Latin West. But it seems to be generally assumed that the channel had no effect whatever on the contents or form of what it transmitted. Yet the attitude of these Arab authors, especially Averroes, had a pervasive influence upon Latin readers. Averroes, it is generally agreed, was a major component in the intellectual heritage of the Middle Ages. Now when scholars inquire into the influence of Averroes, they are apt to be looking for evidence of "rationalism," "skepticism," or "free thought," or for specific doctrines such as the eternity of the world or the unity of the intellect. But surely medieval readers were not looking for "-isms" in Averroes, or for original doctrines, for he was, after all, a commentator on Aristotle ("the" Commentator, in fact), and one does not look for a fresh outlook in a commentator. Originality in a commentator is a vice, not a virtue. One wants sound interpretation, not fresh thought, "free" or otherwise. Latin readers of Averroes were not looking for revisionist doctrines; revisions in Aristotle's thought would have been abhorrent to them as well as to him. What Averroes transmitted, I believe, was not so much a startling new development in Aristotle's system as a certain attitude toward his master, whom he considered a "rule and exemplar in Nature," so perfect that he deserved to be thought of as a "god rather than a man." In Averroes's view, most of his (Arab) contemporaries failed to appreciate Aristotle's greatness, and so Averroes dismissed them as unworthy of philosophical consideration – especially those "Moderns" (the word is conspicuous in the Latin translations of Averroes) who study the commentaries of Alexander of Aphrodisias rather than the works of the master himself. The same thing "happens to many Modern philosophizers" ("pluribus accidit Modernis philosophantibus"), who are content with Avicenna's books rather than the corpus of Aristotle's writings.

Surely it can be no accident that a disparaging attitude toward "the Moderns" can be found in a writer so steeped in Arab lore as Giovanni Dondi. I am not suggesting that Dondi was a confirmed "Averroist" in any of the conventional senses of that much-overworked term. On the contrary, it is quite clear that Dondi was a "loyal Christian," to use his own phrase. What I am suggesting is simply that in his attitude toward the Great Men of Ancient Science, Dondi is far closer to Averroes than to Petrarch. A peculiarly hostile tone toward "the Moderns" is a conspicuous feature of the Latin translations of Averroes. It would not be long before the slur-word applied by hostile outsiders was taken over in a positive sense by the victims of the slur: a process that is very familiar to anyone conversant with religious history. Medieval philosophical literature from the time of the impact of Averroes on to its close is sprinkled with a standard rejoinder to Averroes's characterization of Aristotle: he was, after all, "not a god but a man like us" ("homo ut nos"). A similar reaction was to take place with the term *moderni*, which in Averroes's vocabulary had a disparaging tone ("fleeting," "transitory," "of the present moment only") but subsequently was taken over by those (now Latin rather than Arabic writers) whom it was initially intended to disparage. As we have seen, neither Petrarch nor Dondi thought much of "the Modern." The adversary, in Petrarch's case at least, was not a crowd of Fourteenth-Century boosters (Europe at the time of the Black Death did not have many boosters), but, it would seem, certain younger contemporaries who agreed that the fourteenth century was miserable, but thought that this was the normal condition of mankind.

In Dondi's case, we do not have the writings of the adversary (Fra' Guglielmo), but only Dondi's report of his views. When Giovanni says to Fra' Guglielmo, "Ego vetera prefero tempora, tu moderna defendis" (line 45), can we assume that he is reporting the latter's usage precisely? If so, there are some interesting points to be made. For one thing, Giovanni does not say that his friend *preferred* modern times, simply that he "defended" them against denigration (that of Giovanni, no doubt). For another, Guglielmo would be adopting a favorable stance toward "the modern" that was quite contrary to the prevailing attitude of medieval piety, which viewed this present world as a transitory vale of sin. Finally, we must examine the possibility that Fra' Guglielmo, in defending "the modern", was putting himself on the side of those who were deliberately forging the new and consciously adding to the heritage from the Ancients. It is a common maneuver in medieval scholarship to consider every occurrence of the word *modernus* to be a reference to William of Ockham and his followers (usually, "in logic"). Yet it must be emphasized that before the Council of Constance or a little earlier (say, about 1400), the term *modernus* meant, for the most part, simply "contemporary" and could be found in all fields of medieval thought including those, like law and medicine, that were remote from any influence of Ockham. To be sure, a contemporary of Dondi and Centueri who taught law at the University of Pavia, the famous Baldo degli Ubaldi, was called one of "the moderns" in a fifteenth-century speech.[35] Yet by this time the linguistic situation had changed: *modernus* had acquired a new and favorable connotation, as the orator was at some pains to show.

In the fourteenth century, the word *modernus* had no such nuances.[36] It may very well be that during his lifetime Fra' Guglielmo was witnessing the start of a subtle change in men's attitudes toward the times in which they lived, and that this was beginning to be reflected in a new willingness to accept the "modern" or "contemporary" as something to be cherished rather than despised in the fashion that had prevailed hitherto, particularly in religious writings. In this sense, Giovanni Dondi, paradoxically enough, was probably closer to the past mood of medieval religiosity than was his Franciscan correspondent. A concrete comparison may help to illuminate this point. As a characteristic expression of piety from the period, we may select *The Clock of Wisdom* by Heinrich Seuse (Suso), which was probably written between 1333 and 1341. In this treatise Suso complains bitterly about the coldness of men's love of God "in these modern times, when the world is already senescent."[37] The fourth chapter of this extremely influential book was entitled "Planctus super extincto fervore devocionis in diversis personis utriusque sexus modernis temporibus, quos Cristus per suam passionem revocat ad verum amorem." With its appeal for fervor and devotion, for a return to the simplicity of apostolic times, and for "conformity to Christ," Suso's writing is very much in the spirit of Francis of Assisi, but it also looks forward, of course, to the *Devotio moderna*, which represents in many ways the achievement of the fervor that Suso found lacking in *his* "modern times," and to which Suso bequeathed the phrase "modern devotion."

Dondi's attack on the mores of his day has much in common with Suso's; even the

[35] By the chancellor of the University of Heidelberg in 1469: "Civiles leges prudentissime ac dissertissime editas (et) digestas esse quis neget? Attamen opera Bartholi, labor Baldi, industria Dini non fuit inanis, quos cum suis similibus facultatis modernos appello." Stephan Hoest, Speech in defense of the *Via moderna, Reden und Briefe,* ed. F. Baron (Munich 1971) 174.

[36] A work by one of Baldo's direct disciples, Giampietro Ferrari, a lecturer in law at Pavia from 1389 to 1400, was said to be entitled *Opusculum modernae iudicialis practicae*, the intent being simply to indicate that this manual was accommodated to the needs of the present, according to Pietro Vaccari, *Storia della Università di Pavia* (Pavia 1957) 57. However, Cenci (n. 3 above) 48 gives many manuscript locations for the work and reports the title as *Practica iudicialis papiensis.* The word "modernae" may, as so often happens, be the contribution of the editor of a printed edition. The work in any event was written between 1412 and 1425 (Cenci 63).

[37] "Sed heu modernis temporibus mundo iam senescente, hic amor divinus in multorum cordibus tantum refriguit, ut pene sit extinctus, et pauci inveniantur qui devocioni studeant . . ."; *Henrici Susonis seu fratris Amandi (†an. 1365) Horologium sapientiae,* ed. J. Strange (Cologne 1861), prologus, 9.

language is similar. The two men differ, however, in the Antiquity to which they appeal: Suso harks back to the *primitiva ecclesia*, Dondi to the principate of Augustus. Suso regards "the world" as senescent ("mundo .... senescente"), while Dondi speaks of the senescence of "human nature" ("nature .... senescentia humane," line 86). It seems remarkable that these two very diverse writers of the fourteenth century should have been, in however different ways, so preoccupied with time-pieces and clocks: Dondi as a designer and astronomer, Suso as a writer self-consciously using the clock as a figure of speech. We see a similar contrast in their handling of another entity: the ruins of an ancient city. Where Dondi sees in Rome the ruins of a city once the seat of empire and the fatherland of virtuous citizens, Suso transforms the "ruined City" (not necessarily Rome) into a vision of the pitiable condition of *mater religio Christiana.*[38]

The religious convictions of Fra' Guglielmo are not so easily discerned. If one took his treatise *On the right of monarchy* as a full statement of his views, it would be tempting to write him off as an apologist for the religious and political establishments of his day. This would not be quite fair, for Fra' Guglielmo did not uncritically accept the authority of the pope as absolute, nor did he believe that the pope was incapable of sinning.[39] Yet when all is said and done, it does sound as if Guglielmo, in defending "modern times," might have been entering a plea for the *status quo* under Giangaleazzo Visconti, whose cause he promotes assiduously through the *De iure monarchiae.*[40]

It would certainly be misleading to view Fra' Guglielmo's defense of modern times, however he expressed it, as in any way an anticipation of that surge of Renaissance confidence to which Hans Baron has given the name," Civic Humanism." Such an association would be *prima facie* unlikely, since, in Baron's terms, the court of Giangaleazzo was the chief adversary of Florence, and Fra' Guglielmo, as a member of that court, was an explicit opponent of Florentine republicanism.[41] It has been pointed out[42] that the word *modernus* was used conspicuously by supporters of the papacy but eschewed by men favoring the emperor in the investiture strife. Thus we might have expected Fra' Guglielmo, as an ardent papist, to have followed suit – but in fact he does not use the term *modernus* at all in his treatise on monarchy. Although Fra' Guglielmo holds that "Peter, the first pope, was the true monarch, in temporal as well as in spiritual matters, and so were his successors," he

[38] Suso 43-44.

[39] Cenci (n. 3 above) 196.

[40] This is convincingly spelled out by Cenci in his valuable notes to Fra' Guglielmo's treatise.

[41] Centueri argues that the Florentine republic had declined from previous times and would have been incapable of defending itself had it not been for its allies ([n. 3 above] 156-157). In general, Fra' Guglielmo believes that republics are less capable than monarchies of promoting the peace and well-being of a community, since they tend to be ruled by "most vile and abject persons" (157).

[42] Walter Freund, *Modernus und andere Zeitbegriffe des Mittelalters* (Cologne 1957) 63-66; see also Elizabeth Gössmann, *Antiqui und Moderni im Mittelalter* (Paderborn 1974) 41.

does not apply the word *modernus* to the contemporary successor of Peter. Thus it seems unlikely that Fra' Guglielmo would have transferred a favorable tone for the term *modernus* from its usage in Guelph propaganda to "modern times" generally. In short, there seems no reason whatever to associate Fra' Guglielmo, the enthusiast for things modern, with the attitudes that developed so suddenly, in Baron's view, a few decades later in Florence. Guglielmo's defense may in any event have consisted simply in pointing out the disadvantages of life under Caesar Augustus: this is strongly suggested by Dondi's characterization of his views in line 42 ("nor did those times, *as you say,* lack misery"). Moreover, there may have been no recognition of fresh artistic or scientific creation in Fra' Guglielmo's apologia. So far as political sympathies go, it would seem that the two friends were in favor of rule by responsible princes. We find no sign of republican sympathies in the published writings of Giovanni Dondi. He deplores those who are too inert or cowardly to fight for their freedom, but the freedom he admires seems to be freedom from external servitude rather than freedom from the internal rule of a tyrant. In a well-ordered princedom, true merit would find its reward; to judge from the financial rewards that Dondi reaped from his association with Giangaleazzo, it would seem to follow that he must have been eminently satisfied with the justice meted out by the Visconti.[43]

INFLUENCE OF DONDI'S LETTER. The letter of Giovanni Dondi to Fra' Guglielmo Centueri is not widely distributed in existing manuscripts, and it would be foolish to claim that it exercised much direct influence. But Dondi expressed similar views about the superiority of Antiquity in a letter[44] to Pasquino de' Capelli, Giangaleazzo's chancellor, who had asked him for a set of his letters. This letter was undoubtedly seen by Giovanni Manzini of Motta, who was tutoring Pasquino's son at the time, and who had humanistic pretensions. In 1388, Manzini wrote a long epistle to Giovanni Dondi in which he speaks of a letter of Dondi that "deservedly extols the more outstanding excellencies of the minds of the Ancients."[45] The tone of

[43] Dondi's expectations for Giangaleazzo and his justice are the topics of Sonnets XVI and XLVIII, ed. Medin (n. 27 above) 18, 50.

[44] This letter is also contained in the Venetian miscellany: for a description, see Morelli, *Operette* (n. 1 above) 2.293: "Epistolas a Dondio scriptas ad diversos Pasquinus petierat, cui suadere Dondius conatur quod tanti eae non erant, ut conquiri mererentur: deinde multa scribit de pravis hominum aetatis suae moribus, philosopho apprime digna." Lazzarini (*Scritti* [n. 13 above] 257) gives the following quotation from this letter: "Pridie, vir insignis, epistolarum mearum, si modo nomen merentur huiusmodi seu melius nugarum mearum, copiam exigebas, quas pro variis propositis olim ad amicos vel socios destinavi, quarum paucas admodum ex multis ad alterius indutionem, paulo prius sparsis ex cartulis hic inde retentando colegi . . . Ad Ticini ripam idibus Julii." This was published from the Venetian miscellany, fol. 68. This passage certainly suggests that Giovanni himself collected his letters – but also that copies of the collection were made, whether for Pasquino or for others. It would not explain why the poems of Lovato, Boccaccio, Mussato, and Quirini were added to such a collection of letters, so as to form the Venetian miscellany.

[45] "Veridica quadam tua nec non facunda epistola, quae priscorum merito intellectum praestantiores prius natis excellentias praeconizat"; letter of Johannes Manzinus de Motta to

Manzini's letter is obsequious: obviously he hoped to curry favor with this influential member of the entourage of the Conte di Virtù. Thus he assures Dondi that his clock will "never be constructed, or at least not surpassed, by any of posterity."[46] He encouraged the elderly Dondi to pursue his lately-begun study of poetry, assuring him that if he persisted, he would become no less a poet than Hesiod or Homer, or than Virgil, Statius, or Petrarch.[47] Manzini's letter shows how contagious the attitudes of a literary hero are: taking his cue from Dondi's own letter, Manzini complains of the corruption of his age: "We degenerate too much, and every age falls in speedier and worse fashion from the height of virtues into the abyss of vices."[48] He continues his indictment: "Everyone is concerned with ambition, with money, or with prevailing by fraud and violence, so that you can well see how the world goes, and the religion of Christ."[49]

IS THE VENETIAN MISCELLANY AUTOGRAPH? We now turn to the main manuscript in which Dondi's epistle is found. The letter occupies several folios of a precious codex of the Biblioteca Marciana in Venice, MS lat. Cl. XIV, 223 (4340). This codex contains a collection of literary materials "of outstanding importance for the history of Italian literature in the Trecento."[50] It is usually thought, without much detailed consideration, to have been written by Giovanni Dondi himself, and thus to reflect his literary tastes. Our letter occurs as one among twenty-eight Latin letters, in a grouping that might possibly be thought to have been modelled upon Petrarch's *Epistolae rerum familiarium*, except for the fact that the letters do not even pretend to be in chronological order. Actually the model at work is undoubtedly Seneca.[51]

Johannes de Horologio, 11 July 1388, in Pietro Lazzeri, *Miscellaneorum ex MSS libris Bibliothecae Collegii Romani Societatis Jesu*, 2 vols. (Rome 1754) 1.195-208 at 195. The original MS has apparently not survived.

[46] "Nec per posterorum quemquam credo unquam factibile erit, vel saltem superabile; cum non videamus in aetatum successione tam excelsas ingeniorum auctelas." *Ibid.* 199.

[47] "Ad haec studium poesis et amorem, quomodo nunc in senectute sectaris, quantas laudes mereantur, explicare non possem . . . Quod si non perfunctorie sed dedita opera fuisses Poeticam executus, profecto non opinor, te minorem Hesiodo vel Homero; utque de nostris adjungam, Virgilio, Statio, vel Petrarcha fuisse." *Ibid.* 204. It is as though Manzini were saying, "Whether you agree or not, Giovanni, you could be the equal of the Ancients! "

I might add parenthetically that the tone in which Manzini speaks to Dondi about his "old age" would perhaps have been offensive to a man of 58, but not to a man of 70, and so may constitute one more bit of circumstantial evidence for an earlier birth date for Giovanni Dondi than 1330 (though not necessarily for the exact date of 1318).

[48] "At nimis degeneramus, et omnis aetas declivius deteriusque praecipitat a colle virtutum in vitiorum abyssum." *Ibid.* 207.

[49] "Curat quisque de ambitione, curat de pecuniis, vel de fraude et violentiis inferendis, unde qualiter mundus eat et Christi religio, bene vides." *Ibid.* 208.

[50] Giuseppe Billanovich, *Petrarca letterato 1: Lo scrittoio del Petrarca* (Rome 1947) 345.

[51] An interest in Seneca had been a hallmark of Paduan humanism since the days of Lovato and Mussato: see the references in Gangazza-Billanovich (n. 33 above) 26. It would seem that Giovanni Dondi wrote some notes or glosses on Seneca's *Epistulae morales*: they are mentioned by the author of a commentary on Seneca's letters in a Cremona MS, Bibl. Gov. MS 128. The

The "Venetian miscellany," as we may call this codex, includes the following components: poetry by Petrarch, Giovanni Quirini, Francesco Vannozzi, Boccaccio, Giovanni Dondi, Lovato de' Lovati, and Albertino Mussato; a eulogy of Petrarch by Boccaccio; Dondi's notes on Roman inscriptions and antiquities, followed by the collection of his Latin letters, and finally the last two books of Pier Crescenzi's work

---

author, who may very well be Gasparino Barzizza (1359-1431), lists a number of men who had tried to unravel a difficult passage in the very first letter of Seneca – a letter that deals, interestingly enough, with the "use of time, or Time itself," as the commentator remarks (fol. 121). The list includes Petrarch, who at one time had been heard to remark that Seneca himself, if he were to be revived, would not be able to explain his text. It continues with Lazarus de Conigliano, Giovanni Dondi, Marsilius de Sancta Sophia, Giraldus Vincentinus, and Albericus de Rosciate: "Quantum ad primam partem, pro expositione illius nodose littere, scilicet, 'maxima pars vite' etc., Petrarca, interogatus de hoc passu, illud asseruit se opinari ipsum Senecam, si revivisceret et interogaretur quid sibi voluerit in ea parte, non satis posse explicare textum suum. Verum, ut sibi videbatur, illud 'tota aliud agentibus' debebat exponi 'aliud agentibus,' id est, inconstantibus, qui in nullo bono fundamento possunt unquam sibi consistere. Hec opinio in eo peccare videtur quod nil agentes aut male agentes certe maiorem vite perdunt partem quam non perseverantes in bono, ut per se patet. Hanc Petrarce sententiam memini me legisse libro 2° *De remediis utriusque fortune* [MS: *De remedijs fortuitorum*], ubi remedia contra adversam fortunam pertractat. [The reference is to the following passage: "Dolor: Fluctuo et in diversum agor. Ratio: Maximum argumentum male se habentis animi, fluctuatio est, ut enim aegrum saepe thoro volvitur, sic aeger animus consiliis agitatur, de quo vix ulla mihi spes salutis, parumper abest, quin melius sperem de homine vitiis pertinaciter inhaerente, qui si conversus fuerit ad virtutes, in his forsitan constans erit, quam de homine vario, nullis se consiliis applicante, qui et si boni aliquid incoeperit non consistet, neque perseverabit docilis instare. Et fieri potest ut de hoc intelligere liceat Senecae illud obscurum, quod 'tota vita (elabitur) aliud agentibus,' modo enim hoc, modo illud, agentes, nunquam idem aliud agere sunt dicendi, quamvis et alios sensus locus ille recipiat." Franciscus Petrarcha, "De remediis utriusque fortunae," *Opera quae extant omnia*, 2 vols. (Basel 1554) 1.190. The mistaken title is that of Petrarch's model. Ps.-Seneca *Ad Gallionem fratrem de remediis fortuitorum.*]

"Forte in alia fuit alio tempore opinione. Refert enim magister Lazarus de Conigliano, professor grammatice, se audivisse ab ore ipsius Petrarce exponi passum istum, 'aliud agentibus,' id est, aliena negocia facientibus sicut sunt famuli, qui stant ad servicia dominorum pro pretio, et isto modo perdunt tempus suum faciendo facta aliorum, dum deberent studere, et vacare virtuti, sicut sunt etiam armigeri qui suorum ducum bella gerunt. Hinc est quod de militibus Cesaris scribitur a Lucano, libro V: 'Usus abit vite, bellis consumpsimus evum' [Lucan, *De bello civili* 5.276]. Cui adheret in quibusdam apostillis vir ingeniosissimus et suo tempore insignis physicus Johannes de horilogio, tractans eandem particulam. Dicit enim 'tota aliud agentibus,' id est, nunquam suis sed semper alienis intentis negociis, ut sunt servi, lixe, et ceteri, qui ad alienum somnum dormiunt, ad alienum appetitum comedunt, et sic de singulis ponentes suas actiones in alterius potestate. Huic etiam sententie concordabat famosus doctor huius nostre etatis facile medicorum princeps, Marsilius de Sancta Sophia, hanc addens rationem, quod pro re vilissima, id est, pro corpore servi facti sunt. Idem sentiebat Giraldus Vincentinus physicus. Que sententie quamvis auctoritate tantorum virorum stare videantur, tamen non patet quomodo hoc relativum diversitatis 'aliud' exponi possit, cum mutantes hoc genus vite non faciant aliud a male agentibus. Est propterea multorum vita deterior, ut predonum et paricidarum.

"Albericus de Roxiate, utriusque iuris peritissimus, dicebat 'tota aliud agentibus,' id est, ypocritis, nam ypocrite agunt aliud ab eo quod exterius ostendunt. Sed certe ubi ypocrita non intendat aliud per suam ypocrisin quam gloriam ambitiosam. Multi sunt qui maiorem vite partem amittunt. Ratio autem eius erat quia Scriptura Sacra dicit receperunt enim mercedem suam, ex quo patet quod totam vitam amiserunt." Anonymous "Commentum super epistulas Senecae," Cremona, Biblioteca Governativa MS 128, fol. 121r-v. In Giuseppe Mazzatinti, *Inventari dei*

on agriculture, the *Liber commodorum ruralium*. Some of these items (for example, the poems of Quirini) are not identified in the manuscript, and it has required literary sleuthing to establish their authors. The miscellany has received a great deal of attention from literary scholars, who usually focus their attention[52] upon the particular section of the codex that interests them, whether it be poetry by one of the other authors, or poetry or prose by Dondi himself. This compartmentalized scholarship has tended to neglect the character of the codex as a whole. Is it entirely an autograph from the hand of Giovanni Dondi, or is it partly autograph, partly the work of a scribe or secretary? Moreover, when was it written? Was it copied at one time, or over a period of years? These questions have seldom been raised, much less systematically investigated. Jacopo Morelli, librarian of the Marciana, writing in 1818, said of the manuscript that it had formerly belonged to "the author," meaning Giovanni Dondi, and subsequently to Roberto Pappafava (born 1617), a member of a leading Paduan noble family.[53] As the only information available in print, this brief

manoscritti delle biblioteche d'Italia 50.96, two possible authors are suggested: Sicco Polentone (ca. 1375/76-1447) and Gasparino Barzizza. Sicco's claim seems to rest mainly on the fact that other commentaries in the same codex (on Cicero's orations) are by him. On the other hand, Barzizza is known to have given a course on Seneca's *Epistles* at Padua in 1408 (G. Martellotti, art. "Barzizza, Gasparino," *Dizionario biografico degli Italiani* 7.36).

Lazzaro Malrotondi da Conegliano was a professor of grammar at Padua; he tutored the sons of Francesco Novello da Carrara in 1405 (Billanovich [n. 50 above] 11). He was also an acquaintance of Giacomo Zanetini, the doctor, who owned several copies of Seneca's letters (Billanovich 40). We note that Barzizza was awarded the doctorate in grammar and rhetoric at Pavia in 1392 by Fra' Guglielmo Centueri (Cenci [n. 3 above] 33). Marsilius de Sancta Sophia, of a renowned Paduan medical family, moved to Pavia as did Giovanni Dondi. Some of Petrarch's books passed into the hands of the Santa Sofia family: Paolo Sambin, "Libri del Petrarca presso suoi discendenti," *Italia medioevale e umanistica* 1 (1958) 359-369. Thus an interest in this particular letter of Seneca could be found in doctors (Marsilius and Giovanni Dondi) and lawyers (Albericus de Rosciate) as well as in professional grammarians (Lazzaro Malrotondi and probably Gasparino Barzizza).

In view of all these associations, it is not surprising to find Seneca mentioned or quoted in almost every letter of Giovanni Dondi (including the one published here, line 197). Even in his very short and friendly letter to Guido da Bagnolo, Dondi manages to refer twice to Seneca: letter of Dondi to Master Guido, 26 Dec. 1366, published by P. O. Kristeller in "Il Petrarca, l'umanesimo, e la scolastica a Venezia," in *La civiltà Veneziana del Trecento*, ed. V. Branca (Florence 1966) 171-172.

An interest in this specific passage of Seneca's letters may be taken as a possible clue that the writer might have had connections of some sort with this group of scholars in Padua or Pavia: Petrarch's mention of the passage in one of his most widely-read works would also, of course, have propagated an interest in it. When we learn that the logician Petrus de Mantua wrote an "Exposition of the first letter of Seneca to Lucilius" (P. O. Kristeller, *Iter Italicum*, 2 vols. [London 1963-1967] 2.372, describing MS Vat. lat. 5223), we might look for such a connection with the scholarly community of Padua or Pavia. The fact that Petrus de Mantua was an admirer and expositor of British logic and physics need not prevent us from recognizing that he had humanistic interests as well (a point that is well argued by Vasoli [n. 19 above] 15-18). In Petrus de Mantua, the humanistic interest in Time and the analytical interest derived from Oxford and Paris meet.

52 As Billanovich remarks (n. 50 above) 345.

53 "Ad animum hisce studiis [i.e., the study of Roman antiquities] excolendum Petrarchae, qui in iisdem eminebat, exemplo et familiaritate Dondius adductus, monumenta eius rei

description held the field until the end of the nineteenth century, when Salomone Morpurgo gave the most complete description of the codex. (The official description by Valentinelli was disappointingly sketchy, and is seldom mentioned in the literature.) Morpurgo listed the contents carefully and ventured the hypothesis that the entire book was copied by "a single Venetian" *in the early fifteenth century.*[54] With respect to the dating of the manuscript as fifteenth century, a similar verdict had been reached a little earlier by Luigi Padrin, who edited from it the poems of Lovato de' Lovati and Albertino Mussato, the Paduan proto-humanists. Padrin asserted that it was written in a fifteenth-century hand, "with abbreviations and letters that are scarcely intelligible, so that it would try the patience of a monk to read them."[55] Morpurgo's description has been accepted as definitive by most Italian scholars. Yet many who cite Morpurgo's description persist in asserting, contrary to his own explicit affirmation, that the manuscript was written in the *fourteenth* century, and by Dondi himself. There seems to be an almost irresistible impulse to characterize manuscripts as autograph, and the impulse has been at work in this case. Giuseppe Valentinelli, who compiled the printed catalogue of the manuscripts of the Biblioteca Marciana, elsewhere characterized the Venetian miscellany as a "splendid cartaceous codex of the fourteenth century, put together with loving care by Giovanni Dondi dall' Orologio."[56] Roberto Weiss also assumed that the Venetian miscellany had

---

certissima scriptis tradidit ac post se relinquit; at ea inedita vixque nota in codice chartaceo eiusdem aetatis, ab ipso auctore olim possesso, fortasse uni mihi videre obtigit apud Rubertum Papifavium, Albertini filium ex primaria apud Patavinos nobilitate, patriciumque Venetum, qui singulari me comitate complectebatur: quo quidem in codice scripta Dondii inedita, sine indicio alio, ordine, quo hic refero, ipse legi." Morelli, "De Joanne Dondio ab Horologio Medico Patavino, deque monumentis antiquis Romae ab eo inspectis, et scriptis eiusdem quibusdam ineditis," *Operette* (n. 1 above) 2.285-312 at 289. Besides the notes on Roman inscriptions, Morelli also here published six sonnets of Dondi, including the one given above in n. 25 (although without the heading "viro M^{O} G^{O}").

[54] "Pregevole miscellanea di varie cose volgari e latine, in prosa e in verso, le più del trecento a d'origine veneta, tutte copiat . . . da un veneto nei primordi del secolo XV." Salomone Morpurgo, "Dante Alighieri e le nuove rime di Giovanni Quirini," *Bullettino della Società Dantesca Italiana* 1 (1894) 134-139 at 135.

[55] "Questo prezioso manoscritto . . . è cartaceo, di mano del sec. XV, con abbreviature e con lettere poco intelligibili ed uniformi tanto da stancare la pazienza di un cenobita." Luigi Padrin, *Lupati de Lupatis, Bovetini de Bovetinis, Albertini Mussati necnon Jamboni Andreae de Favafuschis Carmina quaedam ex codice Veneto nunc primum edita*, per nozze Giusti-Giustinian (Padua 1887) xii. (Padrin was mistaken in identifying the judge of this poetic contest with Bovetino de Bovetini, who lived about a century later). Francesco Novati, who was able to publish a more correct text of this poem by collating the Venetian miscellany with a manuscript in Leiden, applauded the courage of Padrin: "Egli dimostro una certa dose di coraggio, perchè, veramente, lo stato in cui que' componimenti offrivansi nel codice, unico, a quanto si credeva, che li avesse conservati, era così miserando da metter a dura prova ed in parte anche mandar a vuoto l'ingegnosità e l'amore del più sperimentato conoscitore di testi medievali." Francesco Novati, "Nuovi aneddoti sul cenacolo letterario padovano del primissimo Trecento," *Scritti storici in memoria di Giovanni Monticolo* (Venice 1922) 171. The editor of the present text hopes that others will be as charitable!

[56] "Uno splendido codice cartaceo (L. XIV, 223) del secolo XIV, posto assieme con cure amorose da Giovanni Dondi dall' Orologio, amico intimo del Petrarca, contiene un brano del *canzoniere*, indicato a suo luogo, come pure scritti vari riguardanti la persona e le opere così dell'

been transcribed by Dondi himself: "Dondi's humanist activity was somewhat remarkable for his time. His Latin style may have been undistinguished, just as his Italian poetry remained flat and uninspired, but on the other hand, the classics were represented in his library, and it is to him that we owe the rescue of a substantial amount of Latin poetry by the early Paduan humanists and of Boccaccio's biography of Petrarch .... *thanks to his transcript of them*, now part of MS Lat. XIV, 223 (4340) of the Biblioteca Marciana, Venice"[57] (my italics). With casual references of this sort, it is difficult to tell how seriously the author has weighed the evidence for and against the attribution. I have in fact found only one scholar who has given detailed arguments for the autograph nature of the Venetian miscellany. Aldo Massèra has argued that it must be autograph because it contains a note in the first person ("Hec retuli dum de Roma redii in tabellis scripta," speaking of reproduced inscriptions).[58] But could not these words have been copied as well as any others?

It must be admitted that arguments against the miscellany's being autograph have not been very well developed either. There is one argument that perhaps deserves to be reexamined. It concerns the inventory of Giovanni Dondi's effects that was compiled after his death. The inventory was drawn up in Padua on 22 June 1389, and seems quite complete. It lists Dondi's books in some detail, but there is no item in it that can be assigned with certainty to the Venetian miscellany. It is possible, of course, that the miscellany had left Giovanni's hands before his death, but this seems unlikely. Vittorio Lazzarini, who edited this inventory, attempted to correlate items in the inventory with extant manuscripts, beginning with those that he regarded as autograph. Item 67, for example, Giovanni's consideration of the Paduan baths "and certain of his letters" ("et epistule quedam sue") is clearly the present MS 358 of the Seminary in Padua, with only one of the letters, that of 24 October 1370 to Petrarch (inc. "Debui nec ignoro. . . ."), remaining. There are other listings of letters: item 102, "Some letters covered in green" and item 154, "Some letters without binding," but they are not specifically said to be by Dondi. The only possible candidate in the inventory is item 96, "libelus quidam in quo sunt sonnecti vulgares et aliqua alia," which Massèra thinks may refer to the Venetian miscellany. On the other hand, Lazzarini thought that this "libelus" may be just the sonnets and *ballate* of Dondi, inserted later into the Venetian miscellany, since these folios (fols. 27-36) have a watermark different from that of the rest of the codex, as Morpurgo had observed.

---

autore che del Petrarca." Giuseppe Valentinelli, "Codici manoscritti d'opere di Francesco Petrarca od a lui riferentisi posseduti dalla Biblioteca Marciana di Venezia," in *Petrarca e Venezia,* ed. Valentinelli (Venice 1874) 91.

[57] Roberto Weiss, *The Renaissance Discovery of Classical Antiquity* (Oxford 1969) 49. This also seems to be the view of Giuseppe Billanovich, *Prime ricerche Dantesche* (Rome 1947) 64.

[58] Aldo F. Massèra, "Di tre epistole metriche Boccaccesche," *Giornale Dantesco* 30 (1927) 41-42. Massèra's interest is in the verses on Petrarch's *Africa* written by Boccaccio and contained in the Venetian miscellany: thus he is not troubled that an Oxford manuscript gives a better reading for them. But what of the clumsy or mistaken readings in Dondi's own letters: should we not be disturbed by them?

Lazzarini does not specifically say that these sonnets and ballads are in Giovanni's own hand. However he does commit himself with respect to the Latin letters of Giovanni Dondi contained in the Venetian miscellany: he says that they were "fortunately transcribed into a Marcian codex in the very first years of the Quattrocento."[59] (Why "the very first years"? We are not told). Since Lazzarini must have had the date of Dondi's death (1389) firmly in mind, it follows that he did not believe that the Latin letters are autograph. Thus we have the following situation: the two authorities most universally deferred to in this matter ascribe the Venetian miscellany to the fifteenth century. And of one thing we can be absolutely sure: the Venetian miscellany cannot have been (1) written in the fifteenth century and (2) written by Giovanni Dondi himself, for these are incompatible statements. At the present time, we have no very firm evidence for either of them; but only a careless scholar would assert them both.

Obviously what is called for is a thorough examination of the handwriting of the Venetian miscellany, comparing it with all other manuscripts suspected to be from the pen of Giovanni Dondi. Such a comparison would have to begin, in my judgment, with (1) a letter from Giovanni Dondi to Ludovico Gonzaga presently in the state archives in Mantua.[60] It is a routine letter in which Dondi recommends a former student to the Mantuan prince, yet it hardly seems likely that Dondi would have allowed someone else to write such a letter.

We have already mentioned another presumed autograph of Giovanni Dondi: (2) MS 358 of the Seminario in Padua, "Consideratio Johannis de Dondis de fontibus calidis paduanis," considered autograph by Lazzarini, who regards the letter "Debui nec ignoro . . .", previously mentioned, as also autograph.[61]

[59] "Altre ventisette lettere latine [sic: actually there are twenty-eight] sono per fortuna trascritte in un codice marciano dei primissimi anni del Quattrocento," Lazzarini, *Scritti* (n. 13 above) 257.

[60] "Magnifice et potens domine. Suadet michi caritas et dilectio singularis quam ad me humilem servitorem vestrum geritis, non tam de meritis meis quam de vestri bonitate atque benignitate procedens, ut egregium virum et singularem medicum Magistrum Johannem franciscum de padua, filium dudum et nunc fratrem et socium, sua exigente virtute ac suficientia recomende(m). Nempe vir bone et supra mediocritatem scientie est, bonorum morum et probate fidelitatis, quorum omnium ego testis sum. Bene consultum est, Magnificentie vestre, ipsum apud vos habere et ad servicia vestra accepisse. Quotidie enim magis atque magis, ut arbitror, dominationi vestre sua facta placebunt, et quod de eo scribo experientia confirmabit. Si qua autem per me, humilem servitorem vestrum, fieri possent vel hic vel alibi vobis grata, paratus sum preceptis vestris in omnibus obedire. Altissimus protegat statum vestrum.

"Servitor vester humilis, magister Johannes de dondis de Padua dictus ab horologio. papie, xxviij, Januar."

Mantova, Archivio di Stato, Archivo Gonzaga, Busta no. 1619. My attention was drawn to this letter by its listing in Kristeller, *Iter Italicum* (n. 51 above) 1.267. A different hand has added a date which I was not able to read with confidence: it could be 1382, which is the year when Lodovico Gonzaga died (Cenci [n. 3 above] 18). Guglielmo Centueri was also a friend of Ludovico Gonzaga, according to Cenci. Worth noting is the exact form of his signature: "johs de dond de Pad dict9 ab horologio."

[61] Lazzarini, *Scritti* (n. 13 above) 256.

(3) MS D. 39 of the Biblioteca Capitolare of Padua contains Dondi's *magnum opus*, the *Tractatus astrarii*. Armando Petrucci, one of the editors of the recent sumptuous edition, argues that only the marginal notes come directly from Dondi's own hand.[62] Lazzarini thought that the whole treatise was autograph.

(4) There may very well be other letters of Dondi in other Italian libraries that should be considered. Publication of the entire set of Latin letters in the Venetian miscellany would expedite the search for their originals.

Until a thorough paleographic study of this kind has been completed, the status of the Venetian miscellany (that is, autograph or apograph?) must be in doubt. Probably no one would seriously question the assumption that these materials derive in some way from Giovanni himself. But unless it is established that the miscellany is undeniably autograph, a shadow of suspicion must fall, for example, upon the titles of the poems, which might have been added by a compiler rather than by the author. It is somewhat disturbing to find that the sonnet in note 25 above appears, in part, in another Marcian codex with the title "Idem in deploratione morum nostrae aetatis" rather than with the dedication to Fra' Guglielmo.[63] Even should the Venetian miscellany turn out to be autograph, it need not follow that the Latin letters are exact replicas of the missives actually sent: Dondi would have the precedent of Petrarch himself for altering the letters with a view to their "publication" or circulation.

At any rate, I believe that the burden of proof lies heavy upon those who persist in claiming that the Venetian miscellany was actually copied by Giovanni Dondi himself. To be sure, there are serious questions that have to be asked about what we may call the Morpurgo-Lazzarini hypothesis, that is, that the Venetian miscellany was copied in the first years of the fifteenth century. For example, what assurance do we then have that the selection of contents was made by Dondi himself? Are we to assume that whoever then copied the miscellany had before him components that had been selected by Giovanni before his death? Also, whether we make this assumption or not, it seems to me that we should ask what principles governed the selection. We observe that apart from the Dondi correspondence, the archaeological notes, and possibly the Crescenzi work on agriculture, the interest displayed is

[62] Giovanni Dondi dall' Orologio, *Tractatus astrarii, Biblioteca capitolare di Padova, Cod. D.39* (Vatican City 1960) 50-51. The body of the text, in Petrucci's view, was written by an amanuensis employed by Dondi for writing this copy and also the one contained in MS Marc. Lat. VIII, 17 (2819). Petrucci speculates that the amanuensis was a Paduan working under the direct supervision of Dondi and executing for him various copies of the work. Furthermore, Petrucci suggests (51) that our Venetian miscellany must also be considered autograph – or, at least, the section of it that contains the Roman inscriptions, which occupies fols. 45r to 46v of the Venetian miscellany. Petrucci does not explain why he does not consider the rest of the Venetian miscellany to be autograph as well. It should be noted that Lazzarini (*Scritti* 255) considered the whole of the Paduan MS D.39 to be the work of the author's own hand. The notes on Roman inscriptions were published partially by Morelli, but subsequently by De Rossi under the title, "Ioannis Dondii Iter Romanum anno fere MCCCLXXV e codice Veneto Mar. Lat. XIV, 223," in *Inscriptiones Christianae Urbis Romae*. . . 2.1 (Rome 1888) 329-334.

[63] See Medin's note on this sonnet, no. IX in *Le rime di Giovanni Dondi* (n. 27 above).

overwhelmingly literary, indeed, poetic. It would be natural to suppose that the items that are not by Dondi represent the non-professional interests of his old age, interests developed as a result of his association with Petrarch, and that the poetic works of others were collected by him as models for his own efforts at poetic composition. On the other hand, it is at least possible that these poetic memorabilia were family heirlooms, some of them pre-dating Giovanni's late-blooming interest in poetry. Lazzarini has pointed out that Giovanni's father could have known Albertino Mussato while both were residents of Chioggia.[64] Is it so unlikely that an interest in contemporary Latin poetry might have been manifested in the Dondi family before Giovanni came in contact with Petrarch? And if so, would it be at all surprising to find that such an interest remained alive with Giovanni's descendants or relatives? Is it not possible that some enterprising younger member of the Dondi family (one of Giovanni's many sons, or even one of his brothers?) might have put together a miscellany containing poetry associated with Jacopo as well as with Giovanni? This is sheer speculation, but once we are freed from the *idée fixe* that the Venetian miscellany must have been actually copied out by Giovanni Dondi himself, it becomes imperative for us to develop other plausible hypotheses to account for the existence and contents of this crucial codex. In fact, it is a scholarly duty.

THE TRANSCRIPTION. I have been able to compare the text of this particular letter of Dondi to Fra' Guglielmo with another version that exists in the monastery in Schlaegl, Austria: Cpl. 76. This codex has been described[65] as having been written in 1451, of Italian origin, and as having formerly belonged to Joannes de Rabenstein. The catalog description of one item, "Centuaria Guillelmus (O. Min. episcop. Papiensis 1386-1402): Epistola ad Joannem de Hordogia (*sic*), quae praestantiora sint ingenia an praesentia an antiqua," leads one to expect that it is Fra' Guglielmo's rejoinder to the letter of Giovanni Dondi. This turns out, however, to be a mistake: the letter is actually Giovanni's, with a few variants from the reading of the Venetian miscellany. There is something more than a little tantalizing about the similarity between the wording of this description of the contents of the letter (which indeed occurs in the manuscript itself, but in the following precise form: "Epistola magistri Guillelmi de Centueriis ad magistrum Iohannem de horologio que prestantiora sint ingenia an presentia an antiqua") and the description given by Morelli in his *Operette* (2.291): "Antiquorum ingenia vel praecipuis novorum praestantiora fuisse demonstrat, etc.," but the resemblance may be purely fortuitous. In any event, it is unlikely that Morelli had seen another version of the letter than the one in the Venetian miscellany (which lacks this heading and simply has the address to Fra' Guglielmo, "famous professor of Sacred Scripture"), or surely he would have mentioned it.

If the actual missive received by Fra' Guglielmo should ever turn up, it would be

[64] Lazzarini, *Scritti* (n. 13 above) 105.

[65] Godefriedus Vielhaber and Gerlacus Indra, *Catalogus codicum (Cpl.) manuscriptorum . . .* (Linz 1918) 178-188 at 178.

extremely interesting to learn how it compares with the version in the Venetian miscellany, and the comparison could even help to decide the issue with respect to the autograph nature of the codex. With this in mind, I have chosen to present, in the critical apparatus, indications that will enable the reader to reconstruct the exact spelling of the letter as it appears in the Venetian miscellany. Dondi's orthography can be compared with what we now know of Petrarch's. In his spelling of ancient proper names, for example, Dondi follows the orthography of the younger Petrarch (that is, general medieval practice) rather than the more refined spelling that his friend later adopted and made into the standard of subsequent scholarly Latin usage.[66]

[66] In line 132, for example, Dondi (or his scribe!) mentions "Pirro Epirrote" where the mature Petrarch would have used "y" instead of "i" in both names Dondi also omits the "H" in "Hanibal" as did the youthful Petrarch. On Petrarch's spelling, see G. Billanovich, "Petrarch and the Textual Tradition of Livy," *Journal of the Warburg and Courtauld Institutes* 14 (1951) 137-208 at 146.

THE LATIN TEXT OF DONDI'S LETTER

Fratri Guilielmo de Cremona Sacrarum Scripturarum
eximio professori

Quid ego nunc vir eximie, quid presentantissime doctor agam? Nempe perplexus sum dum me nuper inter duo adversa pariterque suspecta constituis, quorum quoniam alterum eligere oppositionis natura compellit, diu quid hic [56v] consilii caperem hesitavi. Propositum fuerat pridem dum scriberem stilo vulgari iocari tecum quo animus multiformis cure fasce pergravis nugis inanibus velut quibusdam solaciis levari posset ad solita. Tu interim, vir amice, nec dum excuso mentis onere nec imminuto quidem, imo si verum dici opporteat, non mediocriter aucto superadiectis curis novis et gravibus, me a propositis iocis vocas ad seria, et dicere aliquid quod prodesse possit exposcis? Tacebo ne igitur obstruamque peticionibus aures tuis, an loquar potius et obmissis quibus luximus iocis dicere aliquid utile prout exigis attentabo? Sentio utraque in parte quod terreat. Nam primum si cepero, vereor ne aut insolencie et arogantie arguar et tue despector vel neglector peticionis acuser, quamquam ea labes

M = Codex Marcianus Latinus, Cl. XIV, 223 (4340) P = Codex Plagensis 76

Epistola magistri Guillelmi de Centueriis ad magistrum Iohannem de horologio que prestantiora sint ingenia an antiqua P 2 constituis] constitutus M 3 oppositionis] preponis P 3 quid hic *bis* M 5 fasce] fasse M solatijs M levari] levaretur et M lavaretur P 6 nec] ne P 7 super] sed P 7 novis curis *tr.* P 8 gravidis P locis P feria P 9 obsinamque P 10 lusimus P Sensio P ni fallor perraro meis asuerit habitare cum moribus. Aut supra modum noter ignavie, que quamvis preter dubium plurima mecum sit (utinamque non esset!), quis tamen nesciat hinc michi fore cavendum, non dico a te, viro optimo et mei amantissimo rerumque mearum, at a dentibus lividorum quos frequens ut scis hodie angulus omnis habet, qui dum inficere quemquam posse verbis detractoriis arbitrantur, alienoque nomini nubem obducere, id facere sibi oblectamenti permaximi loco docunt. Ideoque hoc primum super illis studium, hec supra alias omnes diligentior cura est. Cavendum inquam ne si requirente te forte siluero, audentius hi loquantur et astruant ignorantiam meram imperitiamque dicendi causam esse silencii. Quod si partem vertar in alteram et quod postulas utile aliquid coner exponere, ambigo ne in irritum cadat intentio. Quis enim dubitat non modo non serium ac prorsus ridiculum et inane futurum nuliusque momenti quicquid id fuerit quod ab animo occupato prodierit et nubilo ac ab ingenio pene ut ita dixerim alienato? Itaque quoniam ut cernis neuter michi sat tutus est callis, si hactenus hesi et tantisper dilata res, non est quod aut mireris aut aliqua indignatione tangaris. Potius equum est indulgere perplexo et libenter pretacta pericula declinanti. Verum quoniam tui me urget autoritas in partem tuam venio, et certus quod longe cautius est silentium quam insulsa locutio, propono tamen dicere quicquam tecum eo fidentius quod apud te nisi bene loqui me posse non arbitror. Quicquid enim id fuerit et qualecunque quod ab amico processit tu non dubito magnipendes, aut ego non satis humanitatem et patientiam tuam novi. Quatenus autem dictis dicenda conveniant et stilus ludos hic prehabitos decentius subsequatur, ad quod postremo alter sermo pervenerat recensebo. Igitur cum hinc inde vulgaribus ritimis lusissemus et ego novissime illo stilo nostri presentis evi defectum atque miseriam simulque infelicitatem nostram aliorumque quibus hac tempestate mortalem vitam agere datum est gravi animo deplorassem, illos praestantioris sortis faciens quibus obtigit priscis fuisse temporibus, presertim sub Augusti Cesaris principatu, quo terrarum orbe pene pacato latina maxime ingenia floruere et meritum virtuti pretium datum est, tu argutissime vir, si tuorum verborum sat sensum elicui, pro nostris temporibus partem summis nec pateris priscorum temporum memoriam anteponi, quoniam nec ea ut ais suis caruere miseriis, quando ambiciosi glorie atque cupidi dominandi et ob id vincendi flagrantes ardore semper in armis frequenter miserabilibus cladibus sunt afflicti. Sic tu et ego aliud hac in parte sentimus. Ego vetera prefero tempora, tu moderna defendis. Qua de re quid sit non infructuosum forte fuerit percontari, sed si unum prius pro intentionis mee apertione pretulerim, videlicet quod ea que dixeram de predictorum colatione temporum

13 assueverit P 16 at] et P scis] sis P hodie *om.* P 17 quemquam] quemque (?) P alienoque] alieno quoque P 20 hij loquentur P 21 causam dumtaxat *add.* P 22 irritum] reritum P cedat intensio P 23 dubitet P ac] aut P et] sed P 24 ocupato M prodierit] produxit P 26 res] . . . *add* P 27 equm M 28 pretacta] previsa P auctoritas P

31 non arbitror posse *tr.* P id *om.* P processerit P 33 Quatenus] Ut P hic ludos *tr.* P quod] quid P 34 pervenerat] brevibus *add.* P 35 rithimis P 39 quo] quorum P 40 verborum tuorum *tr.* P 41 summis] sumis P priscorum temporum memoriam] priora quorum memineram P 45 sentimus] sotimus P 46 sed *om.* P apertione] fundamento P

queque deinceps dicturus sum ad partem divine religionis seu fidei non trahantur. Neque enim adeo delirus sum nec tam leviter fidei catholice religionis inhereo ut ignorare vel dubitare aliquomodo queam densam [57r] atramque errorum caliginem circha religionis fidem, in qua mersi priores ambulavere per devia et qua perstricti eorum oculi verum numen agnoscere nequiverunt, nostre luci, quam nobis salvator noster Dei filius yhesus cristus apperuit, non magis quam cecitatem visui seu privationem aliquam habitui posse conferri. Ideo hac in re infeliciores nos esse illis negaverim et cristiana tempora illis postponenda dixerim, verum infelices illos qui in perditionem cum suis tenebrarum ducibus abierunt, nos vero felices quibus verum lumen ostensum est et datum noscere si velimus, callisque patefactus est quo ad veram felicitatem valeamus si illo incesserimus pervenire. Hic nulla tecum diversitas, nullum litigium, nulla omnino disonantia, verum omnis concordia summusque consensus. At unde sermo noster ceperat revertamur, si ad virtutum cultum, si ad officiorum premia, si ad robus efficaciamque animorum, denique si ad ingeniorum prestantiam intentio nostra feratur, audacter asseverare non desinam nos a prioribus magnifice superatos et moderna tempora ab antiquis notabiliter deffecisse. Et o utinam michi posset contrarium demonstrari! Sed hoc intellectu videtur esse tam facile ut latere nequeat quempiam advertentem, ideoque ad finem sui argumenti patrocinio non egere, quoniam palam sit sola presentium observatione et recognitione priorum. Mores huius temporis sunt patentes etiam si parumper palpebras errigamus. Quis nunc virtuti qualisque sit cultus nisi cecus sit nemo non videt. Quibus artibus hodie principum gratie vendicentur, quibus meritis sublimiores honores sperari queant et affluentiores divitie, tandem qui qualesque homines prestare sensu atque prudentia communiter censeantur, que res apud Cassiodorum rebus omnibus preponenda est, quoniam in homine feliciter [?] invenitur, iam omnes intelligunt et meminisse me piget. Ad tantum enim erroris mortalium devenere iudicia ut hoc indicio michi sit nature ut sic dixerim senescentia humane et propediem in decrepitum ac tandem in hichilum abiture, ni forte aliter divina bonitas miserata providerit. Iam vides ubique genus hominum, cuius maxime est sociari convivere atque communicare civiliter, insidiari proximo et undique laqueos tendere, in quos si forte incautus quispiam vel fidenter ambulans inciderit supplantetur. Et heu heu hoc hodie pene unum studium omnibus est, si diligenter observas, hic fere tota versatur intentio, hec sunt nostri virtutes evi. Ille melior sibi, ille sapientior atque prudentior esse videtur, nec sibi videtur tantum, sed quod amplius indignandum est, sic etiam esse ab aliis reputatur, qui quidcumque ingenium sibi celitus datum est in alieni eris subreptione, in socii delusione bene de se fidentis exercet. Et qui abominandarum machinamenta artium subtilius atque perspicacius meditatur, favores sibi principum

51 circa P qua mersi] quam universi P 52 nequivere P 53 seu] si P 54 illis esse *tr.* P 55 Xriana P 57 patefactus] prefactus P 60 At] ut *add.* P 63 antiquis] valde *add.* P 64 posset michi *tr.* P 65 quempiam] quelibet P finem sui] fidem suis P 67 prioris P

70 queant] possint P homines *om.* P 71 Cassidorum P 73 mortalium] iam *add.* P 74 decripitam M 75 abiture] pro itinere *add.* P 76 communicari P 80 prudentior et sapientior *tr.* P 81 esse *om.* P 82 reputatur] ruptatur P qui *om.* P est *om.* P 83 subreptione] susceptione P ab hominandarum P

facile comparabit, largitiones habebit et premia, et brevi dominantium dominium optinebit. At quondam qui qualesque viri fuerint, quibus convixerint moribus, quibus virtutibus inheserint, quibus ex actibus premia meruerint, et qualia bene meritis donarentur, quoniam elapsi omnia temporis sunt, non veluti presentia coram observare oculis aut manibus palpare valemus, recognoscere tamen testimoniis magnis licet et tam fide dignis indiciis, ut intendentem subtiliter dubitare non sinant. In primis indicio sunt scripture quas eximia ingenia ad posterorum memoriam edidere, quarum quibusdam tanta est auctoritas atque maiestas ut eisdem fides negari non possit. Apud me autem si queras tam grandis hercle fides ut quodam modo illa putem vidisse que legi. Adeo michi impersuasibile est tam autenticos viros nisi vera scripsisse et nisi que ipsi presentes viderant vel a presentibus acceperant vel magnis ab auctoribus perscripta didicerant, quos potissimum scripturos ystoriam, non poema, in quo forte scribendi genere liceret res aliter scribere quam fuissent, veritatem rerum summopere quesivisse omneque mendacium declinavisse non dubito. Huiusmodi scripturas seu earum precipuas quasdam legisse te aliquando [57v] studiose crediderim et in eis mores et actus preteriti evi multis in partibus non sine admiratione aliqua notavisse, quibus si illos quos in presentia cernimus salvo iure contuleris, iustitiam fortitudinem temperantiam atque prudentiam altius profecto illorum animis insedisse fatebere, illisque qui earum ductu virtutum magnificum quid egerunt longe digniori-bus premiis fuisse provisum. Ceterum eiusdem rei indicio sunt ea que de decretis olim ob actus egregios honoribus usque hodie Romana in urbe perdurant. Quamquam enim plurima ex eis et magnificentiora iam tempus consumserit, et quorundam ruine tantummodo que vestigia quedam prebent eorum que antea steterant ostendantur, illa tamen pauca minusque magnifica que supersunt abunde testantur nisi magne virtutis esse non potuisse illos qui eadem decreverint, magnumque aliquid laude gesisse dignum illos quibus illa in perennem honorem et gloriam pro premio dona-bantur, statuas dico que vel ere conflate vel marmore cese usque in diem duravere presentem et frusta plurima passim iacentia diruptarum, arcusque marmoreos magni operis triumphales et columnas insculptas grandium gestorum ystorias indicantes, aliaque quam plurima generis huius in honorem viris insignibus publice fabricata vel quia pacem fundassent vel quia patriam imminenti periculo liberassent vel imperium subactis gentibus ampliassent prout in aliquibus eorum legisse me memini non sine quadam notabili voluptate et te similiter pretereuntem aliquando auguror notavisse et

---

84 perspicacius] se (?) *add.* P 86 qualescumque P
87 inheserint] inserint P 88 temporis omnia *tr.* P 89 aut] et P volemus P 90 ut] et P 91 quas] quid P memoriam] noticiam P 92 ut] et P 93 ut *om.* P illa putem] presente aliquando illa P 95 nisi] vel. *add.* P 96 didicerunt P 97 fuisset M 98 sumopere M quesuisse M declinasse P 99 scriptas P 100 eis] eos P
102 altius] alicuius P 104 sunt] super P de decretis] de certis P 105 ob] ab P egregios] M *has crossed out* ostendantur. . . . virtutis *from* 107-109 106 eis] hiis P consumserit] assumpserit P 107 que] quo M ostendancia P 109 non *om.* P 110 illa in perennem] ea in perhenniem P gloram M 112 frustra P 113 trihumfales M 114 plura P fabricatas P 116 memini] *M has the following crossed out*: periculo li-

substitisse paulisper aliquo cum stupore ac intra te met forte dixisse; hec profecto sunt magnorum argumenta virorum. Talibus similia ob similes causas hoc nostro evo non fiunt. Et quare putas nisi quia desunt tam hi qui illa agant quibus talis premia debeantur quam hi qui sic agentibus si forent faverent quo talia largirentur? Ad animorum vigorem atque eficaciam transeamus, qua in re nostros comparare prioribus abusio magis quam comparatio dici potest cum constet illos robustos atque validos animos habuisse, nostros vero (quod silerem libentius, sed locus cogit et veritas) sic agentes iudicamus ut de se faciant opinari non modo parvos et imbeciles animos habere sed nullos. Non petam hodie ut michi des Cocliti similem quempiam aut Curtio Scevoleque aut Regulo vel Deciis duobus et innumerabilibus aliis tam ex Romane urbis civibus quam externis qui vel ob patrie salutem vel libertatem, ob fidem servandam etiam hosti certe morti incunctanti animo se dedere, et illam subire sano atque deliberato consilio decrevere. Nec petam ut duces ostendas Scippionibus similes aut pares Catonibus atque infinitis aliis ex Romanis, nec ex exteris Alexandro Macedoni Pirro Epirrote vel Anibali Peno, qui ut aliis imperitarent, ut imperia propagarent, ut sibi suisque gloriam compararent, vel totum vite spatium vel plus utiles annos in armis egere et modo expugnando opida modo acie confligendo cum hostibus magnis incomodis ac indeffessis laboribus, integro tamen semper atque invicto animo perstiterunt. Non petam quidem talibus animis similes, quoniam hac etate non sunt, qua perraro audis expugnari munitiones et vinci et paucos id audere, audentium vero paucissimos nisi fraus quepiam intervenerit optinere. Sic non est querendus in nostris vigor quem constat habuisse priores, inter quos paucos reperies quibus animi tantum sit ut adventantem hostem operiri audeant aut cum expectatione decernere. Scio quid a pluribus hoc solet loco dici, videlicet quod ea que de verterum animis dicta sunt potius fuere furoris atque imprudentie quam virtutis, quem furorem inanis glorie suaserat apetitus atque ambitio dominandi. Sed quicquid de hoc veritas habeat, puta an indubiam mortem dictas ob res eligere sit virtutis et an liceat gentes liberas atque quietas invadere salve iustitia [58r] et hostiliter molestare sibique subicere, non querimus pro presenti nec est nunc in animo terminare, unum ex dictis querimus, quod negari non potest, hoc scilicet, tam magnos et interritos ausus a magnis prodiisse spiritibus et tam difficiles aggressus nisi a robustioribus animis quam hi sunt quos inesse nostris contemporaneis experimur tanta geri perseverantia nequivisse. Tandem ut sermo ab animis ad ingenia transferatur, cui non

---

119 virorum sunt argumenta virorum *tr.* P hoc nostro evo] evo nostro non *tr.* P

120 Et quare. . . .debeantur *om.* P 121 forent] fovent *corrected to* forent P 125 iudicamus] videamus P imbecillos P 126 quampiam P 128 libertatem] vel *add.* P 129 incontanti M et] ut P 130 atque] ac P Scippionibus] sapientioribus P 132 anibalo P 134 expugnanda P acie *om.* P 135 hostibus] acie P indefessis P

138 obtinere P querendum P 140 animi] anni P ut] ad *add.* P cum expectatione decernere] quid etiam petentem P 141 Soleat P veterum animis] veteris annis P 142 fuere *om.* P 143 suaserat] servat P et] atque P 144 indubiam] dubiam P dictas ob res *om.* P 146 nunc *om.* P 148 tam] tamen P agressus M 150 ut] noster P

satis liquet nisi sit penitus insensatus, moderna ingenia a prioribus defecisse adeo quidem multum, ut illis fere nulla in re equiparari queant et in multis quam maxime superentur? Cum enim hominum ingenia nullo magis quam ex eorum operibus innotescant, quantum sit inter hec et illa discriminis nequaquam melius quam admotis invicem eorum operibus palam fit. Opera humani ingenii precipua sunt artium atque scientiarum inventa puta sapientie et liberalium doctrinarum quas volunt ad veram sapientiam preparare et ut verum sit dicere scripture omnes et monimenta librorum. Preter hec sunt artificia que ab inato rationis ingenio et acquisito artis habitu preconcepta per ipsas manus artificum ex exposita materia fabricantur. Horum operum primo liberales artes sive doctrinas reliquasque scientias et universas sapientie partes humanitus adinvente non est dubium adinvenisse priores easque inventas tradidisse posteris conscriptas in libris tam claris et indubitatis principiis, tanto cum ordine et inexpugnabili ratione ut in dies presentes magna fere cum omni admiratione atque veneratione permaneant atque nunc a nostris vestigentur ingeniis. Que vere de novo inveniantur scientie absurdum est querere, tam exigue sunt aut nulle. Satis est et abunde modernis si illorum queant tantum superficies attingere, que veteres illi altissime tractavere. Quod si forte ex his quisquam sibi fidens aliquid invenire studuerit seu de prius traditis mutare presumserit, ut diebus nostris non nullos fecisse dyalecticos non ignoras, quanti illa fuerint quantumque permanserint satis constat. Vix ea etate qua fuerint edita duravere suisque cum auctoribus periere. Ut vero hac in re qualis sit comparatio veterum cum modernis luce clarius ostendatur, nobilissimum et excellentissimum huius etatis ingenium, studiosissimum atque abundantisimum omnium scriptorum, exercitatum in quolibet dicendi genere atque scribendi in medium adducamus, dominum dico Petrarcam, quem ut arbitror nosti et sepe vidisti, sed ego familiaris fui multumque domesticus presertim in posteris eius annis. Hoc ego audacter ingenium pro mera loquens veritate omnis amicitie excluso respectu ceteris nostri evi ingeniis que ego noverim antepono et habuisse censeo apud priores locum si illorum etate vixisset habiturum etiam cum venturis multo amplius gratiae ac precii quam cum suis. Huius viri opera, que plurima edidit et aliqua forte vidisti quavis in parte si legeris placebunt tibi non mediocriter, certus sum. Quid ni placeant? ponderosis enim referta sententiis dulcisono stilo et artificioso ordine sunt confecta. Si eadem legas iterum iterumque relegas, plus placebunt, quod magni operis et auctoris indicium est. At si sepositis illis ad legendum aliquid ex maiorum veterum monumentis accesseris, senties hauddubie

---

151 moderna] mundana P adeo] ade P 154-156 nequam . . . scientiarum] palam fiant opera humani ingenij precipua sunt artium atque scientiarum P

157 sapientiam veram *tr.* P verum] ad unum M 159 aquisito M ex *om.* P 161 adinvente] adinventas P 162 tradisse M 164 permaneat M 165 Que vere] queve M 166 aut] vel P quent] queunt P 167 superficies tantum *tr.* P veteres] inventores P his] hijs P 169 dyaleticos M 170 qua fuerint] qui fuerunt P fuerit M 171 auctoritatibus perire P 173 scripturarum M 174 scribendi *om.* P

175 Petrarcham P ut] uti P 176 posterioribus P 178 censeo] senseo P 180 legeris] ligeris P 181 referta] res sue P dulcissimo P 183 et] aut (?) PM auctoris] autorum P 184 accessire P

si animum intenderis quam altius sonum mittant. Quod ego cum aliquando facerem recordatus sum verbi quod semel ex ore viri illius adhuc viventis audieram. Cum enim bucolicum carmen quod ipse dictaverat post Maronis bucolicam uno in volumine coligasset et librum illum se meque presentibus tertius quidam vir nobilis manu prehensum obiceret, et quisnam liber esset percontaretur, hoc ait, "in libro consutus est pannus griseus cum scarleto," tali responso aperte testatus sua opera non parumper a veteribus superari. Ubi igitur tam singulare et unicum ingenium inter nostros cedit [58v] nec cedere se inficiatur prioribus, relinquitur ut non magis habeamus cum veteribus de ingenio disceptare quam Aranea cum Minerva. Sic est profecto. Nostra ingenia inferioris sunt note, e quibus si quidquam historicum habeamus, est absque dubitatione Livio atque Crispo remissius, si oratorem, longe est inferior Cicerone, si poetam, Maro illum, Oratius atque Naso precedunt, si philosophum, Varro prestat ac Seneca. Neque hi tantum modernos ex prioribus superant, sed innumerabiles prope quos sileo, paucos autem hos ex omnibus atuli quoniam una pene habuit etas simul et se coram in urbe vidit Augustus. Si vero divinorum eruditum canonum sit reperire quempiam inter nostros et sacrarum interpretem scripturarum, multum infra Augustinum atque Yeronimum et alios innumerabiles ex veteribus ambulabit, quod tam manifestissimum est ut sermonem in hoc producere vitium sit. De artificiis ingeniorum veterum quamquam pauca supersint, si qua tamen manent alicubi, ab his qui ea in re sentiunt cupide queruntur et videntur magnique penduntur et si illis hodierna contuleris, non latebit auctores eorum fuisse ex natura ingenio potiores et artis magisterio doctiores. Edificia dico vetera et statuas sculpturasque cum aliis modi huius, quorum quedam cum diligenter observant huius temporis artifices obstupescunt. Novi ego marmorarium quendam famosum illius facultatis artificem inter eos quos tunc haberet Ytalia presertim in artificio figurarum. Hunc pluries audivi statuas atque sculpturas quas Rome perspexerat tanta cum admiratione atque veneratione narrantem, ut id referens poni quodammodo extra se ex rei miraculo videretur. Aiebat enim se quandoque cum sociis transeuntem inde ubi alique huiusmodi cernerentur ymagines intuendo fuisse detentum stupore artificii et societatis oblitum substitisse tam diu donec comites per quingentos passus et amplius preterirent, et cum multa de illarum figurarum bonitate nararet et auctores laudaret ultraque modum commendaret ingenia ad extremum hoc solebat addicere, ut verbo utar suo, "Nisi illis ymaginibus spiritus vite deesset, meliores illas esse quam vivas", ac si diceret a tantorum artificum ingeniis non modo imitatam fuisse naturam, verum etiam superatam. I nunc, magister optime, et facultates nostras tam humiles magni pende et si quo potest modo hodierna tempora adversus priora

---

185 intenderes P quam] quasi P 186 adhuc *om.* P 187 buccellicum P post Maronis] contra mara onis P 189 quisnam] qui P esset] est P 190 respunso M

192 nec] ne P 193 disseptare MP cum] cumcum M 194 Nostrum (?) M quidquam] quemquam (?) P 195 dubitatione est *add.* M remissior P lunge M 196-197 filosophum M 197 Varo M prestat] presto P 199 pene] omnes eos *add.* P vidit] radit P 201 Yeroni (?) P 204 manent] nutrient (?) P 205 illis *om.* P 208 obtupescere P

211 id *om.* P 213 inde ubi] per partes quibus P intuendo] movendo (?) M 216 ingenia] ingenti P 219 I] Quam P 220 magnipendere P

defende, quod o utinam posses, ut ego desinerem indignari et inciperem in gratiam cum nostris venire diebus. Sed videre videor quod non poteris, tam manifeste omnibus patet oppositum. Nec tamen latet me doctorem prestantissimum Augustinum hac in causa tue partis videri posse patronum in eo videlicet libro qui *De Dei* dicitur *civitate,* quo presertim pro Christiana religione decertans antiqua gentilium tempora infelicia fuisse multisque miseriis repleta demonstrat.[1] Quod etiam coetaneus eius atque discipulus Paulus Orosius ex temporum ystoriis conatur ostendere in libro quem ad Augustinum ipsum scripsit contra infamatores temporum Christianorum.[2] Sed his profecto Christianissimi viri atque doctissimi illos quos cecos fuisse ac miseros voluerunt, non a virtutum moralium cultu nec ab animis atque ingeniis pensaverunt in quibus eos multum valuisse monstravimus. Neque id negasset Orosius, qui sepissime eorum gesta referens admiratur, nec Augustinus qui plane eorum extollit ingenia, dum primo illius operis libro Virgilium scribit magnum et omnium preclarissimum fuisse poetam.[3] Et secundo eiusdem antiquos philosophos divinitus adiutos magna invenisse testatur,[4] quamquam errores aliquos suis inventis admiscuerint humanitus impediti. Quarto vero libro dixit acutissimum atque doctissimum virum fuisse Varronem.[5] Veram religionem pro qua agunt cognitionemque vere divinitatis aspiciunt et ad illam se refferunt qua in re erravisse eos qui ante Salvatoris adventum diis falacibus inheserunt et propter id miseros atque cecos esse dicendos. E contra vero felices eos qui orthodoxam fidem catholicam profitentur. Cum Augustino atque Orosio omnis fidelis proculdubio sentiet Christianus, quod iam a principio protestatus sum. Multas etiam grandesque calamitates tempora habuisse priora cum Orosio hoc deducente concesserim, imo neque unam unquam etatem ab illius modi miseriis atque afflictionibus penitus vacavisse, quoniam sic huius temporalis vite natura, que tota miseria est et afflictio; videtur exigere morbos, dico epidimias [59r] pestilentiasque letales, ex quarum numero teribilissimam multum late longeque protensam pluries euntem atque redeuntem nostra etate probavimus non minus fideles Christicolas quam plagas infidelium affligentem. Fames insuper inedias bellorumque clades et hominum quotidianas supra omnem numerum cesiones, quas nec tam grandes neque tam frequentes nostram etatem habere confiteor. Sed ratio prompta est. Illi anime magnitudine et viribus concitati in armis

---

222 videre] videte P quod] negare *add.* P 224 parte tue cause *tr.* P patronem P videlicet] predictum P 224-225 *De Dei* dicitur *civitate*/ *dicitur de Trinitate* P

229 cecos] P 231 multum eos *tr.* P 235 divinitus] diviniter (?) M quamquam *om.* P 236 admiscuere P

237 cognitionemque] cognitionem P 239 salvationis P 240 orthodosam M catholicum P 243 hoc] hec P neque unam unquam] nec unquam unam P 244 miseriis *om.* P penitus *om.* P 244 aflicio M 246 epedimias P ex quarum numero] atque (?) quarum numero (?) M de quorum numero P

250 nec] non P 251 promta M

[1] *Aurelii Augustini de civitate Dei, Lib. III (Corpus Christianorum* [CC] 47.65-98, passim).

[2] *Pauli Orosii adversum paganos libri VII*, ed. Zangmeister (Vienna 1882), *Corpus Scriptorum Ecclesiasticorum Latinorum* 5.3 and passim.

[3] Augustine, *De civitate Dei* 1.3 (CC 47.3, lines 6-9).

[4] Augustine, *De civitate Dei* 2.7 (CC 47.39, lines 9-11).

[5] Augustine, *De civitate Dei* 4.1 (CC 47.98, lines 26-27).

semper agebant vel uti infirmioribus imperarent vel uti animose tuerentur propriam libertatem aliis subici recusantes. Nos refrigeratis animis vim subiciendi alios non habemus et tam facile subesse didicimus ut omne quantumcumque fedum jugum sine molestia preferamus libertatis obliti. Quantumcumque tamen illo priori evo innumerabiles quotidie marte seviente deciderent, ut sepe legisti, illi tamen nos semper magno numero superarunt. Namque Augusti tempore civium Romanorum copia nonagies centena milia trecenta et octoginta milia censa sunt teste Martino[6] quem civium numerum vix tota hodie exhiberet Italia. Claudii quoque principatu descriptione habita iterata Rome fuisse inventa civium copia sexagies novies centena quadraginta quatuor millia Cesariensis Eusebius libro de temporibus autor est.[7] Sic non tantum ut prius deduxeram virtutibus animis ingeniisque defecimus, sed etiam non minus numero personarum. Solo marcore quodam seu inhertia prevalemus, quamquam Christiana religione felices. Unde fit ut admirari et indignari non desinam quod in lumine vere religionis editi atque nutriti tam multum a priori virtute discessimus, tam viri esse desinimus ut multis in partibus pene agamur ut pecudes. Sed iam satis superque ex doloris impetu in longum abii. Ideo parce, precor, vir optime, modum enim dolor nescit habere. Scio me nimia et inania maleque congesta scripsisse, sed tulit indignatio calamum et ego amice atque confidentia tecum egi. Vale.

---

252 infirmioribus imperarent vel uti *om.* P tuerentur] tenerentur P 253 subici] subito P refigeratis M recusantes. Nos *om.* P 254 quantumque P 257 copia] capita P 258 otuaginta M 259 hodie tota *tr.* P 260 habita] habetur P copia] capita P

262 dedixeram M minus] parvo P 265 discensimus P 266 agemur P 267 lungum M 268 congesta] agesta P confidentia] cum fiducia P

6 "Tempore Augustii conputata sunt civium Romanorum nonagies 300 milia et 80 milia." *Martini Oppaviensis Chronicon pontificum et imperatorum,* ed. Wieland, MGH Scriptores 22.444. Among the books left by Giovanni Dondi at his death was a "cronica Martiniana," Vittorio Lazzarini, "I libri, gli argenti, le vesti di Giovanni Dondi dall' Orologio," in *Scritti di paleografia e diplomatica*, ed. 2 (Padua 1969) 268.

7 The Greek original of this passage in Eusebius is lost. There exists a Latin translation by Jerome, given by Migne as follows: "Descriptione Romae facta sub Claudio inventa sunt civium Romanorum 68 centena et 44 milia." Eusebius Caesariensis, *Chronica* (PL 27.581). The figure given in PL (= 6,844,000) does not, however, correspond to that given in the Latin ed. of Eusebius by Fotheringham: "Descriptione Romae facta sub Claudio inventa sunt civium Romanorum LXVIIII centena et XLIIII milia." *Eusebii Pamphili Chronici canones, Latine vertit, audauxit, ad sua tempora produxit S. Eusebius Hieronymus* (London 1923) 263. The correct figure seems to be that used by Dondi (= 6,944,000), which is also found in a Greek paraphrase of the original by Georgius Syncellus (Cf. PL 27.581). Aucher gives a Latin translation of an Armenian version of Eusebius, which varies only slightly (6,941,000) from Dondi's figure: "Censu Romae a Claudio agitato, inventae sunt civium descriptae DCXCIV, et M. unum." *Eusebii Pamphilii . . . Chronicon Bipartitum . . . Pars. II*, ed. Aucher (Venice 1818) 271.

TRANSLATION OF THE LETTER

To Fra Guglielmo da Cremona, distinguished
professor of theology

What should I do now, distinguished sir and most excellent doctor? For I am indeed perplexed, since you have lately placed me between two opposed and equally suspect courses of action. Since the nature of the opposition compels me to choose one or the other of them, I have hesitated for a long time as to what counsel I should take in this matter. Some time ago it was proposed that I should joke with you, writing in the vernacular, so that your mind, weighed down by the manifold cares of office, could be lifted up by inane trifles, by way of relief, so to speak, from your usual concerns. Meanwhile, my friend, though your mind's burden is not yet cast off or diminished – indeed, if I may speak truly, it is even considerably increased by new and important duties – you call me from the proposed jests to serious matters, and you beg me to say something useful. Should I then keep quiet and close my ears to your request, or should I speak, and, having given up the jokes that we used to enjoy, try to say something useful, as you ask? I feel something frightening about both courses. For if I take the first, I fear either that I would be condemned for insolence and arrogance and accused of despising or neglecting your request – although such a failing, if I am not mistaken, has only very seldom characterized my behavior – or, that I should be condemned for excessive cowardice, and although I have no doubt more than enough of that trait (would that it were not so!), still who could fail to see that I should be on guard against this – not from you, best of men, always most concerned for my welfare – but from the teeth of the envious, who lurk everywhere today, as you well know. When they think that they can poison anyone with derogatory words and bring a cloud over another's name, they consider this their ultimate in enjoyment. And hence this is my primary task, this above all else my most diligent concern. I must beware, I say, lest in not obeying you I perhaps keep silent and these people speak more boldly, and ascribe my silence to mere ignorance and inexperience in speaking.

But if I should turn to the other option (or course) and try to expound something useful, as you suggest, I suspect that my intention might be defeated. For who would doubt that whatever emerges from a mind preoccupied and overcast, and from an intelligence almost alienated, so to speak, will be not only not serious but completely ridiculous, empty, and of no consequence as well? And so because as you see, neither course is sufficiently safe for me, if I have hitherto hesitated and the matter has been so long delayed, you must not be surprised or even a little indignant. Rather it is fair to indulge someone who is perplexed and gladly shuns the perils mentioned. But since your authority urges me, I shall come over to your side; and, though I am sure that silence is much safer than foolish talk, I nevertheless propose to say something to you, with more confidence, since I feel that I cannot help but speak well with you. For whatever it is, and of whatever nature, if it comes from a friend, you, I have no doubt, will consider it worthwhile, or I am mistaken as to your humanity and patience.

So that what I am going to say to you will agree with what has been said before, and in order that my present style will follow more decently the former jests, I shall review the upshot of our previous exchange. When then we had amused ourselves on various subjects in vernacular verses, I ended up, still in that style, by deploring with heavy heart the defect and misery of our present age, and at the same time our unhappiness and that of others to whom it has been given to conduct this mortal life in these times; and I made out those of an early age to have been a more fortunate lot, especially during the principate of Caesar Augustus, when the world was almost pacified and the Latin genius flourished to the greatest extent, and when due reward was given to merit. But now you, most sagacious man, if I have sufficiently caught the sense of your words, take the part of our age, nor will you give preference to the memory of Ancient times – since, as you say, those times did not lack in miseries, when men were ambitious of glory and keen on dominating, and hence for that reason were burning with the ardor of conquering, and were always in arms and frequently afflicted with miserable disasters. Thus you and I differ with respect to these matters. I prefer the Ancient times, you defend the Modern. Hence it might perhaps be of some use to discuss this matter thoroughly.

Yet I must advance one proviso to the development of my theme: what I have said in previous comparisons of ages and what I am now going to say do not refer to divine religion or the Faith. I am not so insane, nor do I cling so lightly to the faith of the Catholic religion, that I can ignore or doubt in any way that the dense and black cloud of errors concerning the faith of religion in which the Ancients were immersed, as they wandered from the main path, and which blinded their eyes so that they could not recognize the true divinity, can be compared with the light which our Savior the son of God, Jesus Christ, opened up to us, any more than blindness can be compared with sight, or any privation with possession. And so in this respect I shall deny that we are more unhappy than they, and I shall not claim that Christian times ought to be rated below those; indeed those people who went to damnation along with their benighted leaders were unhappy, and we are rather the happy ones, to whom the true light has been shown, and given to us to know if we so wish, and for whom the way is opened on which we may come to true felicity, if we walk upon it. Here there is no divergence, no quarrel, no disagreement whatever, but complete harmony and total agreement.

But to return our discussion to the point where it began: if we think of the cultivation of virtues, the reward of duties, the robustness and efficacy of minds, and finally of the excellence of minds, I shall not cease to claim boldly that we are greatly outdone by our predecessors, and that Modern times have notably declined from the Ancient. Ah, would that I could demonstrate the opposite! But this seems so easy to understand that it cannot escape anyone who attends to it, and hence does not need any defense to conclude its argument, since it should be clear just by observation of the present times and recognition of the former. The customs of this age are obvious even if we just open our eyes a little. Unless he is blind, there is no one who does not see what cultivation there is now of virtue, and what kind it is.

Today everyone recognizes, and I find it disgusting to recall, by what arts the favor of princes is sought, by what merits higher honors and greater riches can be hoped for, and finally who and what sort of men are commonly believed to excel in sense and prudence, which, according to Cassiodorus, is to be preferred above all else, since in a happy (?) man it is found. To such a degree of error has the judgment of mortals declined that this to me is a sign of the senescence, if I may use the term, of human nature, and a sign that it will very soon decline into decrepitude and finally come to nothing, unless perhaps Divine Goodness in its mercy provides otherwise. Now you see everywhere a mankind whose greatest aim it should be to mingle with others socially, to live together and communicate in a civil way, cheating one's neighbor and setting traps everywhere, by means of which any careless or unsuspecting person who walks by may be tripped up. And alas! alas! today this is nearly the only concern of all men, if you observe carefully, this is almost the whole preoccupation, these are the virtues of our Age. A man seems to himself superior, he seems wiser and more prudent, not just to himself, but, what is still more to be deplored, to others as well, who uses whatever mind heaven has endowed him with for the embezzlement of another's wealth, or for the betrayal of a trusting associate. And he who deploys the machinery of the abominable arts more subtly and shrewdly will easily gain the favor of princes, will receive gifts and rewards, and in a short time will gain dominion over those who dominate.

But who and what sort of men those Ancients were, by what customs they lived, what virtues they had, what sorts of actions gained reward, and what sorts of things were given to those who deserved well, all belong to a bygone age and cannot, like present things, be seen by our eyes or touched with our hands; they can, however, be recognized by great testimonies and reliable evidence, so that no one who looks carefully can doubt them. The best evidence consists of the writings which outstanding minds have left to the memory of posterity; their authority and majesty is so great that no one can fail to trust them. If you should ask my own opinion, their credit is so great, believe me, that I seem somehow to have seen those things that I have read. To my way of thinking, then, it is out of the question that such genuine men could have written anything except the truth, and what they had seen themselves or had accepted from those who were present, or from what they had learned from what was written by great authors – who, I am sure (especially those who were intending to write history, not poems, in which kind of writing perhaps it might be permitted to describe matters otherwise than they were), sought the truth of things above all else and eschewed every falsehood. I am sure that you have diligently read writings of this kind, or certain of the more important ones, and have in many parts of them noted customs and actions of a past Age with some admiration. If you in all fairness compare what we perceive at present with these, you will admit that justice, courage, temperance, and prudence really dwelt more profoundly in their souls, and that they who did great things by the guidance of these virtues were provided with far more worthy rewards. Moreover, proof of this is given by those objects which remain in Rome to this day as testimony to the honors that used to be conferred upon outstanding actions. For although time has consumed many of them – even many of the more magnificent – and only ruins of others appear, which present certain traces of what formerly stood, still, those things that remain, fewer and less magnificent, testify abundantly that those who decreed them must have been of great virtue, and that something great and worthy of praise must have been enacted by those for whom they were being given for their lasting honor and glory. I mean the statues which, either cast in bronze or chiseled in marble, have lasted to the present, and the many fragments of those that have been shattered lying about everywhere, the marble triumphal arches of impressive workmanship and the sculptured columns showing the histories of great deeds, and so many other things of this kind publicly built in honor of men who were distinguished, whether because they had established peace or because they had liberated the fatherland from imminent peril or had extended empire over subjected peoples, as I recall having read in some of them, not without a certain notable pleasure. And you similarly, I suspect, have noticed in passing sometimes and have stopped a little while with some amazement and perhaps have said to yourself, "Surely these are proof of great men." Such proof for such reasons is not forthcoming from our own time. And why, do you think, unless that there are lacking those who should act in such a way as to deserve such rewards, as well as those who would favor men acting in this way, if such there were, by whose means such rewards would be given?

Let us move along to the vigor and effectiveness of minds, in which matter it can be called an abuse rather than a comparison to compare ours with those of the Ancients, since it is clear that they had robust and strong minds, whereas (I would willingly keep still on this theme, but the topic compels me, and truth as well) we should judge the action of ours to be such as to make us think that we have not only weak and feeble minds but none at all. I would not ask that you provide me today with anyone like Coclites, or Curtius, or Scevola, or Regulus, or the two Decii, or innumerable other men, from the citizens of Rome or from foreigners, who either for the safety of their fatherland or its liberty, in order to keep faith, even to the enemy, gave themselves to a certain death with unhesitating mind, having determined to endure it by a sound and deliberate resolution. Nor should I require that you show me leaders like the Scipios or the equal of Cato and many, many others of the Romans, nor of men among the foreigners such as Alexander of Macedonia, Pyrrhus the Epirote, or Hannibal the Carthaginian – who in order to rule others or promote their empires or gain glory for themselves and their followers, would spend either the whole of their lives or the most useful years of them in arms, now storming cities, now rushing the enemy battleline, and who persisted at the cost of much trouble and ceaseless labors, always however with an uncorrupted and unconquered mind. I would not require such minds, since there are none in these days, in which only very rarely do you hear of defenses being stormed and taken, and few attempting it, indeed of those attempting it very few succeeding at all unless by some fraud. And so one should not look for the sort of vigor in us that our ancestors had. Among us you find few who would dare to await the advancing enemy and do so with eargerness. I realize what many people are accustomed to say on this topic, namely, that those deeds which are told of the character of our Ancients were derived rather from rage and imprudence than from virtue, and that they were led to this fury by a desire for empty glory and by ambition for domination. But whatever the truth may be in this matter – that is, whether you say that it is virtuous to choose an undoubted death for such reasons, or whether it should be permitted to invade free and quiet peoples without violating justice and aggressively disturbing them and subjugating them – I do not presently inquire. Nor am I concerned to decide these matters: we ask that you grant only one thing of those mentioned, which cannot be denied, namely, that such great and fearless deeds proceeded from great spirits, and that such difficult attacks could not have been waged with such great perseverance except by more sturdy minds than those which we find in our contemporaries.

Finally, to turn the discussion from character to genius, there can be no one to whom it is not transparently clear, unless he is completely insensitive, that Modern powers of mind have declined from those of the Ancients. Indeed so much so that they be equated in hardly any respect, and indeed in many aspects are overshadowed to the greatest possible degree. For since the minds of men are known through nothing so much as their works, the magnitude of difference between them and us can be shown in no better way than by comparing the works achieved by us respectively. The special achievements of the human mind are the discoveries of the arts and sciences, e.g., of wisdom and the liberal doctrines which are desired as preparation for true wisdom and, needless to say, all writings and literary remains. In addition to these, there are the works of artistry, which are preconceived by the innate genius of reason and by acquired habits of art, and fabricated by the very hands of the artisans from raw materials. Of these works, there is no doubt that the liberal arts or teachings and the other sciences and all of the aspects of wisdom that are humanly derived were first discovered by the Ancients, and once discovered were transmitted by them to posterity in books written with such clear and indubitable principles, with so much order and impregnable method, that they remain to the present day the wonder and veneration of nearly everybody, and are now studied by us still. For it is absurd to ask what sciences are now found out from scratch, they are so meager or non-existent. It is enough and plenty for Moderns if they can just touch the surface of what those Ancients treated in the greatest depth. So that if by chance some Modern should have the confidence in himself to try to invent something or presume to change what has been handed down before (as in our days some dialecticians have done, as you know), it is sufficiently clear how much their results are worth, and how much has endured. They have scarcely lasted past the age in which they were produced, and have perished along with their authors.

Indeed in order to show more clearly what sort of comparisons can be drawn in this matter between the Ancients and the Moderns, let us adduce the most noble and excellent mind of this Age, the most studious and prolific of all writers, proficient in every kind of speaking and writing. I mean Master Petrarch, whom I think you know and have often seen; but I was on close terms with him and was very much a member of his household, especially in his last years. Speaking boldly and in simple truth, without any regard for friendship, I would put his mind first above all others of our age that I know, and I think it would have had a place among the Ancients if he had lived in that age, and also that it will have in future generations even more consideration and esteem than with his contemporaries. The many published works of this man, some of which you may have seen, will please you considerably if you read any part of them, I am sure. For how could they fail to please, filled as they are with such weighty opinions and composed in such a sweet-sounding style and methodical order? If you read them and re-read them again and again, they will please you still more, which is a sure sign of a great work and author. But if, having laid these aside, you turn to read something from the literary remains of the greater Ancients, you will unquestionably feel, if you apply your mind to it, how much deeper a sound they produce. Once when I myself was doing this, I remembered a statement that I heard on one occasion from the mouth of Petrarch himself while he was still alive. For he had had his own *Bucolicum Carmen* bound in together with Virgil's in one volume. I was present with him when a third person, a nobleman, took this book and held it out to him, and asked what the book was. Petrarch answered, "In this book some grey rags are bound in with scarlet,"* indicating clearly by this response that his work was considerably surpassed by the Ancients. Thus when so singular and unique a mind among us yields, and admits that it yields, to the Ancients, it follows that we have no more right to contend with the Ancients than a spider with Minerva. And this is truly the case. Our minds are of inferior quality: if we have anything historical from them, it is without a doubt more careless than Livy or Sallust, if oratorical, much inferior to Cicero, if poetical, Maro precedes and Horace and Ovid, if philosophical, Varro outshines and Seneca. Nor are these the only Ancients who excel the Moderns; there are almost innumerable others whom I do not mention. I only adduce a few from all of these because they were together in one age and Augustus saw them before him in Rome. If you even find anyone among us who is at all learned in the divine canon and in the sacred scriptures, you will find that he walks far below Augustine and Jerome and innumerable others of the Ancients. This is so obvious that it would be criminal to prolong our discourse on the subject.

Of the artistic products of ancient genius, few survive. But those that do remain anywhere are eagerly sought and seen and highly prized by those who feel strongly about such things: and if you compare them with those of today, it will soon become obvious that their authors were by nature more powerful in genius and more learned in the mastery of their art. I am speaking about ancient buildings and statues and sculptures, with other things of the sort. When some artists of this time scrutinize the productions of that age carefully, they are struck with amazement. I knew a certain

*Or "some plain cloth has been sewn in with velvet" (the Latin lends itself to either interpretation).

well-known worker in marble who was famous for his ability in that art among those whom Italy had at the time, especially in the creation of figures. I have heard this man tell many times about the statues and sculptures that he had seen at Rome, with such admiration and veneration that he seemed in recalling it to be transported beyond himself from the wonder of the thing. For he used to say that sometimes, passing with his friends by a place where some images of this sort could be seen, he had held back, looking in astonishment at their artistry, and, forgetting his company, had stood still so long that his companions had passed on five hundred steps and more. And when he would tell of the great excellence of these figures, and praise their authors beyond measure, he used to add in the end (in his own words): "If only these images did not lack life, they would be better than living ones," as if to say that nature had been not only imitated by the genius of such artists but even surpassed.

Now go, best master, weigh our so humble capabilities, and if you can, defend in any way present times against the former (would that you could!) so that I might stop being indignant and would begin to become reconciled with our times. But I suspect that you will not be able, so manifestly does the opposite appear to all. Nor am I unaware that that outstanding doctor, Augustine, may seem to be a supporter of your cause, particularly in the *City of God*, in which, doing battle for the Christian religion, he shows that ancient pagan times were unhappy and full of much misery. His contemporary and disciple Paulus Orosius also tries to show this in his histories of the times, in the book that he wrote to Augustine against the defamers of Christian times. But actually these most Christian and learned men did not weigh those times as blind and miserable by the cultivation of moral virtues or by their minds and genius, which we have shown to be of great worth. Orosius would not deny this, for he very often admires their deeds in telling them, nor would Augustine, who plainly extolled their genius when he writes in Book I that Virgil was a great poet, the most outstanding of all, and in Book II he testifies that the ancient philosophers found out great things with divine aid, although, handicapped by their humanity, they mixed certain errors in with the things they found. Indeed in Book IV he said that Varro was the most acute and learned of men. Obviously they were considering the true religion on whose behalf they wrote, and the knowledge of the true divinity. They refer to it when they say that those who lived before the advent of the Savior clung to deceitful gods and thus wandered astray, and are accordingly to be called miserable and blind. On the other hand, only those who profess the orthodox Catholic faith are to be called truly happy. No doubt every loyal Christian agrees with Augustine and Orosius, which is what I have been claiming from the start. I would concede to Orosius that ancient times had many great calamities; indeed no age was ever completely free from misery and afflictions of this kind, since such is the nature of this temporal life, which is all misery and affliction and seems to demand diseases. I mean the deadly epidemics and lethal pestilences, one of which, very terrible and extensive, many times going and returning, we have experienced in our time, afflicting faithful Christians no less than the territories of the infidel. Moreover, as for famines and deprivations and the destructions of wars and daily killings of men beyond number, I must admit that our age seems not to have them so much or so frequently as others. But the reason is obvious. Those who were aroused by greatness of soul or by strength in arms always acted so that either they should rule the weaker or, unwilling to submit, passionately guard their liberty against others. We, with our failing souls, do not have the force to subject others, and we have learned to submit so easily that we all prefer the foul yoke with its burden and have forgotten liberty. Yet no matter how many multitudes were killed every day in that former age by raging wars (as you have often read), still they always exceeded us by a great number. For at the time of Augustus, the number of Roman citizens was tallied at 9,380,000 persons according to Martinus Polonus, which number the whole of Italy scarcely has today. And in the reign of Claudius, according to the census then repeated, there were found at Rome 6,944,000 persons, on the authority of Eusebius of Caesaria in his book on times. Thus we are lacking, not only in virtues of soul and genius, as I have previously claimed, but in the number of persons as well. We prevail only by a certain sluggishness or inertia, although we are happy in the Christian religion. And so I never cease to wonder and become indignant at the fact that we, brought up and nourished in the light of the true religion, have departed so much from former virtue; we have so ceased to be men that in many respects we are driven almost like sheep. But now I have gone on long enough, indeed too long, from the force of grief. Forgive me, I pray you, best of men, for grief has no measure. I know that I have written too much, inanities badly put together, but indignation drove my pen, and I have acted with you in a friendly and confidential fashion. Farewell.

Department of Philosophy
University of California
Davis, California 95616, U.S.A.

FROM "MIMESIS" TO "FANTASIA": THE QUATTROCENTO VOCABULARY OF CREATION, INSPIRATION AND GENIUS IN THE VISUAL ARTS

•

by Martin Kemp

Students of the Renaissance will be familiar with interpretations of fifteenth-century art which stress the development of a "creative elite" comprising those painters, sculptors and architects who had begun to lay claim to the status of geniuses and who newly exploited the intellectual formulations of art theory to edge their professions into the sanctified realm of the *artes liberales.*[1] This picture contains elements which can be illustrated from the primary sources, but there is a considerable degree of historical discrepancy between the notions of *ingenium*, inspiration and creativity to be found in Renaissance literature on the accepted *artes liberales*, poetry for example, and the actual ideas expressed in *quattrocento* art theory. And if caution is required in applying the principle *ut pictura poesis* to fifteenth-century art and theory, even greater care should be exercised in imposing essentially modern notions of artistic creativity on the period. Such care has all too rarely been apparent in modern accounts of Renaissance ideals in the visual arts.

Renaissance writings on art are not notably characterized by notions of individual creativity but are dominated by the ideal of *mimesis* – imitation of nature or Antiquity or preferably of both, because Antiquity and nature are in no sense opposing factors in a Renaissance context. Thus Landino described Masaccio and Donatello in complimentary fashion as "optimo imitatore di natura" and "grande imitatore degli antichi." But as early in 1564, Landino's editors deemed it necessary to promote Masaccio to the status of "optimo inventore."[2] This tendency to move

[1] A recent if somewhat different usage of the term "creative elite" and analysis of its membership is provided by P. Burke, *Tradition and Innovation in Renaissance Italy*, rev. ed. (London 1974) 49ff. and 349ff.

[2] C. Landino, *Comento di Cristoforo Landino Fiorentino sopra la Comedia di Danthe . . .* (Nicola di Lorenzo della Mappa, Florence 1481) "Proemo . . . Fiorentini excellenti di pittura et scultura"; and *Dante con l'espositione di Cristoforo Landino et di Alessandro Vellutello . . . per Francesco Sansovino* (Venice 1564) fol. 8v. Landino's art criticism is discussed by M. Baxandall, *Painting and Experience in 15th Century Italy* (Oxford 1972) 114-153; O. Morasini, "Art Historians and Art Critics III – Cristoforo Landino,"*Burlington Magazine* 95 (1953) 267-270, and P. Murray, letter on 391-392.

away from the image of the artist as *imitatore* towards an image as *inventore* became increasingly pronounced during succeeding centuries.

Any historical judgment of attitudes towards what we would now call individual creativity and artistic inspiration must be founded upon the meaning of the terms used during the period to denote the production of a painting, sculpture, building or any other artefact. The concepts exploited in connection with this process, such as "invention" and "imagination," in their Latin and Italian forms, and the less obvious but highly significant *fantasia* (or *phantasia*), require careful analysis within the framework of mimetic theory, in conjunction with each other, in relation to associated ideas like *ingenium* and above all in their proper contexts. For the purposes of this study it will be most convenient to begin with the term which could be most readily harmonized with *mimesis*, namely invention.

The following analyses are based upon sources earlier than 1500, with the exception of early sixteenth-century examples which have been introduced to clarify earlier usages. I have deliberately excluded any extended discussion of the impact of Ficino's individual variety of Neoplatonism on the theory of the visual arts, though Platonizing notions of the ideal will appear in one guise or another. Ficino's own impact is a predominantly *cinquencento* phenomenon which warrants a full-scale study in its own right. The present study makes no claims to completeness; in view of the volume and variety of potential sources it would not be surprising if some significant references have escaped my attention, particularly in relation to other fields of study, such as music and dance, of which I can claim no detailed knowledge. And the imponderable of general, colloquial usages remains a factor which is tantalizingly unsusceptible to the historian's methods of analysis. Any discussion focussed upon just one facet of the many-sided diamond of Renaissance culture will inevitably suffer from some degree of one-sidedness, but I hope that any general impression which emerges from this study will be sufficiently free of gross distortion to provide a valid basis for future adjustment and amplification.

The Artist as Inventor

Invenzione was a key concept in Renaissance art theory, as it is in modern ideals of creativity, but it was generally exploited in a manner very different from its present sense. Renaissance conceptions of *invenzione* were broadly of two main types, both of which grew from the same classical roots, but became increasingly differentiated during the course of the *quattrocento*. The first of the categories is associated with the tradition of natural philosophy and is closely related to the discovery of truth; while the second is dependent largely upon a literary-poetic tradition in which invention is less wholly identified with rational processes of discovery.

* * *

At its strictest, the first sense is used as in the almost obsolete phrase "the invention of truth" and can embody both inductive and deductive components with no clear separation between them. Something of this sense survives, quaintly, in the title generally accorded to one of Piero della Francesca's frescoes at Arezzo, *The Invention and Proof of the Cross*. This usage linked invention intimately with the verb *excogitare* (to discover and devise), an association which could find support in rhetorical theory. Renaissance philologists like Lorenzo Valla drew upon Cicero's statement that "Inventio est excogitatio rerum verarum aut verisimilium" (invention is the discovery of things true or probable) to justify their using invention and "excogitation" almost interchangeably.[3] For example, when Guarino discusses the Muses he refers to Clio as the *inventrix* of history, while Uranae and Melpomene respectively *excogitaverunt* astrology and song.[4] The manner in which Filarete uses the verbs *inventare* and *trovare* as synonymous is entirely in the same spirit of invention as discovery or finding.[5]

Invention in this sense can be used in close conjunction with the term *dottrina* (or *doctrina*), which lies at the very heart of Renaissance artists' claims to intellectual respectability. Giotto in Ghiberti's eyes was responsible for having invented or discovered (*fu inventore e trovatore*) "the *dottrina* of art which had lain buried for six hundred years."[6] Similarly Brunelleschi as the originator of perspective, that most important artistic *dottrina* of all during the *quattrocento*, is credited as its *ritrovatore o inventore* (Landino) and its *inventrice* (Manetti).[7] In much the same manner of scientific discovery, Filarete refers to "Athalas" as the *inventore della sphera*, just as Vitruvius had praised Pythagoras and Archimedes as "inventors."[8]

The clearest account of the manner in which this "excogitative" form of invention could operate in the practice of the visual arts is contained in Alberti's version of the original discovery of column proportions. The architect begins by an inductive discovery that the fractions of one sixth and one tenth are innate in the human body. Our equally innate sense of *concinnitas* (harmony) judges that the first is too thick and the second too thin for comfortably proportioned columns. The intermediate fractions are subsequently deduced and judged to be aesthetically satisfying. The middle proportion of one eighth becomes the norm for the handsomely elegant Ionic

[3] Cicero, *De inventione* 1.7; and L. Valla, *De linguae latinae elegantiae* 5.2, for the definition of *invenire*.

[4] Guarino quoted by M. Baxandall, *Giotto and the Orators* (Oxford 1971) 89 and 158-159; also his "Guarino, Pisanello and Manuel Chrysoloras," *Journal of the Warburg and Courtauld Institutes* 28 (1965) 183-204.

[5] *Filarete's Treatise on Architecture* (Florence, Biblioteca Nazionale, MS Magl. II, 1, 140) facsimile and trans. J. Spencer 2 vols. (New Haven 1965) fols 3, 4v, 151v, 152 and 184v. An edited version of the same MS is provided by A. M. Finoli and L. Grassi, 2 vols. (Milan 1972). For convenience all subsequent references are to the folios in this MS in Spencer's facsimile.

[6] L. Ghiberti, *I commentarii*, ed. J. von Schlosser (Berlin 1912) 8v (p. 36). Giotto had previously been credited with "scientia et doctrina" in 1334, when appointed "governor" of the *Opera del Duomo* (C. Guasti, *S. Maria del Fiore* [Florence 1887] 43). A Renaissance definition of *doctrina* is provided by G. Manardi in his exposition of Galen's *Ars parva* quoted by N. Gilbert, *Renaissance Concepts of Method* (New York 1960) 104.

[7] Landino (n. 2 above) *proemo*; and A. Manetti, *The Life of Brunelleschi*, ed. H. Saalman (University Park, Pennsylvania 1970) 43.

[8] Filarete (n. 5 above) fol. 151v; and Vitruvius, *De architectura* 9 pref., 6 and 9.

order, one seventh for the virile Doric and one ninth for the slender femininity of the Corinthian.[9] In actual practice such procedures of "excogitation" are more difficult than this outline might suggest – Alberti stresses that man is subject to error and that his inventions must be diligently refined according to mathematical truth and the lessons of the ancients[10] – but he leaves no doubt that the basis of the inventive process is the interaction of man's innate judgment with the underlying design of nature. Nor does he leave any doubt that the process is of the utmost importance; it is the vital first stage in a five-part system (invention, deliberation, judgment, composition and skill), just as it is the first stage of five in Ciceronian rhetoric.[11]

* * *

In addition to this predominantly "scientific" form of invention, Alberti, Manetti and Francesco di Giorgio all acknowledge a more free-ranging compositive power of inventing *cose nuove e belle* in architecture – new ground-plans, elevations and ornaments. This is not to say, however, that this power is any less part of a rational process than the more inductive forms of discovery. The tone for the Renaissance was set by Vitruvius who indicated (in a passage closely studied by Francesco di Giorgio) that the inventive architect cleverly arrives at an original and correct solution to a new or old problem: "Inventio autem est quaestionum obscuram explicatio ratioque novae rei vigore mobili reperta."[12]

A typical Renaissance instance of the harmony between new inventions and one form of *ratio* is contained in Manetti's account of S. Maria degli Angeli. Though "tutto al modo antico," Brunelleschi's centralized church nevertheless shows great originality in its "invenzioni di qualita."[13] Filippo's inventions are said to surpass the *precetti* of antique methods; but there is no suggestion that Manetti sensed the slightest tension between the imitation of antiquity, the laws of nature and the artist's originality in invention. These three components act with a unity which lies totally outside the frames of reference of Romantic and post-Romantic ideas of creativity.

There is evidence to suggest that Brunelleschi's own values and priorities were directly responsible for the insistent manner in which the early sources (including the

[9] Alberti *De re aedificatoria* 9.7; ed. and Italian trans. G. Orlandi and P. Portoghesi, *Leon Battista Alberti: L'architettura*, 2 vols. (Milan 1966) 2.835-837. For *concinnitas*, see 9.5 (2.815-817).

[10] *Ibid.*, 9.10 (2.861-863).

[11] *Ibid.* 9.10 (2.855): "Ingenio igitur inveniat, usu cognoscat, iuditio seligat, consilio componat, arte perficiat opertet." Cf. Cicero, *De inventione* 1.7.

[12] Vitruvius, *De architectura* 1.2.2. Cf. Francesco di Giorgio, *Trattati de architettura civile e militare* (Cod. Torinese Salluziano 148; Laur. Ashburn. 361; Senese SIV. 4; and Bib. Naz., Magl. II, 141), ed. C. Maltese and L. Maltese Degrassi, 2 vols. (Milan 1967) 1.39 (hereafter *Tratt.*). The editors provide a good discussion of the dating of the various MSS.

[13] Manetti (n. 7 above) 103.

epitaph by Marsuppini to be discussed later) emphasize his powers of invention. Mariano Taccola's entirely credible report of a meeting between Brunelleschi and himself at some time between 1427 and 1430 lays continual stress upon the jealous care which Brunelleschi took to guard his inventions against piracy. "Do not share your inventions [*invenzioni*] with many," the great architect is reported as saying; "share them only with the few who understand and love the sciences. To describe too much of one's inventions and achievements is one and the same thing as to debase your *ingegnia* "[14] A reflection of such intellectual possessiveness can also be discerned in Manetti's assertion that his hero's *invenzioni* are "cose propie del maestro."[15] All this suggests that architecture in Brunelleschi's mind was justly subject to the same kind of elevated elitism as characterized the literary ideas of Petrarch and Boccaccio.

Alberti shares his fellow pioneer's reported esteem for the architect's power of inventing new things. The architect, according to Alberti, must strive to produce something specifically of his own invention, and any achievements in this respect, on whatever scale, are to be prized over and above sheer size in building for its own sake; a clever building is greater than a colossal one. *Inventio*, which he also considers is a power of the artist's *ingenium*, is a vital requirement but, like all other characteristics in his thought, it must be subject to constraint, decorum and discipline. Inventions which outstrip feasibility are unacceptable.[16] Such restraint is entirely consistent with the advice given by Cicero, Alberti's decorous mentor in such matters, who outlines three components of invention – *acumen, ratio* and *diligentia* (or *ars*), of which diligence is given special emphasis as the factor through which *ingenium* may bear fruit.[17]

Similar associations between invention, *ingegno*, diligence and skill abound in Francesco di Giorgio's treatises, and Vitruvian *ratio* is always close at hand. In other respects, however, Francesco's account of invention goes far beyond that of Alberti or anything to be found in their mutual sources such as Vitruvius. Francesco achieves the most deeply considered and philosophically astute analysis of invention in *quattrocento* theory (Leonardo's included).

Francesco begins by setting the arts firmly in the context of the macro-microcosm of cosmological design. "The human mind," he argues, taking as his precedent the opening paragraphs of Aristotle's *Metaphysics*, "moves with the greatest fervor

[14] Munich, Bayerische Staatsbibliothek Clm 197, fols. 107-108v. See F. Prager, "A Manuscript of Taccola, quoting Brunelleschi on Problems of Inventors and Builders," *Proceedings of the American Philosophical Society* 112 (1968) 131-149. Here, as elsewhere, I have taken the advice of Michael Baxandall and avoided translating *ingegno, ingenium* etc. as "genius" which carries too many later associations. Perhaps "innate brilliance" would be the best rendering. "Talent," itself, does not convey adequately the intellectual importance of the faculty in the classical tradition.

[15] Manetti (n. 7 above) 55: "Le invenzioni, che sono cose propie del maestro, bisognia, che nella magiore parte sieno date dalla natura o dalla industria sua propria" – that is, invention embracing both induction and composition.

[16] Alberti (n. 9 above) 9.10 (2.857-859).

[17] Cicero, *De oratore* 2.35.

towards natural philosophy and metaphysics."[18] Francesco then proceeds to discuss the nature of the "incorporeal" soul and the "prime mover," quoting such authorities as Averroes, Cicero, Plato, Augustine, Paul and his favorite source, Aristotle.[19] Even his method of exposition – "dalle cose universale in le singulari nelle scienzie bisogna procedere" – is founded upon Aristotelian principles.[20] The intellectual edifice of knowledge which Francesco erects then provides the basis for the architect's activities. Acting under the traditional influence of Mercury, "signore di quelli che nelle arti . . . sono atti a venire eccellenti," the artist bases his architectural inventions on the underlying design of the universe.[21] Accordingly, *scienzia* takes a prominent place in his requirements for good design.

The manner in which Francesco places the architect in the context of cosmological knowledge is more explicit than anything in Alberti or Vitruvius, in spite of his predecessors' mutual emphasis upon the necessity of the architect being learned in a wide variety of disciplines. An excellent example of Francesco's subtlety in defining the role of the artist in relation to the laws of nature is provided by his cunning adaptation of the famous story of Alexander's architect, Dinocrates. The story, as gleaned from Vitruvius and Plutarch (who gives the architect's names as Stasicrates), can be summarized as follows.[22]

By masquerading as Hercules in a lion's skin, the Macedonian architect, Dinocrates, succeeded in capturing the attention of Alexander the Great in order to present the Greek leader with his novel idea for a new city: "I have shaped Mount Athos into the form of a statue of a man, in whose left hand is shown a very extensive city and in his right a bowl to receive all the rivers in that mountain which pour into the sea."[23] Alexander enjoyed the concept but doubted its feasibility since the city could not be self-supporting in terms of food and other essentials. It is to illustrate this latter point that the story is first exploited by Alberti in *De re aedificatoria*, though he misnames the architect "Polycrates."[24] Later in the same treatise, with a care more characteristic of his high standards of scholarship, he uses the story as an illustration of inventive *ingenium*, basing his account more on Plutarch than on Vitruvius: "Who would be so daring as to undertake, like Stasicrates, as he is called by Plutarch, or Dinocrates, according to Vitruvius, to make Mount Athos into a statue of Alexander and in one of the hands build a city big enough to contain ten thousand men?"[25]

The Alexander-Dinocrates anecdote occurs again and again in Rennaissance litera-

[18] Di Giorgio, *Tratt.* (n. 12 above) 2.369. Cf. Aristotle, *Metaphys.* 1.1.

[19] Di Giorgio, *Tratt.* 2.293ff.

[20] *Ibid.* 2.299. Cf. Aristotle, *Physica* 1.1.184a. The same precedent is cited by Thomas Aquinas, *In II metaphysicorum*, lect. 1, n. 278.

[21] Di Giorgio, *Tratt.* 2.294.

[22] Vitruvius 2, pref.; and Plutarch, *Life of Alexander* 72.4f.

[23] Vitruvius 2, pref.

[24] Alberti (n. 9 above) 1.4 (1.35).

[25] *Ibid.* 6.4 (2.459). The number of inhabitants is quoted from Plutarch, *Life of Alex.* 72.5.

ture on the arts – Villani cites it even before the *quattrocento* "discovery" of Vitruvius, Francesco Colonna found it highly appealing to his sense of wonder, and Filarete produces characteristically eccentric versions[26] – but only Francesco develops it in terms of the macro-microcosm. To do so, he adopts a less literal attitude than his fellow theorists, interpreting Vitruvius to mean that Dinocrates showed Alexander "uno disegno nel quale aveva comparato uno Aton Monte ad uno corpo umano." Francesco goes on to say that Alexander subsequently praised the architect's conception of "la similitudine della citta al corpo umano."[27] Francesco, with characteristic sanity, sees Dinocrates's city design in terms of an anthropomorphic parallel rather than as an improbable project to sculpt the whole mountain into the shape of a man.

Dinocrates himself is ingeniously illustrated as a composite image in the margin of Francesco's treatise (fig. 1), wearing his Herculean fancy dress, but also shown "in the guise of" Mount Athos holding the city and water-bowl (or fountain as he elsewhere calls it), like the actual design of the city presented to Alexander.[28] This image cleverly exploits a three-part analogy between the body of the earth, the body of man and the form of the city, all embodied in the appearance of the architect himself. In the case of the rivers which flow into the bowl the bodily analogy is explicit: "Nella mano sinistra [*sic*] teneva una tazza che tutte le vene del corpo in essa corrivano."[29] Such microcosms abound in Francesco's own city projects.

This is the context in which excogitative invention takes place, the architect basing his principles upon his study of natural systems in the universe and making inventions in harmony with these. However, the actual power of *invenzione*, "without which it is impossible to be a good architect," cannot be learned, precisely codified or described, according to Francesco, but is an innate gift relying upon the artist's "discrezione e giudizio."[30] It is, as acknowledged by Taccola and Alberti, to be attributed to the faculty of *ingegno*. Thus it is with some pride that Francesco describes his wide range of plans for temples and houses as his own *invenzioni*, albeit he modestly adds, of "il mio debile ingegno."[31]

The power of invention is a key concept in his thought, and his philosophical examination of it leads him to adapt Aristotle's doctrine of intellect in a fascinating manner. He twice quotes the authority of Aristotle's *De anima* that the soul is not a

[26] F. Villani, *De origine civitatis Florentie et de eiusdem famosis* (Vatican, MS Barb. lat. 26 fol. 71) in Baxandall, *Giotto* (n. 4 above) 69 n. 71 and 147; F. Colonna, *Hypnerotomachia poliphili*, Aldus Manutius (Venice 1499) fol. 11r-v (written in 1467 according to a note in the first ed.); Filarete (n. 5 above) fols. 9r-v and 156.

[27] Di Giorgio, *Tratt.* (n. 12 above) 2.362. See also 1.4: "Aton monte a guisa d'omo."

[28] *Ibid.* 1.4 for "una tazza," and 2.362 for "una fonte." The image is analyzed by W. Lotz, "Eine Deinokratesdarstellung des Francesco di Giorgio," *Mitteilungen der Kunsthistorisches Institut in Florenz* 5 (1940) 428-433.

[29] Di Giorgio, *Tratt.* 1.4.

[30] *Ibid.* 2.484.

[31] *Ibid.* 2.297.

virtù of the body but is incorporeal.[32] This fact, he continues, is apparent in the operations of the human soul, compared to those of animals. Various animals can act in a natural manner to produce "architectural" works – "like all swallows build nests and like every bee and spider [*aranea*] makes dwellings [*domifica*]" – but these animal products are invariable and stereotyped, unlike the inventions of man's intellect which are "quasi infinite, infinito varia."[33] In the specific case of castle design he states that the invention of "tutte le fortezze che nella mente occorrano continuamente, sarebbe un processo in infinito."[34] The notion of the continuous flow from the human mind of limitless inventions corresponds splendidly to the boundless fertility of Francesco's own ideas; his crowded pages of designs, such as those for "piante di case private," are only rivalled in their "almost infinite" inventiveness by the drawings of his sometime colleague, Leonardo.

The three particular animals (swallow, bee and spider) cited by Francesco had been busily active throughout classical Antiquity and the Middle Ages, building their nests, cells and webs at the behest of the many philosophers who had been concerned with the vexed problem of animal intelligence. These three, together with the industrious ant, were discussed in various permutations by Aristotle, Galen, Maximus of Tyre, Philo, Plutarch, Seneca, Tertullian, Roger Bacon and Reisch, to mention but a few.[35] Plutarch's treatise *On the Cleverness of Animals* plausibly credits Democritus with the original notion that human beings imitated "the spider in weaving and mending, the swallow in architecture and the clear-voiced swan and nightingale in *mimesis* of their song."[36] Vitruvius echoes this when he asserts that the first houses were begun "in imitation of the nest and habitations of swallows."[37] Of the architecturally minded animals, Filarete adopts the bee as his personal symbol of industriousness and *ingegno*, while Alberti characteristically takes the circular nests of birds and hexagonal cells of bees as evidence of the innate geometry of natural forms.[38]

Francesco's particular contrast between stereotyped products of animals and the limitless variety of man's inventions seems to be uniquely his own, though there can be little doubt that the general pedigree of his argument is Aristotelian. His contention that "animals always operate naturally" (that is, according to natural causality) is evidence of this pedigree; and his odd vocabulary – *aranea* and *domificare* from the Latin *aranea* and *domus* – confirms that a classical source was not far from his mind.

[32] *Ibid.* 2.482-483 and 505-506.

[33] *Ibid.* 2.505. On p. 483 the spider is omitted.

[34] *Ibid.* 2.483.

[35] R. Bacon, *Opus majus* v (ii) 3, viii; G. Reisch, *Margarita philosophica* (Freiburg 1503) 10.2.23; Vitruvius 2.1. The others are discussed by S. Dickermann, "Some Stock Illustrations of Animal Intelligence in Greek Psychology," *Transactions of the American Philological Association* 42 (1911) 123-130.

[36] Plutarch, *De sollertia animalium* 20.974a.

[37] Vitruvius, *De arch.* 2.1.

[38] Filarete (n. 5 above) fols. 45 and 136; and Alberti (n. 9 above) 7.4 (2.549-551).

Aristotle's *Physics* contains a statement that "the arts, either on the basis of nature carry things further than can nature, or they imitate nature. If . . . artificial processes are purposeful, so also are natural processes; for the relationship of the antecedant to the consequent is identical in art and nature."[39] He then states that "the works of spiders and ants and so on" should not be attributed to the active intelligence manifested in man's works, but to the teleological principle of natural causality. If this differentiation is allied to his arguments in the opening section of the *Metaphysics* that the inventions and discoveries of man are evidence of his superior mind (compared to the bee which is granted some small measure of intelligence but cannot learn because of its deafness), something close to Francesco's interpretation begins to emerge. And Thomas Aquinas takes us a step nearer when he amplifies Aristotle by stating that "every swallow makes a nest in the same way and every spider a web in the same way, which would not be the case if they acted by intellect and art [intellectu et arte]. For not every builder makes a house the same way, because the artisan judges the form of the thing built and can vary it."[40] But nowhere does Aquinas (nor, to my knowledge, any subsequent Aristotelian) specifically formulate Francesco's differentiation between the intellectual capacities of man and animals on the grounds of infinite inventiveness. At first sight, Francesco's use of philosophical concepts might appear to be naive and eclectic, but as this instance shows he is not without genuine powers of originality in his philosophy of the arts.

* * *

So far our discussion has centered almost entirely upon examples drawn from architectural theory; even perspective is intimately associated with architectural practice. The type of infinite invention of form mooted by Francesco could readily have been applied to painting and sculpture. But this did not occur. The painter's production of form was generally assigned to the realm of "composition" and "disposition," in the sense of the manipulation and arrangement of the parts in relation to each other and to the whole. When Fazio compared the inventive power of the painter with that of the poet – "Almost equal attention is given both to the *inventione* and *dispositione* of their work" – he was not referring to formal invention of Francesco's type but thinking of invention in terms of content while granting the formal aspects of a work of art to *dispositione.*[41] This division of labor is a general rule in the literature on painting; when Boccaccian ideas of poetic invention are applied to *quattrocento* painting, only content is generally considered. This essentially literary application, imposed on the visual arts from outside, provides the

[39] Aristotle, *Physica* 2.8.199a.

[40] *Physicorum Aristoteles Commentaria* 2.13 (259). I am grateful to David Summers for this reference. Cf. F. di Giorgio, *Tratt.* (n. 12 above) 2.414.

[41] See Baxandall, *Giotto* (n. 4 above) 101f. For a later use of *inventio, dispositio* and *colorito* by Dolce, see R. W. Lee, "Ut Pictura Poesis: The Humanist Theory of Painting," *Art Bulletin* 22 (1940) 264.

second main category of invention and is remarkably separate from the Brunelleschian form of "excogitative" invention as developed by Alberti and Francesco di Giorgio.

The literary-poetic form of *invenzione* is concerned with "topics" for paintings – original iconographical schemes, new allegories, fresh variations upon mythologies and histories and fresh ornaments for the main theme. This sense is closely linked to rhetorical theory as transmitted to the Renaissance by Aristotle's *Topics* and Cicero's rediscovered treatises. We have already noted Cicero's equation of invention and "excogitation," but have not studied it in the context which Cicero intended, that is, in terms of content for rhetorical discourse.

He formulated a five-part scheme for rhetoric: *inventio, collocatio, elocutio, actio* and *memoria,* sometimes with slight variations in terminology and order.[42] The division of labor is quite clear; invention is concerned with subject-matter, *collocatio* deals with formal organization and *elocutio* with such matters as the application of detailed ornament in execution. During the Middle Ages, partly as a result of sophistic practice, invention lost its prominence in rhetorical theory, tending to become more closely associated with logic and general cognitive processes (as reflected in the scientific sense of "excogitation" discussed above).[43] It is thus used by Avicenna.[44] Renaissance rhetorical theory strove to reverse this trend and Cicero's scheme was fully reinstated – to such an extent that *inventio* is literally engraved across the bosom of "Rhetoric" in *Margarita philosophica*, Georg Reisch's tidy compendium of Renaissance knowledge (fig. 2). Cicero's reinstated scheme was transferred wholesale to humanist art criticism, as Michael Baxandall has shown; Bartolomeo Fazio, for example, develops a system of *inventio, dispositio* and *expressio* which runs precisely parallel to the first three stages in Cicero's process.[45]

Alongside the rhetorical tradition, there existed the poet's form of *invenzione*, a matter of passion and imaginative inspiration according to Boccaccio. In his *Genealogia deorum gentilium*, he formulates his famous definition of poetry: "Poesis . . . est fervor quidam exquisite inveniendi atque dicendi, seu scribendi quod inveneris." This, with its quality of *fervor*, which "ex sinu Dei procedens," is markedly different from a methodical process of "excogitation."[46]

[42] Cicero, *De inventione* 1.7 and the Ciceronian *Ad Herennium* 1.2.

[43] See C. Baldwin, *Medieval Rhetoric and Poetic* (to 1400), ed. 2 (Gloucester, Mass. 1959) 91 and 191-192, and *Renaissance Literary Theory and Practice* (New York 1939); also D. Clark, *Rhetoric and Poetry in the Renaissance* (New York 1922).

[44] Avicenna, *De anima* 1.4-5, where "adinvenire artes" and "discernere inter pulchrum et foedum" are powers which distinguish the soul of man from that of animals. "Imaginare" is a lowly power, shared with beasts.

[45] Baxandall, *Giotto* (n. 4 above) 101f. Further comparisons between painting and rhetoric are made by J. Spencer, "Ut rhetorica pictura," *Journal of the Warburg and Courtauld Institutes* 20 (1957) 26f.

[46] Boccaccio, *Genealogia deorum gentilium,* bks. 14 and 15, particularly 14.7. Cf. C. Osgood, *Boccaccio on Poetry* (Princeton 1930) 39, and F. Tateo, *"Rhetorica" e "poetica" fra medioevo e rinascimento* (Bari 1960) 68f.

These two traditions, the rhetorical and poetic – the one stipulating a division of labor between invention of content and composition of form, the other interpreting invention in terms of divine inspiration – become increasingly inseparable in Renaissance discussions of the poetic faculty. This process is well under way in Salutati's *De laboribus Herculis* and is fully realized in Landino's introduction to his Dante commentary.[47] And both traditions lie behind the *quattrocento* conception of a literary *invenzione* for a painting or cycle of paintings.

Alberti, who used "excogitative" invention in *De re aedificatoria*, had earlier exploited the term *invenzione* in the more specialized manner of content for painting. In *De pictura* he advises the painter to consort with "literary men, who are full of information about many subjects and will be of great assistance in preparing the composition of a *historia*, and the great virtue of this consists primarily in its *inventio*. Indeed, *inventio* is such that even by itself and without pictorial representation it can give pleasure."[48] The example subsequently cited is the iconography of Apelles's *Calumny*, as conveyed by Lucian's ekphrastic description which itself "excites our admiration when we read it."[49] The intellectual conception of the *inventio* thus possesses an aesthetic quality in its own right, independent of the pictorial *compositio* of form.

Examples of literary *invenzioni* become increasingly common in the second half of the *quattrocento*. When Filarete presents an elaborate and novel scheme for the representation of *Virtue* (fig. 3) and *Vice* in single figures, he relates that he is praised by his patron for "la inventiva."[50] One of his most important requirements for the artist is that he should be capable of making "belle inventioni" like "Appelle che trovo la calumnia."[51] For this it is necessary that the artist should be learned "in lettere" in order to investigate new "fantasie" and "varie moralita e virtu."[52] This Albertian requirement is precisely echoed in 1501 by Jacopo de' Barbari, who believes that in addition to philosophy and music the painter should understand "la poesia per la invention de la hopere."[53]

The fullest documentation of the literary form of *invenzione* occurs immediately after the end of the *quattrocento* in the correspondence of Isabella d'Este. Though technically outside the scope of this study, her terminology can with some justice be regarded as the culmination of earlier trends. From 1502 onwards in her letters to

[47] C. Salutati, *De laboribus Herculis* 1.2-3; and Landino (n. 2 above) proemo.

[48] Alberti, *De pictura* 3.53; ed. C. Grayson, *Leon Battista Alberti, On Painting and On Sculpture* (London 1972) 94. Cf. E. Verheyen, *The Paintings in the Studiolo of Isabella d'Este at Mantua* (New York 1971) 22-29.

[49] Alberti, *De pictura* 3.53 (pp. 94-96). Cf. Lucian, *De calumnia* 5.

[50] Filarete (n. 5 above) fol. 69.

[51] *Ibid.* fol. 184v.

[52] *Ibid.* fol. 114.

[53] Jacopo de' Barbari, *De ecelentia de pittura*, sent to "Federigo Ducha di Sansonia" in 1501; in L. Servolini, *Jacopo de' Barbari* (Padua 1944) 105-106. Later usages of invention in the sixteenth century are discussed by C. Ossola, *Autumno del Rinascimento* (Florence 1971).

the dilatory Perugino, she continually emphasizes the importance of her own "poetic *inventione*" (also called a *fantasia* or *historia*), namely the *Battle of Chastity and Lasciviousness.*[54] She further sends the painter a small drawing to show clearly her ideas and probably also a written account of the iconographical details composed by her court humanist, Paride da Ceresara.[55] After taking such care she not unreasonably exhibits considerable anxiety when she later learns that Perugino is "perverting the whole sentiment of the *fabula.*"[56]

There clearly was a strong feeling among Renaissance patrons that subject matter and meaning were too important to be left to the painter or sculptor. Thus it was that Leonardo Bruni, a master of rhetoric who was professionally skilled in *invenzione*, sought to provide a program for Ghiberti's second set of Bapistry Doors.[57] Such situations would inevitably persist when erudite patrons like Leonello d'Este continued to make (according to Angelo Decembrio's credible account) a sharp division between the cerebral qualities of the writer's *ingenium* and the limited mimetic powers of the painter's hand.[58] In keeping with this attitude, Leonello himself furnished the original idea for the decoration of his studio at Belfiore with paintings of the Muses, while the famous humanist, Guarino, assisted in 1447 with a detailed description of how each Muse should be represented. Guarino deferentially refers to Leonello's concept as an "*inventione* worthy of a Prince."[59] Few such programs drawn up by the patron or his humanist advisers have survived, but the practice of presenting the artist with a cut-and-dried *invenzione* was probably the general rule in the case of new or difficult subjects, particularly those of a classical nature.

The habit of mind which could so readily assign invention of content and composition of form to different individuals was probably a powerful factor in the persistence of the chronological principle of "disjunction" between classical form and classical content in painting. The inventor/executant dichotomy would probably have been particularly strong in the commissioning of a *cassone* from the craftsmen in a specialist *bottega*, and it is in the realm of *cassone* painting that the principle of "disjunction" is indeed most pronounced.[60]

Later in the century certain artists challenged strongly to be credited with their

[54] Letter of 15 September 1502 and "contract" of 19 January 1503. See P. Kristeller, *Andrea Mantegna* (London 1901) doc. 67, and F. Canuti, *Il Perugino* (Siena 1931); trans. D. Chambers, *Patrons and Artists in the Italian Renaissance* (London 1970) 134-138.

[55] "Contract" of 19 January 1503 and letter of 19 February 1505, the latter mentioning Paride in this connection. See Canuti–Chambers 135-141.

[56] Letter of 19 February 1505. *Fabula* or *fabella* is a Boccaccian term.

[57] For Bruni's 1424 program, see R. Krautheimer, *Lorenzo Ghiberti* (Princeton 1956) 372, doc. 52.

[58] See M. Baxandall, "A Dialogue on Art from the Court of Leonello d'Este: Angelo Decembrio's *De politia littaria, pars LXVIII*," *Journal of the Warburg and Courtauld Institutes* 26 (1963) 304-326.

[59] See Baxandall, *Giotto* (n. 4 above) 89 and 158.

[60] See E. Gombrich, "Apollonio di Giovanni," *Norm and Form* (London 1966) 11-28.

own powers of literary *invenzione* – perhaps having taken heed of the advice proffered by Alberti and Filarete. Already Filarete himself had claimed the power of iconographical *invenzione*, having the temerity to point out the shortcomings of both Antiquity and the Christian tradition in failing to formulate single images of Virtue and Vice.[61] Even Isabella d'Este was forced to recognize this trend and learn to live with it. Although she endeavored to shackle Perugino with a precise program, she had previously permitted Giovanni Bellini a freer reign. In 1501 she hopefully requested something from Giovanni of his own invention: "Qualche istoria o fabula antiqua aut de suo inventione ne finga una che rapresenti cosa antiqua e de bello significato."[62] Yet some four and a half years later, Pietro Bembo has need to remind her that the *inventione* which she has sent him in the form of a drawing must be adapted to Bellini's own *fantasia;* rebelling against standard practice, Bellini "does not like to be given many written details which cramp his style; his way of working, as he says, is always to wander at will in his pictures, so that they can give satisfaction to himself as well as the beholder."[63]

Isabella's agent, Lorenzo di Pavia, formed a less favorable impression of Bellini's power of invention than the painter claimed for himself. He praised Bellini's abilities as a colorist, but stated that "in *invencione* no one can rival Mantegna, who is truly the most excellent."[64] A similar opinion of Mantegna had been expressed earlier by Giovanni Santi, who used such terms as *inventione, fantasia* and *concepto* to convey the erudite nature of Mantegna's works.[65] But artists like Mantegna who appeared legitimately able to be accorded humanist powers of literary invention were still a tiny exception to the general rule in the late *quattrocento.* And Villani's *trecento* praise of Giotto's art, "which stood out as a rival to poetry" because "he had a full knowledge of the stories," is unique in earlier literature on the visual arts.[66] Generally, "full knowledge of the stories" was regarded as the prerogative of the patron and his advisors.

Attitudes towards the inventive role of the patron in architecture are harder to define, because the division of labor between the "architect" and the patron was less clearly established than in the case of painting. Was the architect an "ideas man" or merely a technical executant? Any answer to this question is complicated by the fact that the patron might in a very real sense assume important aspects of the architect's

[61] Filarete (n. 5 above) fols. 142v-143.

[62] Letter of 28 June 1501. See J. Fletcher, "Isabella d'Este and Giovanni Bellini's *Presepio*" *Burlington Magazine* 113 (1971) 704 (trans. Chambers [n. 54 above] 127).

[63] Letter of 1 January 1506. See G. Gaye, *Carteggio inedito d' artisti* 2 (Florence 1840) 71-73 (trans. Chambers [n. 54 above] 131-133).

[64] Letters of 6 and 16 July 1504 and 16 October 1506. See Kristeller (n. 54 above) docs. 70, 71 and 83.

[65] *Cronaca rimata*; ed. H. Holtzinger, *Federigo di Montefeltro, Duca di Urbino* (Stuttgart 1893) 22.96.74f. (pp. 187-188).

[66] Villani, *De origine*, in Baxandall, *Giotto* (n. 4 above) 71 and 147, and J. Larner, *Culture and Society in Italy 1290-1420* (London 1971) 278-282.

role and might even be considered the architect of his own buildings. Cosimo de' Medici is one such patron. Not only is there a common quality in all his buildings regardless of their architects – something which can be called the "Cosimo style" – he is also reported to have asked rhetorically in connection with the Badia at Fiesole, "Should I not make an image drawn from my brain or mind, which would secure long memory for my name?"[67]

The patron's conceptual role in architecture is explicitly acknowledged in Filarete's elaborate biological metaphor for the birth of a building, in which the patron is said to conceive (*generare*) the original notion, while the architect is regarded as a mother whose role is to bring the conception to the stage at which it is born (*partorire*).[68] In practice, however, Filarete portrays the pattern of the relationship rather differently. His role is shown in many sections of the treatise as that of the inventor, developing and expounding his own conceptions of Sforzinda, while his master hovers approvingly at his shoulder asking questions and occasionally making constructive suggestions.[69] Just as he credited himself with the ability to make an iconographical *inventiva,* so he regards his architectural function as more than that of a skilled executant.[70]

Whereas no practicing painters before Leonardo and Bellini are on record as having made similar claims to high-flown inventive powers, a number of architects consciously assumed the roles of "ideas men" – if, that is, one can speak in any real sense of the profession of "architect" in the fifteenth century.[71] The practice of architecture lacked both an established system of apprenticeship and a clearly-defined guild of professional executants who could be recognized as "architects." Probably none of those whom we now regard as typical *quattrocento* architects, such as Brunelleschi, Alberti, Filarete and Francesco di Giorgio, assumed identical inventive roles vis-à-vis their patrons on one side and their technical workers on the other. But they did share a common demand for the recognition of their intellectual capacities. It was in this specifically architectural context that the artist laid claim to a command of "excogitative" invention – discovering and devising. Invention for the architects meant something within their realm of action; *invenzione* for most painters meant a story provided by someone else.

The only major exceptions in the *quattrocento* to this habit of compartmentalizing the two main usages of invention are provided by Filarete and Leonardo, but they achieve their ends in very different ways. Whereas Filarete develops an interpre-

[67] E. Gombrich, "Alberto Avogadro's Description of the Badia of Fiesole and of the Villa of Careggi," *Italia medioevale e umanistica* 5 (1962) 217-229, esp. 223: "Non faciam a cerebro extractam aut a mente figuram. Quae mihi, et si moriar, nomina longa dabit." Gombrich's translation (*Norm and Form* [n. 60 above] 46) – "should I not create . . ." – is misleading in tone.

[68] Filarete (n. 5 above) fol. 7v.

[69] *Ibid.* fol. 11.

[70] *Ibid.*; compare fols. 69 and 171v.

[71] Cf.. N. Pevsner, "The Term 'Architect' in the Middle Ages," *Speculum* 17 (1942) 549-562.

tation of formal invention in terms akin to poetic invention of content – both falling under the embrace of *fantasia* – Leonardo unites invention of content and form by according the faculty of imagination a rational potential similar to Francesco di Giorgio's "excogitative" process in architecture. Both these developments will be examined in subsequent sections of this study.

THE ROLES OF IMAGINATION AND FANTASIA

The definition of imagination as the image-forming capacity has remained reasonably constant since classical times, though attitudes towards it fluctuated widely. The Greek term *φαντασία* was generally translated as "imagination" (*imaginativa* or *immaginazione*), though it sometimes also gave rise to the more phonetic transcription, *fantasia* (or *phantasia*). A suitable starting-point is Aristotle's definition – "Imagination is that in virtue of which an image arises for us" – which underwent a process of continual redefinition in the hands of early Christian and medieval philosophers, such as Nemesius, Augustine, Avicenna, Albertus Magnus and Roger Bacon.[72] Aristotle's discussion of the mind in Book 3 of *De anima* was later developed into a functional psychology of perception in which each mental faculty or internal sense was accorded a particular location in the ventricles of the brain and credited with responsibility for a particular stage in the progression from sensory impression through cogitation and cognition to eventual memorization.

One of the most commonly consulted sources for Renaissance psychology was Avicenna's *De anima* which made explicit much that was barely implicit in Aristotle's difficult account. The section on the brain in Mundinus's influential *Anathomia* is closely related to Avicenna's treatise, and a broadly comparable system is succinctly illustrated at the beginning of the sixteenth century in Reisch's *Margarita philosophica* (fig. 4).[73] The first of the three ventricles was generally believed to contain the *sensus communis* (where sensory impressions are gathered together), *fantasia* and *imaginatio*. The division of labor between these faculties was variable and not always

[72] Aristotle, *De anima* 3.3.428af and *Rhetoric* 1.11.6. Discussions of the internal senses are provided by: L. Ambrosi, *La psicologia della immaginazione* (Rome 1898); J. Soury, *Le système nerveux central: Structure et fonctions* (Paris 1899); M. Bundy, *The Theory of Imagination in Classical and Medieval Thought,* University of Illinois Studies 12 (1927) and "Invention and Imagination in the Renaissance," *Journal of English and Germanic Philology* 29 (1930) 535-554 (erroneously placing "fantasy" in the second ventricle, 537); W. Pagel, "Medieval and Renaissance Contributions to the Study of the Brain and Its Functions," in *The History of the Theory of the Brain and its Functions*, ed. F. Poynter, Wellcome Symposium 1957 (Oxford 1958); E. Clarke and C. D. O'Malley, *The Human Brain and Spinal Cord* (Berkeley 1968); E. Clarke and K. Dewhurst, *An Illustrated History of Brain Functions* (Oxford 1972); L. Norpoth, *Der pseudo-augustinische Traktat, De spiritu et anima*, dissertation, Munich 1924 (Cologne 1971); F. Rahman, *Avicenna's Psychology* (Oxford 1952); P. Michaud-Quantin, *La psychologie de l'activité chez Albert le Grand* (Paris 1966). I am grateful to Katharine Park for the references to Soury and Pagel.

[73] *Avicenna latinus: Liber de anima*, ed. S. van Reit and G. Verbeke, 2 vols. (Louvain 1972) 1.5.87-90; Mundinus, *Anathomia,* Papie per Antonium de Carcano (1478) fol. 19f.

very clear. Avicenna identified *fantasia* with the *sensus communis* in the anterior of the ventricle, while Bacon used *fantasia* as a collective term to embrace both the *sensus communis* and *imaginatio.*[74] The more intellectual internal senses, cogitation, cognition, apprehension, estimation, reason and (most relevantly for this study) invention were generally seen as operating in the second ventricle, while the major function of the third cavity was the storage capacity of memory.

Avicenna distinguished between two different types of imagination, which may not unfairly be characterized as sensory (or representative) and deliberative (or active). The former was merely an early stage in the perceptive process whereby an impermanent image was preserved on the bases of impressions transmitted from the *sensus communis.* This was *imaginatio.* The active component, *imaginativa* in relation to the *anima vitalis* and *cogitativa* in association with the *anima humana,* operated more positively with cognition to produce compound images and dreams, and even to simulate sensory experience.[75] In the *Canon* he indicates that "cogitation uses the precepts which have been stored in the imagination and then proceeds to combine and analyze them, constructing quite different images, for instance a flying man or an emerald mountain."[76] *Imaginativa/cogitativa* is located by Avicena in the second ventricle, thus emphasizing its differentiation from the more lowly *imaginatio* in the first. An interesting development of the dual imagination theory is to be found in *Del poema heroico* by Torquato Tasso, who speculates that there is a variety of imagination "beyond that which is a power of the sensory soul" and that this second imagination is responsible for higher symbols such as those which denote the four evangelists.[77]

In humanist literary theory during the two centuries preceding Tasso's *cinquecento* formulation, imagination plays a less prominent role than its image-forming capacity might lead one to expect. Sensory *imaginatio* was only of relevance insofar as an artist might be interested in the actual process of perception, while the properties of active *imaginativa* were either ignored or regarded with suspicion by humanists such as Petrarch who exhibited a marked distrust of fantasy images and hallucinations. Imagination, named as such, finds no prominent role in the inspirational theory of poetry advocated by Boccaccio. It was Dante, alone of the *tre coronati*, who credited imagination with a major creative function.

A large part of Dante's *Vita nuova* is concerned with the inner world of emotional experience, a context in which dreams, visions and related phenomena are as real to the author as perceptions of an empirical kind and often contain more profound truth. Dante's creative process, as subsequently developed in the *Divina commedia*, relies heavily upon the visionary and dream-like qualities for which imagination is the agent. In the *Vita nuova* he describes, in a manner broadly consistent with medieval

[74] R. Bacon, *Opus majus*, V (i), I, 4. Cf. Reisch (n. 35 above) 10.11.21f.

[75] Avicenna, *De anima* 1.5 and 4.2.

[76] Avicenna, *Canon* 1.176-182.

[77] See E. Gombrich, *Symbolic Images* (London 1972) 157-158.

faculty psychology, how such hallucinatory experiences might occur: "I close my eyes and begin to wander like a person who is delirious and to imagine [*immaginare*]." The product of his delirium is a *fantasia.*[78] He makes it clear that imagination was capable of giving the emotions complete dominance over the mind: "Love ruled my soul . . . and began to assume such mastery over me, owing to the power given by my *immaginazione*, that I was obliged to fulfil all his works perfectly."[79] As an artist he attempts to exploit this power to the full, but in the *Divina commedia* even the visionary capacities of imagination ultimately fail to capture the final vision of heavenly truth, because compared to heaven "le fantasie nostre sono basse."[80]

Dante's conception of *fantasia* provides an important source for later usages, but his characterization of imagination as an agent of visionary truth and as an important weapon in the creative artist's armory had a limited impact upon his later admirers, before Lorenzo de' Medici's reinstatement of Dante's attitude and Michelangelo's subsequent assimilation of it. During the first half of the *quattrocento*, the leading humanists tended to stress the learned, philosophical and civic aspects of his life and works, largely at the expense of *immaginazione* and *fantasia*. When the recanting Niccolò Niccoli praises Dante in the second of Leonardo Bruni's *Dialogues*, he does so on the grounds that the poet commanded the three requirements for great poetry: "Fingendi artem, oris elegantiam multarumque rerum scientiam." The first of these is the prerogative of poets, the second is shared with oratory and the third with philosophers and historians.[81] The special figurative (or fictional) element of poetry is associated with metaphors, similes, analogies, allegories, myths and such-like, but this sense of *fingere* is hardly equivalent to Dante's visionary imagination.

In view of this reluctance to accommodate imagination even in poetic theory, it is not surprising that the humanists fail to analyze this faculty in relation to the visual arts. An apparent exception is the discussion of translations of Greek and Latin classics in Matteo Palmieri's *Della vita civile*, in which he compares modern vulgarizations of ancient texts with attempts to copy Giotto. Translations resemble the originals no more than "a figure copied from the most perfect of Giotto's by one whose hand has never worked with pen or brush . . . . Although it has nose, eyes, mouth and all its parts, it would nevertheless be different to the extent that it would be separately imagined by each person."[82] We would be unwise, however, to believe that Palmieri's intention was to credit painters with advanced powers of imaginative

[78] Dante, *Vita nuova* 23. Cf. Bundy (n. 72 above) 225-256.

[79] Dante, *Vita nuova* 2.

[80] Dante, *Paradiso* 10.43-44.

[81] *Leonardo Aretini ad Petrum Paulum Istrum dialogus II*, in T. Klette, *Beitrage zur Geschichte und Literatur der Italienischen Gelehrtenrenaissance* (Greifswald 1888) 74.

[82] M. Palmieri, *Della vita civile*, ed. F. Battaglia (Bologna 1944) 4: "Una figura ritratta dall più perfetta di Giotto, per mano di chi mai non avesse operato stile nè penello . . . avessi naso, occhi, bocca e tutti i membri, nientedimeno sara tanto diversa, quanto ciascuno in sé stessi imaginare potere." Cf. Bruni's parallel between literary translations and defiled paintings (Baxandall, *Giotto* [n. 4 above] 41-43).

individuality: rather, he is resorting to a typical humanist ploy by illustrating his point with a pictorial analogy, without intending to make a considered statement about the nature of the visual arts themselves.

In specialist literature on the visual arts before 1450, references to imagination are no less rare than in humanists' accounts of poetry. "Imagination" as such plays no role in Alberti's theory. When he uses the term at all, he does so merely to introduce an argument, as in "Let us imagine that [*ac immaginari*] . . . ."[83] The nearest he comes to using another term which can be translated as "to imagine" is when he applies *fingere* to Zeuxis's representation of living things – "fingendis aut pingendis animantibus." However, *fingere* as used by Bruni, Valla and Alberti might more properly be rendered as "to form an image of" or even "to fabricate," with no special reference to faculty psychology or Dantesque *immaginazione.*[84]

Manetti later refers on one occasion to imagination in Brunelleschi's inventive procedures, but he largely divorces it from its usual sense by allying it to experience and knowledge. Brunelleschi's experience with clocks and mechanical gadgets is said to have "gli detto grandissimo aiuto al potere immaginare diverse macchine."[85] This reference to imagination in the *Life of Brunelleschi*, isolated though it is, may well reflect the tendency for invention and imagination to move into closer association during the later half of the *quattrocentro*; this process is first fully apparent in Francesco di Giorgio's *Trattati*, to a large extent paving the way for Leonardo's marriage of the concepts.

The reader may already have sensed that Francesco di Giorgio's notion of infinite inventiveness contains a factor which cannot be entirely encompassed by a methodical process of cognition. Francesco appears to acknowledge this in his statement of the intellectual qualifications for architecture; the architect requires "prespicace e singulare ingegno e invenzione" because architecture "e solo una sottile immaginazione concetto nella mente la quale in nell'opra si manifesta."[86] The three components in architectural design, *icnogrofia, ortogrofia* and *scenogrofia*, are "born of *immaginazione* and *invenzione*," the former of which is defined as "cura piena di diligenzia e effetto d'industria della cosa proposta con volontà." This statement is a translation of Vitruvius – "Hae nascuntur ex cogitatione et inventione. Cogitatio est cura studii plena et industriae vigilantiaeque effectus propositi cum voluptate" – with the substitution of *immaginazione* for *cogitatio.*[87]

In adopting Vitruvius's definition of *cogitatio* for his exposition of *immaginazione*, Francesco is giving imagination an unusually rational slant. But he does not

[83] Alberti (n. 48 above) 1.5 (p. 40); cf. 2.32 (p. 68).

[84] *Ibid.* 2.25 (p. 60). Lorenzo Valla applies *fingere* to "things formed with *ingenio* and human artifice, especially if they are unusual or new," but he nowhere hints that it could be associated with "imagination" (*De linguae latinae elegantiae* 5.43).

[85] Manetti (n. 7 above) 50-53.

[86] Di Giorgio, *Tratt.* (n. 12 above) 1.36.

[87] *Ibid.* 1.39; and Vitruvius 1.2.2.

drain it entirely of its variable qualities, as is proved by his later discussion of how to convey architectural images to the mind of the reader of a treatise. Drawings convey the form as intended through the eye, but verbal descriptions pass "drieto alla imaginativa."[88] Imagination subsequently reforms the image of the original *invenzione*, making "varie composizioni" rather than a single definitive image corresponding precisely to the appearance of the object described. In addition to acting as the agent responsible for a variety of images, imagination is also responsible for an inventive man's access to the concept of infinity: "La mente . . . immagina numero infinito in modo che a ogni numero far addizione."[89] The ability to imagine thus aids human comprehension of macrocosmic design and results in microcosmic infinity of invention. Imagination, for Francesco, appears to be an extension of rational thought towards infinite potentiality rather than a negation of the rational process of "excogitation."

Only once during the *quattrocento* is imaginative invention in the visual arts conceived in such a way that it stands in direct opposition to "excogitation." The odd man out is Francesco Colonna, whose extraordinary architectural romance, *Hypnerotomachia poliphili* (1467?), is not only a monument to its author's own fertility of imagination but is also an important milestone in the promotion of invention as a transcendent power of the mind. One of his favorite phrases to convey the fantastic wonder of the marvels fabricated in his dream world is *inventione inexcogitabile*; the strange hollow elephant is an invention "inexcogitabile sencia existimatione," and the porch of the immense pyramid is designed "cum inexcogitabile subtilitate dello intellecto, & arte."[90] Such a positive separation between the rational limits of "excogitation" and the unaccountable power of invention is altogether new in Renaissance writing on the arts. This novel form of "inexcogitable" invention is on one occasion associated by Colonna with imagination, though he nowhere explicitly develops this into a full-scale theory of the role of imagination in the artistic process.[91]

Colonna shares with Filarete, that other architectural eccentric of the *quattrocento*, an infectious joy for curious inventions, marvels, oddities, conundrums and hieroglyphs; and both indulge in the kind of fantastic inventiveness disparaged by Alberti as beyond the limits of feasibility. Filarete's implausibly revolving tower, capped by a rearing equestrian monument, is a case in point, though he is at pains to legitimize his bizarre invention by providing it with an antique pedigree; the "Golden Book," discovered by Filarete and translated by the Greek scholar "Iscofrance Notilento" (that is, Francesco da Tolentino, called Filelfo) names the original *inventore* as "Onitoan Nolievra," Antonio Averlino's (that is, Filarete's)

[88] Di Giorgio, *Tratt.* 2.489.

[89] *Ibid.* 2.482.

[90] Colonna (n. 26 above) fols. 16v and 10.

[91] *Ibid.* fol. 14: "Stupefacto dunque non poco, ruminando e cum summo dilecto curioso riguardando tale ingente machina conflata in animale da humano ingenio, dignissimo imaginato."

anagramatic precursor from ancient times.[92] This procedure of creating a pedigree is essentially similar to the manner in which Colonna gives a sense of reality to his architectural fantasies by supposing them to be products of an older, golden age. Neither author, in theory at least, has lost sight of the principle of imitating Antiquity.

Like Colonna, Filarete implies that the inventive process is to be associated with imagination. When discussing the *invenzione* of the figures of Vice and Virtue he says that he had already often been "immaginando" how they might be represented.[93] However, *immaginare* is not a verb which occurs regularly in Filarete's treatise. He is far more concerned with *fantasia*, a notion which he quite exceptionally applies to both form and content in a work of art.

* * *

Fantasia has already been briefly encountered in the context of medieval faculty psychology. Since the single term *φαντασία* as used by Aristotle could be translated both as "imagination" and *fantasia*, any separation between them is difficult in a medieval context. But in Renaissance art theory some degree of separation was achieved, largely because theorists could draw upon a classical tradition of specialized artistic usage of *fantasia*, whereas "imagination" remained largely within its psychological context. Only once, to my knowledge, is *φαντασία* used in terms of Aristotelian perception in *quattrocento* art theory; this occurs in the exceptional writings of the Greek scholar, Manuel Chrysoloras, who speaks of the "image which it [the mind] grasped through the soul's imagination (*φανταστικὸν*)."[94] This role for *fantasia* in a process of artistic perception is amplified neither by Chrysoloras himself nor by any other author before Leonardo. Indeed, *fantasia* in its strictly Aristotelian sense of "faded sensation" seems to offer little promise for a theory of art. Nor did the Stoic sense of *φαντασία* as an "impression," "presentation" or "visual percept" prove to be a more fertile idea in the context of the visual arts, in spite of the passage in Diodorus Siculus's *Library of History* (known to Alberti) in which the Egyptian artists' use of absolutely fixed measures for figure sculpture were contrasted with the Greeks' reliance upon the "impression [*fantasia*] presented to the artist's eye."[95]

The Platonic tradition, however, provided ample ground for the application of *fantasia* to artistic matters. Plato's own attitude betrays some of the same inconsistencies as his attitude towards poetry, which was banned from the *Republic* but

[92] Filarete (n. 5 above) fol. 171v. On all other occasions the surname is "Nolivera."

[93] *Ibid.* fol. 142v.

[94] See Baxandall, *Giotto* (n. 4 above) 82 and 151.

[95] Diodorus Siculus, *Library of History* 1.98 (cf. E. Panofsky, "History of the Theory of Human Proportions," *Meaning in the Visual Arts* [Harmondsworth 1970] 98), reflected by Alberti, *De statua* 5 (ed. Grayson [n. 48 above] 124-125). Zeno's usage of *fantasia* is recorded by Cicero, *Academica* 1.11.

praised as a "light and winged and holy thing" in the *Ion.*[96] *Fantasia* in Plato's philosophy was a faculty of the lowly "appetitive soul" which resided in the liver. Its insidious action was such that the mind could "easily fall under the spell of images or phantasms day or night," but it also more desirably gave man the power of prophecy: "When the power of understanding is inhibited in sleep or when we are in abnormal condition owing to disease or divine inspiration we form *fantasmata* (*φαντάσματα*)," which can be utilized by the intellect to provide remarkable insights.[97] This is the species of "insane" inspiration which Shakespeare later acknowledged: "The lunatic, the lover and the poet are of imagination all compact."[98]

Fantasia, identified as a form of inspired insight, not only entered literary theory but was also adapted for use in the context of the visual arts, most notably by the Philostrati and Quintilian. Philostratus begins by baldly asserting that "painting is *μιμησίς*," though he adopts a broad definition of *mimesis* which embraces images of "centaurs and heraldic animals" such as can be discerned in the irregular massing of clouds.[99] Later he is challenged to explain the images of gods sculpted by Phidias and Praxiteles; did they go "to heaven and take a copy?" Philostratus's answer is *fantasia*: "Μιμησίς can only create handiwork which it has seen, but *φαντασία* equally that which it has not."[100] The process of conceptual insight in the visual arts is specifically stated in the *proemium* to the *Imagines* to be equivalent to that of poetry: "The art of painting has a certain kinship with the art of poetry . . . an element of *fantasia* is common to both."[101] This formulation gives *fantasia* a vital role in the equation *ut pictura poesis*.

Quintilian writing later and in Latin acknowledges that *fantasia* is a Greek notion: "There are certain experiences which the Greeks call *φαντασίας* and we call *visiones*, whereby things absent are represented to our mind with such extreme vividness that they seem to be before our eyes."[102] Though the process of *ἐνφαντασίωτον* is basically a vice, he nevertheless suggests that it can be turned to good account. It can be utilized to conceive any past or future event – a gift which is extremely useful for the orator, author or painter. When he subsequently discusses the great artists of the

[96] Plato, *Ion,* 533-534. Cf. R. Harriot, *Poetry and Criticism before Plato* (London 1969) 78-91.

[97] *Timaeus* 38.

[98] *Twelfth Night* 5.1.2-8.

[99] Philostratus, *Life of Apollonius of Tyana* 2.22. Is this the source of inspiration for the cloud images in Mantegna's Vienna *St. Sebastian* and *Minerva Expelling the Vices* (Paris, Louvre)? It is known that Isabella d'Este, the patron of the *Minerva*, was greatly interested in the *Imagines.* A Latin edition of the *Life of Apollonius* was published in Bologna in 1501. See also n. 152 below.

[100] Philostratus, *Life of Apoll.* 6.19. *Fantasia* in Greek theory is discussed by B. Scheitzer, "Mimesis und Phantasia," *Philologus* 89 (1934) 286-300; and J. Pollitt, *The Ancient View of Greek Art: Criticism, History and Terminology* (New Haven 1974) 53-55, 293-297.

[101] Philostratus the Younger, *Imagines*, proemium, 6.

[102] Quintilian, *Institutio oratoria* 6.2.29f. (rediscovered in 1416).

past, he credits various painters with different qualities – *cura* (Protogenes), *ratio* (Pamphilos and Melanthios), *ingenium* and *gratia* (both in Apelles) – while one, Theon of Samos, was famed for his power in forming visions, "quas *φαντασίας* vocant."[103] A similar judgment of Theon's art had been provided by Aelian, who stated that the artist ordered a bugle to be sounded in front of his painting, *Soldiers Hurrying to War*, in order to enhance the vividness of the *φαντασία*.[104] These references suggest that the use of *fantasia* in the context of the visual arts may well be dated to the period of Theon, that is, the first half of the fourth century B.C.

In spite of the classical tradition, *fantasia* appears only erratically in Renaissance art theory. Even its increasing use towards the end of the century stops short of giving it a major role as a consistent component in the vocabulary of art. The story of the introduction of *fantasia* in the fifteenth century is far from tidy, and the major source of untidiness is to be found precociously in the introduction to Cennino Cennini's *Libro dell'arte*.

Painting, Cennini considers, requires "fantasia e hoperazione di mano." These qualities are required "to discover unseen things, hiding under the shadow of nature, and to fix them with the hand, demonstrating what does not actually exist."[105] The source for his conception lies ultimately within classical poetics, most notably Horace's *Ars poetica*, as transmitted through medieval intermediaries. Cennini considers that painting "deserves to be placed in the next rank to science and to be crowned with poetry. The justice lies in this: that the poet is free to compose and bind together or not as he pleases, according to his will. In the same way the painter is given freedom to compose a figure standing, sitting, half-man, half-horse as it pleases him, following his *fantasia*."[106] This statement of artistic license closely resembles Horace's assertion that "pictoribus atque poetis quidlibet audendi semper fuit aequa potestas." though Horace himself was reluctant to extend the liberty so far as to include improbable combinations of human and animal forms.[107] Horace's formulation was undoubtedly influential during the Middle Ages; Durandus, for example, acknowledged that in composing "diverse histories" from the Old and New Testaments, "pictoribus atque poetis quidlibet addendi semper fuit equa potestas."[108] This substitution of *addendi* (adding) for *audendi* (daring) also characterizes Cennini's freer paraphrase and suggests that he was using just such a medieval version.

[103] *Ibid.* 10.3-9.

[104] Aelian, *Variae historiae* 2.44.

[105] Cennino Cennini, *Il libro dell'arte*, ed. P. Thompson (New Haven 1932) 2: "Trovare cose non vedute, chacciandosi sotto ombra di natura, e fermale con la mano dando a dimostrare quello che nonne sia."

[106] *Ibid.* 2: "E con ragione merita metterla in second grado all scienzia, e choronarla di poesia. La ragione e questa: che'l poeta ellibero di potere comporre elleghare insieme, si e non, come gli piace secondo suo volonta. Per lo simile al dipintore dato e liberta potere conporre una figura ritta, a sedere, mezzo huomo, mezzo cavallo, si chome gli piace, secondo suo fantasia."

[107] Horace, *Ars poetica* 9-10.

[108] Durandus, *Rationale divinorum officiorum* 1.23.

Cennini also uses *fantasia* and a strange derivative, *fantastichetto*, when later discussing the advantage of studying from the works of one master rather than many. If you copy one master today and another tomorrow "verrai per forza fantastichetto per amor, che ciaschuna maniera ti traciera la mente."[109] On account of its eccentricity, *fantastichetto per amor* is not an easy phrase to understand; perhaps its sense may best be rendered as "bewildered through enthusiasm" (for different styles). If the artist copies one master, however, his style will eventually gain its own individuality through the faculty of his own *fantasia* – providing that "nature has conceded him any."[110] *Fantasia* thus appears to be a variable factor; capable of confusion and delusion, but also responsible for individuality under favorable circumstances.

Cennini's remarkable exploitation of *fantasia* almost certainly takes its immediate inspiration from medieval rather than first-hand classical sources. Horatian poetic license, as disparaged by medieval authorities such as Isidore of Seville, Saint Bernard and the anonymous author of *Pictor in carmine*, had become associated in the visual arts with that facet of medieval style which may be called "gargoyle grotesque" – the style which received supreme late expressions in Schongauer's *Temptation of Saint Anthony*, the Erasmian *phantasmata* of Dürer's *Knight Death and the Devil* and Leonardo's monsters.[111] The *Pictor in carmine* (ca. 1200), for example, takes up Saint Bernard's diatribe against the adornment of churches with monsters such as "centaurs with quivers," concluding that "it is the criminal presumption of painters that has gradually introduced such *phantasmatum*."[112] Against these disapproving voices, Cennini could have drawn comfort from the qualified approval of Durandus and the poetic enshrinement of *fantasia* by Dante. However, such possible medieval sources for Cennini's ideas in no way diminish the precocity and novelty of his far-reaching claims. At least half a century was to elapse before *fantasia* began to appear with any regularity in the literature on the visual arts, and by that time original Greek precedents were becoming more familiar.

The only sustained attempt to exploit *fantasia* as a major element in creative theory after Cennini and before Leonardo is to be found in Filarete's *Trattato*. Just as Francesco di Giorgio's concepts of imagination and infinite inventiveness are so appropriate to his artistic personality, so Filarete's personal predilection for *fantasia* is extremely apt for his own architectural speculations. *Fantasia* for Filarete is an

[109] Cennini (n. 105 above) 15.

[110] ". . . poi atte interverra chesse punto di fantasia la natura l'ara concieduto, verrai a pighare huna maniera propia per te e non potra essere altro che buona." *Ibid.* 15.

[111] I am grateful to David Summers for generously providing me with advance information regarding medieval sources from his forthcoming book, *Michelangelo and the Theory of Art: Fantasy and Order.* See Isidore of Seville, *Etymologiae* 19.16: "Pictura autem dicta quasi fictura." The *Pictor in carmine* has been edited by M. R. James, "Pictor in carmine," *Archeologia* 94 (1951) 142-166. Erasmus and Dürer's *phantasmata* are discussed by E. Panofsky, *The Life and Art of Albrecht Dürer*, 2 vols. (Princeton 1943) 1.152.

[112] James 143.

all-pervasive factor, embracing every facet in the conception of a work of art or architecture.

The initial idea for the work is a *fantasia*. He characteristically uses the now-familiar Macedonian architect, as an illustration; when he first begins to think about Sforzinda, he expresses confidence that his "fantasia" of the new city will please his patron "like the one made by Dinocrates for Alexander the Great."[113] Even his biological parallel for the production of a building – the patron conceiving the germ of the building while the architect is responsible for "parturition" – permits the faculty of *fantasia* a vital role. During the "nine or seven" months of pregnancy, the mother architect's task is "fantasticare e pensare e rivoltarselo per la memoria." As a result of these cerebral processes, various designs are formed "nella sua mente sopra al generamento," after which the architect gives birth to a baby building, an architectural model![114] A practical if mundane instance of the "father and mother" in action is when the *signore* conceives the idea for the kitchens, an idea which is then subjected to Filarete's own process of "fantastication" before the birth.[115]

The *fantasticare-pensare* coupling is common in his treatise. Clearly they are not one and the same thing. Filarete's usages suggest that *fantasticare* is a form of imaginative conception which complements and extends the rational procedures of thought. As a conceptual process it is active during the exercise of geometrical design; Archimedes was killed while "disegnando e fantasticando circuli e tri-angholi."[116] Elsewhere he couples it with the rational procedure of measuring.[117] And the "Golden Book" records one of the artist's roles as "investigare e cercare nuove fantasie e nuove cose."[118] All this conveys the impression that *fantasia* is not wildly irrational; it acts in conjunction with thought, deliberation, investigation, research and discovery, extending the boundaries of rational intellect.

Filarete's couplings are interestingly consistent both with earlier usages in the theory of dance and with later musical terminology. Domenico da Piacenza's dance treatise (ca. 1440) uses *fantasmata* as a technical term defined as "una prestezza corporale laquale e mossa cum lo intelecto."[119] The chances are that Domenico's usage was not isolated and that further research in this and other little-known fields of Renaissance literature on the arts will yield further examples. Later, when musical compositions called *fantasie* begin to appear during the sixteenth century, they are often interchangeably termed *recercari* (or *ricercari* and other spellings). These musical pieces are not to be identified as free flights of improvised fancy but are compositions which embody a process of musical discovery in the development of

[113] Filarete (n. 5 above) fol. 11: "Credo che la fantasia gli piacera come fece quella di Democrate ad Alexandro magnio."

[114] *Ibid.* fol. 7v.

[115] *Ibid.* fol. 70.

[116] *Ibid.* fol. 151v.

[117] *Ibid.* fols. 7v and 46v.

[118] *Ibid.* fol. 114.

[119] I am grateful to Michael Baxandall for this reference.

themes and variations, closely equivalent to Filarete's development of his own or his patron's original ideas.

Fantasia, for Filarete, is concerned with formal invention in architecture. It is also vital in the *invenzione* of content in the figurative arts. It may be exercised either by the patron – the image of a bull lead by a *putto* is one of the patron's *fantasie* – or by the artist or both in cooperation. The idea for the images of *Reason and Will* (fig. 5) originated from the patron's suggestion, while the complex iconographical details were developed by Filarete: "pensato e fantasticato sopra acqueste fantasie."[120] On the other hand, the Houses of Vice and Virtue – "la mia fantasia" – and most particularly his novel representation of *virtus generalis* are claimed as entirely the responsibility of Filarete from start to finish.[121]

He is not unjustified in his claims for originality in this respect. The tradition of individual representations of each cardinal and theological virtue and vice was well established – Giotto's versions on the *basimento* of the Arena Chapel are probably the most famous examples – but there was no established format for the depiction of virtue and vice as general concepts, each embodied in a single figure. A partial precedent was provided by the competing maidens in the story of Hercules at the crossroads, as related by Xenophon and Cicero, and retold by Petrarch and Salutati. Also, an isolated *trecento* forerunner could have been found in Francesco da Barbarino's *Documenti d'amore* (1314), but this seems to have exercised no influence during the *quattrocento* and was only recently discovered as a result of the researches of Mommsen and Panofsky.[122]

Filarete was aware of the classical precedent, but justifiably did not regard the classical images as sufficiently convincing outside the context of the Hercules narrative; the images "did not satisfy my mind [*mente*], to such an extent that I began with my talent [*ingenio*] to conceive imaginatively and deliberate [*fantasticare e pensare*], so that finally it came into my mind to present vice and virtue [each] in a single figure."

To our eyes, the resulting images (fig. 3) contain a certain element of the "fantastic," and they must have appeared somewhat improbable in their *quattrocento* context, when it is remembered that *Virtue*, perched precariously on his righteous diamond, was to be realized on a huge scale as a sculptural form at the summit of the House of Virtue. But their designer's intention was certainly not that they should be amusing and improbable fantasies, but that they should lucidly present true symbolism of worthy ideas. This attempt to capture truth explains why

[120] Filarete (n. 5 above) fols. 44v (bull and *putto*) and 69r-v (will and reason). Cf. fols. 67 and 110.

[121] *Ibid.* fols. 142v-143.

[122] E. Panofsky, *Hercules am Scheiderwege und andere antike Bildstoffe in der neuren Kunst* (Leipzig 1930) esp. 187-196; and T. Mommsen, "Petrarch and the Story of the Choice of Hercules," *Journal of the Warburg and Courtauld Institutes* 16 (1953) esp. 179-182. Also Spencer's footnote to Filarete (n. 5 above) p. 246.

the complicated images of *Reason and Will*, suggested by the patron and "fantasticated" by Filarete, are later astonishingly discovered (or rediscovered) in identical form on the covers of the ancient "Golden Book."[123] The principle in operation is that great minds of the Renaissance and Antiquity think alike. The process of "fantastication" thus involves a kind of miraculous insight, which is in no way in conflict with *mimesis* of Antiquity – both were striving to conceive the true and the beautiful.

The concept of *fantasia* is no less prominent in the "Golden Book" than in his "own" section of the treatise. The ancient author indicates that the artist must be learned "in lettere" in order to invent "nuove fantasie," and he recommends that the artist should be awarded a sum of one hundred ducats, what might be called a research grant, in order that he should be free "to investigate and search for new *fantasie* and new things."[124] "Fantastication" not only takes time, it also makes strenuous demands upon the mental capacities; he requires "arompere il capo a fantasticare."[125]

The fictitious source in the "Golden Book" serves to highlight the problem for the actual source of Filarete's knowledge of *fantasia* and for his remarkable use of the verb *fantasticare* with its derivatives. The all-embracing role of *fantasia*, which includes conception and development of both artistic form and poetic content, is paralleled most closely in Greek theory, though we would be wrong to make too sharp a separation between classical ideas and their medieval translations. In Filarete's case, I suspect that original Greek rather than medieval sources are paramount. He does indeed appear to have acquired knowledge of some Greek literature little known in his time. For example, he draws his information concerning the costumes of the maidens in the story of Hercules at the crossroads from Xenophon's *Memorabilia* rather than from Cicero's more accessible Latin version in *De officiis,* though he mistakenly refers the reader to Seneca.[126] Filarete's errors in recording classical stories, the misspelled names and incorrect attributions, suggest that he may often have relied upon a second hand, oral account, which he imperfectly recorded from memory.

Who better for him to have consulted in Milan for detailed knowledge of Greek texts than the translator of the "Golden Book," Francesco Filelfo? The view that Filarete was attempting a Greek revival in theory and practice has recently been advanced by John Onians, who has drawn attention to Platonic derivations in the

[123] Filarete fols. 69v and 108v. The marginal illustration of the "Golden Book" does not conform to the description in the text.

[124] *Ibid.* fol. 114.

[125] *Ibid.* fol. 128v.

[126] Xenophon, *Memorabilia* 2.1.21-34. See Panofsky (n. 122 above) 194, and Mommsen (n. 122) 182 n. 1. Seneca may, as Panofsky suggests, be a mistake for "Senofonte." Or it may well reflect confusion with Seneca's tragedies, *Hercules furens* and *Hercules oetaeus*, in neither of which does the crossroads story occur.

Trattato, almost certainly inspired by Filelfo, and to the *maniera Greca* (that is, Byzantine as much as original Greek) of his architectural style.[127] Such conscious "Greekness" may well explain his enthusiasm for San Marco in Venice.[128] We may also add that Filarete's notion of creativity is on occasions remarkably Neoplatonic in tone, particularly when he expounds the role of love; architectural design is "un piacere volunptario chome quando l'huomo e innamorato," in which the soul moves towards the thing loved.[129] If this precocious Neoplatonism reflects Filelfo's tastes, might not Filarete's conception of *fantasia* and *fantasticare* be attributed to the same influence? Filelfo certainly seems to have been predisposed towards regarding artistic invention as a vivid process of inner cogitation in which artists refer not to actual models "sed ingenii acrimonia et cogitatione sua pro exemplari sunt usi" – an opinion which Filarete would have found sympathetic.[130] Oral transmission of ideas is a perilous field for the historian, but there seems to be no better explanation for Filarete's "Greekness," imperfect though it is.

No other *quattrocento* theorist before Leonardo deals with *fantasia* in such an extended and coherent manner. Francesco di Giorgio appears to use the term only once, in connection with the peripheral delights of garden design; gardens should be planned according to geometrical principles, but the designer should also investigate (*recerca*) fountains, pergolas, "secret places in accordance with the taste of poets and philosophers" and other *fantasie* for the "delectation" of the patron.[131]

Similarly isolated references occur in contracts. In 1469 Antonfrancesco de' Dotti maintained the *quattrocento* patron's customarily strict control over subject matter in commissioning paintings from Pietro Calzetta for the Gattamelata Chapel in the Santo at Padua. But having stipulated the subjects, he stated that the artist was free to exercise his *fantasia* in the production of a drawing: "Petrus facere unum disegnum cum fantasia seu instoria ei danda et dare ipsi domino Antonio Francesco." The drawing would thus be submitted to the donor for approval, ensuring that the painter's *fantasia* had not obscured Antonfrancesco's intentions.[132] The impression is that *fantasia* is to be exercised on minor matters only, probably on ornaments or details of a secondary or decorative nature. This certainly is the sense in which *fantasia* is used in the 1502 contract for Pinturrichio's work in the Piccolomini Library; the painter was "obliged to render the ceiling of the library with *fantasie* and colours and small panels as lovely, sumptuous and beautiful as he judges best," in

[127] J. Onians, "Alberti and ΦΙΛΑΡΕΤΗ," *Journal of the Warburg and Courtauld Institutes* 34 (1971) 104-114.

[128] Filarete (n. 5 above) fols. 17, 64r-v, 182v. His praise of the mosaics in the vaults and on the floors is consistent with the Byzantinizing elements in his bronze doors for St. Peter's.

[129] *Ibid.* fol. 8.

[130] Filelfo, *De morali disciplina* (Venice 1552) 12 (kindly provided by Michael Baxandall).

[131] Di Giorgio, *Tratt.* (n. 12 above) 2.348 (the text is illustrated, pl. 2).

[132] V. Lazzarini, "Documenti relativi alla pittura padovana del secolo XV," *Nuovo archivio Veneto* 15.2 (1908) 82. See also Baxandall (n. 2 above) 8.

the style "known today as grotesque."[133] Such *fantasie* were probably more in the nature of decorative whimsies rather than the vehicles of truth and beauty intended by Filarete.

Fantasia exploited in connection with content, as synonymous for poetic *invenzione*, is rather more consistent than its application to formal composition. As early as 1441, Matteo de'Pasti was referring to his Petrarch illustrations as *fantasie*: "I warmly beg you [Piero de'Medici] to send me the *fantasie* for the others . . . please send me your instructions to complete that of Fame, because I have this *fantasia* already."[134] Sometimes it is difficult to tell whether the literary or formal sense is intended, as when Bramante is ordered to produce "qualche digna fantasia da mettere in spettaculo" to celebrate the birth of the Milanese duke's heir in 1492.[135] But there is little doubt that it is the poetic usage that appears prominently in the letters of Isabella d'Este and her circle, as in 1493 when Beatrice d'Este wrote to Isabella seeking permission to use her "fanatasia del passo cum li vinci" – an interlock motif invented for Isabella a year earlier by her close literary friend, Niccolò da Correggio and on which she obviously held a kind of patent.[136] The *fantasia dei vinci* is unlikely to have been a merely formal pattern or costume decoration but rather a heraldic *divisa*, that is, a symbol or emblem with an allusive meaning. Its importance for her is confirmed by the intertwined strips which conspicuously form the intricate fabric of her dress in the portrait by Guilo Romano (Hampton Court). The meaning may lie in the associations of *vinco* (osier or willow-strip as in basket-weaving) with *vincolo* as used in the phrases *vincolo d'amore* (bond of love) and *vincolo di sangue* (blood-tie). The love knots of Angelica and Medoro in *Orlando Furioso* by Ariosto (the greatest of all the d'Este court poets and a friend of Niccolò da Correggio) are symbols of this kind, and humanist portraits abound in such allusions; an example is provided by the ivy clinging lovingly to the tree in Correggio's portrait of *Ginevra Rangone* (Leningrad, Hermitage).[137]

Later, in connection with the *studiolo*, Mantegna, Costa and Perugino were each provided with a detailed *fantasia* (or *inventione, historia, fabella*) while Bellini promised to make "una bela fantasia" on his own account – "una fantasia a suo modo."[138] And Mantegna himself, writing in 1506, informs Isabella that he will

[133] G. Milanesi, *Documenti per la storia dell'arte senese* 3.9 (trans. Chambers [n. 54 above] 26).

[134] G. Milanesi, "Lettere d'artisti italiani dei secoli XIV e XV," *Il Buonarotti* ser. 2, 4 (Rome 1968) 78-79.

[135] M. Levey, *High Renaissance* (Harmondsworth 1975) 145.

[136] A. Luzio and R. Renier, "Il lusso di Isabella d'Este," *Nuova antologia* ser. 4, 67 (June 1896) 462. As late as 1512, Susanna Gonzaga still deemed it prudent to ask permission to use Isabella's "inventione." Luzio and Renier provide a number of references indicative of Isabella's fame as an *inventrix* of costume. See also J. Shearman, "Raphael at the Court of Urbino," *Burlington Magazine* 112 (1970) 76.

[137] Ariosto, *Orlando furioso* 19.36. Correggio's sitter was identified by G. Finzi, "Il ritratto di Gentildonna del Correggio all'Ermitage di Leningrado," *Nuove lettere emiliane* 1 (1962).

[138] Letters of 27 August 1501 and 10 September 1502. See Fletcher (n. 62 above) 707-8.

proceed further with the design for his *Comos* "when *fantasia* comes to my aid." [139] The notion that the artist needs to await an almost involuntary burst of *fantasia* before he could work had previously been recorded by Michele Savonarola, who noted that excellent artists were melancholic in temperament (thus anticipating Neoplatonic theories) and that they were dependent for motivation upon *fantasia*. This temperamental peculiarity resulted in artists commonly being called *bizari.* [140] In accordance with this attitude, Federigo Gonazga advised the duchess of Milan to bear in mind when dealing with Mantegna that "communemente questi magistri eccelenti hanno del fantasticho" (1480).[141] The term *fantasia* had in fact first been associated with Mantegna's art in Giovanni Santi's endearingly personal account of contemporary artists in his *Cronaca rimata*, written during the early 1490s; that is when Giovanni was coming into increasingly close contact with the de'Este-Gonzaga circle.[142]

The popularity of the term in Isabella's circle may well have been directly due to her keen interest in Philostratus, as manifested by the translation of *Imagines* made for her by Demetrius Moschos, her resident Greek scholar, and by her efforts to regain this translation after lending it to Alfonso in connection with the decoration of his Ferrara *camerino.* [143] An alternative or complementary source may lie within her knowledge of dance theory which she would have gained as a pupil of Ebreo and Lavagnolo.

Of all the instances cited, only Filarete uses *fantasia* as an *indispensable* part of his vocabulary of art, and only he seems to be moving towards a notion of artistic genius working platonically with inspired insight like the poet. The related concepts of genius and creative inspiration will be the subject of the last section of this study. Before moving on to these, it is appropriate that we should examine the other major instance in *quattrocento* art theory in which an imaginative process is applied equally to the form and content of a work of art. The theory is that of Leonardo.

[139] Letter of 13 January 1506: "seguitando quanto la fantasia me adiutera." See Kristeller (n. 54 above) doc. 76, and Verheyen (n. 48 above) 19.

[140] M. Savonarola, *Physionomia* (probably written 1442), Paris, Bibliothèque Nationale MS lat. 7357, fol. 14va: "Nam in arte aliqua excellentes certe aliquid melancholie habere videntur eo quod tales aliqua ex parte prudentia carere a vulgo dicuntur. Sunt enim ut melancholici in opinionibus fixi neque precibus ad exercendum artis operationes molliuntur ut in cantoribus et fidibus doctis sepe contingere videmus, neque eas operationes non nisi propria a fantasia moti perfectas conficiunt. Et hos bizaros vulgares nominant aitque vulgus neminem artificem excellentem esse posse nisi aliqua ex parte bizaria vexetur a qua culpa Bizarie excellens medicus omnino vacuus est debet." See L. Thorndike, *A History of Magic and Experimental Science* 4 (New York 1934) 196. For the pedigree and sixteenth-century developments of these concepts, see Panofsky (n. 111 above) 165-170.

[141] Kristeller (n. 54 above) doc. 36.

[142] *Cronaca* 22.96.74f. (n. 65 above) pp. 187-188.

[143] See A. Luzio and R. Renier, *La coltura e le relazioni letterie di Isabella d'Este Gonzaga* (Turin 1903) 22. Ariosto, *Orlando Furioso* 7.19: "Non vi mancava chi cantando, dire/d'amore sapesse gaudii e passioni,/ o con invenzione e poesie/rappresentasse grate fantasie."

LEONARDO: INVENTION, IMAGINATION AND CREATION

Leonardo's greatest aspiration for painting was that it should become the primary vehicle for the demonstration of natural truth. As the "sole imitator of all the apparent works of nature," painting is "a subtle *inventione* which with philosophy and subtle speculation considers the natures of all forms."[144] He further defines the role of the inventor as the interpreter between nature and man, an intermediary whose mind must "transmute itself into the very mind of nature."[145] Such an all-embracing vision of invention and art mitigates against any sharp division between invention of content and composition of form. This is not to say that he is unaffected by humanist interpretations of *invenzione*, but his discussions are rarely framed exclusively in humanist terms or limited by humanist compartmentalization of critical vocabulary. This gives a welcome flexibility to his vocabulary of art, but it often less desirably results in imprecision and ambiguity of expression.

Leonardo comes closest to the humanist tradition in his earliest attempts to formulate a *paragone* of painting and poetry. On a number of occasions he joins with gusto into the Horatian debate on artistic license. He states that "in questa tal finctione libera esso poeta se equiparato al pittore."[146] And in the Ashburnham Codex he grants that the poet is "libero come'l pittore nelle inventioni."[147] On the verso of the same sheet from this early codex he answers the poet's claim to make a "fintione che significava cose grande" with the immaculately humanist reply that the painters of Antiquity possessed similar powers – "come fecie Apelle la calumnia."[148] The verb *significare* is itself thoroughly humanist; it had been used by Bruni in connection with his program for Ghiberti's doors and by Isabella d'Este in her efforts to extract a painting of consequence from Bellini.[149]

Although Leonardo once exceptionally claimed that the invention of *fintioni* was "the least part of painting," his attitude towards subject-matter generally seems to have corresponded to Alberti's high regard for *istoria.*[150] Perhaps after 1500, when he appears to have restudied Alberti's *De pictura* with particular care, he argues that "inventione o conponimento di storia" is the "fine di tale scientia" (that is, painting), and that the *inventione* and *misura* which comprise the poet's *scientia* are precisely paralleled by the painter's *inventione* and *misura*: "inventione della materia

[144] Leonardo da Vinci, *Treatise on Painting* (Vatican Library, cod. Urbinas lat. 1270), ed. P. McMahon, 2 vols. (Princeton 1956; hereafter McM.), fol. 4v, McM. 6; and G. Richter, *The Literary Remains of Leonardo da Vinci*, ed. 2, 2 vols. (Oxford 1939) para. 652 (B. N. 2038 fol. 20r, ca. 1492; all MS references abbreviated as in Richter's concordance, pp. 402-421).

[145] Richter 11 (C. A. fol. 117), and Urb. fol. 24v (McM. 55).

[146] Urb. fol. 19 (McM. 41).

[147] Urb. fol. 8 (McM. 30, B. N. 2038, fol. 19, ca. 1492).

[148] Urb. fol. 9 (McM. 30, B. N. 2038, fol. 19v, ca. 1492).

[149] For Bruni, see Krautheimer (n. 57 above) doc. 52; and Isabella's letter of 28 June 1501 (Fletcher [n. 62 above] 704: "Qualche istoria o fabula antiqua aut de suo inventione ne finga una rapresenti cosa antiqua e de bello significato").

[150] Urb. fol. 19 (McM. 41).

[subject-matter?] che lui debbe fingere e misura nelle cose depinge."[151] It might even appear possible to read into these statements an Albertian usage of invention in connection with content alone; that is, if *inventione della materia* applies to subject-matter and *misura* to formal composition. But his other accounts of invention leave no doubt that his conception of the *materia* for painting is not as exclusively literary as Alberti's *inventione* which can give intellectual pleasure independently of its painted representation. Above all, his famous accounts of *inventioni* in stains upon walls should dispel any doubts on this matter. His process of projecting "varie inventioni" into the irregular patterns of wall stains inevitably embraces form and content alike, since the forms in the stains will simultaneously suggest new subjects.[152] The limitless results are "infinite cose" – battles, figures in action, demons, dragons as well as more obvious landscapes.

Leonardo takes great pains in his early writings to emphasize the infinite inventiveness of the artist. Whether he is following Francesco di Giorgio in this, or vice versa cannot be decided certainly, given the inadequate state of our present knowledge of their relationship. But the similarity in their attitudes is as striking as it is unlikely to be coincidental. Leonardo boldly claims that the painter's works are "more infinite than those made by nature" and similarly that the painter invents an infinite number of works that "nature never created."[153] How he is able to reconcile these assertions with his repeated opinion that the works of nature are also infinite is not at all clear.[154] He obviously is not using the term "infinite" in an accurate or precise manner, as his phrase *infinite piu* neatly illustrates. But whatever the imprecisions of his early statements, the similarity to Francesco's views is undeniable.

I suspect that Leonardo's colleague takes priority in this matter. This is suggested by the fact that Leonardo only succeeds some twenty years later in defining the relation between the inventions of man and nature as lucidly as Francesco (though in a slightly different manner): "Nature is concerned only with the production [*produtione*] of elementary things [*semplici*] but man from these elementary things

[151] Urb. fol. 13r-v (McM. 33). For a use of *materia* as "subject-matter" (as well as "medium"), see Rudolf Agricola's *De inventione dialectica* (1479), as quoted by M. Baxandall, "Rudolf Agricola and the Visual Arts," in *Intuition und Kunstwissenschaft: Festschrift für Hans Swarzenski*, ed. P. Bloch et al. (Berlin 1973) 410.

[152] Richter (n. 144 above) 508 (B. N. 2038, fol. 22v, ca. 1492), Urb. (n. 144 above) fol. 35v (McM. 76, B. N. 2038, fol. 22v) – "Modo d'aumentare e destare l'ongegnio a' varie inventione" – and Urb. 33v (McM. 93). See E. Gombrich, "Leonardo's Methods of Working Out Compositions," *Norm and Form* (n. 60 above) 58-63. David Summers has kindly drawn my attention to Leonardo's probable source in Lorenzo de' Medici's account of imaginative projection written in the early 1480s ("Comento ad alcuni sonetti d'amore," in *Scritti scelti*, ed. E. Bigi [Turin 1955] 371), and to the ultimate source in Aristotle (*Parva naturalia: De somnis* 2.460b). For other examples see H. W. Janson, "The 'Image Made by Chance' in Renaissance Thought," repr. in his *16 Studies* (New York 1975) 55-69.

[153] Urb. fol. 50 (McM. 102) and Urb. fol. 15v (McM. 28): "Natura mai le creo." Cf. Urb. fol. 16 (McM. 34) and Urb. fol. 6v (McM. 24).

[154] Richter (n. 144 above) 653, Urb. fol. 8 (McM. 30, B. N. 2038, fol. 19, ca. 1492) and Urb. fol. 38v (McM. 236, B. N. 2038, fol. 26, ca. 1492).

[*semplici*] produces an infinite number of compounds, though he has no power to create [*creare*] any elementary thing except another like himself, that is his children."[155]

Generally in his later writings, discussions of speculative or compositive invention become less common, in accordance with the tendency for his artistic and scientific theories to become more wholly inductive. The kind of inventions with which he is later concerned are often predominantly scientific in nature, like perspective which is an "inventione sottilissima delli studij matematici."[156] This contrasts with his early vision of painting as "ornata d'infinite spectulationi" and embracing all manner of fantasy images: "If the painter wishes to form images of [*fingere*] animals or devils in the inferno, with what abundance of *inventione* his mind teems."[157] Not surprisingly it is during this earlier phase that he is most concerned with *immaginazione* and *fantasia* in the production of a work of art.

That he regarded invention as a component of imagination at this time is confirmed most clearly by his early statement that the artist should "demonstrate in the form of a design the notion [*intentione*] which the *inventione* first made from your *imaginativa.*"[158] Similar statements that *imaginatione* or *fantasia* (using the terms interchangeably during this early period) has a vital conceptual role abound in his early manuscripts. Just as the poet records "manually with the pen those things which are found in his *ingiegnio*," so in painting "the hands represent [*figurano*] that which is found in the *fantasia*."[159] And, in a similar vein: "Whatever exists in the universe through *essentia, presentia* or *imaginatione*, he [the artist] has it first in his mind [*mente*] and then in his hands."[160] The productive process is thus divided into two components, imaginative conception and manual execution, the first of which is given a clear priority: "To devise is the work of the master; to execute the work of the servant."[161]

Some aspects of his early science are characterized by a strongly speculative flavor, as I have attempted to show elsewhere, and his early art theory similarly allows speculation to play a significant role in invention; painting brings "subtle

[155] Windsor 19045, ca. 1510. The text, to be analyzed more fully later, is as follows: "E questo non e in alchuno altro senso perche s'astendano nelle chose che al chontinuo producie la natura la qual non varia le ordinarie spetie delle chose da lei create chome sivariano di tempo in tempo le chose create dall'omo, massimo strumento di natura perche la natura sol s'astende alla produtione de'semplici. Ma l'omo chon tali semplici producie infiniti composti, ma non ha potessta di creare nessuno semplici se non un altro se medesimo cioe li sua figlio." Trans. E. MacCurdy, *The Notebooks of Leonardo da Vinci*, 2 vols. (London 1954) 1.137.

[156] Urb. fol. 27v (McM. 54, Libro A17, ca. 1510; see C. Pedretti, *Leonardo da Vinci on Painting: A Lost Book, Libro A* [London 1965] 38-39).

[157] Urb. fol. 28v (McM. 53; the MS source, B. N. 2038, fol. 24v, ca. 1492, Richter [n. 144 above] 656, is overlooked in McM.'s concordance), and Urb. fol. 6v (McM. 24).

[158] Richter 502 (B. N. 2038, fol. 26, ca. 1492).

[159] Richter 654, Urb. fol. 8v (McM. 30, B. N. 2038, fol. 19v, ca. 1492).

[160] Urb. fol. 5 (McM. 35).

[161] MacCurdy (n. 155 above) 1.85.

speculation to bear on the nature of all forms"; it is "ornata d'infinite speculazzioni" and the painter should avail himself of "notable things composed by subtle speculations."[162] Along with this emphasis upon speculation, he regularly invokes the aid of *fantasia*, particularly in painting as compared to sculpture, because "painting is more beautiful, has more *fantasia* and greater variety."[163] And an applied art, like that of the copper-smiths, is little esteemed because it permits even less scope to *fantasia*.[164]

This use of *fantasia* might at first sight seem equivalent to Filarete's ideas, and some knowledge of Filarete's treatise on Leonardo's part is not out of the question, but on closer examination fundamental differences of approach appear. Whereas Filarete uses *fantasia* in a manner which may predominantly depend upon a distant knowledge of Greek art theory, Leonardo views *fantasia* and *immaginazione* within the context of medieval faculty psychology. A comparison of his cross-section of the human head (fig. 6) with Reisch's version indicates the extent to which Leonardo was operating within traditional concepts, though he radically adapts the Aristotelian division of cerebral labor to his own ends.

He accepts the idea that the *sensus communis* and *fantasia* are closely linked, but after some early experimentation with various arrangements he removes them from the first ventricle and places them with the faculties of intellect in the second cavity.[165] The first ventricle is then given the role of *imprensiva* (or *inprensiva*), a receptor of impressions. Unnamed authorities are cited for this arrangement – he writes that *antichi speculatori* located the *sensus communis* and judgment "in the middle of the head between the *imprensiva* and the memory" – but his system actually seems to be an important departure from the mainstream of Aristotelian theory as transmitted by Avicenna and Mundinus.[166] By means of this arrangement, Leonardo is able more realistically to bring all the cerebral activities into closer conjunction and it provides him with an anatomical justification for the close relationship which he forges between imagination and intellect in his art theory.

Imagination operates in conjunction with the artist's intellectual understanding of the laws of nature to produce an imagined *historia* which obeys natural truth in every

[162] Urb. fol. 4V (McM. 6, B. N. 2038, fol. 20v, ca. 1492), Urb. fol. 28v (McM. 53), and Urb. fol. 36 (McM. 65, B. N. 2038, fol. 26).

[163] Richter (n. 144 above) 656, Urb. fol. 28 (McM. 53, B. N. 2038, fol. 24v, ca. 1492).

[164] Richter 654, Urb. fol. 9 (McM. 30, B. N. 2038, fol. 19v, ca. 1492).

[165] See M. Kemp, "*Il concetto dell'anima* in Leonardo's Early Skull Studies," *Journal of the Warburg and Courtauld Institutes* 34 (1971) esp. 132-134. On 119 I underrated the amount of common ground in the accounts of Avicenna, Albertus Magnus, Bacon and Mundinus, and failed to stress the radical nature of Leonardo's relocation of the *sensus communis* and *fantasia*. Prof. Pedretti has kindly indicated to me that "comocio" (119) should read "como[n] se[n] so." See also K. Keele, "Leonardo da Vinci's Research on the Central Nervous System," *Atti del simposio internationale di storia della neurologia* (Varenna 1961) 12-30.

[166] Richter (n. 144 above) 836 (C. A. fol. 270v). Cf. the similar statement on C. A. 270v (MacCurdy [n. 155 above] 1.192). The *imprensiva* is also discussed in the late MS D.

part. The artist must learn "to make the effects of nature through his *fantasia*." [167] This translation of *fantasia* into a conceptual faculty which can operate in harness with reasoned judgment separates it from its generally lowly status as a source of impermanent impressions in medieval theory and goes much further than Filarete's *fantasticare-pensare* coupling. This does not mean, however, that he entirely discards all the traditional functions of imagination; he still interprets one of its roles as a kind of intermediate memory in the perceptual process and he follows Avicenna in believing that it is responsible for the formation of images in dreams and delusions during illness.[168] But his emphasis upon the rational role of imagination in the production of a work of art is a substantial extension of Avicennian *cogitativa* and lies outside the Arab interpretation of *fantasia* and *imaginatio*.

He also tries to press imagination in his conjectural brain system into the service of his *paragone*. For a time he considered adopting arrangements in which sight possessed some physiological privilege, such as alone passing directly to the intellect; but as he increasingly adopts the notion of the *imprensiva* in the first ventricle, he discards the idea that any of the senses can bypass the *sensus communis*.[169] Instead he proceeds to formulate an argument, again notably close to Francesco's ideas, that an image described in words must be reconstituted by the imagination whereas a visual image requires no such processing. The reconstituted image is far less certain than one received by the eye, because *immaginatione* is to *effetto* as a shadow is to the body casting the shadow.[170] This interpretation of imagination as the former of shadowy images during the process of perception is closer to traditional theory than his early emphasis upon its rational role in the production of a work of art. I believe that this may reflect a shift in his opinion concerning imagination after 1500 – a shift which seems to have occurred at the same time as the *imprensiva* becomes more firmly established in his system. In this context it is worth noting that his definitive illustration of the *imprensiva* dates from the period of the centenarian dissection; that is to say 1508-1509 (fig. 7).

As his art theory becomes more inductively inclined and less involved with speculation, so the *imprensiva, sensus communis* and faculty of judgment become more important to the artist, while the positive role of imagination or *fantasia* appears progressively to decline in prominence. Discussions of imagination are notably rare in his later manuscripts. A late reference to imagination discusses it only in the context of the vividness of images produced in dreams, while *fantasia* fades from the picture altogether.[171] When he discusses invention in the late Libro A (as

[167] Urb. fol. 24v (McM. 48).

[168] Urb. fol. 1v (McM. 21), Urb. fol. 6 (McM. 23), Urb. fol. 36 (McM. 65), Richter 839 (W. 19019v) and Br. M. fol. 278v: "Perche vede piu certa la cosa l'ochio ne' sogni che colla imaginatione, stando desto?"

[169] Kemp (n. 165 above) 119.

[170] Urb. fol. 1v (McM. 21).

[171] Br. M. fol. 278v (see n. 156).

reconstructed by Carlo Pedretti), "judgment" is now seen as the dominant faculty in directing the formation of images.[172] The artist must strive to make his judgment as accurate as possible through a scientific study of natural law. "Subtle speculation" and *fantasia* have no role in achieving this in his late theory.

The concept of invention itself remained with Leonardo throughout his career, and at no point did he feel that there was any possible conflict between the artist's inventiveness and the guiding principle of his art, namely the imitation of nature. That this was so was due in no small part to his particular interpretation of imitation, which for him was no servile procedure of superficial copying but an active ability to remake natural effects in the work of art through a deep understanding of natural causes. In his later theory invention is largely synonymous with the controlled process of remaking, and even in his earlier writings, where he gave *fantasia* freer reign, the faculty of invention still operated in close association with scientific truth – or at least within the context of natural plausibility. Even images of demons and dragons should be based upon a careful study of natural forms.[173]

He always showed a far greater concern with the scientific foundation and rational control of invention than with the origins and nature of the process itself. This is reflected in the fact that he never settled upon a consistent vocabulary to denote the production of a work of art, whereas his conception of the controlling factors, most notably judgment and understanding, remained relatively constant. He used at least seven verbs to indicate the "creation" of a painting. Unexceptionally, the one which occurs with sufficient regularity to be called his standard usage is *fare*, the standard verb of production and, as such, almost invariably used in contracts. What may be called specialized terms of artistic production occur occasionally in his writings. *Fingere* (already encountered in Bruni and Alberti) and *figurare* may be said to fall into this category, and are not surprisingly associated with *fantasia* and the production of *fintioni* in the early period.[174] His other verbs of artistic production – *creare, partorire, nascere* and *generare* – all carry biological or natural associations which convey his attitude more clearly than any other factor.[175] The artist, in a sense, gives birth to works of art, and in common with such processes of

[172] Libro A 15, Urb. fol. 157 (McM. 437, Pedretti [n. 156 above] 35) and Libro A 28, Urb. fols. 44-54 (McM. 274, 86-87, Pedretti 53). Leonardo's conception of judgment is analyzed by M. Kemp, "*Ogni dipintore dipinge se*: A Neoplatonic Echo in Leonardo's Art Theory?" *Cultural Aspects of the Italian Renaissance: Essays in Honour of P. O. Kristeller,* ed. C. H. Clough (Manchester 1976) 311-323. My brief statement (316) of medieval interpretations of imagination is oversimplified, particularly with regard to Avicenna.

[173] Richter (n. 144 above) 585 (B. N. 2038, fol. 29). See Kemp (n. 165 above) 133.

[174] E. g., Urb. fol. 6v (McM. 24), Urb. fols. 13-4 (McM. 33), Urb. fols. 8-9 (McM. 30) and Urb. fol. 12v (McM. 42). For Valla's definition of *fingere*, see n. 84 above. *Fictione* (*finctione* and other variants) is mentioned on Urb. fol. 9 (McM. 30), Urb. fol. 18v (McM. 41), Urb. fol. 12v (McM. 42) and Urb. fol. 15 (McM. 28).

[175] *Creare*: Urb. fol. 15 (McM. 28, re. proportion in art), Urb. fol. 16v (McM. 39), Urb. fol. 124 (McM. 396), Libro A 15, Urb. fol. 157 (McM. 437), W. 19045 (McCurdy [n. 155 above] 137) and cf. Urb. fol. 16 (McM. 34) where the art of painting is praised as "eccellentissimo sopra

reproduction the offspring will tend to resemble their parents. This principle is reflected in auto-mimesis in painting; that is the tendency of all artists to produce figures resembling themselves in appearance, as expressed in the aphorism *ogni dipintore dipinge se.*[176]

Artistic creation thus takes its place in the natural order of microcosmic things; the universal creative force of nature generates all natural species of things, and man produces his works in a broadly analogous manner. During the last decades of the *quattrocento* Lenoardo tends to assume that the macro-microcosmic parallels are exact. Although he later analyzes the correspondences more critically – as we noted when quoting from Windsor 19045r, he stresses that man makes infinite compounds from elementary (or "natural") things but cannot produce any natural elements on his own account except his own children – but the general parallel is still taken to hold good.[177] Indeed, the definition of microcosmic principles is often sharpened by the more precise comparison between similarities and differences in the constituent parts and processes of the universe.

His later analyses of the relationship between the productive powers of man and nature allow him to provide a clear statement of what he sees as the "divine" power of man's production of "infinite things." A note on W. 19030v, closely related to 19045r and similarly datable 1508-1509, explains that "man does not vary from the animals except in accidental things [*accidentale*] and it is in this that he shows himself to be a divine thing [*cosa divina*] ; for where nature finishes its production with its species [*spezie*] , there man begins with natural things to make with the aid of this nature infinite species of things, which [ability] is not necessary for him who governs himself adequately (?) as do the animals and for which it is not the custom of these animals to seek."[178] These natural things (or *semplici* as they are called on 19045r) include all species of plants and animals and all the elements which are regarded in Aristotelian fashion as the basic units of nature. He cites as an example of man's inability to produce *semplici* the inevitable failure of alchemists to "create" gold; while as an instance of man's ability to compose infinite things from the basic *semplici* he discusses the enormously diverse sounds and languages which arise from the combined actions of the lips, tongue and windpipe.[179] Man's creative powers are

---

tutte l'oltre cose create da dio." *Partorire*: Urb. fol. 4v (McM. 6), Urb. fol. 2v (McM. 5), Urb. fol. 7v (McM. 15) and Urb. fol. 19 (McM. 19). *Nascere*: Urb. fol. 15 (McM. 28) and Urb. fol. 19 (McM. 19). *Generare*: Urb. fol. 5 (McM. 35), and see Urb. fol. 27v (McM. 987) for *generare* and *creare* as synonymous in a natural process, the production of clouds. The above is merely a list of examples, not a comprehensive concordance.

[176] Libro A 15 and 28 (Pedretti [n. 156] 35 and 53). See Kemp (n. 172 above).

[177] See n. 155 above.

[178] A translation is provided by McCurdy (n. 155 above) 116. The last section presents some difficulty: "Le quali non essendo necessarie a chi ben si corregge, come far li animali, e essi animali non e disspositione cercane."

[179] W. 19045-6 and 19070v. Cf. Urb. fol. 16 (McM. 34): "Li semplici naturali sono finiti e l'opere che l'ochio commanda sono infinite."

thus not precisely God-like, but operate in their own manner on a different level of the microcosm. It is in this unique kind of creativity that the "divinity" of the artist rests. Not surprisingly, this considered and original statement of man's "divine" productivity occurs during the period when he achieved his most coherent definition of the relationship between divinity and man in the context of nature.[180]

The verb *creare* is used on three occasions in the passage on 19045r.[181] A related use of *creatione* also occurs in the late Libro A, and he similarly talks about the *creatione* of painting (and by implication of music) in a section of the *Trattato* probably dating from after 1500.[182] No such specifically artistic uses of *creare* or *creatione* appear to occur in his earlier writings. The later instances are not sufficiently numerous to justify a claim that *creare* is a standard term of artistic production in his late theory, but its transference from the processes of God and nature to man's activities is undoubtedly significant in that it reflects his growing sense of man's unique place in the natural order of things.

The picture of divine creativity in man which emerges from his earlier writings is far more speculative and less precisely formulated. At one point he expresses a particularly high-flown notion of the painter's role: "The divinity which is the science of painting transmutes itself into a semblance of the divine mind in such a manner that it discourses with free power concerning the generation of the diverse essences of various plants, animals, and so on."[183] This probably reflects the same Neoplatonic influences as are apparent in his assertion that whatever exists "in the universe through essence, presence or imagination, he has it first in his mind and then in his hands."[184] He even goes so far as to claim that painting is more than a science – "not only a science but also a divinity, the name of which should be duly revered and which repeats all the works of God the most high" – and that the artist is "*signore e dio* of all the things he wishes to generate."[185] These interpretations of creativity, with their emphasis upon inner invention which is "made first in your *imaginativa*," are wholly consistent with the weight which he places upon "speculation" in his early definitions of art, noted above.[186]

In the early phase, therefore, invention, *fantasia*, speculation and divine creativity go hand in hand. Although Leonardo himself moved away from this approach

[180] See M. Kemp, "Dissection and Divinity in Leonardo's Late Anatomies," *Journal of the Warburg and Courtauld Institutes* 35 (1972) esp. 211f.

[181] See note 155 above.

[182] Libro A 15, Urb. fol. 157 (McM. 437) and Urb. fol. 18v (McM. 39). See also note 164 above. Panofsky's statement that Leonardo uses *creare* in an artistic context on only one occasion (*Renaissance and Renascences in Western Thought*, rev. ed. [Uppsala 1965] 188n.) is therefore incorrect.

[183] Urb. fol. 36 (McM. 280). Cf. the related statements regarding the divinity of painting on Urb. fols. 19v-20 (McM. 25), Urb. fols. 15v-16 (McM. 34), Urb. fol. 12v (McM. 42) and Urb. fol. 15 (McM. 28).

[184] Urb. fol. 5 (McM. 35).

[185] Urb. fol. 50r-v (McM. 102), and Urb. fol. 5 (McM. 35).

[186] Richter (n. 144 above) 502 (B. N. 2038, fol. 26, ca. 1492).

towards a more disciplined interpretation of invention and judgment, more in line with his later scientific method, the manner in which he insists during the 1490s upon the divine power of painting is nevertheless of considerable historical importance in the context of *quattrocento* notions of divine creativity in the various arts. This context will occupy much of our attention in the subsequent section.

A DIVINELY-INSPIRED GENIUS?

In the important branch of classical poetics derived from Platonism and recorded by Cicero, Horace and Seneca, no easy separation can be made between concepts of *ingenium*, inspiration and divine insight. Renaissance poetic theory was at various times so deeply influenced by this tradition that it is equally unrealistic to discuss fifteenth-century interpretations of *ingenium* and divine inspiration in isolation from each other.

We have already touched upon the ideas of *fantasia* and prophetic madness in Plato's philosophy. These are most fully exploited in poetic theory in his *Ion*: "Poets compose their beautiful poems not by skill but because they are inspired and possessed." In other words, "not in their right minds"; and similarly, "The poet is a light and winged and holy thing and there is no invention in him until he has been inspired and is out of his senses."[187] In the *Phaedrus*, Plato again contrasts mere "technical skill" with the inspiration of "those who are mad," referring to the required quality of insanity as "the Muses' madness."[188] This serves to remind us that classical Antiquity invariably attributed inspiration not to a wholly inner agency but to the Muses' divine power.

The clearest reflection of Plato's ideas, and by far the most influential source for the Renaissance, is to be found in Cicero's *De oratore*: "I have often heard it said, as they say Democritus and Plato have written, that no man can be a good poet who is not on fire (*inflammatione*) and inspired by something like frenzy (*afflatu quasi furoris*)".[189] This formulation, again attributed to Democritus and Plato, is repeated in Cicero's *De divinatione* where he claims that *afflatus* is a "divine power within the soul."[190] The association between this form of inspiration and *ingenium* is made explicit by Seneca: "There never has been any great *ingenium* without some touch of

[187] Plato, *Ion* 533-534.

[188] Plato, *Phaedrus* 245a. Cf. G. Grube, *The Greek and Roman Critics* (London 1965) 46f., and Harriott (n. 96 above) 78-91. See also J. Atkins, *Literary Criticism in Antiquity*, 2 vols. (Cambridge 1934), and R. Lodge, *Plato's Theory of Art* (London 1953).

[189] Cicero, *De oratore* 2.46.194.

[190] Cicero, *De divinatione* 1.37.80. Democritus's importance in formulating the notion of poetic madness is confirmed by Horace, *Ars poetica* 295-301.

madness."[191] Renaissance interest in this last passage is illustrated by its direct quotation in the *De secreto conflictu* of Petrarch.[192]

Ingenium was the inborn characteristic without which highest achievements were impossible, but Cicero is at pains to stress that it cannot on its own result in perfect works. The Romans, for example, innately possessed *ingenium* and *cogitatione* but these factors could only bear full fruit as his ancestors gradually acquired learning, rationality and understanding of rules.[193] In classical theory *ingenium* is associated unquestioningly with the literary and rhetorical arts, but it is rarely even mentioned in discussion of painting, sculpture and architecture. Pliny provides one of these rare instances when he assesses the abilities of Timanthes, "in whose works more is always implied than depicted and whose skill [*ars*], though consumate, is always surpassed by his *ingenium.*"[194] But neither Pliny nor any other classical author extend a fully poetic concept of divinely-inspired genius to any practitioner of the visual arts. This form of exclusion sets the pattern for Renaissance attitudes and only late in the day do humanists begin to relax their outlook to a significant degree.

Renaissance assimilation of Cicero's accounts of inspiration and genius was extremely thorough. Petrarch was characteristically cautious in his attitude towards "creative insanity," but even he quoted with approval Cicero's statement that "poetry depends solely on an inborn faculty, is aroused by a purely mental activity and is inspired as if with a divine spirit."[195] This same quotation was adopted as a statement of principle by both Boccaccio and Salutati.[196] Boccaccio aligned himself more explicitly than Petrarch with classical concepts of divine inspiration when he defined poetry as "fervor quidam exquisite inveniendi atque dicendi, seu scribendi, quod inveneris. Qui ex sinu Dei procedens, paucis mentibus, ut arbitror, in creatione conceditur, ex quo, quoniam mirabilis sic, rarissimi semper fuere poete."[197] Salutati equally follows the Ciceronian lead by opening his *De laboribus Herculis* with an extended account of *afflatus* and poetic genius.[198] This tradition is also reflected by

[191] Seneca, *De tranquillitate animi* 17.10-12: "Nullum magnum ingenium sine mixtura dementiae fuit." A history of genius is provided by E. Zilsel, *Die Entstehung des Geniebegriffes* (Tübingen 1926).

[192] Petrarch, *De secreto conflictu curarum mearum*, in *Francesco Petrarcha Prose: La letteratura italiana* 7 (1955) 174.

[193] Cicero, *De oratore* 1.5.

[194] Pliny, *Historia naturalis* 25.36.74.

[195] Cicero, *Pro Archia* 8.18; and Petrarch, *Invective contra medicum* 1.286-289, ed. P. G. Ricci (Rome 1950) 33: "A summis ... hominibus eruditissimisque sic accepimus: ceterarum rerum studia et doctrina et preceptis et arte constare; poetam natura ipsa valere, et mentis viribus excitari, et quasi divino quodam spiritu inflari."

[196] Boccaccio, *Genealogia deorum gentilium* 14.7 (Osgood [n. 46 above] 41); and Salutati, *De fato et fortuna*. See Tateo (n. 46 above) 70.

[197] Boccaccio, *Gen. deorum gent.* 14.7.

[198] Salutati, *De laboribus Herculis* 1.3-4.

Gianozzo Manetti, who speaks of "poetae divino quodam spiritu afflati," and by Antonio de Ferraris who quoted Virgil's *Georgics* to illustrate that the poet is "inspired [*afflatus*] by a divine spirit" which makes man "similar to God."[199] An early and weighty precedent for belief in the divinity of poetry was provided by "Statius" in Dante's *Purgatory*, who credited his inspiration to that "great fire divine whence many another, thousand by thousand, fetched their light and flame; I mean the Aeneid [of Virgil]."[200]

However, it should not be forgotten that an important intellectual challenge to all this rapture for Ciceronian *afflatus* came from Leonardo Bruni, who was particularly severe upon Boccaccio's interpretation of Dante. There are two kinds of poet, according to Bruni. The first, of whom Saint Francis is an example, rely upon their "own genius, excited and aroused by some inward and hidden force termed frenzy and possession of the soul . . . whence some say that poetry is divine."[201] The second group, amongst whom Dante is supreme, base their poetry upon knowledge, study, discipline, art, forethought, philosophy, theology, astrology, arithmetic, geometry, history, and so on. The second type is greatly to be preferred in that their poetry is neither "poor nor fantastic."[202] Bruni's attitude would not have been hard to reconcile with Alberti's or Ghiberti's Vitruvian requirements for the knowledgeable artist, but there is no clear evidence to suggest that this happened – perhaps largely because the groundswell of poetic theory moved against Bruni, most of all when Ficino introduced his brand of Neoplatonism.

While *ingenium* was automatically associated with all the pursuits close to the humanists' hearts, law included, few humanist critics were prepared to grant *ingenium* to a professional painter, sculptor or architect.[203] To be sure, there were few statements specifically to the effect that *ingenium* and the visual arts were inimical, but this is because most humanists tacitly assumed that it was so. Probably the most explicit exclusion of the painter was voiced by Leonello d'Este in Angelo Decembrio's *De politia littaria*. In answer to the Horatian claim that the painter may "venture as freely in his pictures as a poet does in his songs, and paint a guilded ram flying with wings," Leonello challenges the *manus* of the painter to evoke the passing seasons or capture the depth of human emotions in the manner which can be accomplished by the mind of the poet. In short, he concludes that the "*ingenium* of writers . . . is a divine thing and beyond the reach of painters."[204] However, the fact

[199] I. (Gianozzo) Manetti, *Vita Dantis* (Florence 1747) 42 (written ca. 1440-1445); and A. de Ferraris, *Il Galateo*, ed. E. Garin, *La disputa delle arti nel quattrocento* (Florence 1947) 156-157 (composed during the 1490s?). Cf. Virgil, *Georgics* 2.475.

[200] Dante, *Divina commedia, Purgatorio* 21.95-97.

[201] *Le vite di Dante e di Petrarca*, ed. H. Baron, *Leonardo Bruni Aretino* (Leipzig 1928) 59.

[202] "Lo studio principale fu poesia, ma non sterile, nè povera, nè fantastica, ma fecundata ed inricchita, stabilita da vera scienza e da moltissime discipline." *Ibid.* 59.

[203] For an assertion of *ingenium* with regard to law, see P. Bracciolini in Garin (n. 199 above) 11 and 14.

[204] Baxandall (n. 58 above) 310-319.

that Decembrio's Leonello feels compelled to make such an assertion probably reflects the growing claims for *ingenium* from partisans of the visual arts. Slowly but surely these claims were becoming more common, though the accolade of *ingenium* was more likely to be accorded to an artist in a relatively limited manner to mean "innate cleverness," rather than with connotations of divine inspiration.

I am aware of only one possible instance of a medieval artist being acclaimed for his *ingenium*; an inscription on Modena Cathedral in praise of the architect Lanfranco open with the words, "Ingenio clarus Lanfrancus doctus et aptus/est operis princeps hujus rectorque magister."[205] But the inscription as it now exists is at best an accurate copy of an earlier version and its origins cannot be assigned unquestionably to the eleventh century. A second medieval example is provided by Ristoro d'Arezzo (*La composizione del mondo*, ca. 1282), who openly associated "disegnatori e scolpitori et dipintori" with "ingiegnio" in the section devoted to the influence of Mercury.[206] But for the first generally accredited *ingenium* in the visual arts we have to wait until the century of Giotto, around whom humanist art criticism began to take root. Petrarch discerned qualities of "manus et ingenium" in one of Giotto's works, and Boccaccio granted him an "ingegno" of excellence; but neither author suggested that the painter's qualities should be regarded as fully equivalent to those of literary men.[207] Later in the century, Villani more wholly equated Giotto's abilities with those required for the humanist's own pursuits; not only did he praise the painter's works as rivalling poetry in profound content, but he also accorded him "alto ingenio tenacique memoria," and more generally spoke of "nobilissimi ingenii singularisque memorie" in connection with the visual arts.[208] The faculty of *ingegno* also provides a similar basis for the equation of artists, most notably Giotto, with the Greek masters in a strange passage in Giovanni da Prato's *Il Paradiso degli Alberti* which records conversations supposedly held in the late 1380s but which was probably not written until about 1426.[209]

[205] G. Crichton, *Romanesque Sculpture in Italy* (London 1954) 4.

[206] R. d'Arezzo, *La composizione del mondo* 4.6, ed. E. Narducci (Rome 1859) 225-227: "Et significa secondo et savi. Tucti coloro kanno lanima soctile ad intendere in suctilita perkel regno sia bene fornito dogni ingiegnio et suctilita come sono disegnatori e scolpitori et dipintori" (ref. kindly provided by Michael Baxandall).

[207] Petrarch, *Itinerarium Syriacum,* cited by Baxandall, *Giotto* (n. 4 above) 51; and Boccaccio, *Decamerone* 6.5.

[208] Villani, *De origine*, quoted from Baxandall, *Giotto* 70-71 and 146-147. Villani's emphasis upon *memoria* is probably the first instance of a Ciceronian requirement for rhetoric being exploited in art criticism. Cf. Bruni's criteria for Ghiberti's doors; they should be *illustri* and *significanti*, the latter of which is based upon "importanza degna di memoria" (Krautheimer [n. 57 above] doc. 52). Cf. Cicero, *De invent.* 1.7.

[209] G. da Prato, *Il Paradiso degli Alberti*, ed. Wesselofsky, 16 (Bologna 1867) 185-186: "No' ci acostano su a queste stelle/ E mia donna mi disse 'Mira bene / L'alme che raggian che paion facelle: / Fidia, Apollo et Pulicreto viene / Con Giotto e Tamaris la dolce figlia, / E Micheon sue padre per man tene. / L'altro che vedi ch 'uzza si le ciglia, / Taddeo é quello, e Andrea é co' lui / Della citta della 'nsegna vermiglia, / che nel taglio mostro gl' ingegni sui' " (ref. kindly provided

Trecento references to artist-*ingegni* remain, however, the exception rather than the rule. More regular claims for *ingenium* in the visual arts did not occur until the era of Brunelleschi and Alberti. If Taccola's account may be regarded as substantially reliable, it would seem that Brunelleschi was self-consciously valuing and guarding the fruits of his own *ingegno* as early as 1427-1430.[210] And certainly during the following decade Alberti exhibits no reluctance to credit Brunelleschi with "ingegno maraviglioso." In his Italian dedication to *Della pittura* he boldly claims that the *ingegno* possessed by Brunelleschi, Donatello, Ghiberti, Luca della Robbia and Masaccio is in no way inferior to that of the acients, though he had once believed that tired nature no longer produced *ingegni* – a belief expressed in terms derived from Pliny's *Letters*.[211] Alberti was not only promoting the intellectual merits of the visual arts, but aiming also to promote them socially. To this latter end he ingeniously exploits the similarity between *ingenium* and *ingenuus* (free-born or liberal) when he dedicates the Latin version to Francesco Gonzaga.[212]

However, in true Ciceronian fashion, he reminds the reader that a man's *ingenium* is not on its own sufficient to produce perfect works of art. And he exploits the famous Zeuxis anecdote to prove his point. The story of Zeuxis's selection of the best parts of various beautiful figures to produce an ideal form had been pressed into the service of a variety of disparate causes: Cicero had used it as an analogy for his eclectic method of "culling the flower from various geniuses;" for Boccaccio it had been an illustration of the power of *ingegno* in forming images; while Alberti now uses it to exhort artists to refer constantly to nature herself and not to "rely upon one's own *ingegnio* in setting about painting as do most of the painters of the present day."[213] The kind of external, natural factors with which *ingenium* must interact are the rules of nature, such as perspective and proportion. Thus it is that *ingenium* must be closely associated with *doctrina*; that is, "doctrine" in the sense of true knowledge rather than as a mindless set of rules.

Later, in *De re aedificatoria*, Alberti claims that three factors contribute to beauty and ornament: *ingenium* gives the work its fundamental *dignitas* (profound worth) by the exercise of *electio* (selection), *distributio* (division), *collocatio* (arrangement), and so on, all intellectual acts of composition; the physical act of execution is carried out by *manus* which provides the quality of *gratias* (grace) through skills such as *acervatio* (building up), *affictio* (attaching), *amputatio* (reducing), *circumcisio*

---

by Michael Baxandall). For its dating, see H. Baron, *The Crisis of the Early Italian Renaissance* (Princeton 1966) 333-334.

210 See Prager (n. 13 above) 131-149.

211 Alberti (n. 48 above) p. 32. The derivation was noted by E. Gombrich, "A Classical Topos in the Introduction to Alberti's *della Pittura*," *Journal of the Warburg and Courtauld Institutes* 20 (1957) 173 (Pliny the Younger, Letters 6.21). *Ingenium* is subsequently used throughout *De pictura* on numerous occasions.

212 Alberti (n. 13 above) p. 34.

213 Cicero, *De inventione* 2.1.3-4; Boccaccio, *Il comento alla divina comedia*, ed. D. Guerri, 2 (Bari 1918) 128-129; and Alberti (n. 13 above) 3.56 (p. 98).

(trimming) and *expolitio* (polishing); *Natura* herself contributes the inherently admirable qualities of the materials, as expressed in *gravitas* (weight), *levitas* (lightness), *densitas* (thickness), *puritas* (purity) and so on.[214] *Ingenium*, as in Cicero's system for rhetoric, stands at the head of the attributes for the architect, but it cannot function properly without the other factors and the necessary constraints. Above all, it must not go berserk with its own powers and invent monstrosities.[215] He had already shrewdly observed in *De pictura* that many orators and poets begin works with great enthusiasm, but when the ardor of genius cooled, leave them in a rough and unfinished state; diligence (Ciceronian *diligentia*) and persistence are therefore required no less than *ingenium.*[216] Alberti exhibits a consistent suspicion of inspirational fervor – as of all extremes. Those artists who surrender to the dictates of *fervens ingenium* will paint figures which are excessively histrionic in gesture.[217]

Ghiberti makes many of the same points in his *Commentaries*. The association between *ingegno* and *dottrina* appears prominently in his exposition of Giotto's virtues, and he praises Ambrogio Lorenzetti as "a great *ingegno*, most noble draughtsman and fully conversant with the theory [*teorica*] of his art."[218] In Ciceronian and Albertian fashion he also stresses the need for *ingegno* to be accompanied by *disciplina*. He expresses this view by means of an axiom drawn from Vitruvius and later adapted by Francesco di Giorgio. Their three versions are as follows: Vitruvius: "Neque ingenium sine disciplina aut disciplina sine ingenio perfectum arteficem potest efficere"; Ghiberti: "Lo ingegnio sança disciplina o la disciplina sança ingegnio non puo perfetto artefice"; Francesco: "Lo ingegno senza dottrina o la dottrina senza ingegno l'artefice perfetto far non puo."[219] Francesco's substitute of *dottrina* for *disciplina* is no doubt deliberate; he clearly wishes to exploit the former term's intellectual connotations of learning and knowledge rather than *disciplina's* associations with codes of routine to be followed with unquestioning diligence.

Francesco also extends the axiom by introducing a third factor, *disegno*, which he humanistically weaves into the scheme with neat skill. Many speculative *ingegni* of the past have invented many things, Francesco acknowledges, but these have been difficult to understand because of the lack of visual demonstration in drawings: "Just as we see many who have *dottrina* and do not have *ingegno* and many are endowed with *ingegno* and not with *dottrina*, so many have *dottrina* and *ingegno* but do not have *disegno.*"[220] Nowhere in Renaissance art theory are the three levels of ability

[214] Alberti (n. 9 above) 6.4 (2.459).

[215] *Ibid.* 9.10 (2.857-859).

[216] Alberti (n. 48 above) 3.61 (p. 104).

[217] *Ibid.* 44 (p. 85).

[218] Ghiberti (n. 6 above) fols. 9 (p. 37) and 10 (p. 41). Taddeo Gaddi is comparably credited with *dottrina, arte* and *ingegno* (fol. 9, p. 38).

[219] Vitruvius, 1.1.3; Ghiberti fol. 1v (p. 5); and F. di Giorgio, *Tratt.* (n. 12 above) 1.37.

[220] Di Giorgio 2.489.

which are necessary for the artist – innate brilliance of mind, acquired learning and executant skill – so clearly encapsulated in a single sentence.

As an innate factor, *ingenium* may be possessed by an individual or not, as the case may be; if not, there is nothing he can do about it. The implication is that *ingenium* is an individual factor, but the nature of its individuality is barely even mentioned within the framework of Renaissance art theory, let alone analyzed in detail. Cennini, as we have seen, precociously attributed artistic individuality to *fantasia* and regarded individual style as something to which the painter should aspire. But he does not amplify either of these points. Alberti acknowledges that nature provides each *ingenium* with its own particular gifts, but regards this as a limitation to be overcome by the universal artist rather than as a welcome expression of individuality.[221] A more positive attitude is taken by Lorenzo Valla, who in a chapter of *De vero falsoque bono* devoted to the proposition that "contemplative life is a form of pleasure," writes that he knowledgeably delights in seeing images by either Phidias or Praxiteles because "I understand the diversity of *ingenium* of the two artists."[222] Later Filarete noted what any perceptive observer of painting could hardly fail to see, namely that each artist has his own style ("la sua maniera").[223] But he is at a loss to provide a coherent explanation, falling back upon the lame expedient that God must have done it for the best.[224] Individual variations of form are, he informs us, the gift of a wise God, who has granted man's *ingegno* the power to make forms in man's image and thus to "participate" in godly matters. Why this is so and how it results in individuality we are not told. Filarete clearly has been provided with no established answer from traditional theory.

Only Leonardo, in his well-organized theory of automimesis, provides a logical solution to Filarete's dilemma. Each man's soul is individual, Leonardo claims with impeccable Thomist orthodoxy. Judgment, the power which directs man's invention of forms, is a faculty of the soul and will therefore exhibit corresponding variations from individual to individual. The soul is also responsible for the individual forms of each man's body. Thus it is that the figures invented by the artist and directed by his judgment resemble himself in appearance.[225] Individual style is explained, but is wholly undesirable for Leonardo since it distorts natural truth and beauty; the idiosyncrasies of individual judgment must be overridden by absolute standards

[221] Alberti (n. 48 above) 60 (pp. 102-103).

[222] Valla, *De vero falsoque bono*, ed. M. de Panizza Lorch (Bari 1970) (as *De voluptate* 2.36, *Opera* [Basel 1540] 953): "Et ego quoque plus delector gemino simulachro studiae Phidiae et Praxitilis, quam unus quilibet puerorum, quia utriusque artificis ingenium diversitatem intelligo, quod puer ignorat" (ref. kindly provided by Michael Baxandall). Valla may have taken his cue from Cicero, *De oratore* 3.7.

[223] Filarete (n. 5 above) 2.489.

[224] Cf. Dante, *Paradiso* 8.90-148 for a more profound statement of God's intention in granting individuality to man.

[225] Libro A 15, Urb. fol. 175 (n. 144 above) (McM. 437, Pedretti [n. 156 above] 35), and Libro A 28, Urb. fols. 44-45 (McM. 86-87 and 274, Pedretti 53). See Kemp (n. 172 above).

derived from a rigorous investigation of natural law. Not until the advent of Courbet and Zola were theories of naturalism to be formulated which could happily embrace both individual genius and universal imitation.

* * *

By the end of the fifteenth century the more self-conscious and knowing Renaissance artists, such as Mantegna, did not doubt that *ingenium* was a necessary attribute for the artist. Professional humanists, on the other hand, were not so sure. We have already encountered Leonello d'Este's allegedly negative reaction.[226] I know of no such overt statements in the later *quattrocento*, but many of the humanists who had cause to mention the visual arts fail to acknowledge the claims of Alberti and company. The epitaphs for famous artists are a convenient case in point; they are often as significant for what they omit as for what they actually say. Certain platitudes abound – "a second Apelles," "surpassing even the ancients," "rivalling nature herself" and "figures lacking only speech" – but notions of *ingenium* and divine inspiration are more than uncommon. Poliziano's epitaphs for Giotto and Filippo Lippi, for example, composed at the request of Lorenzo de'Medici, speak of *manus*, *artifex* and the revival of "extinct" painting, but his language nowhere suggests that he credits painters with the same power as poets.[227] To be sure, Poliziano's dedication of *De re aedificatoria* to Lorenzo credits Alberti with "fine genius" and "exquisite learning," but he does so primarily in drawing attention to Alberti's literary and rhetorical gifts.[228]

Against this general pattern of inertia in humanist attitudes must be set a growing trickle of exceptions. The contrast between the reactions of Dondi (1375) and Poggio (ca. 1429) to antique sculpture is symptomatic of this trend. Dondi merely notes the reaction of a contemporary artist who acclaimed classical remains with great fervor, "as if he wanted to say that by the *ingenium* of such great artists, nature had not just been imitated but indeed surpassed."[229] Poggio by contrast is himself "moved by the *ingenium* of the artist" when he sees "how the very forces of nature are represented in marble," and he admits with a hint of guilt that he is himself "forced to admire their *ingenium* and art, since they render a mute and lifeless thing as if it breathed and spoke; often indeed they represent the emotions of the soul."[230]

Architects were the artists most likely to be acclaimed as *ingegni*. Brunelleschi was

[226] Baxandall (n. 58 above) 310-319.

[227] As recorded by G. Vasari, *Le vite de' piu eccellenti pittori, scultori ed architetti,* ed. G. Milanesi (Florence 1906) 1.409 and 2.630.

[228] Alberti (n. 9 above) p. 3: "Baptista Leo Florentinus et clarissima Albertorum familia vir ingenii elegantis, accerrimi iudicci, exquisitissimae doctrinae . . . ."

[229] See Baxandall, *Giotto* (n. 4 above) 52, and Panofsky (n. 182 above) 208-209. For Dondi, see R. Weiss, *The Renaissance Discovery of Classical Antiquity* (Oxford 1969) 49-53.

[230] P. Bracciolini, *Epistolae*, ed. F. de Tonellis (Florence 1831) 4.15 and 21.

twice notably credited with *ingegno* (and, incidentally, with *fantasia*) by Alberti's percipient patron, Giovanni Rucellai, while Alberti himself, Laurana, Giuliano da Sangallo, Aristotele da Bologna, Francesco di Giorgio and Guiniforte Solari were all accorded comparable status in humanist writings or official documents.[231] A combination of a number of factors placed architects in this relatively favorable position. The "rediscovery" of Vitruvius undoubtedly helped, as did the lack of any deeply entrenched notion of the training and role of the architect during the preceding centuries. The necessity of his being skilled as an *ingegnario* and in some aspects of geometry also gave him claims to special qualities. The painter could point to his comparable command of perspective, but by and large the humanists do not appear to have set much store by the painters' new science. When Fazio refers to Pisanello and Gentile da Fabriano as *ingenii* he is typically attracted more by their detailed naturalism than by any command of *doctrina*. His other *ingenii*, Ghiberti and Donatello, could be said to qualify on both counts but Fazio concentrates instead upon their workmanship.[232]

The general impression is that the majority of humanists were insensitive to the new ideals of Renaissance painting, excepting a delight in naturalism. Only when a painter exhibited a quite exceptional grasp of Antiquity in its broader intellectual aspects could he expect to be ranked as an *ingenium*, as was Mantegna in 1484.[233] Beyond such occasional references to individual artists, straightforward statements of principle that painting or sculpture required an *ingenium* equal to that of poetry or rhetoric are rare amongst humanist works. Aeneas Silvius Piccolomini's tidy formulation is the most explicit: "Ingenium pictura expetit, ingenium eloquentia cupit non volgare sed altum et summum."[234] However, even this statement is not intended primarily as an attempt to promote the status of painting but to support his thesis that the arts flourish together at times of general excellence in society, as in classical Antiquity. Generally it is characteristic of the humanists that they find it

[231] Brunelleschi: in G. Rucellai's *Zibaldone Quaresimale*, ed. A. Perosa, Studies of the Warburg Institute (London 1960) 55, where Brunelleschi is given the accolade of "singhulare huomo d'architettura . . . sommo in gieometria e perfetto maestro di scoltura; e in simile chose aveva grandissimo ingiegno e fantasia." Cf. 61 where he is credited with "ingiegnio naturale e fantasia." The *Zibaldone* was begun in 1457. Laurana: the patent granted by Federigo da Montefeltro, 10 June 1468, in P. Rotondi, *Il palazzo ducale di Urbino*, 2 vols. (Urbino 1950) 1.109-110, where architecture is described as an "arte di gran scienza e di grandi ingegno." Sangallo: contract for S. M. delle Carceri, 4 October 1485, in G. Milanesi, *Nuovi documenti per la storia dell' arte toscana* (Florence 1901) 136-139. Aristotele: letter from the lieutenant of Bologna, in C. Gualandi, *Memorie originale risguardanti le belle arte*, ser. 5 (Bologna 1844) 102-104. Francesco di Giorgio: letter of the Anziani, 29 August 1491, in A. Weller, *Francesco di Giorgio, 1439-1501* (Chicago 1943) doc. 99. Solari in L. Beltrami, "Leonardo negli studi per il tiburio della cathedrale di Milano," *Luca Beltrami e il duomo di Milano* (Milan 1964) 362.

[232] Baxandall, *Giotto* (n. 4 above) 164-168.

[233] Kristeller (n. 54 above) doc. 40. For later developments, see E. Panofsky, "Artist, Scientist, Genius," in his *The Renaissance: Six Essays* (New York 1962) 123-182, also R. and M. Wittkower, *Born under Saturn* (London 1963) 60f.

[234] Quoted from Spencer (n. 45 above) 27.

easier to attribute *ingenium* to the safely-deceased artists of Antiquity than to those contemporary painters and sculptors who represented a socially-ambitious group within their own society.

* * *

In this largely restricted climate, it is not surprising that poetic ideals of divine inspiration were little exploited in the literature on the visual arts. Leonardo's loosely-formulated notions of the painter's god-like powers in his notes during the 1490s have been examined in the third section of this study. Before 1490 only Alberti made a serious attempt to establish the "divinity" of painting. In the Italian introduction to *Della pittura* he places painting, sculpture and architecture at the head of the "divine arte e scienze" of Antiquity.[235] Subsequently, in the opening paragraphs of Book 2 he provides four reasons why painting may be considered to possess "divine power." Firstly, painting transcends time by transmitting images of individuals to posterity. In the second place, painted images act as an aid to worship and religious understanding. The third is that painters like Zeuxis, in "forming images of [*fingendis*] or painting living things, appeared as if a god amongst mortals." And finally, "masters who see their works admired . . . feel themselves to be almost like a god" – an argument which may reflect the section in Lucian's *Somnium* in which "Statuary" claims (much to the disgust of "Education") that Phidias, Polykleitos and Praxiteles "are now worshipped along with the gods."[236]

All this stops some way short of an outright portrayal of the artist as a divine creator, whatever modern interpretations of Alberti have suggested to the contrary. Alberti's "as if" (*quasi*) and qualifying "almost" (*paene*) are significant in this respect and are typical of his caution in making extreme claims for the divinity of the artist. This reticence also authentically characterizes the statement attributed to Alberti in the early *Vita* to the effect that the finest achievements of human *ingenium* may be considered "nearly [*prope*] divine."[237]

In his later treatise on architecture he formulates notions of divinity with regard to proportion rather than creativity. Mathematical beauty of proportion is "a quality so great and divine [*divinum*] that in procuring it the full force of art and genius [*artium et ingenii*] must be consumed."[238] Architectural proportion is divine in so far as it reflects God's design of the universe. This conception owes more to classical musical theory than to the notions of divine inspiration which so exercised the poets.

The divinity of proportions was later taken up most conspicuously by Piero della Francesca's *alumnus* and Leonardo's colleague, Luca Pacioli, as the title of Pacioli's book *De divina proportione* (dedicated 1498) graphically illustrates. Similarly,

[235] Alberti (n. 48 above) p. 32.

[236] *Ibid.* 2.25-26 (p. 60). Cf. Lucian, *Somnium* 6-9.

[237] *Vita* in Alberti, *Opere volgari*, ed. A. Bonucci, 1 (Florence 1843) cxiv-vi.

[238] Alberti (n. 9 above) 6.2 (2.447-449).

Filarete's argument that anthropomorphic design methods permit man to "participate" in godly matters is based upon ideas of proportion, though his reasoning is not expounded altogether lucidly.[239] And when Leonardo moves away from his early image of the god-like artist, he is left with mathematics as one of the ultimate foundations for the divinity of painting.

By the second half of the century an individual painter or his works might very occasionally be called divine, in a manner roughly equivalent to that which was not uncommon in the literary arts – witness Petrarch's reverence for Cicero as a *divino ingegno.*[240] Filarete accords an imagined work by Zeuxis the accolade *divina*;[241] Colonna describes the colossus of his dream world as a "divino invento";[242] while Giovanni Santi calls Perugino "un divin pictore," though possibly for his delicate expression of religious gentility rather than for divine genius in Petrarch's sense.[243] The most exceptional, early instance of a "divine" artist occurs in Carlo Marsuppini's 1446 epitaph for Brunelleschi on a memorial tablet in Florence cathedral, which begins, "How valiant Filippo the architect was in the Daedalian art is documented both by the wonderful vault of this celebrated temple and the many machines invented by the divine genius [*divino ingenio*]."[244] There appears to be no comparable acclaim of any quattrocento artist by a contemporary humanist. Landino's estimate of Alberti's books on architecture as "most divinely written [*divinissamente scripti*], replete with all kinds of learning [*tutte dottrine*] and expounded with the highest eloquence" is (like Poliziano's praise of Alberti's *ingenium*) directed more towards his literary gifts rather than to the visual arts themselves.[245] And the introduction to the first (ca. 1486) edition of Vitruvius refers to the "divinum opus Victruvii" – again to a book rather than a work of art or architecture.[246]

Generally notions of *ingenium* in the visual arts stand at some remove from poetic conceptions of divine inspiration. But, in the same way that Aeneas Silvius stood out for his open assertion of similar *ingenium* in painting and poetry, so there is a clear statement from a *quattrocento* humanist that painting and poetry are akin in divine inspiration. This is to be found in a letter from Giustiniani to Chrysoloras, datable before 1446. Giustiniani parades the Horatian *topos* concerning artistic license, but he uniquely works divine spirit into the equation: "Etenim pictoribus, atque poetis,

[239] Filarete (n. 5 above) fol. 5r-v.

[240] Petrarch, *Familiarum rerum libri* 24.2. Cf. Landino's praise of Dante's "divine genius" in the introduction to *Comento* (n. 2 above).

[241] Filarete (n. 5 above) fol. 155v.

[242] Colonna (n. 26 above) fol. 14v.

[243] *Cronaca* 22.96.125 (n. 65 above) 189. In the next passage (126), Signorelli is credited with *ingegno.*

[244] "Quantum Philippus architectus arte dae/ dalea valuerit cum huius celeberrimi/ templi mira testudo tum plures machinae/ divino ingenio adinventae documen/ to esse possunt."

[245] Landino, *Comento* (n. 2 above) proemo.

[246] Vitruvius, *De architectura*, ed. Sulptius (Rome ca. 1486).

quaelibet audendi semper fuit aequa potestas, utrumque certe mentis acumine, et divino quodam spiritu excitari, ac duci constat."[247]

Of earlier humanists only Boccaccio provides a hint that the visual arts were closely linked with divine matters. Introducing his *Life of Dante* he states that sculpture originally arose from the need of man to represent the "essenza divina." This function was subsequently assumed by poetry, which had the advantage of not being mute.[248] The visual arts thus take second place, but he is prepared to grant the painter considerable insight in forming ideal images. The Zeuxis anecdote is exploited to illustrate this conceptual role for the artist; Zeuxis, "assisted by the verses of Homer, formed in his mind a virgin of perfect beauty, which – as far as skill [*arte*] is able to follow *ingegno* – he painted, leaving it to posterity as a celestial resemblance of the true image of Helen."[249] Such a remarkable line of reasoning was not to reappear in mature form until the establishment of Neoplatonic art theory during the sixteenth century.

To an even greater extent than the other factors which we have examined, the notions of divinity and inspiration in the visual arts are, therefore, exploited only exceptionally during the fifteenth century. A few cracks have begun to appear in the venerable dam of intellectual resistance to the visual arts, and a few unorthodox opinions have begun to seep through.

Concluding Remarks

The period we have been studying saw the birth of modern art theory and criticism. The pioneer authors such as Alberti, Ghiberti, Filarete, Francesco di Giorgio and Leonardo were exploring intellectual territory which was virtually uncharted during the Middle Ages and for which surviving classical texts provided only limited signposts. Inevitably there was some superimposition of thought patterns from other areas of learning, most notably rhetoric, poetics and faculty psychology, with varying degrees of relevance and success. The positive side of the situation was that the vocabulary of art had not become fossilized into set formulas which provided an easy excuse not to think. When Alberti and his colleagues wrote, they could not hide a lack of meaning behind a comprehensive shield of established clichés. Even their adoption of clichés from the literature on other disciplines was often a positive act of choice rather than a mindless acceptance of existing ideas. They were faced with the daunting task of saying something new with only the barest hints as to how to say something old.

[247] See Baxandall, *Giotto* (n. 4 above) 98 and 161-162.

[248] Boccaccio, *Origine, vita, studii e costumi del chiarissimo Dante Allighieri,* Bartolomeo Sermartelli (Florence 1576) 46.

[249] Boccaccio, *Il comento* (n. 213 above) 2.128-129.

The authors' response to their task is not surprisingly manifested in a number of individual solutions rather than in uniformity or consistency, but there are clear signs of basic agreement on certain fundamentals as the century progresses. The most powerful unifying factors were the beliefs that *mimesis* of nature was of paramount importance, that art required rational knowledge (*scientia*) and that Antiquity provided the best possible guide. When invention and imagination are granted a significant role they never override these beliefs but operate in harmony with them. Architects provided the lead in this, the ideas of Brunelleschi, Alberti and Manetti helping to insure that no serious writers on the visual arts could afford to ignore the faculty of invention as a necessary attribute of the great architect. In a complementary manner, Cennini, Francesco di Giorgio, Filarete and Leonardo began to establish that imaginative procedures, whether credited to *fantasia, imaginativa* or *cogitativa*, assumed a vital role in artistic invention, taking up a theme which had been fully expressed in Dante's poetry and which had filtered into medieval texts from classical writings.

Invention and imagination were incorporated into each major theorist's thought in guises appropriate to each author's individual proclivities. The pronounced emphasis of Brunelleschi and Alberti upon "excogitative" invention, incorporating discovering and devising, is completely in harmony with their rationally disciplined approach to beauty. Powerful echoes of invention in this sense recur throughout the writings of Francesco di Giorgio, Filarete and Leonardo, but they extended and developed invention in new directions. Francesco developed his own notion of infinite inventiveness, attributing this special quality of imaginative fertility to *ingegno* and ingeniously contrasting man's various inventions with the stereotyped products of animals. To this end he adapted ideas from Aristotle and Aquinas. Filarete has often been interpreted as an eccentric of questionable intelligence, but his advocation of *fantasia* – interpreted in terms of marvellous insight which extends the processes of thought – is very remarkable and original, as is Cennini's earlier usage. If it is likely on one hand that Cennini cleverly adapted medieval ideas of artistic license, it is equally probable on the other that classical sources were important in stimulating Filarete's conceptions. I think that it is no coincidence that *fantasia* received major expression in two centers where Greek studies were enthusiastically pursued – in Filarete's Milan, where Filelfo was active, and Isabella d'Este's Mantua, where she employed a resident Greek scholar.

Just as Dante had transformed the *fantasia* of medieval faculty psychology into the highest inventive force in his poetry, so Leonardo developed *immaginazione* – *fantasia* into the vital image-forming capacity for the painter. To do this, he relocated *fantasia* in the second ventricle of the brain where it could operate in close conjunction with *invenzione* and rational intellect. He also exploited biological analogies for the production of a work of art, eventually using *creare* in this sense.

The poetic sense of *invenzione* in painting remained very much another matter as far as patrons and the vast majority of painters were concerned. The poetic usage is to be found largely in the writings of non-artists, who imposed humanist literary criteria upon painting. *Invenzione* for most painters meant subject-matter provided by a patron or qualified humanist rather than a legitimate aspect of their own role. Major exceptions to this rule were provided by Mantegna, Leonardo, Bellini and Jacopo de' Barbari, but only at the end of the century and the beginning of the next. But even such enlightened patrons as Isabella d'Este remained obstinate in granting this license to painters.

Similar reluctance can be discerned in the very gradual nature of the increase in the likelihood that practitioners of the visual arts would be accorded the status of *ingegni* or *ingenii* – and even then it is likely that some of them were acclaimed as clever men who were also artists rather than as great artists who were therefore clever men. Alberti may well have exercised no small influence in the promotion of the gradual increase in the artists' status. The chronological picture is fairly clear. Within this study only four separate usages of *ingegno* (or *ingenium*) in the visual arts have been cited above from the *trecento*, while those from 1400-1450 are eight in number and the second half of the century has provided no less than thirteen separate authorities who stipulated *ingegno* for the visual arts in general or attributed it to one artist in particular. This list is obviously far from complete, but the relative proportions should not be too misleading. If, however, the thirteen examples drawn from architecture and architectural theory are withdrawn from the list the numbers begin to look extremely thin.

The most advanced and ambitious concepts of all, poetic inspiration and divine power, are found even more exceptionally. *Divino* is applied to art or artists in a few spectacular instances – Marsuppini's epitaph for Brunelleschi and the assertions of the divine power of painting by Alberti and Leonardo – but only Giustiniani fully equates painting with poetic ideals of divine inspiration.

We should not be surprised that there is no unanimity in the usages of *divino, ingegno, fantasia, immaginazione* and *invenzione* in an artistic context during the *quattrocento*, but the trend towards a more widespread and ambitious use of these terms does become pronounced at the end of the century. The appearance and establishment of such terms is of inestimable importance in forming the later vocabulary of art theory and in influencing subsequent thought patterns, but such influences, however strong, should never provide an excuse for assuming that Renaissance authors were then saying what we now mean when we use the same or similar words. It is salutary to realize that the verb "to create" was barely exploited at all in an artistic context before Leonardo, whatever modern translations might suggest to the contrary. The verb invariably used to denote the production of a work of art was *fare*, which could be applied as readily to pasta as painting.

The dominant tone of fifteenth-century writing was that the visual arts were governed by rational procedures of discovery and making, which could be given almost infinite extension by imaginative invention, rather than by capricious creativity of an anarchically modern kind. Surely we would be well advised to bear this continually in mind when looking at the actual works of art produced in this intellectual climate.

Department of Fine Art
University of Glasgow
Glasgow GI2 8QQ, Scotland

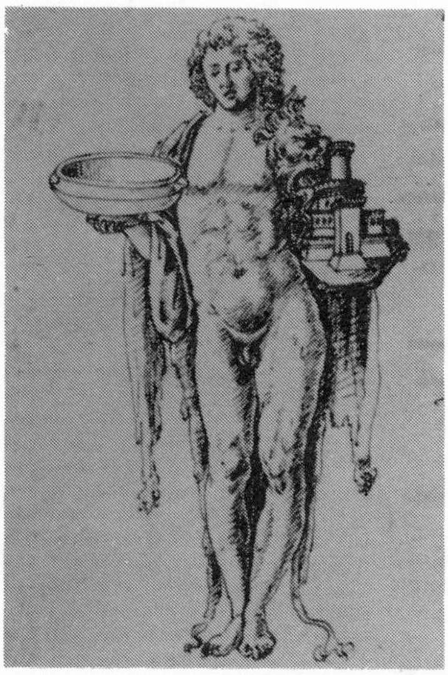

FIG. 1. Francesco di Giorgio, *Dinocrates the Architect*, Florence, Biblioteca Nazionale (cod. Magliabechiano, II, I, 141, fol. 27v).

FIG. 2. G. Reisch, *Rhetoric*, from *Margarita philosophica*, 1503 (d6).

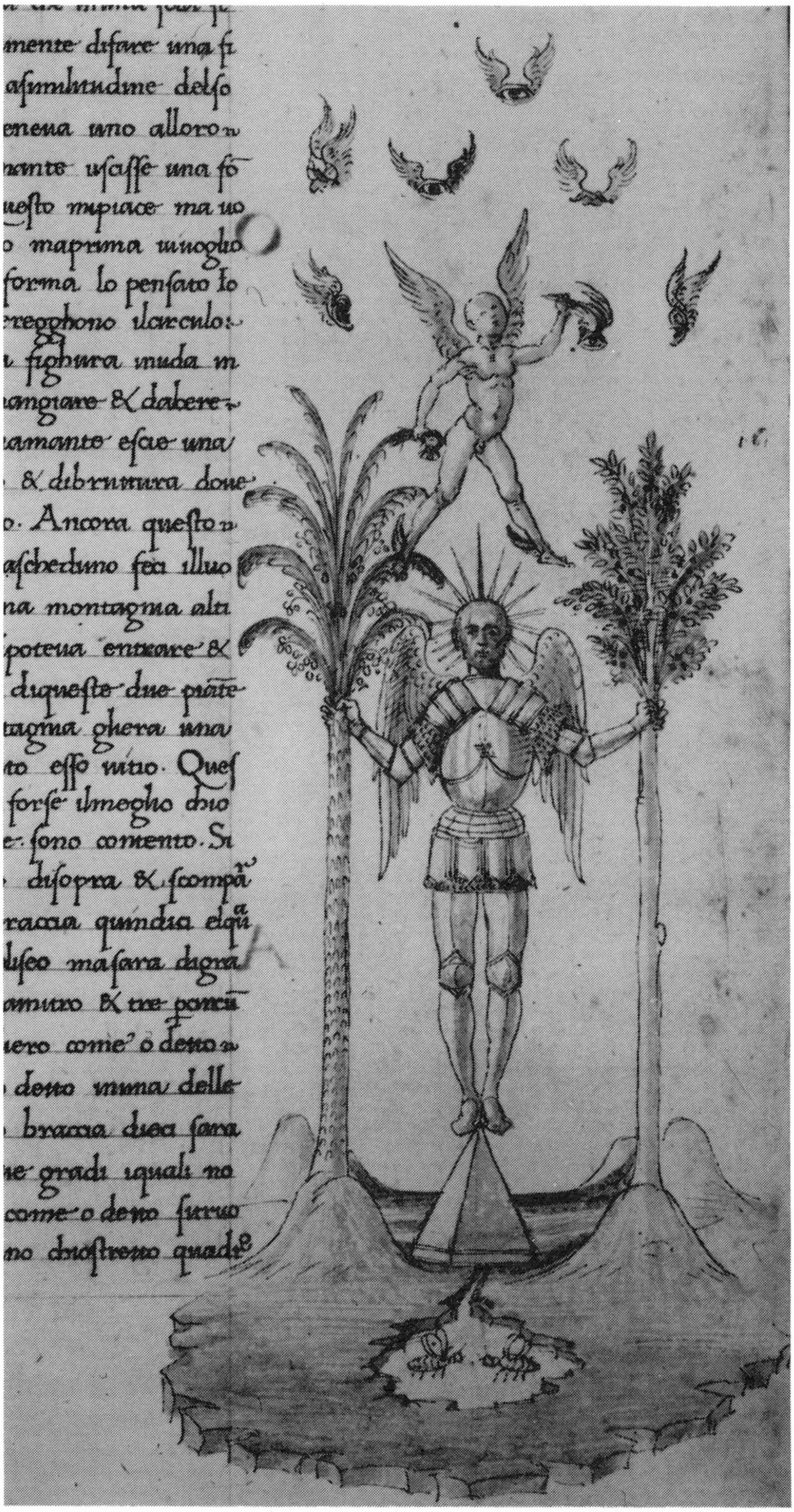

FIG. 3. Filarete, *Image of Virtue*, Florence, Biblioteca Nazionale (cod. Magliabechiano, II, I, 140, fol. 143).

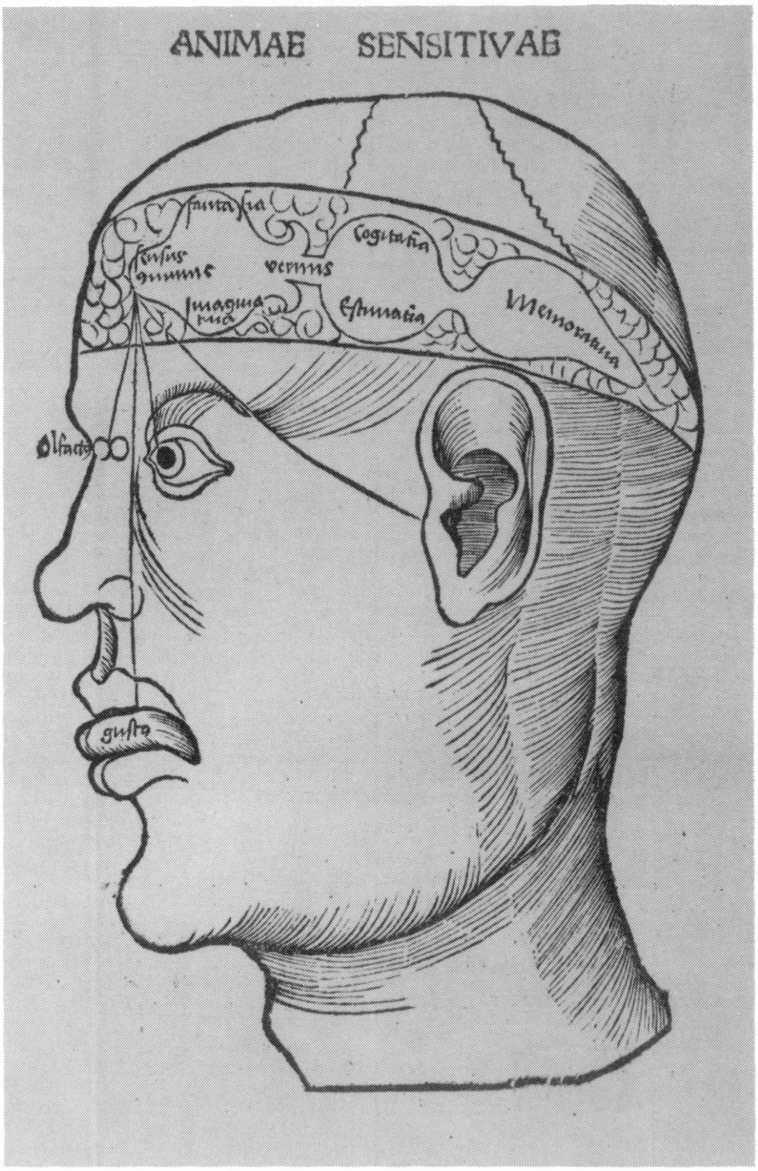

FIG. 4. G. Reisch, *Ventricles of the Human Brain* (h2).

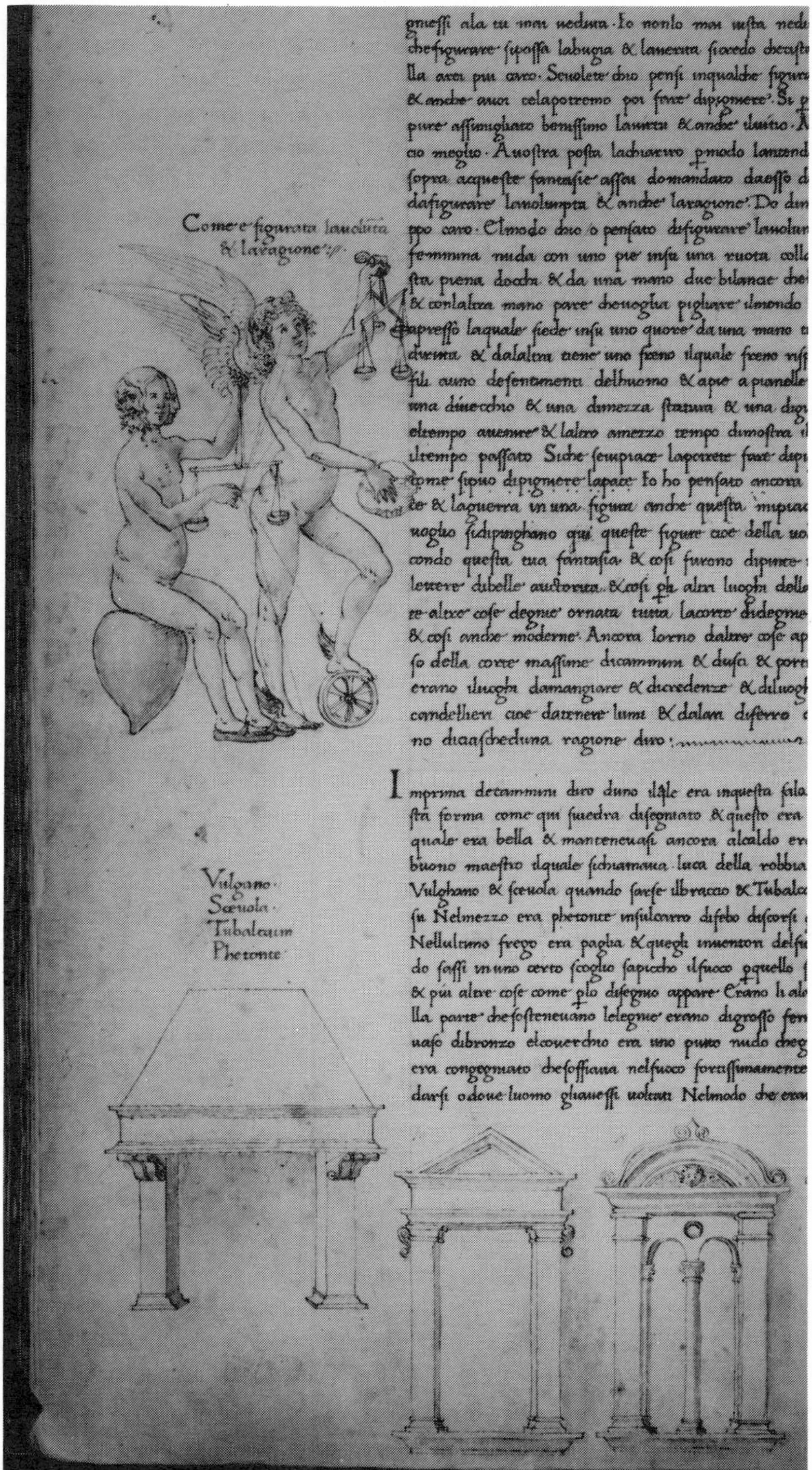

FIG. 5. Filarete, *Image of Will and Reason* (fol. 69v).

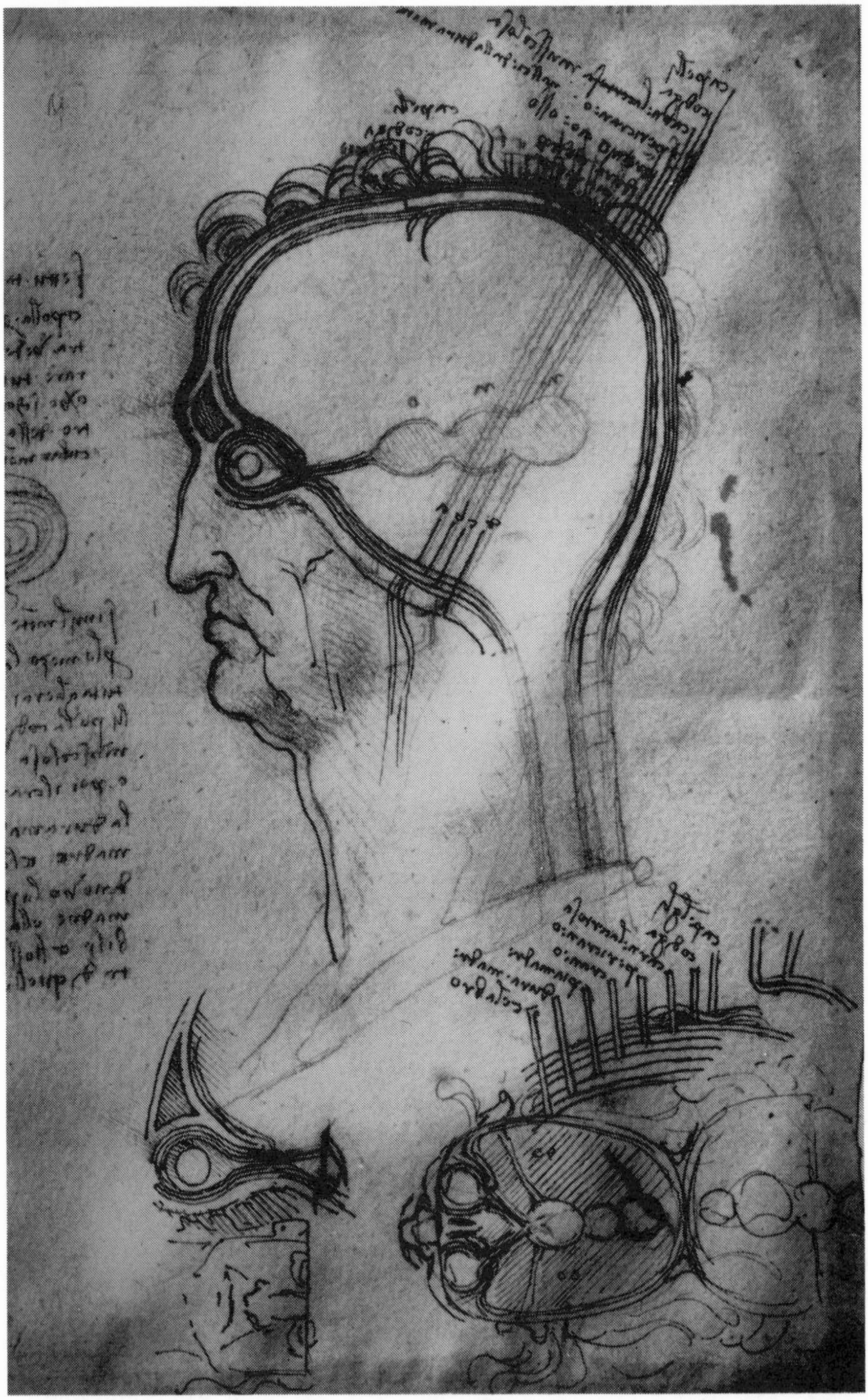

FIG. 6. Leonardo da Vinci, *Sections of the Head to show Ventricles and Membranes of the Brain*, Windsor, Royal Library (12603r). Reproduced by gracious permission of Her Majesty the Queen.

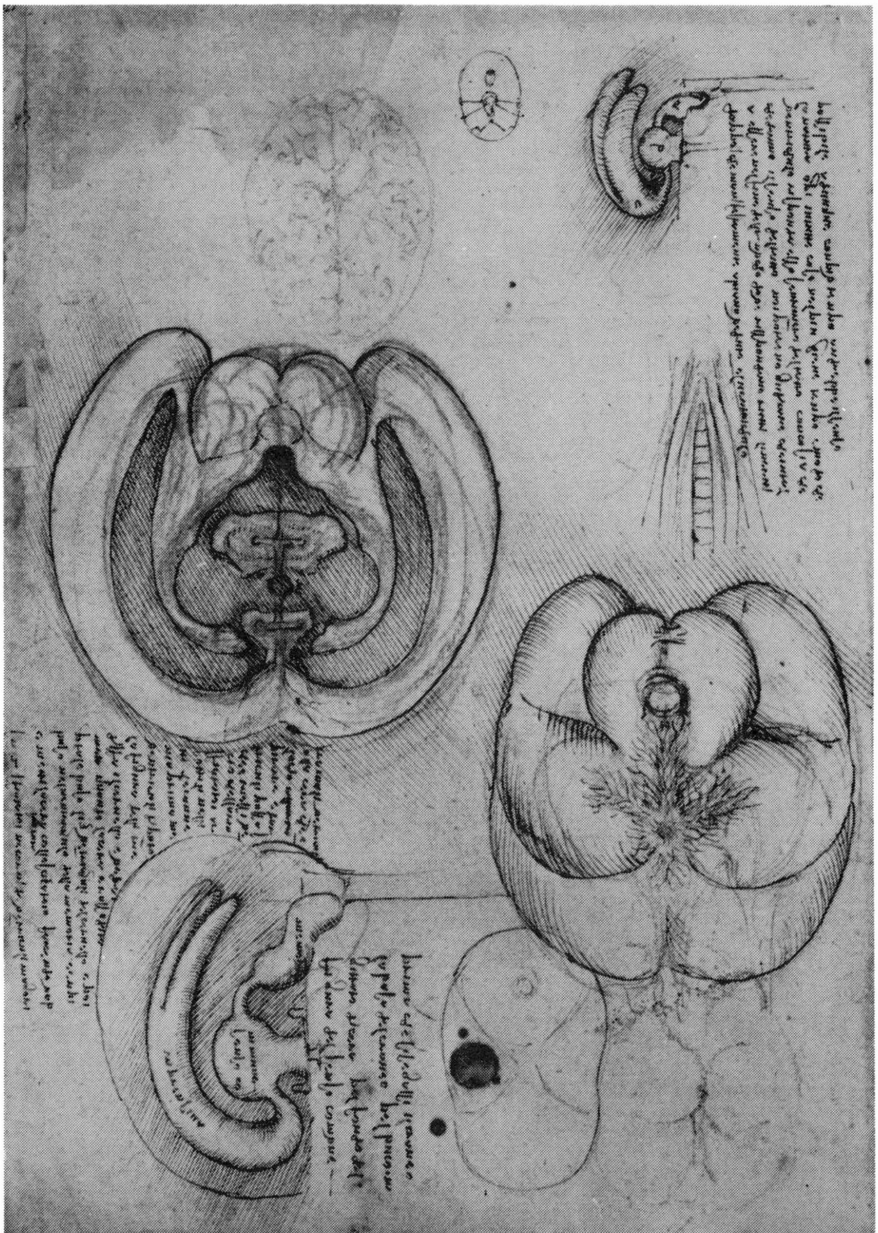

FIG. 7. Leonardo da Vinci, *Studies of the Brain, showing (upper left) the 'Imprensiva, Senso Commune, and Memoria'* (19127r). Reproduced by gracious permission of Her Majesty the Queen.

THE CORRESPONDENCE OF JACQUES DALÉCHAMPS (1513-1588)

•

by Charles B. Schmitt

In previous publications I have dealt with the life and activities[1] of the French physician, botanist, and humanist, Jacques Daléchamps (1513-1588).[2] The center of my focus on those occasions has been, in addition to establishing a firm bio-bibliographical foundation for further studies, to illuminate his interest in the works of Theophrastus, especially his complete Latin translation of the extant works of the Greek author. In addition, however, I have also called to attention the fact that Daléchamps's substantial correspondence remains largely unstudied and, indeed, for the most part unpublished. While on an earlier occasion I was able to cite a few passages from the unpublished letters and to mention some of the names of the correspondents, I was not able to look at the material very closely. Here I shall not repeat the information which I then presented, but hope to make this correspondence better known to scholars and to make it more accessible to those working on various aspects of sixteenth-century intellectual history. In subsequent publications I hope to publish some of the more important letters contained in the correspondence and to discuss their contents more fully. As a first stage in making the letters better known, however, I have here decided to give an inventory (largely from Paris, Bibliothèque Nationale MS lat. 13,063) of the 47 letters by Daléchamps himself (not including the prefatory letters of various books published by him) as well as the 349 letters addressed to him. It is not unlikely that further research will uncover additional relevant correspondence, but it seems useful to make available at the

[1] The abbreviations used in the notes are those indicated in the Appendix. The research necessary for this paper was aided by a Research Grant from the Wellcome Trust. It grew out of a research project supported by United States Public Health Service Grant MH 11,808. Grateful acknowledgement is given to the support from these sources. Thanks are also due to Natalie Z. Davis, who has encouraged and helped my research on Daléchamps over the years, and to Anthony Grafton, who offered many helpful suggestions regarding the present article.

[2] Charles B. Schmitt, "Some Notes on Jacobus Dalechampius and His Translation of Theophrastus (Manuscript: BN. Lat. 11,857)," *Gesnerus* 26 (1969) 36-53. "Jacques Daléchamps," in *Dictionary of Scientific Biography* (New York 1970f.) 3.533-534; and "Theophrastus," in *Catalogus translationum et commentariorum* (Washington, D.C. 1960f.) 2.239-322, esp.257-258.

present time the information which I have thus far gathered. I now feel confident that I have uncovered the major portion of Daléchamps's extant correspondence.

This publication should make more accessible some of the very extensive material which remains hidden away in the extant correspondence of the fifteenth, sixteenth, and seventeenth centuries. While the extant material is voluminous indeed, and contains much important information regarding the intellectual and cultural developments during those centuries, a large percentage has never been published or, if it has, can be consulted only in widely scattered sources. What is more, there do not even exist calendars or inventories for much of the material. The correspondences of major fifteenth-century humanists such as Filelfo still remain scattered and in part unstudied,[3] and only recently has a project been initiated to publish the extant correspondence of so important a fifteenth-century personage as Lorenzo de' Medici.[4] The situation becomes progressively worse as we move to the sixteenth and seventeenth centuries. Though Allen's edition of the Erasmus *Letters*[5] is a model of scholarship, his initiative has not been widely followed in making more such material available. However, in recent years other significant projects include the publication of the correspondence of Amerbach,[6] Beze,[7] Grotius,[8] Mersenne,[9] Oldenburg,[10] and Newton[11] among others. Equally valuable has been the compilation of inventories of various seventeenth-century correspondences of participants of the *respublica literaria,* especially under the direction of Paul Dibon,[12] as well as the publication of various manuscript catalogs which bring to more general attention the existence of various *fonds* containing collections of letters.[13]

The extant correspondence of Jacques Daléchamps is certainly not to be counted as being among the most extensive of the sixteenth century, but is nevertheless of interest for a variety of reasons. It covers the period from 1549 until Daléchamps's

[3] The fullest list is G. Benaducci, "Contributo alla bibliografia di Francesco Filelfo," *Atti e memorie della R. deputazione di storia patria per le provincie delle Marche* 5 (1901) 459-535. This, however, is not complete. I am grateful to Jill Kraye for information on this subject.

[4] Under the general editorship of N. Rubinstein. See P. G. Ricci and N. Rubinstein, *Censimento delle lettere di Lorenzo di Piero de' Medici* (Florence 1964). The first volume of the edition of the letters is now in the press.

[5] *Opus epistolarum Des. Erasmi Roterodami,* ed. P. S. Allen, H. M. Allen and H. W. Garrod (Oxford 1906-1958).

[6] *Die Amerbachkorrespondenz,* ed. A. Hartman (Basel 1942f.).

[7] *Correspondance de T. de Beze,* ed. F. Aubert and H. Meylan (Geneva 1960f.).

[8] Hugo Grotius, *Briefwisseling,* ed. P. C. Molhuysen and B. L. Muelenbroek (The Hague 1928f.).

[9] Marin Mersenne, *Correspondance,* ed. C. De Waard et al. (Paris 1932f.).

[10] *The Correspondence of Henry Oldenburg,* ed. A. R. Hall and M. B. Hall (Madison 1965f.).

[11] *The Correspondence of Isaac Newton,* ed. H. W. Turnbull et al. (Cambridge 1959f.).

[12] Esp. P. Dibon, *Inventaire de la correspondance d'André Rivet (1595-1650)* (The Hague 1971); and P. Dibon, H. Bots, and E. Bots-Estourgie, *Inventaire de la correspondance de Johannes Fredericus Gronovius (1631-1671)* (The Hague 1974).

[13] Especially important in this connection are P. O. Kristeller, *Iter Italicum* (Leiden 1963f.) and L. Denecke, *Die Nachlässe in den Bibliotheken der Bundesrepublik Deutschland* (Boppard a. Rh. 1969).

death in 1588; and in it are letters not only from various parts of France, but also from Spain, Italy, Switzerland, and Germany, as well as a single one from Tripoli. The intellectual breadth of his correspondents is as wide as the geographical range from which the letters came. Daléchamps's subsequent fame is primarily in the fields of botany and medicine and, as one would expect, a large portion of the letters deal in one way or another with these subjects. Many other subjects, including especially religion, philology, and classical humanism, are well represented. The botanical correspondence perhaps dominates, with many letters being concerned with the international exchange of specimens and the discussions of their importance, which marked the sixteenth-century development of the subject. There is also much information relating to the publication of Daléchamps's major botanical work, the *Historia generalis plantarum.* Among those with whom Daléchamps corresponded on botany are Conrad Gesner (1516-1565), Robert Constantin (ca. 1530-1605), and Jehan Robin (1550-1629). His position as the leading medical figure at Lyon during his time is indicated in the rich exchange of letters with eminent physicians such as Jean Fernel (1497-1558), Girolamo Mercuriale (1530-1606), Francisco Micón (fl. 1570-1582), Jérôme de Monteux (ca. 1490-1560), Felix Plater (1536-1614), Guillaume Plancy (d. 1611), and Reinerus Solenander (1524-1601). There is a single letter of astrological interest from Francesco Giuntini (1523-1590). The religious conflicts which divided sixteenth-century Europe come into focus in the letters exchanged with Emond Auger (1530-1591) and Joachim Camerarius the Younger (1534-1598), as well as with Constantin and Gesner. Literary and humanistic contacts include Barthélemy Aneau (d. 1561), Gilbert Cousin (1506-1572), Jacques Cujas (1522-1590), Henri Estienne (1528-1598), Jean Lalement (fl. 1575), Nicolas de Nancel (1539-1610), Guillaume Paradin (1510-1590), Andreas Schott (1552-1629), and Pier Vettori (1499-1585). But these are just a few of the names to be found in this largely unknown correspondence, and the range of topics covered in the letters is far more extensive than can be mentioned in a brief introductory article.

From his base in Lyon, Daléchamps served as a sort of clearing house for information on botany, medical science, and classical studies. Sixteenth-century Lyon was without a university and for many years Daléchamps as Médecin du Hôtel-Dieu, along with his friend Guillaume Rouillé, was at the center of the cultural life there.[14] This is amply illustrated in the letters which are of great potential interest to historians of Lyon. The thriving culture of that city has not been adequately stressed by most historians of sixteenth-century France and, indeed, as a publishing center it was one of the five or six chief cities of Europe during the period covered by Daléchamps's letters. In a way, the letters illustrate as well as anything the preeminent place which Lyon had in the intellectual life of the century.

Daléchamps maintained a number of friendships through letters, some of which

[14] There are many mentions of Rouillé in the letters, including P, 265, 274, 275, 279-280, 284, 443 and frequently in the correspondence with Camerarius.

spanned many years. Perhaps most noteworthy in this respect are the exchanges with Robert Constantin, which covered the years 1558 to 1582, and that with Joseph Justus Scaliger, which continued for the period 1561 to 1587. Some of the epistolary exchanges were quite extensive, more than thirty letters surviving from the exchanges involving Jean Chifflet, Constantin, and Henri Estienne, while others are known to us by a single surviving letter. In addition to the direct information they supply concerning the correspondents themselves, the letters also afford us an insight into the lives of yet others, with whom a direct epistolary contact with Daléchamps is lacking. All in all the letters reveal to us many specific connections which furnish a dimension to intellectual history that is of crucial significance when we come to work out the specific details of the evolution of scientific ideas and the communcation of scientific knowledge. For example, the letters reveal important new information on the relations of Daléchamps to three of the most significant names of sixteenth-century medical and biological thought, Guillaume Rondelet (1507-1566), Jean Fernel, and Conrad Gesner.

Daléchamps had been a student of Rondelet's during his years of study at the University of Montpellier. Though, as far as we have been able to determine, there exist no letters between the two, there are a significant number of references to Rondelet in other letters contained in the correspondence. For example, Pierre Lefevre [Petrus Faber] keeps Daléchamps informed of Rondelet's activities in Montpellier in several of his letters.[15] A letter of Erhardus Zeyselius, dated 1551, indicates that Daléchamps was then already known for his collection of botanical specimens and it is asked that he send some of these on to his former teacher, Rondelet.[16]

Daléchamps's precise relation to Fernel is difficult to judge at the present state of our knowledge. The one letter of Daléchamps to Fernel is somewhat reverent in tone and does not seem to indicate a close friendship between the two. It was written at a time when Fernel was very near death and indeed may have not reached him before he died. It is one of the very few letters addressed to Fernel which survive – perhaps the only one – and for that reason is worthy to be better known. It contains an appeal from Daléchamps for the support of perhaps the most distinguished medical figure in Paris at the time. The physician from Lyon was upset by what he considered to be the quackery of several recent publications in Lyon by Sebastian Colin and Pierre Braillier and apparently was attempting to enlist the help of the prominent Fernel to combat it. In addition to all else it shows the esteem in which Fernel was held in France at that time and sheds important light on the sort of medical debate which characterized the period.[17]

[15] P, 422, 438, 439.

[16] "Tu, vir clarissime, si ex herbatione[?] tua redijsti, simpliciaque et alia habes, quae per me ad attinens meum D. Rondeletium mittere decrevisti." P, 373v.

[17] P, 13-14. This letter will be published with a translation and commentary by James J. Bono and myself in the near future.

With regard to Gesner, the material to be found in the Daléchamps correspondence is far more extensive. In addition to Gesner's letter to Daléchamps published a century and a half ago,[18] with its important discussion of religious issues, there is currently being published the Gesner material contained in Erlangen, which names Daléchamps frequently as a source of information, seeds, and specimens that were assimilated into Gesner's *Historia plantarum.*[19] The letters in the Paris manuscript, however, shed much more light on this important relationship which was marked by an exchange of scientific ideas and numerous botanical specimens.[20] All of the letters, four by Gesner and three by Daléchamps, show the mixture of empirical information with philological discussion concerning the views of the ancients on topics of natural history. This characteristically humanistic approach to natural science often incorporates into one sentence a very accurate and detailed description of a specific plant in its natural habitat (accompanied often by a drawing of some sort, as well as a pressed specimen and seeds), followed by a most erudite discussion of ancient descriptions of the plant in Theophrastus, Dioscorides, Pliny and other writers. In short, here we find very good examples of the humanistic approach to natural history, which reached its full development in the sixteenth century.

In addition to the personal connections which the correspondence illustrates so well, it also provides us with a good deal of specific information about the day to day interests of the circle of intellectuals with which Daléchamps was acquainted. Particularly are the letters from Constantin full of such information. For example, one letter tells us that he has forwarded a packet from Daléchamps to Gesner, that one from J. J. Scaliger is being sent to Daléchamps, that Henri Estienne is ill and hence his edition of Sextus Empiricus has been delayed, that Pierre Lefevre has returned from Italy, and that Denys Lambin has been one of Constantin's friends for a long time, among other things.[21] Nor is this letter atypical of what we find in the long newsy epistles, thirty in number, which Constantin sent to Daléchamps in the course of his extensive travels throughout Europe.[22] During the time when Constantin was in Basel he also furnished much information regarding Gesner and seems to have acted as a sort of intermediary between Gesner and Daléchamps in their exchange both of information and of natural history specimens.[23] From various letters we can also garner many other bits of miscellaneous information. For example we find that Daléchamps sent to Camerarius in Nuremberg the edition of J. C.

[18] MH, 133-150.

[19] C. Gesner, *Historia plantarum.* Facsimileausgabe, ed. H. Zoller et al. (Zurich 1972f.). See n. 32 below.

[20] Until I discovered these letters, they were apparently not known to Gesner scholars. See R. Steiger, "Erschliessung des Conrad-Gessner-Materials der Universitätsbibliothek Zürich," *Gesnerus* 25 (1968) 29-63.

[21] P, 277.

[22] On Constantin see Schmitt, "Theophrastus" (n. 2 above) 271-272, but these letters reveal far more about his interesting personality than can be learned from published sources.

[23] See e.g. the letters in P, 265, 272, 275, 277, 280, 284.

Scaliger's and Constantin's annotations on Theophrastus as soon as it was printed in Lyon in 1584.[24] Indeed, references to the exchange of books sent from one part of Europe to another abound in the letters.

Among the many philological discussions are to be found the communication of textual variants derived from manuscripts not accessible to Daléchamps. Such is the case when Jean Chifflet writes, "Mitto ad te quales notas ad Plinium, quas cursim e codice fratris Claudii Chiffletii et meo rerum[?] scripsi."[25] This material, as well as much other to be found throughout the correspondence on various textual problems concerning Pliny, was incorporated into Daléchamps's monumental edition of Pliny the Younger.[26] On another occasion we find Joannes Faucherius writing from Beaucaire that he is sending to Daléchamps an old manuscript of some of Cicero's works.[27] Many letters, however, including those of Constantin, Cujas, Estienne, Gesner, and Mitalier are devoted to long discussions of humanistic subjects and textual criticism, topics of great interest to the sixteenth-century *respublica literaria* of which Daléchamps was a part.

It is in botany, however, that Daléchamps made his mark and it is his contribution to that science for which he is best remembered. While he cannot perhaps be considered one of the two or three major botanists of the sixteenth century, he certainly has an important place in the second level. Indeed, he played quite an important role in the international development of the science,[28] which, perhaps as no other discipline save philology, progressed as a corporate enterprise during the course of the sixteenth century. The free exchange of botanical specimens and ideas between men of very different national and religious backgrounds characterized the century and we see a genuine community of scientists intent upon sharing their information with one another. The extent to which Gesner benefited is evident in the *Historia plantarum*[29] mentioned above, but it is also everywhere evident in the great botanical compilations of the century and in the letters between the working botanists themselves. As such the letters of Daléchamps are good examples of this interchange of ideas and specimens which marked the sixteenth-century expansion of botanical interests and knowledge. Thus far they have remained unknown, and one has not made use of the insights they provide for an understanding of the development of the natural history subjects which linked scientists throughout Europe.[30]

[24] E (7).

[25] P, 497.

[26] On this edition see Schmitt, "Some Notes" (n. 2 above) 41 n. 19.

[27] P, 401.

[28] In this connection Daléchamps's comments on Cesalpino are interesting. "De Caesalpino nec iudex nec arbiter esse volo. Dicam tamen hoc candide, de multis plantis iudicium eius mihi non probari, et hoc praeterea esse aliquid, sedulo plantas oratione depingere, quod admixtus est ille, sed additas figuras multum afferre lucis ac certitudinis, praesertim in tanta nominum et appellationum diversitate. Accedit et his, quam eius culpam esse non puto, insignis habes vitiosissimae et mendosissimae impressionis." E(8).

[29] See n. 32 below.

[30] For some information on this see my "Science in the Italian Universities of the Sixteenth and Early Seventeenth Centuries," in M. P. Crosland, ed., *The Emergence of Science in Western Europe* (London 1975) 35-56.

In a sense Daléchamps's interests in botany, which predate his arrival in Lyon in 1552, all point toward the publication of his monumental *Historia generalis plantarum* which did not appear until shortly before his death. Already in 1551, he was discussing botanical problems with Hugo Solerius, who was himself at the small town of Raymond near Bourges.[31] Of course the Gesner letters are full of discussions of botanical questions and the influence went in both directions, some of what Daléchamps communicated finding its way into the *Historia plantarum*[32] and information from Gesner finding its way into the *Historia generalis plantarum.*[33] Besides being a source of information on many other things, Daléchamps's close friend, Robert Constantin, also communicated to him much botanical information and many specimens, on one occasion sending "quelques rares simples du mont Jura," but cautioning his friend not to confuse them with other plants similar in appearance.[34] In the next letter an extraneous touch of fate enters when he says: "Je pensois, cher seigneur et ami, vous envoier quelques beaux simples pour ce voiage, mais les grandes pluies que presque chasque iour il ha faict pardeca ont guarde daller aux montaignes et rompu mon deseing. Neant moins ie vous envoie entre autres eryngium ceruleum . . . ."[35] The tone of these letters can perhaps best be seen by giving the entire text of one of the briefer ones.

> Monsieur et entier ami, iai envoie seurement vostre paquet à Mons.r Gesnerus avec les arbres glandiferes. Ie vous remercie humblement du pourtrait d' Ostrya, duquel iai este fort aise et quaies si bien remarque une si belle plante, laquelle iai bien, se me semble examiner et confere les faultes de Pline. A la vostre grace me tiens tout asseure que cest la vraye qu'escript Theophraste. En achevant peu à peu mon dictionnaire, iai commence de longue main ce preparatif pour ledict Theophraste.[36] Ie vous prie a vostre loesir me separer les corrections que penseres que ie nay point les marquant seulement dun traict de plume, et moi, vous

[31] P, 78. Solerius opens the letter by saying: "Gratum fecisti, mi Jacobe, quod Centaurii magni semina aliquot nobis miseris . . . ."

[32] The more interesting examples have not yet been printed in the edition cited above in n. 19, of which only three fascicles have thus far appeared. See Erlangen, Universitätsbibliothek MS 2386, fols. 118 ("Iasmini peregrini nomine Dalechampius misit 1561. Aprilis 21 accepi."), 155 ("Aquilegia minor D. Dalechampius mittebat 1561 Augusto."), 157, 173, 211, 476, etc.

[33] See, for example, *Historia generalis plantarum* (Lyon, 1586-1587) 602, when discussing *lapathum* (sorrel) he says: "Illud est fortasse Lapathum, quod rotundum vocat Gesnerus et circa Friburgum Helvetiorum inveniri ait . . . ." He then goes on to discuss the type called *sanguis draconis,* which had been discussed in Daléchamps's letter to Gesner contained in P, 27-30, at 28.

[34] P, 273.

[35] P, 274. In the *Historia generalis plantarum* (p. 1459) when discussing *eryngium marinum* Daléchamps also includes one "colore quoque caeruleo" which must be the plant referred to in this letter.

[36] The dictionary referred to is his *Lexicon sive dictionarium graecolatinum* . . . (Geneva 1562), which also went through a number of other editions. The work on Theophrastus is Constantin's *Annotationes in libros de historia plantarum,* which was not published until 1584, when it appeared with J. C. Scaliger, *Animadversiones in historias Theophrasti* (Lyon 1584), which was edited by Constantin after Scaliger's death (1558). For further details see Schmitt, "Theophrastus" (n. 2 above) 269-272.

> allant voir les extrairai, ou bien Maistre Vincent Textor[37] le fera fort bien sil vous plaist me faire cest faveur pour adionction de la premiere. Aussi ne vous portant point praeiudice, ie vous requiers encor les plantes rares que iugeres propres pour ce nostre, ou bien vostre oeuvre. Monsieur le febvre[38] part demain pour vous aller voir. Cependant nous ensemble presentons noz humbles, respondons a vostre bonne grace. Si vous plaira noublier faire les miennes au Signeur Roville[39] mon compere. Le Seigneur, tres cher ami et frere, vous conserve et prospere. Ce 15 d'avril 1559.
>
> Vostre humble serviteur frere et entier ami
> Constantin[40]

Other letters are much longer and more informative, but even this brief excerpt gives some idea of the type of information they contain. Very frequently they contain specific descriptions (often accompanied by seed, specimens, and drawings) of particular plants, their habitats and characteristics,[41] precisely the sort of information which Daléchamps could make use of in the compilation of his *Historia generalis plantarum.*

Perhaps some of the most valuable information of this sort to come to Daléchamps was provided by several correspondents in more remote regions. Particularly to be mentioned in this respect were Francisco Micón who sent several letters from Barcelona concerning Spanish flora, and Jayme de Alcalà, who responded from Tripoli with various unusual specimens. In one letter Micón sends "decem herbarum icones cum suis descriptionibus tumultarie conscriptibus."[42] On another occasion we find Micón sending seeds from India, which Daléchamps had requested, as well as further herbs from Spain.[43] In the letter from Jayme de Alcalà we find that Daléchamps had previously asked for various samples and his correspondent has done his best to find them. Jayme then continues by giving a detailed description of various plants which he has procured in Tripoli.[44]

[37] Vincent Textor was perhaps a relative of Claudius Textor, one of Daléchamps's correspondents (see Appendix), and of Benoît Textor, the author of a number of books. The only publication of Vincent Textor which I have been able to find is his *Traicté de la nature du vin* (Lyon 1604) cited in the Bibliothèque Nationale catalog.

[38] For his correspondence with Daléchamps see the Appendix.

[39] See n. 14 above.

[40] P, 278.

[41] A good example is to be found in the letter from Beaucaire dated 28 October 1583 by Joannes Faucherius, one of Daléchamps's most faithful correspondents on botanical matters.

[42] P, 443.

[43] "Vellem profecto aliquid nunc paratum habere, quod mittere possem. Sed spero statim semina, quae ex India ad me polliciti sint, mittere relaguturum: una cum aliis Hispanis herbis, quocunque modo depictis, una eliacum eisdemmet a terra nuper erutibus. Habet enim nostra hec Hispania multa herbarum, fruticum arborumque genera; quanta[?] alia meo iudico [*sic,* iudicio?] regio in tota Europa constituta." P, 444. Micón's contribution to the *Historia generalis plantarum* is most evident. For example, under *Ornithogalum* he discusses a particular species "quod a Mycono habuimus" (p. 1582).

[44] P, 128.

The exchange, however, is not confined to plants, for we find the exchange of information on a variety of other natural history specimens. For example, in one of the letters from Constantin there is a detailed discussion of "la seconde espece de salamandre laquelle a queue danguille." After this he continues, "Je vous renvoie vostre pourtrait de l' insecte que nommes scarabeus longipes,"[45] indicating that the transmission went two ways. The fact that most of Daléchamps's own letters are lost gives us far less information from his end of the correspondence. Since Daléchamps was particularly interested in birds and has left behind a beautifully illustrated *Ornithologie,*[46] it is not unexpected to find the topic arising frequently in the letters. Thus Morosini sent a drawing from Venice,[47] and Claude Textor supplied a variety of information and, on one occasion at least, a bird "en une boite"![48]

Through the letters, especially those exchanged with Camerarius, we can follow the composition of the *Historia generalis plantarum,* including the prolonged misery of finally getting it through the press. We also gain some insight into the nature of the cooperation which went into its composition, including the great role played by various contributors to the edition, especially Rouillé, the printer.[49]

Daléchamps's correspondence thus provides an unusually rich source of information on the exchange of ideas and information which marked the intellectual life during the years after the religious breakdown caused by the Reformation. It is a source of information which deserves to be better known by historians of the period. In the present brief paper I have only been able to touch on some of the highlights to be found in the letters and have not been able to trace in detail any of the numerous points raised, nor have I been able to relate this material in anything but a most superficial way to the historical context of the times. To make these letters more accessible to others, who can make use of them for a variety of different purposes, I shall print a summary inventory of them.

APPENDIX

This inventory is based largely on the materials contained in Paris, Bibliothèque Nationale MS lat. 13,063, of which I gave a brief description in my previous article on Daléchamps. In addition, however, I also incorporate into the list descriptions of other letters which I have found both in manuscript and in printed sources. Undoubtedly, there are others which I have not yet located, but the present list can serve for the time being as a check list of Daléchamps's correspondence.

In describing the various letters I have tried to give the date of the letter, the place

[45] P, 275.

[46] For information see Schmitt, "Some Notes" (n. 2 above) 36 n. 4.

[47] "Ho havuto il disegno dell' ucello che ella desiderava et con queste ve[?] lo mando . . . ." P, 255.

[48] P, 184-186. There is much further discussion in various places including P, 269, 274.

[49] See esp. the Camerarius correspondence. The details of this story are too complicated to deal with here and should be treated fully in a separate study.

where it was written, the incipit, and where the letter is now to be found. Those letters which were written by Daléchamps himself are indicated by the symbol §, while the others were addressed to him. Sometimes the date on which the letter was sent is not indicated, but Daléchamps has noted when he received it. This is indicated by "rec" in parentheses after the date. In many cases, I have not been able to supply all of the information which I had wanted to, either because it is not given in the letter or because it proved to be illegible. Undoubtedly, through further research on Daléchamps and his correspondents and by careful study of the letters themselves, we shall be able to supply some of the missing information. In those cases where there is some doubt concerning a manuscript reading or the interpretation of it, I have indicated this by placing a query in brackets. A particular problem arises with regard to the translation of Latin place names into modern terms. When it is uncertain how a particular name should be translated, I have given the original as it appears in manuscript. With regard to dates, I have changed them all from the Latin form (e.g. "3 Kal. Jul. 1557" is given as "29 June 1557"), but have not altered the year to "new style." With regard to the sources, folio or page numbers are given.

The inventory is arranged alphabetically by correspondent and chronologically (as far as possible) within each group. The names of correspondents are generally listed in the language in which the letter is written and, when necessary, alternate forms are given in brackets. In some cases the full names of the correspondents cannot be ascertained from the letters themselves, and standard reference works have not revealed the identity of the correspondent. This leaves a somewhat untidy result, but perhaps further research by readers of my inventory will clarify some of these details.

The inventory is broken up into three sections. The first contains the bulk of the correspondence; the second contains letters not assignable to a single individual or which seem to be anonymous; the third contains several miscellanous items contained in MS 13,063 which, properly speaking, are not letters, but are included for the sake of completeness. In addition many of the letters in the Paris manuscript contain various notes and annotations by Daléchamps.

Abbreviations

B Jacob Bernays, *Joseph Justus Scaliger* (Berlin 1855) 308-314 (printed from Leiden, Bibliotheek der Rijksuniversiteit MS Burm. q. 19, fols. 50v-52).

E Erlangen, Universitätsbibliothek, Nachlass Trew (see E. Schmidt-Herrling, *Die Briefsammlung des Nürnberger Arztes Christoph Jacob Trew (1695-1769) in der Universitäts-Bibliothek Erlangen* [Erlangen 1940] 139).

L Leiden, Bibliotheek der Rijksuniversiteit MS Burm. q. 19.

M Munich, Bayrische Staatsbibliothek, Clm. 735.

MH *Museum Helveticum ad juvandas literas in publicos usus apertum* (Zurich 1746), part 1 [copy in British Library: 248.c.26].

N *Nic. Nancelli . . . epistolarum de pluribus reliquarum tomus prior . . .* (Paris 1603) [copy in Bibliothèque Nationale: Z.56046].

P Paris, Bibliothèque Nationale MS lat. 13,063.

S *Henrici Stephani epistolae ad Jac. Dalechampium* . . ., printed with *Ad Senecae Proodopoeia . . . autore Henr. Stephano* . . ., (Paris 1586) [copy in Brit. Lib.: 687.c.12].

SD *Henrici Stephani epistola ad Jacobum Dalechampium* . . . (s.l., s.d.; Geneva? 1586?) [copy in Brit. Lib: 621.h.6 (2)].

V *Petri Victorii epistolarum libri X* . . . (Florence 1586).

VB *Cl. Italorum et Germanorum epistolae ad Petrum Victorium* . . ., ed. A. M. Bandini (Florence 1758-1760).

INVENTORY

I. GENERAL CORRESPONDENCE

Jacobus Alcalaus [Jayme de Alcalà] (1)

1 Jan. 1584[?][1] P, 128 Tripoli

Multum diuque est dominus Ambrosius

Bartholomaeus An[n]ulus [Aneau] (3)

30 Nov. 1552 P, 156-157 Bourges

Spectatam erga me et comprobatam

24 Oct. . . . . P, 155 . . . .

Vereor ne absente me uxor

12 Feb. . . . . P, 217 Bourges

Si quid agam scire desideras

Antremons (1)

24 July 1582 P, 80-81 . . . .

Monsieur, lesperance que de jour a aultre

Petrus Areodus [Pierre Aréoud] (1)

29 Nov. . . . . P, 244-245 Grenoble

Effecerunt tuae literae commendatitae

Emond Auger[2] (1)

. . . . P, 154 . . . .

Mitto ad te duos libellos

[1] The MS has "a creatione mundi 5344[?]."

[2] The MS has "Enemundus iesuita."

Claude d'Avesnes [Claudius Davesnes] (2)

.... P, 172-173 ....

Monsieur, jay receu les lettres

.... P, 176-177 ....

Monsieur, il y a si long temps

Ba[i]llif (2)

.... P, 74 ....

Monsieur, Jay veu vos lettres

.... P, 75 ....

Monsieur, ayant en la

Claudius Bal[l]inus (3)

13 Feb. .... P, 132 Montpellier

O me impellit necessaria meae

31 July .... P, 163 Montpellier

Nuncius hîc, praestantiss. doctor

.... P, 168 ....

Non semel (praeceptor observantiss.) mecum

Jacobus Baro (4)

8 Feb. 1559 P, 95 Montpellier

Faber noster in Corsicam hinc

6 June 1559 P, 94 Montpellier

Delectis tuis literis quas

18 July .... P, 96 Montpellier

Quin ad me tue litere

29 Apr. .... (rec) P, 97 Montpellier

Ad 8 Calendas Martias

Antonius Baudanus (1)

25 Nov. 1585 P, 219-220 "E Lemanno"

Redeunt ad se tua exemplaria

Beauvalet (medicin à Bayeux) (1)

§ .... P, 68 Lyon

Memini haud procul istinc

Richardus Bellonaletius (1)

20 July 1563 P, 88 ....

Plurimum tibi habeo gratum

		De la Bessee		(1)
15 May	1586	P, 252	....	
Monsieur, Jay bien voullu				
		Christophorus Blagnius		(5)
....		P, 104-105	....	
Numquam melius aut argutius				
....		P, 106	....	
Nihil unquam pronunciavit				
....		P, 107	....	
Unde [?] mi Dalechampie, quid est				
....		P, 108-109	....	
Medicorum φορικώτατοι genus illud				
....		P, 110-111	....	
Non desinam medicorum praestantiss.				
		Joannes Bonidieus [Jean Bondieu]		(1)
13 Aug.	1569	P, 233-234	....	
Sextus iam primum[?] agitur annus				
		Bos [de Boeuf]		(1)
....		P, 191	....	
Mobilis hic bic[?] maxima				
		Bosquetius		(1)
....		P, 174-175	....	
Mitto ad te, vir praestantiss., de Theophrasto tuo				
		Joannes Bouchardus		(2)
23 Apr.	....	P, 169-170	....	
Medici cum sunt homines nihil				
....		P, 171	....	
Monsieur soub la confidence				
		Ioachim Camerarius [The Younger]		(23)
15 Mar.	1582	P, 344	Nuremberg	
Miraberis procul dubio, vir excellentissime				
§1 Apr.	1582	E (1)	Lyon	
Gratissima sane mihi fuit				
§22 Aug.	1582	P, 51; E (2)	Lyon	
Quod meam ad te literarum scriptionem				

16 Oct.	1582	P, 347	Nuremberg
Humanissimis tuis literis propter			
§18 Nov.	1582	E (3)	Lyon
Non est quod de tardiore scriptione			
§13 Dec.	1583	E (4)	Lyon
Mirabatur stapedius[?] mecum			
§7 Mar.	1584	P, 47-48; E (5)	Lyon
Redditae mihi quidem sunt literae tuae			
§16 Apr.	1584	E (6)	Lyon
Nondum erant allati codices tui			
§7 July	1584	E (7)	Lyon
Redditi mihi codici tui			
1 Sept.	1584	P, 350-351	Nuremberg
Superiore vere praeter omnem meam			
§16 Oct.	1584	E (8)	Lyon
Gravissimam aulicae vitae			
§1 Dec.	1584	E (9)	Lyon
Remitto libros quos commodasti			
§15 Mar.	1585	P, 49-50; E (10)	Lyon
Revocatum fuisse te ab illustrissimo			
§30 Sept.	1585	P, 45-46	Lyon
Reddidit tuas literas affinis			
20 July	1586	P, 345	Nuremberg
Clarissime vir et amice observantissime, cum tibi multis			
12 Sept.	1586	P, 346	Frankfurt
Clarissime vir et amice observantissime, speraveram me hoc			
§16 Sept.	1586	E (11)	Lyon
Paulo serius ad tuam epistolam			
§13 Feb.	1587	E (12)	Lyon
Et iusta et vera causa est			
13 May	1587[3]	P, 511-512	Nuremberg
Rursum debeo responsionem ad tuas			
§22 June	1587	E (13)	Lyon
Plinium nostrum ad vos nondum pervenisse			
1 Sept.	1587	P, 349	Nuremberg
Vincis me, doctissime vir, tua humanitate			
1 Nov.	....	P, 343	Nuremberg
Athenaeum tuum tandem nactus sum			
....		P, 348	....
Clarissime vir et amice observantissime, vide quam celeriter			

[3] There is no indication of Camerarius's name on this letter, but it is written in the same hand as the other letters from Camerarius in the Paris collection.

Claudius Campensius [Des Champs] (1)

. . . . P, 137 "Ex Castellione Dombasum" [?]

Cum hisce diebus evoluerem

Gulielmus Cappellus (medicus Parisensis) (1)

23 July . . . . P, 79 Paris

Quod apud antiquos in communi usu

Joannes Chiffletius [Jean Chifflet] (42)

29 Apr. 1577 P, 447 Besançon

Scripsi, monsieur, ad te

19 Dec. 1580 P, 485-486 Besançon

Monueram [?], monsieur, animum meum

§16 Apr. 1581 P, 42-43 Lyon

Respondeo paucis ad gratissimam

3 July 1581 P, 459 Besançon

Selegi fas ex motis Plinianis aliquot

18 Jan. 1582 P, 497 Besançon

Mitto ad te quales quales [sic] notas ad Plinium

4 Mar. 1582 P, 457 Besançon

Vere menses [?] liborum . . . penuria

2 July 1582 P, 502 Besançon

Firmasti more tuo docte

30 July 1582 P, 461 Besançon

Gaudeo vehementer receptum a te

27 Aug. 1582 P, 495 Besançon

Recepi Ammiani vitam cum literis Gryphii

4 Sept. 1582[4] P, 498 Besançon

Dolui vehementer casus adolescentuli

20 Sept. 1582 P, 455 Besançon

Nunc nunc [sic] tardus ut solet

2 Dec. 1582 P, 492-493 Besançon

De hordeariis gladiatoribus fidem

9 Jan. 1583 P, 458 Besançon

Respondissem, monsieur, ad

31 Jan. 1583 P, 487-488 Besançon

Ad ea quae de Scaligeri

7 Mar. 1583 P, 505 . . . .

Tabellarius, monsieur [?], rettulit [?] mihi datas

[4] The date is written "4 Eid. Sept."

21 Mar.	1583	P, 451	Besançon
Accepi Athenaeum tuum, hoc est			
10 July	1583	P, 481-482	....
Noli indignari, si ad binos			
12 Aug.	1583[5]	P, 450	Besançon
Quae ex ista impudentia est			
18 Aug.	1583	P, 491	....
Respondeo typographo multo quam mihi			
5 Sept.	1583	P, 490	....
Mitto primas quaterniones seu titulos			
18 Oct.	1583	P, 489	Besançon
Vidi ante triduum editionis Tertulliani			
31 Oct.	1583	P. 483	....
De Spondano de scribis [?]			
8 Feb.	1584[6]	P, 503-504	Besançon
Nolo esse [?] longus ad urbanissimos tuos			
20 Feb.	1584	P, 449	Besançon
Expecto quid obtinueris a Junta			
16 Apr.	1584	P, 499	Besançon
Valde miror Juntas			
30 Apr.	1584	P, 500	Besançon
Gaudeo vehementer absolutum librum			
8 July	1584	P, 496	Besançon
Recepi binas tuas literas			
23 July	1584	P, 480	Besançon
Prodierunt hoc anno mustea duo opera			
5 Aug.	1584	P, 479	Besançon
En tibi duo volumina Lipsii			
31 Oct.	1584	P, 462-463	Besançon
Deplorabat, monsieur, me			
27 Nov.	1584	P, 456	Besançon
Accepi literas tuas et quas mittit			
10 Dec.	1584	P, 454	Besançon
Accepi consilium tuum et quae			
23 July	1585	P, 501	Besançon
Venit ad nos messer Antonius Rogerius			
15 Jan.	1586	P, 484	Besançon
Dudum [?] nullas ad te dedi literas			

[5] The date is written "IIX eid. Aug."
[6] The date is written "8 Eid. Febr."

5 Feb. 1586 P, 452 Besançon
Gratulor tibi de tuo Plinio
18 Feb. 1587 P, 460 Besançon
Accepi ingentia duo munera
1 Apr. 1587 P, 448 Besançon
Nunc tuum Plinius meus
30 Sept. 1587 P, 494 Besançon
Ecce . . . vinis et vines
19 Jan. 1588 P, 453 Besançon
Amicum nostrum non potui
§. . . . P, 38-39 Lyon
Ingenio magno tuum fratrem
§. . . . P, 40 Lyon
Egi cum Gryphio de eo quod mandasti
§. . . . P, 41 Lyon
Nihil rescribere liquido possum

Joannes Clericus (1)
13 Jan. 1570 P, 240-243 Poitiers
Praeter nominis tui splendorem

Gilbertus Cognatus [Gilbert Cousin] (1)
19 Apr. 1564 P, 216 "Nazerethi"
Vehementer sum veritus, eximie vir

Robertus Constantinus (30)
6 Dec. 1558 (rec) P, 290 . . . .
Monsieur et meilleur ami, je n'introduiray
9 Dec. 1558 (rec) P, 296 . . . .
Monsieur et meilleur ami, je vous ay escript
24 Feb. 1559 (rec) P, 285 . . . .
Monsieur, mon meilleur amy encore
25 Apr. 1559 P, 278 . . . .
Monsieur et entier ami, iai envoie
2 Dec. 1559 (rec) P, 281 . . . .
Monsieur et singulier ami, le seigneur
16 July 1560 P, 293 . . . .
Monsieur et tres parfaict amy, je vous envoye
7 Mar. 1561 (rec) P, 280 . . . .
Monsieur et singulier ami, ie vous envoie
12 Mar. 1561 P, 279 . . . .
Monsieur et singulier ami, ie vous mercie

25 Apr.	1561	P, 269-270	. . . .
	Tres solicite, trescher seigneur		
7 Apr.	1562	P, 291	Geneva
	Tres cher seigneur et fidelle ami		
31 Dec.	1562	P, 265-266	Basel
	Legi tandem literas dignissimas		
25 Dec.	1567	P, 286	Venice
	Monsieur et entier amy, ie soubhaiterois		
26 Apr.	1582	P, 289	Castres
	Monsieur et tres honoré ami		
§1 Dec.	. . . .	P, 71	Bourg en Bresse
	Prudentissimum consilium tuum arbitror		
4 July	. . . .	P, 271	. . . .
	Monsieur et entier ami		
8 Nov.	. . . .	P, 275-276	Geneva
	Monsieur et entier ami, le present		
2 Apr.	. . . .	P, 277	. . . .
	Cher seigneur et ami, i'envoirai		
10 May	. . . .	P, 284	. . . .
	Monsieur et trescher ami ie vous escri [sic]		
13 Feb.	. . . .	P, 287	. . . .
	Monsieur et tres parfaict ami, je suis		
13 Jan.	. . . .	P, 288	. . . .
	Il ni ha doubte, tres cher seigneur		
21 June	. . . .	P, 292	. . . .
	Je vous envoie, cher seigneur		
24 May	. . . .	P, 295	. . . .
	Monsieur et meilleur ami, ie ne vous escripuis		
. . . .		P, 263	. . . .
	Rogo te, amice charissime		
. . . .		P, 267-268	. . . .
	Monsieur et singulier ami, j'acquiesse		
. . . .		P, 272	. . . .
	Trescher seigneur et ami		
. . . .		P, 273	. . . .
	Cher seigneur et ami, i'hay envoie		
. . . .		P, 274	. . . .
	Je pensois, cher seigneur et ami		
. . . .		P, 282	. . . .
	Monsieur, je crains fort que		
. . . .		P, 283	. . . .
	Monsieur et parfaict ami		

....		P, 294	Castres	
Seigneur et meilleur ami, le voiage				
		Cornuti		(1)
1 Feb.	1580	P, 138	Paris	
Epistolam a te habeo unicam				
		Germanus Courtin		(1)
....		P, 127	Paris	
Saepius in animo fuit				
		Courtois (student at Padua)		(2)
13 Dec.	1583	P, 99	Padua	
Monsieur, estant maintenant en ceste ville				
14 Feb.	1584	P, 98	Padua	
Monsieur, si la vertu n'avoit				
		Joannes Andreas à Croaria		(1)
18 June	1552	P, 135	Montpellier	
Memini cum in te nescio				
		Jacobus Cuiacius [Jacques Cujas]		(8)
23 Oct.	1573	L, 53	Valence	
Et si raro ad te scribo				
11 Mar.	1584	L, 53	Bourges	
Monsieur, C'est pour remercier				
15 Sept.	1584	L, 53	Bourges	
Monsieur, ie n'ay gueres bien				
25 Aug.	1587	L, 53-54	Bourges	
Monsieur. Je loüe Dien et m'en				
.. Sept.	1587	L, 54	Bourges	
Monsieur. I'ay reçeu M. Rene Gros				
2 Nov.	1587	L, 54	Bourges	
Monsieur. Vostre nepueu estant arrivé				
§....		P, 15	....	
Athenaeum qui me diu				
		Dreuille		(1)
23 Apr.	1586	P, 256	....	
Monsieur, ce nest la commodité				

		Jean Le Duc		(1)
19 July	1587[?]	P, 85-86	....	
Monsieur, quelques bons peut estre				
		N. Dulcis (medicus Divionensis)		(1)
14 Apr.	....	P, 421	Dijon	
Nervi puncturae de qua tibi				
		Petrus Faber [Pierre Lefevre]		(20)
5 Jan.	1556	P, 424	Montpellier	
Nae mihi malum omen				
27 Nov.	1556	P, 438	Montpellier	
Immortales tibi gratias agendas				
1 Jan.	1557	P, 434	Montpellier	
Quoniam hac tibi misit				
4 May	1557	P, 429	Montpellier	
Quandoquidem scire cupis in literarum fasciculi				
13 Aug.	1557	P, 426	Montpellier	
Etsi tua te fortasse magis				
25 Jan.	1558	P, 430	Montpellier	
Decrevi hinc in Sorsicam[sic.:Corsicam(?)] brevi profecisti				
2 Feb.	1558	P, 425	Montpellier	
Nihil est gratum tibi				
30 May	1558	P, 436	Montpellier	
Scripseram postremis[?] hisce				
24 Aug.	1558	P, 439	Montpellier	
Literae tuae et Gesneri				
1 Sept.	1558	P, 433	Montpellier	
Nam[?] . . . literis meis negotia				
22 Sept.	1558	P, 435	Montpellier	
Qui hac ad te				
5 Oct.	1558	P, 422	Montpellier	
Accepi literas tuas 25 Septembris				
3 Nov.	1558	P, 423	Montpellier	
Incomparabilia que[?] in me tuus amor profecto				
31 Dec.	1558	P, 440	Montpellier	
Eiconium anatis a te mittit				
1 Apr.	1559	P, 428	Padua	
Expostular non dubito et non				
13 Apr.	1559	P, 441	"Ex Diacra Sorsicae"[7]	
Qui mihi literae tuae				

[7] In this and the following letters, the reading may (and probably should) be "Corsicae," though an "S" is clearly written.

30 May	1559	P, 432	"Ex Diacra Sorsicae"
Toto . . . pacis inter principes nostros			
20 July	1559	P, 442	"Ex Diacra Sorsicae"
Scripseram ad te nuperrime			
17 Sept.	1559	P, 437	"Ex Diacra Sorsicae"
Ex literis ab Eugenio nepote			
12 Oct.	1561	P, 431	. . . .
Quantum olim fuerit adiuvandi[?]			

Ioannes Faucherius (24)

31 Dec.	1575	P, 385-386	Tarascon
Cur tuis votis non usquequaque			
29 June	1576	P, 384	Beaucaire
Binas iam a Bimestri ad te			
31 Oct.	1576	P, 382	. . . .
Mitto iam tertio thapsiam			
22 June	1578	P, 394	Beaucaire
Hac aestate varias cum seminibus plantas			
18 Oct.	1578	P, 383	Beaucaire
Ne mirere si bellicis tumultibus			
1 Feb.	1579	P, 396	Tarascon
Perlectis literis tuis quam quam diligentissime			
6 July	1579	P, 397	. . . .
Ex quo ad te plantam			
13 Jan.	1580	P, 402	Beaucaire
Ex quo novissime ad me scripsisti			
31 Oct.	1581	P, 405	Beaucaire
Vertor ne eadem toties scriptitando			
4 June	1582	P, 404	Beaucaire
Lycii succum quam tantopere tibi			
7 Aug.	1582	P, 398	Beaucaire
Gaudeo plurimum succum Lycii			
30 Dec.	1582	P, 379	Beaucaire
Quereris iusta occasione quod Lycium			
27 June	1583	P, 400	Beaucaire
Mitto ad te rursus Lycium			
31 July	1583	P, 407	Beaucaire
Literae tuae me summa delectatione			
14 Aug.	1583	P, 399	Beaucaire
Mitto ad te portionem cuiusdam herbae			
28 Oct.	1583	P, 378	Beaucaire
Non permittam ut tuum in scribendo			
8 Jan.	1585	P, 406	Beaucaire
Per hunc negotiatorem Lugdunum			

19 Mar. 1585 P, 401 Beaucaire
Mitto ad te quem tantopere

19 June 1586 P, 381 Beaucaire
Anxius diu quaesivi cui tuto litteras

25 Apr. .... P, 408 Beaucaire
Si literae meae postremae ad te

.... P, 380 ....
Mitto ad te nunc denuo Lycium

.... P, 395 ....
In dies te magis atque magis

.... P, 403 Beaucaire
Expectavi hucusque volumen illud si forte

.... P, 409 Tarascon
Reprehensionis notam effugere non possem

Joannes Fernel[l]ius [Jean Fernel] (1)

§.... P, 13-14 ....
Non sine iustissima quadam fati

Paul de Foix (1)

14 Mar. 1583 P, 247-248 Rome
Monsieur Dalechamps, jay receu un Athenae.

Britannus Forsterus[8] (1)

.... P, 238-239 "Ex Hestritro"[?]
Quod bonorum hominum semper

Petrus Froissart (1)

7 May 1558 P, 129-130 "Polyguii"[?]
Cum tam varia eaque praeciosissima

François Fron . . . [?] (1)

.. Oct. 1549 P, 227 ....
Monsieur, j'ay resceu[!] vostre lettre

Iacobus Fulgonius (1)

31 Mar. .... P, 377 Paris
Nihil mihi gratius unquam accidit

[8] The signature to this letter reads: "Brih. Forsterus." Daléchamps's note has "Britannus Viator."

		Jean François Gambalde		(2)
8 Apr.	1584	P, 371-372	Montbrison	
Monsieur, je suis estremement marri				
12 May	1584	P, 369-370	Montbrison	
Monsieur, desirant de tout mon pouvoir				
		Andreas Garbotus		(2)
1 May	1557	P, 158-159	Paris	
Tuis ad praeceptorem meum				
29 June	1557	P, 160	Paris	
Pridie Non. Junii accepi tuas literas				
		Alexis Gaudinus [Godin]		(2)
15 Oct.	1556	P, 133	Blois	
Qui has tibi reddidit				
20 Feb.	....	P, 101	Blois	
Nostris hunc bibliopolam, qui has tibi				
		Conradus Gesnerus [Conrad Gesner]		(8)
6 Jan.	1560	P, 264	Zurich	
Nuper ad te scripsi per iamprimum				
20 Jan.	1560(rec)	P, 261-262	Zurich	
Est (inquit) et rubeus lilium				
24 Jan.	1561	P, 259-260	Zurich	
Ante paucos dies ad te scripsi				
§4 Feb.	1561	P, 31-34	Lyon	
Dentellariae vim et facultatem intelligere				
§27 Mar.	1561	P, 27-30	Lyon	
Ad postremas literas tuas respondi				
6 Sept.	1561	P, 257-258	Zurich	
Literas quas 25 Iunii ad me dedisti				
8 Jan.	1562	MH, 133-150	Zurich	
Salus et pax a Domino				
§....		P, 35-36	....	
Humanitatis summae tuae potius est				
		De Godefroy		(1)
§....		P, 59-60	....	
Monsieur, ie vous remercie tant				
		Pontius Golerius		(1)
14 Aug.	1561	P, 117-118	....	
Antiquus ille noster Hippo.				

		Joannes Goyerius		(1)
23 Oct.	1574	P, 139	Paris	
Ex quo transumus Lugduno in comitatu				
		Joannes Guarinus		(1)
....		P, 115-116	....	
Iam pridem factum est				
		Guichard		(1)
§....		P, 65	....	
Epistolam tuam sane gratissimam				
		Rivodeus Guilloterius		(1)
7 Mar.	....	P, 142	....	
Salui et incolumes in patriam				
		Antonius de Harss[?]		(1)
11 Dec.	1585	P, 112	....	
Monsieur, ce que je vous				
		Franciscus Iunctinus [Francesco Giuntini]		(1)
....		P, 221	....	
Del nascimento et occaso delle stelle fisse				
		Joannes Lalemantius [Jean Lalement]		(8)
25 Jan.	1574	P, 355	Autun	
Ad 12 Calend. febru. mihi				
21 Jan.	1575	P, 360-363	Autun	
Mitto tibi, Dalechampi doctiss., paginas aliquot				
2 Aug.	1577	P, 358	Autun	
D. Jo. Albosius sororius meus				
7 Aug.	1579	P, 367-368	Autun	
Anatomicarum Administrationum libros graecos				
15 May	....	P, 354	Autun	
DD. Dandozileus medicus nostras				
2 Aug.	....	P, 359	Autun	
Verborum multitudine non avertam				
1 May	....	P, 364-366	Autun	
Non licuit per occupationes				
§....		P, 66-67		
Nihil in praesens ad te rescribo				

		Petrus Lambertus [Pierre de Lambert]		(1)
22 June	1582	P, 251	. . . .	
Monsieur, affin qu'a				
		Lect. [?]		(2)
22 Feb.	1585	P, 198	. . . .	
Monsieur, i'ay receu vos deux lettres				
13 Dec.	1586	P, 197	. . . .	
Monsieur, i'ay sceu que				
		De Luc [?]		(1)
15 Mar.	1585	P, 134	Pont de Cheruy	
Monsieur, je vous prie mexcuser				
		Leonardus de Marchief		(3)
14 Mar.	1563	P, 188-189	"Cabilrui" [?]	
Binas tuas accepi litteras				
15 Mar.	1563	P, 178	"Cabilrui" [?]	
Cum regius apud res advocatus				
15 Nov.	1565	P, 190	"Cabilrui" [?]	
Scripturus tibi de magis nostris				
		Joannes Marquisius [Marquis]		(2)
30 Sept.	1587	P, 141	Vienne	
Rogatus sum, vir clarissime, a cognato meo				
24 Feb.	1588	P, 224	Vienne	
Uxor cognati mei (vir clarissime)				
		Jean de Mayerne Turquet		(2)
1 Jan.	1585	P, 211-212	D'Avalon in Lauxois	
Jusquea a [sic] jourduy puis				
17 Oct.	1587	P, 210	Geneva	
Monsieur, ie vous renvoye le livre				
		Hieronymus Mercurialis [Girolamo Mercuriale]		(1)
§. . . .		P, 44	. . . .	
Mihi quamvis nulla tecum				
		Franciscus Miconius		(5)
2 Jan.	1570	P, 445-446	Barcelona	
Aunque no conoza a v. m. de vista				
§24 May	1576	P, 52-57	Lyon	
Mirabar simul et dolebam				

26 Dec. 1576 P, 444 Barcelona
Ex his quas superioribus diebus
§.... P, 58 Lyon
Tam diu nihil abs te literarum
.... P, 443 ....
Accipe, mi Dalanchapie [sic], interim

Claudius Mitalerius [Claude Mitalier] (20)
15 Sept. 1576 P, 307-310 ....
Lectis tuis literis quibus a me
§.... P, 61-62 Lyon [?]
Primum ego gratias quod temporis

There are also eighteen letters in Greek from Mitalerius to Daléchamps, written in a hand that is very irregular and difficult to read. They are to be found in P, 311-327, 342.

De Montfort (1)
24 Dec. 1587 P, 225-226 "De Courlesaulnier" [?]
Monsieur, ayant entendu que

Antonius Montellus (1)
1 Apr. 1559 P, 136 Montpellier
Sic [?] estis, scio coniuncti benevolentia

Hieronymus Montuus [Hierosme Monteux] (1)
§.... P, 72-73 Lyon [?]
Nisi tibi plusquam notum foret

André Mornieu (1)
13 Nov. 1582 P, 103 Paris
Natura fax [?] comparatum est

Gaspar Mornieu (1)
13 Nov. 1582 P, 102 Paris
De Cassii olim iudicie integritate

Giovanni Francesco Morosini (1)
12 Feb. 1574 P, 255 Venice
Ho havuto il disegno

Joannes Munsterius (1)
20 June 1569 P, 119-120 ....
Cum me Januario mensi

Mauricius Nachomius (1)

12 Dec. 1560 P, 82 . . . .
Cum primum Monspessulum veni

Nicolaus Nancelius [Nicole Nancel] (4)

13 Sept. 1581 P, 162 Tours
Emisi in lucem proximis diebus
5 Apr. 1584 P, 161; N, 115-118 Tours
Et candor ille tuus
13 Apr. 1587 N, 168-169 Tours
Proximis meis ad te literis

§. . . . P, 70 Lyon [?]
Vellem, doctissime Nanceli et equidem libentissime

Joannes Palleron (2)

5 Oct. . . . . P, 143 "E nostro alobrogum lavinio" [?]
Literas tuas munusque tuum
20 June . . . . P, 222 . . . .
Iuvamenta [?] princeps rudes in statu

Gulielmus Paradin (1)

18 Nov. 1583 P, 215 . . . .
Monsieur, vostre lettre m'est venue

Petrus [?] Pichot (1)

31 Oct. 1577 P, 140 Montpellier
Scilicet ingeniis aliqua est concordia

Gulielmus Plantius [Guillaume Plancy] (1)

3 June 1555 P, 223 . . . .
Jacobus Vigerius medicus cardinalis

Jacques Plateau (3)

11 May 1587 P, 90 Tournai
Monsieur, estant [?] la renommee [?]
20 July 1587 P, 92 Tournai
Monsieur, iay receu vostre lettre
19 Aug. 1587 P, 93 Tournai
Monsieur, il ya quelques semaines

Felix Plater (1)

22 Apr. 1572 P, 228 Basel
Cl. atque ornatiss. vir, facit nominis

Joannes Platetus (1)

7 Jan. 1579 P, 91 "Aven"[?]
Cum neque de quinta essentia

Jacobus Pons (1)

. . . . P, 113-114 . . . .
Ad questionem mihi perpolitam

Pandulphus Prateius [Pardoux DuPrat] (1)

. . . . P, 232 . . . .
Ea fuit antiquorum medicorum

Jehan Prevost

3 Sept. 1561 P, 152-153 . . . .
Trescher et honoré seigneur jay
24 Sept. 1561 P, 151 . . . .
Monsieur, je me vous envoye[?]

Gulielmus Puteanus [Dupuis] (1)

. . . . P, 83-84 . . . .
Accepi litteras tuas, Jacobe doctissime

A. Rassius [Rasse] (4)

13 June 1565 P, 164 . . . .
Ne tu omnium officiorum in amicum
5 Feb. 1566 P, 183 Paris
Quod prior amice me enim
12 Feb. 1566 P, 182 Paris
Perlegi hoc sero ternas litteras tuas
2 June 1576 P, 165 . . . .
Monsieur, non moins de plaisir

Jan Regnauld (3)

13 Jan. 1573 P, 125-126 Paris
Monsieur, *τὸ μισέω μναμονα*
8 Aug. 1573 P, 413-414 Paris
Monsieur, je retournay il y a huit
17 May 1574 P, 415 Paris
Monsieur, *ἰοκειαι*[?] *κειριτες*

		Hugo Richerius		(1)
7 Nov.	....	P, 123	"Ex Vienna"	
Quum famulus meus chartam illam				
		Jehan Robin		(4)
1 Mar.	1584	P, 507-508	Paris	
Monsieur, le prescrite souis[?]				
10 Sept.	1584	P, 513	Paris	
Monsieur, le prescrite souis[?]				
1 Sept.	1586	P, 514	....	
Quae virorum illustrorum				
30 Dec.	1586	P, 509-510	Paris	
Monsieur, pour satisfaire si la				
		D. de Rochefort		(1)
§....		P, 37	....	
Ad priores literas tuas non respondi				
		T. de Rochefort		(1)
2 Apr.	1560[or 1580]	P, 214	Padua	
Cum Gabriele Fallopio Mutinensi				
		Stephanus Rodetus		(2)
....	1563[?]	P, 181	....	
.... ut promissa haud ita				
..Feb.	1564	P, 179-180	....	
Facit tua in me humanitas				
		Franciscus Rossetus [François de Rousset]		(1)
....	1574	P, 131	"Montregii"	
Mitto ad te, vir doctissime				
		Rousselet [Rousseletius]		(2)
2 Feb.	1582	P, 410	....	
Monsieur, importunité est aux				
27 Dec.	1583	P, 411-412	....	
Varie sum affectus iis libris				
		De Rymon		(5)
13 July	1585	P, 201	....	
Importuna petax perfructe				
1 Sept.	1585	P, 199	....	
Desunt quae placeant Burgundo				

2 Dec.	1585	P, 202-203	....
	Monsieur, par tous bons offres		
.. Jan.	1587	P, 204-209	....
	Monsieur, et la calamité du temps		
....		P, 200	....
	Que penes est teipsum sic		

Michael Saborinus (1)

5 Feb.	....	P, 124	Sancerre
	Tametsi in negotiis meis persequendis		

Matthias Sasbontius (1)

....		P, 76	....
	Non sano malum malo		

Joseph Justus Scaliger

10 Apr.	1561	B, 308	Agen
	Monsieur, ie n'eusse iamais		
7 Sept.	1571	B, 309-310	Valence
	Monsieur, mon frère m'a escrit		
22 Jan.	1583	B, 310-311	Grenoble
	Monsieur, ie vous remercie très humblement		
30 Jan.	1583	B, 311-312	Valence
	Monsieur, il ne me souuient iamais		
24 Oct.	1584	B, 312-313	Abain
	Monsieur, ie pense qu' aurez reçeu		
6 Jan.	1587	B, 313	Chasteau de Trouffou près Poitiers
	Monsieur, si faut il que uous		
23 Mar.	1587	B, 314	Abain
	Monsieur, ie uous remercie très humblement		
....	Vigil of Easter	B, 308-309	Chantemille en la Marche
	Monsieur, i'ay reçeu vostre lettre		

Andreas Schottus [Andreas Schott] (6)

§24 July	1586	P, 19-20	Lyon [?]
	Caesar Augustae scriptae literae tuae		
§....		P, 16-17	Lyon [?]
	Accepi binas tuas, quod ad priores		
§....		P, 18	Lyon [?]
	Ad editionem paratus est Seneca noster		

§. . . . P, 21-22 Lyon
Cum Buissonio cuius fidei capsam tuam
§. . . . P, 23-24 Lyon [?]
Siquid literarum a Rovilio et Bussonio
§. . . . P, 25-26 Lyon [?]
Literas tuas Baptista Rovilius

Seracenus (2)
5 Oct. 1560 P, 416-417 Grenoble
Quod ad me decim [?] quarto
1 Oct. . . . . P, 418-419 . . . .
Eo ad te tardius litterae

Io. Serranus (1)
29 Oct. 1584 P, 218 Nîmes
Clariss. vir, Platonem tuam habui apud me

Reinerus Solenander (2)
20 Sept. 1559(rec) P, 166-167 . . . .
A meo discessu, Dalechampi doctissime
. . . . P, 150 . . . .
Medicamentum [?] quo vidi resinae [?] lapidem

Hugo Solerius (2)
5 July 1551 P, 78 . . . .
Gratum fecisti, mi Jacobe
4 Sept. 1551 P, 121-122 Raymond
Acceptis lectisque diligenter ambabus tuis

Petrus Sosius (1)
. . . . P, 192 . . . .
In myrtei folii speciem cutis

Henricus Stephanus [Henri Estienne] (38)
. . . . SD, 2-5 . . . .
Epitaphia mea in Petrum Victorium
. . . . S, 3-6 . . . .
Superioribus literis novum tibi
. . . . S, 7-11 . . . .
Si Seneca essem, mi Dalechampi
. . . . S, 12-14 . . . .
Quandoquidem in te consolando Seneca esse
. . . . S, 15-16 . . . .
Meministi (opinor) saepe me

. . . . S, 17-20 . . . .
Senecam nostrum mira fuisse
. . . . S, 20-23 . . . .
Audaciae eiusdem, id est
. . . . S, 23-26 . . . .
Ecce alius a superioribus
. . . . S, 27-30 . . . .
Tempus est ut quod me tibi
. . . . S, 30-34 . . . .
Expectabas fortasse ut si quam
. . . . S, 34-39 . . . .
Reliquit Roma, reliquit tibi
. . . . S, 39-44 . . . .
Accidit, mi Dalechampi, epistolae
. . . . S, 44-52 . . . .
Quo nomine hanc epistolam
. . . . S, 52-56 . . . .
Sicut proxime praecedentem epistolam
. . . . S, 57-60 . . . .
Idem facio, mi Dalechampi, quod
. . . . S, 60-64 . . . .
Miror, mi Dalechampi, tam multos
. . . . S, 65-66 . . . .
Memoriae meae imperare non possum
. . . . S, 67-72 . . . .
Non possum mihi temperare
. . . . S, 73-79 . . . .
Epistolae proxime praecedentis argumentum
. . . . S, 79-82 . . . .
Senecae lectores plerisque locis
. . . . S, 82-85 . . . .
Senecam quo magis lego
. . . . S, 85-101 . . . .
Inter partim suspecta, partim reprehensa
. . . . S, 101-106 . . . .
In aliquot superioribus epistolis
. . . . S, 106-113 . . . .
Seneca (si eiusdem Senecae sunt . . .)
. . . . S, 114-119 . . . .
Sicut in Aristotelem inquisivit Seneca
. . . . S, 120-122 . . . .
Parisinae meae in Aulum Gellium

....		S, 122-124	....	
	Πολλὰ μεταξὺ γραφῆς			
....		S, 124-127	....	
	Quemadmodum in aliis quas suscepimus			
....		S, 127-129	....	
	Nescio an tibi, mi Dalechampi			
....		S, 130-132	....	
	Parodiarum moralium a me scriptum			
....		S, 132-136	....	
	Ecce quousque paulatim audacia mea			
....		S, 136-137bis	....	
	Quoties aliquid inveni, non expecto			
....		S, 173bis-140 bis	....	
	Dissentit ab Horatio et caeteris poetis			
....		S, 140bis-144	....	
	Fabio cum Seneca, si uterque			
....		S, 143-149	....	
	Graecis vocabulis valde fuisse			
....		S, 149-153	....	
	Vereor ne me tua iam			
....		S, 153-[158]	....	
	Non differo te (ut Seneca noster loquitur)			
....		S, [158]-[160]	....	
	Statui, hac epistola, mi Dalechampi			
		Cephas Tervius[9]		(1)
....		P, 246	....	
	Misit ad me iam ante menses aliquot			
		Claudius Textor		(2)
1 Feb.	1561(rec)	P, 186-187	....	
	Honnore Seigneur, ie vous envoye un oyseau			
14 Apr.	1561	P, 184-185	....	
	Cher seigneur et ami, neuste este			
		Monsieur Thou		(1)
14 Apr.	1557(rec)	P, 87	"In Radicibus Palatini Montis"	
	Qui ambas insidias moliri			

[9] Daléchamps's note to this letter has "Tarvius."

Jacobus Tussanus [Jacques Toussain] (1)

13 Mar. .... P, 89 Nîmes
Qui tibi has reddet

Federicus de Valimbert (1)

28 Apr. 1575 P, 236-237 Besançon
Consuluit me quidam de inveterato gallico morbo

Petrus Victorius [Pier Vettori] (2)

§1 Mar. 1583 VB II, 155-156; P, 69; M 167 Lyon
Paulo Minutio cive tuo
11 June 1584 V, 217 Florence
Litterae tuae K. Martiis datae fuerunt mihi

Ludovicus Villanovanus (2)

.. Nov. 1574[10] P, 193-194 Grenoble
Accepi, vir eruditissime, que potissimum
12 Nov. 1583 P, 195-196 Grenoble
Memini me superioribus annis

Jacobus Vize (1)

2 June 1574 P, 235 La Raiasse
Bifolium, tum recenter emergens

Willeminus (1)

25 Apr. 1574 P, 229-231 ....
Non voluntate aut proposito

Erhardus Zeyselius (2)

13 July 1551 P, 373-374 Tour-du-Pin
Pulchre philosophi probant, vir clarissime
17 May 1554 P, 375-376 "Ex Thermis Esensibus"
De negotio [?] nostro Montispessulensi ita

II. LETTERS NOT TO A SINGLE INDIVIDUAL, OR BY OR TO INDIVIDUALS UNKNOWN

Ad Academiam [Medicinae] Parisiensem

§8 Apr. 1557 P, 1-2 Lyon [?]
Immortales gratias vobis agimus

[10] The letter has the date as "6 non." of November, which is impossible.

§. . . . P, 3-4 Lyon [?]

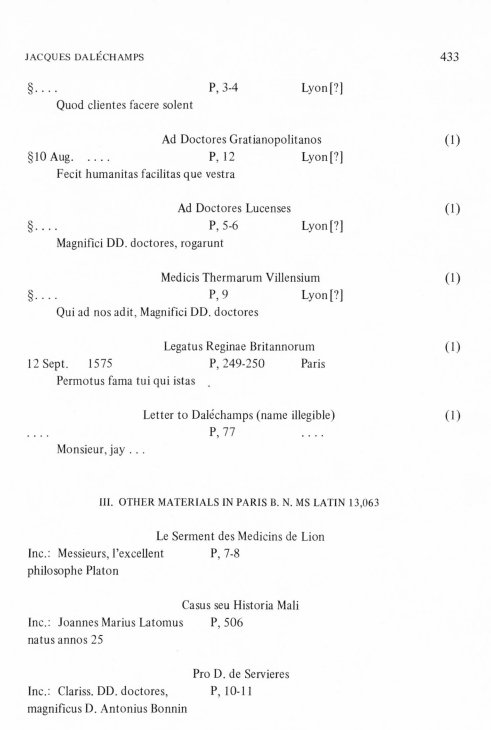

Quod clientes facere solent

Ad Doctores Gratianopolitanos (1)

§10 Aug. . . . . P, 12 Lyon [?]

Fecit humanitas facilitas que vestra

Ad Doctores Lucenses (1)

§. . . . P, 5-6 Lyon [?]

Magnifici DD. doctores, rogarunt

Medicis Thermarum Villensium (1)

§. . . . P, 9 Lyon [?]

Qui ad nos adit, Magnifici DD. doctores

Legatus Reginae Britannorum (1)

12 Sept. 1575 P, 249-250 Paris

Permotus fama tui qui istas

Letter to Daléchamps (name illegible) (1)

. . . . P, 77 . . . .

Monsieur, jay . . .

III. OTHER MATERIALS IN PARIS B. N. MS LATIN 13,063

Le Serment des Medicins de Lion

Inc.: Messieurs, l'excellent philosophe Platon P, 7-8

Casus seu Historia Mali

Inc.: Joannes Marius Latomus natus annos 25 P, 506

Pro D. de Servieres

Inc.: Clariss. DD. doctores, magnificus D. Antonius Bonnin P, 10-11

Pro Domino Foucheo Dolensi

Inc.: Quae praeter naturam in clarissimum virum P. 63-64

Letter of Alexis Gaudinus to Denis Saivaige

28 Apr.	....	P, 100	Blois

Monsieur et bon amy, ie receu

The Warburg Institute
University of London
Woburn Square
London WC1H OAB, England

THE HISPANIC ORIGIN OF OUR PRESENT NUMERAL FORMS

•

by Richard Lemay

In the present article I wish to present some facts observed in medieval manuscripts, Latin as well as Arabic, principally of Hispanic origin or influenced by Hispanic tradition in the circumscribed fields of astronomical, astrological and mathematical sciences. These facts will illuminate the origins of the forms of our present numerals.[1] But first, let me make a few clarifications about the naming of our present system of number symbols.

Despite its long standing in the Western tradition, the appellation "Arabic," or Hindu-Arabic for that matter, is neither the earliest nor the commonest one to be used in the Middle Ages, for the nine symbols and the zero. In the earliest period, they were diversely called by names normally showing an awareness of their foreign

[1] The best general account of the historiography of the problem and of the preferred solutions in recent times remains that of D. E. Smith and L. C. Karpinski, *Hindu-Arabic Numerals* (Boston 1911), on which Smith's own later *History of Mathematics* (1925) mainly depends (Dover Publications 1958 [1925]) 2.36-88. Yet, on their own admission (cf. Smith, *History* 2.68) some basic factors in this long history still remained entirely unknown and little hope was entertained that they might some day receive a final solution.

Gonzalo Menéndez Pidal has made a recent attempt to renew the investigation by concentrating on the traditions of medieval Spain (G. Menéndez Pidal, "Los llamados numerales árabes en Occidente," *Boletín de la Real academia de la historia* 145 [Oct.-Dec. 1959] 179-208). Here is a commendable approach, for it concentrates the research in a limited area of close contact between Eastern and Western science and a close time sequence so as to offer better prospect for concrete results. When, in addition, the whole complex of general cultural traits, historical conditions of acculturation, local traditions and usages, as well as paleographical remains are all taken into consideration, solid evidence may be expected to come to light at the end of the inquiry. Two conclusions of Menéndez Pidal seem already established and deserve special mention. One is that neither the "Hindu" origin nor the *ghubār* tradition provide the right answer to Hispanic tradition: "No puede satisfacernos ni la procedencia india que proclamaron los tratadistas medievales, ni tampoco el origen gubār que le attribuyen los historiadores de hoy" (205). The second is that each numerical symbol seems to have its own separate history: "No existe genealogia única para la serie completa actual, casi puede decirse que cada cifra y cada figura tiene su historia" (208). Menéndez Pidal's own conviction about their introduction into Europe stresses the role of Toledo in the process: "Fue Toledo la puerta per donde penetró en Europa el nuevo sistema de cálculo basado en los nueves cifras y el cero" (188). This study will supply further evidence of the soundness of this approach.

origin. We find the expression *figurae* modified by the addition of *indicae* or *toletanae*;[2] we also find *cifrae*, or *algorismi* or *numeri de abaco. Cifrae* is a Latinized form of the Arabic *ṣifr(un)* meaning null or void, the Arabic name for *zero.* To some, the zero stood out as the most notable novelty and advantage of the system and its name passed on to designate the entire series of symbols in the system. *Ṣifr(un)* became *zero* in the Italian language[3] but late enough when it had become clear that it represented only the null sign. In other European languages (French: *chiffre*; German: *ziffer*; Spanish: *cifra*) the appellation remained general for the entire system, while in English the word *cipher* has retained both meanings. The more generally accepted Latin form was *algorismus* popularized by the treatises of John of Sacrobosco (thirteenth century) and Alexandre de Villedieu (thirteenth century), while in Italy, *numeri de abaco* became more common after the celebrated work of this title published in 1202 by Leonardo Fibonacci of Pisa.[4] *Algorismus* (or algorism, augrim, and so on)[5] of course is a garbled rendering of the name of the Arab author al-Khwārızmī whose book of *Arithmetic,* translated into Latin in three different versions during the twelfth century, along with his *Algebra wa'l-muqabala* and his *Astronomical Tables*, was the most notable single channel through which the "Hindu-Arabic" system of numerals was made known to the West. The appellation *indicae figurae* for these symbols originated in the West probably from the opening statements of al-Khwārizmī's *Arithmetic*, where the invention was credited to the genius of the Indians.[6]

Among the Arabs, the symbols were also called "Indian letters" or "figures" (*al-ḥurūf al-hindī*)[7] and arithmetical operations performed with them were labeled *al-ḥisāb al-hindī.*[8] Another special expression, *jummal,* is sometimes stated by recent historians to have designated the system of alphabetical numerals in use among the

[2] See fig. 1, from Munich, CLM 18927.

[3] *Zero* is a contraction of *zephiro,* the early Italian pronunciation for the arabic *çifrun,* meaning null or void. Cf. Smith, *History* (n. 1 above) 2.71.

[4] The *Liber abaci* of Leonardo was first published in 1202 and revised in 1228 with a dedication to Michael Scot. It was published by B. Boncompagni, *Il liber Abbaci di Leonardo Pisano* (Rome 1857). Leonardo in turn seems indebted for the appellation "abacus" given to the numerals by the tradition issued from Gerbert of Aurillac who died as Pope Sylvester II in A.D. 1003. About A.D. 980, this renowned scholar introduced from Spain into Lorraine (Rheims) intermediary forms of Arabic numerals which he inscribed on counters (apices) for use in reckoning with the abacus. A school of new abacists flourished after him for some time.

[5] Modern *algorithm* is a derivative from this medieval tradition.

[6] John of Seville makes the following statement in the beginning of his *Liber alchorismi*: "Numerus est unitatum collectio, quae quia in infinitum progreditur (multitudo enim crescit in infinitum), ideo *a peritissimis Indis* sub quibusdam regulis et certis limitibus infinita numerositas coarctatur, ut de infinitis difinita disciplina traderetur et fuga subtilium rerum sub alicuius artis certissima lege teneretur." Paris B. N. MSS lat. 7359, fol. 85; and lat. 15461, fol. 1. Cf. B. Boncompagni, *Trattati d'aritmetica. . . .* (Rome 1857) 26.

[7] Cf. the nine "letters" (ḥurūf) of the Indians in *The Fihrist of al-Nadīm . . .*, ed., trans. Bayard Dodge (New York 1970) 1.34.

[8] Al-Nadim, author of the *Fihrist* (ca. A.D. 987) has an entire section (2) of his chapter 7 on "geometricians, arithmeticians, musicians, calculators, astrologers, makers of instruments, and persons interested in mechanics and dynamics." Cf. *The Fihrist* 2.634-672. Among the mathe-

Arabs.[9] Evidence from medieval manuscripts, however, shows a certain inappropriateness of this designation, at least in the above mentioned sense; for the expression *jummal* was equally used, with the accompanying qualifications of *al-kabīr* or *al-ṣaghīr: jummal al-kabīr*, a collection of numbers forming a certain series for use in mystical play with numbers, was written with Hindu numerals, while the *jummal al-ṣaghīr* was its counterpart using the alphabetical numerals.[10] Hence, *jummal,* which means a sum, a series, could be used equally with the Hindu and the *abjad* numerals, of which I shall speak in a moment.

Finally, the term *ghubār* (dust) applied to numerals and used principally and originally in the Maghreb (western Islamic lands) does not designate an independent or original system of symbols, but the "Arabized" version of the numerals originally developed in Spain, or better yet, the "Toledan" numerals, as I shall soon explain, which spread into the western Arabic lands in contrast to the genuine "Arabic" numerals of the Arabs themselves. Hence it seems historically incorrect to state that "the Arabs had two systems of number representation, and characterized each one by a special name: The Hindū and the Ghubār numerals."[11] In fact, "Hindu" and *ghubār* numerals in use among the Arabs belong to one and the same tradition, namely the system of nine symbols and the zero used in value position. Its generic name among the Arabs was *al-ḥisāb al-hindī*, to which the *ghubār* numerals belong. The alternate system, in much wider use, was the alphabetical numerals system properly called the *abjad* (from the first three letters of the alphabet). Calculation in this system was called *ḥisāb al-arabī*, while calculation in the nine symbols and the zero was called *ḥisāb al-hindī*.

I. NUMERALS IN ARABIC MANUSCRIPT TRADITION

A. SCRIBAL PRACTICES

Since we call the figures of our number notation "Arabic" numerals, one is naturally led to assume that these figures were in general use among Arabs, at least among

maticians and calculators mentioned, many treated of the calculation according to the Indians (ḥisāb al-hindī), in particular: Sanad ibn 'Ali, 652; al-Ṣaydanānī, 662; Sinān ibn Fath, 665; al-Karābīsī, 665; al-Anṭakī and al-Kalwadhānī, 670. All wrote especially on Indian arithmetic, some on the *Taht,* presumably the abacus. Al-Nadīm's information is far from exhaustive, however, since for al-Khwārizmī, 2.652, he omits to mention his *Arithmetic* and his *Algebra* although he mentions several authors who commented on al-Khwārizmī's *Algebra* (e.g., al-Ṣaydanānī, Sinān ibn Fath, Abū'l-Wafā'). Al-Nadīm is generally reliable in the information he supplies.

[9] E.g., Smith, *History* (n. 1 above) 2.73 n. 2; Hans Wehr, *A Dictionary of Modern Arabic,* ed. J. Milton Cowan (Wiesbaden 1966) 137b.

[10] See below, p. 441.

[11] S. Gandz, "The Origin of the Ghubar Numerals", *Isis* 16 (1931) 393. Concerning *ghubar* numerals see also F. Woepcke, "Mémoire sur la propagation des chiffres indiens," *Journal asiatique* (1863), and Smith, *History* (n. 1 above) 2.73-74.

their men of science. In reality, scribal practices, especially in the earlier periods, seem wide of this mark. We may consider in turn three categories of Arabic manuscripts to illustrate this point: manuscripts of astronomical-astrological contents, manuscripts of pure mathematics (arithmetic and algebra), and manuscripts of works dealing with number symbolism and magic.

First are the manuscripts of astronomical-astrological contents. The several such manuscripts which I had the opportunity to study in some detail represent a scattered tradition stretching from the tenth to the eighteenth centuries of the Christian era. In such manuscripts I practically never encountered in any section of their bulky volume a regular use of the "Hindu-Arabic" numerals.[12] The universal practice of the scribes of such manuscripts is either to spell out the names of the numbers, or to employ the system of the *abjad.* Historical grounds for this peculiar situation are not difficult to find. The *abjad* is an arrangement of the letters of the Arabic alphabet with numerical value in imitation of the Greek usage. It seems very likely that the Arabs borrowed their *abjad* system from the Greeks.[13] Two basic lines of argument, with an additional corollary of a historical nature, make this more than probable. First, a fully developed Arabic script hardly existed before the rise of Islam. What means of written transmission had existed earlier among the Arabs corresponded to a level of communication much inferior to and much more imperfect than oral transmission.[14] The Qur'ān itself was essentially an oral revelation, later set down in writing in a very unsystematic and haphazard way.[15] Little of a system of numerical notation could be devised or developed in such conditions.[16] Later, however, during the early years of Islamic growth and Arab empire, political expediency inspired the 'Umayyad caliphs to maintain unaltered the

[12] With one exception at least, that of a text by Maslama al-Majriti contained in Vatican, MS arab. 955. The exception, however, belongs to the Hispanic tradition and confirms some of our later assumptions; cf. below.

[13] Some Western orientalists thought that the order of the letters in the *abjad* was the ancient Semitic one such as in the Phoenician alphabet (Silvestre De Sacy, *Grammaire arabe,* rev. ed. [Paris 1841?] 89-91; G. Gaudefroy de Mombynes and R. Blanchère, *Grammaire de l'arabe classique* [Paris 1952] 20). Smith, *History* (n. 1 above) 2.53 thought it was the ancient Hebrew order. Cf. also the article *Abdjad* in *Encyclopedia of Islam.* On Greek ingenuity in adapting the letters of the Phoenician alphabet to their own needs, see T. L. Heath, *A Manual of Greek Mathematics* (Dover Publications 1963 [1931]) 15-19; Smith, *History* 2.47-53.

[14] For instance, the *Mu'allaqat* or pre-islamic Odes, after long oral transmission were collected, written down and heartily commented by a number of *literati* in the eighth and ninth centuries, as is shown in the *Fihrist,* chapter on Poetry (n. 7 above) 1.344-378.

[15] Cf. Nöldeke, Schwally, Bergsträsser and Pretzl, *Geschichte des Qorans,* 3 vols. (Leipzig 1919-1938); R. Blachère, *Introduction au Coran* (Paris 1959) esp. 4-102.

[16] Earlier contacts between pre-Islamic Arab tribes and the world of Byzantium or Persia, in the form of vassalage of the Ghassan tribe in southern Syria, or of the Lakhmids in Mesopotamia, did not reach a level that could have produced significant results on the scientific plane. The only manifestation of Arab culture in pre-Islamic times (*jahliyya*) was in the field of poetry. Cf. C. Brockelmann, *History of the Islamic Peoples* (1939), Engl. transl. J. Carmichael and M. Perlmann (Capricorn Books 1960) 10-12.

earlier Byzantine and Persian administrative structures: Greek and Persian language and script were normally used in the administration of the newly won empire from Mesopotamia to Egypt.[17] A one-way stream of cultural borrowing by the Arabs from the conquered peoples began to flow until the early years of the eighth century. When the caliph Walīd (705-715) ordered his administration to cease using Greek, he made one notable exception: that the notation of numbers in the Greek style could be continued.[18]

Secondly, we notice that the Arabic *abjad* shows traces of some original Phoenician letters soon discarded from their alphabet by the Greeks but kept by them in their numerical system. This was the case with the *episemon* or *digamma* (or *stigma*) ϛ for number 6, of koppa ϙ or ϟ for 90 and sampi ϡ for 900. The Greek *episemon* or *digamma* is found in turn as waw=و , even for 6, in the Arabic *abjad.* This was the closest Arabic letter and sound to stand for the sound of the Greek *digamma;* yet its order in the Arabic alphabet was the twenty-seventh letter. Why place it sixth in the Arabic *abjad* if not in adaptation of the Greek numerical order of letters – as the adaptation of other Arabic letters to the Greek numerical order holds nearly unfailingly for numbers 1 to 80. The same analogy holds for the 5=o in the Arabic *abjad.* The letter h=o was twenty-sixth in the Arabic alphabet, becoming fifth in the *abjad,* to correspond to the soft sound of *epsilon* standing for 5 in Greek numerical order. The Greek koppa ϙ or ϟ stood for 90. This sound approximated a *k* or *q.* In the Arabic *abjad,* we see it transferred to stand for 100 = qaf, and sad ص was used instead for 90, for what reason we cannot perceive. That the position of *q* for 100 in the *abjad* is still in imitation of the Greek order is shown by the nearly uninterrupted correspondence of symbols from 1 to 80 in both systems, and resumed with three more corresponding letters of ra=200 for Greek rho=100, shin=300 for sigma=200, and ta=400 for tau=300. After 400 in the Arabic, and 300 in Greek, the correspondence comes to an end, the Arabic *abjad* taking up in natural sequence the unused pointed letters whose simple equivalents were employed in the earlier portion. The Greek *sampi* could be left out at 900 in favor of the natural sequence of pointed letters in Arabic. The Arabic *abjad* is clearly an artificial system, sophisticated in its distinguishing between corresponding simple and emphatic sounds of the Arabic letters, but it is most unnatural and uncongenial to the spirit of the Semitic alphabet, with clear foreign borrowings. The Hebrew alphabetical number notation[19] parallels roughly the Arabic *abjad.* It is itself probably later than the Greek numerical

[17] Cf. The *Fihrist of al-Nadīm,* chap. 7.1 (n. 7 above) 2.581-583 states that the records of administration in the East had been kept in Persian till the time of *al-Hajjāj* when they began to be kept in Arabic; and in Damascus the records were kept in Greek till the time of the caliph Hisham (724-743 A.D.). So, in both cases, the foreign languages were used by the Arab administration till the beginning of the eighth century, or nearly one full century after the rise of Islam and the creation of the Arab empire.

[18] Cf. Theophanes's *Chronographia* quoted in G. Libri, *Histoire des sciences mathématiques en Italie,* ed. 2 (Halle 1865) 1.375.

[19] Smith, *History* (n. 1 above) 2.53.

letters and also imitated from it; its final form so close to the *abjad* seems to have been fixed only at the time of the Massoretes.[20]

A corroborative argument could be found in the well-established fact that the Arabs received a major stimulation of their interest in sciences and mathematics from translations of Greek works. In those translations the number notation accompanying arithmetical or geometrical demonstrations was usually reproduced unchanged, thus adding impetus to and confirming the system of the *abjad* in imitation of Greek number notation. An Arab author quoted by Carra de Vaux[21] states that the astronomers among them "who are great mathematicians" did not adopt the "Indian" figures in their works because the numbers to be expressed in astronomical research (degrees, seconds, minutes, signs) are small numbers, whereas the usefulness of the Hindu system was most apparent in its capacity to represent large numbers. The astronomer in question may well be the celebrated as-Soufi (tenth century), according to whom the Arab translators of the works of Ptolemy preferred to use the letters of the alphabet (the *abjad*) to express their numbers.[22]

While the astronomers and astrologers among the eastern Arabs do not seem to have made much use, if any, of the "Indian" figures, what of the mathematicians such as al-Khwārizmī who described the whole Hindu system in their arithmetic? Unfortunately the Arabic text of al-Khwārizmī's *Arithmetic* is lost. On the other hand, the twelfth-century Latin translations or paraphrases of it contain the western forms of these numerals, namely the "Toledan" forms to be explained shortly. Since nearly one half of these western figures are of Hispanic origin, as I shall attempt to demonstrate, these cannot have been present in al-Khwārizmī's original. At best, al-Khwārizmī may have used the "Indian" figures like those exemplified in the *Fihrist*,[23] perhaps in a form closer yet to the original "Hindu" style since he wrote more than a century and a half before al-Nadīm.

Al-Khwārizmī's two other important mathematical works, the *Algebra wa'l-muqabala* and the *Astronomical Tables according to the Sindhind* are of little help in the present state of our knowledge. The Arabic text of the *Algebra* published by Rosen[24] contains indeed the Hindu figures. But, as already remarked by G. Libri,[25] the manuscript used by Rosen is of late date; its system of figures is most likely to be attributable to the scribe himself reproducing the forms known in his time. Libri further noted that, of the three twelfth-century Latin manuscripts of the *Algebra*

[20] *Ibid.* In a Paris manuscript of a twelfth-century algorism, B. N. lat. 16208, fol. 70 (fig. 2), the Hebrew system of letters is presented alongside the algorism. Its form corresponds to the one ascribed to the Massoretes in Smith.

[21] Baron Bernard Carra de Vaux, "Sur l'origine des chiffres," *Scientia* 21 (1917) 277. De Vaux does not supply the name of the Arab astronomer.

[22] Cf. Libri (n. 18 above) 1.275.

[23] We shall present the case of the *Fihrist* shortly; see the figures given (n. 7 above) 34-35.

[24] F. Rosen, *The Algebra of Mohammed ben Musa* (London 1831).

[25] Libri (n. 18 above) 1.374

known to him, none contained any "Hindu" numerals.[26] The evidence, he rightly concludes, strongly suggests that the figures were not present in the Arabic original used by the Latin translators of the *Algebra.* As for the Latin translations and adaptations of al-Khwārizmī's *Astronomical Tables,* almost without exception they use the "improved" Roman system described below. It is strange, indeed, if the "Hindu" numerals were in the original of these tables,[27] that the Latin translators did not transfer them into their Latin texts.[28]

There is a third category of Arabic manuscripts that I examined directly in European libraries, which do show an extensive use of "Hindu" or "Arabic" numerals.[29] They are usually late manuscripts, with texts dealing with the magical properties of numbers and their use in judgments of nativities (horoscopes). The principles and rules proposed are based on a correspondence between series of "Hindu" numbers and of numbers from the *abjad.* Such rules are called *jummal* (series, total, arrangement), each one being further specified as the "great series" (*jummal al-kabīr*) which has the particular characteristic of using the "Hindu" numerals (*bi-ḥisābi'l-hindī*), and the "smaller series" (*jummal aṣ-ṣaghır*) proceeding

[26] L. C. Karpinski in 1915 gave an edition of the Latin version of the *Algebra* by Robert of Chester (1145 A.D.): *Robert of Chester's Latin Translation of the Algebra of Al-Khowarizmi,* reprinted as Part I of L. C. Karpinski and J. G. Winter, *Contributions to the History of Science,* University of Michigan Studies, Humanistic Series (Ann Arbor 1930). Karpinski's text contains the "Hindu" numerals; yet, as in the case of Rosen's Arab publication, Karpinski's manuscripts are late (fourteenth, fifteenth, sixteenth centuries) and their figures are likely to have been introduced by the late scribes.

[27] In the Vatican Library there is an Arab manuscript of a work by Maslama of Madrid that contains the "Hindu" numerals; an example that points to the special interest shown these numerals in the maghrebi tradition. See n. 12 above.

[28] An important distinction would have to be made between scholars or authors of scientific treatises or translations on the one hand, and the Latin scribes producing copies of these works. Scholars might know the "Hindu" numerals but might not be able to enforce their use by ignorant scribes. Some early Latin manuscripts suggest this distinction: the scribe has produced a copy with either Roman numerals (including their modified twelfth-century forms) or garbled "Hindu" numerals, and the author, in interlinear or marginal corrections, has specified the exact value by inserting their expression in "Hindu" numerals. Cf. Oxford, Corpus Christi College, MS 283 (O. Neugebauer, *The Astronomical Tables of Al-Khwārizmī: Translation with Commentaries of the Latin Version edited by H. Suter, supplemented by Corpus Christi College Ms 283* [Copenhagen 1962] plates). Cf. also British Library, Harley MS 3631, fol. 34v (fig. 3 below).

[29] I examined some of these manuscripts in the Vatican Library and in the library of the Escorial, but mostly in the Bibliothèque Nationale in Paris. Such manuscripts are obviously numerously represented among great collections of Arabic manuscripts in European and Oriental libraries as shown by catalogue descriptions. Among the Paris Arabic manuscripts of this type may be included MS 2582 (sixteenth century), MS 2584 (seventeenth century), MS 2587 (seventeenth century), MS 2595 (A.D. 1631), MS 2718 (A.D. 1642). The last manuscript, on fol. 219v, has a colophon which betrays the uncertainties still prevailing at this late date in the correct use of the Hindu system among Arabs. The scribe wrote the date in letters, for 1052 Heg. (1642/43 A.D.); another hand added the Hindu form in the margin (1000 + 50 + 2). Errors of this type were also frequent among earlier Latin users of the system: cf. Smith and Karpinski (n. 1 above) 150: 1000, 300, 80 and 4 for 1384.

with the numbers of the *abjad* or "Arabic" calculation (*bi-ḥisābi'l-'arabī*). For example, in Paris, Bibliothèque Nationale MS arabe 2582, of the sixteenth century, the scribe presents on fol. 2 a table of correspondence between the *abjad* on the one hand, in a series progressing regularly by units and tens from *alif* and so on to 1000 (*ghain*); and on the other hand, two sets of figures arranged in similar series: the first set presents "Indian" figures while the second contains an approximation of the *ghubār* figures. But in the last two sets, instead of a regular progression as in the first series, the cycle culminates with ten, after which it declines by even intervals until it reaches a kind of zero position here called *sāqaṭ* (rest), located under the figure *sin* of the *abjad* line. The game is explained in the following terms: "The form of the knowledge of the *jummal al-kabīr* to know the horoscopes of men, whether they be male or female." This gives the real tenor and tone of such speculations with number notations of different traditions. They have obviously little to do with mathematics, although they make abundant use of "Hindu" and *ghubār* numerals.[30]

B. THE "HINDU" NUMERALS IN THE FIHRIST

An unmistakable sign of belatedness in the adoption of the "Hindu" numerals among the Arabs, together with the outlandishness still attaching them toward the end of the tenth century is the passage concerning these "Hindu" figures in the *Fihrist* of Ibn al-Nadīm (ca. 987 A.D.).[31] The full significance of this bit of evidence about the knowledge and diffusion of the "Hindu" numerals among the learned Arabs until late in the tenth century does not seem to have been fully grasped by either Karpinski or Dodge. It should be clearly understood that the "letters" (*ḥurūf*) of al-Nadīm's text were meant for the numerical symbols of the Indians. In using the expression *ḥurūf,* al-Nadīm makes an unwarranted extrapolation from the *abjad* system, better known to him, into the Indian system with nine symbols which he tends to consider as letters. The nine "letters" in examples 14, 15 and 16 of the *Fihrist,*[32] for instance, clearly are the nine Hindu symbols representing the numbers

[30] For instance, Paris B. N. MS arabe 2595 contains at least three different works in a total of 154 folios (308 pages of text); the first work is a treatise by al-Jīlī dealing with the names of the spirits of the seven planets, of the "secret virtues of the Indian ciphers and of the Arab ciphers," of white magic, talismans and magical alphabets, all this in 58 folios. The next treatise is an *Astrology* by Tomtom the Indian (a much quoted authority among early Arab astrologers) in 30 folios. The last work treats of the *rūḥaniya* or demonology (spirits) in 65 folios. Throughout the codex one meets innumerable instances of Hindu figures, *abjad* letters and plain magical alphabets. On this subject, cf. P. Casanova, "Alphabets magiques arabes," *Journal Asiatique* 17-18 (1921) 37-55 and 19-20 (1922) 250-267. Also H. A. Winkler, "Siegel und Charaktere in der muhammedanischen Zauberei," *Studien zur Geschichte und Kultur des islamischen Orients* 7 (Berlin 1930).

[31] See nn. 7-8 above.

[32] Al-Nadīm (n. 7 above) 1.34-35. Cf. also L. C. Karpinski, "Hindu Numerals in the *Fihrist,*" *Bibliotheca mathematica,* ser.3, 11 (1911) 121-124.

from one to nine. In translating *ḥurūf* by "letters" without further explanation, therefore, both Karpinski and Dodge leave unmentioned al-Nadīm's error of representing the Hindu system as a system of letters, which implies in addition some ignorance of the position value in the Indian system by al-Nadīm. At any rate, his method of explaining the Hindu system through comparison with the letter system of the *abjad,* and the omission of any example of use of the nine symbols in value position (other than the whole tens or hundreds, which only required one or two dots below the simple symbol for units), indicate that in al-Nadīm's time the *abjad* was the predominant, and nearly exclusive, system of number notation among learned Arabs. The Indian *ḥurūf* in al-Nadīm should consequently be translated as "characters" or "figures," while the *ḥurūf* of the Arab system of the *abjad* are really "letters."

A further remark on al-Nadīm's passage is that his Indian "letters" are not the real Hindu symbols, as can be shown by comparison with the tables in Smith's *History of Mathematics,*[33] but are in fact the symbols already Arabicized, another indication that the specifically Arab phase of the transmission of the "Hindu" symbols had been but little observed by the Arab learned men themselves. In addition, al-Nadīm gives no hint of the usefulness of the Indian system in arithmetical calculations, showing that he is little familiar with it, despite his extensive readings of Arabic books of science which form a substantial portion of his listings in the *Fihrist.* For this extremely well-read bookseller in Baghdad in the late tenth century to be so confused about the "Hindu-Arabic" system of number notation and arithmetical operations can only be interpreted as a proof that the system was hardly familiar, let alone in general use, among the Arab scientists till the late tenth century.

In a later work published jointly with D. E. Smith,[34] Karpinski collected further evidence of the slow diffusion of "Hindu" numerals among the Arabs. He noted the ninth-century publication by al-Kindī of five books on arithmetic and four books on the Hindu method of calculation,[35] the work of Sanad ibn Ali, who worked under al-Ma'mun, and of as-Soufi who died in 986 A.D. – yet all these examples were listed by al-Nadīm in the *Fihrist* as indicated before[36] with little evidence that the tradition was widely known. One would need to make a systematic examination of the works on "Indian" arithmetic mentioned by al-Nadīm among the Arabs to elucidate the exact significance of the tradition. However, Karpinski recalled the testimony of al-Bīrūnī in the middle of the eleventh century, to the effect that even among the Indians the system of the nine figures and their use in position value was far from universally practiced, since it had to compete within the Indian tradition with two rival systems, the sexagesimal one and the letter system.[37]

[33] Smith, *History* (n. 1 above) 2.70.
[34] Smith and Karpinski (n. 1 above).
[35] *Ibid.* 9.
[36] See n. 8 above.
[37] Smith and Karpinski (n. 1 above) 7.

As for the late adoption of the Hindu system among the Arabs, Karpinski and Smith further note the testimony of a tenth-century Arab author, Motahhar ibn Ṭahir, who considers it a "curiosity" to write a large number of astronomical years in Hindu ciphers.[38] To sum up, then, from the evidence both of manuscript experience and of the bibliographical and historical information already available to us, a surprising degree of neglect or confusion prevailed as late as the tenth century among the eastern Arabs, as illustrated in the example of al-Nadīm in his description of the "Hindu" system of numerals and arithmetic. The earliest transmission of the "Hindu" numerals to the Arabs had taken place under al-Mansur sometime about the year 774 A.D., with the arrival at Baghdad of the Indian philosopher and astronomer who carried the Siddhanta Tables with him; in the late ninth century, Mas'udi reported that the *Sindhind* contained an exposition of Hindu arithmetics. Later on under al-Ma'mun, al-Khwarizmī's *Arithmetic,* his reworking of the *Siddhanta Tables,* and his *Algebra* signalled an interest in Indian arithmetical methods which is also exemplified by several entries in the *Fihrist.* And yet, al-Nadīm's confusion, together with the evidence from Arabic manuscripts in astronomical, astrological, and mathematical sciences, show scant awareness of the Hindu system of arithmetic or of the principles and usefulness of the nine symbols and position value, and rarely any use of them in scientific activity.[39]

In Muslim Spain, on the other hand, as G. Menéndez Pidal has pointed out,[40] the Indian system became known as early as the ninth century. It seems to have prospered more immediately there, although in a significantly different cultural context marked by the opposition of the Spanish 'Umayyads to the Abbassid culture of Baghdad.[41] Starting at least with the tenth century under the first caliph of Cordoba, Abder Rahman III, an indigenous scientific and cultural tradition flourished in al-Andalus where astronomy, astrology and mathematics in particular were intensely cultivated.[42] In view of its potential impact upon western Europe, as shown by the example of Gerbert in the late tenth century, al-Andalus thus becomes a more natural focus of attention for the transmission of the "Hindu" numerals to western Europe in the Middle Ages.

[38] *Ibid.*

[39] F. Rosenthal, "The Technique and Approach of Muslim Scholarship," *Analecta Orientalia* 24 (1947) 16, in a remark on Ruska's article "al-ṣifr" in the *Encyclopaedia of Islam,* writes: "I know of no detailed palaeographical treatment of the Arabic numerals used in Arabic and Persian manuscripts." The same holds true to-day.

[40] Menéndez Pidal (n. 1 above).

[41] Cf. G. F. Hourani, "The Early Growth of the Secular Sciences in Andalusia," *Studia Islamica* 32 (1970) 143-156, esp. 148.

[42] Ibn Juljul, *Tabaqāt al-aṭibbā' wa'l-ḥukamā',* ed. Fuad Sayyid (Cairo 1955); Sa'id al-Andalusi, *Tabaqāt al-umām,* ed. L. Cheikho (Beirut 1911); French trans. R. Blachère (Paris 1935). Cf. J. Vernet, "La ciencia en el Islam y Occidente," in *L'Occidente e l'Islam nell'alto medio evo,* Settimane di Spoleto 12 (1965) 537-567.

II. THE MEDIEVAL HISPANIC EXPERIENCE: THE TOLEDAN CIPHERS

The indigenous scientific culture fostered in al-Andalus under the patronage of the new caliphate of Cordoba spread to many other cities which shared in this cultural blooming. Seville, Almeria, Granada, Toledo, Saragossa, Valencia, Jaen, Murcia simultaneously or in turn took part in the creation of a scientific tradition which continued under the kingdoms of the Taifas after the collapse of the caliphal structure in the early eleventh century. Contacts with Baghdad and Egypt on the one hand, and with Byzantium on the other, were maintained for a while, allowing the Andalusian scientists to participate in the wider movement of learning in Byzantium and Islam during the tenth and eleventh centuries, while western Europe, caught in the grip of narrow feudalism and monastic learning, lived outside of this world culture. A precocious Ottonian Renaissance failed to establish scholarly communication with the outside world, save in isolated and marginal instances like the contacts of Gerbert with Spain, and the mission of Liutprand of Cremona to Byzantium.

Among the three major centers of scientific activity in al-Andalus, namely Cordoba, Seville and Toledo, the latter soon took the leadership in astronomical knowledge and became internationally known for the manufacture of astrolabes. After the reestablishment of Christian rule in 1085, Toledo became the center of diffusion of this knowledge toward Latin Europe, including Italy.

The astronomical works of Ptolemy, together with his astrological *Quadripartitum* or *Tetrabiblos* were well known and intensively studied in Spain, along with the enormous astronomical production of the Arabs from the eastern portion of the Islamic Empire. The *Astronomical Tables* of al-Khwārizmī in particular, embodying Greek, Persian and Indian experience, attracted the greatest attention; and efforts to adjust them to the novel theory of the motion of the eighth sphere issued by Thabit ibn Qurra resulted in many original forms of these tables. The *Khwarizmian Tables* were adapted to the meridian of Cordoba by Maslama of Madrid,[43] and to the meridian of Toledo by al-Zarqali to become the *Toledan Tables*[44] later translated

[43] Commentaries on these Tables of Maslama were written by Ibn al-Mutannā, which in turn were translated into Hebrew (recent edition by B. R. Goldstein [New Haven 1967]) and into Latin by Hugh of Santalla (recent edition by Eduardo M. Vendrell [Madrid 1963]).

[44] Cf. A. Berry, *A Short History of Astronomy* (1898) 3 par. 61 (Dover ed., New York 1961) 80-81 and 84. Smith, *History* (n. 1 above) 2.609 and 616, relying on Braunmühl, says Zarqali lived in Cordova. On al-Zarqali the study by J. Millas y Vallicrosa, *Estudios sobre Azarquiel* (Madrid 1943-1950), gives ample information. But on the influence of Zarqali among the twelfth-century Spanish astronomers and translators, especially on John of Seville, see J. Millas y Vallicrosa, "Una obra astronómica desconocida de Johannes Avendaut Hispanus," *Osiris* 1 (1936) 451-475, esp. 465ff. Cf. G. J. Toomer, "A Survey of the Toledan Tables," *Osiris* 15 (1968) 5-174. The textual problems raised by the various stages of these Khwarizmian Tables in their Spanish mutations are very intricate and have occupied the attention of editors for nearly a hundred years. Cf. H. Suter, *Die astronomischen Tafeln des Muhammad ibn Mūsā al-Khwārizmī in der Bearbeitung des Maslama ibn Ahmed al-Madjrītī, und der lateinischen Uebersetzung des*

many times into Latin and variously adapted to meridians of other European cities such as Marseilles, Cremona, Pisa, London, Malines, Paris, and so on. Of course, astrology was equally cultivated among Muslims, Mozarabs and Jews alike in the works of Ptolemy, Abu Ma'shar, Ma'sha'llah, Sahl ben Bishr (Zahel), al-Qabizi (Alchabitius), Ali al-Imrani, Almansor, Hermes, all authorities popular in the East in the ninth and tenth centuries and imported into Arab Spain shortly. Many of these works were later to be translated into Latin and diffused to the West mostly from Toledo.

It was probably in Toledo or its region that three works of al-Khwārizmī on mathematics and astronomy were translated into Latin during the early twelfth century: the *Arithmetic* which became known as the *Algorismus* from the name of its author, the *Algebra* (*kitāb al-jabr wa'l-muqabala*), and the *Astronomical Tables.* The *Arithmetic* was translated probably directly once,[45] then paraphrased at least twice, once apparently by Pedro Alfonso,[46] and another time by John of Seville,[47]

Athelard von Bath (Copenhagen 1914); J. J. Burckhardt, "Die mittleren Bewegungen der Planeten im Tafelwerk des Khwārizmī", *Vierteljahrschrift der Naturforschung Gesell. Zurich* 106 (1961) 213-231; Neugebauer (n. 28 above).

[45] This is the text entitled *Algoritmi de numero indorum* in Cambridge, University Library MS Ii 6.5 of the fourteenth century published by Boncompagni (n. 6 above) 1.1-23. It was recently reproduced in facsimile by Kurt Vogel, *Mohammed ibn Musa Alchuarizmi's Algorismus: Das früheste Lehrbuch zum Rechnen mit indischen Ziffern* (Aalen 1963).

[46] This is my conjecture concerning the author of the *Algorismus* of "Magister A." tentatively identified, though without much conviction, by Haskins as Adelard of Bath, merely on the strength of this inscription found in but one copy (Paris BN lat. 16208) among the five and possibly six copies of this text. Haskins was perhaps also moved by the coincidence that Adelard had translated the *Astronomical Tables* of the same al-Khwārizmī. Yet the title "magister A." would as well fit Pedro Alfonso (or Petrus Anfusus in many manuscripts). This Spanish Jewish physician, formerly called Moses Sefardi, accepted baptism in 1106 and took the Christian name of his godfather King Alfonso I of Aragon. As a physician he visited the court of Henry I of England ca. 1110. Pedro is known to have written in Latin at least two works addressed to European (Frankish) scholars of his times. One was the famous *Disciplina clericalis* that contains a number of moral tales borrowed from *Kalila wa Dimna.* The second was a *Letter to the Peripatetics of France* (Frankland, i.e. Europe) in which he recommends the study of Arab science which he knew very well himself.

The reason for my ascription to him of the paraphrase of the *Algorismus* in question is twofold: for one, the dates included in a table of eras in this *Algorismus,* namely October 1116, correspond to a similar set of dates met in an Oxford manuscript (Corpus Christi College MS 283) of the adapted Tables of al-Khwārizmī clearly attributed to him there (cf. Neugebauer [n. 28 above]). Secondly, this *Algorismus* in the Paris copy attributed to Master A. includes toward the end an explanation of the Hebrew system of number notation by letters. Both these details fit Pedro Alfonso much more aptly than they do Adelard of Bath who is not otherwise known to have used the system of the algorismus in any of his works, nor to have paid special attention to the Hebrew system of number notation. The date 1116 of this *Algorismus* on the other hand seems too early for Abraham ibn Ezra (see n. 48 below), and probably also for Abraham bar Hiyya (see n. 49 below) whose scientific activity in conjunction with Plato of Tivoli is dated around 1130 and later.

[47] This text, almost everywhere ascribed in the manuscripts to John of Seville, was also published by Boncompagni (n. 6 above) 27-135 from the Paris manuscript BN lat. 7359 (see fig. 6). It contains a prologue by John himself, the text beginning with "Incipit liber algoarizmi

both Spaniards, the one certainly a former Jew and the second probably so also. In addition, Jewish scholarship contributed one more instance of interest in the algorism by the publication of Abraham ibn Ezra's *Sefer Ha-Mispar,*[48] while Ibn Ezra's teacher Abraham Bar Hiyya (Savasorda) shows similar interests a generation earlier.[49]

In Arab Spain, surely, an interest in the "Hindu" numerals and in their use for calculation antedates by far the twelfth-century production of Latin translations. A direct evidence of this appears in the forms of the numerals present in the twelfth-century translations or adaptations: nearly identical in these later works, the figures however are markedly different from either the "Arabic" or the "Hindu" forms. Moreover, John of Seville's examples testify to long-existing variations in the forms of three of these figures in Western or Hispanic usage: namely, the 4, the 7 and the zero.

Astronomy, astrology and mathematics, besides many other natural sciences, thus flourished intensely in twelfth-century Spain among Muslims, Mozarabs and Jews, who pursued their philosophic and scientific activities in a symbiosis that eventually attracted the attention and stimulated the curiosity of their Latin neighbors and visitors from Europe. The Latin production of so many works of science done in Spain in translation from the Arabic during the twelfth century merely points to this newly aroused interest in Arab, and specifically Spanish, science, among Latin newcomers drawn to Spain by the Crusade of the Reconquista. The large number of foreigners, at first French knights and ecclesiastics of the Cluniac obedience,[50] later scholars (English, Italian, Slav) who were attracted to Spain at that time, some to settle permanently,[51] is responsible for this sudden increase of interest in Arab

---

de practica arismetrice." However, the complex question of what was the very nature of al-Khwārizmī's *Arithmetic* and of how far the Latin versions or adaptations diverge from it cannot be solved in the absence of the original which is lost. Perhaps an exhaustive examination of the Arab imitators and commentators of al-Khwārizmī's *Arithmetic* mentioned in the *Fihrist* of al-Nadīm and in El-Qifti may help advance the inquiry. With respect to John of Seville's text G. Enestrom in *Bibliotheca mathematica* ser. 3, 6 (1905) 114 sways between the qualifications of *Uebersetzer* and *Bearbeiter.* Besides the manuscript utilized by Boncompagni, there are extant at least six other copies of this version: cf. Vogel (n. 45 above) 43 n. 10.

[48] Abraham ibn Ezra, *Sefer Ha-Mispar: Das Buch der Zahl, ein hebräisch-arithmetisches Werk des R. Abraham ibn Esra (XII. Jahrh.),* ed. and trans. Moritz Silberberg (Frankfurt a. M. 1895). Cf. D. E. Smith and Y. Ginsburg, "Rabbi ben Ezra and the Hindu-Arabic Problem," *American Mathematical Monthly* 25 (1918) 99-108.

[49] Cf. M. Levey, "Abraham Savasorda and His Algorism: A Study in Early European Logistics," *Osiris* (1954) 50-64.

[50] Cf. M. Desfourneaux, *Les Français en Espagne aux XIe et XIIe siècles* (Paris 1949); P. Boissonnade, *Du nouveau sur la Chanson de Roland* (Paris 1923).

[51] The first archbishop of reconquered Toledo in 1085, Bernard, was a French monk; so, too, was Jerome of Périgord, the fiery companion of the Cid Campeador who made him bishop of his Valencia. Archbishop Raymond of Toledo (1126-1151) was also a Frenchman. Two princes of the House of Burgundy, Henry and Raymond, who had accompanied crusader recruits into Spain ended up by marrying the daughters of Alphonso VI, the conqueror of Toledo. Henry married the illegitimate Theresa and became the father of Alphonso Henriques, first king of Portugal;

science, a movement much more diffused and much more lasting in its effects than the brief adventure of Gerbert a century and a half earlier.

We shall examine briefly the two sets of Western numerals in Pedro Alfonso's and John of Seville's works, comparing them with one another and with the Hindu-Arabic numerals; and finally we shall examine the appearance of separate symbols for some of the nine digits in the Roman numeral system in Spain, which were later coopted for use in the Hindu-Arabic system of value position.

A. THE ALGORISM FIGURES OF PEDRO ALFONSO AND JOHN OF SEVILLE

Both the *Algorismus* of Pedro Alfonso ("Magister A.") and the *Liber algoarizmi de practica arismetrice* of John of Seville have been preserved in several manuscript copies, a good number of which are of the twelfth century.[52] This is a decided

---

Raymond married Urraca, the last heiress of Alphonso VI. Both Burgundians thus ensconced themselves at the heart of Christian politics in twelfth-century Spain. King Alphonso VI himself was married to the French princess Constance, the mother of Urraca. Among the translators, Gerard of Cremona came to Spain about A.D. 1145 and spent the more than forty last years of his life in Toledo where he died. Another bishop of the early twelfth century, Michael of Tarrazona for whom Hugh of Santalla translated so many works of science from the Arabic, was also of French origin.

[52] At least five manuscripts of the *Algorismus* of Pedro Alfonso are extant in European libraries. However, their text and arrangement of materials differ widely from one copy to another and the problem of their mutual relations has not been studied as yet. That one copy might be a remake of another, or that one only of these varying forms might be ascribable to Pedro Alfonso or the mysterious "Magister A.," or that several interpolators might have interfered in the total transmission of this text, all these hypotheses must be envisaged. Yet since all copies carry substantially the same matters, proofs and calculations, and all ascribe the system to al-Khwārizmī, we may assume for the sake of the present demonstration that they form one single tradition of the algorism in the twelfth century. At least the forms of their numerals are nearly identical as will be shown. The manuscripts are the following:

A: Munich CLM 18927, twelfth century. Possibly the original redaction, and hence of the year 1116 A.D. (fig. 1).
B: Munich CLM 13021, late twelfth century, written ca. 1165-1168 by Sigebotus of Prüfening. (fig. 4).
C: Paris BN lat. 16208, twelfth century (seems anterior to 1163).
D: Milan, Ambros. A. 3 supra, twelfth century.
E: Vienna, Nat. Bibl. palat. MS lat. 275 (fragment, fol. 27r), twelfth century.

There is possibly a sixth copy, but of the fifteenth century in Genoa, Bibliotheca Universitaria MS E.III.28, "Ysagoge in artem Alchorismi," which I have not yet examined. E was briefly presented by A. Nagl, "Ueber eine Algorismus-Schrift . . . ," *Zeitschrfit für Mathematik und Physik* 34.4.129-146 and 161-170. A and B were later studied by M. Curtze, "Ueber eine Algorismus-Schrift des XII. Jahrhunderts," *Abhandlungen zur Geschichte der Mathematik* 8 (1898) 1-27 where the first three books are printed (17-27). The work of John of Seville is also extant in at least seven manuscripts (cf. Vogel [n. 45 above] 43), one of which is probably of the twelfth century (A), three are of the thirteenth century, two of the fourteenth and one of the fifteenth century. In three copies (A, F, G) the text is anonymous, in three others it is ascribed

advantage, since the scribes, little familiar at first with these newfangled figures, would tend to reproduce their model as closely as possible, though clumsily. When the figures had become better known, later scribes often substituted the forms used in their own times, thus depriving us of the all-important traces of earlier forms on which we have to base our interpretation of their origin. This essential methodological rule was already alluded to by L. Rodet in the nineteenth century;[53] and a more careful study of the early Latin manuscripts of the twelfth-century algorisms was undertaken by Nagl, Cantor and Curtze, among others,[54] to apply this method. The aim is to find the most ancient forms in the early manuscripts that transmitted the numerals to the Latin West, and to trace their development in a close succession

---

nominally to John of Seville (B, C, D) and in one it is ascribed to Gerard of Cremona (E). The text of D has been printed by Boncompagni (n. 6 above) 2.25-136, unfortunately without any attempt to reproduce the actual forms of the numerals (save for the casual mention of the different usages for 4 and 7 on p. 28). On the basis of this printed text, it appears that E, F and G are incomplete. Here is the list of manuscripts:

A: Paris, BN lat. 16202, fols. 51-81, twelfth century (against Vogel who gives it as thirteenth century. The script is rounded, with particular abbreviations and ligatures proper to late Carolingian, pre-gothic).
B: Paris, Mazarine 3642, fols. 105-117, thirteenth century.
C: Paris, BN lat. 15461, fols. 1-14, second half of thirteenth century (fig. 5).
D: Paris, BN lat. 7359, fols. 85-111, thirteenth century (fig. 6). Edited by Boncompagni.
E: Erfurt, Amplon. 4°. 355, fols. 85-115, fourteenth century (Boncompagni 25-127).
F: Vatican, Reg. lat. 1285, fols. 14-20, second half of fourteenth century (Boncompagni 25-93).
G: Dresden, C 80, fols. 129-134, fifteenth century (Boncompagni 25-49). Cf. Karpinski (n. 26 above) 53-55.

As was already noted, the failure of Boncompagni to reproduce the numeral forms in D makes his edition useless in our present investigation; all other copies have been neglected by historians in this matter of numerals. The only manuscript extant which contains what may be the direct Latin translation of the *Arithmetic* of al-Khwārizmī (the *Algorismus* proper), as distinguished from the works of both Pedro and John which are considered as paraphrases, is Cambridge, University Library MS Ii, 6.5, of the fourteenth century. It was published as the first part of Boncompagni (n. 45 above) 1-23. This manuscript of a late date omits all forms of number symbols for which it regularly presents a *lacuna.* It was again reproduced, this time in facsimile, by Vogel in 1963, who tried to stress its importance for the history of arithmetics in the West. Since this manuscript is late, since it gives no example of numerals, and since, moreover, the only examples of numbers it contains are written in Roman numerals, it remains a mystery to me why so much credit could be attributed to it. Boncompagni's edition served the purpose entirely; besides, Vogel's transcription contains a sizable number of misreadings: in addition to the 26 misreadings he corrects in addendum, I have counted 40 more which are not acknowledged.

A point of clarification may be necessary here. When we speak of the various twelfth-century *algorisms,* we mean to distinguish them from the thirteenth-century Latin remakes of a totally different nature, namely the celebrated *Algorismus* of John of Sacrobosco (Holywood, or Halifax) and its commentary by Peter of Dacia, and also the *Algorismus* in verses of Alexander of Villedieu which was introduced as a school manual and was therefore known by everybody who had some schooling. The mere mention of *Algorismus* (Augrim of Chaucer) after the thirteenth century very nearly always designates the poem of Alexander Villedieu, or Sacrobosco's work.

[53] L. Rodet, "Sur les notations numériques et algébriques . . . ," *Actes de la Société de philologie* 8 (1878) 126 n. 1.

[54] Cf. n. 52 above.

of examples fitted into an organic pattern constituted by related fields of interest, genealogy of manuscripts, regions of diffusion and local conditions, scribal traditions and idiosyncrasies.[55] These methodological requirements have yet to be applied systematically before any solid conclusion concerning the origin of our numerals can be reached.

We have several twelfth-century copies of the *Algorismus* of Pedro Alfonso, and at least one of John of Seville's text. What are the forms of the "Indian" numerals that they offer?[56]

The first thing to note in the two specimens of the *Algorismus* (figs. 1 and 4) is that their number symbols, though cruder and clumsier in figure 1 than in figure 4, are very nearly similar to one another, but certainly differ in several instances (namely 4, 5, 6, 7, 8 and zero) from either the "Arab" or the "Hindu" numerals. The changes from fig. 1 to fig. 4 involve the reversing of the right-to-left sequence as in the Arabic, to the left-to-right order in fig. 4. This may be taken as a chance occurrence, perhaps attributable to a release of inhibition in the scribe (the monk Sigisbotus of Prüfening), but not repeated in the other copies of either Pedro's or John's texts. Another variant is the different shape of the second zero: Pedro's as well as John's texts testify to the existence of alternate forms of zero: a circle (O) or a .t. The crossed ∅ instead of .t. in fig. 4 seems a scribal misreading, since all other copies have O and .t. We may also note the disappearance of the tail in the form 3 of fig. 4, while this tail is normally very characteristic of fig. 4 and of the other copies. Again the loss of this tail is a sign of scribal deviation from the original form. In the course of the works examples of arithmetical operations often contain in fig. 4 a form .t. for 3 which has baffled Nagl and Curtze.[57] We shall later have the key for this .t.=3.

[55] The common practice among students of this problem has been to pick up at random from all sort of sources the examples of numerals which are afterwards arranged according to shape and chronological order, irrespective of their context, regions, and individual scribes' characteristics. What is worse, penmanship, of a very esthetical nature indeed, has most of the time replaced actual photographic reproductions. Thus the very earnest work of G. F. Hill, *The Development of Arabic Numerals in Europe, Exhibited in Sixty-four Tables* (Oxford 1915), loses much of its proof value. If we consider the penmanship of those medieval scribes, who are remote from the origin, to be a source of uncertainties as to the ancient forms, evidence presented through the medium of modern penmanship is still less admissible. The excellent studies of Nagl and Curtze (n. 52 above) greatly suffer also from this defect; and what is worse, they tended, like Boncompagni, to reproduce most of the numbers in their manuscript in modern printing types. These defects in methodology are still present in as recent a book as G. C. Neill Wright, *The Writing of Arabic Numerals* (London 1952). We cannot except from this criticism even the excellent work of Smith, *History* (n. 1 above) in which it suffices to compare the type of evidence given in facsimile on p. 79, line 17, with the earlier examples on 70-76.

[56] The copies of John of Seville's text being somewhat later, they will be used with the proviso that their numerals must always be read within the perspective of a slight evolution in the forms.

[57] Nagl (n. 52 above) 134: "Ich vermag die graphische Abstammung dieses zeichens nicht aufzüklaren." Curtze (n. 52 above) 9, noted that his two Munich manuscripts had forms like those shown in Nagl's Vienna manuscript; both noted that .t. stood for three as well as for zero.

The figures in the *Practica arismetrice* of John, being in more recent manuscripts (figs. 5 and 6), show a developed form more nearly resembling the thirteenth- and fourteenth-century numerals, especially in the definite loss of the tail for the 3 and the inclination to the right and on the line of the initial tail of 2. Also in John, the .t. for zero seems discarded and we have the circle as the sole form. Basically, however, the nine symbols and the zero in both Pedro and John constitute a single series quite different from that of the "Hindu" and the "Arabic." Let us see whether we can account for these differences.

THE CASE OF THE ZERO, THE FIVE AND THE EIGHT

We may take up first the zero form: a circle according to both Pedro and John, to which Pedro adds an alternate form .t. The early "Hindu" and the "Arabic" systems represented the zero by a mere point or dot placed under the digit by the Indians, and on the line with the digit by the Arabs; as for the circle, it was used for representing 5, at least in later Arab tradition probably under the influence of the *abjad* (in which 5=letter *ha*).[58] The existence of two forms for zero in the Western numerals in the twelfth century indicates two independent traditions. The circle for zero in Spain in the twelfth century may or may not be a survival of the ancient Greek usage in which a vacant place in a series of data was indicated by the initial "o" for *ouden* (null or void). Greek influence is known to have survived for some time in Andalucia and the southern and eastern coast of Spain after Justinian's reconquest, even into the Arab occupation after 711. Did the mathematical and scientific works of the Greeks have any currency or influence in pre-Arab Andalucia? Or was the Byzantine administration rooted sufficiently to produce an impact on the system of reckoning?[59] The evidence on this is very slim indeed unless it be on the "notarial" figures sketchily presented by Menéndez Pidal.[60] As to a possible influence of the Indian tradition of the circle for zero, it must be noted that this usage appeared late (tenth century, probably) in India; and it is hard to imagine a direct contact between India and Spain over the vast intermediary span of the Arab empire. It seems more natural to think of the development of the zero as a circle within Spain's own cultural activity.

The form .t. for zero, on the other hand, is a typically Western usage since it appears within the Roman system and in a distinctly traceable context, independent

[58] See Smith, *History* (n. 1 above) 2.70.

[59] According to Maimonides, the symbols and figures employed "for computation on the registers of the accountants" were called *al-'uqud al-rumi*. Cf. Gandz (n. 11 above) 400. This reference to Rumis in medieval Arabic texts is usually to the Byzantines. Now what does Maimonides mean by his "uqud": the ghubār numerals or the "notarial" figures mentioned by Menéndez Pidal? We are not clear on this question.

[60] See n. 1 above.

of the nine symbols.[61] In the thirteenth century John of Sacrobosco and his follower Peter of Dacia accredited the theory that .t. for zero stood for the abbreviation of the Latin word *teca,* the name of a circular-shaped iron with which to brand thieves.[62] Among the earlier writers on algorism, the identification of .t. as *teca* is never met with, but they always interpret .t. as the equivalent of *nihil* (nothing). Its appearance is signalled in the representation of the zero value in the sequences of numerical data in astronomical tables, as with the start and the finish of the periods of planetary motions.[63] Since much of the early arithmetical knowledge in the Latin West, (and this applies of course to pre-Arab Spain) was learned in the *Arithmetic* of Boethius, that is where we must look for this expression. Indeed, Boethius's *Arithmetic* uses the expression *terminus* to designate the beginning or end in a series of numbers connected in some fashion, and it is more than probable that the .t. for zero as used in early astronomical tables is an abbreviation of the *terminus* of Boethius. At any rate, these astronomical tables made much use of the symbol .t., within a system of Roman notation, and this must have slowly suggested the further meaning of zero in its absolute sense.

Alongside .t., the expression *circulus* and the representation of this neutral value as a circle must have suggested itself early, since it is well established at the time of Pedro Alfonso's and John's algorisms. John even uses *circulus* exclusively, both in his denomination of the figures and in his examples of calculations, while in the *Algorismus* of Pedro .t. for zero frequently slips in during the operations performed.

The origin of the present Western forms of 5 and 8 is closely related to the history of the zero. The medieval Latin shapes were ч for 5, and 8 for 8. Both forms can be traced paleographically to the Visigothic script[64] and to the stages of improvement in the Roman system of numerals as will be explained shortly. The ч =5 is merely the Roman V written in its archaic, stylized Visigothic form and little by little appearing as an independent symbol for the digit 5, independently from the Hindu system of nine numerals. The same may be said of 8 which, for a long time was represented by a mere o, the initial of *octo* = eight.[65] Other initials, especially q for four (*q*uatuor) and n for nine (*n*ovem) were similarly introduced in the Roman system to lighten the cumbersome forms. This is the same tendency that had created .t. (*t*erminus) for zero in the astronomical tables.

[61] Here I disagree with Smith, *History* (n. 1 above) 2.69, on the origin of the zero. He writes: "There is no probability that the origin will ever be known, and there is no particular reason why it should be".

[62] Quoted by Curtze (n. 52 above) 9: "Teca enim est ferrum figurae rotundae, quod ignitum solet in quibusdam regionibus imprimi fronti vel maxillae furis seu latronum." Note the "in quibusdam regionibus" which shows that the practice was not to be seen everywhere. Was Peter of Dacia familiar with the customs in Spain at the time that the .t. was used there for zero? Besides, his explanation seems particular with him. Sacrobosco, whom he is commenting here, merely wrote: "Decima vero O dicitur teca, vel circulus, vel cyfra, vel figura nichili."

[63] See fig. 7.

[64] See fig. 8.

[65] See fig. 7 – e.g., col. 5 line 26. This particular tradition will be explained below.

Now, the habit of using a point or dot for zero, common to both Hindu and Arab systems, could have meaning only within a system of value position. The Western scribes were in the habit of using dots on each side of a roman number in order to isolate it from the text (for example, .mccxxii. for 1222, or even .m.cc.xx.ii.). When the "Hindu" system was slowly introduced into Spain, the dot for zero must have appeared utterly improper and confusing. Similarly the circle used for five in the "Arabic" system (both the *abjad* and the Hindu figures) must have appeared as a source of confusion to savants who already disposed of an independent ч =5 and of a circle for 8. This situation seems to have suggested the natural substitution of ч =5 in place of the circle in the "Hindu" system, and the improvement of the o=8 into a double o as an abbreviation by contraction (*octo*): ȣ .[66] The two circles were finally joined to give the medieval and our 8. After these improvements, in which the ч =5, 8 and 0, of independent Visigothic origin, were substituted for their counterparts in the "Hindu" system, the Western numerals came to have a distinctly original aspect. The circle could then definitely be acquired for zero, although the earlier, independent .t. was preserved for a while. By the beginning of the twelfth century, at the very latest, these acquisitions were stable as shown by the *Algorismus* and the *Practica arismetrice.*

THE FIGURES FOR ONE, TWO, THREE AND NINE

These four come in a straight line from the Arabic numerals. There is obviously no problem concerning the figure 1, since in all reckoning systems this is the most natural and unavoidable representation of the unit. The figure nine is identical in the Arabic and the algorism. One must note, however, that, owing to the fact that the "hindu" figures seem to have been first used in the abacus in the West (hence also *ghubār*=dust of the abacus tablet of the western Arabs),[67] namely in the form of

[66] An abbreviation by contraction wrote only the first and last letters of a word; the other type of abbreviation was by suspension, writing only the first letters of a word. MS A of John of Seville's text seems to contain a trace of this process; its 8 is sometimes represented in this form: ʒ (fols. 28 bis). Woepcke (n. 11 above) 58 quotes from a commentary by al-Qalaṣādi (copy used by Woepcke is dated 1229 H / 1814 A.D.) on the *Talkhis* of Ibn al-Bannā a passage which explains the form of 8 ghubār as being made of two zeros (*ṣifrāni*) connected by an *alif*: 9 . This seems to confirm the suspicion that the origin of our 8 was the combination of two Os for the abbreviation of *octo,* which came to be connected into one single form. A faint reminiscence of this origin still shows in al-Qalaṣādi's explanation of the form of ghubār 8.

[67] This is the more general use of the system of the nine symbols, as exemplified by Gerbert ca. 980 who had brought this knowledge from Spain into France. The use of the nine figures simplified the operations with the abacus, without implying a knowledge of the zero, since the columns of the abacus determined the relative value; see fig. 9. The full implications of the Hindu system, especially through its value position, were slow to be recognized. Actually, we have to depend on these twelfth-century translations of al-Khwārizimī's *Arithmetic* and its imitations by Pedro and John to fix a certain date when the whole system was fully understood. Parallel to the growing awareness of the utility of the Hindu system, the desire to improve the Roman system rather had possessed the astronomers for a long time.

movable counters that could be turned inadvertently upside down,[68] the 9 could thus easily take the form of our 6. In the Hindu-Arab figures this was not inconvenient since there was but one figure of this sort. But among the Spaniards, as will shortly be indicated, a nearly similar figure for 6 had developed from the Visigothic script (as in the case of  =5). In order to avoid confusion, the *ductus* of the 9 was stressed,[69] while the superior stroke of the 6 was emphasized.[70]

The figures for 2 and 3 were transferred from the Arabic script into the Latin with a slight modification that can be fully accounted for paleographically.[71] In transcribing these figures, a Western scribe used to writing from left to right had to interrupt the regular movement of his hand and arm, jump a few spaces forward and start tracing these figures in a backward motion. To avoid this inconvenience, the scribes naturally lifted the loops of the 2 and 3 upwards so as to draw them in an uninterrupted movement of his hand from left to right:

 became 

 became 

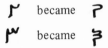

Hence these seemingly awkward tails hanging from the loops in the early Western forms of the 2s and 3s.[72] They are however, absolutely normal, given this process of paleographical evolution in known circumstances and under known motivation.[73] Later, the tail of the three was suppressed since the double loop appeared characteristic enough and could not be confused with any letter of the Latin alphabet. As for the 2, its tail was eventually bent to the right so as to fit within the line of script. These stages of evolution are so manifest in the various Latin manuscripts that one may use the transitional forms of 2 and 3 as dating landmarks within a margin of less than 50 years.[74]

[68] The situation has been described by G. Beaujouan, "Etude paléographique sur la rotation des chiffres et l'emploi des apices aux Xe-XIIe siècles," *Revue d'histoire des sciences* 1 (1948) 303-313.

[69] See fig. 9.

[70] Probably a trace of an original stroke or bar placed above this figure in earlier times, and eventually absorbed into the symbol itself. See however fig. 8 line 20, and fig. 10, col. b, line 4.

[71] Smith's statement (n. 1 above) 68, to the effect that our 2 and 3 are the Arabic forms on their side, does not explain the reason. Nor is the principle of "rotation of the apices" of Beaujouan the proper explanation.

[72] See fig. 1, fol. 1v.

[73] Hence the astonishment of Hill (n. 55 above) 11: "Here we have in use, alongside a fully developed form of 2, a form like a pruning hook , of which the only other instances which I have found are in manuscripts of the twelfth, or at the latest early thirteenth century. Then there is a very curious form of 3, like the pruning hook 2 with an added line through it: ". These "curious" forms are merely the most ancient and the most genuine ones for the twelfth century.

[74] This is obvious when we compare for instance fig. 1 and fig. 4 of the same text. Fig. 4 appears nearly 50 years younger than fig. 1 and the 3 in it often loses its tail.

THE FOUR, SIX AND SEVEN

These three numeral figures of the Western algorism evidently diverge widely from their counterparts in either Hindu or Arabic:, , and V. The  =4 and Λ =7 can be shown, through a series of intermediary forms, to have been borrowed from the Arabic after undergoing notable alterations under the stress of the particular conditions of scientific development in Spain. The other figure  =6 is of distinctly Visigothic and Spanish descent.

The Latin text of al-Khwārizimī's *Arithmetic*[75] expressly states the existence of variations in the forming of several among the nine "Hindu" symbols. Unfortunately, the unique manuscript copy gives no example of these various forms, as it omits nearly all the actual symbols, and resorts to Roman numerals in the mathematical operations. Moreover, it seems more than probable that this statement about the variations is an interpolation by the translator or the scribe, just as the *Algorismus* of Pedro has been tampered with by the scribes or scholars who reproduced it. What the situation alluded to in the *Arithmetic* may have been, becomes somewhat clearer from a similar situation in John of Seville's *Practica arismetrice.* Here, two different forms for the 4 and three or perhaps four for the 7 are mentioned to be current "according to the variety of place."[76]

Naturally, the original figures, whether borrowed from the Arabic-Hindu system or developed independently in the Latin West, underwent significant alterations as the centuries wore on, so that our attention must be focused on the forms in the earliest manuscripts. Of the three copies of John of Seville's text which I have examined in detail, namely A, C and D,[77] the earliest, A, presents two forms of 4: , , the first being the preferred one, appearing in the basic list of the nine figures and being used throughout the text. In C the two forms are:  and 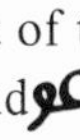, and in D they are:  and . The latter form in each case is presented as a variant still in use in John's times, but clearly they do not seem as universal as the first form, which in fact is nearly identical and standard in the three copies and became soon the only one in use.[78] Yet, in all its uncertain shapes, the second form in all these manuscripts shows clear trace of an immediate descent from the Arabic 4. One can follow the evolution of this figure from an imitation of the Arabic one, through the displacing or the outright dropping of the hook at the upper right section of the figure, leaving the mere loop  as the characteristic form of 4 in the medieval algorism. Other intermediary examples may be found in a Parisian copy of the twelfth-century

[75] Text published from the unique manuscript by Boncompagni (n. 6 above) and later in facsimile with transcription by Vogel in 1963 (n. 45 above).

[76] See fig. 6 (fol. 85vb, lines 5-7) and fig. 5 (fol. 1rb, lines 27-30).

[77] See above, n. 52, for sigla of manuscripts.

[78] All the copies of Leonardo Fibonacci's *Liber abaci* (1202) which I have examined have this prevalent form of the single loop for 4.

translation of Alfraganus by John of Seville: Bibliothèque Nationale MS lat. 14704 fol. 215rb:[79] 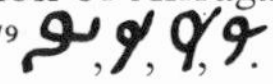. In the first instance, the scribe has transferred the initial hook from right to left in the figure, with a hint that the original figure was more elaborate than the mere loop  , which dominates throughout this text. Another distinctly Spanish tradition probably helped in selecting the pure loop as the core of the figure 4 in this 12th century algorism. In an earlier, separate evolution of the Roman system in Spain, which we shall explain shortly, a special symbol  had stood for the Roman xl=40. This was merely a Visigothic ligature of the two letters, and is attested very early in Spanish epigraphy and paleography.[80] During the penetration of the "Hindu" system in Spain, this symbol for Roman xl soon became obsolete since, in the position value, there was no need for a special figure beyond the basic nine numerals and the zero. Thus the looped  =40 of the improved Roman system in Spain became available as a clearer, simpler figure for a digit than the complicated Arabic =4, though the latter was clearly maintained for some time, as the example of John of Seville shows.

The avatars of our 7 from the Arabic V to medieval Λ, and finally 7, can be linked up in order and give an explanation of our present form. John supplies one regular form along with the other eight figures: .Λ. in C and .7. in D. The variants immediately listed by John show the transitional stages which were apparently still in use in John's time, about 1130 A.D., since he writes: "Est autem in aliquibus istarum figurarum *apud multos* diversitas . . . *pro varietate locorum*".[81] The three variant forms of 7 are nearly identical in all three copies examined:  or  or . It will be immediately noticed that the V shape is present, in some form or other, in all three: in figures one and two, we have an upright and upside down V combined in two different ways, while in figure three, the V is merely upside down. Whichever way we look at them, the V shape is basic in all. The first two alternates betray the instability of the transition from Arabic V to algorism Λ : a mere turning upside down of the same figure. What led to this reversion and stabilization of the upside down form? The theory of the "rotation" of the apices on an abacus may have helped, but the dual forms in which both the upside and downside forms are combined seem to postulate another explanation. First, we must remember that in the Arabic sequence of the nine figures, both forms followed one another: V for 7, and Λ for 8. (Hence the "rotation" alone becomes pointless.) In fact, the Arabic V for 7 was so similar to Latin capital V that its eventual elimination could be foreseen with the slightest pressure from the progress in the use of the system in scientific works. On the other hand, as we have already shown, the Western tradition in Spain had previously developed an original form of 8 which, being introduced (like the 5, 6 and 0) into the "Hindu" system, displaced the Arabic upside down Λ for 8. Of the two forms of V,

[79] Fig. 10.

[80] Cf. the works of Mallon, De Navascues, García Villada and Millares Carlo (nn. 82 and 84 below).

[81] "For some of these figures, we meet some variety among many writers . . . according to the diversity of regions." The place of this quotation is cited in n. 76 above.

this one was less confusing for Latin readers than the upright V for 7. It seems then that the discarded Arabic Λ =8 was soon transferred to 7 instead, and the upside V could be discarded. This process seems to be still operating at the time John was writing and he left us clear indications of the hesitations in the transition.

With respect to the 6 =6 of the algorism, it is no less evident that its shape is a far cry from the Arabic one: ٦ . Its origin is to be found in the ancient Visigothic script of Roman numerals, as was shown by J. Mallon[82] who brought examples from Spanish or Visigothic epigraphy to bear on the explanation. The drafters of "minutes" for monumental inscriptions as well as the engravers on stone have always shown tendencies to conservatism in the writing of dates, and hence of the figures. When written in two letters (VI) as a Roman numeral, the 6 came to be represented in ligature thus: ϥ, so that the symbol was eventually confused with a G in the later forms of the Visigothic script.[83] Possibly to avoid confusion with the figure 9 when both were used in the abacus or *ghubār,* a stroke was added over the G and later fused with the upper stroke of the symbol 6 to give this characteristic medieval algorism 6.

In conclusion of this section, it may be said that close scrutiny of the early forms of the algorism figures in the West, comparative study of pre-algorism traditions of number representations in Visigothic and Mozarab Spain, show that among our ten basic symbols of numbers, the figures of 4, 5, 6, 7, 8 and 0 have all developed in one region, medieval Spain, and acquired their shapes – widely different from and much clearer than either the Hindu or the Arabic ones – during a slow and obscure traverse among the mathematicians and astronomers of medieval Spain.

B. THE IMPROVED ROMAN NUMERAL SYSTEM IN SPAIN

The appearance in Visigothic script of separate symbols for some among the nine digits antedates the adoption of the Hindu-Arabic system of nine figures and value position. The original Spanish symbols for 5, 6, 8 and 0 developed within the system of Roman numerals. The reason for their continued vogue until the rise of Spanish science is obscure: we find them mostly in the dating of documents or in lists of chapters or in inventories.[84] In the cultural atmosphere of Arab Spain in close relation with the scientific activity of eastern Islam (Baghdad and Egypt), the *Arithmetic* of al-Khwārizimī traveled early to Spain but does not seem to have

[82] J. Mallon, "Pour une nouvelle critique des chiffres . . . ," in *Emerita* 16 (Madrid 1948) 22 and figs. 1, 3, 7, 13, 16, and p. 45 n. Also J. M. de Navascues, *La Era . . . AS* (Madrid 1951) 11.

[83] See fig. 8, line 20, fig. 10, col. b, line 4, and fig. 11, lines 14, 16, 18, 19 and 20.

[84] Abundant examples may be found outside of the scientific fields in the paleographic albums of Visigothic script, such as Z. García Villada, *Paleografía española* (Madrid 1923); A. Millares Carlo, *Paleografía española* (Barcelona 1929); and in the works of Mallon and De Navascues (n. 82 above). See also A. González Palencia, *Los Mozárabes de Toledo en los siglos XII y XIII,* 4 vols. (Madrid 1926-1930).

obtained general acceptance, at least in the earlier stage. Instead, with the rise of interest in astronomical science in Spain, principally with the tenth and eleventh centuries, we witness attempts to improve the system of Roman numerals in order to make it more manageable, easier to handle. The inspiration behind these efforts may be detected when one compares an earlier *computus*[85] loaded with clumsy Roman numerals, with an example of the improved situation in a set of later astronomical tables:[86] the nature of the progress sought is immediately obvious. The data that I have collected in this area[87] are all taken from manuscripts of astronomical, astrological and mathematical science originating in the Spain of the eleventh and twelfth centuries, which soon became the home of astronomical study in European eyes.

While preparing my edition of the Latin translations of Abu Ma'shar's *Great Introduction to Astronomy,* I had to examine in detail some fifty manuscripts of this bulky text and a host of others of similar content. During the early stages of my investigation I was frequently detained by the occurrence of queer forms of numbers, which I considered as errors and tended to blame on the scribes. Yet at some point I was forced to realize that my impressive lists of "errors" occurred in the earliest and otherwise best manuscripts of my text. Something had to be done to test the validity of my initial evaluations and I began to note minute details that had escaped me before. The "errors" usually related to the degrees of the circle and of its regular division into hemicircle, quadrant, sixth and so on. The recurring readings X for XL, or LX for XC were errors on my part, arising from my inadvertence to a special symbol for XL hardly perceptible to the untrained eye: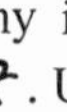. Used in combination with the L for 50, this peculiar symbol also gave me the clue for the interpretation of the numbers in the 90s which I had previously read as 60s. Further on, examination of astronomical tables in the same manuscripts revealed the use of equally unfamiliar symbols such as q, o and n, mixed up indiscriminately with normal notations of Roman numerals. The cyclical character of data in astronomical tables enabled me to decipher these symbols as standing for the initial letter or abbreviation of the numbers represented: q=4, o=8 and n=9.[88] More examples from some of the manuscripts of Pedro Alfonso's *Algorismus* indicated that the practice of using initial letters of the digits tended to be generalized, leading to a system as follows:

t = tres[89]
q = quatuor
Q = quinque
s = sex

[85] See fig. 11.

[86] See fig. 7.

[87] I have already presented some of this experience in the paper submitted at the *XIIe Congrès international d'histoire des sciences* in Paris in 1968. See *XIIe Congrès . . . Textes des rapports* (Paris 1968) 111-113, and the results of the Discussions on this subject were published *XIIe Congrès . . . Actes 1* (Paris 1971) 94-113.

[88] See the embarrassed interpretation of E. Poulle in his discussion of my paper, *Actes* (n. 87 above) 104-108. Poulle failed to recognize mere letters in these symbols.

[89] Hence the puzzling form of t=3 met with by Nagl in the Vienna manuscript; see n. 57 above.

S = septem
o = octo
n (also no) = novem[90]

More normally, however, in the astronomical tables the system remained limited to only the more cumbersome numbers like iiii=4, viii=8 and viiii=9, which had resulted from an almost universal abandonment of the traditional subtractive forms in the roman system: iv, ix, xl, xc, cd, cm, which became respectively: iiii, viiii, xxxx, lxxxx, cccc and dcccc. On this principle, a number like 44 was expressed xxxxiiii, 99 was written lxxxxviiii, and so on. The combined use of the initials for the digits, and of the ligature of x and l (xl) for 40:  allowed one to lighten considerably the more cumbersome numbers. 99 could be expressed: 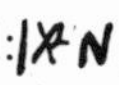; 49 as 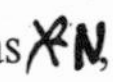 and so on. All such improvements, however, remained confined within the system of Roman notation, namely, the total value is expressed by addition and not by position.

The important conclusion emerges, then, that we find this usage of an improved Roman system to prevail among Spanish astronomers and mathematicians until the middle of the twelfth century, while during the crucial period from the tenth to the twelfth centuries, the Hindu system and its symbols obscurely made their way in some as yet little explored fields or areas that led to the creation of a typically Spanish set of "Arabic" numerals, the ones Europe finally inherited.

The exact moment of transference of some of the Visigothic and Mozarab symbols into the Hindu system to take the place of several among them, is not known. The full-blown system of nine numerals and the zero of Spanish origin emerges suddenly into clear light with the *Algorismus* of Pedro Alfonso and the *Practica arismetrice* of John Seville. The European scholars of the twelfth century were told that the idea of nine basic numerals originated with the Indians: both Pedro and John are specific about this. Yet the scribe of our figure 1 knew the difference between real "Indian" figures and the Western ones: he calls the latter the "Toledan ciphers" (*toletane figure*). We should probably follow him and do the same: as regards their form, our so-called "Arabic" or "Hindu-Arabic" numerals are in fact *Toledan numerals.*

The "Hindu-Arabic" numerals, as inherited by medieval European scholars, must be credited to a large extent to the Spanish experience. What was received by Latin European scholars in the middle of the twelfth century had been concocted in its full form in the precincts of Arab and Mozarab Spain, where a fusion of the Visigothic, Roman, and Arab traditions all worked together to create this marvelous instrument of modern mathematics.

Graduate Center
City University of New York
33 West Forty-Second Street
New York, New York 10036, U.S.A.

[90] One example of this fully developed system may be found in manuscript C of Pedro's *Algorismus.*

Figure 1. Munich CLM 18927 (twelfth century), fol. lr and fol. lv. Toledan astronomical tables. The three lines of figures inserted above the text in fol. lr, but before the table of contents above, are labeled respectively "toletane f(igure)" in the first line and "indice f(igure)" in the second line; the third, unnamed line, is giving the figures as used in the following tables in the codex. A fourth line reads: "o et t sunt cifre" showing the scribe's knowledge of the zero and of variations in its representation. The figures used in the Toledan tables on fol. lv and following are of the crudest and earliest twelfth-century type very near their Arabic origin especially for the 2s and 3s with their surviving tail. The o for zero is used in complex numbers while *t* is used in isolation. = 40 is used as well as = 4 in position value, despite some redundancy as when 40 is written 0 (columns 4, 5, 9 and 10).

Figure 2. Paris BN lat. 16208, fol. 70v. End section of *Ysagogai Alchorismi* by "Magister A." (Anfusus or Pedro Alfonso?). Name of Hebrew months and Hebrew system of the *abjad.* This is not present in al-Khwārizmī's *Arithmetic* as edited by Boncompagni (Rome 1857), nor in John of Seville's translation or adaptation of the same work. This Hebrew addition does not seem likely to be Adelard of Bath's idea. Moreover, the date 8 October 1115 A.D. on which the table of eras is based well suits Alfonso's literary activity destined to the Latins between 1110 and 1115 while he sojourned for a while in England. A similar date is at the root of the Khwarizmian astronomical tables ascribed to Pedro Alfonso in an Oxford manuscript, Corpus Christi College 283, recently studied by O. Neugebauer.

Figure 3. London, British Library Harley 3631, fol. 34v (Abu Ma'shar's *Maior Introductorius*); reproduced by permission of the British Library Board. In col. b, improved Roman numerals are used in the text with =40, although not very different from a mere X = 10. The scribe (or a later hand?) has inserted into the interlinear margin the equivalents in Arabic numerals in order to eliminate any possible confusion (a confusion frequently met with in other copies of Abu Ma'shar's text when the scribe was not familiar with the "improved" Roman numerals). Improved Roman numerals here met with are vii = (47), line 4; viiii = (49), line 5; vi = (46), line 15; XXN = 29, line 16.

Figure 4. Munich, CLM 13021 (twelfth century). *Algorismus* (Same incipit as in Paris BN lat. 16208, fol. 67, but the two texts have very important differences in variants, in contents and in arrangement). Codex studied by M. Curtze. Fol. 27r-v. Early types of "Toledan" figures with 2 and 3 preserving their tail. Fol. 27r, line 22 of col. b contains the nine figures; the zero is Ø and O (the Paris text still has "O vel t"). In fact, the scribe of the Munich manuscript uses *t* for 3. (See multiplication table: 4 X 9 = t6; 5 X 7 = t5; 7 X 9 = 6t; there are several errors in this multiplication table: e.g., 2 X 6 = 11; 2 X 7 = 15; 2 X 9 = 14; 3 X 6 = 14; 6 X 7 = 45; 6 X 9 = 58. Since many of the errors involved a 4 instead of an 8 or vice versa, it appears that the scribe was not clear about the real form of 8, as if for him the 8 was a mere closing of the inferior loop of the 4=.) On fol. 27v also, *t* is frequently used in the operations for a 3, never for zero – in such a way that his presentation of the two forms of zero "Ø vel O", ignoring the t=0 symbol, appears deliberate.

Figure 5. Paris BN lat. 15461 (thirteenth century), fol. 1. Beginning of John of Seville's adaptation of al-Khwārizmī's *Arithmetic.* His figures are of a late model, without the tails in 2 and 3. The series of numerals is presented in col. b, lines 25-26; variations in the forms of 7 and 4 are here: , , for 7, and for 4 (lines 28-29).

Figure 6. Paris BN lat. 7359, fol. 85 r-v. Another copy of John of Seville's adaptation of al-Khwārizmī's *Arithmetic.* List of numerals is presented on col. b line 2 of fol. 85v. Their form is late thirteenth century. Variations for 7 and 4 here are somewhat altered, especially for the 4 (lines 5-6).

Figure 7. Paris BN lat. 14704 (twelfth century), fol. 121 (continuation of tables of Raymond of Marseilles). Numerous examples of "improved" Roman numerals with use of initial letters: 4 = q; 8 = o; 9 = n; 0 = t and 40 =. These are intermingled with numerous old forms for the same numerals.

Figure 8. Paris BN lat. 14754 (twelfth century), fol. 157v. Extract from Martianus Capella. Pre-gothic capital V is written, the form that has given the=5 of the "Toledan" numerals (see lines 1, 13). The present example appears to be a transitory stage in the evolution, since V is also written (lines 7, 15); the instability of the hand is certain since the same word "vel" (lines 13 and 15) is rendered once with a and once with a. Instability extends to other letters like A and Q.

Figure 9. Paris BN lat. 15461 (thirteenth century), fol. 50v. Abacus table. A good instance of the passage from the abacus to independent "Arabic" numerals. No zero was needed in the abacus, but here, in the designation of the value of each column, the zero is employed for 10, 100, 1000. The rest of the enumeration however still relies on initial letters, like 10^{m} for 10,000, 100^{m} for 100,000, M^{m} for 1,000,000 and so on; also the position value is so faintly perceived that the order of the columns has to be indicated on the very top from 1 to 10. The figure for 3 still carries a faint trace of its original tail at this late date, while the 8 seems to be distinctly perceived as initial o with superscript o (octo), namely: two Os one upon the other; this is especially visible in the number designating the eighth column on top.

Figure 10. Paris BN lat. 14704 (twelfth century), fol. 215r-v. A passage from Alfraganus. Very early forms of "Toledan" numerals. The 2s and 3s still have their long tail, 5, 6 and 8 have their typical "Toledan" shape, some still resembling letters from the same script (e.g. 6=G, fol. 215rb, line 4; when writing the tyronian "et", fol. 215rb, line 5, the scribe here has noted the possible confusion of his "et" with figure 5 and has consequently inserted "ac" for "et" between the lines). It will also be noted that at this early stage, numbers are enclosed in boxes to separate them from letters of the script, while later the numbers will be isolated from the line by a dot before and after them.

Figure 11. Paris BN lat. 14069, fol. 19. A computus of pre-twelfth-century epoch showing the cumbersome character of Roman numerals in astronomical calculations. Line before last in the table must be read: (lunatio) 228: 6726 d(ies), 6612 m(inuta), 79,344 ath(omos).

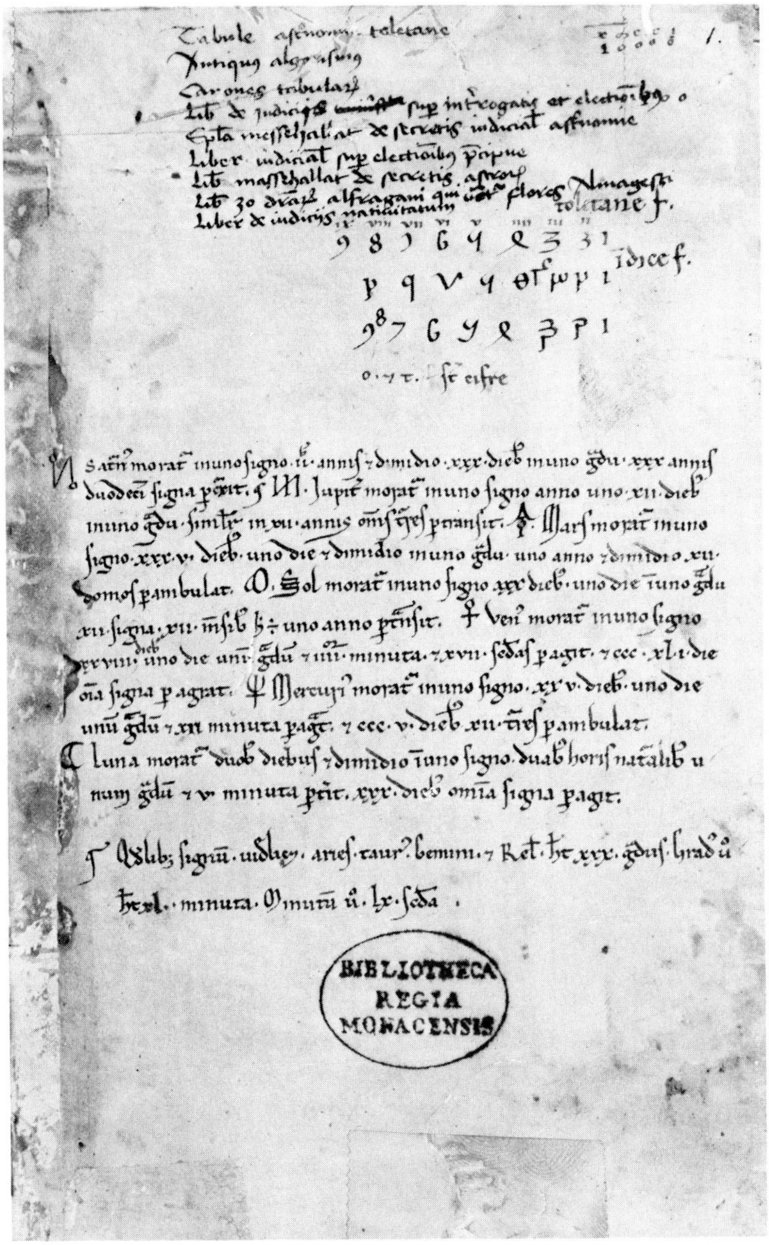

FIG. 1a. Munich, CLM 18927, fol. 1r

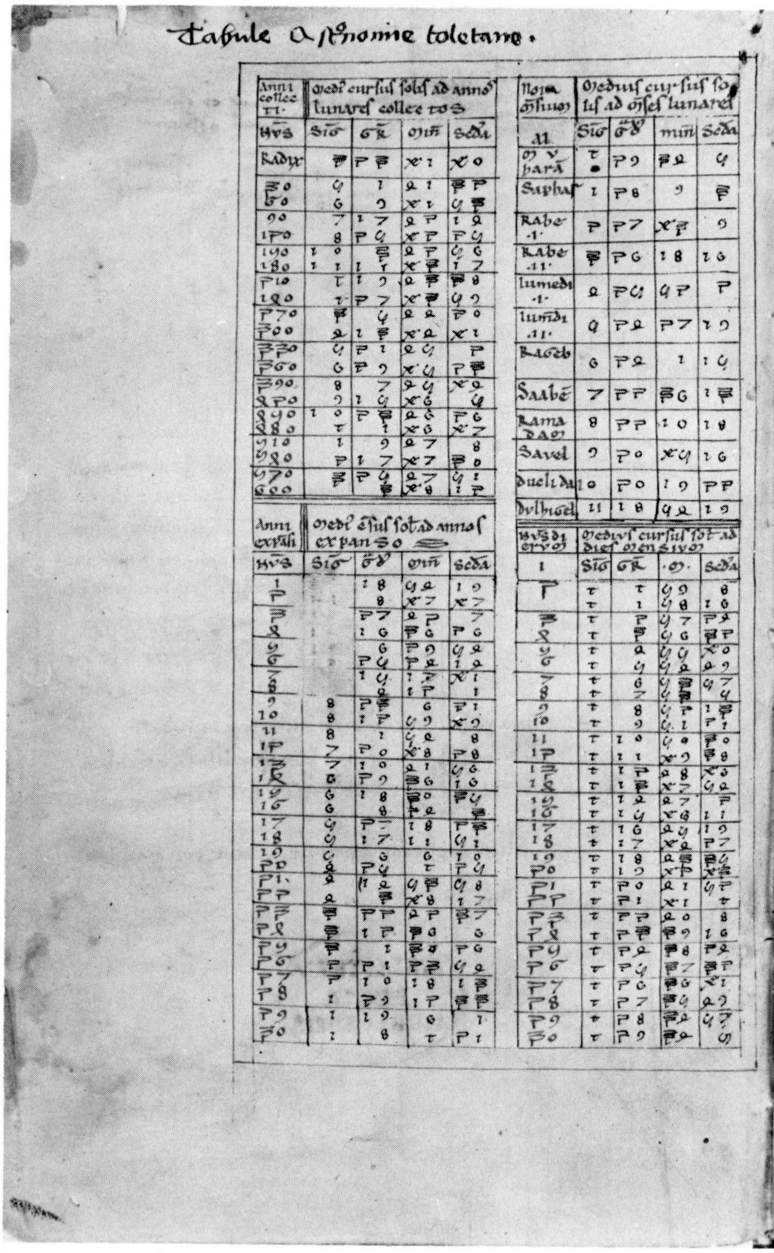

FIG. 1b. Munich, CLM 18927, fol. 1v

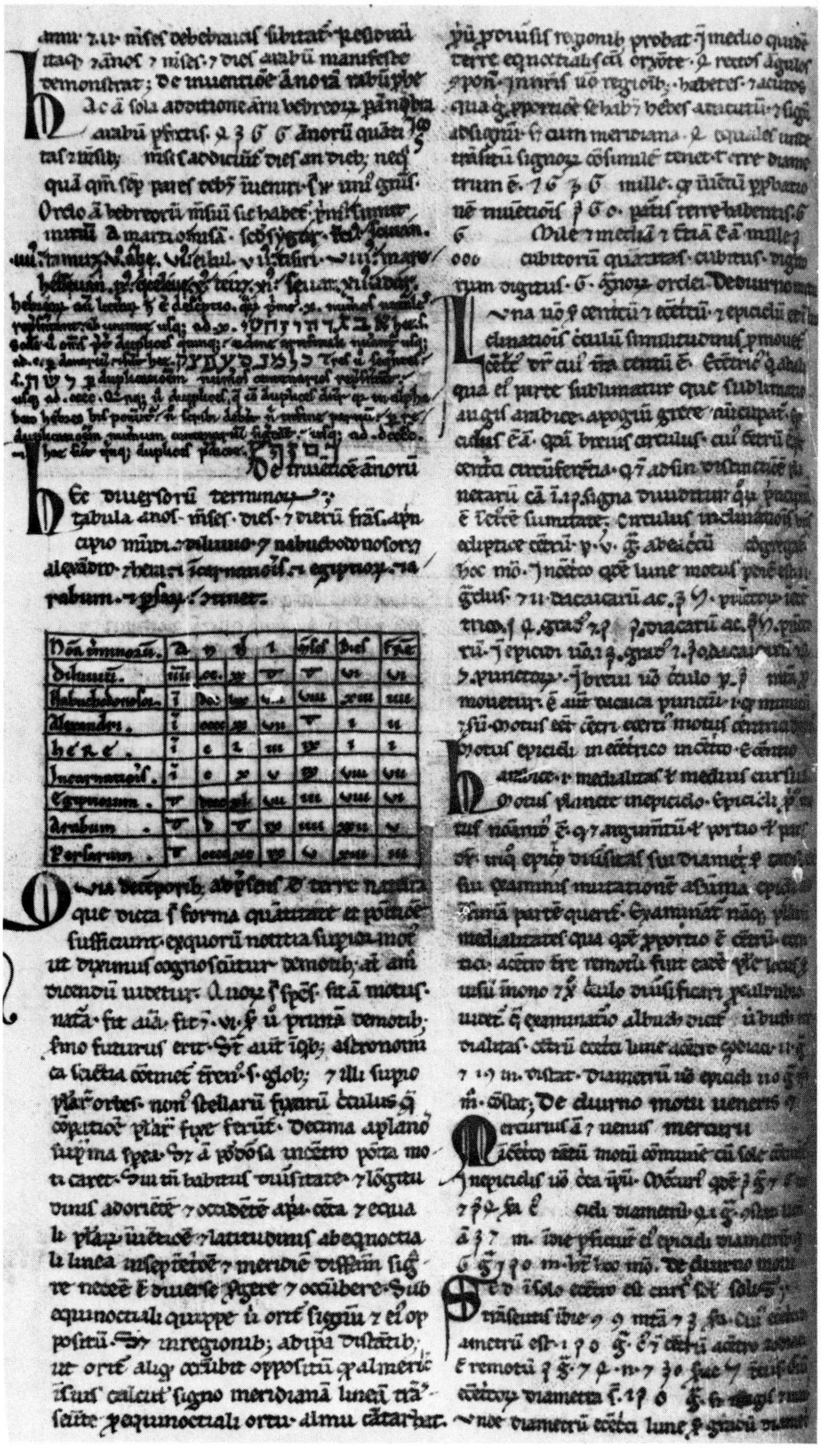

FIG. 2. Paris, BN lat. 16208, fol. 70v

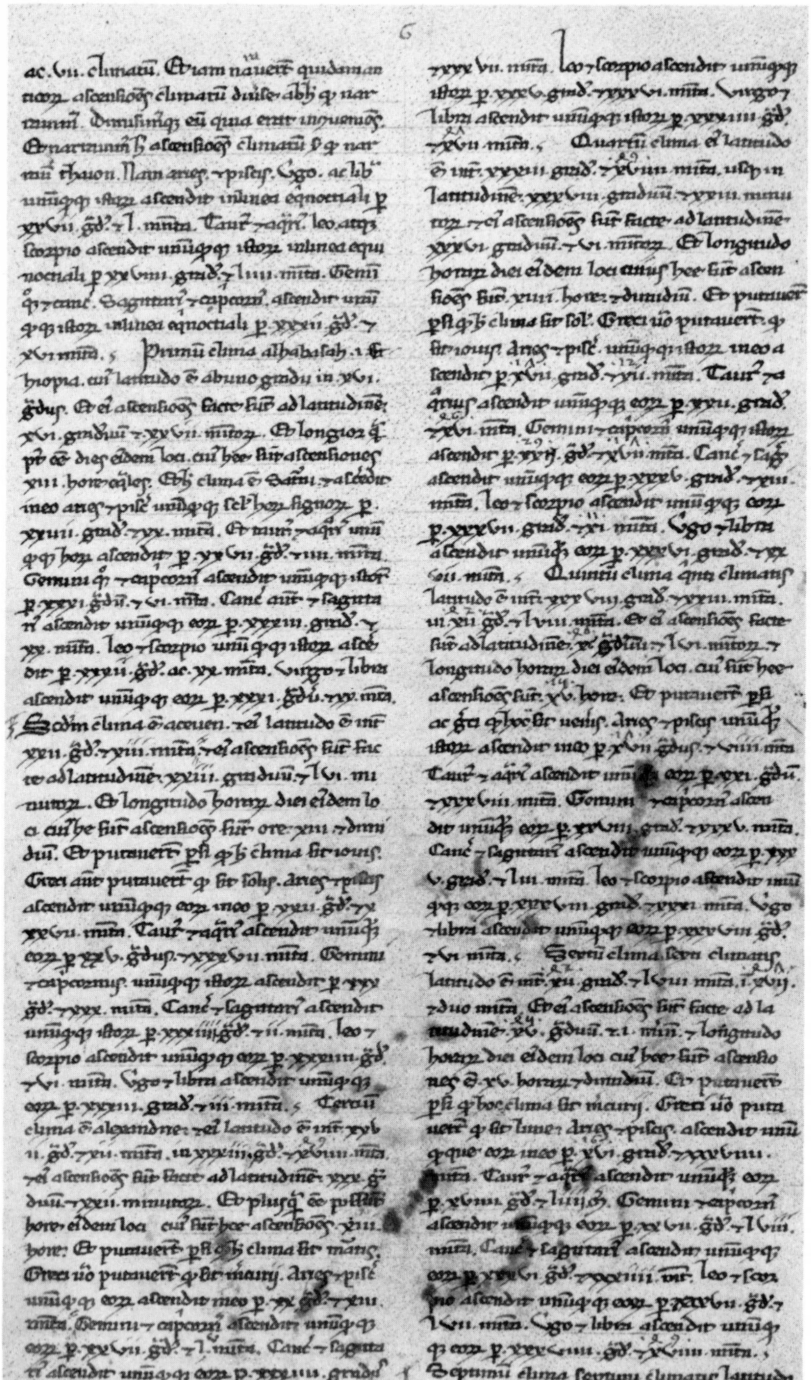

FIG. 3. London, British Library, Harley 3631, fol. 34v

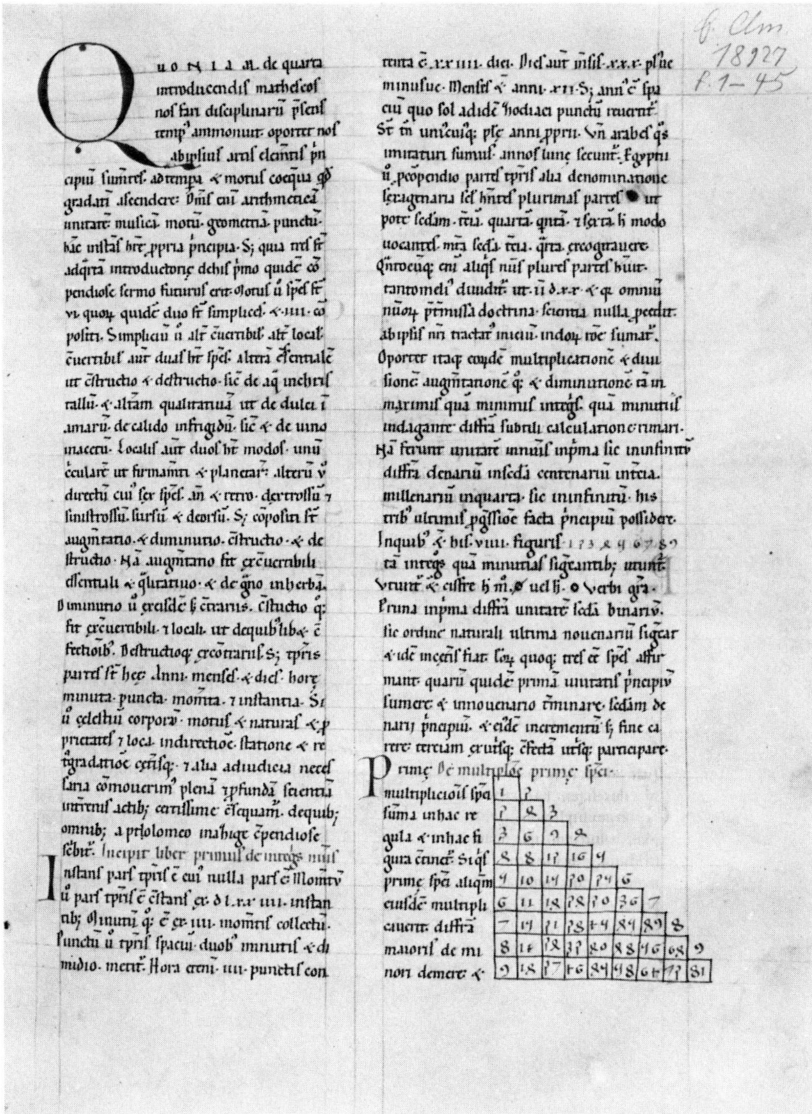

FIG. 4a. Munich, CLM 13021, fol. 27r

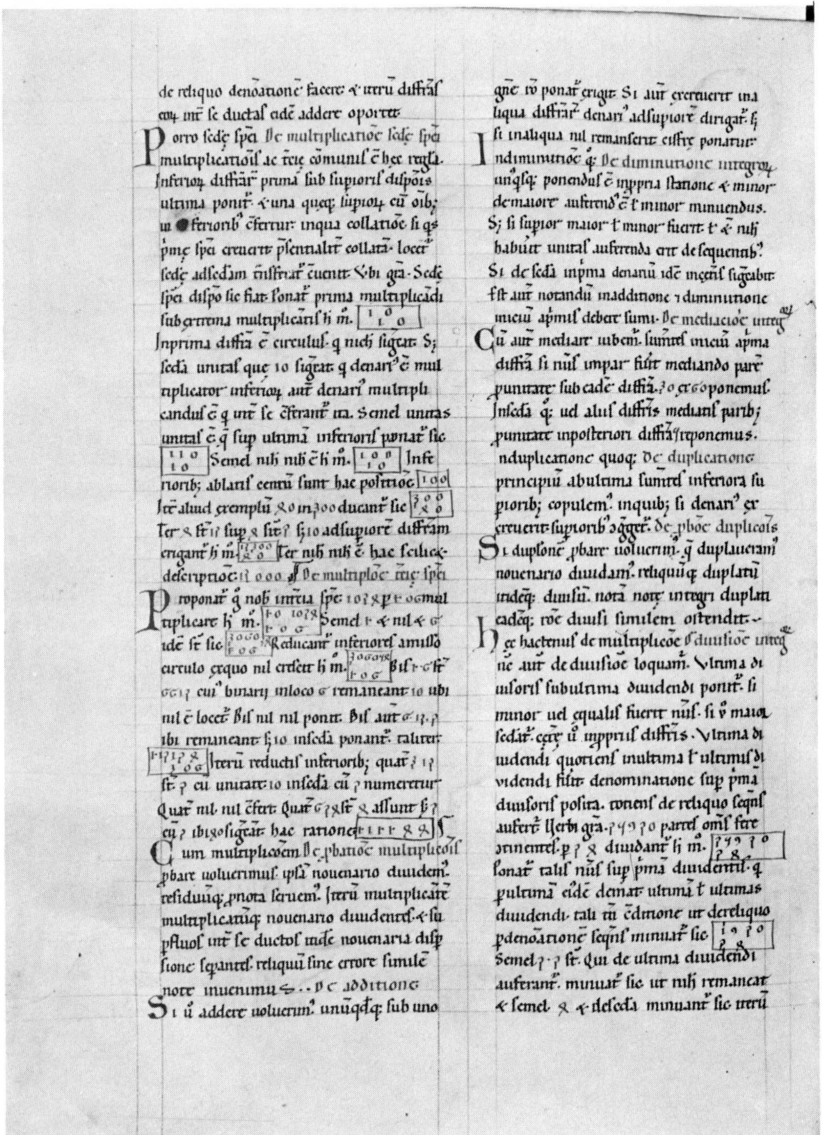

FIG. 4b. Munich, CLM 13021, fol. 27v

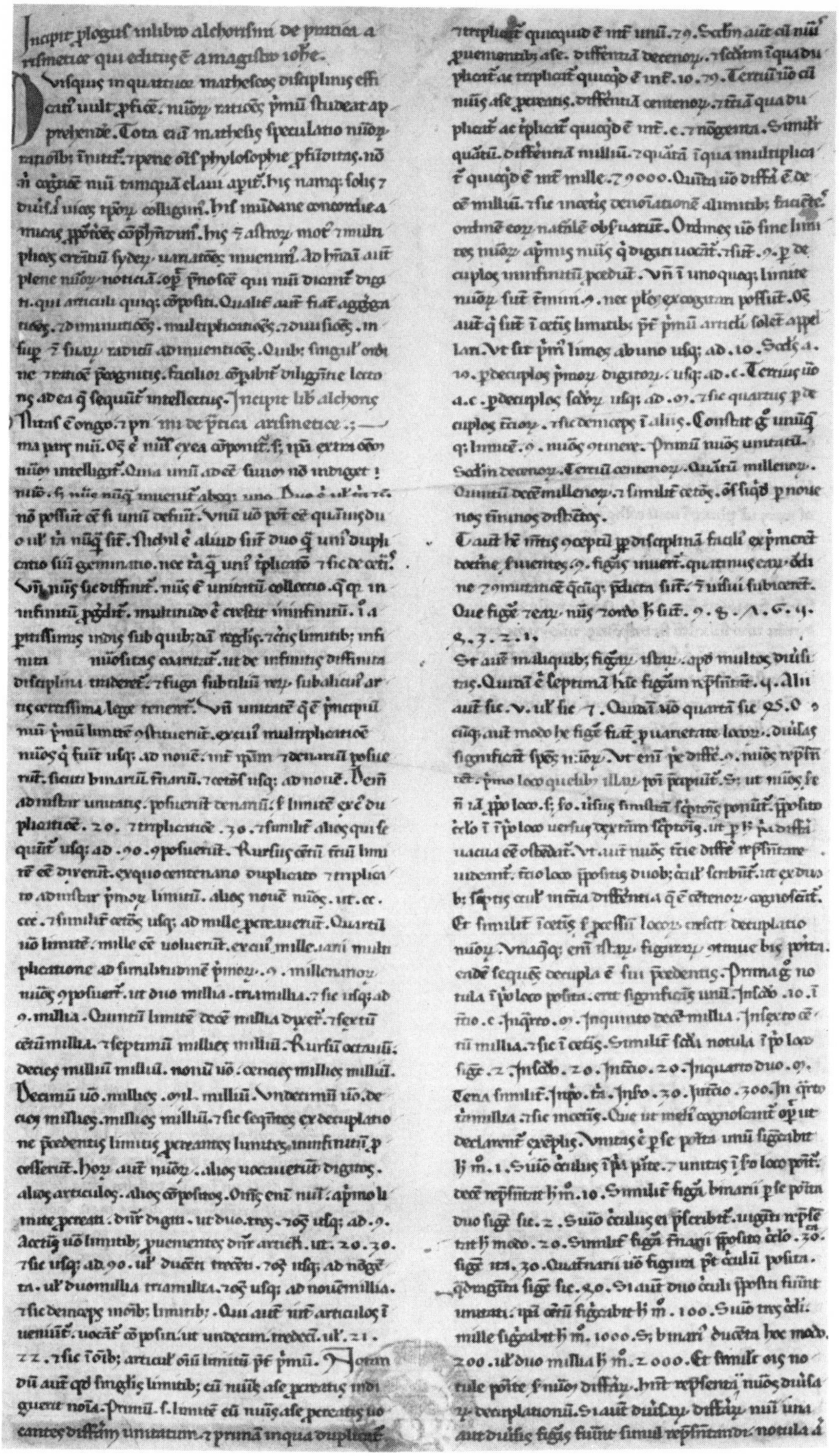

FIG. 5. Paris, BN lat. 15461, fol. 1

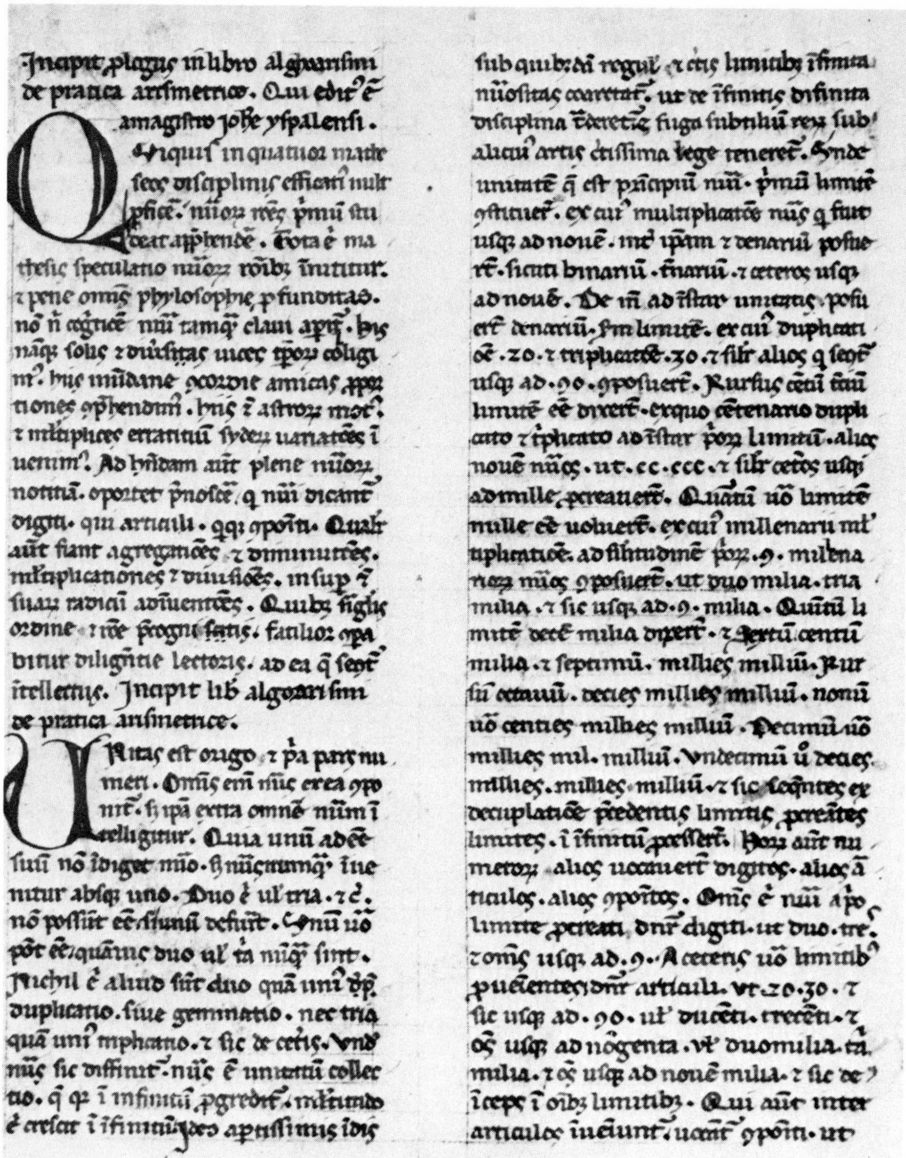

FIG. 6a. Paris, BN lat. 7359, fol. 85 r

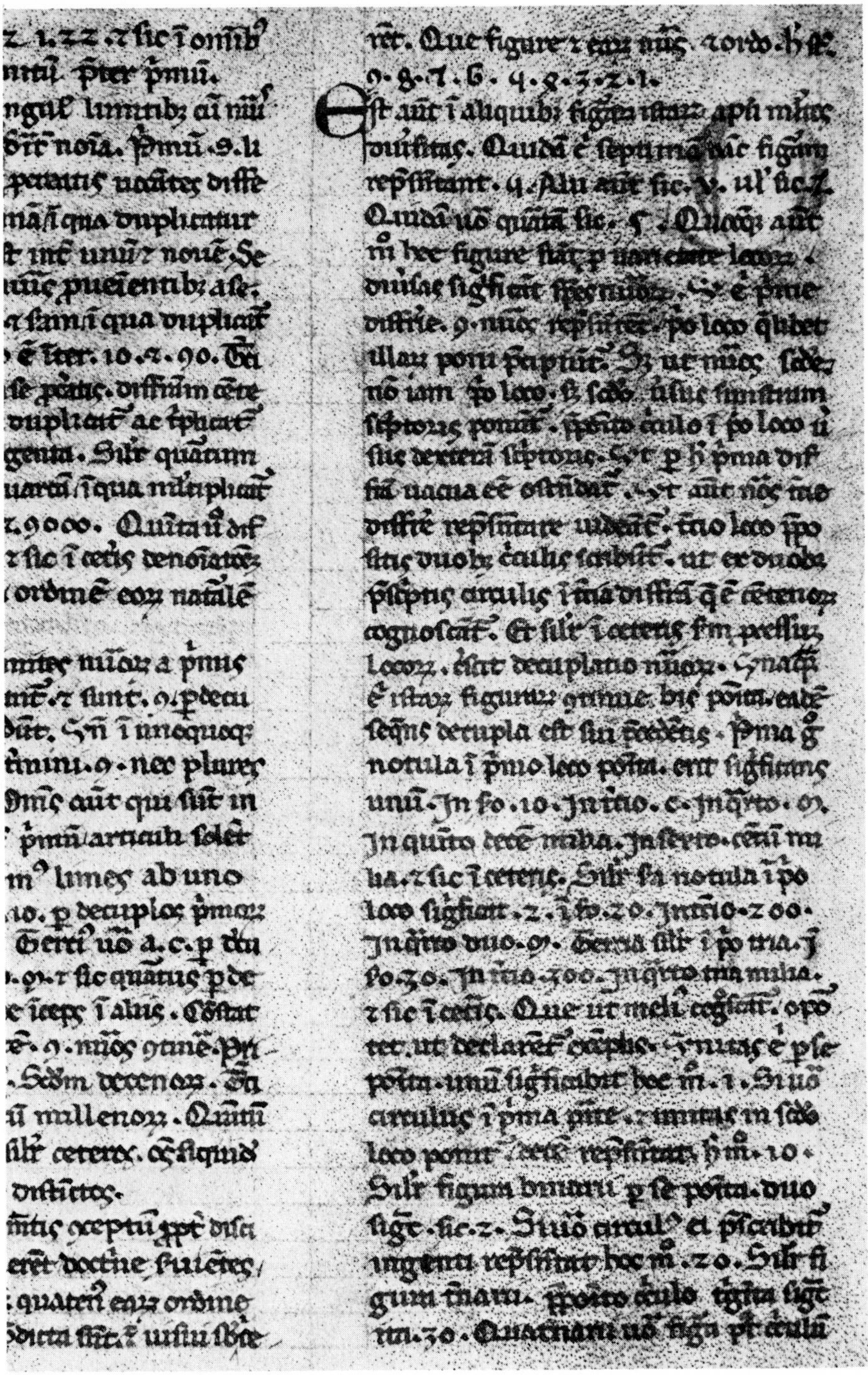

FIG. 6b. Paris, BN lat. 7359, fol. 85v

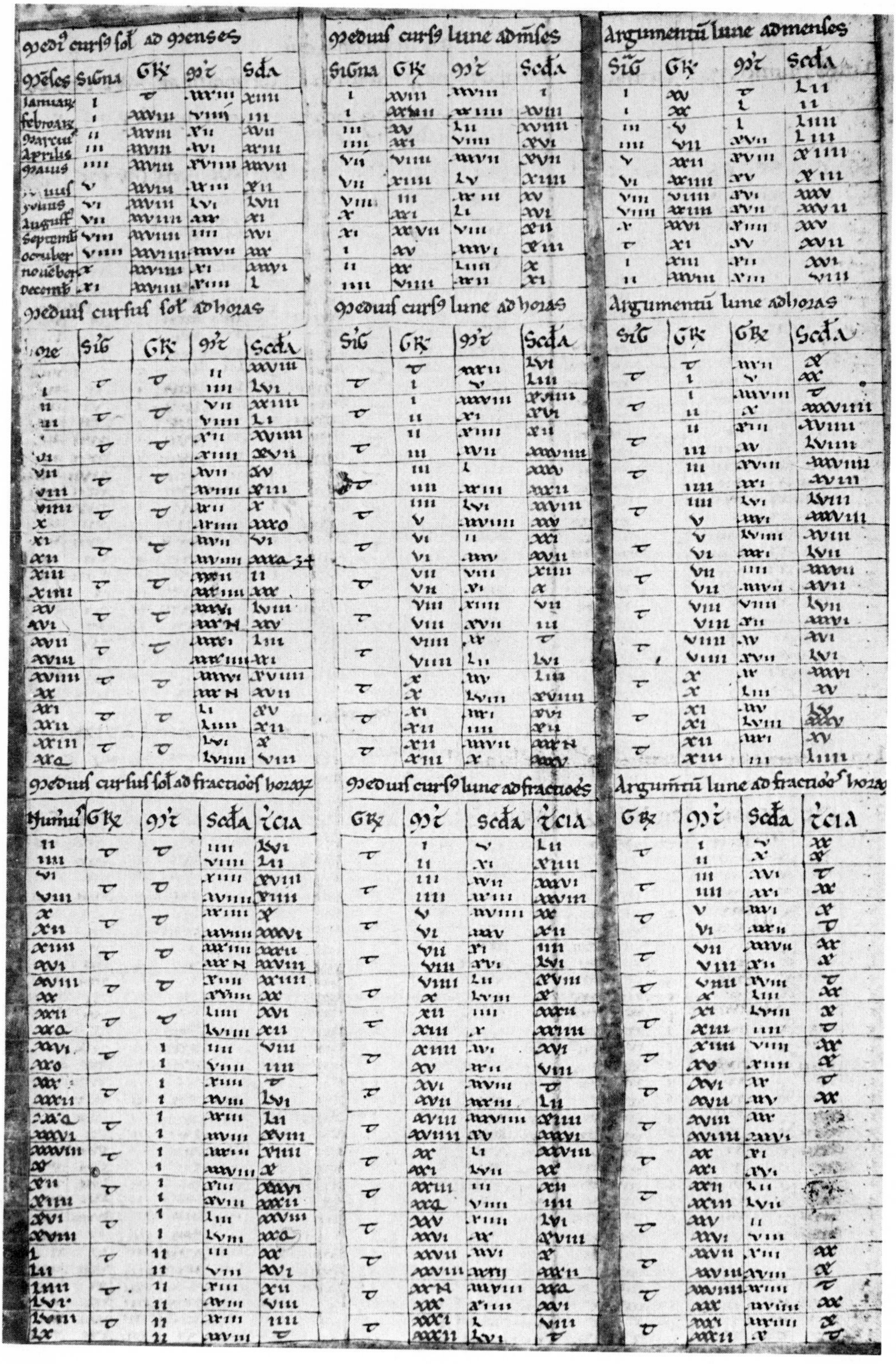

FIG. 7. Paris, BN lat. 14704, fol. 121

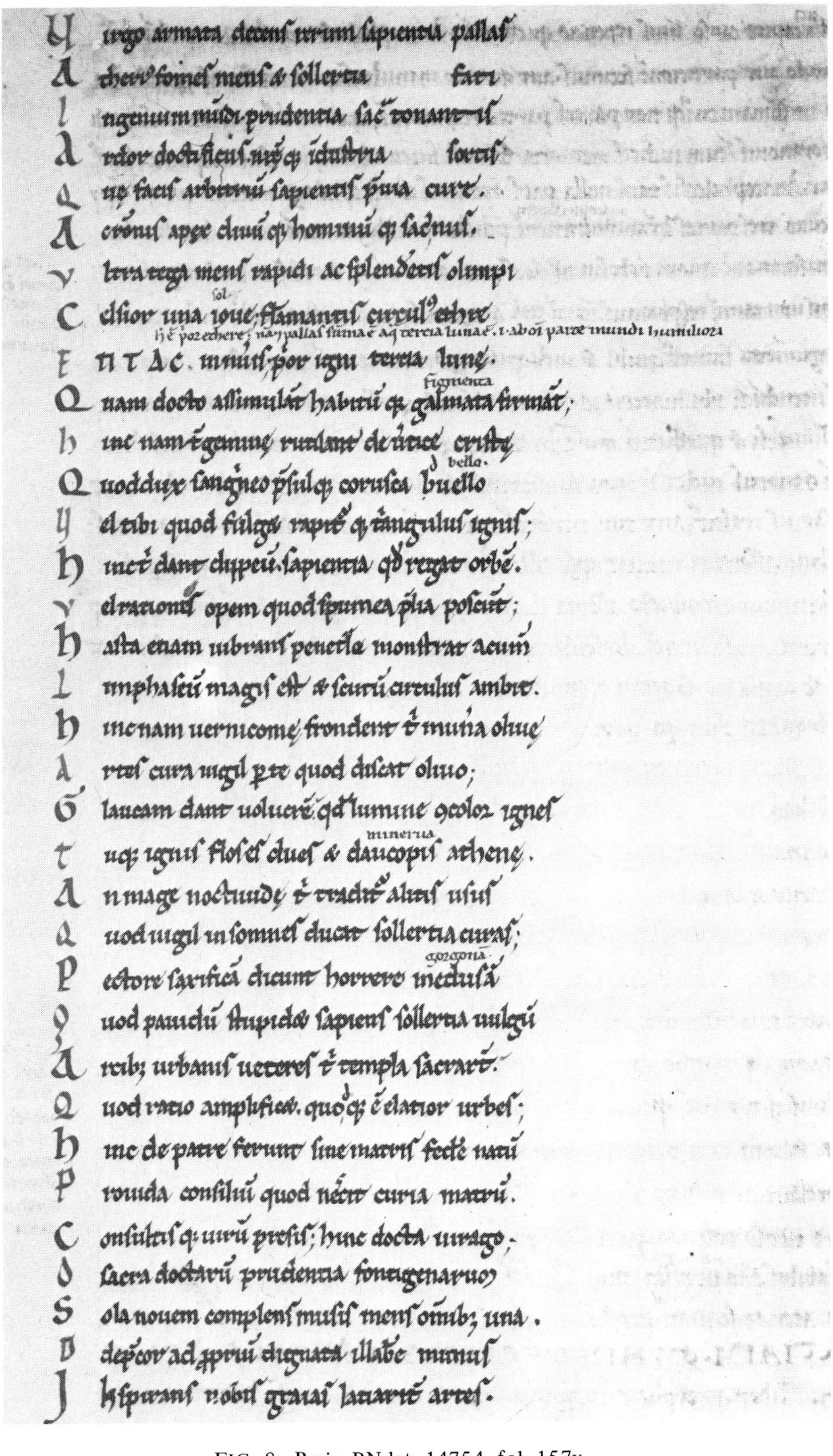

FIG. 8. Paris, BN lat. 14754, fol. 157v

FIG. 9. Paris, BN lat. 15461, fol. 50v

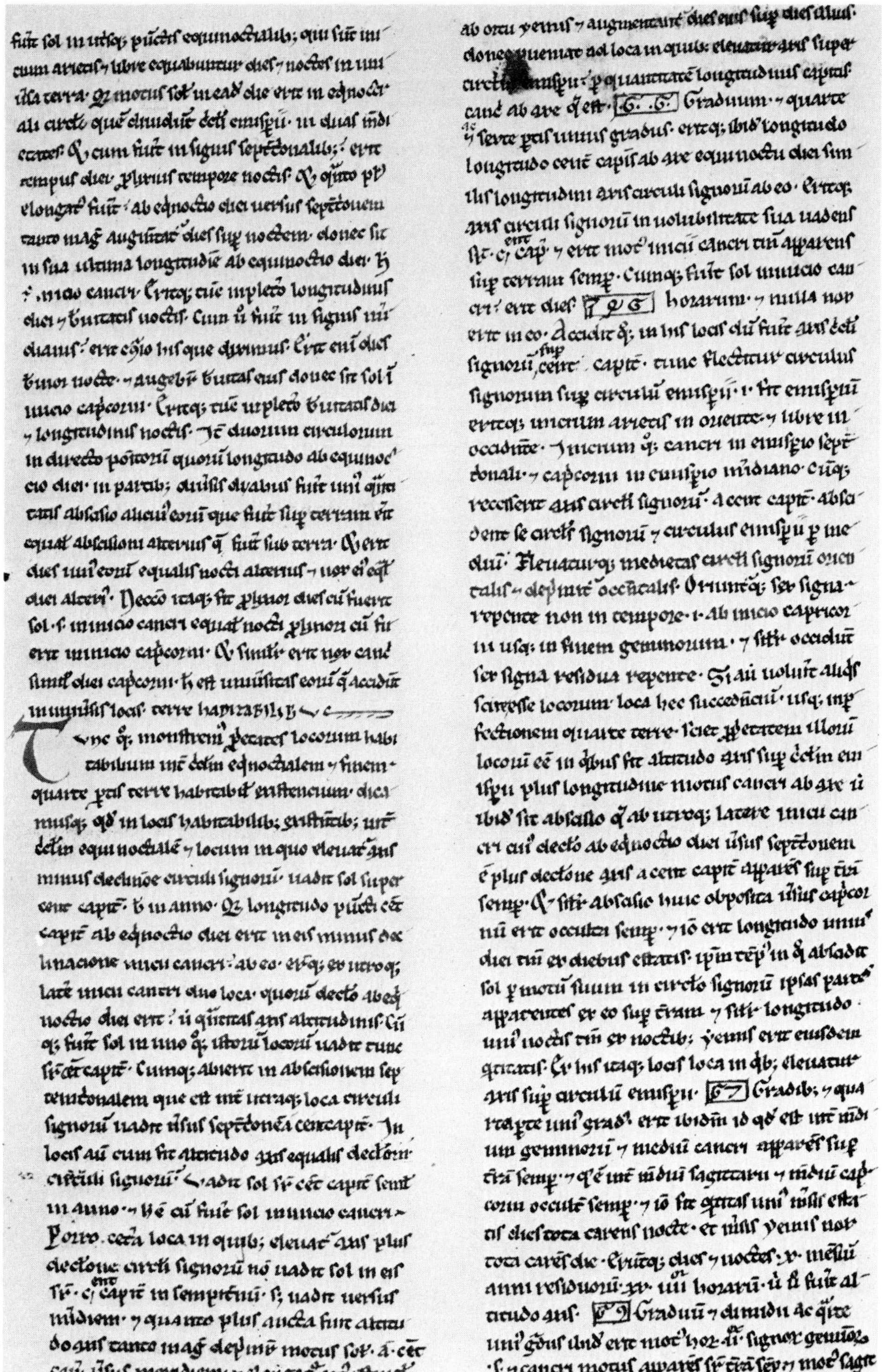

FIG. 10a. Paris, BN lat. 14704, fol. 215r

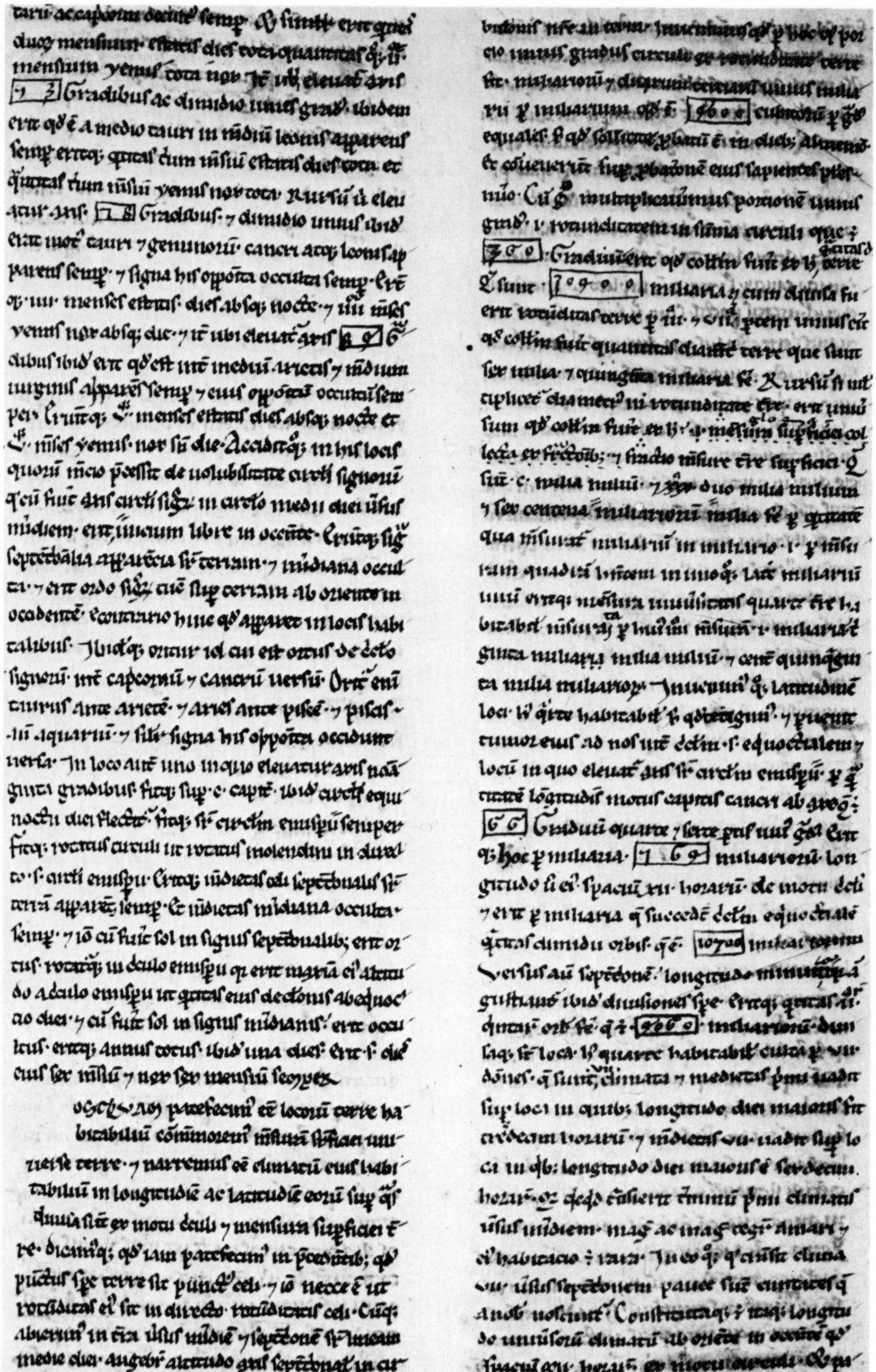

FIG. 10b. Paris, BN lat. 14704, fol. 215v

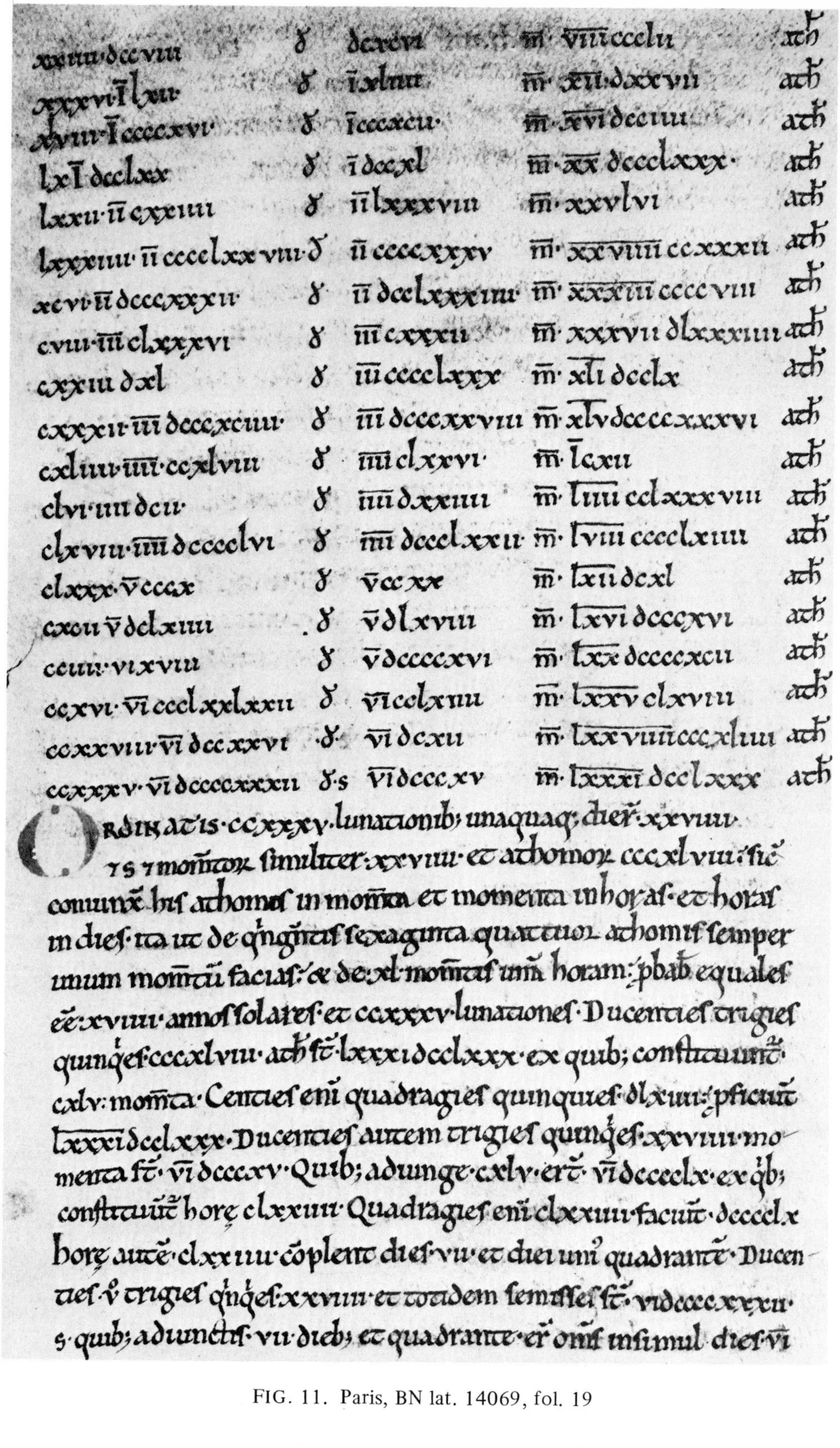

xxiiii dccviii	δ	dcxcvi	m	viii ccclii	ach
xxxvi I lxii	δ	I xliiii	m	xii dxxvii	ach
xlviii I ccccxvi	δ	I ccccxcii	m	xvi dcciiii	ach
lx I dcclxx	δ	I dccxl	m	xx dccclxxx	ach
lxxii II cxxiiii	δ	II lxxxviii	m	xxv lvi	ach
lxxxiiii II cccclxxviii	δ	II ccccxxxv	m	xxviiii ccxxxii	ach
xcvi II dcccxxxii	δ	II dcclxxxiiii	m	xxxiii ccccviii	ach
cviii III clxxxvi	δ	III cxxxii	m	xxxvii dlxxxiiii	ach
cxx III dxl	δ	III cccclxxx	m	xli dcclx	ach
cxxxii III dcccxciiii	δ	III dcccxxviii	m	xlv dccccxxxvi	ach
cxliiii IIII ccxlviii	δ	IIII clxxvi	m	L cxii	ach
clvi IIII dcii	δ	IIII dxxiiii	m	Liiii cclxxxviii	ach
clxviii IIII dccclvi	δ	IIII dccclxxii	m	Lviii cccclxiiii	ach
clxxx V ccx	δ	V ccxx	m	Lxii dcxl	ach
cxcii V dclxiiii	δ	V dlxviii	m	Lxvi dcccxvi	ach
cciiii VI xviii	δ	V dcccxvi	m	Lxx dccccxcii	ach
ccxvi VI ccclxxii	δ	VI clxiiii	m	Lxxv clxviii	ach
ccxxviii VI dccxxvi	δ	VI dcxii	m	Lxxviiii cccxliiii	ach
ccxxxv VI dccccxxxii	δ s	VI dcccxv	m	Lxxxi dcclxxx	ach

ORDINATIS · ccxxxv · lunationib; unaquaq; dierum xxviiii · et s et momentorum similiter xxviiii · et athomorum cccxlviii : sic coniunxi his athomos in momenta et momenta in horas · et horas in dies · ita ut de quinquagintis sexaginta quattuor athomis semper unum momentum facias : et de xl momentis unam horam : probabis equales esse xviiii annos solares et ccxxxv lunationes · Ducenties trigies quinquies cccxlviii · ath fiunt · lxxxi dcclxxx · ex quib; constituuntur cxlv · momenta · Centies enim quadragies quinquies dlxiiii · perficiunt lxxxi dcclxxx · Ducenties autem trigies quinquies xxviiii · momenta fiunt · vi dcccxv · Quib; adiunge · cxlv · erunt · vi dccclx · ex quib; constituuntur horę clxxiiii · Quadragies enim clxxiiii faciunt · dcccclx horę autem clxxiiii cōplent dies vii et diei unius quadrantem · Ducenties vero trigies quinquies xxviiii et totidem semisses fiunt · vi dcccxxxii · s · quib; adiunctis vii dieb; et quadrante · erunt omnes insimul dies vi

FIG. 11. Paris, BN lat. 14069, fol. 19

VIATOR Style Sheet

1. All contributions must be typewritten in *double space,* with ample margins. This applies to text, quoted material, and footnotes. Please do *not* use corrasible paper.

2. Footnotes should be typed in *double space* on separate sheets at the end of the article and numbered consecutively.

3. Bibliographical references ordinarily belong in the notes rather than in the text; the first reference to an item should contain the complete data:

Book: J. K. Brown, *Book Title* (City 1879) 234-236.
Title [Translation of title] (City 1877) 34.
Title, ed. John Doe and Jane Doe (City [etc.]).
ed. 2 (City [etc.]).
trans. John Doe (City 1876) fol. 15v.

Monograph: John G. Black, *Monograph Title*, Title of Series (ABBRV) 21 (1786) 34.
C. J. Smith, *Monograph in Same Series*, ABBRV 22 (1787) 345-346, esp. 345 n. 4.

Article: John Doe, "Article," *Journal* 76 (1879) 1-22, 34ff., 50.
Undated Journal 76.1-22.

Manuscript: Augustine, *De musica* 3.4, Paris, Bibliothèque Nationale lat. MS 9320, fols. 4., 5v, 6rv.

4. Subsequent references may be shortened as follows, always with a view to brevity without ambiguity.

a. Smith 24-25. (Only one Smith is cited, in a recent footnote, and there can be no possible ambiguity.)
b. Jones (n. 2 above) 245-246. (Complete reference is in n. 2 above.)
c. Jones, "The Blue Book" (n. 2 above) 34. (Jones has more than one reference in n. 2, so short title is necessary.)
d. Augustine 3.6 (7v).

5. Sigla: *Acta sanctorum*: AS Apr. 3.420.
Patrologia graeca: PG 37.96A.
Patrologia latina: PL 129.432.
Monumenta Germaniae historica: MGH Auctores antiquiores 5.1 (Berlin 1882) 130.

6. Titles of foreign books and articles should be capitalized according to the usages of the respective languages. In Latin and the Romance languages, only the first word and proper nouns should be capitalized.